[From the American Journal of Science, Vol. XXXIV, Nov., 1862.]

ON THE

SALIFEROUS ROCKS AND SALT SPRINGS

OF

MICHIGAN.

BY ALEXANDER WINCHELL.

The perfectly dish-shaped conformation of the strata of the lower peninsula of Michigan, has prevented the escape to the sea of such soluble substances as were originally embraced in the marine deposits from which the rocks were formed. Were there any point in the margin of one of these rocky basins, lower than its central portions, chance for escape of all its soluble contents would have existed; and it is doubtful whether in such case, brines could have been retained to the present day, in any considerable quantity. Our subterranean peninsular basins are comparable with the superficial basins in which the salt lakes of the world are located. Neither class of basins has an outlet. The basin of lake Superior was once filled with water as salt as that of the Great Salt lake. Both have received accessions of fresh water; but while one has been drained by an efflux which has continually carried away some portions of the chlorid of sodium, the other has been drained only by evaporation. The salineness of one has been reduced almost to an infinitesimal quantity;* that of the other is unimpaired, if it has not

* Given the time required for the efflux through the Straits of St. Mary, of a volume of water equal to the usual contents of Lake Superior; given also the minute percentage of chlorid of sodium still remaining in the water of the lake; it is required to determine how long the processes of dilution through meteorological precipitation and drainage through the Straits must have been continued to reduce the sea-water which originally filled the lake basin to the degree of weakness which it has now attained: disregarding the chlorids derived from the drainage waters flowing into the lake.

actually been strengthened by the loss of more water than it has received.

The subterranean basins of Michigan furnish us with three "great salt lakes." The principal one of these is shown, for the first time, in the "First Biennial Report" of the geology of the State (1860), to occupy a position between the Carboniferous limestone and the sandstones at the base of the Carboniferous system—being on a parallel with the gypsiferous formation of Nova Scotia. It is a mass of argillaceous, gypseous and pyritous shales, with thin beds of arenaceous and magnesian limestone, and beds of pure gypsum from eleven to twenty feet in thickness. The aggregate thickness is from 180 to 200 feet. Its outcrop describes an irregular circle, embracing the central portion of the peninsula. It underlies an area of 17,000 square miles, embracing the whole of 19 counties and at least half of 16 others. This assemblage of strata, though probably included in the American representation of the Mountain Limestone of the Old World, has received the local designation of Michigan Salt Group.

Seven hundred and fifty feet below this is the Onondaga salt group, the circuit of whose outcrop is traced from Monroe county to Galt in Canada West, thence to Mackinac island, Milwaukie and southward. The supply of brine in these strata has not been ascertained. They are well stocked with gypsum and are known to be saliferous.

The third saliferous horizon has but recently been recognized. It was indeed known that brine of feeble strength exists in the coal measures, but only within a few days has it been proved that the salt wells at Bay City and vicinity on the Saganaw river, are supplied from this source. It *might* have been known from the first existence of these wells, if those having the boring in charge could have been induced to preserve specimens of the rocks. The Parma sandstone below the coal measures is the reservoir of this brine, as the Napoleon sandstone beneath the Michigan salt group is the reservoir of the brine from this group. It is now known that the Bay City wells terminated at the bottom of the Parma sandstone though bored to nearly as great a depth as the wells of East Saginaw and vicinity, which pierce the Napoleon sandstone. This fact being established, a new well near Bay City has been sunk to a greater depth, and at 916 feet the Napoleon sandstone has been struck as predicted; and at the depth of 74 feet in this rock, brine has been brought up *completely saturated.* This occurrence, no less than the success of the first well bored in the valley, becomes a very gratifying confirmation of geological inferences drawn from observations extended over thousands of square miles, and in great part, hundreds of miles distant from the points where success has been attained.

When the first geological survey of the state was organized in 1837, Dr. Houghton, the superintendent, was instructed to direct his attention to the development of the "State salt springs." In pursuance of his investigations, and with the liberal coöperation of the legislature, he began, in 1838, two salt wells—one three miles west of Grand Rapids, and the other in Midland county on the Tittabawassee river. The latter, after being prosecuted at intervals for four years, had reached the depth of only 139 feet when the work seems to have been obstructed by a "quartzose" boulder. The Grand Rapids well was sunk 473 feet but without success. In the mean time Hon. Lucius Lyon of Grand Rapids sank a well 661 feet at a point further east; and, obtaining water about one-fifth saturated, succeeded in manufacturing salt for a few years, at a time when salt was selling for $3.00 per barrel.

The cause of these early failures is now apparent. Dr. Houghton entertained erroneous views of the structural geology of the peninsula. He expressed the opinion (Report, 1839, p. 9) that the strike of the rocks was northeast and southwest across the peninsula—that Saginaw bay occupied a denuded space along the outcrop of "the sandstone" just where it comes in contact with "the limestone of the north"—that the coal on the Illinois river was on the strike of the coal-bearing rocks of Michigan—and the galeniferous limestone of Wisconsin and Illinois a prolongation of "a portion of the rock formation in the northern part" of Michigan. He further supposed that the brines of the state rose to the surface through fissures in the strata overlying the salt rock (Rep., 1838, p. 21; also special Rep., 1839, pp. 2 and 3), and that the geological positions of the state wells on the Tittabawassee and Grand Rivers were about the same (Spec. Rep., 1839, p. 6); while the latter was at least 360 feet below the former and separated from it by the whole thickness of the coal measures (see also Hubbard's Geol. Rep., 1841, pp. 132, et seq.).

It now appears that while the well on the Tittabawassee was located far within the salt basin, that on the Grand River was upon the thinning out edges of the strata. The brine at the latter point, as well as in Macomb and Washtenaw counties is caused by a sort of exudation over the rim of this basin, and does not rise through fissures from a deeply seated rock.

When it became apparent that the deepest portion of the great salt basin was probably beneath the neighborhood of the confluence of the Cass, Shiawassee and Tittabawassee rivers, a boring was commenced at East Saginaw, which at 742 feet had passed through the Coal measures, Carboniferous limestone and Napoleon sandstone, and afforded a plentiful supply of brine nine-tenths saturated. This success was the signal for a general onset; and within two years, twenty-three wells have been bored along the valley of the Saginaw, and new ones are continually undertaken.

The following is an average section of the rocks passed through in the borings in the vicinity of east Saginaw:

Alluvial and Drift materials, ...	100 ft.
"Woodville sandstone," brown and coarse, ...	65 "
Coal measures, consisting of shales with some sandstones and limestones and coal, ...	130 "
"Parma sandstone" white and porous, ...	115 "
Carboniferous limestome, often highly arenaceous; generally so below, ...	75 "
"Michigan Salt Group,"	170 "
"Napoleon sandstone," light buff, rather coarse and porous,	110 "
Total,	765

The Napoleon sandstone is underlaid by a red shale which has been pierced 64 feet.

From East Saginaw the depth of the wells increases southward, toward the center of the general basin; and also northward, so that in the vicinity of Bay City the bottom of the Napoleon sandstone is found at the depth of 1000 feet. We seem therefore to have a local basin toward the mouth of the Saginaw river, although the vicinity is ten or fifteen miles nearer the outcropping margin of the salt basin, which is found at the mouth of the Pigeon river and in Tawas bay, on opposite shores of Saginaw bay.* This local basin is filled by an extraordinary thickening of the shales of the Coal measures, almost exclusively. As the Parma sandstone, which furnishes the brine of the first wells at Bay City, is probably the equivalent of the saliferous "Conglomerate" of Ohio, it seems that the supply of brine at this horizon, bears a relation to the thickness of the overlying shales of the Coal measures. It also suggests that in the deeper portions of the general basin, the Coal measures must be found similarly augmented in thickness, and the Parma sandstone similarly charged with brine. This condition should be looked for, west and northwest into Gratiot and Midland counties.

The following are analyses of Saginaw valley brines. The first is by Prof. DuBois of the University of Michigan, from the Napoleon sandstone; the second by Jas. R. Chilton & Co., from the Parma sandstone.

* On page 72, vol. i, Geolog. Rep. Wisconsin, Prof. Hall states, undoubtedly through inadvertence, that the "Hamilton group is known upon Saginaw bay." The Hamilton group strikes the lake shores in Thunder and Little Traverse bays many miles further north.

	Saginaw City.	Bay City.
Specific gravity,	1·180	1·163
Chlorid of sodium,	19·246	19·692
" calcium,	2·395	0·742
" magnesium,	1·804	0·432
" potassium,	0·127	
Sulphate of lime,	0·534	0·145
" soda,		0·116
Bromid of magnesium,		0·013
Compounds of iron,	0·064	
Total solid matter,	24·170	21·140

The difference in the composition of these brines is in accordance with their difference of origin.

The average supply of the Saginaw wells is at least 25,000 gallons each, in 24 hours.

The creation of this new branch of local industry is destined to become a matter of very great general importance. Although but two years have elapsed since the production of the first bushel of salt in the Saginaw valley, there are now (Aug. 1st) no less than 22 blocks of kettles in actual operation, turning out 1210 barrels of salt per day, or, making an allowance for the effect of winter weather, 1,980,000 bushels per year. Here is a growth, at the end of two years, equal to that attained by the Onondaga Saltworks in 1834, at the end of 38 years after the salt springs passed under the superintendence of the State. In two months, seven more blocks will come into operation, increasing by nearly one third, the foregoing figures.

Such is the strength and abundance of the brine and cheapness of fuel, that a barrel of salt is made at a cost of 64 cents. The cost of a barrel at Syracuse is at least 95 cents, so that Saginaw salt would pay the manufacturer 48 per cent of profit if the price were put down to the prime cost of the article at Syracuse. Moreover the quality of the article has proved so superior, that the market is actually clamorous for an adequate supply.

When we consider the cheapness and quality of Saginaw salt, the inexhaustibleness of the supply of brine and the excellent facilities for shipment, it would appear that there is little danger of over estimating the future development of this new resource.

University of Michigan, Aug. 4, 1862.

STATEMENT

Of Operations in the Museum of the University of Michigan in the Department of "Geology, Zoology and Botany," and the Department of "Archæology and Relics," for the year ending September 24th, 1868.

Rev. E. O. Haven, D. D., LL. D., President of the University.

Sir:—I have the honor to submit the following report on those departments of the Museum under my charge.

I. DEPARTMENT OF GEOLOGY, ZOOLOGY AND BOTANY.

Everything has been accomplished in this department which the limited resources at my command have permitted. Some very material assistance has been rendered by Mr. M. W. Harrington and Mr. J. B. Steere, members of the last senior class, and now graduates of the University. Mr. Harrington, in particular, devoted a considerable portion of nearly every week to work in the laboratory or museum, and, though without any compensation, rendered service which could not be dispensed with. It gives me pleasure to say that Mr. Harrington, by authority of the Board of Regents, granted in September, 1867, is now employed, at a moderate remuneration, to assist me in the details of this department.

I. Geology.

Four new cases have been constructed, extending across the south end of the old library room, at an expense of $175.

In the arrangement of the geological collection I have effected great improvements. Changes were rendered necessary in providing a suitable location for the collections from Lake Superior, to which reference was made in my last report; and the re-arrangements became now, for the first time, possible, by the construction, this year and last, of several new cases. The want of these had long prevented me from giving the geological collections anything like a systematic distribution. Under the present arrangement, the room attached to the Gallery of Mineralogy is devoted exclusively to the Lithological section, while the old library room is appropriated exclusively to the Paleontological section. In the Lithological section there are twenty-four cases assigned as follows:

A. *Azoic and Eozoic.*

1–2. Metalliferous—Michigan Copper.
3–4. " " Iron.
5. " Other Metals.
6–7. Plutonic Rocks and Rock-constituents.
8–9. Schistose Rocks and Rock-constituents.
10–11. Eruptive Rocks and Rock-constituents.

B. *Paleozoic.*

12. Potsdam Rocks.
13. Trenton and Nashville Rocks.
14. Niagara, Salina and Lower Helderberg Rocks.
15. Oriskany, Corniferous and Hamilton Rocks.
16. Chemung, Waverly and Lower Carboniferous Rocks.
17. Coal Measure Rocks.
18. C. *Mesozoic.*

D. *Cenozoic.*

19. Tertiary Rocks.
20. Post-Tertiary Rocks.

E. *Students' Lithological Cases.*

21. Illustrating Rocks and Rock-constituents.
22. " Rock-structures.
23–24. F. *Economical Geology.*

The plan of the Paleontological section is shown in the lithographic diagram and printed explanations appended to this

Statement. The plan proposed cannot be completely carried into execution until all the cases for this section are constructed. To each case I have attached a description, in book form, of the geology of that age of the world illustrated in the case. These several explanatory volumes have been made by taking to pieces a volume of Dana's Manual of Geology, and binding the parts up sepatately. Each part is prefixed by a diagram of the Hall with the requisite explanations.

Some very important contributions to the geological cabinet have been received from Ile Royale and the north shore of Lake Superior through Dr. A. E. Foote, Assistant in the Chemical Laboratory. Dr. Foote, with unusual, and extremely creditable zeal for science, organized, at his own risk, an extensive expedition to the north shore of Lake Superior and the adjacent islands. The expedition left in the latter part of April and returned during September. The geological department of the University furnished the party with a tent, a camp-chest and utensils, and, in return for these facilities, as well as in recognition of the claims of his Alma Mater upon the services of her Alumni, Dr. Foote has furnished my department with a complete set of the geological, zoölogical and botanical specimens collected. These will be found more particularly enumerated below:

Additions to the Geological Cabinet.

Dr. A. E. Foote. Twelve varieties of porphyry, mostly from island St. Ignace, mouth of Neepigon Bay, north shore of Lake Superior.

5 varieties of amygdaloidal trap. N. Shore.

Amygdaloidal trap with agates. St. Ignace.

" " " jasper. "

" " " chalcedony. "

Tufaceous trap. St. Ignace.

Slate. Thunder Cape.

Chloritic Schist with iron pyrites. Champion Mine, North Shore.

2 Conglomerates. N. Shore.

2 " Ile Royale.

1 Conglomerates. Eagle River, Keewenaw Pt.

2 Metamorphic sandstone. Ile Royale.

2 Porcelain jasper. " "

1 Sandstone, St. Ignace.

1 " Bayfield, Wis.

1 Chlorastrolites in amygdaloidal trap. Ile Royale.

1 " gangue rock.

1 Basaltic column weighing about 80 lbs. Simpson's Island.

2 segments of basaltic columns.

WILLITS, HARRINGTON AND FOOTE (Alumni). Several slabs of Corniferous limestone with glacial grooves, from Stony Point, Lake Erie.

M. W. HARRINGTON. Rare lithological specimen.

J. H. BURLESON. Compressed peat, from Dexter, Mich. Talc, from a quarry in North Carolina. Iron Ore, from Brewster's Station, Putnam Co., N. Y.

L. B. POTTS (Student). Rare lithological specimen.

CHARLES POOR (Student). Rare lithological specimen.

B. R. CHAFEE (Student). Fossils and rocks from Marcellus, N. Y.

W. L. OGE (Student). Fine specimen of *Tentaculites*.

C. H. PLANT (Student). Compressed peat, from Chelsea, Mich.

P. M. BARKER. Salt from crude brine, from well at Bennington, Shiawassee Co., Mich. Depth 680 feet—apparently in "Napoleon sandstone."

WILLIAM BRISCOE, Esq. Travertin from near Sheppardsville, Mich.

D. MONROE (Class of 1865). Black oxyd of manganese, from Moléje, Lower California. Plumbago, from Sonora, Mexico.

AYRES, LARNED AND WISWALL (Salt Manuft'g Co., Port Austin, Mich.), through Rev. George Taylor. Samples of coarse and fine salt, in bottles.

J. MONTGOMERY (Alumnus). Fossil coral (*Syringopora Hisingeri*), from near Woodstock, Ontario.

MRS. H. M. REDFIELD, Cambridge, Lenawee Co. Pure and fine specimen of Kidney Iron Ore—long mistaken for an aërolite.

Philadelphia Academy of Natural Sciences (By purchase of Prof. E. D. Cope for $15). A set of Maryland Miocene fossils, consisting as follows:

11	species of	sharks' teeth	17	specimens.
39	"	Molluscs	198	"
1	"	Articulate (*Balanus proteus*)	5	'
1	"	Radiate (*Madrepora palmata*)	2	"
52	"		222	"

II. Zoölogy.

Two pediment cases for large specimens have been constructed at an expense of $45.

Mr. Harrington has identified and labeled 25 species of Unionidæ presented by T. Entrekin; also the considerable collection of shells left to the museum by my former geological assistant, A. D. White, to whom acknowledgements were made in my Report of 1863, p. 10. The collection consisted of about 60 species of Unionidæ, Cycladidæ, Helicidæ and Lymneidæ. He has also relabeled and placed on exhibition our entire collection of Cycladidæ, besides acting as general assistant during the year, but without compensation. Mr. J. B. Steere, also a student, bestowed considerable labor upon the Lymneidæ and Helicidæ—having relabeled and arranged 134 species. A considerable portion of our domestic Pulmonate Molluscs has been relabeled according to an improved arrangement which I have devised. It is my intention to begin immediately the relabeling of the ornithological collection by the introduction of a new label-holder or clamp which I have invented. This clamp is already in use in some other museums, and has been highly approved by the best judges in some of the larger museums of the country.

The zoölogical results of the expedition to the north shore of lake Superior, under Dr. Foote, have added considerably to our collections from that region, especially in the families of Fishes, Reptiles, Insects and Molluscs, as will be shown below. A complete series of the zoölogical specimens is pledged to the University.

Additions to the Zoölogical Collection.

DR. A. E. FOOTE. Specimens from Ile Royale and the north shore of lake Superior, as follows:

Common Hare (*Lepus sylvaticus*).

Common Mink (*Putorius vison*).

14 Bird skins.

12 Eggs of *Larus argentatus.*

1 Carapace of turtle.

5 Serpents in alcohol.

7 Batrachians in alcohol.

50 Fishes in alcohol.

250 Species of Insects.

Unio dilatata and *Anodonta Pepinana.*

22 Species of *Planorbis*, *Valvata*, *Amnicola Sphaerium*, *Pisidium*, *Helix*, *Succinea*, *Lymnea*, *and Physa.*

HOLMES AND WILTSIE, Ann Arbor. Hen Hawk (*Buteo borealis*).

E. P. AUSTIN (Alumnus). 3 small Rodents' skulls. 1 skin of Shrew Mole (*Blarina talpoides*).

J. T. COLEMAN. Mud Hen (*Fulica Americana*), mounted.

W. J. ENGLISH (Student). Large Water-bug (*Belostoma Haldemanum.*)

W. H. MARTIN, Deerfield, Livingston Co. Large Hornets' Nest.

MRS. S. A. DELONG. A remarkable native fly.

WILLIAM VAN OSTRAND. Large Water-bug (*Belostoma Haldemanum.*

A. WINCHELL. Maple limbs cut transversely by an unknown insect larve.

Specimens of *Anoplitis suturalis* which has just commenced ravaging the locust trees of central Kentucky.

Labeled specimens of small fishes from Ann Arbor. Labeled by Prof. E. D. Cope.

M. W. HARRINGTON. Three species of *Helix* to supply deficiences in the Museum. Male and female seventeen-year Cicadas, and larva-cases.

J. B. STEERE. Eight species of *Helix*, to supply deficiencies in the Museum.

MESSRS. PLANT AND CHAFEE (Students). Fish Lizard (*Menobranchus lateralis*).

W. J. ENGLISH (Student). Apple tree branches pierced by the seventeen-year Cicada (Very abundant and general in June, 1868).

The following duplicate bird-skins, in a fair state of preservation, are offered for exchange, viz.: 8 *Querquedula discors*, 2 *Aix sponsa*, 6 *Anas boschas*, 6 *Fulix collaris*, 2 *Aythya Americana*, 1 *Dafila acuta*, 4 *Anas obscura*, 1 *Nettion Carolinensis*, 3 *Mareca Penelope*, 1 *Bucephala albeola*, 1 *Spatula clypeata*, 1 *Croicocephalus Philadelphia*, 2 *Larus glaucus*, 2 *Ardea Herodias*, 4 *Fulica Americana*, 2 *Bubo Virginianus*, 7 *Haliaëtus Leucocephalus*, 1 *Pandion Carolinensis*, 1 *Ortyx Virginianus*, 1 *Botaurus lentiginosus*, 1 *Buteo borealis*, 1 *Accipiter fuscus*.

Also 1 *Sciurus Ludovicianus* and 1 *Sciurus Carolinensis*.

In my Statement of 1866 I credited, through wrong information, a remarkable specimen—the Double Crested Cormorant—to the wrong person. It should be credited, H. N. FRENCH (Alumnus), of Homer, Calhoun Co.

I deem it but an act of justice to a gentleman of science who, I am sure, would never ask the correction for his own sake, to state that the entire collection of Insects obtained for the University some years since through the agency of Mr. R. Kennicott, and presented as a portion of the "Trowbridge Collection," should be credited to Mr. P. R. Uhler, of the Peabody Institute of Baltimore. This information reached me indirectly and without the agency of Mr. Uhler. It has been ascertained, however, that these specimens were selected, labeled and pinned by Mr. Uhler from his private collection as a donation from himself directly to the University, and that he had no knowledge that they were to be credited to the "Trowbridge Collection." It is claimed by Mr. Uhler's friends that this acknowledgement should be made. In gladly rendering tardy justice to a naturalist of so unpretending superiority, I desire to state that I had no other agency in the transaction referred to than to receive the specimens as they purported to be—a part of the "Trowbridge Collection," with no particular mention of Mr. Uhler's name.

Lest this statement should seem to reflect upon the memory of Mr. Kennicott, I ought to say further, that I believe, if this zealous and conscientious young naturalist were living he would show that his honesty is not in the least implicated in this misunderstanding.

III. Botany.

Mr. Harrington has labeled and placed on exhibition the collection of seeds presented by Mr. Austin and myself, as also the truncheons of wood presented by students of botany. He has also completed the catalogue of the Houghton Herbarium, from which it appears that this collection contains 612 species, and about 2000 specimens. The Sager Herbarium catalogued by Dr. Lyons, is found to contain 878 species and 1555 specimens.

Mr. Harrington has also looked through the entire collection of duplicate plants and rectified the labeling according to the modern nomenclature. The duplicate specimens number 4259, and belong to 643 species. These have been arranged, under my direction, in ten labeled sets, of each of which a complete catalogue has been made out. The sets are composed as follows:

No. 1, 643 species; No. 2, 578 species; No. 3, 503 species; No. 4, 440 species; No. 5, 372 species; No. 6, 310 species; No. 7, 274 species; No. 8, 243 species; No. 9, 202 species; No. 10, 179 species. There are besides 367 specimens of 108 species not included in the sets.

The foregoing plants are mostly in good condition and I shall endeavor to use them in making exchanges for foreign specimens. Nearly all were collected in the Lake Superior region.

The expedition under Dr. Foote made extensive collections in the Vegetable Kingdom, embracing Phænogams, Equiseta, Ferns and Lycopodiace. The Flora of Ile Royale was pretty thoroughly studied during a stay of about ten weeks. The number of species observed on the island belonging to the types just indicated was 560. The total number of species of the same orders reported by the expedition conducted some years since by Prof. L. Agassiz, was 386.

Additions to the Botanical Collection.

DR. A. E. FOOTE. Two hundred and seventy-five species of dried plants from Ile Royale, numbering about 350 specimens, embracing half a dozen of the rare fern *Allosorus acrostichoides* and the same number of *Aspidium fragrans.*

A. WINCHELL. Sixty-two varieties of garden seeds.

4 Bolls of Cotton from Louisiana.

1 sample of Chinese cotton.

W. MERRILL, East Saginaw (Class of '71). Specimen showing a wound of a Hickory tree by an axe, grown over and filled up by the growth of seven years.

E. W. WHITMORE, Ann Arbor. Stick of wood showing stump of a limb (cut off by the axe) overlaid by twelve years of annual growth.

E. P. AUSTIN. Fifty-five species of seeds of wild plants.

D. R. SHOOP (Alumnus). Fifty-nine species of dried plants from Tennessee and North Carolina—mostly new to the collection.

C. H. PLANT (Student). Specimens of the Teasle (*Dipsacus fullonum*), foom Marcellus, N. Y.

SUMMARY OF ADDITIONS.

Geological,	117	entries,	322	specimens.
Zoölogical,	354	"	468	"
Botanical,	457	"	536	"
Total,	938	"	1326	"
Grand totals last year,	21591	"	70303	"
Grand totals this year,	22519	"	71629	"

II. DEPARTMENT OF ARCHÆOLOGY AND RELICS.

The following additions have been made:

A. WINCHELL. Hickory cane from near the tomb of Andrew Jackson, Hermitage, near Nashville, Tenn.

Leaf of *Magnolia grandiflora* from the tree growing by the tomb of Andrew Jackson.

Pieces punched from the rivet holes of the plates of the iron-clad "Ram" built by the government at Carondelet, Mo.

Virginia Treasury Note for 225 pounds, of date 1781. Presented to A. Winchell by Regent John B. Bowman, of Kentucky University.

Bill of account bv Abram Bowman, 1779. From the same.

Receipt of Benjamin Roberts, Louisville, Ky., 1785. From the same.

J. H. BURLESON (Steward). Limestone, from door-post of Fort Ticonderoga.

Fragment of brick from Fort George.

Musket-ball and gun-flint from battle-field of the American Revolution, Caldwell, Lake George.

Fragment of the Cathedral of Notre Dame, Montreal.

EX-GOV. ALPHEUS FELCH, Ann Arbor. A Hindoo Idol made of metal.

WILLIAM J. WATERS (Student). Harpoon and seal-skin thong used by the Esquimaux of Greenland

REMARKS AND RECOMMENDATIONS.

A Register for the names of visitors to the Museum was opened on the 24th day of October, 1867. The total number of names registered to September 24th, 1868, is 3349. It is thought at least one-third of the visitors fail to register their names. If so, the Museum has been visited by not less than 5000 persons during the last eleven months, which is at the rate of 5400 per year. Of these, it is ascertained that 60 per cent. are people of Michigan.

The registrations have been distributed through the several months as follows:

October (from 24th), 138; November, 410; December, 282; January, 257; February, 242; March, 346; April, 222; May, 151; June, 501; July, 187; August, 502; September (to 24th), 183. Total, 3349.

I beg respectfully again to call attention to the Rominger Collection. In courtesy to Dr. Rominger some definite action should be taken without further delay.

I have the pleasure to transmit for the consideration of the Board of Regents the offer of Prof. James Orton, of Rochester University, to place in our Museum a collection of 127 specimens of lavas from the Andes, for the moderate sum of $100. These specimens were collected by himself during the last year.

I would also respectfully urge the importance of completing the cases in the Paleontological Hall, and constructing another cabinet of drawers for specimens kept in the laboratory.

I should be pleased to see some steps taken toward the founding of a Botanic Garden and Green House. I believe, after considerable inquiry and observation, that much could be done without permanent expense to the University. Once founded, such an accessory to the University might be made self-supporting, and would perhaps produce a small revenue. On this subject I would be pleased to confer with the Board of Regents.

Respectfully submitted,

A. WINCHELL,

Prof. Geol., Zoöl., and Bot.

UNIVERSITY OF MICHIGAN,
Ann Arbor, 28 Sept., 1868.

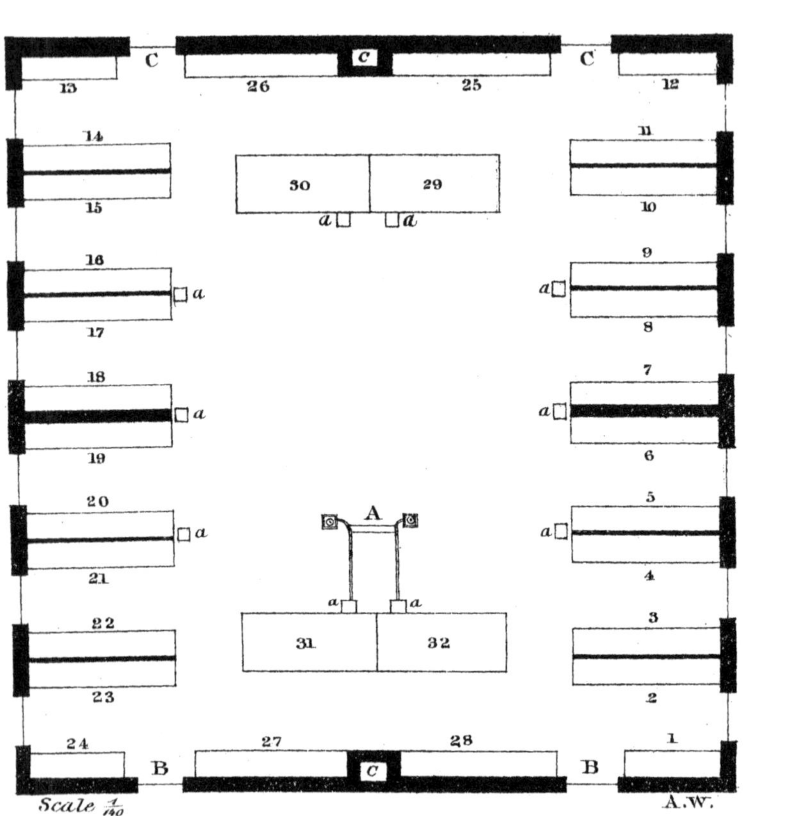

PLAN
OF THE GALLERY OF PALEONTOLOGY
University of Michigan

The Calvert Lith. Co. Detroit.

Explanation of the Plan.

A. Foot of Stairway to "Hall of Lithology."

B, B. Entrance Doors.

C. Entrance to the Department of Fine Arts.

a, a, a. Pillars supporting the Gallery of Mineralogy.

c, c. Chimneys.

PALEOZOIC TIME.

SILURIAN AGE.

1. Potsdam Period.
2. Trenton "
3. Nashville "
4. Niagara "
5. " "
6. Salina "
7. Lower Herderberg Period.

DEVONIAN AGE.

8. Oriskany Period.
9. Corniferous "
10. " "
11. Hamilton "
12. " and Chemung Periods.

CARBONIFEROUS AGE.

13. Waverly Period.
14. Mountain Limestone Period.
15. " " "
16. Coal Measure "
17. " " "

MESOZOIC TIME.

TRIASSIC AGE.

18. Triassic Period.

JURASSIC AGE.

19. Liassic Period.
20. Oolitic "

CRETACEOUS AGE.

21. Earlier Cretaceous Period.
22. Later " "

CENOZOIC TIME.

TERTIARY AGE.

23. Tertiary Period.

POST-TERTIARY AGE.

24. Post-Tertiary Period.

25., 26. } STRATIGRAPHICAL SERIES,

27., 28. } ZOÖLOGICAL SERIES.

29., 30., 31., 32. } *Large Specimens.*

REPORT

OF OPERATIONS IN THE

MUSEUM OF THE UNIVERSITY OF MICHIGAN,

IN THE DEPARTMENT OF

GEOLOGY, ZOÖLOGY AND BOTANY,

AND THE DEPARTMENT OF

ARCHÆOLOGY AND RELICS,

FOR THE YEAR ENDING SEPT. 21, 1869.

BY ALEXANDER WINCHELL,
Professor of Geology, Zoölogy and Botany.

ANN ARBOR:
DR. CHASE'S STEAM PRINTING HOUSE, 41 & 43 N. MAIN STREET.
1869.

REPORT.

No year in the history of the University has been marked by a more rapid growth of the Museum, a greater amount of work performed, or a greater interest in its contents, on the part of the public. Two large collections have been added, the one by bequest, the other by purchase. Dr. George L. Ames, late of Niles, a man of high standing in his profession, had attained a conspicuous position among the naturalists of the country. He had devoted an immense amount of labor to the collection and study of the plants and animals of the United States, when he was stricken down by valvular disease of the heart. A portion of his collection of insects had been placed in the Union School at Niles. The remainder, together with his vast magazine of dried plants, was presented by Mrs. Ames to the University. These specimens have been received; and the plants have been thoroughly invoiced and arranged. The total number of specimens of all kinds is about 22,500. The details are given in their proper place.

David Van Vechten was a practical man, who went from western New York to California and Nevada, where he spent several years among the mines, and accumulated a large mass of material, much of which was valuable, while some of the specimens possessed unique interest. Returning, about three years since, he deposited his collection in the University, with a view to sale. He removed to Michigan, was taken sick and recently died. The executors of his estate finally consented to take $200 for the collection. It contains about 1000 entries and 1788 specimens.

Other interesting additions will be specified in the sequel.

The rooms of the Museum are daily thronged with visitors from all parts of the country. Though it is estimated that not more than one-half of them register their names, the following have been recorded during the year ending with August last:—September, 314; October, 541; November, 376; December, 304; January, 407; February, 446; March, 512; April, 278; May, 317; June, 391; July, 299; August, 355. Total, 4,540. It is probable there have been not less than ten thousand individual visits to the Museum during the year.

The efficiency and usefulness of the Museum have been

greatly promoted by the assistance which has been furnished in the multiplied details of its management. Mr. Harrington's services have been of immense value. His rewards pecuniarily, have been so meagre that I feel it to be equally a duty and a pleasure to testify to his knowledge, skill, fidelity, prudence and patience in the performance of his work. Considerable aid has been received from Messrs. J. B. Steere, A. B., E. L. Mark, H. W. Montrose, H. C. Markham and S. T. Chamberlain, A. B. W. J. English, A. B. and E. L. Mark have acted as janitors.

I. DEPARTMENT OF GEOLOGY, ZOOLOGY, AND BOTANY.

I. GEOLOGY.

Eight cases, holding 192 drawers, have been constructed for the accommodation of duplicates and specimens awaiting investigation; and provision has been made for the completion of the series of exhibition cases in the Paleontological Hall.

Some exchanges have been effected during the year with the duplicates of the Museum. The usual number of presentations has been made. The University has purchased the Van Vechten collection. The resumption of the State geological survey, under improved auspices, will result in a great augmentation of authentic specimens from Michigan and contiguous regions. The University has very properly been made the headquarters of the survey.

The investigations in geology and paleontology have made some progress. In these I have been assisted by Mr. M. W. Harrington and Mr. T. C. Chamberlain. Among the more important results may be mentioned the determination of the existence of the "Marshall Group," in Tennessee, and in Venango County, Pennsylvania — a region which the highest authorities had asserted to be occupied exclusively by the "Chemung." Another interesting result is the discovery of abundant specimens of the peculiar genus *Syringothyris* throughout the Marshall sandstones of Ohio and Pennsylvania. This genus was originally founded on specimens known only in our Museum. These determinations have been based on collections submitted by Prof. James M. Safford of Tennessee, and Prof. E. B. Andrews and Rev. H. Herzer of Ohio. The scientific interest and importance of these discoveries will be understood by the geologist. They tend to settle, if they do not completely settle, a great geological controversy.

Additions to the Museum in Geology.

THE VAN VECHTEN COLLECTION. This was accumulated by David Van Vechten, an amateur geologist, during a residence of several years on the Pacific coast. It embraces the usual classes of specimens from the mining districts, and some very interesting mammalian remains from Table Mountain, Cal., among which are teeth and bones of *Mastodon;* tooth of an Elephant; skull and horns of *Bos* (*latifrons?*); bones and teeth of a fossil Horse, and fragments of the skull and femur of man. These specimens acquire interest in connection with the questions relating to *fossil man* in California. The following is an analysis of the collection:

	Entries.	*Specimens.*
Ores, including gold, silver, lead, copper, manganese. a little antimony, and very little tellurium	350	700
Minerals	150	300
Lithological specimens	50	50
Fossils, Mammalian	15	25
" Invertebrate	70	80
Geological specimens, unlabeled	300	500
Zoölogical	35	50
Botanical	25	75
Relics	8	8
Totals,	1003	1788

J. F. STEWARD, Plano Ill. Fifty-one entries of fossil plants from concretions in the Coal Measures of Mazon creek, Grundy county, Ill. In exchange for Lake Superior specimens collected by A. Winchell.

J. T. SCOVELL, M. D., Denver, Cal., (Alumnus.) Fifty-four entries, (65 specimens,) illustrating the mining geology of Colorado.

JOHN PEACH, Washtenaw county, Mich. A box of specimens of cannel and bituminous coals, galena, calcite, limonite, potter's and fire clays and associated rocks, from the mines of H. & T. Simpson, Mountain Co., Mo.

NATURAL HISTORY SOCIETY OF ST. JOHNS, N. B. (Through the Smithsonian Institution). Thirteen species of "Devonian Plants, collected by Prof. C. F. Hartt, at the 'Fern Ledges' near St. Johns, New Brunswick, and described in Jour. Geol. Soc., London, Vols. XVIII and XIX; and in Dawson's Acadian Geology, 2d edition. Set No. XXXIII."

JOHN H. HALL, Oxford, Chester Co., Penn. Twenty-one entries, (60 specimens) of minerals from Lancaster and Chester counties, Penn. In exchange for Lake Superior specimens collected by A. Winchell.

A. E. Foote, M. D. (Alumnus.) A small vial of Chlorastrolites from Ile Royale.

C. W. Durham. (Alumnus '69.) Specimen of Galena.

George W. Lawton, A. M., Lawton, Mich. Gray calciferous sandstone from Bangor and Antwerp, Van Buren Co., Mich.

M. N. Brewster, Houston, Texas. A large specimen of silicified wood from Texas.

William Freeman, Milton, Canada. Plaster cast of a Lower Silurian trilobite (*Asaphus gigas.*)

M. W. Harrington, Assistant. (1.) Section of a gypsum bed, "Salina group," Camillus, N. Y.

(2.) Two specimens of travertin, Camillus.

E. S. Dewey. (Alumnus '69.) Ten geological specimens from southern Michigan.

Joseph Brown, Lemont, Ill. A box of specimens of building stones from the quarries at Lemont.

Mrs. S. B. Olney, Ann Arbor. Snowy gypsum from Fort Dodge, Iowa.

J. B. Steere, A. B. (Alumnus.) Glass sand from Monroe, Mich.

T. Montgomery. (Alumnus.) Twenty-one specimens of Devonian fossils from Ontario.

C. T. Harris, M. D., Ann Arbor. Fragments of a scoriaceous meteorite, which fell in May, 1869, on the farm of D. F Harris, Elkhorn, Wis. An analysis of this by Prof. A. B. Prescott, gives:

Silica	0.578
Sesquioxide of iron	.130
Alumina	.096
Lime	.024
Magnesia	.020
Potassa	.099
Loss, (including traces of Manganese and soda)	.053
	1.000

II. ZOÖLOGY.

Arrangements have been made for the construction of a new case in the south-west corner of the zoölogical gallery.

The entire collection of Birds has been rearranged and relabelled, so that the visitor can now read both the scientific and popular names of the species. The labels are supported by a new device which seems to be very effective.

The rearrangement and relabeling of the land and fresh-water univalves has been completed; and the visitor can now read distinctly the name of each species. Many marine shells and other specimens have for the first time been arranged and placed on exhibition. Among these are the last deposite of shells from the Smithsonian Institution; and the specimens from the coast of Maine, received some years since from Dr. J. DeLaski. A collection of forty species, (400 specimens) of duplicate shells—mostly marine—has been brought from the attic, where they had lain since the life-time of Dr. Houghton, and worked over and packed away. The zoölogical specimens of the Foote collection, 40 in number, so far as received, have been worked up.* The Cicadas have been investigated and arranged; and the diurnal Lepidoptera further studied and catalogued.

Mr. Harrington, assisted, to some extent, by T. C. Chamberlain, and Messrs. Mark, Markham and Montrose, has collected the following fresh specimens: Mammals, 14; Birds, 350; Reptiles, 15; Articulates, 1250; Molluscs, 350; total 1979 specimens. Most of these have been identified and labeled.

Mrs. S. E. Becraft, a lady of Ann Arbor, has been occupied nearly four months as taxidermist to the University, and has given good satisfaction. She is still on duty. She has been principally engaged in renewing the illustration of our common species of birds and quadrupeds. Something over 200 specimens of birds have been mounted, and numerous skins preserved for exchanges. Mr. J. Hobson, the taxidermist of the Audubon Club, of Detroit, was employed to mount a fine panther and a Boa constrictor.

Additions to the Museum in Zoölogy.

C. HAYNES, ESQ., Toronto, Ontario. A case of nine mounted birds, under glass, with the following inscription: "This case of birds from Guatemala, Central America, is presented to the University of Michigan by a member of the Young Men's Christian Association of Toronto, Canada, in grateful remembrance of the Detroit Convention of Associations in June, 1868, and of the visit then paid, by invitation of the authorities of the University, to Ann Arbor.

Toronto, Sept., 1868."

The following is a list of the birds, so far as identified: 1. Trogon resplendens; 2. Dacris atricapilla; 3. Trogon Mexicanus; 4. Rámphocelus sanguinolentus; 5 and 6. Unknown; 7. Thamnophilus; 8. Cœreba cyanea; 9. Ramphocelus passerinii.

WILLIAM B. SAGER, Cheyenne, Neb. (1.) *A Boa constrictor*, seven feet in length, from South America.

* The *Insects* reported last year were subsequently taken by Dr. Foote, and sent to Philadelphia for determination; since which none have been returned.

(2.) Skin of a Panther, (*Felis concolor*,) shot near Cheyenne, Neb. These were presented through Professor Sager, M. D.

ESTATE OF GEORGE L. AMES, M. D., late of Niles, deceased. A collection of about 5000 specimens of insects—mostly Coleoptera and Lepidoptera—pinned in close, glazed, portable cases.

HIS EXCELLENCY, DOMINGO F. SARMIENTO, President of the Argentine Republic, S. A. (1.) A fine specimen of the Condor of the Andes, (*Vultur gryphus*,) which, when living, probably measured nine feet from tip to tip of the wings. (Not yet mounted.)

(2.) *Chlamyphorus truncatus*, (Harlan.) A unique species of the family of armadillos, from the mountains of Chili, of which only one specimen is known to have hitherto reached North America, while only one exists in Europe.

FORD COLLECTION. Attached to the Ford Anatomical Collection, purchased by the Board of Regents, were two or three hundred specimens of shells, mostly marine, which have been transferred to the cabinet of zoölogy.

DR. C. B. PORTER, Ann Arbor. Plastron of tortoise, (*Emys meleagris*,) carved with his initials in 1838—found again in 1867, and found a third time in 1868. In thirty years this individual had varied but very little in size, as was demonstrated by the fact that one of the figures was still quite close to one of the sutures separating the shields of the plastron.

A. B. WOOD. Cutting by Beavers through the trunk of a Yellow Birch tree fourteen inches in diameter. The cut is diagonal, and measures sixteen inches in length. A fine specimen.

E. A. ELLSWORTH, La Fayette, Ind. *Storeria Dekayi.*

H. S. JEWETT, A. B. (Alumnus and Chemical Assistant.)

(1.) *Epeira insularis*, (Hentz,) from Dayton, Ohio.

(2.) Ten species of land and fresh water shells from Dayton.

(3.) Fifty specimens of insects from Dayton.

T. C. CHAMBERLAIN, A. B. *Storeria Dekayi*, Ann Arbor.

C. P. GILBERT. (Student) Lower Jaw and teeth of a Walrus, (*Trichecus rosmarus*,) from an inland lake, Newfoundland. Perhaps should be regarded *a fossil.*

J. B. STEERE, A. B. (Alumnus.) Two weasels, (*Putorius Noveboracensis*,) from Ionia, Mich.

J. C. STARKEY, M. D. (Alumnus.) Bob-o-link, (*Dolichonyx oryzivorus*,) in winter dress—having been kept in a cage.

REV. L. D. BURCH, Ann Arbor. Skin of a very large specimen of the Wild Cat, (*Lynx rufus*,) from near Rochester, Oakland Co.

M. Kellogg. Deer mouse. (*Hesperomys leucopus.*)

J. T. Scovell, M. D. (Alumnus.) Larves of grain moth (*Tinea granella.*)

E. Henderson, Homer, Mich. Lake-fly, (*Corydalis cornuta.*)

Mrs. Prof. Frieze. Nest and Eggs of a Canary Bird.

M. W. Harrington. Skull of Skunk, (*Mephitis chinga.*)

F. H. Lewis, Adrian. A double-headed turkey chick.

III. BOTANY.

Mr. Harrington has expended a large amount of labor upon the botanical cabinet. The 300 specimens from Lake Superior, furnished by Dr. Foote, have been investigated, labeled, and arranged. The entire collection of plants has been looked over, emumerated, and classified; exchanges of duplicate specimens have been effected; a collection of 100 species of seeds remaining from the Houghton Survey has been bottled, labeled, and placed on exhibition, and seeds of 40 species of plants have been added; the 7,000 specimens in the serial collection of plants of the Ames Herbarium have been catalogued, and the 10,500 specimens of duplicates have been carefully and laboriously identified, catalogued, and put away. Mr. Harrington has also collected and preserved 500 fresh specimens from the vicinity of Ann Arbor, making 2,519 specimens in zoölogy and botany added by him during the year.

Additions to the Museum in Botany.

The Ames Herbarium. The total number of specimens in the serial collection is 7,000. The total number of duplicates, 10,500. Grand total of specimens 17,500. Total number of species 1,375. Number of species new to the University Cabinet, 400.

This is a very important acquisition to the Museum. The Herbarium comprises, 1. A collection of New England plants, including some from the summits of the White and Green Mountains, most of which are new to the University. 2. A collection from the pine barrens and salt marshes of New Jersey, including a large number of rare plants new to the University. 3. A collection of Tennessee plants, among which are a few not mentioned in Gray's Botany, and new to the University. 4. A collection of plants from the vicinity of Niles, a few of which are new to the Flora of the State, as published, and also new to the University. Among these are *Stylophorum diphyllum* (Nutt), *Draba Caroliniana* (Walt.), *Silene nivea* (DC.), *Desmodium ciliare* (DC.), *Conioseli-*

num Canadense (Torr. & Gray), *Stachys hyssopifolia* (Mx.), *Carex Steudelii* (Kunth.), *C. decomposita* (Muhl.), *C. adusta* (Booth), *C. aperta* (Booth), *C. panicea* (L.), *C. Careyana* (Torr.), *C. retrorsum* (Dew.), and others.

Among the duplicates of the Ames Herbarium are many desirable species, among which may be enumerated, *Atragene Americana*, *Lechea major*, *Hypericum ellipticum*, *Desmodium ciliare*, *D. sessifolium*, *Eryngium yuccæfolium* *Polytænia Nuttalli*, *Archemora rigida*, and var, *ambigua*, *Eupatorium teucrifolium*, *Solidago thyrsoidea*, *S. Muhlenbergii*, *Coreopsis tripteris*, *C. palmata*, *Stachys hyssopifolia*, *Onosmodium Carolinianum*, *Frasera Carolinensis*, *Scheuzeria palustris*, *Goodyera repens*, *Liparis Lœselii*, *Aplectrum hyemale*, *Carex Steudelii*, *C. adusta*, *C. aurea*, *C. plantaginea*, *C. Careyana*, *C. Schweinitzii*, *C. oligosperma*, *Glyceria acutiflora*, *Poa debilis*, *P. nemoralis*, *Eragrostis poœoides*, *Andropogon macrourus*, *Woodwardia Virginica*, *Ophioglossum vulgatum*, and many others.

A. Winchell. A collection of 151 species (63 specimens) of European plants.

H. S. Jewett, A. B. Limb naturally grafted into a crotch of the same tree.

M. W. Harrington. (1.) Forty species of seeds of wild plants from the vicinity of Ann Arbor.

(2.) Cone of *Pinus strobus* from Ile Royale.

Rev. A. P. Foster, Springfield, Mass. Fifty-seven species of dried plants new to the University. Obtained by exchange.

George H. Briggs, Vicksburg, Mich. Fruit of the Yellow Nelumbo (*Nelumbium luteum*)—erroneously reported the Egyptian Lotus—from Vicksburg, Kalamazoo county.

Mrs. Crosby. Seeds of an unknown plant from Cuba.

George O. Fry. (Alumnus.) Fungus of the Tribe Gasteromycetes, genus *Nidularia* (?) from Freeport, Ill.

Miss Mary H. Clark, Ann Arbor. Specimens of *Triticum dasystachium* from the Grand Traverse region.

Mrs. Rev. Seth Reed, Ann Arbor. Seed of "Shrub Palm," (probably the Fan Palm, *Corypha umbraculifera*) from Ceylon.

(2.) Spike of seeds of another Ceylonese (?) plant.

SUMMARIES.

(1.) Additions during the year, (approximate.)

Geological,	1163	entries,	2062	specimens.
Zoölogical,	1185	"	5358	"
Botanical,	1556	"	17845	"
Totals,	3904	"	25265	"

(2.) Grand aggregates (approximate). In 1863, and again in 1866, I presented approximate estimates of the total number of specimens in the Museum under my charge. To exhibit the continued growth of this Department, I submit the following comparative statement:

	GEOLOGY.		ZOÖLOGY.		BOTANY.	
	Entries.	*Specimens.*	*Entries.*	*Specimens.*	*Entries.*	*Specimens.*
1863	7,268	26,044	4,895	12.598	1,530	9,035
1866 *	10,318	32,562	6,318	15,261	3,447	15,629
1869	12,398	36,966	8,194	22,403	5,536	34,235

Grand Totals: Entries, 26,128. Specimens, 94,604.†

II. DEPARTMENT OF ARCHÆOLOGY AND RELICS.

Sixty entries of relics of the late war, have been labeled and placed on exhibition. The following additions have been made:

* The numbers for Botany, in 1866, as given, are less than originally reported, in consequence of a former over-estimate of one of the collections.

† It will be borne in mind that these numbers do not set forth the magnitude of the entire Museum; since they do not embrace the cabinet of Mineralogy, nor the specimens (even in Zoölogy and comparative Osteology) in the Museum of the Medical Departm ent,nor the specimens of the Art Collections.

Van Vechten Collection. About eight specimens from Alaska and California, besides the human remains already mentioned.

Mrs. S. E. Becraft, Ann Arbor. Two Indian arrowheads from southern Michigan.

REPORT

OF OPERATIONS IN THE

Museum of the University of Michigan

IN THE DEPARTMENT OF

GEOLOGY, ZOÖLOGY AND BOTANY,

AND THE DEPARTMENT OF

ARCHÆOLOGY AND ETHNOLOGY,

For the Sixteen Months ending January 14, 1873.

By ALEXANDER WINCHELL.
Professor of Geology, Zoölogy and Botany

ANN ARBOR, MICH.:
COURIER STEAM PRINTING HOUSE, MAIN ST.
1873.

REPORT

Of Operations in the Museum of the University of Michigan, in the Department of Geology, Zoology and Botany, and the Department of Archæology and Ethnology, for the sixteen months ending January 14, 1873.

BY ALEXANDER WINCHELL,
Professor of Geology, Zoölogy and Botany.

To the Honorable, the Board of Regents of the University of Michigan:

The Report which, in accordance with my custom of several years' standing, should have been submitted at your last September meeting, has been deferred to the present occasion, through a desire that the last Report which I shall have the honor to make in my present capacity, should extend the history of my connection with the Museum, to the last day of my connection with the University.

The principal accessions to the material of the Museum since my last Report, have been made through the labors of Alumnus J. B. Steere, in South America, and Assistant M. W. Harrington, in Alaska. Mr. Steere sailed from New York, September 17, 1870, for Para, Brazil, bearing the credentials of the University and of the Smithsonian Institution, with the view of making collections in geology, zoölogy, botany, archæology and ethnology, in the countries which he might visit. All the collections were to be sent directly to the University. Mr. Steere began his work immediately on landing at Para, visiting the numerous islands of the lower Amazon, especially in search of birds. By favorable stages, he continued his journey up the Amazon, collecting in the waters and upon the land, and exhuming from ancient mounds a large quantity of more or less broken pottery. He also collected articles of food and implements and utensils employed by the various native tribes, which he interested himself in visiting and studying; and by this means, and through the notes collected, furnished large facilities for extending our knowledge of the ethnology of the valley of the Amazon. At Pichana, Pebas, Old Pebas and other localities, he collected large quantities of the interesting fossils which, it is supposed, reflect much light on the geological age of the Amazonian deposits. Other geological specimens were collected at Yquitos and in the Andes. On the west side of the mountains, he has made very considerable collections of Peruvian antiquities, which have been shipped, but not yet received.

The specimens announced as sent, have all been received, except three boxes, and also three boxes were recently announced from Callao. The boxes overdue are as follows:

No. 12. Said to contain skins and skulls, bottles of alcoholic specimens, a monkey, a bag of cotton, specimens from shell-heaps, etc. Collected at Obidos, Brazil, and shipped Aug. 17, 1871, from Santarem.

No. 19. A tin trunk, said to contain ferns, lichens, clubmosses, and skins. Shipped December 10, 1871, from Manaos, Brazil, care of U. S. Consul A. Watrin, Para. It is possible that this package has been received, since we have what answers to the contents, but without anything properly called a "tin trunk."

No. 27. A small box of fossils ordered sent from Yquitos, Peru. Announced in letter of March 18, 1872.

We are under obligations to Mr. J. B. Gager, of 67 South street, New York, for the pains he has taken to hunt up these and other boxes held a long time in the various government storehouses, in New York. Mr. Gager is now regular consignee and forwarding agent for the University; and no similar detentions or losses are to be expected hereafter. Mr. Steere's shipments, for a year past, have gone to the care of Mr. Gager.

The specimens received are generally in excellent condition. Box No. 13, containing pottery from the mounds, had been opened (probably at the U. S. Custom House, New York,) and very shabbily repacked. The contents were much damaged.

The contents of Box 30 were nearly destroyed by water. It contained plants, butterflies and bird-skins. It was shipped May 30, 1872, from Tarapota, Peru, and was received in September. The shells, fossils and gypsum, in the same box, were, of course, uninjured.

The collection of bird-skins sent by Mr. Steere is large and fine. His numerous butterflies have arrived in excellent condition. All the alcoholic specimens were secure. The mosses and lichens are an interesting feature of his collections, as also the large assortment of Brazilian and Peruvian woods. I feel that it is but justice to an enthusiastic, indefatigable and intelligent collector, to bear testimony to the able and satisfactory manner in which he has executed the plans announced to us when he left with our credentials. I deem it a matter of general interest, and worthy of record, to state, also, that Mr. Steere has been a regular correspondent for the Ann Arbor *Courier*, to which he has contributed about 60 lengthy letters of great interest. These serve as an invaluable commentary upon the specimens, and it is to be hoped that their republication, in a permanent and accessible form, will secure for the "Steere Collections" those detailed histories and explanations so essential to a full interpretation of the specimens. It is indeed to be hoped that Mr. Steere, on his return, may find the University in a position to set him at work in the thorough elaboration of the results of his journeys, in one or more of the departments.

It ought to be stated that the principal part of Mr. Steere's expenses has been defrayed by Mr. R. A. Beal, of this city, and that means have been forwarded to enable the explorer to extend to New Zealand, Australia and the East Indies.

All the specimens received have been examined, registered, secured from damages by insects or mould, registered, and either placed upon the shelves of the Museum or carefully repacked. The following is a classified summary of specimens thus far received:

Summary of Steere Collection.

	SINCE LAST REPORT.
Total number of boxes received.......... 27	18
Total number announced................. 33	22

			SINCE LAST REPORT.	
	Entries.	Specimens.	Entries.	Specimens.
Mammalian specimens..	49	65	25	26
Ornithological " ...	450	642	241	273
Reptilian " ...	50	93	42	79
Fishes..................	47	179	46	178
Insects..................	225	978	172	870
Crustaceans.............	5	13	4	5
Shells..................	251	238	185	1582
Total Zoölogical......	1077	4351	715	3013
Total Botanical.......	229	822	166	559
Total Geological......	157	1283	139	1245
Archæ. and Ethnol....	203	265	181	231
Grand Totals.....	1666	6721	1201	5048

The original letters and lists of specimens will be found deposited among the papers of this Department; and all the requisite entries and detailed tabular statements have been recorded in the JOURNAL.

Assistant M. W. Harrington connected himself, in July, 1871, with a government expedition to Alaska, under command of Captain W. H. Dall, and has very recently returned to duty in the University. During his absence, his efforts for the Museum have been unremitting; and though his relations to the public service were such that comparatively few of his collections remained under his own control, the University has been made the recipient of many valuable specimens; and it is expected that others, through the favor of Captain Dall, will be received, after passing through the hands of the Smithsonian Institution. While in California, both on the outward trip and the return, he secured specimens in geology and botany; and, on the Aleutian islands, obtained rare examples, now very difficult to procure, of the products of native industry. Some of these, like the geological specimens from California, were purchased; while a few were presented by native Aleutians, on being informed of the nature of their destination.

A most interesting result of Assistant Harrington's expedition, is the introduction of a native and full-blooded Aleut boy, 15 years of age, into the surroundings of American civilization. This young man, contrary to prevalent impressions respecting his race, possesses a marked degree of intelligence, and voluntarily seeks expatriation for the purpose of securing the advantages of an education. This Aleut is an ethnological specimen of unique interest; and by the similarity of his physiognomy to that of the Japanese, confirms strikingly the opinion, long held by some, that our northwestern shores were peopled from the orient.

The following is a summary of specimens recently received from Assistant Harrington.

	Entries.	Specimens.
Geological..............................	87	92
Botanical, (estimated)................	150	250
Ethnological..........................	16	16

The ethnological specimens, though not numerous, are unusually fine and rare, as the detailed statement will show.

Lieutenant F. D Baldwin has forwarded the Museum a donation which deserves especial mention. It consists of the skeletons of three buffaloes from the vicinity of Fort Hays, Kansas—a bull, a cow, and a calf. Lieutenant Baldwin has also presented a specimen of the "Jackass Rabbit."

Principal S. N. Sanford, of Cleveland, Ohio, at the instance of Alumnus T. R. Chase, has presented a living Cashmere Goat; General

C. B. Comstock, Superintendent of the U. S. Lake Survey, has presented a set of specimens dredged in Lake Superior; and the Geological Survey has contributed 222 Type specimens from the Marquette Iron Region, collected by T. B. Brooks, Assistant, and A. Winchell, Director of the Survey.

Other contributions will be named in their order.

The work in the Laboratory attached to the Museum has been continued as heretofore. Much attention has, of course, been paid to the specimens of the Steere Collection, in cleaning, repairing, discriminating, securing, registering, assorting and repacking. Similar attentions have to be bestowed upon all other specimens; while those deposited upon the shelves of the Museum are by no means placed beyond the need of continued care and watchfulness. A limited number of students have occupied themselves in the Laboratory, under my direction, in studying certain classes of specimens from the Museum; but the facilities for study of this kind, it is hoped, will hereafter be improved. The principal courses of study pursued here since the last Report, are courses in Lithology, Conchology, Palæontology, Ornithology, Herpetology, and Microscopy. Lithology, hitherto a required study of the Senior Class, has been somewhat a specialty here, in consequence of extraordinary facilities for the collection of specimens. Every student is encouraged to secure a series of labeled rock-samples; and the last class in this subject has collected no less than 2,409, which have been authentically labeled, either in the class-room or the Laboratory.

The partial completion of the new building having vacated the suite of rooms hitherto occupied by the Steward in the Museum Building, the operations of the Museum will find needed relief by taking possession of them. This is a relief which I have long anticipated. I would respectfully propose that the west one of the two larger rooms be set apart as a working room for special students in this Department; and that the east one of the two smaller rooms be assigned to the accommodation of the botanical collections. I should hope that the latter might be furnished with the requisite cases, and the former with the requisite tables. Of the other two rooms, the larger, being the room into which the bell-rope descends, could not be advantageously used for a working or study room, but might be supplied with cases for the reception of a certain class of specimens—the bell-rope being boxed and secured by lock and key. The smaller room will be needed for a botanical store room.

The large room known as the "Old Chapel," being no longer needed for lectures in my Department, ought to be regarded as the natural extension of the Museum. I have long looked to this consummation, and the appropriation of this large apartment, on the first floor, to the accommodation of large specimens, like skeletons of the buffalo or elephant, and casts of the megatherium and other gigantic extinct quadrupeds. The ceiling should be cut away in a style uniform with the stories above.

The collections in the Department of Archæology and Ethnology are attaining very considerable magnitude and importance. The interest of the specimens sent by Mr. Steere from Brazil and Peru, can hardly be overestimated; and there is no doubt that many others will be received. I earnestly hope, in the interests of American science, and no less in the interests of the University, that opportunity will present itself for the proper study of all these specimens, and that a creditable volume may yet appear, under some auspices, in which ample justice shall be done to the collection, in descriptions, discussions and illustrations. For the present, our accommodations are insufficient for the display of most of the specimens. Some are, accordingly, shelved temporarily in the Palæontological Hall, and many more are repacked and stored away. If the present room is to be retained for the collections of this Department, two or three new cases ought to be constructed immediately.

It will be readily understood that the Steere Collection has furnished a large amount of work for the hands of a taxidermist, and every consideration prompts to the engagement of his services at as early a day as practicable. The three valuable skeletons of the American bison ought also to be mounted, and thus rendered educationally useful. In a communication placed in the hands of the President in June last, I suggested that the duties of taxidermist and custodian of the Museum might be fitly united in one person. His duties, to be performed under the direction of the Professor in charge, would be—

1. To prepare and mount all zoölogical specimens—including skins, skeletons, skulls and other preparations.

2. As far as possible, to clean and prepare palæontological specimens, and prepare and mount objects for microscopic study.

3. To watch the zoölogical and botanical specimens in the cases—killing insects, replenishing the jars of alcoholic specimens, removing dust, and giving such further attention as the security of the specimens demands.

4. To give instruction in taxidermy when required.

5. To act as custodian of the Museum in all its departments—opening and closing doors at designated hours; noting the conduct of

visitors, and preventing depredations; keeping the curtains closed when visitors are not in, and performing such other kindred service as might be required.

Such an appointment would also secure to the Department the performance of sundry small duties, like the bringing of wood and water, and the kindling of fires, which none of the present janitors regard as falling within their province. Without this provision, some other arrangement needs to be effected, which will secure the performance of such work in a prompt and cheerful manner.

I congratulate the University on the return of Assistant Harrington to duty. Familiar with all the details of the Department, and inspired with a true scientific ardor, I am sure that the opportunities of a few years will render him an ornament to science and an invaluable adjunct to the University. Mr. G. W. Allyn, a graduate of 1872, and a young man of uncommon zeal and industry, has rendered assistance during the present collegiate year, whose efficiency I am glad to acknowledge, with an expression of the hope that the University may continue to be favored with his services.

The following is a detailed statement of accessions to the Museum since the date of my last report:

I. GEOLOGY.

J. B. Steere, (Alumnus).

The aggregate of geological specimens sent from Brazil and Peru, S A., are as follows:

Fossils	77	entries	1068	specimens.
Rocks and Minerals	80	"	215	"
Totals	157	"	1283	"
Total since last report	136	"	1245	"

Many of the fossils from Pebas and vicinity are very small, and there is no doubt the literal aggregate of specimens would much exceed the above.

C. J. Kintner, (Alumnus).
Four fossils from the Cretaceous rocks of Texas.

John A. Talbott, Cassopolis, Mich.
Favosites Niagarensis, a fossil coral from the Drift.

M. Baker, (Alumnus).
Grammysia (n. sp.) Drift, Ann Arbor.

CHARLES N. FOX, San Francisco, Cal.

Two specimens of gold-bearing, and one of silver-bearing quartz.

DELOS MINER, Parma, Mich.

One specimen, Iron Pyrites and 10 specimens Bog Iron Ore.

M. W. HARRINGTON, (Alumnus and assistant).

Box of 78 entries and 95 specimens from California. Ores of gold, silver and copper and the associated rocks and minerals. Of these, 9 were presented by Capt. Mosher, one by George Lamb, and one by W. P. Lamb.

J. A. WOODS, ('72.)

Specimen of rare rock, Ann Arbor.

Prof. J. MONTGOMERY, (Alumnus) Woodstock, Ont.

One *Pentamerus oblongus*, Owen Sound, Lake Huron.

Prof. N. H. WINCHELL, (Alumnus).

Snowy Gypsum from the plaster beds of Ottawa Co., Ohio. Oriskany Sandstone from Otsego, Wood Co., Ohio.

Rev. GEORGE JUCHAN, Robbinston, Me.

Cretaceous fossils, apparently from Nebraska—8 entries, 11 specimens.

STATE GEOLOGICAL SURVEY.

222 type specimens from the Marquette Iron Regions, collected by Major T. B. Brooks under the directorship of A. Winchell. This 115 in addition to specimens heretofore reported.

C. H. WALKER, ('74, Detroit.)

Two specimens, Silver Ore, Silver Islet, L. Superior. 13 spec. veinstones from same locality.

O. C. JOHNSON, (Pharmacy class.)

Two hollow stalactites of pure carbonate of lime, from the cistern of the Chemical Laboratory.

A. H. PARTRIDGE, Ann Arbor.

Specimen of Bog Iron Ore, from South Lyons, Mich.

CAPT. E. B. WARD, Detroit.

2 specimens of ore from Silver Islet, L. Superior. Corundum and Mica from North Carolina. Galena from Missouri. Total, 5 specimens.

PROF. E. HAANEL, (Albion College.)

Plate of immature molar of *Elephus primigenius*, from Mt. Pleasant, Iowa.

J. W. PHELPS, ('72).

Fossil, from near Pontiac, Mich.

MILES RORABACHER, M. D., Smithfield, Mich.

Three bottles, different varieties, of mineral paint, at the instance of Rev. George Taylor, Ann Arbor.

E. P. HANNA, Student, Salina, Kan.

Fossil leaves from the Cretaceous, and shells from the Permian, of Kansas—28 entries, 90 specimens.

PROF. E. A. STRONG, Grand Rapids.

Upper Helderberg Fossils—15 entries, 32 specimens, from Onondaga county, N. Y.

I. C. KIBBEE, Chippawa Falls, Wis.

Kaolin—one entry, 5 specimens.

D. L. GRAVES, Proprietor, Mamouth Cave.

Box of specimens from Mammoth Cave—eight specimens foliaceous gypsum—one compound statactitic form. 2 entries, 9 specimens.

JAMES W. FRENCH, Toledo, O.

Shell marl from central Ohio.

G H. WHITE, Chicago.

Incrustation upon *outside* of tubing in oil well, West Va.

F. W. FARR, ('73).

Oolitic limestone from central Iowa.

G. W. ALLYN, ('72, assistant.)

Sixty specimens of uncommon rocks.

JOSEPH HARPER, Central City, Cal.

Rocks and ores of copper, silver and zinc, from the California Mine, Cal.—5 entries, 27 specimens—2 very large, of which one weighed 60 or 70 pounds.

F. S. DEWEY, ('72.)

Two entries, two specimens of fossil corals. Five lithological specimens. All from Ann Arbor.

Dr. T. J. SCOVELL.

Three Corniferous Brachiopods, Ann Arbor.

M. W. HARRINGTON, assistant.

Fossil wood, thirty feet beneath the prairie soil, Sycamore, Ill.

A. WINCHELL.

Fossil wood sixty feet beneath the surface, Ann Arbor.

II. ZOOLOGY.

J. B. Steere, (Alumnus.)

The following is a synopsis of the collections in zoology sent by Mr. Steere from South America:

	Entries.	Specimens.	SINCE LAST REP'T.	
			Entries	Specim.
Mammals. In alcohol..........	3	3	3	3
Skins...............	27	33	9	9
Skulls...............	10	24	13	14
Totol mammalian.........	49	64	25	26
Birds. Skins....	406	564	222	232
Skulls..................	22	27	10	11
Eggs.......	18	51	9	30
Nests	4	10	0	0
Total ornithological.......	450	642	241	273
Reptiles........................	50	93	42	79
Fishes	47	179	46	178
Insects..........	225	978	172	870
Crustaceans.................. .	5	13	4	5
Shells	251	2381	195	1585
Total zoölogical...........	1077	4351	713	3013

C. J. Kintner, (Alumnus.)
Walking stick (*Diaphemora femorata.*)

Lieut. Frank D. Baldwin, U. S. A.
Three complete skeletons of American bison—a bull, a cow and a calf.

Skin of Jackass Rabbit (*Lepus callotis.*) Fort Harker, Kan.

G. P. Voorheis, ('72, White Lake.)
Snowy Owl (*Nyctea nivea*), Oakland Co.

David L. Blackburn, Dundee.
Water Mole (*Scalops aquaticus*) mounted.

Gen. C. B. Comstock, U. S. Lake Survey.
Twenty-two entries, 40 specimens, drudged from the deep water of Lake Superior n August and September 1871. In alcohol.

Bryant Walker, student, Detroit.
Land and Fresh-water shells—27 entries, 73 specimens.

Rev. George Juchan, Robbinston, Me.
Skull of Dolphin (*Delphinus rostratus*).

Enes J. Warner, Little Cotton Wood, Utah.
Two Lage Hens (*Centrocercus urophasianus.*)

Principal S. N. Sanford, Cleveland, Ohio.
A living Cashmere Goat, since mounted.

Principal C. B. Thomas, (Alumnus) Battle Creek.
Palatal teeth—of Fish (?)

Marcus Baker, ('70)
Two eggs *Hirundo bicolor.*
One *Cicindela sexguttata.*

S. J. Harding, Owosso, Mich.
One Osprey (*Pandion Carolinensis*).

Volney Spaulding, '73, Ann Arbor.
One Shrew (*Sorex cooperi*) Ann Arbor.

Nelson B. Beers, Virginia, Cass Co., Ill.
Hair Ball from stomach of calf.

Max Ten Brook, Ann Arbor.
Cast of skin of snake.

A. Winchell.
Unionidæ from White River, Rockford, in southern Indiana.

III. BOTANY.

J. B. STEEBE, (Alumnus.)

The following is a summary of botanical specimens seceivad from South America :

	Entries	Specimens	SINCE LAST REP'T Entries.	SINCE LAST REP'T Specms.
Dried plants....................	120	336	63	263
Fruits..........................	9	379	..	..
Woods..........................	100	107	..	..
Total Botanical...........	229	822	166	559

The dried plants include many mosses and ferns. The wood-specimens are long enough for at least four samples each.

M. W. HARRINGTON, Assistant.
Dried plants from California—about 150 entries and 250 specimens.

C. J. KINTNER, (Alumnus.)
Receptacle and seeds of Nelumbo, (*Nelumbium luteum.*)

LEVI JOHNSON, Ann Arbor.
Curious malformation of an ear of Maize.

Dr. STEBBINS, California.
Fifteen samples of wood from California and Sandwich Islands—inlaid and polished.

J. C. JONES, ('72.)
Collection of Dried Plants, from north shore of Lake Superior—about 60 entries (species) and 120 specimens.

IV. ARCHÆOLOGY AND ETHNOLOGY.

J. B. STEERE, (Alumnus.)
The whole number of specimens in this department received to

his time from South America, is 203 entries, 265 specimens. Received since last report, 185 entries, 231 specimens.

M. W. Harrington, Assistant.
The following articles were received from Alaska :

1 *Parka* (outer garment) made of ducks' and divers' skins, and edged with hair-seal skin. Aleut, not common. Unalashka, Aleutian Islands.

1 Muskrat-skin *Parka*, with hood, edged with wolf-skin. Esquimaux, St. Michæl's.

1 Pair of *Torbassa* (boots) of reindeer skin. Indian, Nushagak river.

1 Wooden Eye-shade, used in hunting. Aleut, Unalashka.

1 Kamalayka (outer water-proof shirt) made of walrus-intestines, and sewed with whale sinew. Aleut, Unga, Shumagin Ids.

1 Larger Aleut harpoon ; bone-head, Unalashka.

3 Smaller ditto ; bone-heads, Unalashka.

1 Aleut harpoon; iron lance head. Unalashka. This is the killing spear.

1 Aleut harpoon ; glass-head, with wooden sheath. Whaling harpoon, Unalashka.

2 Casting-boards, for directing the harpoon and adding velocity to its flight. Aleut, Unalashka.

Models of the one, two- and three-oared Bidarkas or Kyaks (canoes) of the Aleuts. Made by the Aleuts at Unalashka.

Miss Elizabeth Allmendinger, Ann Arbor.
Specimen of bark from the stockades at Andersonville, S. C.

William Paul, Ann Arbor.
One flint Arrow-head.

SUMMARY OF ADDITIONS SINCE LAST REPORT.

Geological	508	entries.	1766	specimens.
Zoölogical	778	"	3144	"
Botanical	393	"	946	"
Archæological and Ethnological	202	"	249	"
Totals	1882	"	6105	

RETROSPECT.

In concluding this report it seems natural to indulge in a brief retrospective glance. It is now 19 years since I became actually connected with the University, and 18, since my first connection with the Department of Geology, Zoölogy and Botany. Within that time the greater part of the collections in this Department, has been acquired; and the Department of Archæology and Ethnology has first had an existence. At the time of my accession to this chair, the chief part of the collections appertaining to it, consisted of a series of the rocks of the State, collected by the geological survey under Dr. Houghton, and corresponding sets of the birds and plants of the State. None of these series are completed, though that of birds approaches the nearest to completion. No historical records of the museum were known to be in existence; but some information was preserved in tradition, and some was embraced in the proceedings of the Board of Trustees and Regents of the University. With my accession to the chair of Geology, Zoölogy and Botany, I attempted to gather these scraps of information together; and commenced the preservation of a system of historical records, which, from time to time, has been extended and perfected. In October, 1863, I presented a Report to the Board of Regents, in which I embodied all the important information extant, in reference to the sources of the materials of the museum, (I speak always of Geology, Zoölogy and Botany, alone) and included an analysis of its contents, as then existing. In September of each year since that date, I have posted up the history of the museum in a Report of Operations for the year preceding. I summarize, from these published records, the following list of chief sources of the materials of the Museum in every department.

Sources of the Materials in the Museum.

1838—45 collections of the State Survey under Dr. Houghton, consisting of lithological, mineralogical, zoölogical and botanical specimens (for details, see my report of 1863).

1855—"Monds Collection" purchased. Chiefly marine shells.

1859—"Trowbridge Collection" deposited. Donated in 1861. For analysis, see report, 1863. A catalogue was also published.

1859—60 collections of State Survey under A. Winchell, consisting chiefly of lithological and palæontological specimens; but including many fishes, and 278 species of plants not embraced in earlier collections.

1863—"White Collection" purchased. Mostly palæontological. For analysis see report 1863.

1864—Collection of osteological preparations presented by A. Winchell. Smithsonian Institution deposit of rocks and shells.

1865—Smithsonian Institution deposit of fossils from the Upper Missouri region.

1866—Collection of fossils made by Dr. Rominger under an appropriation by the Board.
Deposit of the "Rominger Collection" of European fossils. Afterward purchased by the Board.
Numerous additions to the collection of birds, and replacement of old specimens by J. T. Coleman, taxidermist.
Smithsonian Institution, deposit of marine shells.
W. J. Beal, marine imertebrates from the coast of New England, donated. To these Mr. Beal has added others at subsequent times.
"Sager Herbarium" donated.

1867—A. Winchell and students, collections resulting from an expedition to Lake Superior.
Smithsonian Institution. Ethnological specimens.

1868—A. E. Foot. Dried plants and other specimens from L. Superior.

1869—"Van Vechten Collection" purchased; chiefly geological, from California.
"Ford Collection" of shells purchased.
"Dr. Ames' Herbarium." Donated by the heirs.

1870—Smithsonian Institution deposit of British shells.
Dr. J. T. Scovell, zoölogical, botanical, and geological specimens, from Colorado.
Many old birds replaced by newly mounted specimens, by Mrs. S. E. Becraft, taxidermist.

1871—Commencement of reception of "Steere Collection" from South America.

1869-71—State Geological Survey, under direction of A. Winchell, furnished type-specimens from the iron and copper regions. All the other collections, for two years, remain in the University.
A. Winchell, collection from Sandy Hook, N. Y.
J. C. Jones, Dried plants from north shore of Lake Superior. Others donated in 1872.

1872—J. B. Steere. Large collections from South America, in all departments.

M. W. Harrington. Geological and botanical specimens from California, and ethnological from Alaska.

Lieut. T. D. Baldwin. Three complete skeletons of American Buffalo.

In the details of the foregoing additions will be found in my Annual Reports, together with lists of a large number of minor collections from the friends of the University.

The following table exhibits the progressive growth of the Museum:

DATES.	GEOLOGY.		ZOOLOGY.		BOTANY.		ARCHÆOLOGY.		GRAND TOTALS.	
	Entries	Specim.	Entries.	Specim.	Entries.	Specim.	Entries.	Specim.	Entries.	Specims.
1863	7,268	26,044	4,885	12,598	1,590	9,035			13,683	47,677
1866	10,318	33,562	6,319	15,261	3,447	15,504	50*	50*	20,133	66,377
1867	11,118	35,562	6,628	16,512	3,513	15,629	96	96	21,365	67,829
1868	11,235	35,884	6,982	17,000	3,980	16,165	110	112	22,307	66,161
1869	12,398	36,966	8,194	22,403	5,536	34,235	180	182	26,308	93,786
1870	12,623	37,396	8,897	23,952	5,828	34,660	204	216	27,582	96,224
1871	13,202	38,074	9,318	25,622	6,098	35,437	230	259	28,848	96,392
Jan. 1873	13,718	39,840	10,096	28,766	6,491	36,385	433	508	30,733	105,499

* Estimated for this. The "grand totals" given in my Annual Reports do not include specimens in Archæology and Ethnology. The totals in the above table embody corrections required by latest determations.

The foregoing totals for January 1873, are believed to furnish an unexaggerated statement of specimens now on the shelves of the Museum, or in a state of readiness to be placed there. In addition to these is a large accumulation of uninvestigated specimens, mostly geological, which have accrued from the public surveys of the State.

It will be remembered that the foregoing totals do not embrace the Mineralogical Collection, nor the Art Collection, nor the large collection in Comparative Osteology and other branches of Zoölogy, incorporated in the Museum of the Medical Department.

Notwithstanding the rapid development of the museums of other American colleges and universities, it is believed that only one surpasses our own, as yet, in the number of specimens. It must be confessed, however, that our own Museum is notably deficient, though, by no means wanting, in specimens difficult to obtain, whether domestic or foreign; and that a set of the larger casts of fossils manufactured by Professor H. A. Ward, of Rochester, is a desideratum of urgent importance. Respectfully submitted,

ALEXANDER WINCHELL,
Prof. Geol. Zoöl. and Bot.

JANUARY 14, 1873.

ADAMITES

—AND—

PREADAMITES.

—BY—

ALEXANDER WINCHELL, LL.D.

SYRACUSE, N. Y.:
JOHN T. ROBERTS.
1878.

Price, - - 15 Cents.

ADAMITES AND PREADAMITES.

The reader will please note the following corrections:

Page 5, 13th line from bottom, after "transgression" insert 2. "Transgression" is a violation of "law"; therefore, etc.

Page 16, 11th line from bottom, after "Pruner" *dele* comma.

"	"	10th	"	"	"	for "Bleck" read "Bleek."
"	"	9th	"	"	"	for "decended" read "descended."
"	"	4th	"	"	"	for "archipelego" read "archipelago."
"	18,	7th	"	"	"	for "*and*" read "and."
"	21,	17th	"	"	top	for "Botecuda" read "Botecudo."
"	22,	3d	"	"	"	for "Sidians" read "Sidonians.
"	24,	20th	"	"	"	for "suture" read "sutures."
"	38,	12th	"	"	"	for "has" read "have."
"	"	14th	"	"	"	for "600" read "900."
"	40,	18th	"	"	bottom,	for "glaciations" read "glaciation."

Adamites and Preadamites:

—OR—

A Popular Discussion

CONCERNING

The Remote Representatives of the Human Species and their Relation to the Biblical Adam.

—BY—

ALEXANDER WINCHELL, LL.D.,

Professor of Geology and Zoölogy in Syracuse University, and of Historical Geology and Zoölogy in the Vanderbilt University.

[Originally published in the *Northern Christian Advocate.*]

SYRACUSE, N. Y.:
JOHN T. ROBERTS.
1878.

PRINTED BY MASTERS & STONE,
SYRACUSE, N. Y.

Adamites and Preadamites.

CHAPTER I.

A SAGACIOUS DUTCHMAN.

In 1655 a small book appeared in Paris, which had for its title the unheard-of subject, "Pre-Adamites." It was written in Latin, and its full title was as follows: *Præ-Adamitæ, sive Exercitatio super Versibus duodecimo, decimo tertio et decimo quarto, capitis quinti Epistolæ D. Pauli ad Romanos, quibus inducuntur Primi Homines ante Adamum conditi.*" The book appeared anonymously; and those acquainted with the spirit of the dominant ecclesiasticism of that date will readily divine the motive of its author. It very soon became known, however, that it was written by La Peyrere, a Dutch ecclesiastic, whose name when Latinized was Peyrerius. The work was an attempt to prove from biblical authority that men must have lived on the earth before Adam. Within a year appeared its complement, from the pen of the same author, in which the whole subject was newly argued and more thoroughly discussed. This was a "Theological System based on the Hypothesis of Pre-Adamites." The two works may now occasionally be found in one volume. The Syracuse University possesses a copy.

The following year a book appeared in London, the title of which is a literal translation of that of "Præ-Adamitæ," but it includes also the "Systema Theologicum" of Peyrerius.

In the undeveloped stage of scientific inquiry existing two and a quarter centuries ago, it is certain that no investigation respecting Pre-Adamites could have been conducted on true anthropological principles. In Europe the Bible was the source and basis of all belief. Whatever the ecclesiastical authorities had accepted and sanctioned was held to be taught by the Bible. Whatever the ecclesiastical authorities did not understand the Bible to teach was denounced as heresy. The meaning of the Bible was extracted according to the canons of grammar. There are doctors high in authority amongst us at this day, who maintain that grammatical structure and Hebrew usage are sufficient to light the way to the meaning of the darkest passages of revelation. I suppose a knowledge of Hebrew history and usages is admitted to shed its light upon interpretation, because the text is generally occupied with Jewish affairs. But the inspired writers have sometimes plunged into the midst of the profound and mysterious facts of science; why not, then, summon *all our knowledge* to the task of evoking the meaning of the text? I maintain, against the narrow and pernicious dogma that the Bible is sufficient everywhere to interpret itself, that, on the contrary, it was ordained to be interpreted under the concentrated light of all the learning which has been created by a God-given intelligence in man. I believe that the Bible was written for all time, and that its meaning is so deep and so rich that the accumulated learning of the latest generation of men will be unable to exhaust it.

Not so the contemporaries of Peyrerius. Even where two or more different meanings of the text were equally grammatical and legitimate, that was held to be the true meaning which accorded best with current beliefs. An alternative interpretation, when once promulgated, was held to be divine truth, as absolute and authoritative as if no other interpretation were possible. Perhaps the well-established infallibility of the church had an interest in consistency. No matter if it concerned a fact of a purely scientific or secular character, the verdict was held as binding on the conscience as if the church had been in possession of all possible science.

According to the evidence till then available for the formation of opinion, it had been held that Adam was absolutely "the first being that could be called a man;" and that he was created in the possession of a culture such as we call enlightened. From time immemorial, biblical scholars had understood this to be the meaning of Genesis. It was, therefore, only on biblical grounds that Peyrerius based the new doctrine of Pre-Adamites. St. Paul was held to teach the existence of men before Adam, in the 12th, 13th and 14th verses of the 5th chapter of his epistle to the Romans, ("Wherefore, as by one man sin entered into the world," etc)

Now it is no part of my purpose to exhibit the scriptural argument on one side or the other. Many of my readers can do that better than I. My purpose is to bring forward certain scientific facts having a bearing on that question, and to leave exegesis to summon these important facts legitimately to its aid. But the writings of Peyrerius possess, in the present status of science, an extraordinary interest. He was the first to promulgate to the world the idea of Pre-Adamites. The first enunciator of the idea was prompted only by biblical considerations, and he has given at least an outline of the scriptural argument in support of the hypothesis. Few of my readers intelligently interested in a question deemed by some so fundamental in a theological system have access to the original work; and still fewer would have the patience to decipher, as I have done, the quaint old Latin text. I assume, then, that they will consider it a favor to be put in possession of the learned Dutchman's "points." They are as follows:

1. The "one man" (Romans v. 12,) by whom "sin entered into the world" was Adam; for, in v. 14, that sin is called "Adam's transgression"; therefore "the law" (v. 13) signifies the law given to Adam—natural law, not that given to Moses. 3. The phrase "until the law" (v. 13) implies a time before the law—that is, before Adam; and, as "sin was in the world" during that time, there must have been men in existence to commit sin. 4. The sin committed before the enactment of the natural law was "material," "actual;" the sin existing after Adam, and through him, was "imputed," "formal," "legal," "adventitious" and "after the similitude of Adam's transgression." 5. Death entered into the world before Adam; but it was because of the imputation "backwards" of Adam's prospective sin; and this was necessary, that all men might partake of the salvation provided in Christ. Nevertheless, death before Adam did not "reign." Death was robbed

of its sting. 6. Adam was the "first man" only in the same sense as Christ was the "second man;" for Adam "was the figure of Christ." (v. 14.) 7. All men are of one blood in the sense of one substance –one "matter." The Jews are descended from Adam; the Gentiles from Pre-Adamites. The first chapter of Genesis treats of the origin of the Gentiles; the second, of the origin of the Jews. The Gentiles were created aborigines, in the beginning, by the "word" of God, in all lands; Adam, the father of the Jews, was formed of "clay," by the "hand" of God. Genesis, after the first chapter, is a history, not of the first men, but of the first Jews. 8. The existence of Pre-Adamites is also indicated in the biblical account of Adam's family, especially of Cain, who found a wife amongst some older peoples, and went forth in fear of violence from strange hands. 9. The biblical doctrine is corroborated by the evidence afforded by the "monuments" of Egypt and Chaldea; and by the history of the astronomy, astrology, theology and magic of the Gentiles; as well as by the racial features of remote and savage tribes; and by those discoveries of fossil remains in the rocks, which were then recent events, but which have since become the foundation of the modern science of geology. 10. Hence the epoch of the creation of the world does not date from that "beginning" commonly figured in Adam, but "from a remoter beginning, which is to be sought in ages long since passed." 11. The deluge of Noah was not universal, and it destroyed only the Jews. Nor is it possible to trace to Noah the origins of all the races of men.

Some of these positions were far in advance of the age; and it is only just to say that they were defended with learning and ingenuity, and, best of all, with moderation and candor. But they were all "heretical." Peyrerius was, therefore, made a victim of the intolerance of the times. Numerous replies were thrown upon the world, in most of which, bitterness, contempt and denunciation were employed to supply all deficiencies of argument. Many of these I have been able, through the kindness of Mr. Spofford, Librarian to Congress, to examine in the Congressional Library. The most important, whose translated titles I here present, will serve to convey an idea of the temper of the age.

1. "No Pre-Adamite Being; or a Confutation of a certain emp-

ty dream, in which a certain anonymous author, under pretext of sacred Scripture, has lately attempted to impose on the incautious, pretending that men were in the world before Adam."

2. "Animadversions on the Book of Pre-Adamites, in which a late writer is confuted, and the doctrine is defended that Adam was the first of all men."

3. "Response to a treatise entitled Pre-Adamites."

The writers of these responses have, of course, employed strictly scriptural arguments, but they have brought to their aid the dialectic skill which characterized the scholastic theology, as well as the authority of the older writers and the dicta of councils and ecclesiastics.

Now, the whole controversy concerns a question of fact, and we are at this day in possession of many collateral lines of evidence to place by the side of old scriptural interpretation. We can summon ethnology, archæology and anthropology to bear witness. The truth seems to be that these witnesses are quite as competent to testify as witnesses need to be. It is their business to know all that is knowable about the matter. The answer to the question is a fact of science, sustaining fixed relations to the other facts patent before the eyes of the investigator. Whether the world has been populated by people who spread from Ararat forty-two centuries ago, or even from Mesopotamia fifty-nine centuries ago, is a question of fact, to be investigated strictly on the basis of scientific evidence. I think a great deal of evidence is now accessible, perhaps enough to lead us to a final conclusion. Whatever conclusions may be found to represent the truth, I believe our sacred records will be found in harmony.

CHAPTER II.

DISPERSION OF THE NOACHITES.

In discussing the question of Pre-Adamites from anthropological data, the first requisite is to trace the geographical dispersion of the descendants of Noah. The oldest document available for information on this subject is the Book of Genesis; and, aside from any claim to inspiration, its statements respecting the immediate posterity of Noah have been found so closely accordant with the observed facts, that ethnologists are content to adopt its information as a starting point. It is agreed, then, that the enlightened nations of the world belong to one race. This is the race of white men. By Blumenbach it was styled Caucasian, because our earliest knowledge of the race finds it in the region south of the Caucasus, and the dominant European family, which is the leading type of the race, is first discovered on the north and south of the Caucasus. But recent ethnologists designate the white race as "Mediterranean," because the three families which constitute it have always, since very early times, dwelt around the shores of the Mediterranean.

From the earliest history of this race, it has presented three family types. Since the dispersion of these three families accords with the biblical account of the dispersion of the posterity of the three sons of Noah, science has agreed to designate them Hamites, Semites and Japhetites. The last are more frequently known as Indo-Europeans or Aryans—names which associate the natives of India with the dominant European family.

Now, fortunately, we are able to indicate, with considerable certainty, the regions occupied by the three families of Noachites. The Hamites are known to have distributed themselves through the north of Africa, the Nile-valley, and the east of the continent as far as the straits of Bab-el-Mandeb. They passed from Asia Minor into the south-east of Europe as early as 2500 B. C., and occupied the peninsula of Greece under the name of Pelasgians. To this family belonged the Etruscans, who, at a later date, migrated from Greece and founded a kingdom in Italy, centuries before the building of Rome by another family. The Phœnicians were probably Hamites, instead of Semites. Unexpected and truly wonderful evidence of the common origin of these earliest Greeks, early Phœnicians and early Egyptians has been unearthed by Di Cesnola on the island of Cyprus, where pottery and works of art presenting Egyptian and Phœnician characteristics are mingled with conceptions characteristically Greek. Late researches have shown that the original Chaldean monarchy also (before the 18th century B. C.) was Hamitic and not Semitic, and its written language was Accadian, the parent of the cuneiform character. These are the views of the latest and best recognized authorities—Rawlinson, Lenormant, Oppert, Peschel, Jubainville. The Egyptians were certainly pure Hamites, and they are still represented by the Fellaheen, or peasantry of the lower Nile; and especially by the Coptic Christians of the towns. The Hamitic Berbers, including Libyans, Moors, Numidians and Gætulians are spread, intermingled with Semites and Europeans, through the countries of the Mediterranean, and through the Sahara. Other Hamitic nations, possessing a civilization far beyond that of any of the purely black races, occupy some of the regions about the Nile, especially in Nubia, and are scattered in distinct tribes, united by common linguistic elements, through Abyssinia, and in one direction as far as the heart of Africa, from eight degrees north to three degrees south, and in the other direction, from near Bab-el-Mandeb to Juba on the Indian ocean. The Hamitic dialects and Hamitic civilization, wherever they occur, are readily recognized as superior to any of the indigenous productions of the black races.

The antiquity of Hamitic civilization in Egypt is indicated by the recorded observations of the heliacal rising of the Dog Star. This is the rising of the Dog Star just before the sun, in the first *thoth* or month of the year. This is a conjunction which occurs only once in 1461 years We have a heliacal rising recorded for 1322 B. C. The period, or Sothis, ending at that date began 2782 B. C. As the observations must, apparently, have extended through at least one preceding sothic period, to enable them to know its length, the Egyptian observations must have begun as early as 4243 B. C. This is the opinion of Lepsius (*Chronologie der Aegypter* pt. I. p. 165 seq.) Some other respectable authorities—as Lane, Poole, Brown and Wilkinson—dissent from the inference of so high an antiquity for the first Egyptian dynasty. They maintain that the "era of Menes" reaches back no farther than 2717 B. C.; and some second-hand Egyptologists would bring it down to 2464 B. C. It is impossible to discern the logic, if we could discover the motive, for the prevalent desire to cut down the period of Egyptian civilization, since nearly all the original investigators agree in assigning to it a high antiquity. The most moderate of the German authorities places Menes at 3892 B. C.; and "in his time the Egyptians had long been architects, sculptors, painters, mythologists and theologians." Brugsch (in *Histoire d' Egypte*) has given a chronological canon, in accordance with which the reign of Menes would fall in the years 4455—4395, B. C., and this is in accord with Lepsius. (See also McClintock and Strong's *Cyclopedia*, and Hardwick's *Christ and other Masters*, p. 426, etc.) A similar result is obtained from very elaborate investigations respecting the rate of accumulation of Nilotic deposits. The question of Egyptian antiquity has no relevancy in this discussion; but we deem it a fact of interest that the posterity of Ham, first in the history of the human species, made a record of themselves capable of withstanding the ravages of all time. It is proper also to add that, in spite of English and American incredulity, all the recent archæological discoveries, whether in Egypt, in Assyria, at Hissarlik, Mycenæ or Cyprus, tend to prolong antiquity, and, so far as Egypt is concerned, to strengthen the authority of much suspected and much slighted Manetho. (See Bayard Taylor's *Egypt and Iceland*; Schliemann's *Ancient Troy*, and *Mycenæ*; Di Cesnola's *Cyprus*; George Smith's *Assyrian Excavations*.)

This is the whole of the geographical dispersion of the Hamites. The reader will note particularly that they have not spread over most parts of Africa. The Negroes are not regarded by modern ethnologists as the descendants of Ham.

Now let us follow the track of the Semites. From the earliest records, they have inhabited western Asia. Thence they have taken possession of parts of eastern Africa. They are represented by the Jews, Arabs, Abyssinians and Aramæans. They subjugated the Hamitic Babylonians and Chaldeans at a date earlier than the migration of Abraham from "Ur of the Chaldees." They adopted the Hamitic religion, which, in western Asia, was the worship of God under the names of Baal and Bel. They probably also conquered, and consolidated with themselves, the Phœnician people. They have migrated, to some extent, into eastern and northern-central Africa, and have familiarized the Negroes with a rude Moslem civilization. The facility with which they had intercourse with the Egyptians and affiliated with the primitive Babylonians and Chaldeans evinces their close affinity with the Hamites. The results, also, of linguistic study show that the Hamites and Semites developed their languages in a common primeval home. This is also taught in Genesis (chap. x, 1:15) where (Semitic) Sidon is described as the oldest son of Canaan, who was descended from Ham. This is the extent of the early migrations of the Semites. They have not escaped observation. They have been conspicuous actors in the historic world.

It only remains to follow the track of the Japhetites, Indo-Europeans or Aryans. When first known, they are national neighbors of the Asiatic Hamites and Semites. They dwelt along the slopes of the Caucasus, and through the gorge of Dariel, within reach of both the Euxine and the Caspian seas. According to some of the authorities, they dwelt nearer to central Asia. Their migrations were both southeastward and eastward. In the first direction, they passed over the Hindu Kush mountains, on the northwestern border of Hindustan, and settled in the region of the "Seven Rivers"—the modern Punjab. Here Brahmanism underwent its development and decline. The Vedas they had brought with them from central Asia. These had originated as early as 1400 to 2400 B. C. Moving still farther southward they isplaced an aboriginal population, and drove them to the hills, and to the extreme parts of the Indian peninsula. To this day, Hindustan is populated by the millions of descendants of the Asiatic branch of the Aryan family.

But while these eastward migrations were in progress, another branch of the Aryans moved toward Europe. According to some of the authorities, they passed through the gorge of Dariel into Europe; according to others, they moved along the eastern border of the Caspian Sea. According to all authorities, they appeared in Europe on the north of the Caucasus. Holding communication across the mountains with both Semites and Hamites, they received from them the excellencies of their civilization. From them were obtained wheat, rye and barley; and these cereals, together with the plough and the metals—gold, silver and bronze—they bore with them into central Europe, where they appeared about 2000 B. C.; reached the Adriatic (as Istrians,) and (as Venetes) founded the city of Venice (Venetia). They also held part of the Archipelago; and, as Phrygians, conquered parts of Asia Minor. The Ligurians (including Siculi) dispossessed the Iberians of most of western Europe, at about the same date, and in the time of Hesiod (850 B. C.) they held Gaul. In the sixth century B. C. they also held possession of Spain for eighty years.

Next is the Aryan group composed of the ancestors of the Hellenes, Italians and Kelts. The Hellenic Achæans were in the Peloponnesus in the 14th century B. C., according to Egyptian monuments. They came into Greece by following the eastern coast of the Adriatic southward. Hence they must probably be regarded as an offshoot of the Thracian group. Continuing eastward, they occupied the Ionian Islands. "By these were the isles of the Gentiles divided in their lands." Later they appeared in Thessaly, and in the 11th century B. C. they had returned to Asia and established settlements upon the coast of Asia Minor. The Ombro-Latins wrested most of Italy from the Ligurians, but were, in turn, subjugated by the Etruscans. Subsequently they regained possession. The Kelts or Gauls suddenly appeared along the valley of the upper Danube, driven, probably, by the Scythians, from the region of the Dnieper. In the 7th and 6th centuries B. C., they spread over Gaul, displacing the Ligurians, and passed to the British Islands, where, as Irish and Scotch, they have retained a foothold to this day. At the beginning of the 5th century B. C. they wrested a great part of Spain from the Phœnicians and their Iberian vassals. In the beginning of the 4th century B. C. they extended their authority over the north of Italy and other regions to the Danube and the Black Sea.

The third group belonging to the first Aryan migration into Europe consisted of Slavs and Germans. We first know them as subjects of the Scythians, about 400 B. C. The German stock became differentiated about 182 B. C. under the name of Bastarnians.

A second wave of Indo-Europeans swept from Asia across the European border about 1500 B. C. Under the name of Scythians they seized upon the country bordering on the Dnieper, expelling the Kelts who now proceeded on their conquest of Europe.

Such, in bold outline, is a sketch of Aryan migrations both eastward and westward. In the original site of this family the Iranians still maintain a foothold. From this centre the Brahmanic people spread over India. From this centre a succession of waves of migration tended toward Europe. The first of these we may designate the Thracian; the second, the Hellenic; the third, the Keltic; the fourth, the Scythian. Probably, however, the first three migrations were only ramifications of the first Asiatic invasion, while the Scythians made an independent invasion from Asia.

The facts here set forth are supplied by the very latest ethnological researches. (See Jubainville, *Les Premiers Habitans de l'Europe*, 1877, and Le Hon, *L'Homme Fossile*, 1877.) It is of interest to us to note that the Hindus are members of the same race, and of the same family of that race, as ourselves. They are possessed, then, of similar intellectual and moral characteristics. If we style them "heathen" we must remember that they are wise and thoughtful heathens, armed with science and philosophy far above our contempt.

As to the movements of the Aryan family since the Christian era, history is able to speak with a certain sound. No fragment of the family has escaped observation. It would not be possible to conceal itself in the remotest quarters of the world. The color of its skin would betray it. The tint and texture of its hair would reveal it. The very speech of the rudest peasant would proclaim it. The clang and tone of the Greek and the Sanscrit are in the speech of the most ignorant Suabian and the most servile Slav.

CHAPTER III.

THE BLACK RACES NOT ADAMITES.

We have traced the sons of Noah in all their wanderings over the earth. We have swept over Southern and Eastern Asia. We have pursued the swarms of men across the north and northeast of Africa. We have followed wave after wave over the Caucasus and over the Bosphorus; and have seen all Europe, save Northern Russia and Scandinavia, trod by the feet of Asiatic immigrants. "These are the families of the sons of Noah, after their generations in their nations."

But now we reach an interesting juncture in the progress of

our discussion. These Noachites everywhere found older people in possession of the land. Who were they? In central Asia they bordered on the Mongolians—who were they? On the south of the Hindu-Kush they drove before them, to the confines of the peninsula, the aboriginal Dravidians—who were they? In Greece, the Hamitic Pelasgians drove out the cave-dwelling Cyclopes—who were they? In Italy and Spain the Aryan Ligurians found and expelled the Iberians—who were they? Everywhere, Iberians, Ligurians, Achæans, Ombro-Latins, Kelts and Scythians found a people who dwelt in caves, used stone implements and clothed themselves in the skins of beasts—who were they?

These aborigines were everywhere people whom we cannot trace to the sons of Noah. Between Adam and Noah's flood was an interval of 1656 years. Could these unknown peoples have ramified from the stock of Adam during that interval? Let us look in their faces and see if we can detect any affinity with the recognized sons of Adam.

There, first, was the Dravidian race, dispossessed of the peninsula of India by the eastern branch of the Aryan family. They remain distinct to the present day, and their characteristics agree with the representations which have been made of them from time to time in the progress of history. Their skins are dark; their hair is black and curly; their lips are intumescent, but their jaws are *not* prognathous, like those of the Negroes. They still hold possession of a belt along the east coast of Hindustan, and even stretch far into the interior. They also retain a foothold upon the west coast, and linger in Beloochistan. The northern half of Ceylon is also the seat of a numerous Dravidian population. One of their languages is the Tamul or Tamil, spoken by ten millions of people, and the repository of an ancient literature of surprising richness. These people are *not* the descendants of Noah. We may assume, however, that they are not so divergent from the types of the Noachian race as to preclude the admission that they may be descended from the same Adam. Let us grant that they may be Adamites.

What shall we say of the Mongoloids? This vast race, forming two-thirds the population of the globe, spreads over all eastern and northern Asia and Arctic Europe. It possesses the Japanese islands, and many other islands of Polynesia. The

Chinese and Tartars and Malays belong here, as well as the Siberian tribes, and the Finns and Lapps of Europe. The fierce Huns were of this race; and so, with more or less of intermixture, are the modern Magyars and Turks. More than this, the aborigines of America are Mongoloids—not less the civilized Peruvians and Aztecs than the Chippeways, Iroquois and other North American tribes, and the Aleuts and Eskimo of the extreme north. The Mongoloids encircle the globe. They belt it without interruption, in the frozen latitudes; and the Mongoloid Malays penetrate the tropics of Polynesia, while Mongoloid Americans range through all the zones. No race, save the Mediterranean, has ever had a dispersion at all comparable. Can these be cousins of the Noachites, and brethren of the Dravida? Are these the sons of Adam? The dusky Dravida could not well disown relationship, on the score of complexion, with the dusky Malay. But the Dravidian's curly hair reveals little affinity with the straight, coarse hair of the Mongoloid; and the latter's high cheek bones and generally obliquely set eyes wedge the races apart so far that we feel a little incredulity respecting the claim that the antediluvian period of less than two thousand years could have marked them with such disparity, while the two thousand years of our acquaintance with the two races has witnessed no sensible divergence. Could 1656 years differentiate three races, while the next 4225 years have not increased the number? Must the Mongoloids be admitted as Adamites? Since we have provisionally let in the dusky Dravida, let us also admit provisionally the dusky Mongoloids, and then ascertain what results.

The Negroes are about to cause us trouble. The Negroes have made us a great deal of trouble. The whole group of black races recedes from the white and dusky races. These tropical ebonites are now regarded as comprising four races. The three families of Noachites constitute still, after a lapse of more than four thousand years, but a single race. Compare with this fact the differentiation of black men into four properly characterized races, and we have at once a fact bearing on the antiquity of the black races. These races are (1) Negroes, (2) Hottentots and Bushmen, (3) Papuans, (4) Australians. Besides their black skins, they all have narrow heads (*dolicho-cephalous*—a term which means long heads, but they are only relatively long, because so thin) and projecting jaws (*prognathous*). They possess long thigh-bones, and sometimes, also long arms. The shanks are lean, the pelvis is obliquely set, and the secondary sexual characters are deficient. The Negroes are further distinguished by short, crisped hair, each fibre of which is flattened, like the fibre of wool. The beard is almost wanting, the lips are thick, the fore-head is retreating, the nose flattened. But why describe the Negro? The home of the Negro is all Africa from the southern border of the Sahara to the country of the Hottentots and Bushmen—except some portions on the extreme east which have been possessed by the Hamites, as before stated. The northern tribes are the Soudan Negroes, and embrace numerous peoples speaking many different languages and dialects, and stretching quite to the interior of the continent. The southern tribes are the Bantus, and embrace the Zanzibar and Mozambique nations, and the well known Betchuans and Kaffirs connected with the missionary labors of Livingstone and Moffat.

All the southern portion of the African continent belongs to the Hottentots and Bushmen. They have a leathery brown skin, which becomes greatly wrinkled with age; and their hair is peculiarly matted in tufts. This does not result from ignorance of combs and brushes. The Hottentots—or Koi-Koin, as they call themselves—have sometimes been placed at the foot of the anthropological scale; but this is unjust, as they have very distinct religious ideas, know how to work iron, and possess a language so complete, and marked by such affinities with the Egyptian, that many investigators—Moffat, Lepsius, Pruner, Bey, Max Muller, Whitney and Bleck—have turned our thoughts to the inquiry, whether the Egyptians and the Hottentots have decended from a common stock since the development of language, or have simply lived in contact with each other at some former period.

We turn now to the Papuans and Australians. The former inhabit New Guinea and the other islands of Micronesia, including the Fiji archipelego. Their matted and tufted hair stands out wildly from their heads in shaggy crowns six or eight inches in height. The beard is abundant, and the skin ranges from dark chocolate color to blue-black. The jaws are less projecting than in the Negro, and the nose, instead of being flat, is broad and straight, and sometimes even aquiline. In intelligence, they range from the besotted fetish-worshipers of New Guinea, to the semi-civilized Fijians.

The Australians are so named from the vast island, which, with Tasmania and small contiguous islands, is their exclusive home. Their whole body is thickly hairy. The hair of the head is matted and shaggy, but less spreading than that of the Papuans. Their language is well developed, and the use of the boomerang is another proof of their intellectual capacity. So is their system of religious beliefs and practices. But they use no metallic implements, and their boats are mere logs, which may be regarded as the initial point in the evolution of naval structures.

These four constitute the Black races. We have to consider whether they, too, are descendants of the same Adam as the White and Dusky races. Let us begin with the purely linguistic method, which refuses to invoke collateral aids according to any consistent system, for eliciting the meaning of Scriptural language. Adam is a word which signifies *red.* The man thus designated must have had at least some infusion of red in his complexion. We can readily discover this tint in the skin of the white man. Before the invention of clothing, the summer sun upon the plains of central Asia must have developed in the white man's skin a very visible amount of ruddiness. It is admitted on all hands that the Adam of the Bible was the progenitor of the White race. But now, can the same term be applied to those races which I have designated "Dusky"? The Bible gives no distinct account of the genealogy of these races showing that their progenitor was "red." It is only popular opinion which traces them, with all other men, to the white man's Adam. But as we have assumed that they may, on anthropological principles, be admitted as Adamites, so we may admit that the term "Adam" is capable of sufficient stretching to cover the dusky Mongoloids and Dravida. Is it now thought the word will bear still a farther stretch? My private judgment forbids. I can discover some red in the complexion of the Mediterranean stock, and even in that of the Mongolian and Dravidian; but when you tell me that the Negro has a color which the old Hebrew would have called "red," I feel myself very ignorant of the meaning of terms.

Anthropologically, color possesses less significance than the meaning of the term Adam. It is confessedly one of the less constant characteristics of race. But the strict interpretation of Scripture is very often insisted on, and in this case I would like to pin the strict constructionists to their chosen method; because the strict construction, as will be shown, is the one which corresponds with the entire range of facts.

CHAPTER IV.

THE NEGRO PREADAMIC.

In the attempt to ascertain whether the biblical Adam was the progenitor of all mankind, or only of the White and Dusky races, I pointed out the fact that literal interpretation renders the name Adam inapplicable to races whose complexion displays no noticeable tinge of "red." But in the attempt to make Adam the father of the Black races, I find myself beset by other and graver difficulties. The Adam of Genesis is supposed to date from an epoch less than two thousand years before Noah. There have been almost six thousand years for the posterity of Adam to attain their present amount of divergence, as exemplified in different families and races of man. This has not perceptibly increased since the Christian era. I suppose all will admit, on the evidence of history and monuments, that the Semitic, Hamitic and Aryan features were not perceptibly less marked two thousand years ago than at present. If any one doubts this, he can be easily satisfied by turning over the pages of any work illustrated from the monuments of Egypt and Assyria. (For accessible American digests, see Nott and Gliddon's *Types of Mankind and Indigenous Races of the Earth.*) Better, let him visit the Assyrian and Egyptian departments of the Louvre and the British and Berlin Museums. It is equally true that delineations of Negro features, executed at a date not less remote, are exactly as pronounced as the realities of to-day. Now, I think we may fairly take 2,000 years as the measure of 4,000. If these races and families have not sensibly diverged in 2,000 years, will the reader believe that all the marked divergence which actually exists took place during the previous 4,000 years?

But the negative argument is much stronger. The Egyptian and Assyrian monuments which testify to the distinctness of races and families date back one or two thousand years farther than our era. In these sculptures and mural paintings the stately Semite with his aquiline nose is instantly distinguished from the nimble Hamite with his straight nose, full lips and oblique and languishing eyes. Amongst the other figures the Negro is often discovered by his thick lips, projecting jaws and wooly hair. For at least half of the recognized interval between Adam and us, the Negro has been a Negro; the Hamite, a Hamite; the Semite, a Semite. Archæology and ethnology, therefore, force this alternative conclusion upon us: If human beings have existed but 6,000 years, then the different races had *separate beginnings*, as Agassiz long since maintained—each race in its own geographical area. But if all human beings are descended from one stock, then the starting point was *more than* 6,000 *years back;* as Huxley and the evolutionists generally maintain; and the Duke of Argyll and other anti-evolutionists equally maintain. Accordingly, if the reader insist that Adam was absolutely the first creature which could be called a man, he must admit first that "red," in Hebrew, means "black," and secondly, that the biblical chronology between Adam and Noah omits at least nine-tenths of the time. In such an admission, he will have the excellent company of the Duke of Argyll, (*Primeval Man*).

Now, every person remains free to contemn a logical difficulty, and commiserate the unfortunate facts for being opposed to his belief. But my training has been such that logic and facts still command a degree of respect. Nor am I enough of an actor to play the part of an idiot. If I can avoid a difficulty I shall not dash out my brains against it. Let us consider Adam the father of the White and Dusky races. These, then, are Adamites; and have a chronology extending back about 6,000 years—perhaps all the time we require. The Black races, then, are preadamites; and there is no objection to allowing all the time requisite for their divergence from some common stock. This view recognizes the unity of man; the possession of "one blood" by all the races, one moral and intellectual nature, and one destiny; it recognizes Adam as the progenitor of the nations which form the theme of biblical history; it explains sundry biblical allusions and implications—for instance, the wife found by Cain in the land of Nod; Cain's fear of violence from others when condemned to the life of a "fugitive and a vagabond;" the antithesis of the "sons of God" and the "daughters of men;" it validates the biblical chronology; it satisfies the demands of facts. The only objection outstanding against this view is the authority of an opinion formed two or three thousand years ago, by men who also held the opinion that witches ride broomsticks through the air, and that the stars were created two days before Adam, though some of them are so distant that their light has been a hundred thousand years in reaching us.

Now, let us take up another set of considerations. The Adam of our race is generally regarded, I believe, as a man with natural endowments as good as our own. At least, I shall claim so much for him. His immediate posterity developed all the intelligence and moral characteristics which could be expected of modern men similarly situated, and having absolutely everything to learn. If the same Adam must be regarded the progenitor of the Black races, then these races represent a wide-spread degeneracy, which is not only vast and appalling, but must be pronounced eminently improbable. Now, degeneracy of tribes and fragments of tribes is a phenomenon quite familiar in anthropology. It has taken place where the oppression of superior tribes has driven the weaker into the midst of conditions unfriendly to existence. The Spaniards crushed the spirit out of the Peruvians and the Aztecs. The miserable Fuegians are crowded to the dripping and stormy and inhospitable shores of Cape Horn, where nature begrudges man a stick of fuel, and a crab's claw is a thanksgiving feast. The timid Andamaners are the persecuted remnant of a race driven to the shelters of the mountains, and tormented by the penal colony which England has planted on their lands. The Dyaks of Borneo, skulking in the mountains and jungles of the interior, are despised by the superior border tribes of their own race, and denied a rightful place in the ranks of humanity. Some of the Congo tribes which inhabit the pestilential regions of the west coast of Africa have been degenerated to the last degree. Only the most sluggish natures escape the fatal infection of miasm; and, hence, only the most brutish survive to perpetuate their race. By a process of natural selection, the law of progress is reversed. The law of *progress*, I say, for it is a *real* law of the organic world. Should it be claimed that the white man's Adam had descended from a common stock with the Negro, all nature cries out in assent. But should it be affirmed that the Negro is degenerated from the white man's Adam, every fact in nature shakes its head in denial. The Black man is too numerous. The affirmation would establish a law of retrogression. Progression, I say, is the law. The Black man on the healthful and fertile plateaux of central Africa is not oppressed by miasm, nor starvation, nor cruel neighbors. He is free to roam where he will—like the Digger Indian of North America, or the driveling Botecuda of Brazil. No, these savages exist in a normal condition; they are coming up instead of going down. Their Adam was farther from our Adam than they are. Their long thigh bones, and lean shanks, and projecting jaws are inheritances of a lower, rather than a higher ancestry.

CHAPTER V.

THE NEGRO PREADAMIC,—*Continued.*

The conclusion that the Black races are preadamic is opposed, so far as I know, only on the three following grounds:

I. *The Negroes are supposed to be the descendants of Ham.* This has been the traditional opinion of the Church, and hence of mankind at large. I doubt whether the Church would reach the opinion if the question were now first opened in the light of present knowledge. But because the Church and mankind in general have so long held the opinion, cautious conservatism is reluctant to let go its hold. The opinion, really, is not worthy of scientific consideration. I may summarize the objections to it. 1. Scripture does not sustain the affirmation. 2. We discover the posterity of Ham in the population of Mizraim (Egypt;) and in the compatriots of Nimrod, the son of Cush, the founder of Babel and the other Accadian cities; and in the compatriots of Asshur "who builded Nineveh;" and the compatriots of the Sidians who were descended from Canaan, the son of Ham. This is the plain teaching of Genesis, and there is no space for the assumption that the Negroes represent Ham's posterity. The consequences of Noah's curse upon Canaan must be traced out in some other direction. (See M'Causland, *Adam and the Adamites* and *The Builders of Babel.*) 3. The best ethnological authorities oppose the view. (See especially Rawlinson, *Herodotus* and *Historical Evidences.* Also M'Causland, as above. Dr. Whedon has expressed an inclination to agree with M'Causland. See *Methodist Quarterly Review*, Jan., 1871, p. 153 and July, 1872, p. 526.) 4. The view is opposed by the facts of archæology. The monuments of Egypt display the Negro in a state of complete differentiation at a period little later than the Deluge (2348 B. C.) The absurdity of supposing that this had been accomplished in 1,500 or 2,000 years is glaring. 5. The view opposes the universal law of progression as I have already explained. 6. It does not account for the other Black races—Australians and Papuans. Whose sons are they?

II. *The ethnological list given in Genesis is not complete.* Well, if this is granted, it must tend to help the Negro to an Adamic ancestor in one of two ways: 1. It may mean that the several patriarchs named had other posterity than that mentioned; but this would not help the theory, for *time* is what the case needs, not more brothers and cousins. 2. It may mean that some of the generations are omitted, and hence those mentioned do not cover all the time. Whether such omissions exist, Biblical scholars must decide. Extended time would provide for the whole amount of the race divergences existing a thousand years before Christ. But yet two difficulties would remain. These are the *color* of Adam's skin and the *degeneracy* of the Negro. This leads me, then, to the third objection.

III. *The Negro is not inferior to the white man.* To this I have to reply: 1. If, when the sun is shining brightly, a man tells me it is dark, I can only pronounce him blind. The inferiority of the Negro is a fact everywhere patent. I imply here only inferiority of intelligence, the instrument of self-helpfulness and of all civilization. I need not argue the fact; *circumspice.* But when this inferiority is conceded, we always hear the appeal to "unfavorable conditions." This leads me to note, 2. The African continent has always been *favorably* conditioned. In the first place, it had a land connection with Asia and the seats of ancient civilization. It even had a remote civilization planted within its own borders; and the fires of Egyptian civilization have never been extinct; while for two thousand years the enlightenment of Europe has been within accessible distance. In the second place, the salubrity of the climate, the fertility of the soil, the vast hydrographic system of lakes and rivers, have all conspired to give the interior of the continent natural conditions unsurpassed by those of the site of any civilization which ever existed. Thirdly, the indigenous productions of Africa have supplied other conditions of human advancement. There exist two native cereals, Negro millet and Kaffir corn, which supply material for bread. There are the edible "bread-roots" and also "earth-nuts," which are adequate to supply the daily food of whole villages. As to fruit trees, there are the doom-palm, the oil-palm and the "butter tree." Moreover, for thousands of years the way has been open as wide as the continent for the introduction of the cereals of Asia. In fact, they have long been known to the natives; and maize, the manioc root and sugar cane, as well as wheat and barley, have spread far toward the interior. There, too, have been domesticated animals, received, probably, from the Egyptians in a domesticated state; but no native animal has ever been domesticated. The Aryans of India employed the elephant as a beast of burden; but the African elephant was never utilized. These are not the conditions under which a whole race could be crushed into a process of degeneracy. 3. Comparison with other races shows the Negro's inferiority. The Egyptian civilization was reared on the African continent by the side of the barbarous Negro, and under the same conditions. If the materials of civilization were introduced from Asia, it was certainly easier for the Negro to introduce them from Egypt. America is not naturally superior in its physical conditions to Africa. Its only cereal is maize. Its principal edible roots are the mandioca and the potato; and the feeble llama and vicuna are the only native animals capable of domestication as beasts of burden. Yet the civilization of the Nahuatl nations of Mexico, the Quiches of Central America, the Mayas of Yucatan and the Aymaras and Quichuas of Peru, had become, both in respect to intellectual and industrial advances, and judicial, moral and religious conceptions, almost a stage of true enlightenment. The glaring fact of Negro inferiority in respect to social conditions cannot be explained by any appeal to adverse conditions. Such are the ethnological facts and the co-ordinated circumstances. But in proof of my position I make another point.

5. The anatomical structure of the Negro is inferior. The lean shanks, the prognathous profile, the long arms (which do not always exist) the black skin, the elongated and oblique pelvis—these are *all* characteristics in which, so far as the Negro diverges from the White man, he approximates the African apes. The skull also is inferior in structure and in capacity, and in the relative expansion of its different regions. Among Whites, the relative abundance of "cross-heads" (having permanently unclosed the longitudinal and transverse suture on the top of the head) is one in seven; among Mongolians, it is one in thirteen; among Negroes it is one in fifty-two. This peculiarity is supposed by some to favor the prolonged development of the brain. In any event, it is most frequent in the highest races. Again, the prevailing form of the Negro head is dolichocephalous; that of civilized races is mesocephalous and brachycephalous. That is, it lacks the breadth which we find associated with executive ability. The broadest Negro skull does not reach the average of the Germans nor does the best Australian skull, let me add, reach the average of the Negro. Finally, the capacity of the Negro cranium is inferior. Assuming 100 as the average capacity of the Australian skull, that of the Negro is 111.6 and that of the Teuton 124.8. Now, no fact is better established than the general relation of intellect to weight of brain. Welker has shown that the brains of 26 men of high intellectual rank surpassed the average weight by 14 per cent. Of course, quality of brain is an equally important factor; and hence not a few men with brains even below the average have distinguished themselves for scholarship.

But this does not abolish the rule; nor does it prove that the racial inferiority of the Negro brain, in respect to size, is not to be taken as an index of racial inferiority in respect to intelligence and the capacity for civilization; and this all the more since the quality of the Negro brain is also inferior.

I am not responsible for the inferiority of the Negro. I am responsible if I ignore the facts. I am culpable if I hold him to the same standard as the White man. My appeals to him must be of a widely different character from my appeals to the Aryan Hindu, or the Mongoloid American savage. The ethnological facts have their application in all missionary efforts.

Nor must these statements be set down to the Negro's demerit. If it would help my argument, I could point out the excellencies and capacities of Negro natures, and would take pleasure in doing so. But this would be irrelevant. I have indicated the proofs of the Negro's physical, intellecual and social *inferiority*. I have insisted on the high improbability of a *degeneracy* from the grade of Adamic races to that of the actual Negro; and finally I have maintained that if a complete racial degeneracy were admissible, the *time* between the biblical Adam and the date of ancient monuments depicting the fully developed Negro, is palpably insufficient for the racial divergence.

CHAPTER VI.

SCHEME OF PREHISTORIC TIMES.

In previous chapters, I have indicated reasons for holding that the black races are probably preadamic. I have no doubt that some who have paid these pages the compliment of an attentive perusal have felt a little discomforted at the announcement of such a conclusion. Such views, they think, are calculated to disorganize belief—old and hitherto unassailed belief. Such a result may not be an unmitigated evil. The disorganization of an old belief may be wholly advantageous. Some beliefs need to be disorganized. Built like rude log cabins, in a primeval period, they ought to be taken down as soon as we are able to build better. I have a reverence for old beliefs; but I think they ought to be preserved as relics. What has become of the primitive shanty in this City of Salt? Did anybody refuse to pull it down because it was old? I venture the assertion that the spirit of the age has not even preserved it as a relic. For the old shanties of opinion, which have been a refuge for the ignorance of the past, I have a sentimental regard; but I am not willing to continue to skulk beneath them, when I see the stars through all the roof, and find the sills eaten up by rats.

Allow me to indicate the superstructure of a modern belief, and, therefore, a belief better co-ordinated with the present conditions of human knowledge. Do not think me laying corner stones; they have been laid by Moses; they have been laid by Champollion, and Lepsius, and Sir William Jones, and the Rawlinsons, and Haug, and Max Müller, and George Smith; they have been laid by philologists and archæologists and ethnologists; by zoölogists and geologists, and by interpreters of our sacred histories. I build on such foundations, and the reader shall see if the new edifice is not fairer than the old.

It was many thousand years ago that the first being appeared which could be called a man. Whether descended from a being unworthy to be called a man, is a collateral question which rests on other foundations. We shall return to it. That first of all men did not make his advent in Asia, nor in Europe, nor in America. He appeared either in Africa or in a continental land which stretched from Madagascar to the East Indies; and which has since become reduced to a few relics of itself. His skin was probably black, and well clothed with hair. He had implanted within him the divine spark of intelligence. He listened to the voice of conscience and felt the claims of duty. If not indigenous in Africa, his descendants took possession of that continent. They spread over Australia and Borneo and the lesser islands of the sea. In the course of thousands of years, they disseminated themselves over considerable portions of Asia.

The time arrived, at length, when, under the law of progressive development, a grade had been reached nearly on a level with that of modern civilized man, in respect to native capacities. Now appeared the founder of the Adamic family. His home was in central Asia. Seth and Cain were either his sons, or nations descended from him. He had also "other sons and daughters" in the same sense. The Sethites and Cainites and the other tribes of Adam, as they spread themselves eastward, displaced and at length exterminated the Preadamites of Asia. They overran the peninsula of Hindustan and extended themselves into Ceylon. Under the influences of climate, and other physical conditions, they diverged from the Adamic aspect, and became Dravidians. The northern or Mongolian (also called Turanian) stream of Adamites was more prolific, and more inspired by the spirit of emigration. Continuing eastward till arrested by the Pacific, the stream divided. The southern branch swarmed over the Malayan peninsula and islands, and dispossessed the Preadamites of many of the islands of Polynesia. The northern branch moved toward Behring's Straits. Here a portion of them passed over the isthmus which then connected Asia and America, and in the course of thousands of years extended to Greenland and Cape Horn. Another portion of the northern branch was reflected westward, and followed the northern slope of the continent into Europe, and overran all Europe.

Meantime a great deluge occurred in western Asia. Whole populations were destroyed. The Adamites who had remained near the original seat of the family were swept out of existence. The vacated regions of western Asia were, for a time, occupied by the wandering Mongoloids. But the descendants of Noah crowded upon them. The Mongoloids, though numerous, were inferior. They passed through the isthmus of Suez, before the settlement of the Hamites in Egypt, and ranged along the south coast of the Mediterranean, crowding the aborigines into the desert. At the Straits of Gibraltar, they crossed over into Spain. The straits were then an isthmus. But they found another outlet. The fabled Atlantis, of which the tradition has been preserved by Plato and Theopompus, has been discovered At least, we have found the remnants of it. It lay along the present bed of the Atlantic from the Bay of Biscay to the mouth of the Niger. The Maderia islands and the Canaries are surviving vestiges of Atlantis. Its worn stump has been traced by the soundings of American and British explorers; and the outlines of the obliterated continent have recently been mapped in a scientific publication. (*Nature*, March 1, 1877.) In Atlantis was reared a Mongolian monarchy. Its armies, according to the tradition said by Plato to have been preserved in a poem by Solon, marched eastward and subjugated all the region south of the Mediterranean, as far as Egypt. The valley of the Nile had, by this time, been populated by Hamites, and they successfully resisted the encroachments of the Atlantideans. This was during the reigns of Cecrops, 1582 B. C., and Erechtheus, 1409 B. C.,—dates preserved by the marble of Paros.

Subsequently the Hamitic Egyptians encroached upon the Mongolian territory south of the Mediterranean, and at an early period displaced the Mongoloids from this region and from the continent of Atlantis.

In the course of time Atlantis was swallowed up by the sea. Whether sunken by an earthquake shock or slowly gnawed down by the waves, is matter for conjecture. A relic of the ancient population, the Guanches, survived until recently upon the Canaries—the only islands in the Atlantic ocean which were found occupied by an aboriginal people. Ethnologists regard them as belonging to the Berber branch of Hamites.

According to the evidence of skulls, the troglodytes of Europe were Mongoloids. They were the earliest population of the continent. I suppose they descended from that reflected stream of Mongoloids who impinged against the shores of the Pacific ocean in their eastward movement, and recrossed Asia along the northern boundary of the region held by the Noachites. When they took possession of Europe, the continental glacier was just dissolving. The rivers were flooded with the melting snows. England was joined to the continent. The hairy elephant was ranging over Southern Europe. The two-horned rhinoceros wallowed in the marshes of France. The cave-bear was tenanted in the caverns of the mountains, and the voice of the cave-lion reverberated through the aisles of the primeval forest. This primative European was purely barbarous. He usurped the caverns for his abode. He fashioned stones into implements of warfare and set himself about the extermination of the wild beasts. His more civilized cousins of the Atlantidean branch of his race made an early invasion into south-western Europe. Known to history as Iberians, they took possession of the Spanish peninsula and extended their conquests over Italy, Gaul, Sardinia, Corsica and the British Islands. The Iberians, in turn, were dispossessed by immigrations, first, of Hamitic Pelasgians, and, afterward, of Aryan Illyrians and Ligurians. In our times, all that remains of them is the little nation of Basques in the north of Spain and the south of France; while the troglodyte stone folk have retreated along the track of the retreating glaciers, to the borders of the Arctic ocean and are represented in Europe by the Mongolian Finns and Lapps.

This scheme of prehistoric times, embracing only a few conjectural features, weaves in all the facts of history and science. If it traverses old opinions, we need not mourn. New truths are better than old errors. Fact is worth more than opinion. Certainty is more desirable than confidence. Progressive knowledge implies much unlearning. The loss of a belief, like the death of a friend, seems a bereavement; but a false belief is only an enemy in a friend's cloak. It is only truth which is divine; and, if we embrace an error, we shall not find it ratified in the oracles of divine truth. We who hold to the valid inspiration of the sacred records may feel assured that nothing will be found affirmed therein which collides with the final verdict of intelligence. Nor has the color of the first man any concern with a simple religious faith. If our creed embodies a dogma which enunciates what is really a conclusion, true or false, based on scientific evidence—that is, evidence brought to light by observation and research—that may be exscinded as an excrescence. All such subjects are to be settled by scientific investigation—not by councils of the church. Ecclesiastical faith has had a sorry experience in the attempt to sanctify popular opinions. A faith that has had to surrender the geocentric theory and the denial of antipodes, and of the high geological antiquity of the world, should have learned to discriminate between religious faiths and scientific opinions. Religious faith is more enduring than granite. Scientific opinion is uncertain; it may endure like granite, or vanish like a summer cloud. Religious faith is simple, pure and incorruptible; scientific opinion is a compound of all things corruptible and incorruptible. Let us not adulterate pure faith with corruptible science. An unadulterated faith can be defended by the sturdiest blows of reason and logic; a corrupt faith puts reason and logic to shame.

CHAPTER VII.

RETROSPECT OF PRIMEVAL MAN IN EUROPE.

According to authentic ethnological evidence, the earliest men in Europe were not Noachites. The descendants of the three sons of Noah, in the progress of their dispersion, found older peoples in possession of Europe, and drove them out. The earliest Noachites known to have settled on that continent were of the family of Hamites. These were subsequently displaced by Aryans. (See second chapter.) The primitive tribes encroached upon by Hamitic immigration were, we have good reason to believe, Mongoloids. (See fifth chapter.) These I have assumed to be Adamites. The primitive Mongoloids seem, at one time, to have spread over the entire continent. Indeed, according to the general positions of this discussion, the Mongoloids and Dravida held possession of the greater part, if not the whole, of Asia, in antediluvian times, and even for some ages subsequently. That some uniform race of men populated the Orient from India to Great Britain, in remote prehistoric times, is evinced by the similarity of the monuments left behind in all the intervening countries. I refer especially to tumuli and huge stone structures of a certain style. That these widely distributed monuments were erected by peoples of antediluvian origin, is proven by the fact that the posterity of Noah, wherever they went, found these monuments already in existence. That these antediluvian people were Mongoloids, is shown: 1. By the forms of some of their skulls and the stature and porportions of their skeletons. 2. By the Mongoloid character of the Samoyedes, Lapps and Finns, who are regarded as the remnants of the primitive population displaced by the families of Noachites. The Basques, another remnant, are not definitely recognized as Mongolian.

What was the condition of those remotely prehistoric peoples? Modern researches have been wonderfully prolific in materials illustrating the physical, intellectual, social, moral and religious status of the earliest inhabitants of Europe; and the developments of investigation in Asia, as far as pursued, are entirely in accord. Indeed, it may be said that the prehistoric antiquities of America present so many resemblances that archæology confirms the verdict of ethnology, which assigns the aborigines of America to a Mongolian origin in Asia.

The chief sources of information respecting prehistoric man in Europe are, in addition to the traditions preserved in ancient history, the remains of man found in caverns, river drifts, alluvial deposits, volcanic tuff, peat bogs, kitchen middens, tumuli and megaliths, and, finally, the ancient lake dwellings.

Whether primitive men dwelt to any extent in houses of their own construction, it appears, both from history and archæology, that caverns everywhere have served as human shelters. Nor do they seem to have been temporary refuges; for immense quantities of human remains frequently occur in them, imbedded in successive layers of earth, broken stones and stalagmitic material, to the depth of ten or twenty feet. These remains consist chiefly of stone and bone implements. Sometimes ashes and cinders remain; and in front of the celebrated rock shelter of Aurignac are the relics of an ancient stone hearth, on which was cooked the food which probably served as a funeral repast; for within the cave, which had been closed by a large stone, were uncovered the remains of seventeen human beings. It is seldom that the bones of men occur in the caverns, but the bones of the cave-bear, hyena and lion, as also those of the reindeer, ox, mammoth, rhinoceros and other animals, are often abundant. No metal seems to have been known to the cave-dwellers.

Other human relics, as ancient as the earliest occupation of the caverns, are found imbedded in the gravel and sand which line certain river valleys in France and England. These deposits were at first supposed to be Glacial or even Tertiary in age; but it is now admitted that they were formed by the rivers which occupy the valleys, at a time when they flowed at levels thirty to fifty feet higher than at present. It is a doctrine of geology that this stage of the rivers existed at the time when the continental glaciers were melting. The human relics obtained from these gravels are chiefly articles of rough stone and bone. With these are associated some remains of extinct quadrupeds. Some alluvial deposits near Strasburg, and at Maestricht and elsewhere, have afforded rude flints and human bones. In the volcanic mountain of Denise, in Central France, human bones have been found imbedded in volcanic tuff; and in another locality tuff resulting from the same eruption encloses the remains of a cave-hyena and a hippopotamus.

Again the peat-bogs of Denmark have afforded a rich series of relics chronologically arranged. These bogs are from ten to thirty feet deep. In the lowest portions they enclose remains of the scotch fir, a tree no longer growing in Denmark; and with these are associated implements of flint. Above are found traces of the common oak, now very rare in Denmark, and, associated therewith, implements and ornaments of bronze, as well as stone. But in the highest portions of the peat are found the remains of the beechen forest now living, and mingled with these are relics of an age of iron. The bogs of Ireland have been correspondingly productive.

The kitchen-middens, or kitchen refuse heaps, are piles of earth and human relics occurring along the shores of Denmark, reaching sometimes a height of ten feet, with a breadth of 200 and a length of 1,000. They are largely made up of the shells of the oyster, cockle and other edible molluscs, but these are plentifully mingled with the bones of various quadrupeds, birds and fishes, which have served as food. Interspersed with these offal accumulations are flint knives, hatchets and other instruments of stone, horn, wood and bone, with fragments of coarse pottery. No traces of bronze or iron occur. Such refuse heaps lie upon the shores of many other countries, and have been described in America, from Florida to Maine.

The megaliths or huge roughly hewn blocks of stone, arranged in rude structures, abound in nearly all the countries of Europe. Those called "dolmens" are enormous slabs resting horizontally on upright stones. "Menhirs" are huge stone posts, sometimes standing singly, and sometimes surrounding a dolmen, when they constitue what is called a "cromlech." The "dolmens" were for centuries regarded as the stone altars of the ancient

Druids; but we now know that they were as mysterious to the Druids, two thousand years ago, as to ourselves. Sometimes the dolmen is covered by a mound of earth. That these were burial places is proved by the occurrence of skeletons in some of them. In certain tumulus-dolmens, the crypt inclosed by the stones is divided into several compartments, each enclosing a skeleton. The associated implements are mostly of stone.

The lake dwellings were cabins erected on piles in the lakes of Switzerland and other European countries. Relics of everything connected with the life of the lake-dwellers were, as a matter of course, accumulated in the bottom of the lake around them. In recent times, these have been discovered and dredged up. They consist of such remains as have already been enumerated, with the addition of articles of bronze. They, hence, belonged to a later age. In certain lakes artificial islands were formed of stones and timbers, on which huts were built. In Ireland these are called "crannoges," and are now deeply covered with turf.

The interpretation of these human relics is, of course, greatly helped by the study of modern savages, and the accounts of ancient history. The flint arrow-heads of the American Indian, for instance, are fashioned precisely like some of those found in European caverns and lake-habitations. To understand the ancient lake-dwellings, recall the account by Herodotus of an ancient tribe dwelling in Pæonia, now a part of Roumelia, who erected cabins on piles; and also the narrative by D'Urville of the lake-dwellers of New Guinea. As illustrations of the kitchen-middens, we may turn to the shell-heaps on the north-west coast of Australia, and the city border offal heaps of Guayaquil and Mexico. In India some of the tribes still erect cromlechs. Early historic times also reflect a light on the pre-historic ages. "Jacob took a stone and set it up for a pillar," (Gen. xxxi, 45; see, further, ver. 46–52,) and at Mount Sinai Moses erected twelve pillars—menhirs, (Exod. xxiv, 4; Josh. iv, 21-22.) In connection with tumuli, it may be remembered that Semiramis raised a mound over her husband; stones were piled up over the remains of Laicus; Achilles raised to Patroclus a mound more than 100 feet in diamter; Alexander erected one over the ashes of Hephæstio which cost $1,200,000; and in Roman history we meet with similar instances. So, finally, the small bronze chariot exhumed from a tumulus in Mecklenburg recalls the wheeled structures fabricated for Solomon by Hiram of Tyre. (I. Kings, vii, 27–37.)

From time immemorial, civilized nations have recognized three ages in the history of society—the stone, bronze and iron ages. Archæology justifies this belief. In the stone age, the metals were unknown; in the bronze age, bronze displaced stone to some extent; and in the iron age, iron came into use for cutting instruments. While these are the successive stages in the social development of peoples, they by no means serve as chronological landmarks for mankind at large; since different tribes and nations and races have passed out of their stone age at very different epochs, and many tribes still remain in their stone age. Researches have shown that the stone age must be sub-divided into three epochs:—the Palæolithic or Rude Stone Epoch, the Reindeer Epoch and the Neolithic or Polished Stone Epoch. In the first, human skill was very little developed, and man lived as contemporary with the mammoth, cave-bear, cave-hyena and other extinct quadrupeds, whose bones occur in caverns and river-drifts. In the Reindeer Epoch, human works were of a higher order; the animals just mentioned had chiefly disappeared, and the bones of the reindeer are most abundantly associated with human relics. In the Neolithic Epoch, stone weapons and implements were ground and polished, and some domestic animals had made their appearance.

The physical conditions of Europe on the first advent of the Stone Folk were strikingly different from the present. The continent was then just emerging from a secular winter which had buried all the mountains and plains beneath a mantle of glacier material as far south, probably, as the Pyrenees. England and Scandinavia had been connected with the continent; the English channel and the German ocean had been dry land, and the Thames had been a tributary of the Rhine. A subsidence now took place which made Great Britain an island. An amelioration of the climate caused a rapid melting of the glaciers; the land was extensively flooded and the drainage of the continent now began to mark out and to excavate the river valleys of the modern epoch. The cave-bear, mammoth and other quadrupeds of Pliocene time still survived; and now man appeared in Europe to dispute with them the possession of the forests and caverns. Now the swollen rivers flowed many feet above their present levels, and the relics of the Stone Folk were mingled with the deposits along their borders. The Reindeer Epoch witnessed another elevation and a new invasion of cold. England was again joined to the continent. The cave-bear and mammoth dwindled away. The reindeer and other northern quadrupeds were driven south over the plains of Languedoc and through the valleys of Perigord. The hyena went over to England and took possession of the caverns. But the men of Europe had made a slight advance in the industries. Next, another subsidence resulted in the isolation of England and the Scandinavian peninsula; the climate was again ameliorated, and the reindeer and other Arctic species retreated to Alpine elevations and northern latitudes. Now the modern aspects of the land began to appear, and now appeared various species of mammals destined to domestication—or, more probably, already domesticated in their oriental home. The ages of bronze, iron and authentic history succeeded.

It would, of course, be interesting to trace the physical, intellectual and moral characteristics of these primitive people in the light of the facts whose sources I have pointed out; but a brief article does not furnish the opportunity. A few words must suffice. *Physically* these people were of rather short stature, with roundish heads, and of a Mongoloid type, like modern Finns and Lapps. In the Neolithic epoch, they were not decidedly divergent from the Mediterranean race, while some of the skulls were equal in capacity to those of the very highest modern families. The Neanderthal skull, famous for its low forehead and massive brows, has a capacity of seventy-five cubic inches; and the Cro-Magnon skull a capacity of ninety-seven cubic inches *Socially* and *intellectually*, Palæolithic man existed in the rudest condition, ignorant even of the use of fire. In the Reindeer Epoch, he produced a better style of pottery, and was acquainted with fire. In the Neolithic Epoch cereals were cultivated and ground into flour; cloth was woven; bone combs were used; stores of fruit were preserved for winter's use; garden-tools were fashioned from stags' horns; log canoes were employed in navigation, and many other indications have been discovered of a fair inventive capacity and an extensive system of industries, even while yet every tool had to be constructed of stone, bone or stag's horn. *Esthetically* considered, the oldest Stone Folk had advanced no farther than the use of necklaces formed of shell beads. Some obscure etchings on stones exist. In the Reindeer Epoch, articles of ornament became decidedly abundant. *Religiously*, there is little to be affirmed or inferred of the Palæolithic tribes. Some curiously wrought flints may have served as religious emblems; and the occasional discovery of deposits of food near the body of the dead may very naturally be regarded as evidence of a belief in the future life. In the Reindeer Epoch, this class of evidences becomes very greatly augmented, as shown in the systematic and carefully provided burials in some of the tumulus-dolmens, and in the traces of funeral repasts in these and the rock-shelters of Aurignac, Bruniquel and Furfooz. The numerous specimens of bright and shining minerals found about many settlements may have been used as amulets, and may thus testify to the vague sense of the supernatural, which characterizes the infancy of human society. The Neolithic people add to such indications the erection of megalithic structures, some of which, surrounded by their cemeteries, as at Amesbury, England, must naturally be considered as their sacred temples.

Pre-historic man, in brief, represented, in Europe, the infancy of the human species. All his powers were undeveloped and uneducated. Every evidence sustains us in the conclusion that he was not inferior in psychic endowments to the average man of the highest races; but he was lacking in acquired skill, and in the results of experience accumulated through a long series of generations, and preserved from forgetfulness by the blessings of a written language.

This glance at the scientific facts bearing on the condition and physical relations of primeval man in Europe opens the way for a more intelligible discussion of the antiquity of the race at large.

CHAPTER VIII.

ANTIQUITY OF MAN.

The antiquity of the human species has generally been discussed from a point of view which I hold to be erroneous. It has almost always been assumed that when we have ascertained the antiquity of the oldest historic nations—the Egyptians and the Chinese—or, according to more recent views, of the Stone Folk of Europe, we have ascertained the antiquity of the human species. But, if the Black races are not descended from the progenitor of the White and Mongoloid races, these races are descended from the progenitor of the Black races, and possess an antiquity very much less than that of the Black races. The question, therefore, of the antiquity of the White race is quite different from that of the antiquity of the human species. The white man may have begun to exist six or eight thousand years ago; but the black man, I have reason to think, was thousands of years his predecessor upon the earth. The white man may have made his advent in central Asia; but the black man first appeared in Africa, or, more probably, upon an obliterated continent, of which the Mascarene Islands on the southeast of Africa are a surviving vestige. The first white man may have descended from a remote progenitor of black color; but the first black man could not have descended from a white progenitor.

The search for the antiquity of the human species is, therefore, a search for the antiquity of the Black races. That search must be instituted in the regions which the Black races have occupied—Africa, Australia and obliterated continental lands. These races have left no records, no monuments; and hence the search must become a purely geological one. This task is one which has never been undertaken; but it is one from which science will not shrink; and I anticipate that somewhere in the caverns of Abyssinia, or south Africa, or Australia, or in some of the stratified formations of those countries, we shall discover evidences of the existence of man at a date prior to the general glaciation of Europe and the United States.

For the present, however, we are compelled to restrict ourselves to an inquiry respecting the epoch of the oldest historic nations, and of the prehistoric Stone Folk of Europe. Of the validity of Chinese and Egyptian historic claims to a high antiquity I shall express no opinion. I dissent emphatically, however, from the position entertained by some recent archæologists, that the Stone Folk of Europe carry us back fifty or a hundred thousand years, or even that their antiquity is greater than that of the oldest historic nations. The opinion seems to me wild and fanatical. The obscurity which hangs over the Stone Folk is mistakenly ascribed to remoteness. Like objects seen in a fog, the events of the Stone Age are not so remote as they seem. The latest pile-habitations come down to the sixth century In many instances, the *debris* from the lacustrine villages has yielded Roman coins and other works of Roman art. Homer's epic was composed but 600 years before our era, and the Stone Folk were then in full possession of central and northern Europe.

History declares that among the Lapps and Finns the Stone Age descended to the time of Cæsar. The civilized Pelasgians entered Greece 1400 years before Homer and found the Stone Folk there. We have, then, at least twenty-five centuries of historical time for the duration of the Stone Age. I see no good ground for the opinion that the primeval men of Europe appeared more than 2500 or 3000 years before Christ. But, as a contrary opinion is sometimes expressed, I will proceed to state the grounds on which I understand it to be based, and then offer my reasons for the rejection of these grounds.

I. *Pre-glacial remains of other animals have been mistaken for human remains.* I refer to remains older than the continental glacier of Europe. Some bones found at Saint Prest, France, were observed to bear cuts and scratches which might have been made by flint instruments in human hands. But with them were associated the remains of a species of elephant, known to have lived in later Pliocene time. Hence the mercurial Frenchman made proclamation of *Pliocene man.* But actual experiment proved that precisely similar markings are made upon bones by the porcupine; and as a rodent left his bones in the same bed with the cut and scratched bones, cooler reason promptly ascribed the markings to rodent agency rather than human. Again, certain shell-marks near Bordeaux enclose the bones of a manatee, which bear marks similarly ascribed to human agency. But the manatee lived in the Miocene period; therefore the Frenchman now proclaimed *Miocene man*. Unfortunately a fierce, carnivorous fish lived in the same waters, and was buried in the same cemetery, and his sharply serrated teeth exactly fit the markings on the scratched bones of the manatee. Tertiary man vanishes again. Finally at Thenay, again in France, some flints are found in lower Miocene limestone, which were at first pronounced the work of human hands. But bushels of similar flints may be picked up on any sea-beach of the chalk districts.

II. *Human remains erroneously supposed pre-glacial.* A human skeleton found in volcanic tuff at Le Puy-en-Velay, in central France, was associated with the bones of an elephant known to belong in Pliocene time. *Pliocene man* was again proclaimed, when, alas, some one showed that the elephant-bearing tuff was an *older* eruption than that bearing human bones, while the latter contained in fact the bones of another elephant—the well-known mammoth, which lived *after* the reign of ice. Again, the river drifts of the Somme were set down by the French geologists as pre-glacial or glacial in origin; and hence the flints which they enclose belonged to Tertiary man. The cooler heads of English geologists detected the fallacy, and pointed out several localities where it appears that even the valley of the Somme was not excavated till after the glacial drift was laid down; and the flint gravels are of still later date. In 1856 a human skull and numerous bones of the same skeleton were exhumed from the Calle del Vento in Liguria, and published to the world as "*l'uomo pliocenico;*" but no scientific observer saw the bones in place, and the best anthropologists now declare that the remains are not pliocene. A few years ago a sensation was created by the discovery of a human pelvis at Natchez, Mississippi, in a deposit of undoubted pre-glacial age. This, like all similar finds, filled the newspapers with sensational paragraphs calculated for the discomfiture of old opinions. But Sir Charles Lyell showed that the pelvis had in all probability fallen down from an Indian grave at the top of the bluff. So, from being a relic of pre-glacial man, it suddenly became the pelvis of a modern Cherokee, perhaps a hundred and fifty years old. The human remains of California, reported to be found under a sheet of Tertiary lava, are not sufficiently authenticated to form a subject of profitable discussion.

And this is all. These are the only evidences on which the claims of pre-glacial man in Europe have rested. But if he was post-glacial, what measure of years may express his antiquity? This is equivalent to asking the remoteness of the decline of the glacial epoch, which the Stone Folk certainly witnessed. The following are the grounds of the opinion, current to some extent, that fifty or a hundred thousand years separate us from the men who saw the decline of the continental glaciers.

I. *The astronomical hypothesis of glacial periods.* Recent astronomers have suggested that the glacial period was only the last of a succession, and that changes in astronomical conditions must produce such periods with calculable regularity. M. Adhemar has argued that the northern temperate zone must be glaciated once in 21,000 years by the influence of the precession of the equinoxes. Thus, the secular winter might be supposed to have passed about 10,500 years ago. But Mr. Croll, discrediting Adhemar, appeals to variations in eccentricity of the earth's orbit, and puts down 80,000 years as the time elapsed since maximum eccentricity led to continental glaciations. Accordingly, we might put the decline of the glaciers at 50,000 years ago, and this would indicate the antiquity of the Stone Folk. But I hold that archæology vetoes such a conclusion.

II. *Contemporaneousness of man with animals now extinct.* Geology once taught that all extinctions are remote in time; and hence, when man was found a contemporary with the mammoth and the cave bear, he was held to possess a high antiquity. But geology was mistaken. Extinctions have been recent. Extinctions are in progress. Continued extinctions are the order of nature. The Maories of New Zealand still retain traditions of the extinct gigantic birds of their islands. In Madagascar, the Dodo has lived within 250 years; but it is now extinct, like the solitaire and the Æpyornis. The huge *Rhytina gigas* has become extinct; as also the whale of the Bay of Biscay, which was once the basis of a flourishing industry. Other species are plainly approaching extinction. The Great Auk of Newfoundland has been seen but once in fifty years; and the Labrador Duck, ten years ago so abundant in the Fulton market, New York, has suddenly disappeared, and museums are bidding in vain for relics of the lost species. The Aurochs of Europe, abundant in Cæsar's time, is now saved from extinction only by the care of the Prussian government. The big trees of California will have no successors. In short, every species of animal which cannot occupy the continent with civilized man is clearly doomed to pass away. So extinctions continue, even in recent times, to be the order of nature.

III. *The magnitude of the geological changes since man's advent.* When we say that man was witness of the disappearance of the continental glacier in Europe, or learn that since his advent England and Scandinavia have been joined to the continent, and the North Sea has been dry land, and the Thames a tributary of the Rhine, we seem to sink back into geological time, where anything less than a hundred thousand years for man would be a ridiculous demand. So, too, when we learn that Mongoloid man came to America over an isthmus existing where Behring's Straits now are, and floated his canoe on the waters of a great lake, which spread over the prairie-region of Illinois.

But I believe, on sober reflection, that our imaginations have been excited. The mystery and the magnitude of geological changes seem to relegate them to the remote ages of convulsion and cataclysm. Let us not be frightened. We are in the midst of great changes, and are scarcely conscious of it. We have seen worlds in flames, and have felt a comet strike the earth. We have seen the whole coast of South America lifted up bodily ten or fifteen feet, and let down again in an hour. We have seen the Andes sink 220 feet in seventy years. We are pointed to vast hydrographical changes in China within historic times. As to the glaciers, they are still shrinking. Before our human eyes proceeds that retreat which has left its foot-prints all the way across the valley of Switzerland. We may still gaze on the ancient glaciers. We may still see them at their work. The Stone Folk are drawn down toward our own times. We look over the abyss of years and seize it in our apprehension. They saw the borders of the ice-field perhaps on the Rhine; we see them in Russia, and Siberia, and Greenland. And in our own country their presence has been so recent that their stumps linger in the gulches of the Sierra Nevada; and huge masses remain undissolved in the ice-wells of Vermont, New York and Wisconsin. The truth is we are not so far out of the dust and smoke of antiquity as we had supposed. Antiquity is at our doors. Multitudes of facts might be cited which must tend to convince us that changes are in progress before our eyes, which must accomplish in a few thousand years results as great as those which separate the Stone Folk from us.

But how many years express the interval? This is the point on which it is not safe to be too precise. I can enumerate a dozen of the highest authorities in prehistoric archæology, who bring the epoch of polished stone down to within four to six thousand years of our time; and I could cite historical mention and historical data to show that the Stone Folk were known from a date 4000 or 5000 B. C., when the Iberians found them, down to 3000 or 3500 B. C., when the Iberian Libyans made war on Egypt, and thence down to 2000 B. C., when the Stone Folk were found in Sicily and Peloponnesus.

The Stone Folk had lived somewhere at an earlier epoch. Their Asiatic progenitors were more ancient. If descended from the white man's Adam, he must be removed somewhat further back than we have supposed. If Adam, however, is a divergent twig from the same stock as the Stone Folk, then the Stone Folk may have been in Europe even before our Adam appeared in Asia.

CHAPTER IX.

ORIGIN OF MAN.

The recognition of the descent from one stock, of types of structure as diverse as the European and the Australian, prompts at once an inquiry respecting the extent to which divergencies may have been carried. Whether the Negro has descended from the white man's Adam, or the Caucasian from the black man's Adam, there is implied a degree of physical divergence which is very suggestive of reflection. The more we insist on the blood affinity of the races of man, the more we crowd upon attention the query whether a blood affinity may not exist between the lowest race and some type of being a little too low to be called human.

The different races of men bear zoölogically such characteristics as would be employed to distinguish different species amongst the lower animals. I have heard the elder Agassiz declare that they differ as much as the different families of monkeys. Family distinctions are more profound than specific distinctions. If the various races of men are descended from a common stock, have we not as good grounds for assuming that the domestic dog, the prairie-dog, the wolf, the fox and the jackal are also descended from one stock? If parity of reasoning demands an affirmative response to this question, then the barriers are all down to admission of the derivative origin of organic forms in general. Now, while not affirming a parity of reasoning, it seems appropriate to state the grounds of derivative doctrine, preparatory to pointing out a disparity of an important kind. The general doctrine of the material continuity of organic forms seems to me to rest on the following classes of evidence:

I. *Analogical evidence.* Evolution is a law of thought, and hence a law of activity regulated by thought. An idea or concept is first grasped in its general character, then developed in detail. This is the method of the evolution of a sermon or a book. The longer thought dwells on the concept, the more there is evolved from it, under its general and subordinate divisions. This, however, is rather psychological than analogical evidence. But appropriate proof under this head is at hand. The method in the cosmos is a material continuity. Our earth has been what Jupiter is, and has been annulated like Saturn. It has been a sun, self-luminous; it is destined to become, as the moon, a fossil world. So our sun and all suns are in the midst of a progress of an identical kind. So the features of the earth's surface have become what they are through a continuous series of transitions from older to newer states—from less specialized to more specialized conditions. Again the succession of forms presented by a developing embryo is effected through a material continuity. The embryo retains its identity in passing through phases as diverse as a tadpole and an elephant—as diverse as a cell and a man.

II. *Geological evidence.* The forms of organization which have populated the world in its remote preparatory stages have been as diverse as the successive stages. Types of organization suited to a rude condition of the world demanded improvement when the conditions had improved. Fossil remains indicate that such improvements took place. It was not the displacement of the old type by the new, but a modification of the old type. So the general types of animals with which the world began to be populated in its infancy continue in existence. If we take a particular existing type, as the proboscidian, we learn from the testimony of fossils, that it is a modification of a type which existed in the last geological age before the present. That was a modification of an older one, and that of a still older, and so on. If we take the existing type of ox, or hog, or horse, we discover in each case a series of older modifications of the type reaching back through Tertiary time. In the case of the horse the series of known forms is remarkably full. (See *Reconciliation of Science and Religion*, pp. 166-170.) Now these series of successions receding into the past constantly converge. That is, the ancient proboscidian type differed less from the hog or horse type than the modern one does. All the ancient types approximated each other. In some cases two or three types are found actually merged together. The judgment cannot resist the conviction that some distance farther back they all converge. Thus the modern types of mammals have diverged from a common five-toed, plantigrade, primitive form. But all this is no proof of genetic relationship in the terms of each series. All this might be if each term were a new beginning—an independent creation. This evidence is only a link in the proof.

III. *Variational evidence.* A species is now known not to be "a primordial organic form," as defined by Morton, but only a phase in a series of changes. That species vary to a wide extent has lately been shown by the study of many thousands of American birds. One-fourth of all our recognized species are only geographical varieties. The variations had become so wide that all naturalists recognized these varieties as good species. Something similar is true of our mammals. In short, it is now generally admitted that a large fraction of all hitherto recognized species are only varieties of certain forms which we must continue to admit as species. Some special instances of variation are quite striking. The axolotl of Colorado breathes water throughout life. But Dumeril, Prof. Marsh and others have caused this animal to absorb its gills and breathe air. It thus becomes a salamander, not only of a different species, but a different genus and tribe. So, certain marine crustaceans, gradually habituated to water less and less salt, undergo a transformation to fresh water species. By reversing the process, the transformation is reversed. It thus appears that transitions from one specific form to another are in the order of nature, and we learn that the transition from one modification of the horse type to another, during the lapse of Tertiary time, is a solution of the problem of successional forms which may be legitimately contemplated. The genetic relation of one term to another is not in conflict with nature, but is now strongly suggested by the aptitude of organic forms to vary.

IV. *Embryological evidence.* Every embryo in its course of development passes, by continuity, through a succession of stages, beginning with a cell. My limited space forbids to particularize, but I may state that the human embryo exhibits not fewer than twenty-two stages pretty distinctly marked, each in succession more complicated than the preceding ones. Now the points to be made in view of embryonic stages are the following: 1. The embryonic stages of all animals are, to a certain extent, *identical.* The simplest animals pass through but few of these stages; higher animals more. 2. Embryonic stages furnish a parallelism with the *gradations* of existing animals. The lowest animals having gone through three or four stages are arrested and live as permanent representatives of the last stage reached. Animals successively higher pass through successively more of the stages, and, becoming arrested, stand permanently as pictures of the highest embryonic stages reached. So the gradation of animal forms in the world becomes a series parallel with the series exemplified by the embryonic history of every higher animal. 3. Embryonic stages furnish parallels with the geological succession. That is, the succession of types of animals in geological time presents the same characters and the same order as the embryonic history of any higher vertebrate.

Now the embryonic succession is a demonstrated continuity. Is not the identical succession revealed by palæontology also a continuity? If the analogy does not convince, the aptitude to variation predisposes to conviction; and conviction becomes almost irresistible, when we reflect that a profound similarity—indeed, a physiological identity—obtains between the mode of the continuity in embryonic and genealogical successions. I can do scarcely more than enunciate conclusions; and I fear the reader will wonder, at the end, what is the evidence on which they rest.

Now, we may admit the force of the evidence, and still, with Wallace, hesitate to admit that the body and soul of man fall under the law of evolution; or, with Mivart, admit the principle with reference to the human body, and deny it with reference to the human soul. 1. A great gap exists between man and all other animals. Structurally, his brain and cranium as much surpass an ape's as an ape's surpass an eel's. Psychically, man is equally differentiated from the highest brute. 2. No connecting links between man and the brutes are known. In the living world the fact is patent. In the extinct world we should expect to discover forms immediately below man, but they are not forthcoming. We find neither connecting links nor remains certifying to such antiquity as man must possess, if a derived form. On the whole, the question in reference to man is quite open. We are very far from the possession of evidence that his organism has been evolved; still farther from the proof that his soul is derived from the psychic nature of a brute.

I express myself simply as a scientist. As such, I warn the reader not to be disturbed by any conclusions of science either achieved or impending. It is absolutely immaterial whether God created man by a fiat instantly, or by a fiat derivatively. Whether man has been evolved or not, he is the work of a Creator; and every moment's continuance of his being is a manifestation of power so far superior to the prerogatives of matter as to constitute an ever-repeated creation. There has been a great deal of dogmatism in science, and it is as much to be deprecated as dogmatism in religion. Science is progressive, and it is not the sign of a well ballasted intelligence to be moved with apprehension over any fresh utterance of science. Every theory must be subjected to appropriate tests. If it stands, it becomes a new revelation of God's mind; if it falls, all our trepidation over the supposed consequences becomes ridiculous.

At the meeting of the German Association for the Advancement of Science, last summer at Munich, Professor Hæckel, of Bonn, delivered a lecture in which he indulged in some of his characteristic sneering at spiritualism, and clinched his positions with the customary self-asserting dogmatism. To this lecture fitting reference was made by Professor Virchow, of Berlin, an older, more candid and abler investigator in the same field; and I close by a citation from Virchow's address.

"All attempts to transform our problems into doctrines, to introduce our theories as the bases of a plan of education, [as Hæckel had proposed,] particularly the attempt simply to depose the Church, and to replace its dogma by a religion of descent, these attempts, I say, must fail. Therefore, let us be moderate; let us exercise resignation, so that we give even the most treasured problems which we put forth, always as problems only, and that we say it a hundred and again a hundred times: Do not take this for confirmed truth—be prepared that, perhaps, this may be changed....Only ten years ago, when a skull was found, perhaps in peat, or in lake dwellings, or in some old cave, it was believed that marks of a wild and quite undeveloped state were seen in it. Indeed, we were then scenting monkey-air; but this has died out more and more....But I must say that one fossil monkey skull or man ape skull which really belonged to a human proprietor has never been found. We cannot teach, we cannot designate it as a revelation of science, that man descends from the ape, or from any other animal."

CHAPTER X.

PATRIARCHAL CHRONOLOGY.

In assuming the position that the Black races are Preadamites I have depended chiefly on the two following propositions: 1. The time from Adam (according to accepted chronology) to the date at which we know the Negro type had been fully established is vastly too brief for so great a divergence, in view of the imperceptible amount of divergence since such date. 2. No amount of time would suffice for the divergence of the Black races from the white man's Adam, since that would imply degeneracy of a racial and continental extent, and this is contrary to the recognized principle of progress in nature. At the same time I have *assumed* that the Mongoloid and Dravidian races may have descended from our Adam, both because the divergence in these cases is comparatively slight, and because those races, intellectually and morally, stand nearly on a level with our own. But I have not been *satisfied* with this assumption respecting the Brown races, because I do not think the Usher chronology affords sufficient time even for such a degree of differentiation. I admit the possibility; but I feel that the assumption is a strain upon the evidence.

What we need, then, to relieve us of this difficulty, is more time between Adam and the dawn of written history; and especially between Adam and the Deluge. But this is only one phase of the ethnological data which would be greatly accommodated and relieved by a larger allowance of time. The fourth chapter of Genesis, for instance, appears to have been composed before the Deluge—perhaps in the 500th year of Noah (Gen. v. 32); but at that time there were peoples in existence, descended from Cain, who were celebrated for agriculture, mechanics and music. They were indeed descended from Jabal, Jubal and Tubal-Cain, of the eighth generation from Adam. But, as the ten generations from Adam to the 500th year of Noah cover only 1,526 years, we may assume the eight generations to Tubal-Cain to cover about 1,245 years; and hence from Tubal-Cain to the 500th year of Noah we have only about 300 years, which is insufficient time, in the infancy of the world, for the growth of tribes and nations and culture which seem then to have been in existence.

Take another case. The tenth chapter of Genesis narrates a series of events which took place after the flood and before the division of the land in the time of Peleg. Computing the time in the usual way, the interval from the flood to the birth of Reu, the son of Peleg, was 131 years; and, according to the usual rate of increase, the posterity of Noah must have amounted to about 900 persons. This chapter was written in the time of Peleg, as otherwise the history would have been brought down to a later date, as it is in the eleventh chapter. But note the progress which had been made in the settlement of the world and the building of cities, at the date of this composition. The posterity of Japhet had moved westward and taken possession of the islands of the Ægean and the Mediterranean, and probably the adjacent continental regions, and had spread over the vast territory of Scythia on the north, and penetrated to Spain on the west. They had become separated into distinct "languages, families and nations." This is a glimpse of ethnic events which we cannot reasonably assume to have taken place in 131 years. Again, the descendants of Ham had accomplished even greater results. Egypt had been settled, and its population had become differentiated into at least eight tribes or nations. Phœnician Sidon had been built and the Phœnicians had grown into nine peoples, "and *afterward* the families of the Canaanites spread abroad." But before the Canaanites there were present in Palestine the Rephaim, Zuzim, Emim and others. Who were these peoples? Nimrod, also, or his posterity, had planted cities. Babel, Erech, Accad and Calneh were the "*beginning* of his kingdom." Then Asshur arose amongst the Nimrodites and led away a colony, which built other walled cities—Nineveh, Rehoboth, Calah, and Resen which was "a great city." Thus the descendants of Ham had developed "families and tongues and countries and nations." The posterity of Shem also had become divided into "families and tongues and nations" and dispersed to many "lands." Accordingly the descendants of Noah, in the days of Peleg, had become numerous "nations" and divided the earth amongst themselves. Now it is difficult to believe that these cities and nationalities had come into existence from one family in the space of 131 years.

A similar set of considerations is furnished by the eleventh chapter, which seems to be a distinct document, and begins back at an epoch near the flood, and preserves the history down to Abraham. Journeying westward, the Adamites, as yet one family, attempted to build a tower, and were defeated. Still, it appears a city known as Babel rose into existence, and it would be fair to presume that this and the other cities named as the beginning of Nimrod's kingdom, instead of being built by him or his successors, were already in existence long before the time of Nimrod.

How much, then, beyond 131 years must the time from Noah to Peleg be elongated?

These are simply samples of the exigencies which arise on biblical, ethnological, scientific and linguistic grounds, when we make the attempt to satisfy ourselves with the popular chronology. I think, therefore, I shall do my readers a service by directing their attention to a recent work which undertakes to show that the original text of Genesis, when rightly understood, gives us a much more extended chronology. The work is written by Rev. T. P. Crawford, of Fung Chow, China, and published in Richmond, Virginia, by Josiah Ryland & Co., and is entitled "The Patriarchal Dynasties from Adam to Abraham shown to cover 10,500 years, and the highest human life only 187." The fundamental position assumed by the author is a reformed reading of the genealogical tables contained in the fifth and eleventh chapters of Genesis; of which the first traces the posterity of Adam to Noah, and the second traces the posterity of Noah to Abraham. For the purpose of giving an intelligible explanation of Mr. Crawford's reformed reading, I here reproduce the biblical paragraph touching the family of Adam:

"And Adam lived a hundred and thirty years, and begat *a son* in his own likeness, after his image; and called his name Seth. And the days of Adam after he had begotten Seth were eight hundred years; and he begat sons and daughters: And all the days that Adam lived were nine hundred and thirty years; and he died."

A similar paragraph is recorded respecting each of the antediluvian patriarchs. Now the author maintains that the word Adam is employed, above, in a *personal*, and afterward in a *family*, sense; that the first clause denotes *the whole life* of Adam, and not his age at the birth of Seth; that *yolad*, translated "begat," signifies rather "appointed," and refers to Adam's designation of Seth (in place of Abel) to be his successor; that "likeness" and "image" refer not to personal appearance, but to character and office—the name Seth itself signifying "The appointed;" that "Adam" in the next clause refers to the tribe or family of Adam; that the Adamic family continued to be ruled over by successors not in the line of Seth, for a period of 930 years; that thereafter the representatives of the Sethite line acceded to the kingship for 912 years, when the family of Enos assumed the government, and so on.

These positions are argued with much ability. That the first clause expresses the whole life of Adam is maintained on the following grounds: 1. The Hebrew never employs the verb *lived* with definite numbers to indicate the age of a man at the birth of a son; but it invariably says such a one *was a son* of so many years *when* his son was born, or some other event took place. Many passages are cited, of which see Gen. xxi, 5; xvi, 16; xvii, 24; xxi, 4; Lev. ix, 3; Josh. xiv, 7; I. Kings xiv, 21; xx, 42. On the contrary, the verb *lived* denotes the whole term of a man's life. See Gen. i, 22; xxiii, 1; xxv, 7; xlvii, 28; v, 5; xi, 11; ix, 28; II. Kings xiv, 17; Job xliii, 16. 2. Antediluvian life is substantially asserted to have been one hundred and twenty years, on an average. (See Gen. vi, 3.) 3. There is nowhere in the Old Testament any allusion to such enormous ages as eight hundred and nine hundred years. On the contrary, Abraham, who was promised a "good old age," died at one hundred and seventy-five years. (Gen. xv, 15; xxv, 7, 8.) So Isaac, at one hundred and eighty years, was "old and full of days," (Gen. xxxv. 28, 29.) Other reasoning I have not the space to cite. A paraphrase of the paragraph concerning Adam would, therefore, read somewhat as follows:

And Adam lived a hundred and thirty years. And at the close of his life he appointed his son to be his spiritual heir and successor and designated him Seth, "The appointed." And the duration of the house of Adam after the appointment of Seth was eight hundred years, represented by male and female descendants. And the whole duration of the house of Adam was nine hundred and thirty years, and it ceased to exist.

The paragraphs touching the other antediluvian patriarchs are to be similarly understood. It will thus appear that the average duration of life was then one hundred and twenty years. A similar interpretation of the eleventh chapter gives the average duration of life after the flood at one hundred and twenty-eight. After Abraham, the ages, as stated in the sacred text, range from one hundred and ten to one hundred and eighty years, with an average of one hundred and thirty-five years. Still further, the utmost limit of ancient Egyptian life was one hundred and ten years. The average life of the eight kings of the second Chaldean dynasty was eighty-eight years. Under the first Chinese dynasty of four hundred and thirty-nine years, average life was seventy-seven years; under the second, of six hundred and forty-four years, it was sixty-nine years. These two dynasties extended from the days of Peleg to those of Solomon. Many other facts tend to show that human life, in the most ancient times, had a duration not far from that of the Hebrew patriarchs, if we interpret the first clause of each paragraph as proposed by Mr. Crawford; while the marvelous duration of human life, according to the popular interpretation, is opposed to every item of knowledge which we possess from other sources.

Applying these principles to the genealogical tables of Genesis, we obtain the following chronological data:

Adam to the flood	7,737	years
Flood to the birth of Abraham	2,763	"
Adam to Abraham	10,500	"
Birth of Abraham to Christ	2,000	"
Adam to Christ	12,509	"
Christ to the present time	1,878	"
Adam to the present year	14,378	"

It is to be hoped that Hebrew scholars will give Mr. Crawford's views a candid examination, and I will also indulge the hope that they may find his exegesis valid.

Ubert

Ignatius Donnelly's Comet.

By Prof. ALEXANDER WINCHELL.

Reprinted from the new review, The Forum.
Vol. IV., September, 1887.

IGNATIUS DONNELLY'S COMET.

"HAVE you read 'Ragnarok'?" "What do you think of it?" "Is it a true explanation of the Drift?" "Is the theory there set forth generally held by geologists?" These queries have often been addressed to the writer.

Let us first understand what "Ragnarok" is. The Honorable Ignatius Donnelly, in 1883, gave to the world a volume in which he gravely maintained that the superficial accumulation which geologists know as "Drift" was brought to the earth by a comet. He accompanied his new theory by an array of scientific facts and doctrines respecting the Drift, and respecting comets, and seemed to find an amazing amount of substantial support. Then he turned to the legends of the world, and was equally happy in finding hundreds of traditions which seemed to be indisputable reminiscences of a time of tribulation that ensued after the earth had been struck by a comet's tail. His curious book ends with the discussion of sundry questions more or less connected with the well-sustained story of the conflict between the comet and the earth. The course of the treatment is illustrated by thirty-six wood-cuts, copied mostly from scientific works, and all tending to make the solid truth as obvious to the unaided eye as the text makes it to the understanding. *Ragnarok*, in the Norse legends, means, according to Anderson, "the darkness of the gods," but our author, with characteristic facility, patches up an etymology which makes it signify "the rain of dust," and *presto*, that is just the name for the book.

Undoubtedly this is a work of genius; the writer does not intend to dispute its claims in that respect. It is worth reading; at least, if one wishes chiefly to be amused by an extraordinary association of facts and legends and conclusions. If one never saw a square plug fit a round hole, here is a rare opportunity to see the feat accomplished over and over again, twenty times in immediate succession. Prestidigitation is nowhere in comparison with this "presticogitation." Literature has never been the field of equal jugglery. Keen jokers never smile at their own sallies; so our author is everywhere as grave as a logician, and as earnest as the state's attorney in working out his theory of a capital case. Dead and buried facts are exhumed stealthily from the history of science, and set up for contemplation with an air of triumph which seems to ask, "Who will know that they are mummies?" Misfit facts are set together, and the joints are puttied over with a "doubtless" or a "probably." The feint of argumentation is so consummately done that the unsuspecting reader absorbs the conclusions with avidity, and the trained skeptic asks himself, "Is this man in earnest or is he romancing?" He arrays so much that is true in science, and genuine in legend, and wise in proverb, and excellent in style, that if he means his book for a scientistic romance, it is one of the most successful ever set afloat; while, if he means it as a sober argument for a striking theory, it stands by the side of "Paradise Found" as a phenomenal aggregation of varied learning sundered from its conclusions. To all queries the author remains dumb. I suspect, however, that when he gets by himself he chuckles inordinately.

One almost feels compunction in stepping forward to interfere with the genial author's harmless play upon the public credulity. But there's the rub. Is it harmless to inculcate fable with such gravity that a majority of readers accept it for fact? Does science receive no prejudice from an exposition as attractive and baseless as a romance, but dressed in the conventional guise of genuine science? Since the author has not seen fit to send forth his lucubration in the character of a romance, let us strip off its disguise and give it a passport for what it is.

But before we attempt to take this structure to pieces, let us inspect a little more particularly the method of its building. The gist of its several chapters is about as follows: The Drift of geologists is first synoptically described. Its origin is alleged not to be known; and in proof, the author cites Figuier and an anonymous writer in the "Popular Science Monthly." He names four theories which have been proposed, and disposes of these *seriatim*. The theory of a continental ice-sheet is untenable, because no one has explained where the ice came from. If it were in existence there would be no motion, since the "immense sheets of ice" which cover some mountains to-day do not descend; "they lie and melt and are renewed."

Had there been a continental ice-sheet, the striæ produced would "all run in the same direction," but, "on the contrary, they cross each other in an extraordinary manner." And further, these markings would have been more pronounced on the southern slopes of hills than on the northern; since "the schoolboy toils patiently and slowly up the hill with his sled, but when he descends, he comes down with railroad speed, scattering the snow before him in all directions." But a fatal objection to the theory of continental glaciation is the statement that not all the cold lands have been overspread with Drift. Siberia is not so covered. "There was no Drift in all northern Asia, up to the Arctic circle;" probably not in any part of Asia. Moreover, "it does not extend over all Europe," for Collomb finds "only a shred of it in France," and thinks it "absent from part of Russia." "Even in North America, the Drift is not found everywhere. There is a remarkable driftless region in Wisconsin, Iowa, and Minnesota." "This is now the coldest part of the Union." Why no Drift? "Again, no traces of northern Drift are found in California," and "it did not extend to Oregon." Again, the presence of a continental ice-sheet would have required a temperature "some degrees below zero," says Figuier; and on this information our author concludes that if the climate "to 35 or 40 degrees of latitude, was several degrees below zero," then "the equator must have been at least below the frost-point," and no tropical plants could have survived the great ice-age. This is another fatal objection. But further difficulties. The glacial theory gives no account of the "gigantic masses of clay" which stretch from Minnesota to Cape May, and "from the Arctic Circle to Patagonia." Did the ice grind this out of granite? Where did it get the granite? The granite reaches the surface only in limited areas; as a rule, it is buried many miles in depth under the sedimentary rocks. How did the ice pick out its materials so as to grind nothing but granite? This deposit overlies limestone and sandstone. "Why were they not ground up with the granite?" Another marvel. The Drift clay is red. This results from the grinding up of mica and hornblende. But granite contains feldspar also, the clay from which is yellow or white. Now, by what mysterious process was the feldspar separated from the mica and hornblende, to make "great sheets by itself west of the Mississippi, while the ice-sheet ground up the mica and hornblende and made blue or red clays which it laid down elsewhere"?

Now, not to quote other points made against the continental glacier, let us note that glacier phenomena, according to L. Agassiz and Professor Hartt, occur in Brazil. That country, therefore, must have been clad in ice; and if Brazil, then Africa. Indeed, along the Atlas range, moraines have been reported; while the whole Sahara is "probably" a Drift deposit. Thus it is made to appear that on the American hemisphere characteristic Drift stretches from Arctic to Antarctic, while on the opposite hemisphere Drift is wanting.

The distribution of the Drift was a great and sudden catastrophe. The author quotes Figuier copiously; Charles Martins, who believes in a change in the position of the poles; also Cuvier, an old and extreme cataclysmist. He cites many testimonies as to the deep burial of woody fragments, and mentions the famous Siberian elephants. In further proof that the catastrophe was world-convulsing, our wide-searching author states that in addition to the deposit of clay, sand, and gravel, "the earth at the same time was cleft with great cracks or fissures, which reached down through many miles of the planet's crust to the central fires, and released the boiling rocks imprisoned in its bosom; and these poured forth to the surface as igneous, intrusive, or trap rocks." To what does he refer? "David Dale Owen tells us that the outburst of the trap rock at the Dalles of the St. Croix came up through open fissures." Our author continues: "Where the great breaks were not deep enough to reach the central fires, they left mighty fissures in the surface, which in the Scandinavian regions are known as 'fiords.'" "They are found in Great Britain, Maine, Nova Scotia, Labrador, Greenland, and on the western coast of North America." Let us add, they ought to be in Brazil also, and in the Desert of Sahara, if the Drift is in those regions, and if the fissures are an incident of the Drift.

The author then undertakes to establish the proposition that "great heat was a prerequisite." He has found writers who remind us that copious evaporation precedes copious precipitation; who even hint that a warm climate in southern regions may have favored snowy precipitation in cold ones; and hence —the reader will notice the obvious sequence—intense heat must have actually accompanied the spread of the Drift deposits. Such is the picture given of glacialist opinion.

Next, our genial and humorous friend has found out something about the constitution of comets, and he begins by letting out his secret at once—"a comet caused the Drift." "What is a comet?" he asks. He gives us an orthodox definition, and adds that its constituent parts come to us in some cases as meteoric stones; and we thence learn that the substance of a comet is a mass of stones, sand, and clay, just like that of the Drift. These comets are a reminiscence of the earth's primitive history. They "form a part of our solar system." Our earth was once gaseous, then liquefied, then incrusted. Later cooling resulted in shrinkage of the molten nucleus; and now, this suggestion leads on to an astounding and novel theory of the origin of comets. As the crust grows rigid it no longer subsides with the contracting nucleus, but "a space exists between the two." Suppose the process continued "until a vast space exists between the crust and core of the earth," and that some day a convulsion of the surface creates a great chasm in the crust, and the ocean rushes in and fills up part of the cavity; a tremendous quantity of steam is formed, an explosion takes place, and the crust of the earth is blown into a million fragments. "The great molten ball within remains intact, though sorely torn. In its center is still the force we call gravity. The fragments of the crust cannot fly off into space; they are constrained to follow the master power lodged in the ball, which now becomes the nucleus of a comet, still blazing and burning, and vomiting flames, and wearing itself away. The catastrophe has disarranged its course, but it still revolves in a prolonged orbit around the sun, carrying its broken *débris* in a long trail behind it. The *débris* arranges itself in a regular order; the largest fragments are in or nearest the head; the smaller are farther away, diminishing in regular gradation until, at the farthest extremity, the trail consists of sand, dust, and gases." Constant internal movements, caused "by the attraction and repulsion of the sun," result in collisions, striations, and fine dust. "Magnetic waves passing through the comet might arrange all the particles containing iron by themselves, and thus produce that marvelous separation of the constituents of the granite which we have found to exist in the Drift clays." Then all this theory's substantial "granite" fabric is further strengthened by the solid contributions of the "eminent German geologist, Dr. Hahn." He discovered, just in time for utilization in this cob-house of scientific dreams, "an entire series of organic remains in meteoric stones"—sponges, corals, and crinoids. These are the tale-bearers which clinch the evidence that comets are exploded worlds.

"Could a comet strike the earth?" Certainly; it could not be avoided. Did not Kepler affirm that "comets are scattered through the heavens with as much profusion as fishes in the ocean?" And did not Arago estimate that the comets belonging to our system "number seventeen million five hundred thousand"? And did not Lambert put the estimate at five hundred millions? Now, think of five hundred million comets circling about the sun in a mazy dance, with the earth in the midst of the whirl; can anything prevent the earth from being run over? But, really, the earth has been hit many a time. The consequences, in well-established cases, have indeed been very trifling; but that need not deter us from picturing the consequences of collision with some imaginable comet; the comet, for instance, which sowed Drift over the earth. "Imagine such a creature as the great comet of 1811, with a head fifty times as large as the moon, and a tail one hundred and sixteen million miles long, rushing past this poor little earth of ours, with its diameter of only seven thousand nine hundred and twenty-five miles!" "The earth would simply make a bullet-hole through the tail;" "and yet, in that moment of contact, the side of the earth facing the comet might be covered with hundreds of feet of *débris*." But suppose it to have "struck the earth head on, amidships," as described in some of the legends. "The shock may have changed the angle of inclination of the earth's axis;" "to this cause we might look also for the great cracks and breaks in the earth's surface, which constitute the fiords of the sea-coast, and the trap extrusions of the continents; and here, too, might be the cause of those mighty excavations, hundreds of feet deep, in which are now the great lakes of America, and from which great cracks radiate out in all directions, like the fractures in a pane of glass where a stone has struck it."

These things assumed possible, we may argue consequences. The comet was much larger than Donati's. "It came with terrific force. It smashed the rocks." "It was accompanied by inconceivable winds," which "whirled the Drift materials about in the wildest confusion." It formed long trains and banks, as if of snow. The comet came with a scorching and destructive heat. The earth was lighted up like the temporary star in the Northern Crown. The carbonic oxide and carburetted hydrogen came with it; and these, burning and exploding, baked and rent the earth precisely as the legends narrate. This scene is painted by our author in gorgeous colors. And here were human populations! It is not necessary to follow the stream of eloquence which floats their fortunes into our comprehension. There was burning which dried up the waters; there was a rain of stones; men fled to caves; when this storm was past, men crawled out. Electrical action now began; clouds accumulated; darkness reigned; floods of water descended; snows in the northern regions consolidated into ice; frost gradually invaded more southern latitudes. But when the clouds were exhausted, the sun brought back warmth which melted the snows and flooded the continent.

Then the legends are cited—Hindoo, Persian, Greek, Chinese, Norse, and American, from all parts of the two continents. They are accumulated in great volume. But myths and sagas generally appear in such dubious shape and incoherent texture that our author is able to mold them deftly to the facts accompanying the fearful cometic collision. The mere mass of legends capable of such interpretation is a literary curiosity. Then follow, specially, "legends of cave-life." We have long known that primitive men dwelt in caves; but we never learned till now that a rain of fire and stones drove them to such shelters. Other legends are made to refer to the age of darkness; but, though they generally speak of the beginnings of the world's existence, the author knows how to shape them to his theory. Still others refer specifically to the triumph of the sun, and others to the fall of the clay and gravel. The myths of Arabia and the conceptions of the Book of Job are set forth in much detail. The author then reads Genesis by the light of the comet. We get a unique vindication of the old book. The events of the "six days" are the incidents of the cometic collision.

The concluding portions of this amusing literary circus attempt to show that men before the cometary catastrophe were civilized; that the survivors dwelt upon an island in the Atlantic, and that this had been anciently connected with Europe, Africa, and South America by ridges of land, often in the legends called "bridges." To complete the formalities of scientific argument, this smileless provoker of irrepressible smiles devotes a chapter to the consideration of "objections." But, like the duelists on the stage, he takes care not to hurt.

Now I will mention a few objections not put on parade. I omit the difficulties of making the legends mean what is here pretended, and confine myself to some of the geological objections. Instead of general doubt, geologists are nearly unanimous in ascribing the Drift to glacier action accompanied and followed by water supplied by melting ice. A moving ice-sheet would incontestably act most energetically on the northern slopes of hills. The facts, instead of being a difficulty, are a striking proof of the ice-sheet. It was once by some writers supposed that no Drift occurs in Siberia; but many always held that the real Drift was simply covered by the *tundras;* and this is now known to be a fact. Western America was at first thought destitute of evidence of glaciation; but it is now well known that it exists at altitudes above the thawing influence of Pacific coast temperatures. Figuier's mention of "zero" in connection with temperature of the glacier epoch refers to the centigrade scale, where zero is thirty-two degrees above our zero and Donnelly's. The glacier did not confine itself to granite as material for grinding up; it pulverized limestones and sandstones and quartzites. Nor are Drift clays always red; and hence the selection of mica and hornblende for trituration never taxed its discriminating powers.

Again, Brazilian glaciers were only an inference by Agassiz, based on vast accumulations of incoherent materials, which he supposed to be moraines. But these have resulted from the decay of rocks "in place," especially granites and schists. Professor Hartt himself arrived at that opinion; and the very figure reproduced from Hartt shows clearly the still-bedded character of the pile of loose materials. As to morainic deposits in the southern hemisphere, which are supposed to exist; if real, we have no evidence that they are contemporaneous with those of the north. On the contrary, the best accepted theories imply that the northern and southern hemispheres were glaciated alternately. Hence, we see no such spread of Drift from Arctic to Antarctic as our entertainer pictures; and so far as the two hemispheres are Drift-covered, their coverings were not simultaneous. There are other yawning rents in the theory.

Now, in reference to those rifts in the terrestrial crust which our author attributes to the smashing, head-on collision of the vast comet; it is true, indeed, that the trap of the Dalles of the St. Croix came up through open fissures, like that of Keewenaw Point and Ile Royale; but that was in Palæozoic time, a million years, more or less, before the fiords of Norway and Maine existed. And then those fiords, though perhaps of the age of the Drift, are sinuous, irregular erosions, instead of clefts. The huge cracks radiating from the great lakes are only flaws in the information; they do not exist.

As to the confused state of the Drift materials, I believe the intelligent reader will feel as willing to attribute it to water as to wind; and when we speculate on the agency which placed some large bowlders high up in the water-worked sands, it requires only a good understanding to comprehend the probable agency of ice-blocks or rafts in water torrents, or icebergs in a sea-like expanse; but to comprehend the action of wind in planting such bowlders requires a pure Donnellian imagination.

Next, in reference to the amount of heat required for the accumulation of a sheet of ice; do we not detect here a slip of intelligence? Is it not evaporation which is implied in precipitation? But evaporation goes on at all temperatures, provided that precipitation has taken place which restores the capacity of the atmosphere for the product of evaporation, or, provided a rise in temperature has created such capacity. Whenever the temperature is rising that capacity is increasing; whenever it is falling the capacity is diminishing. These fluctuations often take place while the thermometer is below freezing (zero, centigrade). Evaporation and precipitation proceed in the Arctic regions with the atmosphere forty degrees below freezing; does this imply intense heat in glacier-making? But somebody suggested that climatic heat would facilitate evaporation and promote precipitation; and our keen-eyed watcher for available citations from the pages of science at once sets down: "great heat; that means a comet." And then how slyly he borrows the idea of heat from the glacialists, at the same moment that he rejects the ice-field for which alone the glacialist appealed to heat sufficient for evaporation. For the ice-field, heat. "Yes," he says to himself, "I'll take the heat, but the ice-field is awkward for my story. I don't want any ice-field." And this is all the foundation there is for the author's burning catastrophe.

Speaking of comets, he affords us a sample of the pure wheat which he uses to give currency to his chess. His account of the constitution of comets is approximately quadrate with latest views; but when he gives us his episode on comet-making, he has clearly broken friendship with the scientists. That bulging planetary crust arching over huge vacuities into which the ocean dives, on occasion, is too turgid altogether. Has the author reflected on the enormous pressure exerted by such arches on their abutments; and on the enormous strain about the key-stone. Has he ever studied the rigidity of the crust-materials, and calculated the amount of strain or pressure of which they are capable? He is contemplating an arch broad enough to give capacity for water whose sudden conversion to steam would blow up a planet. Now, the cold fact is, that any such arch would be crushed by its own weight, a hundred times and in a hundred places, before it could be raised. As well fancy the arch made of dough. Granite seems, to our feeble hammer-blows and under our very limited pressures, to be a very hard and resisting rock; but granite, in the presence of cosmic forces, or under the pressure of an arc of the earth's crust, has relatively no rigidity. It might as well be water. These tremendous forces crush and mold and pour the solid granite with the same facility as molten granite. And the conceit of a planet driven from its path by an explosion within itself is another presticogitative fact. As well attempt to steer a steamship by crowding against the guard-rail.

Science, to the question, "Can a comet strike the earth?" says "Yes." And science feels somewhat certain that comets have struck the earth; and even during the life of the present generation this little incident has been experienced. But note, it did not destroy cities, and drive people into caverns. The dire shock was scarcely noticeable. But, then, this was not a huge monster, like the anathematized comet of 1811. Possibly not, but after all, 'tis distance lends the terror to the view. These creatures, while in the distant sky, look large enough and solid enough to "smash" a planet. So does the aurora borealis. One of these comets ran amuck in the family of Jupiter's children, and not a child was knocked from its feet, not an infant was budged.

Men have entertained all imaginable views respecting comets; and Donnelly is not the first to discover the effects of a comet's collision with the earth. Whiston ascertained that the deluge of Noah came from the whisk of a comet's tail; but Donnelly has outdone Whiston, for he has shown that our planet has suffered not only from a cometary flood, but from cometary fire, and a cometary rain of stones.

ALEXANDER WINCHELL.

Press of J. J. Little & Co., Astor Place, New York.

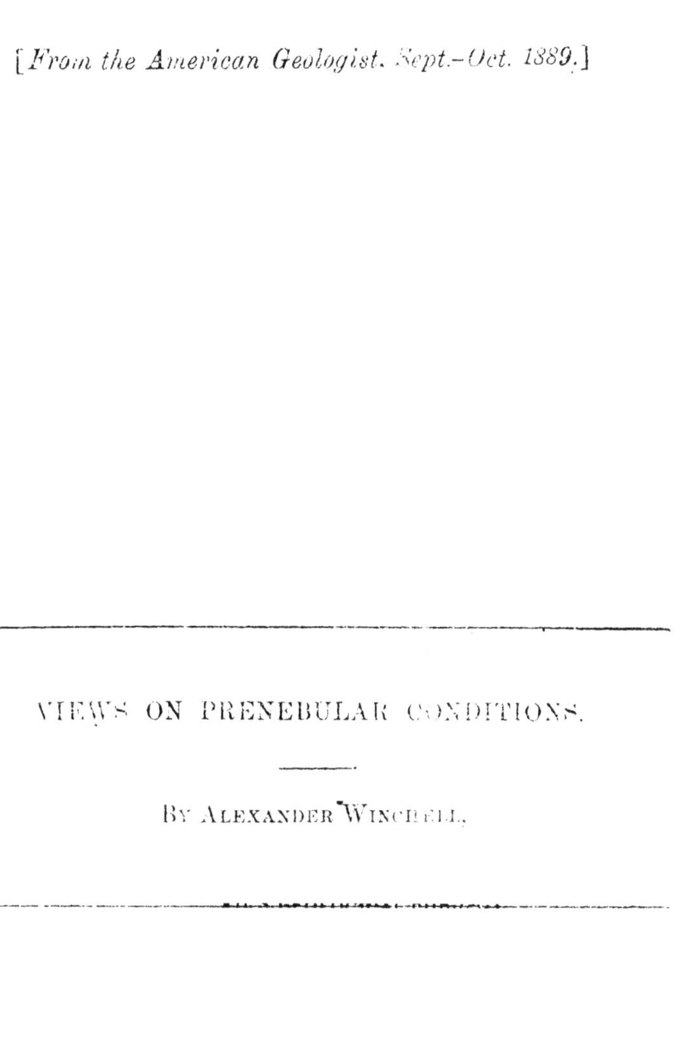

[*From the American Geologist. Sept.–Oct. 1889.*]

VIEWS ON PRENEBULAR CONDITIONS.

BY ALEXANDER WINCHELL.

[*From the American Geologist, October, 1889.*]

VIEWS ON PRENEBULAR CONDITIONS.

BY ALEXANDER WINCHELL.

Geologists interested in the speculative departments of their science will be gratified to know the state of opinion concerning the earliest condition of terrestrial matter on which deductive reasoning sheds any light. That the matter of our planet, in common with that of the Solar System has undergone a physical evolution of the nature first outlined by Kant, in 1755, is now almost universally believed by those who have based their opinions on a rational examination of the evidences. In addition to the familiar proofs, we may mention the new and original elucidations of M. Roche, so highly esteemed by professor Darwin, and the very remarkable photograph of the planetary nebula in Andromeda exhibited to the Royal Astronomical Society, on December 6, 1888. This is regarded by professor G. H. Darwin as affording "something like a proof of the substantial truth of the nebular hypothesis."[1] With reference to the same photograph Dr. Huggins remarks, "The stage of evolution which the nebula in Andromeda represents is no longer a matter of hypothesis. The splendid photograph recently taken by Mr. Roberts[2] of the nebula, shows a planetary system at a somewhat advanced stage of evolution; already several planets have been thrown off, and the central gaseous mass has condensed to a moderate size as

[1]Darwin, *Phil. Trans.* Nov. 15, 1888. Note added Dec. 19, 1888. An excellent engraving from this photograph was published in *Knowledge*, Feb. 1, 1889, and another on a larger scale Aug. 1889. Both reveal an annulated structure in the accompanying smaller nebulæ (Added Sep. 7, 1889.

[2]Monthly Notices, Royal Astronomical Society.

compared with the dimensions it must have possessed before any planets had been formed.[3]

The nebulæ have long been suspected to belong to the order of cosmic existence which served as the starting point of those rotations, annulations and planetations which marked the history of our system. The constitution of the nebulæ and their antecedent history, have, however, been involved in great mystery. The irresolvable nebulæ—to which the present reference is restricted—have been generally conceived to consist of tenuous matter heated to luminosity. Whether in the condition of a luminous gas, or that of a firemist, or that of the rings of Saturn and the matter of the zodiacal light, remained a question. The publication, in 1864, of Mr. Huggins' results of spectroscopic studies of certain nebulæ,[4] seemed to demonstrate that at least some of the luminous matter of certain nebulæ exists in the condition of a gas. Hydrogen, it was thought, was quite certainly identified, while the brightest line in the spectrum was exceedingly close to nitrogen.[5] Huggins' later researches throw doubt on the identification of nitrogen, and tend to suggest the presence of lead.[6]

While making this brief reference to elementary matters indicated in the nebulæ, it may be stated that Mr. Lockyer, in a paper read before the Royal Society in 1887,[7] stated that only seven lines in all had been recorded to that time in the spectra of the nebulæ, three of which coincide with lines in the spectrum of hydrogen, and three correspond to lines in magnesium. Dr. Huggins, in his late memoir, has made a very critical examination of the claims of magnesium for recognition in the nebulæ and concludes, against Mr. Lockyer, that the coincidence of the lines is not sufficiently exact.

Aside from the identification of substances, the recognition of gaseous states of very high temperatures is considered es-

---

[3]Huggins, Memoir read before the Royal Society, May 2, 1889. A beautiful delineation of the nebula of Andromeda is given by Father Secchi in *Le Soleil,* VOL. II., PL. I. Fig. 2. He remarks, "One circumstance deserves to arrest our attention. Certain planetary nebulæ seem to offer luminous points. * * * Meantime the planetary nebula of Andromeda presents two spectra superposed" p. 464.

[4]"On the spectra of some of the Nebulæ." *Phil. Trans.*, 1864.

[5]"On the Spectrum of the Great Nebula in Orion," etc. *Proc. Roy. Soc.* VOL. XX. See the results summarized by Le Padre Secchi, "Le Soleil," vol. II. pp. 461-466.

[6]In a memoir read before the Royal Society May 2, 1889.

[7]*Roy. Soc. Proc.* vol XLIII. p. 111.

tablished. Huggins, Lockyer and others believe that some of the matter exists in a state of dissociation. At the same time, some of the nebulæ, notably that in Orion, present also, a continuous spectrum, as if matter existed in them in a condition different from gaseity, though Huggins cautiously suggests that under most favorable conditions the continuous spectrum may be found to consist of bright lines. The evidence as observed, however, is in accord with the presumption which may be offered on other grounds, that matter may exist, in aggregations as vast as the nebulæ, in all conceivable conditions—dissociated, gaseous, liquid, and solid; luminous and non-luminous.

We once felt that in tracing the genealogy of our system to the nebulous condition of matter, we had attained what might fairly be denominated a beginning. But as the nebular theory becomes less speculative, the speculative spirit is tempting science to inquiries about *pre-nebular* conditions. If matter was not created in nebulæ, they have had an antecedent history which it remains to disclose by observation and reasoning. If the data of science enable us to reason out antecedent conditions along a line of evolution, then we may rest in the sure conviction that the nebula itself represents only an ulterior stage. Matter was not originated in nebulæ.

The discovery of the cosmic nature of meteorites through the researches of Newton, Schiaparelli, Oppolzer and others; the establishment of the existence of meteoroidal swarms revolving in orbits about the sun; and especially the identification of the August and November swarms with certain comets[9] furnished indications that comets generally are constituted of masses of matter analogous to those which reach the earth as meteorites. The present writer, as early as 1877, generalizing from the recognized facts of meteorites, announced in a public lecture reported in the daily papers of various cities, his theory of the universality of "cosmical dust," and its slow aggregation into cometary and nebular masses.[10] In a subsequent

[9]The writer has given an elementary exposition of this chapter of science in "World-life," pp. 3-23.

[10]It is stated by Mr. Lockyer, that a similar theory was published by Prof. Tait in "Good Words"; but of that the writer had no knowledge. The coincidence of views, if it exists, must be regarded as lending confirmation to the theory. The late professor R. A. Proctor (in "Other Worlds than Ours," 1870) conceived of the growth of cosmic bodies "under the continued rain of meteoric matter;" but his purpose was

work, he explained with considerable detail, his conception of the mode of aggregation of "cosmical dust" into nebular and cometary assemblages.[11] In this he spoke in particular of the necessary collisions of constituent parts, the development of intense heat, and the formation of an elongated train, in the case of comets moving within the Solar System.[12]

This theory of the origin and constitution of comets has been heartily endorsed, and discussed with ample learning, in a series of papers published by Prof. Lockyer, in Nature, in volumes XXXVII, XXXVIII, XXXIX, but more specifically in the latter volume. Here (page 402), he mentions professor Tait, and without quoting, explains his views. He says professor Tait's researches have not been published *in extenso*, but a summary of results appeared in "Good Words" "some time ago."[13] These Mr. Lockyer presents in language from which the following are extracts: "In the case of comets of but small masses, the component materials would be small and far apart. * * * While the swarm which builds up the

---

to explain the formation of worlds antagonistically to the Kantian conception, while that of the present writer was to gain a starting-point for the unfolding of that conception. Sir William Thomson is said to to entertain the opinion that the "origin of the planets was through a gradual accretion of meteoric matter."

[11] "World-Life," 1883, pp. 71-75, 482-3.

[12] It seems necessary, as will appear, to make special citations from the work mentioned. After speaking of the aggregation of nebulæ, the author continues: "In the nearer neighborhood of some great attractive centre, the velocity of one of these swarms is accelerated. Its form becomes more elongated. The internal movements of the parts become more vigorous, collisions are sharper, and flashes of light are evolved, and the posterior train is expanded. Further influence exerted by the central body increases all those consequences. The head of the swarm becomes permanently luminous. The long gathering swarm is now a comet" (p. 75). The contingencies happening to a cometary aggregation once introduced into our system, are next traced, "A cannon-ball moves 1400 to 2000 feet in a second, and yet its impact upon a solid body always develops a flash of light. But this velocity is mere rest when compared with that of a comet in its flight. Now in case of these mutual collisions among the parts of a comet, the velocities of some will be accelerated, and those of others retarded. Those retarded are liable, of course, to be accelerated again by other collisions, so that the total amount of motion in the assemblage should remain constant, so far as actions in the system are concerned. Nevertheless, the changed velocity of a part results in a change of intensity of action from without," etc. Thus, not to quote at length, the comet tary aggregation is partly pulverized, and gradually torn asunder—disintegrating into the meteoroidal stage (pp. 482-3). These principles are applied to the slow contraction of Saturn's rings, and to the zodiacal light.

[13] From Dr. Croll the writer learns that this was in the volume for 1875, p. 861. The date of publication does not appear.

comet is coursing round the sun as a whole, the individual members will themselves gravitate toward each other. * * * The stones colliding will generate heat, and some gas will be evolved; some members of the mass will be quickened, while other constituents of the mass will be retarded in their motion. * * * The result of these collisions would be such a smashing up of the constituents of the swarm that much finely attenuated material would be left behind, sufficient to reflect sunlight and to give rise to phenomena of the tail".[14]

Thus the suggestion came into existence that some of the nebulæ, as well as comets, are simply aggregations of stones, sand, fire mist and gases. This at least, was specifically enunciated by the present writer. Professor Lockyer inclined to adopt such a view of the constitution of nebulæ, as is shown in the ample and interesting series of papers referred to. In one of these he says: "The brighter lines in the spiral nebulæ, and in those in which a rotation has been set up, are in all probability, due to streams of meteorites with irregular motions out of the main streams, in which the collisions would be almost *nil*. It has already been suggested by professor G. Darwin [*Nature* volume XXXI, 1884-5, p.25]—using the gaseous hypothesis—that in such nebulæ "the great mass of the gas is non-luminous, the luminosity being an evidence of condensation along lines of low velocity, according to a well known hydrodynamical law. From this point of view, the visible nebula may be regarded as a luminous diagram of its own stream-lines."[15]

The question naturally arose whether a swarm of discrete meteoric bodies, in an aggregation of nebular dimensions, would manifest the behavior of a cooling and shrinking spheroid of gas. The essential conception of the nebular theory of the Solar system involves an elastic fluid and the conservation of an equilibrium figure, while the meteoroidal aggregation presents at first view, a discrete condition of solid constituents quite lacking the distinguishing properties of a fluid. As soon, however, as we conceive the constituents in a perpetual state of collision and rebound, the physical movements of fluid molecules are at once suggested, and we perceive that within certain limits of distance of the meteoric constituents, the meteoric aggrega-

[14] Nature, XXXIX, 402. Feb. 21, 1889.
[15] Nature, Nov. 17, 1887; *Roy Soc.*, Nov. 15, 1887.

tion is essentially a gross fluid, and might manifest the behavior of a fluid.

Professor G. H. Darwin undertook the analytical investigation of this question,[16] and in a memoir of extraordinary interest, established the following conclusions :—As far as frequency of collision is concerned, the hydrodynamical treatment of a swarm of meteorites is justifiable; the aggregation may be treated as possessing a coëfficient of viscosity such that if rotating, it would revolve nearly without relative motion of its parts, other than the motion of agitation; but in later stages the viscosity would be diminished to such extent that the central portion would probably rotate more rapidly than the outside—as some phenomena suggest to have been the case in our system. A further conclusion is, that the larger and less frequently colliding meteorites will gradually settle toward the centre, leaving the smallest and most frequently colliding meteorites—or fragments, particles or molecules—disposed at and near the surface, thus creating a maximum density about the centre, though its distribution is not according to the law of an elastic gas. It is further suggested that in the late stages of evolution, the meteors would be mostly absorbed by the central sun and planets, that their relative motion of agitation would be largely diminished, and that they would probably move in clouds—"the dust and refuse of the system"—with so infrequent inter-collisions that it might not be permissible to treat the cloud as possessing the mechanical properties of a gas.

A very different conception of the prenebular history of matter was suggested by Dr. James Croll, twenty-one years ago.[17] This supposes "that our sun was formed from a hot gaseous nebula produced by the colliding of two dark stellar masses, and that as the stars are suns like our own, they in all likelihood, had a similar origin." The considerations

[16] His results are embodied in a memoir "On the mechanical Condition of a Swarm of Meteorites, and on Cosmogony," read Nov. 15, 1888, before the *Royal Society*, and published in the *Transactions*, vol. 180, A. pp. 1–69, with notes by the author to Dec. 19, 1888. The writer is indebted to professor Darwin for a copy.

[17] *Philosophical Magazine* May, 1868. The thought has been several times reproduced. "Climate and Time" chap. 21; *Quarterly Jour. Sci.* July, 1877; *Phil, Mag.*, July, 1878; "Climate and Cosmology," chaps. XVII, XVIII and XIX; "Stellar Evolution," 1889, 12mo, 218 pp. For the last two works named the writer acknowledges his obligations to their author.

which favor the theory are well set forth in Dr. Croll's recent work on "Stellar Evolution." The motion of the colliding masses is not supposed to be entirely due to the action of gravity—as according to the more recent conception of Sir William Thomson.[18] "If the masses were created, they may as likely have been created in motion as at rest; if they were eternal, they may as likely have been eternally in motion as eternally at rest. Eternal motion is just as warrantable an assumption as eternal matter." "A mass equal to that of the sun, moving with a velocity of 476 miles per second, would possess, in virtue of that motion, energy sufficient, if converted into heat, to maintain the present rate of the sun's radiation for 50,000,000 years."

"The collision of two bodies each half the mass of the sun would result immediately in a chaos of fragments. The enormous heat generated would further shatter and disperse the fragments. Much of the matter would be transformed suddenly into the gaseous condition. In the course of time, the whole would assume the gaseous condition, and we should then have a perfect nebula[19]—intensely hot, but not very luminous. As the temperature diminished, the nebulous mass would begin to condense, and ultimately, according to the well known nebular hypothesis, pass through all the different phases of rings, planets and satellites, into our Solar system as it now exists."

Here then, are two distinct conceptions of prenebular history:—First, The Meteoric Theory, as reasoned out, it is represented, by professor Tait, and independently by the present writer, and also, with convincing and admirable fullness, by professor Lockyer; Second, The Impact Theory, of which Dr. Croll's form postulates initial motion and Sir William Thomson's assumes initial rest. Under the first theory, the nebular mass undergoes a prolonged aggregation, heat resulting from the impact of descending contributions. Under the impact theory, dark bodies exist in immensity[20] whose move-

---

[18] *Nature*, 27 Jan. 1887; *Proc. Roy. Institution*, vol. XII.

[19] Whether "a perfect nebula" is entirely gaseous is the question at present in doubt.

[20] Lambert conceived the existence of dark bodies as centres of the great cosmic systems. "Kosmologische Briefe ueber die Einrichtung des Weltbaus," Augsburg, 1761. Newcomb affirms that "not the slightest evidence favoring the existence of these opaque centres has ever been found."

ments, whether initial or gravitational, bring them occasionally into collision.

But there are prenebular inquiries prior to those reached by these theories. What was the antecedent history of matter which had attained the condition of meteoroidal masses? In the work already quoted, the present writer set forth the theory that the "universal world-stuff" postulated by Grove, Brodie, Hunt and many others, or generalized from the phenomena of meteors, is, in its state of ultimate attenuation, the ethereal medium conceived by Newton, Young, Saigey, Macvicar, Lodge and others.[21] He suggested, in other words, that out of this semi-spiritual substance may have germinated the molecules of common matter, and that the so-called ethereal medium may thus have been the ultimate condition of the matter of nebulæ.[22] Further considerations confirmatory of the doctrine of the continuity of planetary atmospheres with the interplanetary medium, were based, at a later date, on the fact that the gaseous atmospheric constituents fixed in coal-beds, carbonates and other forms, during the progress of rock-formation have been many times greater than could have been yielded by a terrestrial atmosphere of determinate volume and mass.[23]

The recent memoir of Dr. Huggins, "On the Spectrum, Visible and Photographic, of the Great Nebula in Orion"[24] is thought by some "to go a good way to overturn the views held by Mr. Lockyer, and recently advocated by professor Darwin, on the meteoric constitution of nebulæ." The present writer does not share in that impression. Dr. Huggins' researches confirm the presence of hydrogen, throw some doubt on the presence of nitrogen and perhaps still more doubt on Mr. Lockyer's contention for the presence of magnesium at a comparatively low temperature. Had he shown that the nebula is exclusively gaseous, the

[21]Dr. Croll in allusion to this says: "Professor Winchell has advanced views similar to those of Tait and Lockyer regarding the nature and origin of nebulæ. But he, in addition, discusses the further question of the origin of these swarms."—"Stellar Evolution," p. 23.

[22] World-Life, p. 533, and more specifically, pt. I. ch. I §7.

[23]A. Winchell, "Secular increase of the Earth's Mass," *Science*, II. 820-1, Dec. 28, 1883. *Chemical News*, London, March, 1884.

[24]Read before the *Royal Society*, May 2, 1889, but not yet published—an uncorrected proof copy having been received from Dr. Croll by the present writer.

showing would have been adverse to the theory of a meteorics constitution of that part of the Orion nebula investigated. But the spectrum studied chiefly was a bright line spectrum, and of course revealed only gaseous conditions of matter. Such gases may have been merely an atmosphere bathing other portions of matter in liquid and solid states. This being so, the facts stated are quite compatible with either the meteoric or the impact theory of prenebular states. Moreover, Dr. Huggins himself supplies statements which indicate the existence of matter in other than the gaseous condition. He speaks of a "continuous spectrum," which, however, he attributes to the two of the four bright stars of the Trapezium which fell upon the slit. But he detects evidence that the stars *belong to the nebula*, in the fact that the bright nebular lines crossing the steller spectrum can be traced for some little distance into the nebula, showing that those stars are not merely optically connected with the nebula, but are physically bound up with it, and are very probably condensed out of the gaseous matter of the nebula. It may be mentioned that other nebulæ affording the bright lines of gaseity, exhibit stronger continuous spectra, while in the nebula of Andromeda, the continuous spectrum supersedes that of bright lines.

This is all intelligible without ignoring the probability of pre-gaseous conditions, and still more without denying non-gaseous matter of pre-gaseous origin, coëxistent with a conspicuous amount of gaseous matter. If the meteoric theory implies the aggregation of cold stones and sand, it implies equally the evolution of intense heat and resulting gases. So a nebula resulting from impact of single masses would consist similarly of solid and liquid fragments immersed in a gaseous atmosphere of high temperature. If under either theory, the temperature should reduce to a gaseous state, the entire matter of the nebula, that would furnish no reason for assuming that the nebula had been gaseous from the beginning of its existence.

To the writer, the present state of knowledge seems to justify the opinion that some nebulæ exist in a condition entirely gaseous, and others in a mixed state, while a few seem to have attained throughout, the condition of fire-mist—borne up probably, by a faintly luminous residual gas. It seems further, to justify the theory that all nebulæ have had a prenebular history—a growth or development from cold, non-luminous states of matter. The difficulty of admitting vast, dark cosmic bodies, whose existence is entirely conjectural, leads the writer to prefer the meteoric theory, which finds the requisite cold matter in all-pervading "cosmic dust," whose existence is actually revealed in the meteorites which course about the sun, and descend in "star-showers" to the planet on whose surface we dwell.

Ann Arbor June 15, 1889.

FROM THE PROCEEDINGS OF THE BOSTON SOCIETY OF NATURAL HISTORY, VOL. IX., FEBRUARY, 1865.

NOTES ON SELANDRIA CERASI HARRIS, AS IT OCCURS AT ANN ARBOR, MICHIGAN. By PROFESSOR ALEXANDER WINCHELL.

[Condensed, with a few additions, from a paper read before the Michigan Scientific Association, June 24, 1863.]

This destructive insect made its first appearance at this place in 1859: its depredations were, however, not generally observed till 1862, when it caused the death of many fine cherry-trees. Its increased ravages during the present year have attracted general attention, and induced the writer to extend his observations previously begun, and to determine what relations exist between the Michigan insect and that described by Peck and Harris.

The fly commenced to deposit its ova the present year on the 5th of June. It selected for this purpose the leaves of the pear and cherry; though, in the course of the season, it was observed that the mountain-ash and the plum had also suffered to a limited extent. The ova were deposited through rectilinear incisions in the epidermis of the upper side of the leaf; and the chlorophyl, for a small distance around each egg, was changed to a brown color, and deadened, giving the leaf, where the eggs were numerous, a strongly mottled appearance. Trees in open situations were most infested; and the outer portions of the foliage of a tree were preferred to the more shady.

The ovipositor is attached at a distance of .025 of an inch from the extremity of the body of the female. When at rest, it is lodged in a slit which reaches nearly to the tip of the abdomen. It has the form of a butcher's knife, a little bent upwards near the point. Toward the other extremity, the organ is curved in the opposite direction into a right angle with the main axis, and is furnished internally with a couple of apophyses for the attachment of the muscles which move the instrument in the execution of its office. The upper margin of each blade is worked into a series of low, sharp teeth, turned from the point of the blade; the lower side is furnished with a series of erect teeth, whose margins are themselves serrate. The muscular action which moves this instrument thrusts it entirely through the leaf, cutting with the serrated teeth of the lower side as it enters in the act of being drawn; while the backward turned teeth of the upper margin do the same work while the instrument is being withdrawn, and resuming its place in the slit. The straight gashes made by the ovipositor can be invariably seen on the under side of the leaf, close by the position occupied by the egg. The length of the ovipositor, to the internal bend, is .042 inch; and its width, .001 inch.

The habits of these saw-flies are sluggish. In damp or even cloudy weather, they stand motionless on the under sides of the leaves. When approached by the hand, they are apt to drop as if dead, and thus escape. They never, in such weather, attempt to fly away. In sunny weather, they may be seen on both surfaces of the leaves; and, on taking alarm, will sometimes fly away. The insect is willing to alight on the leaf of any tree, but makes a strict selection in depositing its ova.

These flies were first observed on the 5th of June. By the 8th, they had apparently diminished in numbers; on the 9th, they were moderately numerous, and active on some of the trees; on the 10th, very few were to be found; on the 11th, none. Nevertheless, one or two were observed near the close of June, and one or two in July.

The following observations were made on the development of the embryo: —

June 7. The ovum is .03 of an inch in its longer diameter, and .014 in its shorter. The form is a prolate ellipsoid, flattened on one side. The contents are simply granular.

June 8. Under a power of 230 diameters, the contents of the egg-cell consist simply of small globules, the whole mass of which, under a compressor, seems to be divided into large irregular areas. On certain sides, also, are presented some inequalities, like convolutions, as if the embryo were beginning to receive shape.

June 9. The embryo can be discerned doubled together, and presenting already distinct traces of articulations.

June 10. Embryo appears clearly as an articulate, doubled together with its back next the periphery. The place of the eye is a dark-brown spot. The oral organs are clearly developing, and the legs are beginning to protrude in distinct sacs. When slightly compressed, the vitelline membrane bursts, and the traces of organization dissolved at once into a multitude of granules floating in a watery fluid.

June 11. Pedal protuberances well developed, and claws beginning to appear. The head distinctly isolated from the body, and the oral apparatus quite distinct; at intervals, also, the embryo squirms in its nidus, and occasionally a single foot protrudes and retracts itself.

June 12. Movements of the embryo frequent. Aortic contractions quite regular, at the rate of 30 per minute: occasionally they intermit for a minute or two. The contractions are always seen immediately after the efforts at motion.

June 13. Embryo appears stronger, and makes more energetic motions. The claws of the true legs are pretty well developed. The contractions of the dorsal vessel are less violent than yesterday; have increased to 55 per minute; and can be traced through half the length of the embryo. I could not, under any circumstances, detect any movement of a circulating fluid. Bristles begin to appear on the feet, and the pro-legs are developed. The tracheary system is faintly marked out in the vicinity of the head, though the coiled spring could barely be discerned in one of the largest trunks. A mysterious vitality inheres in this forming organism, as the following experiment shows. The egg was put under the compressor, and pressed till the outer membrane burst, and the tail of the embryo was extruded: in this condition, the contractions of the dorsal vessel increased to 80 per minute. On further compression, the contractions near the head were 68, and near the tail 144, per minute. On still further compression, the contractions near the head remained the same; while those near the tail occurred by threes, in which the beats were very quick. The compression was increased as far as the thin glass could allow: the embryo was completely crushed, and its parts extruded in every direction; and yet, where the dorsal vessel lay, the wonderful struggle to perpetuate existence was kept up to the end.

June 14. The ova are beginning to hatch. The slug cuts a semicircular slit through the membrane of the egg and the epidermis of the leaf, forming a lid, which folds back, and allows it to escape. One slug, which had not moved its own length from the trap-door through which it emerged, was .06 of an inch in length. In form, the young slug slightly increases in width from the tail to the region of the head, where it exhibits a considerable enlargement. The head is black, and habitually curled under the shoulders: it is furnished with a powerful pair of serrated mandibles. The eyes can be seen, under pressure, as a pair of small round, clear globules; in front of which is a pair of oval semitranslucent spots. The feet are provided each with a bifid claw and several short bristles. The pro-legs are truncate, smooth, and retractile: a few bristles are seen scattered in clusters of two and three over the exterior, and they become more numerous at the posterior extremity. The external surface is transversely wrinkled, and covered with a small amount of watery slime. The young slug is nearly transparent, but having a pale, olivaceous hue, with a dark spot at one extremity produced by the head, and another at the opposite extremity caused by an accumulation of fecal matter.

The alimentary canal in the new-born larva is by far the largest vessel in the animal. It swells out to its largest diameter just behind the head, and somewhat irregularly tapers toward the hind extremity, near which it is much contracted. In this part of the slug, numerous faint, parallel, longitudinal lines can be seen, which are perhaps muscular fibres, related to the excretory apparatus. The vermicular action of the alimentary canal is constant and rhythmical.

The dorsal vessel is next in size. It can be traced to the region just behind the head, where it shows a disposition to curve downwards; though neither here, nor at the opposite extremity, could I detect the continuity between this vessel and the recurrent vessels or streams.

The ventral or recurrent streams are at least two in the middle region of the larva. There are all the usual indications of vascular walls; but the general doubt entertained amongst anatomists, as to the existence of such walls in any insects, causes me to withhold the allegation of their occurrence here. Posterior to the middle region, these streams pursue a somewhat convoluted course, but do not assume any thing like the sinus-disposition seen in certain worms: the circulating fluid could be distinctly traced, flowing backwards with an irregular movement through nearly the whole length of the larva.

The tracheary system is beautifully distinct. Stigmata occur along the sides at points corresponding to the feet and pedal swellings, and connect by large trunks with a somewhat sinuous longitudinal vessel, which runs from the head quite around the animal, being somewhat reduced in size in the neighborhood of the hinder extremity. These longitudinal trunks are connected, in each segment, by a single transverse trunk; but, in the segments which bear the three pairs of feet, the transverse trunks are in pairs. From the trunks arising from the stigmata, but especially from the longitudinal trunks, arise branches which ramify throughout the body. The transverse trunks are also somewhat branched.

No trace of a nervous system was detected.

Immediately after the slug escapes from the egg, it begins to feed upon the green pulp of the leaf, and thus by degrees covers the leaf with small, round, faded spots. The brood began to attain the full growth and to disappear about the middle of July. It would seem that their retirement to the chrysalis state may be somewhat hastened by external circumstances. The stem of a small dwarf pear-tree, which had been completely denuded by these depredators, was seen to be covered with slugs of various ages, all alike winding their way toward the ground. Dozens of the larvæ were seen already squirming upon the surface of the soil. The next day, all had disappeared.

The autumn brood of our cherry-slug may be regarded as a complete failure; the fly barely making its appearance early in September, and the slugs being scarely discoverable.

This saw-fly, in reference to which I have offered some facts which I have not found on record, differs as much from the slug-fly of Boston as that does from the *Selandria æthiops* of Europe: whether the three forms are to be regarded as specifically identical, will depend somewhat on the views entertained as to the variability of species. The points of difference thus far observed between our insect and that described by Harris are as follows: —

1. In Harris's insect, the ova are deposited in *semicircular* incisions: in ours, they are in *straight* incisions.

2. In Harris's insect, the eggs are generally on the *under* side of the leaves: in ours, they are always on the *upper* side.

3. In Harris's insect, the embryo escapes on the *fourteenth* day: in ours, on the *eighth* or *ninth*.

4. The first two pairs of legs in the adult insect are not nearly so light colored as in that described by Harris.

5. Perhaps the almost complete failure of the autumnal brood deserves to be mentioned in this connection; though this might be due to a changed climate, as it is well known that the reproduction of many species is materially influenced by climatic conditions. It may also be added, that, unlike the Boston slug, ours emits no odor; and that, contrary to the statement of Norton,* from three to a dozen individuals may generally be found on each leaf, in those parts of the tree that have been visited by the fly.

As to the remedy for this horticultural pest, it may be added to what has been already published, that the odor of coal-tar effectually drives away the fly. This can be smeared over a piece of board, and suspended in the tree, — a resort which I have found effectual against the plum-weevil. It is likely that the odor of petroleum or naphtha would produce similar results.

Contrary to the conjectures of Harris, this disgusting larva is never eaten by birds.

University of Michigan, 15th October, 1863.

* Proc. Bost. Soc. Nat. Hist., Oct. 1861, p. 222. Harris states, however, that sometimes twenty or thirty may be seen on a single leaf (Insects Inj. to Veg., 1862, p. 530).

THE CLIMATE OF MICHIGAN.

A PAPER

READ AT THE

ANNUAL MEETING OF THE STATE HORTICULTURAL SOCIETY,

DEC. 7, 1880,

By ALEXANDER WINCHELL,

PROFESSOR OF GEOLOGY AND PALÆONTOLOGY IN THE UNIVERSITY OF MICHIGAN.

[EXTRACTED FROM THE ANNUAL REPORT OF THE SOCIETY FOR 1880.]

THE CLIMATE OF MICHIGAN.

It is fifteen years since I first endeavored to impress upon the attention of the people of Michigan the beneficial peculiarities of their climate. There is but one physical characteristic of our peninsula which is exceptional, and confers upon us any superior advantages—*that is climate.* Apart from climate, our soil is no more fertile than that of Ohio and Wisconsin; our primitive forests are no more abundant, our timber no more valuable; our water-powers no more numerous; our grasses no more nutritious. But our climate *is* exceptional; and it is exceptional to the great advantage of the agricultural and horticultural capabilities of the State.

My attention was first particularly directed to the influence of the great lakes, and especially of Lake Michigan, in the autumn of 1865, while making an economical and geological survey of the "Grand Traverse Region;" and the convictions first impressed by the vegetation of that region were confirmed by some precise meteorological comparisons published in my report* which appeared early in 1866. In August, 1866, I read a paper on "The Fruit-bearing Belt of Michigan," before the American Association for the Advancement of Science, at its Buffalo meeting.† At the Troy meeting of the same association, in 1870, I presented a more detailed paper, on "The Isothermals of the Lake Region," based on a much wider range of data than I had employed before.‡ In this paper, I embodied the results of all the meteorological observations ever published from within the limits of Michigan, as well as many observations then unpublished. As the object in view required comparisons, I collected similar data respecting more than fifty localities lying outside of the State. The Michigan observations aggregated two hundred and eighty-four years, and those of the other localities, four hundred and ninety-three years. A great amount of labor and research was expended in the compilation of the 132 tables on which the condensed published results were based. It had been my intention to embody these tables in the first volume of the geological survey of the State, which was then in progress under my direction.

With the view of bringing these most interesting generalizations before another class of readers, I drew up a paper on the "Climate of the Lake Region" for one of the most widely read of the literary magazines,|| and this was accompanied by two isothermal charts and other illustrations.

---

* The Grand Traverse Region. A Report on the Geological and Industrial Resources of the Counties of Antrim, Grand Traverse, Benzie, and Leelanaw, in the Lower Peninsula of Michigan, 8vo., 82 pp., with Map, and Appendix of 10 pp. on Palæontolgy. 1866.

† Proceedings American Association, 1866, pp. 84-91.

‡ Proceedings American Association, 1870, pp. 106-117.

|| Harper's Magazine, July, 1871, pp. 275-285.

My memoir read before the American Association in August, 1870, was appended, without charts, to my "Report of Progress," communicated by the Governor to the legislature of 1871, and is included in that report as published by authority.* It was supposed that this general presentation of the peculiar features of our climate would awaken an interest in the minds of the members of the legislature which would easily secure the requisite appropriation for publication. But, for some reason, the interest and importance of these results were not appreciated. There were special active influences at work adverse to the interests of the survey. I presented the subject at an evening meeting of the members, and finally, laid upon the table of every member, a copy of a pamphlet on "The Climate of Michigan," in which the salient points in our climatology were very briefly pointed out, and illustrated by isothermal charts; but, suffice it to say, the appropriation failed, and this, of course, ended my official connection with the effort to publish to the world the great and beneficent facts which constitute the only superior natural resource of our peninsula.

In 1873, I was called upon to furnish several chapters of information concerning Michigan, for Walling's "Atlas" of the State. One of the subjects discussed was Climatology; and in this paper, I presented again the numerical results of the studies which I had before completed. This paper was accompanied by four colored charts of isothermal lines. The first of these gives the isothermals for July and January; the second, for Summer and Winter; the third, for Spring and Autumn, and the fourth, for the year, and for the mean *minima* and extreme *minima.*† This makes, in effect, nine sets of isothermal lines. The memoirs embodied in Walling's Atlas were subsequently reprinted in a thick pamphlet, of 121 pages, accompanied by the same charts as were contained in the Atlas.‡

Though the efforts, of which I have given a sketch, have received no legislative appreciation, I do not rely on my own judgment alone, in declaring that they set forth, on a scientific basis, a body of generalizations possessing the utmost importance for the agricultural and horticultural interests of our State. My report on the Grand Traverse region was circulated during 1866. In the older portions of the State, it awakened some undisguised incredulity. This was participated in by Mr. Sanford Howard, then secretary of the State Board of Agriculture; and accordingly, in 1867, Secretary Howard made a tour of the region, and embodied the results of his observations in a contribution of twenty-four pages to the report of the Board of Agriculture for that year.‖ Departing, as I was informed, with the full purpose of exposing the fabulous character of my report of the year before, he returned with a complete confirmation of all my statements, using very many of the same facts, and associating them with very similar explanations and suggestions. Yet my own name is not once mentioned in the paper, nor would the reader infer that Mr. Secretary Howard was not absolutely the first man to publish these discoveries and conclusions.

My popular paper in Harper's Magazine was re-published in Der Michigan Wegweiser, at Hamburg, Germany, a periodical established to promote immi-

---

* Report on the progress of the State Geological Survey of Michigan. Presented to the State Geological Board Nov. 22, 1870. Lansing, 1871.

† On this chart, the *minus* signs before the numbers denoting mean and extreme minima have been omitted by the engraver. These numbers express, of course, temperatures *below zero.*

‡ Michigan. Being condensed Popular Sketches of the Topography, Climate and Geology of the State. 8 vo., 121 pp. 1873.

‖ Sixth Annual Report of the Secretary of the State Board of Agriculture of the State of Michigan, for the year 1867, pp. 79–102.

gration into our State. It was also re-published in the scientific journal entitled Zeitschrift der öster reichischen Gesellschaft für Meteorologie, or Journal of the Austrian Society for Meteorology, at Vienna, volume viii, p. 40, February 1, 1873. An abstract of my paper on the "Isothermals of the Lake Region" was also published in this journal, volume vii, p. 351.

The report drawn up by Mr. S. B. McCracken on the resources of Michigan,* for use at the centennial exposition of 1876, draws a large supply of facts and generalizations from the papers previously published by myself; and for this indebtedness due acknowledgments are made. The report of the State board of health for 1878, contains an extended and thorough presentation of the "climate and topography" of the lower peninsula of Michigan, by Dr. Henry F. Lyster,† who, while drawing extensively from the published results of my studies in the geology, topography and climate of the State, gives adequate credit for materials used, and accords to myself due priority in the disclosure of the peculiarities of our climate. Dr. Lyster, in a few pages, takes the cream of a body of results which I had based on months of labor and thousands of calculated means.

In numerous other sanitary, pomological and agricultural proceedings, I have found these generalizations cited and re-produced. I am, therefore, encouraged to believe that I have not misconceived their importance. This belief is strengthened by the spontaneous request of the State horticultural society to read a paper on the climate of the State—that factor in the fruit-raiser's operations which is most completely independent of all human control.

The foregoing statements concern the history of investigation on this subject, and are important to be made for the sake of preserving the record; and also, for the purpose of indicating where the members of this society may find fuller details on the climate of the State than it is my purpose to present on this occasion.

Before my own researches on this subject, no one had as much as suggested the great amount of the influence of Lake Michigan upon our climate; and no one, so far as I am aware, had subjected the recognized influence of any of the great lakes to the test of exact statistics. Dr. J. P. Kirtland, of Cleveland, had published a note on the influence of Lake Erie, but aside from the phenomena connected with the growth of vegetation, and the presence of southern birds and insects, he recorded no exact data beyond a few single observations.‡ He states that killing frosts are about a month later on the lake shore than in the interior, and that, in a case of extreme cold, the thermometer marked about six degrees higher at Cleveland than at points some miles back from the lake. Mr. Loren Blodgett, at the commencement of my own researches, had published a "Climatology of the United States,"‖ embodying a vast amount of exact information; but his isothermal lines march across our peninsula, and across the entire lake region, as if the whole surface were one unbroken land-area. Still cruder is the isothermal chart of the United States "as determined by the Smithsonian Institution,"§ and published a year or two earlier than Blodget's work. It will be understood, as a necessary inference, that the

*S. B. McCracken: The State of Michigan, embracing sketches of its History, Position, Resources and Industries, 1876, 8 vo. 136 pp.

†Sixth annual report of the secretary of State board of health of the State of Michigan, pp. 167–250.

‡ J. P. Kirtland, Am. Jour. Sci., II., xiii., 215 and 294.

‖ L. Blodget: Climatology of the United States and of the Temperate Latitudes of the North American Continent, 8 vo. pp. 536, with charts. Philadelphia, 1857.

§ Patent Office Report for 1856. Agriculture, Plate iv.

charts based on the army observations,* as well as all previous attempts at isothermal charts, fail totally to detect the local climatic influence which, as we now know, bends the isothermal lines of our peninsula in the most extraordinary manner.

The peninsular situation of our State is something which arrests the attention of the most casual observer of the map of the northwest. It is not apparent to observation, however, that our State is also a climatic peninsula; and yet, extended observation shows that our climate, in its seasonal means, is a patch taken from the latitude of Ohio; while in the moderation of its extremes, it bears an analogy to the Floridian peninsula. Its climate is cut off from that of Wisconsin and Iowa by a barrier as abrupt and as real as that which limits our territory. That which constitutes the barrier in the one case, creates it in the other.

The nature of our climatic situation is exemplified in the comparative statistics of every cold wave which passes over the northwest. On the 18th of November, 1880, for instance, while the thermometer was 5° at Milwaukee, it stood at 18° at Grand Haven, and 10° at Port Huron. At the same time, it was 8° at St. Louis, 2° at Denver, 4° at Dodge City, Kansas, and 6° as far south as Fort Gibson, Indian Territory. On the 19th of November, while the thermometer marked 29° at Grand Haven, it was 13° at Port Huron; and farther south, it marked 14° at Chicago, 2° at Indianapolis, 11° at Louisville, and 8° at St. Louis.

The rationale of our peninsular climate is easy to understand. It involves only two fundamental factors: 1. The presence of a large body of water on our western boundary. 2. The prevalent westerly direction of our cold winds. Lake Michigan is a body of water 360 miles long and 108 miles wide, with a mean depth of 900 feet, and a superficial area of 20,000 square miles. You could sink, in this lake, the three States of New Jersey, Delaware and Maryland. It contains 18½ millions of millions of cubic yards of water,† or in other terms, 3,400 cubic miles of water. This vast body of water maintains a comparatively uniform temperature. Three months of summer warmth do not suffice to elevate it much above the annual mean, nor three months of winter to depress it much below that mean. While the mean July temperature of the land, in the mid-latitude of Lake Michigan, rises to 74°, that of the lake surface does not surpass 51°. While the January temperature of the land sinks to 19°, that of the water does not fall below 40°. On the land, the whole amount of heat absorbed is accumulated within 50 or 60 feet of the surface; while on the lake, the agitation of the water tends to distribute the summer accumulation through a depth of 900 feet. The average temperature, and therefore the surface temperature, is lower than the surface temperature of the land, and must, consequently, during the warm season, exert a cooling influence. On the contrary, during the winter, the average temperature of the water, and therefore its surface temperature, is much above that of the land, and must, consequently, exert a warming influence on the contiguous regions. In fact, the mass of the water of the lake becomes an immense stove, holding such a store of surplus summer heat, that, during the winter it warms up "all out doors." If the constant radiation of the lake is so perceptible in mean winter weather, it becomes truly striking when the land temperature sinks to

---

* Army Meteorological Register, 1855. It is impossible to overestimate our obligations to the army officers who planned and executed the extended series of observations taken at the military posts of the United States.

† 18,536,038,400,000 cubic yards.

its minimum point, and the difference between the land and the lake amounts to 50° or 60°.

Observations have shown that even the annual means of the regions contiguous to the lakes are somewhat raised by the lake influence. The cooling effect in summer is not equal to the warming effect in winter. In other words, the mean temperature of the lake is a few degrees higher than that of the land. As this fact cannot be attributed to an influx of river water from more southern latitudes, and would seem to be only partially explicable from the probably higher temperature of river-waters in the same latitudes, it remains to seek an explanation of the higher mean temperature of the lake. Now, let it be remembered that the waters of the lake penetrate 900 feet toward the heated interior of the earth; and that it has been ascertained that on the land every 55 feet of descent beneath the plane of constant temperature brings us one additional degree of heat. It will thus appear that if the depth of constant temperature in the mean latitude of Lake Michigan is 60 feet, the water of the lake reaches to a depth where the terrestial temperature should be 15° higher than the constant temperature beneath the land, which would probably be about the mean annual temperature of the locality. I have ventured to suggest, in former papers, that though the cooling influence of the local annual mean must have been felt by the earth, in the bottom of the lake, it must be still true that the bottom of the lake has felt somewhat the warming influence of the normal terrestrial temperature at that depth. It seems to me entirely reasonable, therefore, to maintain that the heat of the earth's internal fires contributes something to the excess of the lake's mean warmth over the mean warmth of the land. The great lake may, therefore, be conceived as held in a vast natural dish, which is warmed over the imperishable fire which we know to be imprisoned within the earth. When the temperature of the land sinks to -20° or -30°, that of the lake is sixty or seventy degrees higher; and the vapor which ascends from its surface is the literal similitude of the steam rising from a kettle heated over a domestic fire.

The other factor in our peninsular climate is the prevailing direction of the wind. Were the atmosphere perpetually calm, the contiguous land and superincumbent atmosphere would only be very feebly warmed by direct radiation; and this effect would be more than counterbalanced by a perpetual land breeze as long as the lake should remain warmer than the land. But the general atmosphere is always in motion. Warmed in winter, while passing over the surface of the lake, it conveys some part of the lake-warmth to the land, and the rigor of the cold becomes ameliorated, on the principle of a hot-air furnace. As the wind, by turns, moves from all directions, the lake exerts some warming influence on all the surrounding land. This is illustrated by the isothermal lines for the cold months, which are bent southward, on approaching the lake from either side. Evidently, that side of the lake which receives most wind from the lake-surface, will be most impressed by the lake-influence. Now, it happens that the Michigan side of Lake Michigan receives most lake winds during the cold season, because, as is well known, our cold winds approach from a westerly direction. Thus, in January, at Chicago, according to eleven years' observations, the winds from the west of the meridian are to the winds from the east of the meridian as 72:5=14.4; at Milwaukee, for thirteen years, as 60:18=3.33; at Manitowoc, for eleven years, as 67:11=6.09; at Grand Haven, for one and a half years, as 34:16=2.1. A similar excess of westerly winds is shown for all the months of the year, except April and May, and especially the month of May.

In consequence of this prevalence of westerly winds, the east side of the lake is warmed in winter and cooled in summer. While, therefore, the winter mean at Chicago is 24½°, that of New Buffalo, in the same latitude, is 28°. While that of Milwaukee is 22°, that of Grand Haven is 26°. While the winter mean of Fort Howard is 20°, and that of Appleton 19°, the winter mean of Traverse City, farther north than either, is 23½°. In autumn also, the preponderance of westerly winds raises the mean temperature one to two degrees along the south half of the lake shore, and three to four degrees along the northern half of the shore. This is illustrated by the chart which hangs before us, where the red lines pass through localities having the same autumnal means. To the west of the lake region, the lines conform approximately to the parallels of latitude, but over and east of lake Michigan, they bend abruptly northward. The autumnal isotherm of 46°, which passes through Fort Winnebago, bends northward nearly to the extreme point of lake Michigan, a difference of latitude of about 185 miles. The isotherm of 47°, which passes through Fort Atkinson, bends northward to the Beaver islands, 192 miles. The isotherm of 48° is deflected northward an equal distance. The isotherm of 49° sweeps from Evanston, near Chicago, to the mouth of the Manistee river, a difference of latitude of 152 miles. The isotherm of 50° bends from Kensington, south of Chicago, to Grand Rapids, a difference of latitude of 97 miles. The favorable contrast diminishes in the southern portion of the eastern shore, since in November the cold southwesterly winds either miss the lake entirely, or are held at a lower temperature by mingling with wind which has not traversed the lake. To put the subject in another light, an investigation of the monthly means on the opposite side of the lake, during autumn, shows that the temperature attained at Milwaukee, Oct. 15, is not reached at Grand Haven until Oct. 20. The Milwaukee temperature of Nov. 15 is only reached at Grand Haven Nov. 23. The Chicago temperature of Sept. 15 is the same as the New Buffalo temperature of Sept. 21. These comparisons show that the warm season is lengthened, on the east side, about six to eight days, in the autumn. In 1865 the first killing frost in the Grand Traverse region was Dec. 2; in 1866, Nov. 15; in 1867, Nov. 18.

By a singular and happy exception, in the prevailing direction of the wind, we find that during the month of May, winds from the east of the meridian preponderate. This is shown from the tables again; since at Manitowoc the easterly winds in May are to the westerly as 37:26=1.42; at Milwaukee, as 62:24=2.58, and in April as 52:33=1.6; at Chicago, including north winds, which are her lake winds, the ratio of lake and land winds is, in May, as 44:40=1.1. Now, in May, a lake wind is a chilling influence, except when the thermometer is sinking below the growing temperature for vegetation. It is then an influence which prevents frost. It follows, therefore, that during the mild days of May, the eastern shore of the lake is exempt from the chilling and retarding influence of westerly winds; while, during a cold period, when, as a rule, the wind is westerly, the eastern shore receives the benefit of protection from frost. Thus on the 16th of May, 1868, a destructive frost occurred throughout Illinois, Indiana and Ohio, but did no damage in the Grand Traverse region. This unique arrangement seems to have been prompted by a beneficent regard for the interests of early vegetation on our side of the lake. Westerly winds cease to predominate only in that month when they cease to be beneficial to Michigan. And yet even in that month they exist whenever the interests of vegetation demand. Not only do westerly winds cease to predominate at the juncture when they cease to be beneficial, but at the same juncture the warmer land winds from the east of the meridian become predominant. Both causes accelerate vegetation on the east side of the lake. A study of the means for a series of years, at places on opposite sides of the lake, shows that the temperature of Grand Haven, March 15th, is equal to that of Milwaukee March 21st; that of Grand Haven, April 15th, is equal to that of Milwaukee April 24th; that of Grand Haven, May 15th, is equal to that of Milwaukee May 28th. Remember that these are not comparisons of single instances; they are comparisons of the results of many years of accurate instrumental observation. They show that in May, Grand Haven is thirteen days in advance of Milwaukee. Add the thirteen days of growing weather gained in spring to the five days gained in October, and we perceive that the growing season is eighteen days longer at Grand Haven than at Milwaukee. Every practical cultivator knows that eighteen days often make all the difference between a crop well-ripened and perfect, and a crop immature and savorless, if not ruined by an untimely freeze.

This contrast is the same in kind as exists along the whole length of the two shores; but we find it qualified by two influences. First, the northern portion of the western shore receives a warming influence from northerly winds approaching over Green Bay; but at the same time, the greater expanse of water passed over by westerly and southwesterly winds approaching the Grand Traverse region imparts to that region a greater relative influence than is felt by the Grand Haven region. Secondly, the southern portion of our lake shore is exposed to the unmitigated sweep of southwest winds which, in the northwestern States, are often the coldest of all; but, on the contrary, this region receives northwesterly and even north winds which have swept over a vast expanse of lake surface.

It is not to be supposed that these climatic influences are confined to the immediate shore of Lake Michigan. Undoubtedly, they reach there their greatest development; but the tables which I have compiled, and place before you, and the isothermal charts which I exhibit, demonstrate that the whole of our peninsula receives a similar kind of influence. The President of our local horticultural society will inform you how many car-loads of peaches, grapes and other fruits have been sent out of Ann Arbor during the past season. Nor is it to be assumed that the western borders of our great lakes receive none of their equalizing effects. My own charts show that the northward deflection of the winter isothermals begins on the west side of Lake Michigan, many miles from the lake. This is also shown on the climatic chart of Wisconsin, published by Dr. I. A. Lapham, in 1865. My charts also show that a similar influence is exerted upon our peninsula by lakes Huron, St. Clair and Erie. I include Lake St. Clair, because it is always filled with water of the same temperature, except in the stagnant portions, as that of the great lakes beyond, and never cools down in winter, like a small isolated body of water. Moreover, the Huron peninsula lies in the lee of Saginaw Bay, and is another Michigan on a smaller scale. Thus, also, the south shore of Lakes Erie and Ontario are known to be greatly protected from unseasonable frosts and extreme winters, in spite of the preponderance of westerly winds along those shores.

I have thus far directed your attention almost exclusively to mean temperature—to the averages of months and seasons. These suffice, indeed, to indicate the length of the growing period and the average severity of the winter. But there is another aspect of climate which possesses at least equal importance;

though in climatic discussions it has been largely overlooked. Published tables give us means of the year, and of the several seasons; and their authors seem to think that in this they have brought to view all the important elements of climate which bear on health and production of crops. A little reflection, however, shows that the *extremes* of climate are of equal importance with the means. It signifies little that the growing season begins in March, if liability to killing frosts continues to the middle of May, as in Tennessee. A mean October temperature of 60° is comparatively valueless after a September freeze. The mean temperature of a season may be mild, or even delightful at the same time that one or two days have brought a destructive cold. One killing frost is as bad as a dozen, for vegetation has but one life to destroy. It is the liability to these exceptional temperatures which we must know before forming final judgment on the adaptability of a district for a particular crop. A winter which averages mild may be marked, like the climate of St. Louis, by one, two or three mornings destructive to everything which would triumphantly survive all the rest of the season. Every fruit-raiser knows that it is not the average weather of winter or spring which endangers his buds or his trees. It is the one or two nights of the whole season which brings him apprehension—especially if accompanied by high wind. It is of no consequence that the winter mean of St. Louis is 33°, and that of Grand Haven 21°, or of Traverse City 24°, if the thermometer falls sometimes to -22° at St. Louis, and never sinks below -16° at Grand Haven or Traverse City. It is precisely against these exceptional extremes that lake Michigan exerts its most striking influence.

There are two ways to consider extremes of climate. We may consider the mean minimum of a locality, or its extreme minimum for a series of years. There is a lowest point reached by the thermometer at each locality every winter. Different winters may vary greatly in the severity of the coldest day, but we may take the average of a series of winters. This is the mean minimum. It indicates the lowest temperature which the locality is as likely to experience as to escape. Now, from this point of view, the Michigan climate stands forth singularly favored. I have with me a chart of mean minima, which members of the society are at liberty to inspect. You will be surprised to notice how the lines passing through points having the same mean minimum are bent northward along the region of the lakes. They do not trend east and west, as they must under the normal influence of latitude, but they run literally north and south in the vicinity of lakes Michigan and Huron. The isothermal of -15° strikes from Mackinac through Manitowoc, Milwaukee, and New Buffalo to Fort Riley, in Kansas, near the parallel of 39°. Here is a deflection over nearly seven degrees of latitude, or about 480 miles in a straight line. The meaning of this is that the most excessive cold at Mackinac, for a period of twenty-eight years, is not, on the average, greater than at Fort Riley, 480 miles further south. It is one degree less than at Chicago for a term of eleven years. There is but one feature about our climate which is more striking, and that is the isotherms for extreme minima.

Suppose we note the lowest point reached by the thermometer in a series of years, at each of fifty localities. These points are the extreme minima of the several localities. Now, drawing a line, on a map, through all the localities which have the same extreme minimum, we have an isothermal chart for extreme minima. Such a chart I present before you on an enlarged scale. Its features are similar to the chart of mean minima, but still more pronounced.

By a glance at this chart, we percieve that the lowest point reached at Mackinac, in 28 years, is but two degrees lower than the extreme minimum of St. Louis. Extreme weather at Chicago is twelve degrees colder than at New Buffalo. The lowest extreme of Milwaukee is fourteen degrees below the extreme minimum of Grand Haven; while the extreme of Fort Howard is twenty degrees below that of Northport. In general, while the mean minimum along the west side of lake Michigan is -16°, that along the east side is -6°; while the extreme minimum on the west side is -22° to -30°, that of the east side is -10° to -16°, as far north as Little Traverse Bay. On that day of memorable cold, Jan. 1, 1864, the thermometer sank to -30° at Milwaukee, but only reached -14° at Northport and Traverse City. At the same time it was -29° at Chicago and -20° at Kalamazoo. It sank to -24° at St. Louis and -16° at Memphis, Tennessee. This point was two degrees colder than Northport, 640 miles further north in a direct line. The isotherm of -24° bends from the latitude of Alpena through Grand Rapids, Battle Creek and Coldwater, and thence to St. Louis, 452 miles further south. Cincinnati is reported to have an extreme minimum of -29°, a degree of cold not known in our peninsula, and but little exceeded along the south shore of Lake Superior. At Ann Arbor, the lowest point reached in 28 years, according to my own observations, is -24°. The area of this extreme minimum seems to cover all the central portion of the peninsula east of Grand Rapids, west of Bay City and south of Otsego Lake, and stretches southward into central Kentucky. Compared with Traverse City, the extreme minimum of Hazlewood, Minn., is 22° lower; that of St. Johnsbury, Vt., 28° lower; that of Gardiner, Me., within 30 miles of ocean, 19° lower; and of Montreal, P. Q., 26° lower.

These illustrations of the general principles announced must suffice for the present. This is not an occasion for entering into greater detail. The details must be conned over deliberately, in the presence of the charts which represent them graphically. For this purpose, I must refer you to the papers whose titles have already been cited. Better and more satisfactory still would be the study of the full tables of mean and extreme results on which these discussions have been based. Meantime, I hope I have made it clear that in our exceptional climate, we possess a natural resource which ought to be studied both by the public and the private citizen, and which, utilized to the fullest extent, will enable us to produce the crops suited to the lower Ohio valley, with a more certain exemption from unseasonable frosts than is enjoyed by Kentucky, Missouri, northern Texas, or the much-coveted Indian Territory.

THE ISOTHERMALS OF THE LAKE REGION

IN NORTH AMERICA.

BY ALEXANDER WINCHELL,

PROFESSOR OF GEOLOGY, ZOÖLOGY, AND BOTANY,

IN THE UNIVERSITY OF MICHIGAN.

From the Proceedings of the American Association for the Advancement of Science at the Troy meeting, August, 1870.

The Isothermals of the Lake Region. By Alexander Winchell, of Ann Arbor, Michigan.

It may be remembered that four years ago, at the Buffalo meeting of this Association, I read a paper on the "Fruit Belt of Michigan," in which I presented some statistics, illustrating the influence of Lake Michigan upon the climate of the contiguous regions on the east side. More recently I have had occasion to continue my investigation of the climatology of the Lake Region, and to prosecute it to a much greater degree of thoroughness and detail. For this purpose I have accumulated all the meteorological observations ever published from within the limits of the State of Michigan, as well as many observations yet unpublished. For purposes of comparison, I have collected similar *data* respecting more than fifty selected localities lying outside of the State of Michigan. The Michigan observations aggregate two hundred and eighty-four years, and those of the other localities four hundred and ninety-three years. The result of this discussion is to establish from extensive inductive *data* the existence of very remarkable influences exerted by the great lakes upon the temperature of the regions adjacent. A general statement of these results is here presented.

For the purpose of exhibiting the thermometric generalizations to the eye, I have constructed nine isothermal charts, covering the area between the fortieth and forty-eighth parallels of latitude, and between the eightieth and ninety-seventh meridians. This embraces the region within the influence of Lakes Superior, Michigan, and Huron, and the valley of the Mississippi as far west as Kansas and Nebraska.

It is well known that these great bodies of water exert a cooling influence in summer, and a warming influence in winter. The isothermal charts for July and January, to which I direct your attention, present these influences in strong contrast. Turning our attention first to the chart for July, we are at once impressed by the magnitude of the deflections of the isothermals in passing the great lakes. These deflections are toward the south, in consequence of the cooling influence of the lakes. In the lower peninsula of Michigan the lines all form loops opening southward, showing that the mean temperature of July, in the interior, is much higher than along the lake borders. And yet, within the peninsula

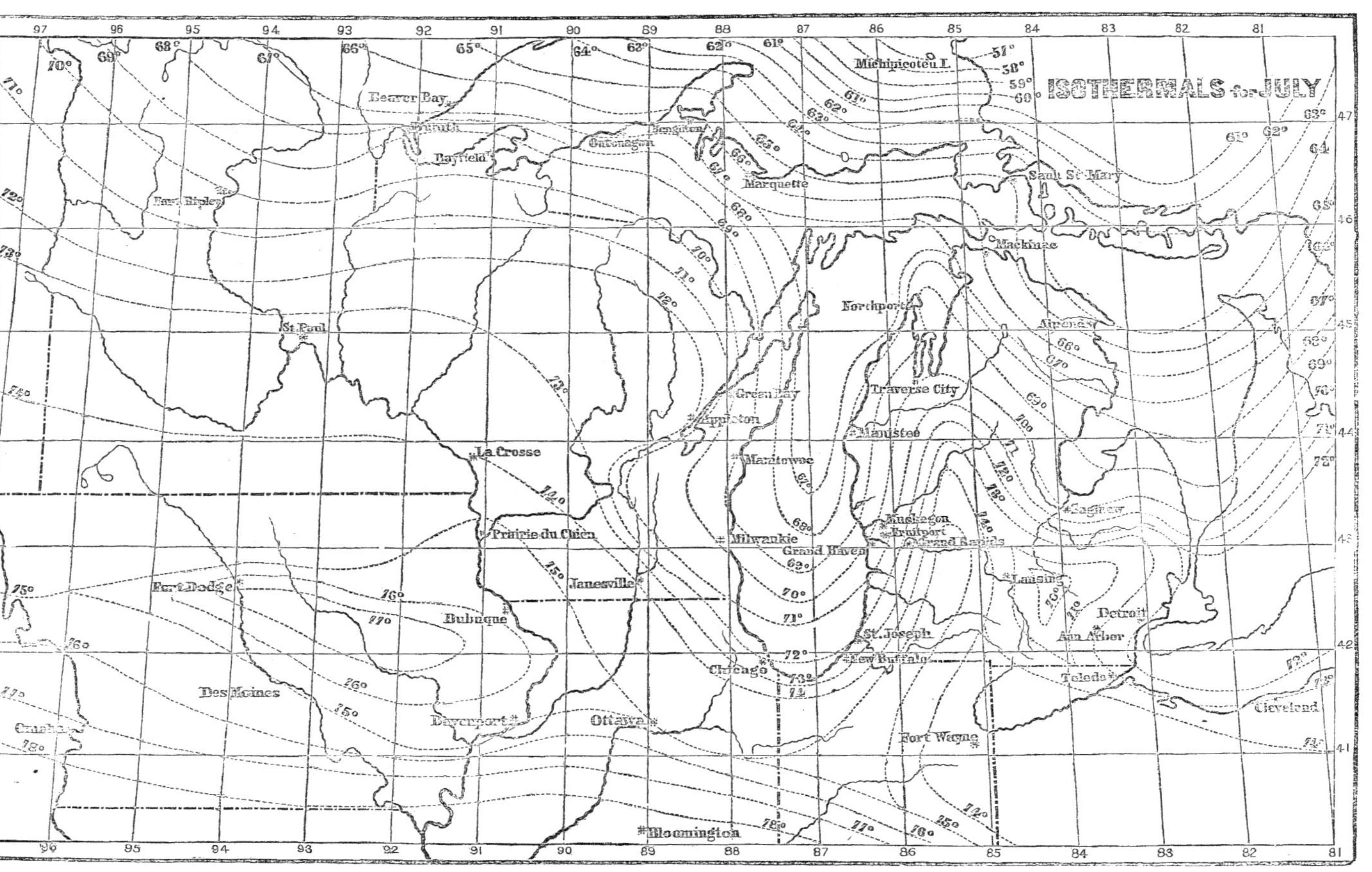
ISOTHERMALS for JULY
Michipicoten I.
Beaver Bay
Bayfield
Ontonagon
Marquette
Sault St. Mary
Mackinac
Fort Ripley
St. Paul
Northport
Alpena
Traverse City
Green Bay
Appleton
Manistee
La Crosse
Manitowoc
Muskegon
Fruitport
Grand Rapids
Prairie du Chien
Milwaukie
Grand Haven
Janesville
Fort Dodge
Lansing
Dubuque
Detroit
Ann Arbor
St. Joseph
New Buffalo
Chicago
Toledo
Des Moines
Davenport
Ottawa
Cleveland
Fort Wayne
Bloomington

of Michigan, the isothermals do not attain so high a northern limit as in the continental region west of Lake Superior. The isotherm of seventy degrees, for instance, first appears within the limits of the chart in the latitude of forty-eight degrees in the valley of the Red River of the North. Passing south-eastward and eastward to the valley of the Menominee River, it comes within the influence of Lake Michigan, and bends directly southward through Green Bay and Milwaukie to latitude 42° 40′, and thence trends northward to Traverse City in latitude 44° 40′. Here it is deflected southward again under the influence of Lake Huron, and, passing Saginaw and Sanilac, finally bends north-eastward to attain its normal position, striking Penetanguishene on Georgian Bay of Lake Huron. West of Lake Michigan, this isotherm sweeps across a latitudinal belt of five and a half degrees. Within the peninsula of Michigan, it is deflected first northward two degrees, and then southward one and a half degrees.

Similar deflections are experienced by the isotherms between 67° and 72°. The isotherms of 73°, 74°, and 75°, appear to escape much of the influence of Lake Huron. The isotherm of 74° divides in Southern Michigan, — one branch passing eastward through Northern Ohio, and the other southward through Central Indiana and Southern Ohio. The State of Ohio consequently constitutes an area of uniform temperature in July, which is identical with the mean temperature of Central Michigan to the limit of four and a half degrees of latitude, or three hundred miles, further north.

An area in the south-eastern part of the peninsula of Michigan seems to be an area of cold; since the temperature is two or three degrees colder than it is on either side. There exists a region in this part of the State which is topographically elevated about three hundred feet above the general level of the peninsula. It is the region of outcrop of the sandstones of the Marshall Group, but it is not entirely coincident with this area of cold. An area of warmth seems to be indicated in Northern Iowa.

It will be observed that the cooling effect of Lake Michigan is somewhat greater on the west side than on the east. Not only are the isotherms deflected from a higher latitude on the west side, but they likewise attain a somewhat lower latitude. The lowest deflection of the curve of 75°, for instance, is at Ottawa, Ill., to the west of the meridian of the lake. The curves of 71° and 72° are also somewhat more southern on the west side than on the east. This circumstance is undoubtedly accounted for by the slight preponderance, during July, of winds from the east of the meridian. Thus, at Chicago, this preponderance is as 60 : 33 = 1.82; at Milwaukie, as 48 : 37 = 1.30. But at Milwaukie, and further north, northerly and even north-westerly winds feel the influence of Green Bay.

Contrasting with these results those represented on the isothermal chart for January, we are at once struck with three phenomena: 1st, the great deflection of the isothermal lines; 2d, their northward deflection; and 3d, the exertion of an excessive amount of lake influence upon the east side. All this is illustrated by tracing the isotherm of 22°. Coming within the limits of the chart, a few miles south-west of Omaha, it pursues an undulating course eastward to Ottawa, in Illinois, when it bends abruptly northward, passing west of Chicago, and east of Milwaukie, to Northport, at the mouth of Grand Traverse Bay, whence it bends southward to Corunna, in the middle of the lower peninsula of Michigan, and northward again to Thunder Bay Island of Lake Huron, and thence east to Penetanguishene on Georgian Bay. The isotherm of 23° reaches almost as far north; but, in crossing the peninsula of Michigan, it strikes southward into Northern Indiana and Ohio, thence northward again almost to Thunder Bay Island. The sinuosities of this isotherm spread over a belt four and one-half degrees, or three hundred miles in width. In other words, the influence of the lakes is such that the mean temperature of January at Northport and Thunder Bay Island is identical with that of Omaha, Peoria, Chicago, and Fort Wayne. The January temperature of Mackinac and Marquette is the same as that of Green Bay and Fort Winnebago.

An island of cold is again indicated in the south-eastern part of the peninsula of Michigan. In this case its form and position correspond quite exactly with a region of elevation. The area in Northern Iowa, which in July is an island of warmth, appears to be in January an island of cold. A similar one exists in the elevated region of Southern Wisconsin, while a remarkable axis of cold stretches through Northern Wisconsin and Minnesota. This axis is not entirely coincident with the crest of the ridge dividing the tributaries of Lake Superior from those of the Mississippi; since the warming influence of Lake Superior crowds it about sixty miles southward.

One of the most striking phenomena exhibited by the chart for

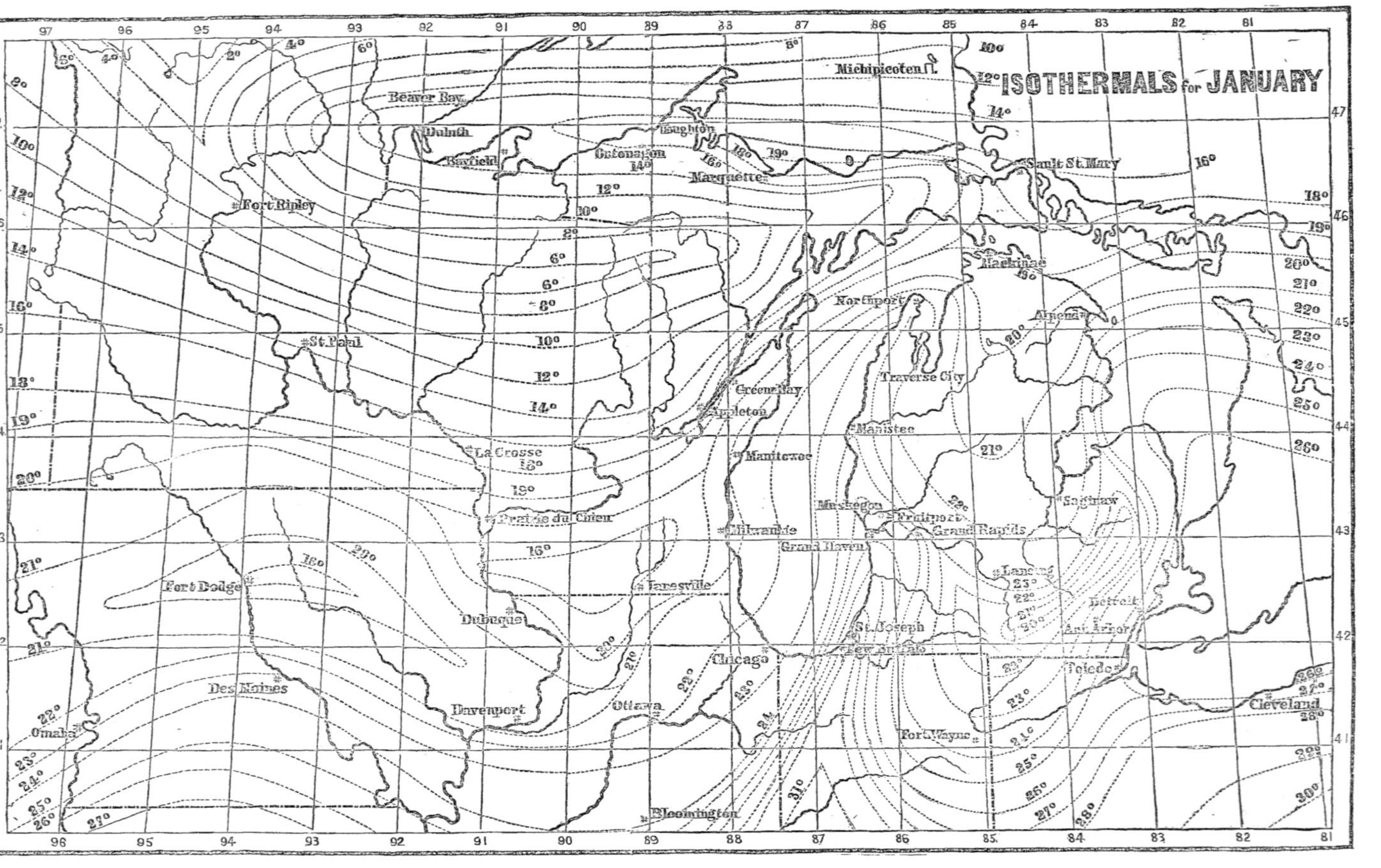
ISOTHERMALS for JANUARY
Michipicoten I.
Beaver Bay
Duluth
Bayfield
Houghton
Ontonagon
Marquette
Sault St. Mary
Fort Ripley
Mackinac
Northport
Alpena
St. Paul
Traverse City
Green Bay
Appleton
Manistee
Manitowoc
La Crosse
Saginaw
Muskegon
Fruitport
Grand Rapids
Prairie du Chien
Milwaukee
Grand Haven
Lansing
Fort Dodge
Janesville
Detroit
Dubuque
St. Joseph
Ann Arbor
New Buffalo
Chicago
Toledo
Des Moines
Davenport
Ottawa
Cleveland
Omaha
Fort Wayne
Bloomington

January is the excess of the warming influence along the eastern side of Lake Michigan. The isotherm of 23½° strikes from Chicago directly to Northport, almost at the opposite end of the lake. The contrast in January temperature between the opposite shores of the lake is, for the northern half, four degrees, and for the southern, six degrees. This circumstance is due to the fact that the cold winds of the region come from the west and south-west. The precise ratios of the winds from the east and the west of the meridian in January are at Chicago, according to eleven years' observations, as 72 : 5 = 14.4; at Milwaukie, for thirteen years, as 60 : 18 = 3.33; at Manitowoc, for eleven years, as 67 : 11 = 6.09. These results embody all January winds, except those directly from the north or south. The reason why the excess of warming influence on the east side is greater toward the south than toward the north is evidently because north, and even north-west, winds coming from Green Bay add their warming effect to that of Lake Michigan in all the region north of Milwaukie.

The isothermal charts for the summer and winter contrast in the same way as those for July and January. From the summer chart we perceive that the isothermal of 72° makes its advent upon the northern limit of the chart, and disappears upon its southern limit only 12° of longitude further east. Coming from the Winnipeg country, it passes near Dubuque and Ottawa, thence into the centre of the peninsula of Michigan. Sweeping around this region, it strikes directly south to Germantown and Portsmouth, in Ohio. The summer temperature of the Winnipeg region, and of Central Michigan, is identical with that of Northern Illinois and Southern Ohio. Areas of cold exist in South-eastern Michigan and Northern Minnesota; and large areas of uniform temperature in Wisconsin, Indiana, and Ohio.

The excess of cooling influence upon the west side of the lake, during the entire summer, is quite noticeable. The isothermals, in approaching the Lake Superior region, make an angle of 45° with the meridian; and under the influence of Lake Michigan they become quite parallel with the meridian. It does not appear that, in the Lake Superior region, any excess of winds from the lake exists; but, in the vicinity of Lake Michigan, such excess is well established. At Chicago, the winds from the lake are to those from the land, during summer, as 151 : 119 = 1.27; at Milwaukie, the lake winds are to the land winds as 142 : 104 = 1.27; at Manitowoc, the lake winds are to the land winds as 153 : 123 = 1.24.

From the winter chart we notice that the isotherm of 24° undulates over a breadth of more than two hundred miles. Other isotherms are similarly sinuated. The mean winter climate of Mackinac is 20°; and is identical with that of Green Bay, Fort Winnebago, and Fort Dodge.

The excess of the warming influence on the east side of Lake Michigan is most apparent. The winter mean of Chicago is 24½°, while that of New Buffalo, in the same latitude, is 28°. The winter mean of Milwaukie is 22°, while that of its *vis-à-vis*, Grand Haven, is 26°. The winter mean of Fort Howard is 20°, and of Appleton, 19°; while that of Traverse City, farther north than either, is 23⅓°. These contrasts illustrate again the effect of the prevalence, during the cold season, of winds from the west of the meridian.

As to the isothermals for the spring and autumn, it might be expected that they would suffer little deflection under the influence of the lakes. Comparatively speaking, this is the case; but it will be noticed, nevertheless, that a marked cooling influence is exerted in spring; since the isotherm of 43°, for instance, is deflected southward one hundred and fifty miles. It is worthy of remark at the same time, that the maximum deflection takes place on the west side of Lake Michigan. On the east side, the deflection of the same isotherm amounts to no more than twenty miles. In general, we find the mean spring temperature of the eastern side of Lake Michigan to be about three degrees higher than the mean spring temperature of the western side. As this excess is accumulated in April and May, — especially in May, — it is at once apparent that the circumstance has a most important bearing upon the growth of spring crops on the opposite sides of the lake. The effect is such that the temperature of Grand Haven, March 15, is equal to that of Milwaukie, March 21; that of Grand Haven, April 15, is equal to that of Milwaukie, April 24; that of Grand Haven, May 15, is equal to that of Milwaukie, May 28. These contrasts relate to *mean* temperatures. They show that vegetation on the east side secures a start of six to thirteen days. Add to this, protection from *exceptional* cold, in the form of spring frosts, and, to this, the effects of a drier and lighter soil, and we get a clear and demonstrative explanation of the difference in the agricultural and pomological products of the opposite sides of the lake.

This contrast of temperatures in spring is explained, as before, by the predominance, during the cold month of March, of winds from the west of the meridian, and during the warmer months of April and May, of winds from the east of the meridian. Thus, at Manitowoc, in March, the winds from the west of the meridian are to those from the east as 43 : 24 = 1.8; at Milwaukie, they are as 44 : 32 = 1.4; at Chicago, as 57 : 20 = 2.85. On the contrary, the preponderance of winds from the east of the meridian during May is, at Manitowoc, as 37 : 26 = 1.42; at Milwaukie, as 62 : 24 = 2.58; and in April, as 52 : 33 = 1.6; at Chicago, including north winds, which are here lake winds, the ratio of lake and land winds, in May, is as 44 : 40 = 1.1.

In autumn the resultant of the lake influences on the west side is almost zero; while, on the east of Lake Michigan, a warming effect is experienced, amounting, along the southern half of the lake, to one or two degrees, and, along the northern half of the lake, to three or four degrees. This, as before, is caused by a preponderance, during each of the autumn months, of winds from the west of the meridian. This preponderance is shown for Chicago by the ratio of 151 : 70 = 2.16; for Milwaukie, by the ratio of 147 : 94 = 1.56; and for Manitowoc, by the ratio of 160 : 60 = 2.67.

The advantages thus secured to vegetation along the east side of the lake are not less in autumn than in spring. These singular facts depend upon a shifting of the prevalent winds at the end of the cold season, toward the close of March, and again at the end of the mild season near the close of November. An investigation of the monthly means on the opposite sides of the lake, during autumn, shows that the temperature attained at Milwaukie, Oct. 15, is not reached at Grand Haven until Oct. 20. The Milwaukie temperature of Nov. 15 is only reached at Grand Haven Nov. 23. Comparing Chicago and New Buffalo, we find that the Chicago temperature of Sept. 15 is the same as the New Buffalo temperature of Sept. 21. The October and November temperatures seem to be nearly coincident. These comparisons show that the warm season is lengthened, on the east side, about six to eight days in the autumn. This, added to the time gained in the spring, makes the growing season, on the east side of Lake Michigan, from twelve to twenty-one days longer than on the west side, — to say nothing about exemption from unseasonable frosts and a much warmer constitution of the soil upon the east side.

Turning our attention now to the chart of isothermals for the year, we might anticipate that the warming and cooling influences of the lakes would exactly neutralize each other, so that the isothermals would experience no deflection. We find, however, that on the western side the resultant influence is slightly cooling, and on the eastern side decidedly warming. The resultant of these two influences gives a final resultant of a warming character exerted upon the eastern side. This final resultant has a value of one-half to two degrees. In other words, Lake Michigan elevates the mean annual temperature of the contiguous region nearly two degrees above the norm. This results, of course, from the fact that the mean temperature of the lake waters is higher than that of the land. This excess must be considerably greater than the resultant warming influence upon the land. Its explanation is a curious and interesting subject of inquiry. It cannot be caused, as in the case of the Gulf Stream, by great currents moving from tropical regions. Nor can we attribute it to a large volume of river water poured into the lake from regions lying to the southward. Some more occult cause operates to raise the mean temperature of the lake above the normal temperature of the land.

I suspect that the mean temperature of the tributary streams of the lake is somewhat above the atmospheric mean of the year. The greatest volume, perhaps, is poured into the lake during the milder months; but more than this, the waters of the tributaries, by the laws of physics, can never be cooled below a certain limit, while their warming may proceed to the extreme limit of the atmospheric temperature. The same considerations will apply, to some extent, to the shallow bays connected with the lake. Still, I conceive, there must be another cause invoked for the full explanation of the phenomenon under consideration.

I do not hesitate to suggest that this cause may be the internal heat of the earth. Consider the depth to which the basins of the great lakes are excavated. Lake Michigan has a mean depth of nine hundred feet. At this depth in the solid crust of the earth, we should expect to find the temperature some eighteen degrees above the mean temperature at the surface. That is, if the mean land temperature, in the middle latitude of the lake is 44°, the temperature of the lake bottom should be 62°. This heat received from the bottom, however, would be distributed through the whole mass of lake water, so that the average temperature of the mass might not be increased more than nine degrees.* The excess of radiation from the warmer waters of the lake might reduce the

* It is probable that the temperature at or near the bottom is considerably lower than that near the surface.

warming effect of the lake bottom to four or five degrees, in the whole mass of water. It may not be amiss to mention, also, that the lake waters at the depth of nine hundred feet, in consequence of the mingling of the temperatures of the different strata, would be cooler than the land at the same depth. But as the bottom immediately underlying the water must possess nearly the temperature of the water, it is evident that the warming effect upon the water is less than eighteen degrees as first calculated. Still we must argue that the rate of increase of temperature at greater depths beneath the lake would be more rapid than at the same depths upon the land, so that the actual resultant warming influence exerted upon the lake waters at the bottom would be somewhere between the two results already indicated. It would be a positive warming effect, and its reaction upon the temperature of the land would be very nearly such as indicated by our isothermal lines for the year.

In studying the influence of the great lakes upon the climate of the contiguous regions, we should especially note its presence under circumstances of exceptional cold or heat upon the land. For the purpose of illustrating these relations, I have constructed two isothermal charts for minimum temperatures. One of these is a chart for *mean minima*, and the other a chart for *extreme minima*. By the "mean minimum" of a locality, I understand the *average* of the yearly minima for a series of years; and by the "extreme minimum," the *lowest point* attained during that series of years. These charts present results which are truly striking. The isotherms in the vicinity of Lakes Huron and Michigan trend literally north and south. In the chart of mean minima the isotherm of —15° strikes from Mackinac through Manitowoc, Milwaukie, and New Buffalo, to Fort Riley, in Kansas, near the parallel of 39°. Here is a deflection over nearly seven degrees of latitude, or about four hundred and eighty miles in a straight line. The meaning of this is, that the most excessive cold at Mackinac, for a period of twenty-eight years, is not, on the average, greater than at Fort Riley, four hundred and eighty miles further south. It is one degree less than at Chicago for a term of eleven years. By a glance at the chart of extreme minima, we perceive that the lowest point reached at Mackinac is but two degrees lower than the extreme minimum of St. Louis. Extreme weather of Chicago is twelve degrees colder than at New Buffalo. The lowest extreme of Milwaukie is fourteen degrees below the extreme minimum of

Grand Haven, while the extreme of Fort Howard is twenty degrees below that of Northport. In general, while the mean minimum along the west side of Lake Michigan is —16, that along the east side is —6; while the extreme minimum on the west side is —22° to —30°, that of the east side is —10° to —16°.

I cannot forbear directing attention to the important bearing of these additional facts upon the results of soil cultivation. It will be remembered that it is not the severity of the winter mean, but that of the winter *extremes*, which conditions the immunity of exotic plants from destructive frost. One killing freeze is as fatal as thirty. That one killing freeze is as likely to occur at Fort Riley, or Leavenworth, or Peoria, or even St. Louis, as at Mackinac. The whole east shore of Lake Michigan is 15° to 20° more secure than any of the places just named. As grapes and peach-trees require for their destruction a temperature of —20°, it is apparent that peach orchards and vineyards are perfectly secure along the whole extent of the eastern shore of Lake Michigan.

The *rationale* of these remarkable climatic effects is not difficult to discover. It lies in the comparatively low capacity of watery surfaces for absorbing and radiating heat. The mean temperature of the land in the middle latitude of Lake Michigan is about 44½°, and that of the lake a few degrees higher. In July the temperature of the land rises to 74°, while that of the lake is not above 51° or 52°. This difference is partly due to the fact that upon the land the heat from the solar rays is accumulated near the surface, while upon the water it is disseminated through the whole mass by the action of waves and currents. In January the mean temperature of the land sinks to 19°, while that of the water does not, probably, fall below 40°. The atmosphere in contact with the water must partake to some extent of the temperature of the water, and, when moving from the water to the land, must transfer to the land some portion of the heat or cold proper to the lake. The effect is a tendency to equalize the land temperatures. This tendency is most distinctly felt in case of extreme weather. On occasion of our coldest weather, the wind blows generally from the south-west, and, passing diagonally over Lake Michigan for a distance of one hundred to two hundred miles, must necessarily experience a great degree of amelioration.

The influence of the sea in equalizing temperatures has long been understood. The immunity from unseasonable frosts secured by bodies of fresh water to localities in their immediate vicinity has also been universally observed; but the fact that inland lakes, of the size of Lake Michigan, exert an ameliorating agency, quite comparable with that of the Atlantic Ocean, is something which has only been brought to light by recent thorough discussions of a wide range of meteorological *data.* On general principles, it has, indeed, been asserted by Professor Henry, and by Blodgett, and at an earlier period by Humboldt, that the great lakes of North America must exert some influence in deflecting the isothermal lines; but when we come to examine any of the charts which have been published to represent existing knowledge or conceptions, we fail to detect any marked inflection of these lines in passing the region of the great lakes. In fact, the thermometric observations from the fifty-five meteorological stations in Michigan have not heretofore been employed in tracing out the remarkable tortuosities of the isothermals of the lower peninsula of Michigan. I believe these disclosures are destined to take their place among the most remarkable phenomena of climatological science.

NOTES. — The views set forth in the foregoing paper were first foreshadowed in a report on the "Grand Traverse Region," published in 1866. They were again published with a few additions in the Proceedings of this Association for 1866. In 1867, I received from Dr. I. A. Lapham a chart of Wisconsin, bearing date 1865, in which the isothermals for January and July are shown to be extensively deflected in Wisconsin by the influence of Lake Michigan.

I desire to express my thanks to J. F. Grant, Esq., for a full transcript of his meteorological observations at Traverse City, and to General W. F. Raynolds, Superintendent, and C. F. Henry, Assistant, for permission to copy the unpublished results of the observations of the Lake Survey.

SOME EFFECT OF PRESSURE OF A CONTINENTAL GLACIER.

BY ALEXANDER WINCHELL.

[*From The American Geologist, March, 1888.*]

The reader will please correct the following typographical errors:

In the title, for "effect" read "effects."

p. 140, 3rd line from bottom, for "molton" read "molten."

p. 141, 18th line from bottom, for "anticipated" read "anticipate."

p. 143, 3rd line from top, for "glaciation" read "Glacial."

[*From The American Geologist, March, 1888.*]

SOME EFFECT OF PRESSURE OF A CONTINENTAL GLACIER.[1]

BY ALEXANDER WINCHELL.

The terrestrial globe in some of its behavior, may be compared to an India rubber ball filled with water. If indented by pressure in one place, there must be a protuberance equal in volume in another place. In a ball of uniform composition, the protuberance would be spread over the entire surface beyond the region indented, and the effect in one particular spot might be insignificant. Should a small area of the caoutchouc be thinner than the rest, that part would be protruded to a greater extent than other parts of the surface. Should there be small holes or fissures through it, the water would escape and flow over the surface. That is, the protuberance resulting from local pressure would be chiefly on the outside of the shell. As we ordinarily conceive it the water would be squeezed out —like the juice of a squeezed orange.

The analogy of the earth does not depend on the theory of a molten interior beneath a solid crust. Whatever weight or force is adquate to indent the world's exterior develops, by crushing mechanical action, heat enough to fuse the rocks and supply liquid material. The amount supplied is proportioned to the magnitude of the action. It is generally admitted that ocean sediments accumulated on a large scale, have in many cases, produced a subsidence of the bottom on which they rest. In some cases, we can point out the regions elevated as the counterpart to the subsidence. I think in some cases, we may

[1] The views here enunciated were published in the University *Argonaut* in March, 1886.

point out escapes of molten lava as sequences to sedimental pressure; but geologists have not done this in any articulate way; and the principle involved is one of the points at which I aim in this memorandum.

One of the great doctrines of geological science which have found their way into common knowledge and acceptance, is the doctrine of former general glaciation of the north temperate lands. North America, east of the Rocky Mountains, and as far south as Cincinnati, was covered by a sheet of glacier ice, which perhaps averaged a mile in thickness. Its pressure upon the earth's exterior will readily be understood as enormous, and the reader can easily reach a numerical result. It will be borne in mind that the whole weight of the ice assumed the form of a pressure; while in the case of ocean-sediments, whose effects are generally admitted, the buoyant action of the sea-water prevents about half the weight of the sediments from assuming the form of a pressure in excess of that already exerted by the water.

Now where was the region subjected to protrusion in response to the enormous pressure of the great ice-mass? The view which I wish to enunciate is, that some of the region west of the Rocky mountains was the theatre of actions responsive to the great eastern and northern pressure. It is established that those regions were not generally glaciated. They must consequently, have experienced a tendency to become protuberant. Some regions may have been bodily uplifted. If fractures were thus caused, an escape of molten matter may have permitted such regions to subside. There are evidences of simple vertical actions and movements such as would thus result. If, however, fissures existed, or were produced, through which outflows of lava could take plaee, then instead of a vertical elevation of the crust, a flood of lava would cover the country.

Such floods of lava have occurred. Vast sheets of frozen lava are the most conspicuous feature of a region embracing large parts of Washington, Oregon, Idaho, Nevada, California, Arizona and New Mexico. In Oregon and Washington there was an almost universal flood of molton material, which covered and buried the whole original face of the country—hills and dales, mountains and valleys. Its extent is estimated by Le

Conte at not less than 150,000 square miles, with a thickness of three to four thousand feet. The Columbia river at the Cascade Range, has cut through 2,500 to 3,800 feet of lava.

Heretofore the epoch of the outflows has been placed late in the Pliocene—*before* the Glacial epoch. On this assumption, American man has been located in the Pliocene, since his remains have been found in California beneath the great sheet of lava which caps the celebrated Table mountain of Calaveras county. The relation here suggested, but hitherto overlooked between western lava outflows and eastern ice-pressure has therefore, the ulterior effect of reducing the supposed antiquity of man in America, and thus of harmonizing his chronology with that of European man.

This conclusion is indicated on other grounds. Remains of man have been found associated with *Equus occidentalis* and *E. excelsus* Leidy, in Oregon, in beds held by Cope and Marsh, it is true, to be Pliocene; and a similar association is reported from Colorado by Dr. Gilbert. The account of these observations has not yet been published; but from personal information from Dr. Gilbert, I learn that he and Mr. Mc Gee connect the Equus fauna of Oregon with the Glacial epoch rather than the Pliocene; and this result is in accord with what I anticipated on theory, mav be found to be the truth in California, in respect to the gravel beds holding human remains underneath tables of lava.

This method of viewing the subject of continental glaciation leads to another suggestion. If the terrestrial crust, to the east of the Rocky mountains and north of the Ohio river, was deeply indented by the weight of a sheet of ice say five thousand feet thick, a change must have resulted in relative levels of land and sea in the regions contiguous to the ice-boundary. The crustal depression would not be limited strictly to the ice-covered area. The crust's partial rigidity would cause the depression to be experienced along a bordering belt many miles in width. That is, the original Atlantic border of Labrador and New England would be depressed, and so would a belt through New Jersey, Maryland, Kentucky and Illinois lying along the southern limits of the glacier.

Along shores reached by the glacier, the ocean would bathe

the glacier and dissolve it more or less rapidly. On coasts where the glacier's motion was inconsiderable, the action of the sea maintained a bare shore line; and beach history was recorded as if the interior had not been ice-covered. The most important records would consist of beaches. The gulf of St. Lawrence, along the south shore, would have been kept free from ice, and a succession of beaches would record the successive stages of sea-level. Thus genereally, on shores trending meridionally, and more especially on southern shores, a series of beaches would be formed, while probably northern shores, through the constant encroachment of the glacier, might be kept completely concealed. The beaches formed during the progressive relative rise of the water would probably be obliterated, but, as usual, the beaches formed during the receding phase, would remain as records and evidences of the former submergence.

The theory implies that the greatest crustal depression would be experienced northward; the depression would gradually diminish southward. That is, the beaches northward would attain the highest elevations in relation to the preglacial level of the land. On the final dissolution of the continental glacier, and the restoration of the land to its former level, these beach-records would be found attaining progressively higher levels toward the north. The theory implies also that elevated beaches would be formed along all shores bordering glaciated lands—whether American, European or Asiatic.

Now witness the facts. Inland beaches whose geological relations connect them with the last great events of the world's history are actually found along the Atlantic coast from New York to Labrador, and even to arctic latitudes On the southern coast of New England ancient beaches are found from ten to twenty-five feet above present sea-level; on Nantucket, 85 feet; on the coast of Maine, 27 feet; on the borders of lake Champlain,—then a part of the gulf of St. Lawrence—350 feet; at Montreal, 500 feet; on the Labrador coast, 500 to 800 feet; on the arctic shores, 1000 feet. Commander De Long found elevated beaches on Bennett island, at the altitude of——feet.

This theory further implies that the formation of the beaches was *synchronous* with the prevalence of wide glaciation. The common opinion has been that the subsidence followed glaciation, and was a phenomenon of the Champlain epoch rather than the glaciation. Under the views here set forth the beaches which remain date from the commencement of the decline of the glacier.

Croll, who has so ably speculated on the causes of continental glaciation, conceived the icy load as heaped above the former level of the continent.. He viewed the crust as too rigid to be depressed by the weight. A polar ice-protuberance of 5,000 feet, and covering all the north temperate lands, would shift the earth's centre of gravity northward to a certain extent. The oceans would as a consequence, flow northward to restore the proper figure of the earth, and all northern lands would suffer inundation. This reasoning becomes nugatory in the face of much evidence that the earth's crust has many times yielded to the pressure of accumulated sea-sediments, and would much more yield to the weight of a continental glacier.

[*From the American Geologist, Sept. 1889.*]

DOUGLASS HOUGHTON.

Alexander Winchell.

Original Portrait by Alvah Bradish. Copyright 1889, by A. Bradish,

DOUGLASS HOUGHTON,

GEOLOGIST, LAKE SUPERIOR.

[*From the American Geologist, September, 1889.*]

DOUGLASS HOUGHTON.

BY ALEXANDER WINCHELL.

The fourth decade of the present century produced a body of geologic investigators whose brilliant achievements constitute them a galaxy in the firmament of American science. The preceding decade had given birth to Eaton and Dewey and Green, and the lustre of Maclure's name had not yet faded. To a large extent, their example and teaching were the conditions of the advent of the great workers of the fourth decade —Edward Hitchcock, Ebenezer Emmons, Henry D. and W. B. Rogers, William W. Mather, Lardner Vanuxem, James Hall and Douglass Houghton—workers whose labors illuminated still more brilliantly the fifth decade, and one of whom still lingers to set an example of fidelity to a host of younger compeers and aspirants in this ninth decade of the century. Of the distinguished workers of the fourth and fifth decades Douglass Houghton was youngest. His fellow-laborers indeed, considered him young—too young, almost, for the aspirations which animated him, and the independence which characterized his judgments. He was still young when his brilliant career was cut short—not too young to have left an impression on the science of the country, and to have determined a bias in the industries of his adopted State.

Douglass Houghton was the son of Judge Jacob Houghton[1] of Fredonia, New York. His mother was Mary Lydia Douglass, of New London, Conn., from whom he received his name. Judge Houghton had removed to Fredonia from Bolton, Mass., in 1812. His ancestors came to America about 1758. The American family is descended from an honorable English stock residing in Bolton, Lancaster, from the time of the conquest. The name was originally De Houton. The present head of the family is Sir Henry Bold Houghton, a member of Parliament.

The date of Douglass Houghton's birth was September 21, 1809. His early constitution was delicate, but his intelligence was bright, and his nature was sympathetic and sensitive. He was reared amid the influences of books and high ideals. He was destined for an education, in the hopes of both his parents. His father, though settled in the wilderness of Chautauqua county, was able to command the conditions which brought the realization of his hopes. The Fredonia academy was organized in 1824, and Douglass was among its earlier pupils. Though faithful to study during his academic career, tradition represents him as party to many of those pranks to which nature instigates so many of those whom she has chosen for distinction and influence. The boy who leads in pranks is father to the man who leads his State. Douglass, by the educational maxims of his time, was consigned to the usual routine of Latin drill; but by the bent and appointment of a forceful intelligence, he was destined to a life of scientific devotion.

This destination early revealed itself in many ways. Back of the orchard, a few rods from the residence, the Houghton boys made an excavation in the bank, and roofing it over, dedicated the simple structure to the uses of a laboratory and study. After some months, it became also, a powder factory—the requisite machinery and water power having been devised by the young Houghtons. One day an explosion occurred in

---

[1]The sources from which the present notice is drawn are a sketch by his co-laborer Bela Hubbard, in *Amer. Jour. Sci.*, II., v, 217-227, May, 1848; a memoir recently published by Prof. Alvah Bradish (8vo. 302pp., Detroit, 1889); personal communications from Mr. Hubbard who still resides in Detroit, and traditions preserved in the memory of surviving relatives and friends. Of Prof. Bradish's memoir I shall speak more particularly.

this mill. Douglass narrowly escaped total blindness. This accident was coincident, naturally, with a new trend in Douglass Houghton's scientific activity.

At a youthful age, Douglass entered the Van Rensselaer Institute at Troy, then under the charge of Prof. Amos Eaton. This destination was opportune. It suited the nature of the young man, and opened the way to the crowning of his hopes. Graduating as Bachelor of Arts in 1828, he waited but a few months to receive from Eaton the appointment of assistant professor in chemistry and natural history. Such was his standing that in 1830, he was selected by Eaton to deliver a course of lectures on chemistry, botany and geology in the distant and quaint old French town of Detroit. It is worthy of note that a course of scientific lectures had been provided for by the leading men of Detroit—Gen. Lewis Cass, Governor of the territory, Maj. John Biddle, Col. Henry Whiting, E. P. Hastings, Shubal Conant, Rev. Dr. Berry and others—let their names be perpetuated for an example to the leading Detroit gentlemen of the ninth decade of the century. Hon. Lucius Lyon, a delegate in Congress from the Territory, was to call on professor Eaton on this business. Though the youth of the the chosen lecturer dismayed the stately delegate, he soon discerned adequate maturity of thought, and the course of lectures became the resort of the *élite* of the town.

This was Houghton's introduction to the State of Michigan. It was in 1830, and Houghton had just attained his majority. He was destined now to settle in Detroit in the practice of medicine. He had studied under Dr. White at Fredonia, before his departure for Troy, and in 1831 he was admitted to practice by the Medical Society of Chautauqua county. In Detroit, his education, his talents and his affability gained him rapidly many friends whose devotion went with him during life.

A few months after his arrival in Detroit, he received the appointment of surgeon and botanist to the expedition for the discovery of the sources of the Mississippi, organized under the direction of Henry R. Schoolcraft. His report on the botany of the remote and wilderness regions passed over, displayed extensive acquaintance with the science, and constituted a permanent contribution to our knowledge of the flora of the

Northwest, for which he still stands credited in American Manuals.

From 1832 to 1836, he practiced as a physician and surgeon, never relaxing however, his pursuits in natural science. During the visitation of cholera in 1834, he performed many acts of heroism and noble charity, for which he is remembered to this day. In 1836 he matured the scheme for the Geological Survey of the state. To the promotion of the interests of this work he devoted the next nine years of his life. At this date geological surveys had been carried to completion in very few states or countries, but now an interest was arising which extended throughout the Northern States. It is worthy of note, however, that the lead was taken by North Carolina in 1824, and South Carolina in 1826. Massachusetts had furnished an example and a stimulus to other northern States since 1830. The survey of Tennessee had been organized in 1832, that of Maryland in 1834, of New Jersey and Virginia in 1835. Acts were passed in New York, Maine and Connecticut in 1836, and in Ohio, Indiana and Michigan.[2] in 1837. Before the decade was closed, surveys had been ordered in Kentucky, Rhode Island and the mineral lands of Iowa and Wisconsin. There was a wide and active awakening to the importance of that modern form of scientific and economic enterprise which is exhibited in public geological surveys.

An alert intelligence like Houghton's could not fail to enter into the spirit of the time, and there would be little difficulty in conceiving a practicable plan. To induce a population just emerged from a territorial condition to give their practical endorsement to such a plan, demanded gifts which were more than scientific. Only a born public leader could have carried such a scheme into effect. It must be remembered nevertheless, that for obvious reasons, the difficulty was less in those times than would be encountered to-day. Though the State was only a month old, Detroit, its capital, had been settled since 1701. In the missionary operations of the Jesuits, Detroit was long a central post, while in the wars with Indians, French and British, it was regarded as a strategic point. The military establishment was the nucleus of a spirit of intelligence, honor and respect for superior station and worth. Detroit was there-

[2]The bill was signed by Gov. Mason, Feb. 23, 1837. The State was declared a member of the Federal Union, Jan. 26, 1837.

fore already in advance of the average character of the west, or even of western towns. Those too, were days in which the leveling spirit of democracy had not destroyed the rightful influence of superior intelligence. The Legislature assembled at Detroit was predisposed to listen to the judgments of such men as Gen. Cass, Dr. Zina Pitcher, Henry N. Walker, Maj. Henry Whiting, Charles C. Trowbridge, Stevens T. Mason and Dr. Douglass Houghton. Still, nothing less than the tact, urbanity and captivating humor which distinguished Dr. Houghton, could even at that time, have secured an appropriation of $29,000 to be expended during a period of four years.[3] The financial crash which fell upon the country in 1838, was peculiarly distressing in Michigan, in consequence of the lavish scale of general internal improvements which the infant State adopted, and most of which were paralyzed during the years which followed. To sustain the heart of the State in a geological enterprise of such considerable magnitude was a greater achievement than to secure its original assent.

To the geological reader the sketch of the next nine years of Houghton's activity embraces the culminating interest of his biography. It seems appropriate, however, to reduce to a minimum the exposition of the scientific results of his labors, and to restrict the present notice to a history of the man and his personal relations.

Under provisions of the act passed in the beginning of 1837 Dr. Houghton occupied most of the season in investigations relating to the "salt lands" of the State, donated by Congress in 1836. Many salt springs had long been known. Houghton, from surface indications and general principles, argued that the source of supply was a deep-seated formation which might be reached by boring or by sinking of shafts in the vicinity of the salines. Accordingly, the Legislature of 1838 appropriated

[3]The total expended by the State for the survey during the four years, was $31,597. In 1841 the State made another appropriation of $6,219; in 1842, one of $3,703; in 1843, one of $2,020; in 1844, one of $2,535; in 1845, one of $1,832; making total appropriations for the Houghton survey, $52,000. But of this $4,171 remained unexpended. The present writer in June, 1886, by request, transmitted to Director J. W. Powell, for the use of the United States Geological Survey, a pretty full "History of the First Geological Survey of the State of Michigan," embracing memoirs of Dr. Houghton and others. It may here be added, that in November of the same year, he transmitted also a paper on "Public Geological Surveys in Michigan under the Direction of Professor Alexander Winchell."

$3,000 for such experiments, and Dr. Houghton located two wells—one near Grand Rapids and one on the Tittabawassee river. To these enterprises much attention was given, and in them many difficulties were encountered during two or three years, with an expenditure of $45,000 of special appropriations, but without attaining the results expected. The Tittabawassee well was carried down 139 feet and abandoned in 1842. The Grand Rapids well was sunken 876 feet, and abandoned in 1843. Had Dr. Houghton been in possession of modern facilities for boring, he would probably have achieved success in the Tittabawassee well, and salt manufacture would have been commenced in Michigan twenty years earlier than it was.

The Legislature of 1838 placed the survey on a broader basis, authorizing departments of zoölogy, botany and topography, as subordinate to geology. Besides the requisite attention to the salt enterprises just mentioned, Dr. Houghton, this season, made explorations along the shores of lakes Michigan and Huron, and in some limited portions of the interior and southern counties. One cannot peruse the report rendered in 1839, without receiving a vivid impression of Dr. Houghton's geological sagacity. Though he gives expression to certain inferences and suggestions which later studies have not justified, his obvious characteristic as a geologist is largeness of view and a tendency to grasp the geology of Michigan in its correlations with that of surrounding regions. He thinks the rocks of the northern part of the Peninsula "may be regarded as referable to the great Carboniferous group of the state—a position to which their fossil contents are amply sufficient to substantiate their claim."[4] Again, referring to the range of hills a little south of Thunder Bay river which "stretch in a southwesterly direction toward the head of lake Michigan," he says "they follow the line of bearing of the rock formation, and no doubt extend diagonally completely across the state, forming a portion of the summit of the more northern part of the Peninsula" (pp. 6-7.) "The ridges of limerock," in the vicinity of Little and

[4]Such an opinion cannot be considered a disparaging error, since the dividing line between the Carboniferous and the Devonian had not been clearly fixed in American geology. In his *First Annual Report* on the Fourth District of New York, James Hall spoke of the limestones of the Helderberg mountains as "Carboniferous or Mountain Limestone." (*Reports N. Y. Geol. Surv.*, 1837, pp. 290, 300.) A similar reference is made of that at Black Rock, etc. (p. 302, note, 307, 374.)

Grand Traverse bays "are without doubt, a continuation of the line of bearing of the great limestone formation of Wisconsin." On the whole, however, Dr. Houghton reveals in this first glance at the general geology of the Lower Peninsula the tact and sagacity of a skilled observer. This report is accompanied by those of the various assistants.

The report of observations made by Dr. Houghton in 1839, dated February 3, 1840, is devoted to the Northern Peninsula. This and that of the following year, dated February 1, 1841, are the two most important and original contributions made by Dr. Houghton to geological science. In these reports he describes the rocks of the Upper Peninsula under the following divisions: 1. Primary Rocks, 2. Trap Rocks, 3. Metamorphic Rocks, 4. Conglomerate, 5. Mixed Conglomerate and Sandstone, 6. Lower or red Sandrock and Shale, 7. Upper or Gray Sandstone, 8. Sandy Limerock. The Primary Rocks consist chiefly of granite, syenite and syenitic granite. The extended range of Trap Rocks flanking the Primary rocks on the north or northwest (relative positions being reversed on the north shore—hence, he says, proving the basin of the lake synclinal) are themselves flanked on the north by amygdaloids which in part, result from the intense alteration of sedimentary rocks next in order. From the masses of greenstones proceed dykes (so called) which intersect the newer formations in planes conformable with their bedding. The writer gives a careful and particular description of the true veins which intersect the dykes, the amygdaloid and the sedimentary rocks,[5] but, like the dykes, they comform to the bedding of the amygdaloid and the sandstone. These veins, he says contain native copper.[6]

The Metamorphic rocks consist of talcose, mica and clay slates, slaty hornblende rock and quartz rock. These are the rocks claimed by Emmons as representing the Taconic system in Michigan. To these must be added the argillites first reported as included in the "Lower Sandstone and Shales."

---

[5]Besides the descriptions embraced in these reports, Dr. Houghton presented a careful summary touching metalliferous veins, before the "Association of American Geologists" at Philadelphia, in 1841. (See Transactions, pp. 35-38. See also, Amer. Jour. Sci.

[6]A statement which aroused a discussion in the meeting of 1843. *Amer. Jour. Sci.* XLV. p. 160, 1843.) A report was made on the subject in 1844 (*Amer. Jour. Sci.* XLVII, 132, 1844).

The Conglomerate, No. 4, and the Mixed Conglomerate and Sandstone No. 5, (constituting the Keweenawan system of Chamberlin and Irving) are made up of volcanic ejections—the sandstone layers having the same greenstone composition as the conglomerates, but being finer and evidently deposited as sediments in shallow water. The "Lower or Red Sandrock and Shale," No. 6, at first supposed to represent the "Old Red Sandstone,"[7] then in 1843 the "New Red,"[8] was subsequently pronounced the equivalent of the Potsdam sandstone of New York.[9]

In his brief report dated January 25, 1842, Dr. Houghton says the survey has made progress, though the unavailability of funds has been a hindrance. He speaks of duties assigned relative to the boundary line between Michigan and Wisconsin. He makes mention of other detailed work in exploration of the Porcupine mountains, and the rivers in the western part of the Upper Peninsula. Though the field-work on the scale originally contemplated, is now nearly complete, a large amount of laboratory and office work remains, for which he asks and receives a small appropriation. In this work the year 1842 was occupied, as he informs us in the very brief report dated January 3, 1843. This was his sixth annual report. In his seventh, dated February 15, 1844, he simply states that work on the final report is making some progress, but slow. He speaks of progress made on the county maps, and pathetically asks an advance of $1,000 or $1,500, to be reimbursed from the sale of the maps, when completed. This is his last report to the State. Though the office of state geologist was not abolished, no State report is found for the eighth and ninth years of his incumbency.

In the meantime, however, Dr. Houghton, despairing of the ability of the State to complete the work, meditated a connection between the linear and geological surveys of the Upper Peninsula. His plan was fully set forth in a paper read before the Association of American Geologists in Washington, in

[7] In the report of 1838, he says "The Old Red Sandstone in the vicinity of the Porcupine Mountains has been shattered similarly to the limestone of Mackinac island."

[8] *Trans. Assoc. Amer. Geol.*, 1843; *Amer. Jour. Sci.* XLV, 160.

[9] This view was embodied in his notes of 1845, reported on by Bela Hubbard. See Jacob Houghton's *Mineral Region of Lake Superior*, 1846 p. 118.

1844.[10] The advantages of such a combination were at once comprehended, and the project was warmly endorsed, and a committee appointed to "memorialize the proper department of the Government." The land commissioner, however, fearing the ordinary surveyors would not possess sufficient geological information, hesitated, until Dr. Houghton himself offered to take the contract. This was signed June 25, 1844, and the remainder of that season and the season of 1845 were occupied in completing preparations and carrying on the work. His contract with the surveyor general was nearly completed, when the lamentable event occurred which put an end to his zealous and useful activity in the development of the natural resources of his adopted State.

Dr. Houghton's death occurred by drowning, October 13, 1845, on the west shore of Keweenaw point, not far from Eagle river. He was returning in an open boat, with four men, from a trip made to provision one of his parties. Overtaken by a severe snow-storm with high wind, about nine 'oclock in the evening, the boat was thrown endwise by the waves, and dashed on the rocks. Doctor Houghton, with two of his voyageurs, was lost. His remains were recovered in the spring of 1846, and interred in Elmwood cemetery, Detroit. The place is marked by a monument erected by Mrs. Houghton.

It would not be proper to extend this notice; though it would be interesting and edifying to contemplate an analysis of Dr. Houghton's character, and seek to discover the elements of that power by which he commanded the respect, and even the admiration of all who made his acquaintance. This, however, is the less necessary, as his life and character have been so well portrayed by a surviving friend, professor Alvah Bradish,[11] an artist of wide reputation, an appreciator of science, and a member of various learned societies. Mr. Bradish for many years, was Emeritus incumbent of the Chair of Fine Arts in the University of Michigan, and for several years delivered lectures. In this volume the biographical sketch of Houghton occupies 75 pages. It is followed by brief sketches of several

---

[10] *Amer. Jour. Sci.* vol. xlvii, 1844, p. 115.

[11] *Memoir of Douglass Houghton, first state geologist of Michigan. With an appendix containing reports and abstracts of the first geological survey, and a chronological statement of the progress of geological exploration in Michigan.* By Alvah Bradish, A. M., Detroit: Raynor & Taylor, 1889, 8vo, 302 pp.

of Houghton's contemporaries and friends, appreciative notices, details of the final catastrophe, an account of the Houghton portrait, a proposed monument, a memorial window at Marquette, and various memoranda and notes. A selection from Dr. Houghton's letters occupies 20 pages. The Houghton portrait, painted by professor Bradish, hangs in the capitol at Lansing. As a portrait it is said to be faithful and true to life. It represents the geologist as standing on the rocky shore of lake Superior. His dress is that of an out-door explorer—a loose summer coat, without vest, with leather suspenders, trousers of a lighter color, and high-top boots. He is resting and meditative. One arm is extended and rests on his hammer. The other holds his crushed and well remembered hat. A cliff of lake Superior sandstone rises in the background, and in the distance opens "The Portal," which constitutes one of the features of the "Pictured Rocks." A photo-engraved copy of this painting forms the frontispiece of the memoir, and an impression of it accompanies the present sketch.

With the geologist, another feature of the "memoir" will secure a cordial welcome, and that is the reproduction in the appendix, in abstract or in full, of all Dr. Houghton's reports, occupying 160 pages. As these reports have long been out of print, at the same time that they have been in very great request—the demand seeming to increase with lapse of time—these reproductions will be a boon to all geological investigators. They embody abstracts of the reports of Dr. Houghton's assistants. The fourth annual report, dated February 1, 1841, (89 pages) the most important of all, and containing the most matured results, is reprinted in full. The accompanying report of Bela Hubbard, (34 pages) the most important one made on the Lower Peninsula, is also reproduced, and here includes a colored section prepared at the time, but not engraved. The report also of S. W. Higgins, topographer, (26 pages) is fully reprinted

Dr. Houghton died at the age of 36. His brief career was one of intense intellectual activity. He was a leader among men. His life opened with brilliant promise, and was adorned by many honorable successes achieved. Only an act prompted by an excess of enthusiasm and the virtue of personal daring, gave opportunity for the elements with which he had so often toyed, to blot his name, too early, from the list of America's most distinguished devotees of science.

THE DIAGONAL SYSTEM IN THE PHYSICAL FEATURES OF MICHIGAN.

By A. WINCHELL,
CHANCELLOR OF THE UNIVERSITY OF SYRACUSE.

[FROM THE AMERICAN JOURNAL OF SCIENCE AND ARTS, VOL. VI, JULY, 1873.]

THE DIAGONAL SYSTEM IN THE PHYSICAL FEATURES OF MICHIGAN.

IN the study of the topographical features of Michigan, our attention has been arrested by the observation of an interesting method in the disposition of the lines of relief and drainage. This method, which has not been heretofore pointed out, may be enunciated as the *Diagonal System*. By this expression we mean to say that the longitudinal axes of the topographical and hydrographical features of the State, especially of the lower peninsula, lie in directions which are diagonals between the cardinal points of the compass. We propose to cite a few facts for the purpose of illustrating and establishing this generalization.

With reference to the surface configuration of the lower peninsula, we divide it into the northern and southern lobes. These are separated from each other by a depression extending from the head of Saginaw Bay, up the valley of the Saginaw and Bad Rivers, and down the valley of the Maple and Grand Rivers, to Lake Michigan. This, which we have styled the Grand-Saginaw Valley,* nowhere attains a greater elevation than 72 feet above Lake Michigan. The highest elevations of the southern lobe are more than 600 feet, and those of the northern 1200 feet above Lake Michigan.

The southeastern watershed of the southern lobe is an elongated axis of relief, stretching through Huron, Sanilac, Lapeer, Oakland, Washtenaw and Hillsdale Counties. None of the streams of the peninsula cross it, though its easterly and

* See Walling's Atlas of Michigan; also "Topographical Data for Michigan" (nearly ready for publication), by the writer.

westerly slopes are deeply furrowed by the streams issuing at right angles with its main trend.

The northern lobe of the peninsula is divided primarily by the deep valley of the Manistee and Sable Rivers, flowing southwesterly and southeasterly into their respective lakes. The southern division is deeply indented by the basin which holds Houghton and Higgins Lakes. The former has an elevation of 589 feet above Lake Michigan. From this lake the Muskegon River, the largest of the peninsula, takes its rise, and flowing southwesterly, marks the position of a broad, deep valley, having, on the southeast an elongated watershed stretching from Mecosta County through Clare and Roscommon into Ogemaw County. This we have designated the central watershed. It has a general elevation of 700 feet, while some of its summits exceed 800 feet. On the northwest of the Muskegon Valley we note three broad summits ranged in a line parallel with the valley and reaching elevations of 700 feet.

The northern division of the northern lobe of the peninsula, embracing the most elevated land south of Mackinac, being the region of the parting of the waters in all directions except the south, has not preserved any marked longitudinality.

We may now direct attention more particularly to the diagonism to which we have referred.* In the lower peninsula, the southeastern watershed stretches 200 miles from northeast to southwest (euroboreally), and the central watershed, 80 miles in the same direction; while the Grand-Saginaw Valley lies in the midst of the intervening region. To this direction conforms the trend of the water-courses from Lake Huron to Lake Erie, the axes of Saginaw and Green Bays, and Great and Little Bay de Noquet, as well as the northern reach of Lake Michigan. Along the same diagonal lie the valley of the Manistee, Muskegon, White and Crockery Rivers, as well as large portions of the valleys of the Pine, Salt, Shiawassee, Cass, Flint and many smaller streams.

In the northwest and southeast (euronotal) direction lie Thunder Bay and the valleys of the Kalamazoo, Little Manistee, Pine, South Branch of Père Marquette, Sable, Rifle, Tittabawassee, Belle, Clinton, Huron and many smaller streams. Even streams

* As our language does not supply the terms for the convenient and brief expression of some of the following ideas, we venture to suggest a few new terms. Lines lying in the direction of the cardinal points of the compass, may be designated as *cardinal*, or *cardinals;* those lying in the angles between the cardinals may be called *diagonal* or *diagonals.* Of the two cardinals, the north-south one may be designated the *meridional,* and the east-west one, the *transmeridional.* Of the diagonals, the northwest-southeast one may be called *euronotal* (from "Euronotus," a southeast wind), and the northeast-southwest one, *euroboreal* (from "Eurus," an east wind, and "Boreas," the north wind). These terms may be used both adjectively and substantively.

whose outlets are east or west of their sources, pursue zigzag courses to their mouths, in order to conform to the diagonal system. The St. Joseph River, from its sources in Hillsdale County, pursues a general southeasterly course to South Bend in Indiana, and then flows northwest to Lake Michigan. The Cass River flows southwest into Saginaw County, and describes a rounded angle toward the northwest, to pursue its course to the Saginaw. The Flint flows southwest 35 miles to Flint, and then northwest 30 miles to the Shiawassee. The Shiawassee flows northwest 35 miles to Owosso, then northwest 35 miles to the Saginaw. The Raisin, traced from its higher tributaries, is found to flow from the southern part of Jackson County, southeast 15 miles, then east-northeast 7 miles, then southeast 7 miles, then northwest 18 miles, then southeast 15 miles to Lake Erie. The Pine River (of the east) flows southeast 28 miles, then northeast 33 miles to the Tittabawassee. This river, from its source to Saginaw Bay through the Tittabawassee, consists of four sections, two almost rigorously at right angles with the other two, and all lying along the diagonals. The Becs Scies (or Betsie) River flows southwest 20 miles, then northeast 15 miles, into Lake Michigan.

Nor are there any considerable streams not included in the foregoing mention, whose valleys conform to the direction of the cardinals. The river St. Clair and a portion of the Detroit constitute an exception to the statement, to which reference will be made in the sequel. The axis of Grand Traverse Bay trends meridionally, as that of Little Traverse Bay trends transmeridionally. There are also some unimportant streams in the southern peninsula whose general direction is cardinal; but even in these, it is interesting to note to how great an extent the general course is made up from a number of inconsiderable reaches conforming to the diagonal system.

If we look toward the upper peninsula, the attention is immediately arrested by the euroboreal trends of Kewenaw Point and Bay, the copper range, the Porcupine Mountains and Ile Royale. The general watershed of the upper peninsula exemplifies the law in a beautiful manner. Beginning at Pt. Detour it pursues a west-northwest course 23 miles; it then proceeds N.N.W. 13 miles, then W.N.W. 10 miles, then S.W. 16 miles, then N.W. 43 miles, then S.W. 34 miles, then N.W. 6 miles, then a little E. of N. 6 miles, then S.W. 12 miles, then N.W. 37 miles, thence S.W. by zigzag courses 50 miles to the Wisconsin line. The Menominee, Escanaba and other affluents of Green Bay flow southeast. The same is true of the upper waters of the Monistique and all its tributaries, while the main river flows southwest. The Montreal, Presqu'Ile, Ontonagon, Flint-steel and all the streams of Kewenaw Point, have their axes along the euronotal. The Sturgeon River rises near Lake Michigan, flows N.W. 11 miles, then S.W. 8 miles (meeting a tributary from the S.W.), then N.W. 7 miles, then N.E. 25 miles, into Portage Lake, thence S.E. 6 miles through Portage River into Kewenaw Bay--thence finally N.E. through Kewenaw Bay into Lake Superior.

These examples may serve to illustrate sufficiently the law enunciated. But its application is not confined to Michigan. The Maumee River of Ohio, with its tributaries, is a striking reproduction of the Saginaw and its affluents. The Maumee, flowing east-northeast, is fed by the Auglaize and St. Mary's from the southeast, the St. Joseph from the northeast and the Tiffin from the northwest—the last named, in its higher reaches, flowing from Hillsdale County, Michigan, first southeast and then southwest. In Wisconsin, the euroboreal basin of Green Bay is prolonged through the Fox River into Lake Winnebago. The euroboreal trend is seen in the shore-lines about Chegowawegon Bay, the Apostle Islands and the western extremity of Lake Superior. Even the upper Mississippi, whose general course is meridional, divides itself into a succession of reaches conforming strangely to the law of diagonism; while, on the other hand, the river and gulf of St. Lawrence are a further indication that something in the course of events which have fashioned the actual surface, has exerted a greater energy in the direction of the diagonals than in the direction of the cardinal points of the compass.

The causes of these curious phenomena are not difficult to discover. Geological structure will, indeed, be found closely connected with them. The watershed of the Monistique Peninsula follows, in its *general* trend, the strike of the Lower Silurian strata; as the southeastern watershed of the lower peninsula follows nearly the belt of outcrop of the Marshall sandstone. So too, the axes of Lake Michigan and its appendages, Georgian Bay, Kewenaw Point and Lake Ontario, conform to the geological trends. But another force has evidently been operative, for the trends of the physical features of the country have often been deflected from the lines of geological strike. Saginaw Bay trends at right angles to geological strike; and so does Little Traverse Bay. The central watershed and most of the river-valleys sustain imperfect relations to rocky structures. As it is now generally admitted that the whole region under consideration has been extensively glaciated, it seems reasonable to presume that this glaciation is the general cause which has deflected the topographical and hydrographical axes from strict relations to the geological strike. As it has been shown by Prof. N. H. Winchell,* that the glacier probably moved toward

* Proceedings Amer. Assoc., Dubuque Meeting, 1872.

the southwest through Lake Erie and the valley of the Maumee; and as we long since reported this as the direction of the principal set of glacial furrows at the west end of Lake Erie,* it seems equally probable, even without collateral evidence, which we have, that the glacier moved in the same direction along Saginaw Bay and the valley thence to Grand Haven; and in a similar direction in the regions about Green Bay. This movement shaped the southeastern and central watersheds of the lower peninsula, and may have impressed its action upon the relief of regions much farther toward the west and northwest. The euronotal trends of river-courses, alternating with euroboreal trends have been determined by the breakage of the drainage across the euroboreally disposed barriers, down slopes whose general descent is euronotal, or across the euronotally-disposed barriers, down slopes whose general descent is euroboreal.

Not to pursue the discussion further, we think the facts will justify the enunciation of the following general proposition: *The actual topogrophical and hydrographical axes of Michigan are the resultant of two forces—a glacial, acting from the northeast, and a stratigraphical, acting along the lines of strike.*

As a corollary, we shall find that where the rocky formations are most consolidated, the resultant lies nearest to the stratigraphical force; and where the rocky formations are little consolidated, the resultant approximates the line of the glacial force.

As a second corollary, physical features determined by causes which have *obliterated* the glacial and stratigraphical trends, do not necessarily express relations to either force. Of this kind are the small streams whose courses over the diluvial beds have been determined by post-glacial erosions, and river-courses, like the St. Clair and Detroit, marked out across lacustrine or other post-glacial deposits which have concealed the surface features due to geological structure or glacial erosion.

Syracuse University, May 26, 1873.

* Michigan Ge›logical Report, 1861, p. 128.

THE TACONIC QUESTION.

BY ALEXANDER WINCHEL.

[*From The American Geologist, June, 1888.*]

[*From The American Geologist, June, 1888.*]

THE TACONIC QUESTION.

BY ALEXANDER WINCHELL.

CONTENTS.

The following concise statements of the elements of the question concerning the Taconic, may prove helpful to the young student who lacks time or opportunity for consultation of the original documents. The writer undertook the investigation with complete freedom from bias, save that his patriotism was predetermined to claim for American geology all that belongs to it. The research is not continued into the later history of Dr. Emmons' work in this field, because the validity of the name must rest on facts connected with the period of its first proposal.

I. Original proposals of the founder of the Taconic system.

1. *Date of first definition.* The term Taconic system was first employed by Dr. Ebenezer Emmons, in the final report on the geology of the second district of New York, the preface to which is dated January 1, 1842.[1]

The conception of the system existed in his mind, as he tells us, long before. "When, in 1836, I determined that in New York, the Potsdam sandstone was the base of the Silurian system, it seemed that we had at that time, the base of the sediments; but when two years subsequently I had observed the same base resting on sediments still older—as those along the eas ern side of Champlain and elsewhere—it became evident that there was still a series older than the Silurian. The proof of this has been accumulating ever since; and the Taconic system is found to rest upon primary rocks without an exception; and it has now been observed through the whole length of the states, from northeast to southwest. It is worthy of note, that through this whole extent, the base is continuous."[2]

2. *Stratigraphical position.* "A group or system of rocks which belong evidently to a position between the primary of the Atlantic ranges of mountains and the New York system." That is, between the crystalline schists and the Potsdam sandstone. This was a first formative conception of the stratigraphic limits of the system. It would be anticipated that the precise limits would be fixed by subsequent observations. For instance, the rocks naturally referable to the system might not always rest on the crystalline schists; and on the other hand, the upper limit might not finally be fixed at the base of the Potsdam sandstone.

3. *Geographic position and distribution.* The typical rocks "lie along both sides of the Taconic range of mountains, whose direction is nearly north and south, or for a great distance parallel with the boundary line between the states of New York, Connecticut, Massachusetts and Vermont. The counties [in

[1] Constituting chapters VII. VIII, and IX.

[2] American Geology, pt. II., The Taconic System. [Albany, 1855,] pp. 5 and 6.

New York] through which the Taconic rocks pass are Westchester, Columbia, Rensselaer and Washington; and, after passing out of the state, they are found stretching through the whole length of Vermont, and into Canada, as far north as Quebec. It is however, in Massachusetts, in the county of Berkshire, that we find the most satisfactory exhibition of the rocks. They form a belt whose width is not far from fifteen miles, along the whole western border, and which extends clearly to the western base of the Taconic range. The greatest breadth therefore, as will be seen, by an inspection of any map of this section of country, is wider upon the eastern than upon the western side of this range. In Vermont, they range along the upper members of the Champlain group, and thus become connected with the Second District." [p. 136].

The "Black slate" "extends as far as St. Albans in Vermont." The "Taconic slate, with its subordinate beds, occupies almost the whole of Columbia, Rensselaer and Washington counties." The Sparry limestone passes through Ancram, Hillsdale, New Lebanon, Canaan, Berlin, Petersburgh, Hoosic, White Creek, the west part of Arlington, [Vt], and onwards in the same range north, through the eastern townships of Canada East."[1] The magnesian slate forms the highest mountains in the Taconic range, which "extends along the western border of Massachusetts and through Vermont."

In 1846, the occurrence of Taconic rocks was announced in Rhode Island, Maine and Michigan."[2]

In 1855, Dr. Emmons announced that the Taconic system of rocks had "been observed through the whole length of the states from northeast to southwest * * * The most northeasterly point at which I have observed this system is at the Fox islands, off the coast of Maine, but I have good reason to suspect its existence in Newfoundland. If so, it ranks among the most persistent geological formations of the country."[3]

It is not necessary to follow Dr. Emmons' later identification of the Taconic in North Carolina and other regions.[4]

[1] Agricultural Rep., 74.

[2] Report on Agriculture, pp. 90—101.

[3] American Geology, pt. II, pp. 5 and 6.

[4] Geological Report of the Midland counties of North Carolina, Raleigh, 1856, 8vo.

4. *Constitution.* In the first enunciation of the system, Dr. Emmons was not fully persuaded of the order of superposition of the strata embraced in the Taconic belt. Leaving that determination to the future, he described them in geographical order from the west. As the general dip was easterly, this order would be ascending, unless the whole system had been subjected to an overturn. The order was as follows:

Taconic slate, sparry limestone, magnesian slate, Stockbridge limestone, granular quartz.

In the first volume on the Agriculture of New York, the preface to which is dated December 30, 1846, Dr. Emmons describes the members of the Taconic system in the following order:

Black slate, with two species of trilobites. Not here certainly regarded as belonging to the Taconic.
Taconic slate with its subordinate beds, with various markings referred to Nereites. Cited from Brunswick, Rensselaer county.
Sparry limestone.
Magnesian slate. (Talcose slates of 1856.)
Stockbridge limestone.
Brown sandstone or granular quartz.

5. *Palæontologic characters.* In the original characterization of the system, it was supposed to be destitute of fossils. This was made one of the points of distinction from the rocks of the Champlain Division. In the agricultural report, however, the author, besides describing and figuring two genera of trilobites—*Atops trilineatus* and *Elliptocephala asaphoides* (now known as *Conocephalus* and *Olenellus*)—from the Black slate, described and figured eleven species of Nereites and two fucoids; also one crushed tube supposed to be that of an annelid. Subsequently, many more species have been discovered in the rocks embraced by Dr. Emmons in the Taconic system.

6. *Original grounds of the Taconic system.* (1). Lithological: Compared with the palæozoic rocks, they are not the same, nor the same in a metamorphic state. Nor do the different lithological divisions occur in the same order as the divisions of the Champlain group from which they might seem to be derived by alteration. Further, they are distinguished by the presence of hæmatitic masses, while the iron of the Silurian is argillaceous or oölitic. The black oxide of manganese is another

distinction. As expressed in the agricultural report, "The members of the Taconic system have a different arrangement. The sandstones, limestones and slates are nòt only different in their relative position but they are much thicker than those with which they have deen supposed to be identical in the New York system."[1]

Compared with the primary rocks they are less crystalline, and in constitution, the rocks themselves differ, and also inclose a different range of accessory minerals. Actinolite, epidote, titanic and auriferous sulphuret of iron and graphite are confined to the primary. Further, the minerals of the Primary have a uniform connection with the rock masses; they are contemporaneous with them. There are rarely any cavities around them; but they are closely invested on all sides by the materials of which the rock is composed. On the contrary, in aqueous rocks, minerals occur in pré-existing cavities, and they are usually composed of substances more or less soluble under one or more conditions.[2]

(2). Stratigraphic unconformities: These appear not to have been distinctly brought out before 1846. In the agricultural report, page 56, three sections are delineated, in which the Calciferous sandstone is shown to overlie the Taconic strata unconformably. In plate XVIII, six sections are given in detail, showing the unconformable relations of the Taconic and New York systems. The details of the report point out marked unconformities with the underlying Primary masses.[3]

(3). Palæontologic unconformity: In the first enunciation, the Taconic beds were supposed differentiated from the New York system by their complete destitution of organic remains. At the date of the agricultural report, Dr. Emmons' view on this point was embodied in the following conclusion: "The Nereites and other fossils of the Taconic slates are unknown in any of the members of the Champlain group; the mollusca of the New York system are also wanting."[4]

In subsequent publications, the author of the Taconic system

---

[1] Report on Agriculture, p. 168.

[2] Report on the Second District, pp. 138-141.

[3] See, for instance, p. 111.

[4] Agricultural Report, p. 108.

embodied the results of later studies both by himself and others, and the stratigraphic and palæontologic grounds of the system were much more fully, accurately and effectively stated. But it is only necessary in this examination to learn distinctly what was the founder's view in the institution of his system.

7. *Central conception of the founder of the Taconic system.* From a study of the oldest documents treating of the Taconic system, it is not difficult to discover their essential purport. The central conception of Dr. Emmons was a system of sedimentary fossiliferous rocks underneath the Champlain group. To be a system it must possess distinct stratigraphic limitations both above and below, and must contain the records of a system of life unlike that of the overlying system. Quite possibly, the original propounder had not attained exact views in reference to the true limitations of his systems either above or below. He entertained the opinion that the Potsdam sandstone was not embraced in the Taconic; in that he may easily have been mistaken. He seems to have entertained the conviction that his system extended downward to the crystalline schists, and held what he termed "the absolute sedimentary base;" in this he may also have been mistaken. The upper and lower limits concern, however, only the border land of a great conception which with him was entirely original—a vast downward extension, below the base of the New York system, of the records of marine sedimentation and of life.

II. Is there a real sub-Silurian system?

1. That the Potsdam sandstone, the base of the New York system, does not mark the lowest limit of the record of life, is now a fact so notorious as to constitute one of the elementary truths of the science.

2. An extensive fauna of sub-Silurian life has been brought to light within the very area over which Dr. Emmons extended his system. Many of these forms have been discovered in the very strata embraced in the enumeration of the Taconic formation. Most of them have been signalized from strata lying on the eastern side of lake Champlain, and northward toward Quebec—the Swanton slates, the Phillipsburg group, the Georgia slates and the St. Albans group—called collectively

the Georgia group, by Walcott. On the west side of the state boundary, at Bald mountain, in Washington county, and near Saratoga, occur fossils belonging to sub-Silurian types, and therefore Taconic; but the latter are found in the upper portion of the Potsdam group, and hence carry that group into the Taconic, in spite of Dr. Emmons' early opinions. It may be added that fossils of the same significance have been found also by Marcou, at Keeseville in New York; and if the red sand-rock of Vermont is in continuity with the granular quartz, which, according to Walcott, contains primordial fossils, the place of the Potsdam is fixed in the Taconic.

The discovery of sub-Silurian remains in Massachusetts, New Brunswick, Newfoundland, Nevada, Colorado, Mount Stephens, Northwest Territory [recently, by Dr. Rominger], and other regions in America, require no more than the mention.

I quote a single passage from Mr. C. D. Walcott, in one of those careful and elaborate memoirs which have so enriched the literature of American geology: "Of the presence of a well-defined geologic system beneath the strata characterized by the second fauna of Barrande, or the Trenton fauna [including the Chazy and most of the Calciferous] of North America, on the North American continent, there is no question. The geologic sections given in this paper show it to have a total thickness of over 18,000 feet."[1]

It will give a clearer conception of the justness of this verdict of Mr. Walcott to reproduce some of the results embodied in his last and very important memoir,[2] a continuation of which is promised. He gives us a colored map of the original Taconic region through Vermont, Massachusetts and New York. The so-called Georgia group, which is sub-Potsdam, is represented by three colors. These collectively form a band beginning at the northern boundary of Vermont, and extending without a break, through western Massachusetts to Columbia county, New York, where information seems to be wanting. But be-

---

[1] Bull. U. S. Geol. Surv. No. 30, p. 11; also Am. Jour. Sci. (3), xxxiii, 139, Aug., 1886.

[2] Am. Jour. Sci., (3), xxxv, pp. 229-242 and pp. 307-327, with a colored map and a section. To be followed by a memoir on Washington county, N. Y.

yond this it is known with interruptions as far as Litchfield and New Haven counties, Conn., and Dutchess county, New York. From the Canadian border to Columbia county these rocks cover a breadth of eight to twenty miles. Mr. Walcott states that he knows the occurrence of fossils at over one hundred localities within the area of the Georgia terrane. All these rocks and all these fossils are older than the Potsdam. They lie within the area of the original Taconic, and the fossils are all types of the first fauna of Barrande. I consider these results conclusive of the right of the Taconic system to full recognition.

A sub-Silurian is therefore well established at the present day. This is precisely what Dr. Emmons contemplated and anticipated.

III. Was Dr. Emmons anticipated by other investigators?

1. *Limits of the Silurian.* In 1839, Sir R. I. Murchison published his "Silurian System," in which he gave an exposition of a system of fossiliferous rocks underlying what is now known as the Devonian system. The name Silurian had been employed by him since 1835. It was intended to embrace all the known fossiliferous rocks below the Devonian, but at that time little was known of remains below the horizon of the Caradoc. In 1834 Murchison had recognized the extension of the sedimentary series as far down as the "unfossiliferous graywacke of the Longmynd."[1] In his Silurian System, and in Siluria [1854] the Longmynd and Llanberis rocks are excluded from the scope of the Silurian system, because destitute of fossils, so far as known in Great Britain. The Longmynd were characterized as "bottom rocks." But even in 1844 two species of *Oldhamia* had been described from beds in Ireland equivalent to the Longmynd of Shropshire and South Wales. The Silurian therefore, terminated downward in the midst of the fossiliferous column.

2. *Position and rights of Cambrian.* In 1836, the name Cambrian was bestowed by professor Sedgwick on a series of strata occuring in North Wales, believed to occupy a position

[1] Proc. Geol. Soc. London, II, 11, Jan., 1834.

inferior to that of the series designated as Silurian by Murchison. But it subsequently appeared that the upper portion of them was the equivalent of strata in the continguous county of Shropshire, which Murchison had already annexed to his Silurian, under the designation of Lower Silurian—assuming that one systemic designation could properly include a palæontologic and stratigraphic break as abrupt as that between the "Upper" and "Lower" Silurian. The Cambrian of Sedgwick extended from the top of the Bala rocks to the bottom of the Llanberis. Their position was below the Silurian of Murchison as first conceived by himself, but was embraced in what may be called the Silurian annex.

3. *Stratigraphical relations of the Cambrian.* Meanwhile, M. J. Barrande was at work on the geology of Bohemia. In 1851, appeared his publications in the *Bulletin de la Societe geologique de France*, and in 1852, the first volume of his *Systeme silurien de la Boheme.* In these was introduced his classification of older rocks into stages denoted by the letter A, B, C, etc., and the more important recognition of certain great palæontologic breaks, separating a succession of distinct systemic faunas, thus:

E to H.	Third fauna, 900 feet.
D.	Second fauna, 6,000 feet.
C.	Primordial fauna, 1,200 feet.
A and B.	Azoic schists, 9.000 feet.

When the same strict principles of palæontologic classification came subsequently to be applied to the oldest rocks of Great Britain and America, the following conclusions were apparent:

(1). The true primordial fauna had not been embraced in the proposals of either Murchison or Sedgwick. The rocks containing this fauna in Bohemia extend "on an average, ten thousand two hundred feet" below any fossiliferous strata then known to Murchison or Sedgwick. Barrande embraced this entire extension under the name "Silurian," because he had then (1852) no knowledge of what had been done and proposed by Sedgwick in 1836, or by Emmons in 1842.

(2). The "sedimentary base" of the Taconic system signalized by Emmons in 1842, and synchronized with his "palæozoic base," fixed in 1844, did reach down to the primordial fauna of Barrande, and included it. So that Emmons was guided by a true insight in 1860, when he wrote: "The upper part of the Taconic is equivalent to Barrande's primordial group."[1] The Cambrian, therefore, laid no claim to the chief ground covered by the Taconic.

4. *Stratigraphical relations of the Huronian of Logan.* The Huronian system was proposed by Sir W. E. Logan, in 1855, for some Canadian strata located north of lake Huron, and supposed to extend from the base of the Potsdam sandstone downward to the crystalline schists. His conception was therefore identical with that of Dr. Emmons in proposing the Taconic system. In the case of the Taconic, strata containing primordial fossils older than the Potsdam have been found within the geographical limits originally assigned to the system. In the typical region of the Huronian, no fossiliferous strata have as yet been discovered, and it remains to show what part of the Taconic they correspond to. In saying this, I employ Taconic as originally conceived by Emmons — a great system extending down to the crystalline schists. It may be said, however, as the Huronian strata are now known to rest unconformably on lower strata which overlie the crystalline schists,[2] so, undoubtedly, adequate knowledge of the base of the Taconic, will show the inadmissibility of its claim to extend down to the crystalline schists. At its base, the Huronian stands, therefore, at the present time, precisely in the position of the Taconic, and is superseded by it. Above, it remains to determine whether the typical Huronian reaches up into the zone of the primordial fauna, which, as stated, the Taconic includes. In the basin of lake Superior, the so-called Kewenian series intervenes between schists identified with the Huronian and strata believed to belong to the age of the Potsdam sandstone. These hold, therefore, the stratigraphical position of the St. Albans, Phillipsburg and Swanton groups, with their primordial fauna. As beds having an igneous history, they may sustain some such relations to primordial life as the porphyry of Bohemia, whose eruption terminated the existence of the primordial fauna, before it had

---

[1] Letter to M. J. Marcou, in *The Taconic system and its position in stratigraphical geology*, by Jules Marcou, Proc. Am. Acad., new ser., vol. xii, p. 184.

[2] A. Winchell, in Amer. Jour. Sci., Oct., 1887, p. 314; *American Geologist*, Jan., 1888, pp. 14-24.

attained so prolonged a history as in some parts of North America. Whatever the facts may be as to the upper limit of the Huronian, the designation commonly employed for the system is clearly superseded by Taconic. This was the understanding of Dr. Emmons, though the contention seems to have dropped almost out of remembrance.[1] In 1860, in a letter to M. Marcou, speaking of a communication to the American Journal of Science, which was refused publication, he says, "I claimed that the Huronian was only the Taconic system." In 1861, he wrote, "It was ten years ago, I think, when I claimed Logan's Huronian system as nothing more than the Taconic." Unless, therefore, we find the zone of the primordial fauna interposed between the typical Huronian and the Lower Silurian, showing the typical Huronian to stand for a zone of truly azoic sediments, it would appear that the name Huronian ought to be dropped out of use.

IV. Validity and Scope of the Taconic.

1. *Grounds of opposition to the Taconic.* It was from the beginning maintained by certain North American geologists, to whose judgment most of the others deferred, that the rocks within the area of the Taconic as defined by Dr. Emmons, were newer than the Potsdam sandstone, instead of older; and that their more ancient aspect than the other strata of the same age was due to metamorphism It is not needful to consider with whom this view originated, nor to recall the discussions which have taken place. It may be granted that palæontological and structural investigations, carried on in the region south of lake Champlain, have succeeded long since, in showing that a considerable mass of strata embraced by Emmons in the Taconic, lies really within the New York system. It is not known, however, that no genuine sub-Potsdam Taconic occurs within the same area. Indeed, it has been shown while I write, that the quartzite series contains sub-Potsdam fossils, and extends from near Bennington in Vermont to Williamstown, Mass., and Stissing mountain in Pine Plains, Dutchess county, N. Y.[2]

[1] This equivalence was urged by N. H. Winchell in his vice-presidential address before the Am. Ass. Adv. Sci. in 1884.—[Ed.]

[2] Walcott: *The Taconic System of Emmons.* Am. Jour. Sci., 3, xxxv, pp. 234-6.

As to the region east and north of lake Champlain, investigations equally assiduous have succeeded in showing that a considerable area is occupied by strata older than the Potsdam; and that they contain a fauna of a truly primordial character, whose geological position is lower than any fossiliferous strata known to either Murchison or Sedgwick. Nothing more is needed than this simple statement.[1]

Thus the investigations of forty years have shown that the central conception of Dr. Emmons was founded on fact. This was simply a system of fossiliferous strata older than the New York system. Such system has been demonstrated by the researches of many investigators — Perry, Barrande, Billings, Marcou, Ford and Walcott. "To him belongs," says Walcott, "the credit of recognizing and describing the Middle Cambrian series of North America, as a distinct formation, both on structural and palæontologic grounds. * * * The central idea of which [Emmons' proposal] that a great series of Palæozoic strata, of pre-Potsdam age, existed east of the Hudson river shales of the valley of the Hudson and lake Champlain, we now know was correct."[2]

It signifies nothing that others — Dana, Dwight, Walcott[3] — have shown that some strata of the New York system are included among those described by Dr. Emmons as Taconic. Any amount of demonstration of such a proposition has no bearing against the conclusion that sub-Potsdam strata do exist, as Emmons alleged, and in the region originally circumscribed by the founder of the Taconic.

Mr. Walcott, who seems disposed to do justice, expresses regret that he cannot apply the term Taconic to the series of fossiliferous strata older than the Ordovician, the middle division of which Emmons distinguished "on structural and palæontologic grounds." But, if we do so, he says, "the great lower division described by Emmons as the typical Taconic, will be dropped entirely, and the Upper Taconic, which is not now

---

[1] The objections urged against the Taconic are discussed seriatim by my brother, N. H. Winchell, in *American Geologist*, March, 1888, pp. 162-72.

[2] Walcott: Bull. U. S. Geol. Surv., No. 30, p. 65.

[3] See especially, Walcott's most recent paper, Am. Jour. Sci., (3), xxxv, 229-42 — still to be continued.

known to occur in the Taconic area, would be taken as the true Taconic, which it does not appear to be, although Dr. Emmons included the Black Slate in it in 1847."[1]

The above paragraph, if I successfully penetrate its meaning, seems to me at variance with good reasoning. If Dr. Emmons characterized well the middle division of Mr. Walcott's Cambrian, it seems to me the two ends must go with the middle into the Taconic, whether Emmon's established a proper order within the Taconic or not. If, in continuing, the writer means that the great lower division of the Taconic was "described as the typical Taconic," I should beg to differ, since the greatest abundance of Taconic characteristics cited by Emmons pertained to the Upper Taconic — as finally he designated it. The Lower Taconic was originally described simply as a part of the Taconic, and if it cannot hold its place a large body of Taconic rocks remains. Lastly, with the statement that the Upper Taconic "is not now known to occur in the Taconic area," I beg again to differ, since the whole" Georgia group," as defined and mapped by Walcott, and ranged in the middle division of his Cambrian, falls within the original Taconic area. The Upper Cambrian of Walcott was excluded from the Taconic, but it appears that its palæontological affinities carry it there.

Mr. Walcott's position will be made plain by the following compilation of results embodied in his last paper, to which reference has already been made:

Parallel with Walcott's stratigraphy I have placed the principal members of Emmons' system, showing the singular stratigraphical disorder into which he fell. At the right hand, the Taconic and Cambrian stand as I would here propose.

It is chiefly in consequence of this unfortunate confusion that Mr. Walcott concludes the term Taconic ought to be dropped out of use. It seems almost presumptuous to differ with so thorough and candid an investigator. Mr. Walcott seems to have completed happily the difficult work on which professor Dana has so skillfully labored for several years. The results possess the highest scientific value, for the labor has been one of exceptional

[1] Bull. U. S. Surv., No. 30, p. 65.

difficulty, requiring palæontologic and stratigraphic skill of the highest order. A flood of light now shines on a question long dark. We can understand that the defenders and the opposers of the Taconic have all had good reasons for their claims—if they had not made them so exclusive. American geology owes

WALCOTT.		Walcott's stratigraphy within the Taconic area.	Emmons' equivalents.	WRITER.
ORDOVICIAN.		*Hudson terrane.* 4. Shales and sandstones. Smooth shales with Graptolites. 6. Red, black and green shales, cherts and sandstones, faulted in between two parts of terrane No. 5. With Graptolites.	*Lower Taconic.* Talcose slates. Essentially a repetition of Lower Silurian.	CAMBRIAN.
ORDOVICIAN.		*Trenton-Chazy-Calciferous.* 3. Limestone and marble, both sides of the Taconic range. Determinations worked out chiefly by Dana.[1] Fossils investigated by Wing, Dana and Dwight, and by Walcott.	*Lower Taconic.* Stockbridge limestone. *Super-Taconic.* Chazy at Bald Mt.	CAMBRIAN.
CAMBRIAN.	UPPER.	*Potsdam group.* 2. Talcose and silicious slates, sandstones and limestones. 2,000 feet. Saratoga county. { 2. Limestone with Potsdam fauna. 1. Massive sandstone, with typical Potsdam fossils farther north. Washington county. { 3. Calciferous, interbedded in shales. 2. Limestone, with Potsdam fauna. 1. Potsdam sandstone. Dutchess county. { Limestone with Potsdam fossils.	*Super-Taconic.* Calciferous. Potsdam. Overlapping by faulting.	TACONIC.
CAMBRIAN.	MIDDLE.	*Georgia group.* 1. Quartzyte series. Shore-line deposit, contemporaneous with No. 5. Not as low as lowest of No. 5. Bennington and Pownal, Vt., North Adams, Mass., Stissing Mt., Dutchess Co., and elsewhere. 5. Georgia terrane. Slates, shales and interbedded limestones and sandstones 14,000 feet. Off shore deposits. Fossils at over 100 localities in the typical Taconic area.	Lower Taconic. = *Upper Taconic.* Granular quartz. | Slates, Shales, limestones, sandstones	TACONIC.
CAMBRIAN.	LOWER.	*Paradoxides fauna belongs below.*		TACONIC.

Mr. Wallcott gratitude and honor for what he has accomplished. But I am inclined to the opinion that it is the very severity of his scientific method which prevents his due appreciation of the bearing of the facts which he has been foremost to bring to

[1] Amer. Jour. Sci., 1872 to 1887.

light. Mr. Walcott has gone farther than a comprehension of the elements of the Taconic question requires. He has followed Taconic history too far, and with too much minutiæ of criticism for a broad, judicial contemplation of the essential problem—though not, I repeat, too far for the ends of science. He has disclosed many egregious errors which, at first view, are rather confounding, and suggest that with so much mixture of error, confusion and truth, it may be best to abandon Taconic to the records of the past. But when we rise from the study of these perplexing and discouraging features of Taconic history, and generalize our field of view again, we observe that after all, they are but details, subordinate to the grand fundamental conception of a sub-Silurian and sub-Cambrian system of rocks and of life. As long as Dr. Emmons' central conception remains valid, we must not be too exacting in reference to the details of his determinations. Nor must we mercilessly hold to the standards of to-day, the conclusions of a research prosecuted over forty years ago, when primordial palæontology scarcely had existence either in America or Great Britian; and when stratigraphic and petrographic methods of research were generally no more thorough than those which Emmons so long, and so patiently, and so full of conviction, pursued. Unfortunate circumstances surrounding him gave an adverse set to opinion, which no efforts of his friends could change during his life-time. Those who knew Dr. Emmons personally can understand some of the reasons of this. But personal dislikes are poor arguments, and they become contemptible when known only as traditions. We are concerned at this day, only for truth and justice. If we can discern the grand outlines of truth and justice, we shall not be frightened away by some details of error and misconception. Viewing the subject in a large way, with a mind free from prejudice and prepossession, I feel borne to the conviction that the Taconic system has a right to stand.

2. *Defenders of the claims of the Taconic.* American defenders I will not cite; but I wish to quote the judgment of M. Barrande, whose competency perhaps none will question:

"At its origin, that is to say, from 1838 to 1844, this Taconic system was presented as founded on petrographic and stratigraphic observations, and constituted simply the *sedimentary base*, according to the American expression. It was still without any characteristic fauna. But in 1844, Dr. Emmons having discovered in this formation fossils before unknown, his Taconic system for him represented the *palæozoic base.*

"This expression, used on the other side of the Atlantic, is evidently equivalent to that of "primordial fauna,' which I have applied to the trilobitic group, the oldest of Bohemia, defined for the first time in my *Notice preliminaire*, in 1846. It is known that the *Lingulæ* which characterize the horizon of Lingula flags in Wales, that is, the Cambrian region of England, were only discovered by Mr. Davis in 1845 [Siluria, 2d ed. p. 43, 1859.]

"In comparing these dates, it is clear that Dr. Emmons had first announced the existence of a fauna anterior to that which had been established in the 'Silurian System' as characterizing the Lower Silurian division, and which I have named second fauna. It is then just to recognize this priority, and I think it all the more fitting to state it at this time, that it has not been claimed to this day."[1]

I agree with Marcou that "it is evident that if Barrande had seen the memoirs of Emmons when they appeared, he would have used the name "Taconic" to designate all that lower part of the most ancient strata of Bohemia which, having nothing better, he called Divisions A, B, and C of the Lower Silurian.[2]

The other judge whom I desire to cite is M. Dewalque, the general secretary of the committee on uniformity of nomenclature. At the meeting of the International Congress at Berlin, in 1885, after giving the opinions of various national committees in reference to the classification of the lowest Palæozoic rocks, M Dewalque said:

"Since the receipt of the reports of the national committees, the question to be decided has become complicated. M. Jules Marcou, in an important work published by the American Academy of Science and Arts, and entitled "*The Taconic System and its position in Stratigrapic Geology*," has vindi-

[1] *Documens anciens et nouveaux sur la Faune primordiale et le Systeme Taconique en Amerique.* Bull. Soc. geologique de France, 2 ser., tom., xvii, p. 225. 1861.

[2] Proceedings Amer. Acad., xii, 252, 1885.

cated the priority of the term Taconic, of which the Cambrian above mentioned [of primordial fauna] would be the equivalent. To us the question seems demonstrated. In such a case, the term Cambrian would be employed to replace the Ordovician, and the name Silurian would come back by right to group 6. If we be not in error, this solution would avoid many difficulties."

3. *Position and Equivalences of the Taconic system.* I forbear the presentation of any extended table of sub-divisions and equivalents of the Taconic system. After the presentation of Mr. Walcott's results, it is scarcely necessary to do more than refer for comparison to the table of M. Marcou in his last publication.[1] I conclude by saying, that in my opinion, the proposal of M. Dewalque is entirely feasible and just. The term Ordovician has no need to appear in American geology. It stands, in England and America, for the rocks first named Cambrian; and Taconic stands for the older strata holding the primordial fauna. I favor, therefore, the following arrangement:

III. Silurian [=Upper Silurian, containing 3d fauna.]
II. Cambrian [=Ordovician, containing 2d faun.]
I. Taconic [Containing primordial fauna.]

[1] *On the Use of the Term Taconic*, Proc. Soc. Nat. Hist., Boston, xxiii, Mar. 2, 1887, pp. 343-55.

GEOLOGY AS A MEANS OF CULTURE.

BY ALEXANDER WINCHELL.

[*From The American Geologist, July and August, 1888.*]

[*From The American Geologist, July, 1888.*]

GEOLOGY AS A MEANS OF CULTURE.

BY ALEXANDER WINCHELL.

I.

1. INTRODUCTORY.

The editorial management of the AMERICAN GEOLOGIST announced in the Prospectus, as an important feature, the intended publication of matter expressly suited to the needs of teachers of geology. Their plans also, embraced the presentation of views setting forth the true relation of Geology to educational work, and to general intelligence. It was believed such efforts would commend the science to all teachers and readers; and enlarge its acceptance and influence in the field of education. In view of the needs of teachers, it is intended to offer synopses, expositions, analyses, tables, schemes and other devices and matters of practical utility in the processes of instruction; and for this purpose, the editorial board anxiously await the accession of sufficient financial support to justify the employment of illustrations on a generous scale. They believe the profession of teachers will respond to their efforts.

The editorial board are aware that a "departure" of this kind may be regarded as compromising the scientific standing of the journal. They hear it said there are too many popularizers dealing with scientific material at second hand; and that we want many more investigators and more original contributions. The writer of this is also of the opinion that original work should be actively and directly promoted; but with the founder of the Smithsonian Institution, he perceives that the best interests of science demand that knowledge be "diffused" as well as "increased." The diffusion of knowledge promotes its increase by multiplying the number brought into position to contribute by money and brains toward effecting the increase. When the diffusion is extended into the ranks of intelligent teachers, the best possible conditions of increase are brought into existence.

In the January Number of THE GEOLOGIST, was inserted under the general head of Editorial Comment a note entitled, "Geology in the Educational Struggle for Existence." It was intended to point out the nature of the rivalry which tends to restrain, especially in certain universities, that advance of geological studies which their inherent relative importance would lead us to expect. That note simply pointed out a state of the facts. How greatly the interests of education and general culture are made to suffer by the existence of such a state of facts the writer did not undertake to show. But the exposure of the facts ought to be followed by an exposure of their wrong and unreasonableness, and the injury which they inflict on the cause of education —an injury inflicted at such a stage of educational development as to result in permanent malformation and deformity. The present writer will attempt, therefore, to carry the discussion to its natural development, and will begin, in the present article, a candid examination of the relation which geological study sustains to symmetrical culture. To the positions here taken he invites the thoughtful attention of all teachers and all geologists.

2. WHAT IS MEANT BY CULTURE?

It is considered educational orthodoxy to maintain that education, as the term itself implies, consists in such training of the human powers—but more especially the intellectual faculties—as will make them of greatest service to their possessor. If this expression means exclusively culture, and does not involve the acquisition of useful knowledge, it should at least be said that the acquisition of knowledge is one of the incidents of culture, and hence culture ought to be so sought as to involve the attainment of *useful* knowledge. For the present, however, the writer wishes to contemplate the purely cultural aspect of education, and to inquire how geological studies stand related to processes of pure culture.

In order that one's faculties may become most serviceable, they must acquire as far as possible, alertness, effectiveness and readiness. In other words, they must act with facility and rapidity; they must accomplish a large volume of their appropriate results in a given time, and must be ever ready to enter into action. They must be like a team which is quick, strong, and in harness.

What in detail, do educators contemplate when they speak of culture? What are the several powers whose alertness, effectiveness and readiness are best promoted by best culture? This is equivalent to asking what are the powers by whose most perfect activity we achieve most successfully the work allotted to us? The obvious answer is, all the powers by which a human agent seeks his ends—powers *physical*, powers *intellectual* and powers *ethical*. Let us restrict the inquiry, for the time being, to the powers intellectual. We will contemplate then, for the present, pure *intellectual culture.*

The term culture is much employed by a class of writers and speakers who extol lines of study demanding the exercise especially of *verbal memory*, and the power of comparison and analysis. The verbal memory is the faculty of retaining and recalling mere words. It is the means of acquiring names and of speaking them on occasion. It fixes phrases and quotations, and puts us in possession of them. It seizes on the words and forms of a foreign language, and makes them permanently ours. It is the spring of the faculty of verbal utterance; it confers effective power of expression. Its function extends to the retention of dates and other numerical expressions. Self-evidently, the verbal memory is an important means in the acquisition and communication of all knowledge, and the attainment of all ends to which knowledge contributes. To add alertness, effectiveness and readiness to the verbal memory is one important factor in intellectual culture.

Verbal memory, however, appears to be psychologically analogous to the memory or reproduction of sounds and sights in general; and thus, for our purpose, the general power of reproducing percepts may be designated the *sense-memory*. This power in its further exercise, is that by which we recall the features of individuals, and attain an extensive acquaintance. It preserves what we have seen in the forms of matter in general—forms of animals, plants, scenery, architecture. Readiness of recognition is conferred by it, and therefore, power of detail in descriptions. It is the chief faculty of story-telling—so far as simple utterance is concerned. Facility in sense-reproductions confers many advantages; and it is often the means of attaining successes which a superior grade of reflective intelligence fails to win. Aside from the store of facts which it sometimes holds at the service of the other powers, it is the most available instrument for what we call popularity. Though the vice of the excessive exercise of sense-memory may be garrulousness, recital of meaningless details, the substitution of anecdote for thought, and general shallowness, yet it is quite manifest that the fullest exercise of the sense-memory can only be productive of advantages, if the judgment and other intellectual powers are brought into symmetrical and restraining development. The whole field of the sense-memory deserves careful exercise and strengthening, and this work must be one of the useful and legitimate elements of broad culture.

Embraced in the order of culture first referred to is the exercise of the power of *comparison and judgment.* Without affirming that these are one faculty, their constant association in activity leads me to speak of them as one process. In detection of likenesses and unlikenesses, we discover grounds for judgments. Every judgment pronounced is an assertion of congruity or incongruity. As every act is the explicit or implicit expression of a judgment, a ready facility in the apprehension of the grounds of judgments is a cultural acquisition of prime importance.

The power of *abstraction* is another factor in that intellectual effectiveness which attaches to the lines of study extolled by the same class of writers about culture. Abstraction is the contemplation of one thing apart from all other things. It is simply an effort of attention carried to complete success. Attention is specially indispensable in the search for relations which are not immediately obvious—relations between things inconcrete, or abstracted from tangible forms. Every continued process of reasoning depends on abstraction. All mathematical relations, mental powers and moral qualities are abstract. The power of abstraction is a faculty in constant demand, but especially in the higher efforts of thought. It is an important power falling plainly within the scope of general culture.

The faculty of *deductive reasoning*, while constantly employed in many familiar modes of mental activity, is also one especially demanded in many of the higher efforts of intelligence. It is preeminently the faculty of mathematics; but it finds constant exercise in logic, in philosophy, in physics, and wherever principles or abstract truths are given, and their consequences or outcome are demanded. Obviously, mental culture must embrace the improvement of this royal power.

But deductive reasoning implies a power of retention of abstract truths or principles. This is often designated the *philosophic memory*. As an accessory and inseparable adjunct of ratiocinative processes, this power is indispensable in the higher mental activities; and its capability of perfect exercise must be one of the conditions of most efficient mental service. In other words, complete culture embraces an improved power of philosophic or thought memory.

It will scarcely be doubted that general culture involves the quickening of the *imagination*, the training of it to moderation and consistency, and the employment of it as an adjunct in the efforts of memory and deductive reasoning. The picturing power of this faculty gives vividness to the reproductions of sense-memory, and readiness in the comprehension of descriptions. It is an invaluable instrument in the attainment of clear conceptions of the results unfolded by deductive processes. The interpretation of the results reached by mathematical reasoning often depends wholly on the illumination of the field of exploration by the light of this faculty. It goes before discovery, and discloses resting-places for thought in the midst of the gloom of the unknown. Its creative powers are often exercised under the promptings of analogy, congruity or contrast, and it thus becomes luxuriant in simile and metaphor. By its luminous apprehension of the forms and details of concrete things inaccessible to perception, it contributes to graphic description; and through its resources of metaphor, both illuminates the thought and garnishes the style. Imagination is therefore a powerful instrument in the creation of new conceptions and the transmission of them to the intelligence of others. A mind well fitted for the creation of new conceptions possesses one of the most effective gifts of culture; and if, in addition, it wields the power of graphic and pleasing elucidation, its cultural gifts are brilliant, attractive and useful. Assuredly, then, the imagination is one of the most important faculties to improve and strengthen by the arts of education.

I have mentioned the intellectual powers and processes somewhat in the order in which they are the subject of disciplinary exercise in the popular systems of "liberal" culture, rather than in the order of their importance or the order of their spontaneous development. Assurdly, however, the sense-memory would receive no content unless the *sense-perceptions* had been previously called into activity; and the picturing power of imagination would remain latent unless sense-perception had supplied the elements of its creations. Perceptions are the antecedents and conditions of sense-memory, of imagination and of induction. They are also the conditions of the awaking from slumber of those intuitive cognitions of necessary truths, which regulate and control all human actions. Perceptions, in other words, are the germinal elements of all knowledge and of all power of knowledge. In a more obvious sense, they are the sole means of communication with the external world. They find therefore a more constant, and more diversified and more essential use than any other of our intellectual powers. The most widely and variously exercised of our faculties are those which most demand the improvement of judicious culture. To learn how to observe most advantageously should be one of the chief ends of education.

The power of *inductive reasoning* should not be omitted from the list of those deserving of culture. Induction from observed data has been pronounced the characteristic modern method of attaining to scientific knowledge; and Sir Francis Bacon, very mistakenly, has been regarded, in cant phrase, as the founder of the inductive method. So far as this is true, it shows with what aim and method we must proceed, if we would enter into the spirit of the modern march of intelligence. So far as induction has been pursued from the earliest dawn of reflective thought, it shows what is the inflexible and changeless mandate of nature in the method of marshalling our powers for the search of truth. In either view aptness and good logic in the drawing out of general truths from many details of observation appear plainly to be essential ends of well balanced modern culture. Without the acquisition of this power, education is glaringly defective. Whether Baconian or Aristotelian, the method of induction brings order out of a universe of discrete facts, and lays the foundations of principles which we build into the fabric of natural science. Induction has more than a service to science to perform. Thousands of the grotesque and unreasoned *nonsequiturs* of daily life are but the outcome of hasty inductions; and some of these, as in the search for petroleum, gas, or coal, are neither harmless nor inexpensive. To train this generalizing power so that it serves us thoroughly and truly is the part of education in its cultural aspect. I emphasize this truth, because it is quite generally ignored in our prevailing forms of education, at the same time that its importance seems to be foremost.

In the advocacy of the popular form of liberal culture, we hear much of the creation of a good *taste*. The study of the ancient languages, it is claimed, with truth, tends to improvement of the taste. If I understand the meaning of this expression, taste is the perception and feeling of congruity or fitness n the realm of sensible things. It seeks congruity, and takes pleasure in it. It knows how to shun incongruities, and is distressed by their occurrence. A good literary taste knows what juxtapositions of thought are consecutive, graduated, and pleasings and it knows what juxtapositions of words and phrases will avoid a jar, and best adapt expression to the thought. In music, it appreciates and seeks such successional relations and harmonic combinations of tones as are congruous with each other and with our musical apperceptions; and such as are congruous with the thought of feeling which the composer seeks to express. A good artistic taste understands what forms and colors harmonize with the common forms of beauty and fitness implanted in the soul. It is preëminently *literary* taste which the prevailing culture claims to shape and perfect. Indisputably, such culture, besides increasing the happiness of its subject, confers a means of influence which improves the scholar's chances of success in the battles of life. Such control of the adversities of situation is therefore, eagerly to be sought in our professed systems of general culture.

The foregoing may be regarded as an enumeration and characterization of all the important powers which fall within the scope of intellectual culture. The term, so far as I know, is not employed, and cannot be employed, in any sense involving more than the educational discipline of these. What our linguistic and literary friends mean by "culture" cannot refer to any occult influences bearing in any other direction than the improvement of these powers. It seems superfluous to emphasize so plain a proposition; but it becomes desirable to bring to the light of day and to the terms of definite statement, the whole secret and mystery of "liberal culture."

It is intended next, to present an analysis of the content of geological science, and then an examination of the nature of the demands which it makes upon the powers of the student.

II.

3. Diversified aspects of Geological Study.

Unlike mathematics and many other subjects of study, the science of geology consists of various ranges and kinds of knowledge. It is not a mere body of facts of observation, like political or physical geography in the ordinary acceptation; nor of facts of record, like history in the scholastic sense. It is not merely a field stocked with the products of imagination and sentiment, like popular literature. It is not merely a realm of abstract concepts and necessary ideas, like metaphysics. It is not merely a system of deductive processes all firmly bound together and to first principles by necessary laws of thought, like mathematics. It is not merely a department of mental activity where conclusions are balanced on probabilities, and moral certitude is the highest satisfaction afforded the aspiration to know, as in many ecclesiastical, political and educational questions. It is all these, and more than these. Geology as the science of the natural world, embraces all which the natural world contains; all with which it is historically and genetically connected, and all the accessories and means whose employment contributes to the attainment of a knowledge of the world in its widest relations. It is the organization of all the sciences in a crusade for conquest in the realm of the unknown. To illustrate and justify a claim so large, I shall venture to recite in brief the processes by which geology advances from the most familiar facts of observation, step by step through generalizations higher and higher, to the grandest doctrines ever enunciated by science; and thence by a reverse, or deductive process, to the details of events from which actual observation is separated by intervals of space and time to finite powers impassable.

The beginning of all this fabric of geological science is what we see by the roadside, in the field, on the mountain slope or the ocean's strand. In our daily observations are the facts which point the way to the loftiest generalizations of the science. Let me confine the reader's attention to a group of phenomena leading toward the fundamental *doctrine of a cooling globe*. About our very doors lie the bowlders whose hard and crystalline character proclaims the agency of intense heat. In the structure of the mountains which we climb, and underneath the lands which we inhabit, are square miles of rock similarly crystalline and vitrified. These are data of observation. They are data of easy and familiar and universal observation. They sustain the inductive conclusion that intense heat has been there. Other observations on ancient lavas—on palisades, dikes and extinct volcanoes, indicate that the heat has been sufficient to fuse the rocks. Has been—but is now no longer. *The heat has subsided.*

Thermal springs, geysers, artesian borings, deep mines, volcanic eruptions supply other observational data from which we induce the doctrine of *a heated interior.* The earth has cooled, but is still hot within. *The earth is in the midst of a cooling process.*

This is a most fruitful principle. If the earth is a cooling globe, two inquiries next press upon us. Through what phases of existence has it passed in its remote history; and what vicissitudes is it destined to undergo in the future continuance of the cooling processes? From what initium did the cooling process set forth, and at what finality will it end? No one can fail to understand that these are lofty inquiries; and that any well grounded responses must lift our thoughts into the realm of sublime truth. But the history of the earth's cooling unrolls a vista through the past eternity. No human intelligence has been witness of the events. The future career of the cooling globe lies in the folded possibilities of events unreal and stretching into the eternity lying in the opposite direction.

But these lofty questions are not unanswerable. The events of terrestrial history succeed according to methods which lie revealed. There is no uncertain caprice in their order and relationships. Physical events run in grooves. What we observe discloses a trend which may be followed in either direction. By observation we have learned the laws of cooling, and the elemental and climatic changes which depend on changes of temperature. If the earth be a cooling globe we may with confidence deduce its conditions and their concomitances in the earlier stages of cooling. Here our reasoning becomes *deductive.* We proceed from the inductive principle of a cooling globe, and from the primary principles of thermodynamics, and retrace the cooling history. We see in imagination as we recede, a warmer terrestrial surface, a more tropical climate, and, in correlation, more tropical plants and animals. We strengthen and verify the deduction by the inductive data afforded by the successively deeper sheets of ocean sediment. Farther on in the retrospect, the sediments are but beginning to accumulate. The mountains are still in embryo; the ocean is universal. As the scroll of terrestrial history continues to unfold, the ocean itself is noticed at its natal epoch; the clouds are discharging the ocean from their bosom. Here the possibilities of inductive confirmation disappear. Earlier than this no enduring rocky forms had existed. The greater heat had reduced all terrestrial matter to a fluid state, which retained no records. This is the starting point of inductive geology.

But this is not the starting point of the process of cooling.

With the eye of imagination under the calm guidance of the reasoning powers, we behold in the remoter past, a world of firemist, with the beginning of a central nucleus of molten matter. In the profounder depths of the eternity past, the firemist is conceivably in the condition of a gas. In a history of cooling, we have learned of no condition antecedent to this. The gaseous state of matter accompanies the highest temperature known. Do not understand me as enunciating the doctrine that the cooling process must have begun at a temperature at which all terrestrial matter existed as a gas. I mean only, that the process of cooling leads always away from that state as the remotest possibility. Actually, it may have proceeded from a condition thermally subsequent to this. The subsequent thermal condition may have been attained from some older state in which the constituents of the world were gathering together, and were yet even at a low temperature. I am not seeking to reason out that condition of the world which was absolutely primordial. I seek only to illustrate how by an inverted deduction, we may recede toward a state of the world which antedates all human observation and even all the rocky records of inductive geology.

Now, having found a starting point — having assumed any remote condition as a starting point, we pursue by direct deduction, the course of events which under the laws of matter, must have ensued in the progressive escape of heat from the terrestrial mass. We reason out the attainment, sooner or later, of the firemist condition, the precipitation of a molten rain and the growth of a molten globe, the condensation of aqueous vapor, the enveloping of the earth in a mantle of clouds, the descent of æonic rains, and the gathering of the universal ocean. Many other events collateral with these, we logically reason out. By the aid of imagination, the scenes enacted become vivid and real, and our understanding of them improved. Now we see how and when marine precipitation must have begun, how the submarine floor by thickening, became melted off by encroachment of heat from below, and how as sedimentary deposits continued, the deep-seated residual heat invaded upward the earlier sea-sediments and transformed them. We see how and when the time arrived for the possible introduction of organic forms, and how they succeeded each other as the rolling æons of cooling wrought the terrestrial surface into changed conditions. Of all these post-crustal events, the crust has retained some records, and the inductive evidences from them check and verify our deductive inferences.

Let us for a moment stand on a higher plane of observation, and rise to a higher generalization. There are other planets within the range of our vision which exist under the same forms and motions and accompaniments as this planet. They are regulated by the same system of laws; they consist of the same matter; they undergo the same visible vicissitudes. Here is a body of data of observation—not indeed, with unaided vision, as when we noted the aspects and conditions of the vitrified and crystalline rocks—but with the aid of the telescope, the spectroscope, the polariscope and the crucible. From these data we formulate the inference that all the planets revealed through our instruments are bound together in one system, have had a common history and are moving to a common destination. This larger generalization produces in our minds a conscious expansion—a larger apprehension of the scope and unity of the cosmic plan. This higher attainment of thought is attended by a grateful emotion, a spiritual delight; and if we are philosopher enough to contemplate plan as the correlative and expression of mind, we feel here, in the presence of this grand disclosure, a higher certitude of Supreme Mind, and a deeper seated and more enduring sentiment of devotion.

At the level of this loftier generalization, we conceive the matter and the forms of all the planets merged in one. Perhaps the common mass is in the state of firemist, and luminous. Perhaps it is a heterogeneous assemblage of mineral particles and masses undergoing condensation, and destined in a later æon, to evolve the heat which will develope luminosity and reduce portions to a state of firemist. As before, I care not to define precisely the actual state of the matter of the solar system which was primordial. We seek only a rational commencement—a condition such as involved all later conditions. There must have been a time—so we reason—when the evolution of heat began to be surpassed by loss of heat. From that epoch cooling and contraction began. Rotation is a primordial, necessary condition of all separate masses of cosmic matter. In a rotating, cooling and contracting spheroid, the changes of form and condition resulting are the subjects of calculation. Even if there be alternative lines of vicissitudes, one of these leads on through processes of annulation and spheration—with possible secondary annulation and spheration—on to such an outcome as we see exemplified in the assemblage of planets and satellites constituting our solar system. And this earth on which we dwell is a particular outcome of such an evolution—so grand, so vast, so ancient. And all that is now of the earth was involved in those æonic vicissitudes. The bone and flesh and nervous matter of our bodies existed in that primordial fire mist—in those annulating spheres—in that fervid atmosphere—in those glowing rocks—in those ancient sediments—in the shells of primeval molluscs—in the framework of generations of reptiles—enduring as matter; and our plans of organization give expression to thoughts no less enduring. Such is the unity of the organism of the planetary system, and such the unity of man with the organism of the worlds.

In this regressus of thought, we rise to a still higher plane. The sun appears as the residuum of a prolonged process of planetation. By the aid of our instruments we learn that the stars are other suns. Imagination kindles and emotion warms at the suggestions of such a fact. The stars then, are so many centres of planetary systems completed. Yes, to the utmost limit of the visible universe, the same modes of world-life prevail as are exemplified in our own system—the same as are revealed in continental masses and granite cliffs and ocean sediments on this orb to which we have been assigned as its inhabitants. There must be then, other planets. There must be other inhabitants. If other inhabitants, their intelligence is akin to ours; for otherwise, the universe around them, so interpretable to us, would be uninterpretable to them; and the fitness of things which reigns everywhere within our cognizance, would be turned into contradiction of the testimony of the universe. Reason refuses to credit this. Other intelligences there are, to whom the universe has the same meaning as to us; who think as we think; who are already familiar with our ideas, or are ready to receive them and to impart to us their own.

Does not the reader find such ranges of thought expansive, ennobling, spiritualizing? Possibly he is saying this is not geology. No—not in the school-book sense. But geology in the stricter sense leads to the high-swung bridges over which thought passes by an uninterrupted continuity of path into the realms of philosophy and theology, whose light tinges the clouds which engirt a primeval world. I suffer myself to follow thought into these remoter realms for the purpose of showing the vastness of the range of geological contemplation, though the ordinary geologist may seldom explore it. Geological facts and doctrines, with which we are all chiefly occupied, lie in a single province of the science.

I said that the grooves of passing events run into the distinct future as into the distinct past over which the reader has been transported by a rapid flight. By direct deductive reasoning from the generalized principle of a cooling globe, we are able to depict future vicissitudes with no less certainty than those past. We anticipate a frozen world and a darkened sun. From the generalized doctrine of slow continental degradation we depict beforehand the destructive work of future ages. From the action of the moon on the lagging lunar tide, we are enabled to foresee a lengthened day, and finally synchronistic rotary and orbital movements of the earth, accomplished by a slower action of the sun on the solar tide. Through the operation of a resisting medium—whether ethereal, meteoric or molecular—we look forward to a general gathering of all the dead planets at a common sepulchre. Then by completing the parallelism already delineated in reference to the past, we learn that the unrolled history of this world represents that of all the worlds of our system; and the unrolled history of the system pictures that of the firmament. And now the grand and culminating inference of all science looms before our intelligence in majesty awful and inspiring: The history of matter is one in all the bounds of all space and in all the æons of time past and time to come. The vicissitudes of yesterday are a paragraph in the annals of universal matter. In that totality every human life is a constituent part. Man stands in the midst, and casting his mental glances backward and forward, affirms and feels his unity with all. *Man only as an organism.* Those glances are not the rays of sun or star—they are the thoughts which imperishable and unchanging mind has written on the forms of star and planet and organism. And thus, out from the forms of matter as they perish and disappear, rises an entity which neither changes nor disappears, nor yet endures as mindless matter—

but endures in self-consciousness and self activity, and constituting my essential self, unveils to vision another universe where suns neither wax nor wane, and the limitations and infirmities of changeful matter never interrupt or ruffle the gentle current of eternal being.

4. The Intellectual Powers which Geology calls into exercise.

These thoughts are presented with no intent to expatiate on the themes of science. My purpose is only to indicate the vastness of the range of cognitions and contemplations to which the study of geology invites. It begins with simple facts of easy *observation.* It calls the *percipient powers* into pleasant exercise. In observing separate facts we *compare* them with each other. By processes of *judgment* we pronounce them identical or similar or diverse. If similar we *abstract* the particular characters in which the similarity consists, and decide whether they are trivial or fundamental. The wide ranges of facts brought under observation are distributed into groups. *Names* for the facts there must be, and thus arises a technical nomenclature, which gives us additional exercise in *verbal memory.* In extending our knowledge of facts beyond the sphere of personal observation, we resort to the records of the observations of others. We are led to the use of *foreign languages.* We obtain the cultural benefits of *linguistic study.* Our various groups of facts lead to various *generalizations* or interpretations. One group points to a former high temperature on the earth, as we have seen. Another convinces us that the lands have been covered by a universal sea, and that the bedded rocks are but its sediments. Another group indicates the magnitude of land erosions in the past, and the complete obliteration of ancient continents. Another group of facts establishes the doctrine that the earliest animals were invertebrates; and that the oldest vertebrates were marine; and in short, that the order of succession in the advents of animal types was identical with the order of rank—thus contributing one of the principles on which we base that higher generalization which expresses the method of Supreme Mind in all the successions of the natural world. Within each of these broader and more obvious generalizations are others of more limited scope. If the first vertebrates were marine, so the first marine vertebrates were not fishes of typical structure, but of archaic forms now long extinct. If land vegetation appeared after marine, it was at first only a flowerless jungle. The great body of geological *doctrines* consists of inductions like these, founded upon facts of observation. Many, very many of the facts are near and familiar; many are remote and unfamiliar. A large part of the body of geolgical science consists of a *record of facts.* The generalizations are not, indeed, postponed till all the facts of the science are catalogued. We begin to draw our generalizations while yet we must hold them as merely tentative. Final generalizations may displace them; and even these in some cases, may prove not to be final; or may prove to be wholly erroneous. By a law of our minds we begin to generalize as soon as two or more cognate facts are brought together; and continually test and revise our generalizations, as long as new facts of the same group prove incompatible with earlier generalizations. Then we have reached a principle or doctrine. Thus it is a doctrine today that Dinosaurs did not survive the close of Mesozoic time. But if tomorrow we find the remains of Tertiary Dinosaurs, that generalization must be rectified.

Thus in dealing with the great body of geological science, we keep the observational faculties in training. With this, we exercise the powers of *sense-memory* and of *language.* This training holds a large place in the exactions of geological study. So far as trained quickness and exactness of perception constitute mental culture, the study of geology is eminently cultural. In dealing with the same great body of the science, we keep the *inductive powers* in constant exercise. Their activity, as I have said, is the characteristic activity of modern intelligence, in distinction from mediæval and ancient thought. If the training of the mind in those methods of activity which tend to identify it with modern thought, and make it master of the characteristic results of modern thought is a useful training and a desirable training, then the habits of inductive reasoning fostered by geology constitute an eminently valuable form of mental culture.

But with these studies come various forms of incidental culture. Many of the facts are recorded in works of travel and description written in style of high literary excellence. Allow me to cite Hugh Miller's "Old Red Sandstone;" Major Powell's "Exploration of the Colorado River of the West;" Captain Dutton's "High Plateaus of Utah," and Miss Bird's "Fire-Fountains;"—or in a different field, the Duke of Argyll's "Unity of Nature." If the student is called upon to record his observations, as well he might be, he may acquire a copiousness of diction and a beauty of style not inferior to that promoted by essays on historical or romantic themes. More indirectly, come the acquisition of languages and the enrichment of the vocabulary.

With these forms of geological study will be noticed an accessory training of the *imagination.* The picturing power is demanded even in bringing into juxtaposition in thought, absent data of observation which have to be compared together. Still more is it demanded in acquiring a vivid comprehension of data presented through descriptions. Especially is this demanded in the study of descriptions of fossil remains unaccompanied by delineations; and not less in the drawing up of such descriptions. I know palæontologists who declare that a mere description of a fossil shell is unintelligible; but, provided the description is good, it would become intelligible with improved picturing power in the imagination. The facts show that in the study of descriptions of fossil remains, and other facts not fully illustrated by drawings, the imagination is kept in constant exercise. The cultural results on this faculty are therefore of great effectiveness and high value.

In an accessory way also, comes discipline in the *art of delineation.* It is impossible for the geological observer to record his observations without the ability to accompany them with drawings. If the student has had no instruction or practice in drawing, he will soon obtain the practice, and then the instruction will be unessential. On almost every excursion, the student or investigator must execute from nature geological sections or geological maps. Not unfrequently, he must delineate some fossil which cannot be removed from the rock, or embody some delineation in a description. I am aware that finished drawings exhaust much time, and are commonly confided to special artists. Still, drawing is one of the demands of geological study and in vestigation; and this artistic acquirement is one of the forms of culture for which the science of geology provides.

The same demand for pictorial illustration leads the field geologist to subsidize for his ends, the superb picturing power of the photographic camera. Topography, mountain forms, rock-structure, details of stratification, water-falls invite to the application of the camera while in the field; and the exact delineation of fossil forms is greatly promoted by photography in the laboratory. Thus the geologist is led still further to diversify his accomplishments, and add to the sources of his efficiency as a geologist, and of his enjoyments as a lover of nature.

These various forms of mental exercise and discipline are incident to the acquisition of the facts and doctrines of geologic science. I have illustrated a higher range of geological truth, and I wish to impress the fact that its acquisition calls into exercise another range of intellectual powers. The faculties of *deductive* or *a priori* reasoning come into play in the attempt to proceed from an admitted principle to the particulars which it involves or necessitates as consequences. Geological investigation very *freqnently* takes the deductive form. It does not often proceed from *necessary* principles, as in mathematical reasoning; but generally from a principle or truth established by previous inductive research. When a distinguished American geologist described a large number of three-toed tracks found in the brown sandstones of the Connecticut valley, and ascribed them to extinct species of birds, the elder Agassiz reasoned deductively when he declared that they could not be bird-tracks, since birds, according to all inductions, had not begun to exist at so early an age of the world. Similarly, the geologist declares that coal will never be discovered in the valley of the Hudson river, however black and misleading some of the slates may be; since all productive coal measures have been found to hold a higher stratigraphic position. More marked and prolonged employment of deductive inference is observed in the treatment of those geological problems which admit of the application of the methods of mathematical analysis. Some of these problems are as follows: The temperature of the earth's interior; the thickness of the earth's crust; the condition of the central matter of the earth; the existence of tidal effects in the earth's general mass; the greatest possible altitude of mountains; the sub-meridional direction of mountain chains; the sufficiency of mountain-wrinkles for the total of mountain folds; the existence and position of a zone of no stress in the crust of a cooling planet. Then in that higher range of geological investigation which may be styled comparative geology, or an application of the doctrines of geology to the conditions and histories of other planets, we find many uses for mathematical methods; as in the study of the moon's atmosphere, and her general physical condition; the conditions of Jupiter, and of Saturn and Uranus, and the light they throw on past and future conditions of our own planet.

Without the application of mathematical analysis, the general processes of deductive reasoning from the principle of a cooling world, afford, as I have shown, large and valuable exercise for the higher intelligence. It is a regal power by which we explore in thought the distant ages of terrestrial history which elapsed before even the race of man existed, or the æons of cosmic vicissitudes undergone before even the world had existence. It is a regal power by which we may stand here and glance down through the æons of terrestrial changes yet future. The past has been real, but the future is unenacted. The intellectual eye, through the telescope of geology, pierces through all potentiality. It is prophetic. It enables us to live alike in the æons of the past and the æons of the future. It confers on us a limited omnipresence and omnipotence. No enlightened man can possibly deny that such exercises of mind are lofty, noble, cultural—cultural and improving to an extent scarcely paralleled in the circle of human thought.

There are those—among them a few geologists—who affirm that these lofty deductive reasonings are little more than flights of the imagination, and that the results do not belong to the body of recognized science. These men conceive geology as properly restricted to its body of facts and generalizations. It is easy to show that such a dogma is impossible of observance, and is violated daily even by those who acknowledge only positive geology. But a thoughtful consideration of the mode of evolution of our grand deductive conclusions will show that they are *reasoned out*, not imagined. The difference between a pure romance and a romantic inference is as wide as the beginning and conclusion of terrestrial history. It cannot be claimed that the particular denouements which we picture have been or are to be actual events. The pathway of reasoning often bifurcates, and we may pursue either road to conclusions. There are always concomitances lying alongside, which are the outcomes of causes acting outside of our trains of reasoning. These may determine whether the actual course of events will pursue the right or the left. We know however, that it will pursue one or the other; or at least some course within the scope of rational anticipation. With all these qualifications and uncertainties of actual detail, the sublime fact remains, that our science enables us to mount into the æons past, and plunge into the depths of the æons to come, and get visions, even if dim, of the stupendous events flowing out of the exercise of infinite power and infinite intelligence in the realms of infinite space and infinite time.

Let me add that if these visions are absolutely unreal, the exercise of the intelligence is still the same. It is an exercise of the loftiest powers of the mind, and if it leaves in our possession no real knowledge, but only culture, it stands on a footing equal with some other studies deliberately pursued simply for their cultural influence—and that, even on a lower range of faculties than those employed in the higher inductions and deductions of geological science.

It must have occurred to the reader that much yet remains to be said of the cultural influence of the higher reasonings of geology. I allow myself a few words further. Imagination, I said, is not the creator of the histories, past and future, which I have depicted in the vicissitudes of the world; but it is the indispensable instrument for securing to the understanding a vivid apprehension of the reality, the nature and meaning of those vicissitudes. These exercises of the higher reason keep imagination in constant and pleasing activity, and thus train a power which sheds over the logical products of the mind a vivid radiance, and often lights the way for the understanding into the dark regions of the unknown.

The loftiness of these themes demands a lofty style. To portray them to the common intelligence—always eager to learn of them—demands such imagery and metaphor and lucidity and earnestness as belong to the higher ranges of polite literature. If a good *use of language* be one of the results of culture, here are examples for imitation, and here are opportunities for scholastic exercise.

In commencing this discussion, I proposeed to confine my treatment to intellectual culture, but the friends of geology might well charge me with remissness, if I should fail to remind the reader again, of the *moral* and *spiritual improvement* which comes from such contemplations as I have pointed out respecting the unity of the realm of nature, and the revelation of Supreme Intelligence which we read everywhere in the plans and methods of nature.

I could not say more within reasonable limits of space. Enough I hope, has been said to establish the proposition that the study of geology is *suited for universal culture.* In its various grades and departments it calls into exercise *every power of intelligence*, and even comes into moving relations with the *ethical susceptibilities.* What more is universal culture? What more is symmetrical culture? Who can claim any discipline of intelligence as not reached by the influence of geological learning? I shall not institute comparisons in detail. I leave it to my readers to seek out other lines of study capable of a wider or more profitable culture. Their efforts will but enforce the truth of my conclusion.

I am not so unreasonable as to maintain that geology is the only science to be studied; or that other sciences or literatures do not afford particular kinds of culture to a greater extent than geology. I only desire the truth to be discerned and acknowledged, and acted upon, that geology is a study capable of culture more diversified than is found in the pursuit of those studies often prescribed exclusively for their cultural value.

I have presented geology simply as a means of culture. I have not considered it as a *means of useful knowledge.* An elucidation of the utilitarian side of geologic study would show that in geology we possess the means of uniting general culture with the attainment of useful knowledge. Thus is doubled the claim of geological study upon our regards as educators and promoters of the best civilization.

These positions being established, it might still remain to examine the relations of geological science to the developing intelligence of the young. Though this also is a field which cannot now be entered, it would be easy to show that many of the observational data of the science are precisely suited to the stage of intellectual development of young pupils; other data, and the inferential principles of the science, to pupils of progressively maturer years. And finally, it would be easy to illustrate practically the observational method of introducing the familiar elements of geology to pupils of tender years, and proceeding by gradual expansion and elevation of the method, to ranges of geological thought suited to pupils of full maturity.

I leave the subject to the reader's reflections. What I have said is true or untrue, or partly true and partly untrue. If true, educators cannot, as reasonable persons, permit the science of geology to remain under their reproach and neglect as a materialistic science—a "bread and butter science." They must act; they must acknowledge the truth, and allow geology to come into the enjoyment of its rights in the field of education. If what I have said is untrue, my positions demand an impartial refutation; for a wide and powerful public sentiment is gathering at my side. If they are partly true, I shall continue to maintain that the true is the larger part, until my numerous and powerful literary friends honor my views with the electric light and heat of their destructive criticism.

[From the American Journal of Science, Vol. XXX, December, 1885.]

SOURCES OF TREND AND CRUSTAL SURPLUSAGE IN MOUNTAIN STRUCTURES.

By Alexander Winchell.

[FROM THE AMERICAN JOURNAL OF SCIENCE, VOL. XXX, DECEMBER, 1885.]

ART. LII.—*Sources of Trend and Crustal Surplusage in Mountain Structures*;* by ALEXANDER WINCHELL.

TWO facts in mountain structure have baffled, hitherto, the attempts made to arrive at a comprehension of the mechanics of mountain formation. The north-and-south trend of the profounder physiographic features of the earth has no light thrown upon it by any of the orogenic theories commonly entertained. It appears also, from calculations made by Captain C. E. Dutton, Rev. O. Fisher and others, that the shortening of the earth's circumference in cooling from the incrustive stage to the existing temperature would be insufficient to supply the folds and plications wrought into the structure of the mountains. Professor E. W. Claypole has reached a similar result from approximate measurements across a portion of the Appalachian chain in Pennsylvania. These determinations, so far as they are valid, reveal an insufficiency in the contractional theory. Still the mechanical principles of the theory cannot be successfully assailed; and it becomes necessary to seek for some coöperative cause which has hitherto been overlooked. I venture to contribute one suggestion toward the explanation of meridionality, and another suited to aid in the explanation of

* Substance of a communication presented to the Geological Section of the American Association, August 27, 1885.

meridionality and supply also an adequate supplement of crustal surplusage to meet the demands of orogenic phenomena.

1. I assume that meridionality in the earth's surface features, will be granted. There are, indeed many transmeridional features; but they have arisen from geological actions comparatively late. The oldest mountain chains and continental lines tend distinctly toward north-and-south trends; and this predisposition has given direction to many trends of later geological appearance. This is the fundamental impress received by the earth's crust. Evidently, it belongs to a primitive formative stage. We must seek for the cause in the early periods of incrustation.

Now, let us consider lunar-tidal action during those periods. This is a cause to which I appealed in a work published as long ago as 1870, and in periodical literature as early as 1858. Were the moon's tidal efficiency no greater then than at present, its deformative influence must have been experienced by the earth. If ever our planet was a molten sphere, a tidal prolateness stretched its axis in the direction of our satellite; and the axial revolution of the planet changed constantly the portion of matter tidally elevated. As the matter of the molten earth possessed some degree of viscosity, there was then, as always, a *lagging* of the tide, and the moon exerted that action now so well understood, which antagonizes the planet's rotation. After incrustation had begun, this action was not materially diminished. The greater viscosity (or partial rigidity) of the crust would, indeed, tend to shorten the prolate tidal axis; but, in proportion to increase of the index of viscosity; the lagging of the tide would also increase and thus augment the moon's retral action on the tidal protuberance. But the tide continued to rise and fall; and would have continued if the earth had become solid granite. Tidal movements of the crust must result in fractures, friction and displacements.

By as much as the moon's tangential pull on the tidal mass was capable of antagonizing the earth's rotation, by the same it tended to displace the tidal mass toward the west. There must have been some *retral slipping.* The power which could deform a planet could move a raft of frozen matter floating on a molten liquid, especially if floating in the midst of a hemisphere of fragments more or less discontinuous. This westward impulse was continually repeated on each meridian as it came in succession into the position of the tidal crest. The effect was such as could result from a westward push of the forming crust, applied successively over the whole surface within the parallels limiting the tidal disturbance. The slight backward slipping of every part in succession of the tidally moved zone must have developed, in the growing crust, internal structures meridionally disposed. These must have consisted of incipient meridional ridges and accumulations, meridional belts of greater and less strength, and belts of differentiated internal elements —either in form, position or material.

Now, while refrigerative contraction would necessarily develop wrinkles in the crust, it would not determine for them a meridional trend. This was pointed out by Captain Dutton. The tidal action instanced would, however, produce this result. Nor can it be pronounced insignificant in amount, since evidently, a force which could move the earth on its axis could move a floating patch of the earth's shattered crust.

It will be readily understood that the retral slipping of the tidal mass would be greatest at the crest, as first shown by Professor G. H. Darwin, and would diminish according to a certain law, toward the north and south. As the mean declination of the moon may be regarded as zero, the greatest mean slipping would be on the equator. The sub-meridional pre-dispositions instituted would therefore trend from the equator eastward of north and south.

If, as is probable, the moon's distance were much less during the incrustive periods, the tidal results cited would become more conspicuous. If, as is equally probable, the earth's rotation were correspondingly more rapid, the tidal results would be correspondingly further augmented.

The actions here considered pertain necessarily to the early forming stages of the crust, and have impressed its profounder features. Later, with increased rigidity of crust, tidally formed predispositions were less controlling; and with the growth of oceans, crustal pressures were experienced from other directions.*

2. Meridional trends would be further promoted by the secular subsidence of the earth's equatorial protuberance. That this accompaniment of the slow retardation of the earth's rotary motion must have exerted geological influences was first distinctly shown by Professor J. E. Todd; and I have elsewhere recorded the fact;† but its determinative influence on the trends

* These views, for the greater part, were first propounded by me in printed form in *World Life*, Nov., 1883, pp. 252–255, 350–355; but were taught in lectures several years previously.

† The ample résumé of W. B. Taylor, in the October number of this Journal will not be overlooked. An abstract of this paper was read before the Geological Section immediately after the presentation of my own communication.

I embrace this opportunity to remind the reader that the first conception of the now accepted cause of the moon's synchronistic motions must be credited to Kant rather than Ferrel, as Mr. Taylor thinks. In 1754, Kant presented to the *Royal Academy of Sciences*, Berlin, a memoir entitled: *Untersuchung der Frage ob die Erde in ihrer Umdrehung um die Achse wodurch sie die Abwechselung des Tages und der Nacht hervorbringt einige Veränderung seit den ersten Zeiten ihres Ursprunges erlitten habe.* After appealing to the action of the tides as a cause of diminution of the earth's rotational velocity, he says: "Dieses legt uns auf of the earth's wrinkles was first conceived by me in the early spring of 1885.* To say that the equatorial protuberance underwent a secular subsidence is to say that the equatorial circumference of the earth, as an effect of retarded rotation, has shortened more than the polar—that indeed the polar circumference has lengthened. That is, the greatest lateral pressure has been experienced from east and west around the equator. An excess of pressure in this direction must develope crustal changes having north and south continuity. Whether the results were foldings or crushings together, or over slippings, their axis-trends would be meridional. This cause then, conspired with early tidal action in predetermining the direction of the longitudinal dimension of the earth's structural features.

3. The same cause produced crustal surplusage around the equatorial zone. Aside from refrigerative contraction of the earth, the equatorial circumference diminished while the polar increased. This cause alone would, therefore, have developed meridional mountain plications over the protuberant belt. If the crustal surplusage resulting from refrigerative contraction was less than existing mountain plications demand, here is a cause which would supplement the supply from that source. Careful measurements may show that the supplementary surplusage needed is not greater than calculations may prove this cause capable of affording. If so, the contractional theory will experience the relief which every physical geologist must have desired, if not anticipated.

4. The meridional predisposition depending on subsidence of equatorial protuberance would be developed north and south of the equator as far as the parallels marking the limits of the protuberance. The meridional predisposition induced by lunar tidal action would be experienced north and south of the equator to the latitude marking the limits of the prolate tidal swell resulting from the moon when over the equator, *plus* the amount of the moon's lunar-monthly declinations. The extent of these actions, therefore, is as great as the actual trends demand; and embraces also, all the strongly plicated portions of the earth's surface.

einmal die Ursache deutlich dar, die den Mond genöthigt hat, in seinem Umlaufe um die Erde immer diesselbe Seite zuzukehren." He proceeds to say that this phenomenon is not due to overloading on the nearer side; that the influence began at the moment when the moon abandoned the earth; that the moon was at first in a fluid state, and that it then rotated with much greater velocity than at present. This historic fact deprives Mr. Ferrel of priority, but does not diminish the credit due him. Kant's memoir was dated at Königsberg, the identical spot where Helmholtz, one hundred years later, put forth the same thoughts as original with him.

* It is but just credit to a sagacious pupil, Mr. W. E. Bond, of Albion, N. Y., to say that he embodied a clear and original exposition of the principle in a thesis presented in June.

PROF. WINCHELL

On the Prairies of the Mississippi Valley.

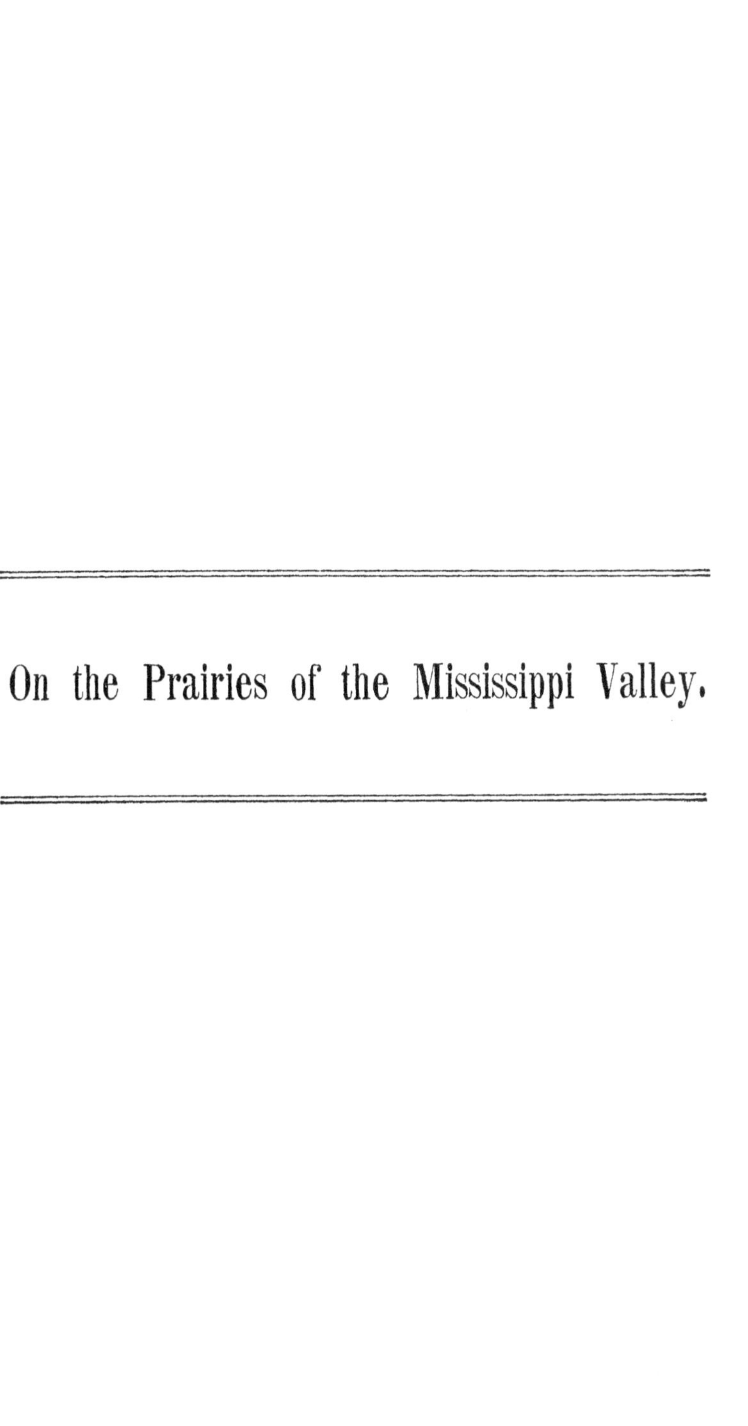

On the Prairies of the Mississippi Valley.

From the American Journal of Science and Arts, 2nd Series, Vol. XXXVIII.—Nov., 1864.

ON THE ORIGIN OF THE

PRAIRIES

OF THE VALLEY OF THE MISSISSIPPI.

BY

PROFESSOR ALEXANDER WINCHELL.[1]

THE diversity of opinions in existence regarding the cause or causes of the absence of trees from the prairies of the valley of the Mississippi is, of itself, sufficient proof that no satisfactory theory of this phenomenon has as yet been advanced. In the mind of the writer, a conviction has for some time been growing up, that we may discover the origin of the prairies in the last great geological revolution of the globe. The boldness of some of the suggestions about to be offered, ought not to prevent the presentation of them to the judgment of the scientific world.

In discussing the origin of the prairies, it is to be borne in mind that there are two facts to be accounted for—1st. The physical peculiarities of the soil and subsoil of the prairies—2d. The absence of trees from these areas, in cases where no obvious

[1] The original views presented in the following paper were first shadowed forth in an article in the *Ladies' Repository* for May, 1863. The theory was more fully elaborated in a paper read before the Illinois Natural History Society, at Springfield, in June, 1863. As this paper has not as yet been published, I embrace the opportunity of presenting a recast of my views in the present form.

cause exists. The first fact is brought into consideration under the first of the following propositions; the other is discussed under the propositions which follow the first.

1. *The soil of the Prairies is a Lacustrine Formation.*

Some of the older writers on the prairies, confining their attention to the so-called "wet prairies," so common in Ohio and Michigan—now usually termed "marshes," "swales" and "bogs" —found little difficulty in discovering the true origin of this class of prairies, and in proving that the humidity and sourness of the soil were the real causes of the absence of ordinary upland trees from their surface. Other writers, whose observations were made upon the dry and rolling prairies of Illinois, saw no immediate evidence of the aqueous origin of the soil, and knew no cause but the annual burning of the grass, for the remarkable absence of arboreal vegetation. It is this class of prairies to which the present discussion applies. They are conceived to have their origin in more general causes than the marshes and swales before mentioned. The latter have not had a simultaneous origin, and the causes which have brought them into existence have been local and limited in their influence. Being produced by the filling of ancient lakes, one has become a prairie at one epoch, another at another; and the work of filling lakes and forming wet prairies of this class is still in progress. For these reasons, a distinction should be carefully made between the wide, rolling prairies of Illinois and contiguous states, and the local swales of that or other states.

The lacustrine origin of the prairie soil is shown, *first*, by its physical characters. Not only has it the fineness, color and vegetable constitution which characterizes such soil, but we actually discover in it abundant remains of lacustrine shells, disseminated hundreds of miles from the present limits of the lakes. If, among older formations, we are permitted to infer the origin of the sediments from the nature of the included organisms, the evidence from testaceous remains is not less conclusive as to the nature of the prairie sediments.

The lacustrine origin of the soil is shown, *secondly*, by the necessary effect of geological changes of level which are generally admitted to have taken place. From the head of lake Michigan, all the way around the lakes to Niagara river, exist the well known evidences of a former higher level of the waters.[3] Even the increased elevation depending on the position of the falls of Niagara at Queenston—that is to say, the level of lake Erie at the time when the falls began to excavate their great

[3] Hall, *Geol. Rep. 4th Dist. New York*, pp. 348, 383; Lyell, *Travels in N. A.*, 1*st Visit*, i, 29, and ii, 85; Desor, *Foster and Whitney's Rep. L. Sup.*, i, 204, 212, ii, 248, 253; Hubbard, *Mich. Geol. Rep.*, 1840, p. 102; Whittlesey, this Journal, [2], x, 31; Logan, *Geology of Canada*, p. 910, &c.

gorge—setting back through the chain of the lakes, would cause a rise in lake Michigan, above its present level, of 25 feet. This small elevation of lake Michigan would probably open an outlet toward the Illinois river. But it is highly probable that the escarpment at Queenston, by extending further north, attained, in consequence, a somewhat higher elevation, at the epoch under consideration. It could hardly be presumed, however, that this was the barrier which dammed the waters of the lakes to the much higher level, of which we have equally the indisputable records. We need but refer to the well known proofs of aqueous erosion along the shores of the lakes, extending from their present levels to the altitude of 200 and 300 feet. Mark them in the escarpments of the south shore of lake Erie; in the lake ridges of Ohio and Michigan;[3] in the caverns and arches and purgatories of Mackinac island[4]—especially in the side of "Sugar Loaf," whose base is now inland and elevated 150 feet above the surface of the water. Whatever may have been the barrier which dammed the waters to these heights, the evidences of their former presence are incontestable. But the moment we grant this ancient level to the waters, they inevitably escape from us toward the south, through the valleys of the Illinois and Mississippi rivers.[5] Turning our attention in this direction we find corroboration of the suggestion. The broad and deep, bluff-lined valley of the Illinois was never excavated by the present inconsiderable river. The deserted river valley discoverable at intervals further north, indicates the former southward flow of a large volume of water. At Lamont, this valley is distinct, with its bounding bluffs and its "pot holes" worn in the solid rock of the ancient river bed. But with the waters of lake Michigan standing one or two hundred feet above their present level, how much of the region south and west of Chicago must have been submerged? The ancient lake must have reached its arms into Iowa, northern Indiana and southwestern Michigan. These, the writer is convinced, were the relative levels of the land and water

[3] We are aware that Col. Whittlesey has attributed the higher ridges to a submarine origin, and that Sir Charles Lyell has advanced the same opinion in reference to the ridges of lake Ontario. In regard to the latter, it will be remembered that lake Ontario is 330 feet lower than lake Erie, and may easily be surrounded by ridges of marine origin, whose level is entirely below the ridges of lake Erie. Further, in reference to the latter, it will be remembered that they have often been found to enclose lacustrine shells. To say the least, even if we do not insist upon the lacustrine origin of the higher ridges, the lower ones, which blend with the terraces of late formation, establish a former altitude of the lakes which is quite sufficient for our present purpose.

[4] Foster and Whitney, *Rep. L. Sup.*, ii, pp. 164–6; Winchell, *Mich. Geol. Rep.*, p. 128.

[5] If the earlier portion of the gorge of the Niagara was undergoing excavation while a large portion of the waters of the lakes was being drained through the valley of the Illinois river, the force and rate of erosion must have been materially diminished below the present standard by the diminution of the volume of water.

for a considerable period immediately following the last great submergence of the continent. This conviction was first reached in the study of the prairies of Alabama, in the years 1851–2 and 3. Shells of *Unio*, *Melania*, &c., are here incorporated with the soil, as in Illinois, but in much greater abundance; and the ancient water-line can be distinctly traced around the bases of the knolls of white limestone, which rise like chalk islands from the bosom of a dark and heaving sea. The aqueous origin of the Alabama prairies was announced by R. W. Withers,[6] and W. W. McGuire,[7] but they both adopted the evidence of *marine* fossils, so abundant in the soil, as proof of the former presence of the sea; and were not at all aware that the submergence of which they saw the proofs had nothing to do with the formation of the prairie soil.

The aqueous origin of the soil of the northwestern prairies was intimated by George Jones in 1836,[9] who compares the prairies and barrens of Illinois to the marshes, dykes and sand flats of Holland. Lesquereux, in 1856,[10] ascribed the general formation of prairies to water, and in 1861[11] reaffirmed his position in reference to the prairies of the Mississippi valley. Prof. J. D. Whitney has distinctly asserted a lacustrine origin for the prairies of the northwest,[12] and Dr. J. S. Newberry[13] has recognized the evidences of a former efflux of the lake waters over the Kankakee ridge in northern Illinois. The indications, indeed, seem to be sufficiently patent to induce the general assent of living geologists to the doctrine of the lacustrine origin of the soil of the prairies.

2. *Lacustrine sediments inclose but few living germs.*

Of the seeds which find their way to a body of fresh water, one portion—embracing the seeds of the grasses and sedges—will float upon the surface, and eventually lodge upon the lee shore. Another portion—embracing the fruits of most arboreal vegetation—will sink to the bottom, and undergo a speedy decomposition. Whenever a lake or a pond has been drained, the bottom remains a naked waste till the germs of vegetation have been gradually introduced *ab extra*. The gradual encroachment of vegetation upon the ancient domain of a lake during the period of its *gradual* drainage or gradual filling up, depends, of course, upon a supply of germs from the main land.

[6] This Journal, xxiv, 187. [7] Ib., xxvi, 93.

[8] So far as the writer is aware, he was the first to assert the lacustrine origin of the Alabama prairies and to maintain it—even in opposition to views then held by Prof. Tuomey.

[9] This Journal, xxxiii, p. 225.

[10] *Bullet. Soc. Nat. Sci. Neuchatel.* [11] See 2d *Geol. Rep. Ark.*

[12] Hall's *Geol. of Iowa*, i, p. 25.

[13] *Proc. Bost. Soc. Nat. Hist.*, vol. ix, May, 1862.

3. *Diluvial deposits, on the contrary, are found everywhere replete with living germs.*

Many of the facts upon which this proposition rests, are matters of common observation, but the broad conclusion does not seem to have impressed itself upon our attention. Nothing is a more common observation than to see plants making their appearance in situations where the same species was previously unknown, or for a long time unknown and under circumstances such that the supposition of a recent distribution of seeds is quite precluded. The following are some of the circumstances under which the sudden appearance of unwonted species occurs.

1st. When a change is produced in the physical condition of the soil. Left to nature, certain perennial grasses secure almost exclusive foothold in our fields, and form a sod in which the ordinary annuals are unable to flourish. Break up the sod, after any number of years, and subdue the perennial grasses, and we shall have a crop of annuals the first season—Veronicas, Chenopodiums, Euphorbias, Portulacas, Ambrosias, Crab-grasses, Fox-tails, Panicums, &c., &c. Cease cultivation, and the Poas and Glycerias will immediately resume possession. Similarly, the pertinacity with which the common Knot-grass (*Polygonum aviculare*) seizes and maintains its position only along the hardest beaten foot-paths is notorious; while the greater Plantain (*Plantago major*) renders itself no less conspicuous growing alongside. Earth thrown out of cellars and wells is generally known to send up a ready crop of weeds, and not unfrequently of species previously unknown in that spot. In all these cases, after allowing for all known possibilities of the distribution of seeds by winds, birds and waters, it still seems probable that germs must have previously existed in the soil.

2d. When a change is produced in the chemical nature of the soil. Illustrations are familiar to every agriculturist. How soon does a dressing of undecomposed muck or peat develop a crop of acid-loving sorrel—and how readily it is again repressed by a dressing of some alkaline manure. Let the waters of a brine well saturate a meadow, and how long before we witness the appearance of *Scirpus maritima*, *Triglochin maritimum* or some other salt-loving plant, whose germs, unless spontaneously developed, must have lain dormant in the soil at a greater or less depth.

3d. The disappearance of dominant species. It is well known that the clearing of a piece of forest and the burning of the brush is almost always followed by the appearance of certain unwonted plants known as "fire-weeds." In many cases it would seem highly improbable that the seeds of such plants have just been transported to such situations, at the moment when the disappearing forest admits the introduction of the conditions essential to their growth. It can hardly be doubted that the germs existed in the soil, ready to germinate whenever free sunlight, warmth and atmospheric air should be permitted to rouse their latent vital energy. Of the same nature is the recurrence of particular forest growths upon the same soil. Not unfrequently the second growth is of a very different nature from the first. In the "old fields" of Virginia and other southern states, the soil, cleared originally of deciduous trees, and then abandoned, after years of continuous cropping, sends up a growth of pines instead of deciduous trees. Many similar examples will suggest themselves to the mind of the reader.

4. *The living germs of the diluvial deposits were buried during the glacial epoch.*

Whence come the germs of that vegetation which is everywhere springing up in situations to which recent seeds could not have been distributed? This question has agitated the mind of many an inquirer who would have shrunk from the proposition which we here venture to enunciate. Let us examine the facts.

(1.) The vegetation which characterized the close of the Tertiary epoch was probably nearly identical with that existing at the present day under the same climatic conditions. Even in the older Tertiary Lignites, we have, according to the investigation of Lesquereux and Newberry, the remains of plants belonging to the following American genera, viz: *Quercus*, *Carya*, *Populus*, *Acer*, *Morus*, *Carpinus*, *Negundo*, *Laurus*, *Persea*, *Cornus*, *Rhus*, *Olea*, *Rhamnus*, *Magnolia*, *Smilax*, *Thuja*, *Sequoia*, *Taxodium* and *Sabal*—identifications made from scanty and defective material, and we may fairly presume that further investigations will greatly increase the number. Yet these plants, probably older than the Claiborne sands, show, according to Lesquereux, "the greatest affinity with species of our own time." From other beds of the middle or earlier Tertiary, we have still other existing genera, such as *Diospyros*, *Fagus*, *Nyssa*, *Aristolochia*, &c. The facts in our possession relative to the vegetation of the middle and later Tertiary epochs, show a most decided approximation to the existing Flora. From a pleiocene deposit near Somerville, Tennessee, Lesquereux identified the following recent species, viz: *Laurus Carolinensis*, *Prunus Caroliniana*, *Quercus myrtifolia*, *Fagus ferruginea*.[14] From the chalky banks of the Mississippi river, near Columbus, Kentucky, a collection was made of which all the species are recent, viz: *Quercus virens*, *Castanea nana?*, *Ulmus alata?*, *Planera Gmelini*, *Prinos integrifolia*, *Ceanothus Americanus?*, *Carya olivæformis*, *Gleditschia triacanthos*, *Acorus calamus*.[15] It is true that Dr. D. D. Owen has assigned the deposit containing these remains to the Quaternary

[14] This Journal, [2], xxvii, 363. [15] This Journal, [2], xxvii, 364.

period;[16] but as their position is 120 feet below the ferruginous sands containing *Megalonyx Jeffersoni*, and as the nature of these species is incompatible with such a climate as we universally associate with the glacial epoch, it is quite likely this assemblage of vegetable remains represents the general nature of the arboreal flora in existence near the close of the Tertiary period.

Although our positive knowledge of the vegetation of the period immediately preceding the advent of the reign of ice is confessedly meagre, it is certain that all the facts in our possession point to close specific correspondence with the modern vegetation of the same regions—modified certainly by the fact that, even in the latest Tertiary, the climate was considerably warmer than in the same latitudes at the present day.

(2.) The general effect of the events which ushered in and marked the progress of the reign of ice was, to destroy the vegetation flourishing over all the northern portion of the continent and mingle its forms with the cubic miles of *debris* detached from the underlying rocks. We find the trunks and limbs of trees buried 50 and 100 feet deep in this diluvial rubbish. It is impossible that myriads of vegetable germs should not also have been stored away. The drift deposits became the vast granery in which nature preserved her store of seeds through the long rigors of a geological winter.

(3.) But what evidences have we that the seeds of plants are capable of retaining their vitality through a geological period?

(a.) The ordinary process of destruction of vegetable tissues is merely an oxydation of the carbon and hydrogen entering into their constitution. It is seriously doubted whether the requisite conditions for such oxydation exist at considerable depths in the soil. It is stated that the piles sustaining the London bridge have been driven 500 years, and are still comparatively sound. Old Savoy Place, in the city of London, is sustained on piles driven 650 years ago, and they are yet perfectly sound. One of the piles taken up from the bridge built by the emperor Trajan across the Danube, was found petrified to the depth of three-quarters of an inch, while the remainder of the substance was unchanged after an interval of 1,600 years. The buried tree trunks already alluded to must have lain since the time of the last great geological revolution. Nor are these rare cases, for the encroachments of the waves upon the shores of the great lakes reveal whole forests of the buried trunks of the White Cedar, (*Thuja occidentalis*), bearing scarcely a trace of the work of destructive agencies upon them. Indeed it is known that well preserved woody tissue has been frequently exhumed from deposits of Tertiary, and even of greater age. The writer has pieces of drift-wood from the Cretaceous sands of Alabama, in

[16] *Kentucky Rep.*, vol. i, p. 22.

which the ligneous tissue is so fully preserved as to be capable of ignition, like recent wood. Even from the coal measures of Michigan the writer has made preparations of the delicate tissue of Jungermannia-like fronds; and from the coal mines of Lasalle in Illinois, he has specimens of exogenous wood of a brown color and not yet carbonized, though partially pyritized. All these examples tend to show the extreme slowness of the process of decay in ordinary vegetable tissues when excluded from the usual conditions of decay by burial in the earth.

(b.) The oily tissues of which seeds are composed are still more capable of resisting the tendency to dissolution; and ought certainly to remain unchanged, under circumstances which permit such perfect preservation of ordinary ligneous fibre. The evidences are very conclusive, that the seeds of ordinary vegetation may lie dormant in the surface soil for half a dozen or a dozen years. The seeds of *Erechthites* and other "fire-weeds" must have reposed in a latent state during the existence of the forest, whose disappearance is the signal for the resumption of their vital activity. The same is true of the seeds of the "old field pines," which have probably lain for an age or more, awaiting the maturity and destruction of the deciduous forest which usurped the soil. How *many* ages may they have lain there? How many more might they have lain and still been found ready for the first opportunity to seize a foothold?

There are some facts in our possession still more specific. It is well known that Dr. Lindley raised three raspberry plants from seeds discovered in the stomach of a man whose skeleton was found thirty feet below the surface of the earth, at the bottom of a barrow, or burial mound, which was opened near Dorchester, England. With the body had been buried some coins of the emperor Hadrian, from which we are justified in assuming that these seeds had retained their vitality for the space of 1,600 or 1,700 years. If they remained undamaged that length of time, their condition was practically fixed; and who shall say that 10,000 years would have produced a greater effect? Again, Lord Lindsay states that in the course of his wanderings amid the pyramids of Egypt, he stumbled on a mummy, proved by its hieroglyphics to be at least 2,000 years of age. On examining the mummy, after it was unwrapped, he found in one of its closed hands, a bulb which, when planted in a suitable situation, grew and bloomed in a beautiful dahlia. The credibility of this story may be questioned, as the real dahlia is a tuberous-rooted, Mexican genus, not known to botanists till the year 1789. That a bulb of some sort germinated under the circumstances alleged is not wholly incredible. It is further asserted, and generally believed, that wheat is now growing in England, which was derived from grains folded in the wrappings of Egyptian mummies, where they must have lain for two or three thousand years. Prof. Gray does not fully credit the account, but Dr. Carpenter, the eminent physiologist, gives it his full endorsement. Dr. Carpenter even goes so far as to give utterance to the following observations, which happen to be extremely pertinent to our present argument.

"These facts make it evident," he says, "that there is really no limit to the duration of this condition, [latent vitality], and that when a seed has been preserved for ten years, it may be for a hundred, a thousand or ten thousand, provided that no change of circumstances either exposes it to decay or calls its vital properties into activity. Hence, where seeds have been buried deep in the earth, not by human agency, but by some geological change, it is impossible to say how long anteriorly to the creation of man they may have been produced and buried, as in the following curious instance: Some well-diggers in a town on the Penobscot river, in the state of Maine, about 40 miles from the sea, came, at the depth of about 20 feet, upon a stratum of sand. This strongly excited their curiosity and interest, from the circumstance that no similar sand was to be found anywhere in the neighborhood, and that none like it was nearer than the sea-beach. As it was drawn up from the well it was placed in a pile by itself, an unwillingness having been felt to mix it with the stones and gravel which were also drawn up. But when the work was about to be finished, and the pile of stones and gravel to be removed, it was necessary also to remove the sand heap. This, therefore, was scattered about the spot on which it had been formed, and was for some time scarcely remembered. In a year or two, however, it was perceived that a number of small trees had sprung from the ground over which the heap of sand had been strewn. These trees became, in their turn, objects of strong interest, and care was taken that no injury should come to them. At length it was ascertained that they were Beach-plum trees, and they actually bore the Beach-plum, which had never before been seen except immediately upon the sea-shore. The trees had therefore sprung from seeds which were in the stratum of sea-sand that had been pierced by the well-diggers."[17] It cannot be doubted, as Carpenter concludes, that the seeds of the Beech-plum had lain buried since the remote period when that part of the state was the shore of the slowly receding sea.

Such a fact, so striking and so circumstantially recorded, is only of the same nature as others less critically noted, which daily pass before our eyes, in the upspringing of vegetable forms from the diluvial materials thrown out of wells, cellars and other excavations.

[17] Carpenter's *Elements of Physiology*, Am. ed., p. 41.

It must be confessed that the crucial observation is yet to be made. If vegetable germs exist in the drift, they can be discovered beforehand. The writer is not aware that any thorough search has ever been made for them; but until they have been actually detected, it is probable that even the convincing facts cited above will fail to secure universal assent to our proposition involving the prolonged vitality of the seeds of preglacial vegetation. While, however, the case is far from demonstrated, it may fairly be submitted that the explanation of certain facts, afforded by our theory, is less presumptuous and improbable than the supposition of spontaneous generation, the fortuitous distribution of seeds by any modern agency, or any other explanation which can be reasonably offered.[18]

5. *In proportion as the diluvial surface became exposed, the Flora of the preglacial epoch was reproduced.*

As the continent slowly rose from its last sea-burial, every portion of its surface, inch by inch, passed under the action of the ocean's surges. Even if the vegetable germs inclosed in the more superficial portions of the drift deposit had yielded to the destructive agencies of a geological period, the action of the sea would have uncovered and brought to light some of the more deeply seated and better protected seeds. If, then, our reasonings are correct, returning spring time vivified into activity the myriads of germs stored away by Nature from before the reign of ice; and the continent was again clothed with those forms of verdure which had adorned it at the close of the Tertiary period. But at this moment in the world's history, the retreating waters paused to brood over the wide region destined to become the garden of the west; perpetual dilution converted them into a vast inland sea of fresh water, upon whose bottom gathered the lifeless sediments that were to be the soil of the prairies. Then, when, in the progress of events, either through the removal of barriers, or the further upheaval of the land, the fresh waters were poured from the wide prairie region, there remained a naked and lifeless expanse of vegetable slime. From the bosom of the slime no plant could start, for the germ was not there. From beneath the load of slime, in the diluvial deposits below, no plant could raise its head, for it was sealed hermetically from air and light and warmth. A shining coat of

[18] With reference to the effect of sea water on the vitality of seeds during the epoch of submergence of the continent, we have not overlooked Darwin's experiments recorded in the London *Gardeners' Chronicle* for May 26th, 1855. While the experiments show a wonderful power of resisting the destructive influence of sea water, it is still apparent that the conditions of the experiments were such as to throw no light on the fate of seeds buried deeply in a submarine sand bed. It will be remembered further, that the filtration of sea water through a mass of sand, deprives it of its saltness, so that this agency in the destruction of vegetable germs embraced in a submarine soil becomes to a great extent eliminated. Compare Cabot, *Proceedings Bos. Soc. Nat. Hist.*, vol. iii, pp. 92, 103.

verdure clothed everywhere the more-ancient surface of the drift; and here and there in the abandoned lake bottom, rose a knoll crowned with its emerald crest—an island perhaps in the former lake. Thus the prairies were at first a naked and herbless waste.

6. *The vegetation which finally appeared on the drained lacustrine areas was extra-limital, and was more likely to be herbaceous than arboreal.*

The natural agencies in the introduction of vegetation from beyond the limits of the prairie region would be winds, running water and animals—especially granivorous birds. In a region so nearly level, the agency of running water would be but feebly exerted. Winds would exert a more important influence in the dispersion of the lighter, and especially the feathered seeds; but granivorous birds, it is believed, would exert a still more important influence. Yet it will be noticed that none of these agencies, and especially the two more important ones, would effect the distribution of any except the smaller and lighter seeds. Numerous quadrupeds, it is true, engage in the transportation of nuts and acorns, but no suitable storage place for such fruits would be found upon the prairies, not to mention the fact that they are transported and stored for consumption rather than for seed. It can hardly be doubted that the humble forms of vegetation producing the lighter seeds would be the first to secure possession of the soil. Sedges and marsh-loving grasses, especially, would eagerly occupy the ground, until the chances of germination of any of the larger fruits, would become exceedingly diminished. Thus the prairie became covered with herbaceous vegetation exclusively, while all around the margins was arrayed a shining fringe of forest trees, and every island knoll stood crowned with its cluster of oaks. Around the borders of the prairie were the ancient sand dunes, blown up while yet the prairie was a lake bottom. A peculiar vegetation would suit itself to so purely arenaceous a soil; and an occasional tree would be able to plant itself along the belt thus destined to become the "barrens."

Thus the prairies were treeless because the grasses first gained foothold and then maintained it. The Indian, perhaps, made his appearance at this time, and formed an alliance with the grasses in their contest against the trees; and thus decided the question in favor of the grasses.

This is our theory of the origin of the prairies, and the absence of trees from their surface. Fatal objections may rest against it, but it is certain that all other theories are untenable.

1. The old and popular belief that the treelessness of the prairies was caused by the annual burning of the grasses by the Indians,[20] is now generally admitted to be inadequate.

2. The supposition that trees have been choked out by the tangled roots of cane, which in turn has disappeared under the influence of a burning sun,[21] has no applicability in a region visited annually by frosts too severe for cane to survive.

3. The supposition that the absence of trees is due to too great dryness of the soil during the summer, is disproved by the fact that trees flourish naturally in drier soils in the same vicinity, while, on being introduced, they flourish equally well in the prairie. The treeless and almost herbless deserts of the far west may have originated in extreme aridity of the atmosphere[22] —as others have from the highly saline character of the soil—but all our discussions have had reference to the prairies of the Mississippi valley.

4. A theory often urged is the considerable humidity of the soil of certain prairies,[23] and especially the wetness of the subsoil in contrast with the dryness of the soil during summer.[24] It is singular that such an opinion could be entertained when it is so well known that there is no situation so wet but certain trees will flourish on it—the willow, the cottonwood, the beach, the ash, the alder, the cypress, the tupelo, the water-oak, the tamarack, the American arbor-vitæ or some other tree—some of them standing joyously half the year, if need be, in stagnant water. It is well known that swales are generally devoid of trees; but the reason for this is to be found in the fact that since a soil assumed the place of the ancient lake, the germs of trees have never been introduced; while the introduction of such germs is delayed by the circumstance that neighboring forests are generally such as are adapted to drier situations. Has it been found that a green willow or poplar twig will not root and thrive in a wet prairie? But further than this, large portions of the treeless prairies are *not wet.* Is there a different cause for treelessness here?

5. Prof. J. D. Whitney[25] has advanced the opinion that the extreme fineness of the prairie soil is the cause of the absence of trees; and the author of the article on "Plains," in the New American Cyclopedia, seems to have adopted this view. Against this theory we see several weighty objections. Many alluvial soils, as pulverulent as that of the prairies, are densely

[20] This Journal, vol. i, p. 331. [21] This Journal, vol. xxiii, p. 40.

[22] Does Prof. Dana allude to the prairies of the Mississippi valley when he says, (*Manual of Geol.*, p. 46), "and where the moisture is not sufficient for forests, she [America] has her great prairies and pampas?" See also Cooper, *Smithson. Rep.*, 1858, p. 276; Newberry, *Ohio Agric. Rep.*, 1859; Lambert, *Pacific R. R. Rep.*, vol. i, p. 166.

[23] Atwater, this *Journal*, i, 116; Bourne, *Ib.*, ii, 30; Lesquereux, *2d Ark. Geol. Rep.*; *Western Monthly Magazine*, Feb., 1836

[24] Engelmann, this *Journal*, [2], xxxvi, 384. [25] *Iowa Geol. Rep.*, vol. i, p. 24.

wooded, and that in the same latitudes and under the same meteorological conditions. Again, partial or complete destitution of trees is observed on the coarser, sandy borders of the prairies, and on all recent sand dunes, even where no lack of vegetable sustenance exists. But the fatal objection to this theory, and all theories which look to the physical or chemical condition of the soil, or even to climatic peculiarities, for an explanation of the treeless character of the prairies, is discovered in the fact that *trees will grow* on them when once introduced—not water-loving trees exclusively, but evergreens, deciduous forest trees, and fruit trees—such as flourish in all the arable and habitable portions of our country. Everybody now knows that trees flourish well on the prairies; and the prairie farmers are actively engaged in their introduction.[26] It seems to us that this fact alone militates fatally against the views advanced by Whitney as well as those of Engelmann, Bourne, Atwater and others, who have attributed the distinctive character of the northwestern prairies to an excessive humidity of the soil.

University of Michigan, Aug. 30, 1864.

[26] Compare Wells, this Journal, i, 331, where the forest is said to be encroaching on the prairies about St. Louis; Engelmann, Ibid. [2], xxxvi, 389; Edwards, *Rep. Dep. of Agric.*, 1862, p. 495.

POSTSCRIPT TO PROF. WINCHELL'S ARTICLE ON THE ORIGIN OF PRAIRIES.

[Page 444 of the November No. of the Journal of Science.]

In my article on Prairies, the belief is expressed that the assumption of the possibility of the almost indefinite suspension of the vitality of seeds, required by my theory, would present the greatest obstacle to its reception. It seems excusable, therefore, to crowd into a postscript, a reference to evidences temporarily overlooked, and especially to testimony and facts collected by Mr. Marsh in his learned work, "*Man and Nature*," page 285, *et seq.* This work has but just fallen into my hands. Mr. Marsh thinks, with Dr. Carpenter, that the vitality of seeds "seems almost imperishable while they remain in the situations in which nature deposits them." He cites numerous instances in which one crop of plants has disappeared on a change of conditions, and another, of different nature, has promptly assumed its place, originating, evidently, from seeds preëxisting for ages in the soil. He says "earth brought up from wells or other excavations soon produces a harvest of plants, often very unlike those of the local flora." He expresses the opinion that earth ejected from considerable depths by a certain earthquake convulsion, to which reference is made and which soon became covered with vegetation "never observed in that region before," must have brought up with it the seeds from which the novel vegetation sprang, under "the influence of the air and sun, from depths where a previous convulsion had buried them ages before." In the same connexion may be quoted a statement by Darwin (*Origin of Species*, Am. ed., p. 69), to the effect that in the midst of a very large and very sterile heath in Staffordshire, some hundreds of acres were planted with the Scotch fir, and, after twenty-five years, not less than twelve species of plants (not counting grasses and sedges) had made their appearance in the plantation of firs, "which could not be found in the heath"—and this, though the fir forest seems to have been visited only by insectivorous birds.

Mr. Marsh quotes from Dwight's *Travels* his account of the appearance of a fine growth of hickory [*Carya glabra* Torr.] on lands in Vermont which had been permitted to lie waste, when no such trees were known in the primitive forest within a distance of fifty miles; also, Dr. Dwight's account of the appearance of a field of white pines, on suspension of cultivation, in the midst of a region where the native growth was *exclusively* of angiospermous trees. "The fact that these white pines covered the field exactly, so as to preserve both its extent and figure," says Dr. Dwight, "and that there were none in the neighborhood, are decisive proofs that cultivation brought up the seeds of a former forest within the limits of vegetation, and gave them an opportunity to germinate."

The existence of a succession of forests of different prevailing species has been satisfactorily established in Denmark by the researches of Steenstrup on the *Skovmose*, or Forest-bogs, of that country (*Mem. Acad. Sci. Copenhagen*, ix, 1842). These bogs are from twenty to thirty feet in depth, and the remains of forest trees in successive layers, prove that there have been three distinct periods of arborescent vegetation in Denmark—first, a period of the pine (*Pinus sylvestris*)—secondly, a period of the oak (*Quercus robur sessiflora*)—lastly, a period of the beech (*Fagus sylvatica*), not yet arrived at its culmination. The dominant species of each period flourished to the entire exclusion of the other two species, (see *Smithsonian Report*, 1860, p. 305, *et seq.*) Cæsar affirms that the *Fagus* and *Abies* were, in his time, wanting in England, but the beech (*Fagus*) is now plentiful, and Harrison tells us in his "*Historicall Description of the Iland of Britaine*" (*Holingshed's Chronicles*, 1807, i, 359), that "a great store of firre" is found lying "at their whole lengths" in the "fens and marises" of Lancashire and other counties, where not even bushes grew in his time. (See further, Marsh's *Man and Nature*, p. 222.) No doubt such extinct forests have flourished in America, even since the Glacial epoch, and have stocked the accumulating soils with their stores of vitalized fruitage, awaiting some future resurrection; and no doubt the "fens and marises" of Lancashire, under suitable circumstances, would reproduce from their granaries of forest fruit, the arboreal vegetation which had flourished and disappeared before the Roman conquest.

Ann Arbor, Mich, Oct. 15, 1864.

From The American Geologist, March, 1889.

Conglomerates Enclosed

IN

Gneissic Terranes.

BY

Alexander Winchell.

The reader will kindly note the following typographical errors and omissions:

Page 157—2d foot note, for "1850, pp. 69-200," read "1850, vol. i, pp. 99-100."

" 158—3d line, for "allusions," read "illusions."

" 159—8th line, for "if," read "of."

" 160—1st foot note, for "264," read "199-204."

" 160—The 2d foot note belongs on p. 159.

" 160—3d foot note, second line, for "1833," read "1835."

" 161—foot note, last line, for "Mar.," read "May."

" 164—2d par., 2d line, for "T. S. Bonney," read "T. G. Bonney."

" 164—2d line from bottom, change * to †, and add foot note as follows:

† Lehmann: *Untersuchungen über die Entstehung der altkrystallinen Schiefergesteine.* 1884, S. 128.

" 165—10th line, change † to * and add note as follows:

* Credner: *Elemente der Geologie.* S. 373.

" 165—1st par., 2d line from end, for "Konigsberg," read "Kongsberg."

The writer embraces the opportunity to refer to a contribution temporarily overlooked, by Prof. W. O. Crosby, in Proc. Bos. Soc. Nat. Hist., 1888, *Geology of the Black Hills*, pp. 494, 498-501; and also to one just published by Dean F. R. Carpenter, on *The Geology, Mineral Resources and Mills of the Black Hills of Dakota*, pp. 17-27, in both of which facts are stated, of the same tenor as those set forth in the present article.

CONGLOMERATES ENCLOSED IN GNEISSIC TERRANES.

By Alexander Winchell.

The region which is the special subject of the present article lies on and near the International boundary, northwest of Lake Superior. It is embraced within the great Archæan area of the North, between the parallels of 47°30′ and 48°30′ north latitude, and the meridians of 90° and 91°30′ west longitude. The surface is occupied by gneisses, crystalline schists and earthy schists, all standing quite conformably, in an attitude nearly vertical, and trending east-northeast. Occasionally, over limited areas, the gneisses appear destitute of bedding or foliation, and for this reason, and also the unimportance, for geological purposes, of the distinction between gneisses and ordinary massive granites and syenites, I have frequently recorded as "granite," the crystalline masses underlying the crystalline schists. For similar reasons, usage has affixed the name "granite" to rocks in which the dark mineral constituent is hornblendic, as well as to those in which it is micacic. With this understanding, it may be stated that the region here considered extends into and embraces portions of three granitic regions which superficially appear to be wholly separated from each other by earthy schists. The most easterly I have elsewhere described as the "Saganaga granite;" the most westerly, as the "Basswood granite," and the more southerly, as the "White Iron granite"—these taking their names from the lakes whose shores they occupy.*

Of the lithological characters of these granites it is not proposed to speak particularly at present, nor of their structural and mineralogical relations to the crystalline and the earthy schists which lie along their borders. It may have a bearing however, on the object of the present article, to state that the Saganaga gneiss holds hornblende for its dominant dark mineral. The same is true of the White Iron gneiss, though augite sometimes usurps the place. The Basswood gneiss is chiefly micaceous, and the mica ranges from muscovite to biotite and hydromica. Not unfrequently however, a hornblendic constituent intervenes, and this is sometimes replaced by a viriditic mineral. A chloritic constituent often appears in all these gneisses, more or less blended with the feldspars. As usual the feldspar is chiefly orthoclase; but generally, a small proportion of plagioclase can be seen. In the Saganaga gneiss the quartz individuals are generally of very large size.

It will have a bearing also, on the interpretation of the phenomena which I propose to describe to state that between the gneisses and crystalline schists no structural discontinuity anywhere appears—a gradual transition in mineralogical and stratigraphical characters being everywhere apparent.† Nor is there any abrupt break between the crystalline schists and the earthy or semi-crystalline schists; and consequently, no such phenomenon as a contact between crystalline and uncrystalline terranes is known to occur. Nor do I find any unconformability between the proper and very distinct bedding of the earthy schists and the foliation of the crystalline schists and gneisses. It could not be expected under these circumstances, that any of the phenomena of local metamorphism should occur along the zone of gradual transition from the crystalline rocks to the uncrystalline.

**Sixteenth Annual Report Minn. Geol. and Nat. Hist. Surv.*, pp. 330–334. These three gneissic or granitic areas appear to be discriminated by Irving in his "Preliminary Geological Map of the Northwest," in the Fifth Annual Report, U. S. Geol. Surv., p. 181.

† These facts have been fully set forth in the XVth and XVIth Annual Reports of the *Geol. and Nat. Hist. Surv. of Minn.*, to which reference may be made.

Throughout the whole extent of these three granitic masses, as far as explored, *rounded pebbles* are found disseminated. They are by no means uniformly distributed; and in the Basswood and White Iron granites they are infrequent. They are however, mentioned in my reports.* The Saganaga granite (syenite, gneiss) is more numerously supplied with them. In coasting along the shores of West Seagull, Seagull, Red-rock, Granite and Saganaga lakes, one or more pebbles may generally be seen at intervals of one or two rods. On the north shore of Seagull lake they become rather abundant.† The pebbles here, as elsewhere, are distinctly limited and fully rounded, presenting the ordinary appearance of shore pebbles, and generally of a dark color. In size they range mostly from two to six inches in diameter. They are sometimes so firmly imbedded in the gneiss as not to be separable from it; at other times, they may be removed. In mineral character, many of the pebbles appear diabasic, chloritic and augitic. Some of them are syenitic, and even approach the Saganaga syenite in character. I found pebbles of this which themselves embraced fine granulite, chlorite rock, chlorite schist and copper carbonate. Other syenitic pebbles were fine-grained and unlike the Saganaga variety; and these in other cases, were stratified. Besides worn fragments, the outlines of large angular masses may be traced in the midst of the usual gneiss. Some of them are a fine-grained granulite with a very little hornblende. They attain a length in some cases of several feet, with a width of a foot or less. In other cases they appear like sheets three or four inches thick. They are all firmly united to the common mass of gneiss.

At another locality on the shore of a large island in the same lake, a real conglomerate occurs. This is chlorito-graywackenitic, and somewhat resembles the remarkable Ogishke-conglomerate, but it is not the same. The groundmass holding the pebbles is not of a syenitic character, but rather graywacke-like, though the whole is surrounded by the prevailing syenite of the region.

A conglomerate is also reported to me from an inland position on the northwest of West Seagull lake.

---

* XVth Ann. Rep. Geol. Minn., pp. 79, 85, 88, 105, 113. In other lakes, XVIth Ann. Rep. Geol. Minn., pp. 227, 229, 241.

† See details of facts in *XVIth Ann. Rep. Minn.*, p. 298.

The most extraordinary occurrence of all is found on a small island which I named Wonder island, near the south-east shore of Saganaga lake, and supposed to be located a short distance beyond the international boundary.* This island lies far within the gneissic region. The contiguous main shores are characteristically gneissic. On the south I have traced the gneissic terrane eight miles, to its culmination in the Giant's range and its southern limit near Gunflint lake; on the southwest, nearly to Frog-rock lake, twelve miles; on the west, to Oak lake, twelve miles; on the north, to the north shore of Saganaga lake, six miles. The point is therefore several miles from any boundary of the great mass of the Saganaga gneiss.

At this place rounded pebbles are accumulated in such abundance as to constitute a real conglomerate. Two patches are exposed to view and disappear beneath the level of the water. One of the patches as far as exposed, is four feet wide, and the other three. The breadth of the intervening gneiss is about ten feet. In neither are the pebbles generally in contact. In one area, the conglomeritic condition disappears gradually around the margin; in the other, somewhat abruptly—except that a single pebble is quite separate. The intervals between the pebbles are filled with the common gneissic material in full possession of its usual characters. The pebbles are of all sizes up to four or five inches in diameter; and they are generally dark green in color. Mineralogically, as far as I could judge in the field, they consist principally of the following species and varieties: Lamellar augite in coarse agglomerations; lamellar augite in fine agglomerations, with a minute quantity of light feldspar disseminated in strings and grains; lamellar augite with conspicuous grains of feldspar; a mixture of augite, feldspar and epidote; a lamellar mineral soft as talc or chlorite; a pale green augite, inclosing lamellar augite; augite hyposyenite or perhaps diorite; greenish transparent augite in slender prisms; lamellar augite in coarse agglomerations, but of a pale green color. There were no pebbles of syenite, none of quartzite, none of jasper, none of any sedimentary rock. In one instance, I saw two or three large grains of quartz imbedded in a large pebble

---

*The location is mapped on page 218 of the *XVIth Ann. Rep. Minn. Geol. Surv.*, and the facts are given in detail on the succeeding pages.

composed of lamellar augite and feldspar. This conglomerate therefore, differs from the Ogishke conglomerate of north-eastern Minnesota both in the mineral character of the pebbles and in the nature of the groundmass.

Though the list of pebbles differs somewhat from that cited from Seagull lake, the general resemblance is noteworthy. The dark pebbles elsewhere scattered through the gneiss of Saganaga lake are also very similar in character; and the evidence is quite clear that the pebble-supply of all parts of the region has had a common origin.

The presence of pebbles so widely disseminated through the gneiss reveals this great Laurentian terrane in quite a new aspect. This character seems especially adapted to awaken reflections in the minds of those who hold to the theory of a purely igneous history for the crystalline rock-masses. No other origin for rounded pebbles possesses any plausibility in comparison with shore action. Such pebbles are everywhere regarded as evidence of fragmental accumulation. The great Ogishke conglomerate, whose borders are not over fifteen miles distant, is stocked with similar pebbles; and no one could entertain other theory respecting them than that of slow fashioning along an ancient shore. The *prima facie* evidence in reference to the Saganaga pebbles is entirely in favor of a similar origin. I shall hold it as incontestable that these pebbles are due to attrition along a shore.

I do not forget the dictum of Von Buch in reference to the eruptive origin of certain conglomerates,* nor the application made of the principle by the founders of the "Azoic System," to the well known conglomerates of the cupriferous region of Kewenaw Point.† But the pebbles in the latter case are associated with amygdaloids of unquestionably eruptive origin; and moreover, they are alleged to consist chiefly of rocky material of the same nature. In both respects the Saganaga pebbles differ. They are not pebbles of the contiguous rock, and it is inconceivable that they have become rounded by friction during projection through it while in a molten state, or by contact

*Von Buch, *Geognostische Briefe*, pp. 75–82.

†Foster and Whitney, *Report on the Lake Superior Land District*, 1850, pp. 69-200; and *Amer. Jour. Sci.*, II, xvii, 1854, pp. 11-38, 181-194. The same view was advanced by Houghton in 1841.

with fissure walls existing in it after solidification. The late Prof. Irving however, may be regarded as dissipating finally, any such allusions in reference to the cupriferous conglomerates,‡ since, as geologists generally have discovered, "the pebbles are only in very subordinate quantity of 'trap' or amygdaloid, being almost wholly of some sort of acid eruptive rock, *i. e.* felsite, quartziferous porphyry, quartzless porphyry, granitic porphyry, augite syenite or granite. The fundamental difference between such pebbles and the associated basic, massive rocks is alone enough to overthrow the theory, even were there not other sufficient arguments against it. Further, the pebbles are just as plainly water-worn as those of any other conglomerates, though they may have, in some cases, had the polish removed by surface alteration."

The evidence for the igneous origin of the Saganaga pebbles is incomparably less than that for the Kewenaw pebbles. An attentive consideration of the case confirms this conclusion. The conglomerate described on Wonder island is not one consisting originally of a mass of pebbles over which a fluid magma has been poured at some date perhaps long subsequent to the formation of the pebble deposits. I have seen a pile of angular fragments over which fluid gabbro had been poured, which flowed into the interstises and filled them. But the preexisting fragments were self-supported—they lay in direct contact with each other. On Wonder island the pebbles are not in contact; they could not have lain where they are before the gneissic magma existed. The gneissic magma was present, and it was this which supported the pebbles and prevented their contact. *The gneissic magma was contemporaneous with the pebbles.* But its condition was not that of molten fluidity, for so vast a molten mass would have fused the comparatively few pebbles immersed in it—still more the single pebbles which we find so widely distributed. It must however, have been sufficiently fluid or plastic for extraneous bodies to be moved in it. But a molten sea would have destroyed the pebbles and obliterated all traces of them. The plasticity therefore, was *low-temperature plasticity*—igneo-aqueous plasticity.

We cannot, to avoid such a conclusion, seek to propound the

‡Irving, *The Copper-bearing Rocks of Lake Superior*, 1883, U. S. Geol. Surv., Mon. v. pp. 9, 31-2.

theory that the conglomerate of Wonder island is one having origin long subsequent to the gneiss, and embraced in it by a process of folding and squeezing together. For, (1) the conglomerate has never been a conglomerate by itself; it never rested on another terrane, and could never have been caught in any sharp fold of the Saganaga gneiss; (2) If it were a formation so caught, we should find it revealing a greater extent along the line if strike; (3) The supposition of a close fold for the Wonder island conglomerate is not applicable to the isolated pebbles scattered through the gneiss across the whole breadth of the belt. These were in some way introduced from without into the plastic mass in all positions along lines transverse to the bedding.

If the pebbles were neither older than the gneiss nor newer than the gneiss, they were of course simultaneous with it. No other view would be conceived unless there were some preconceived theory of the non-sedimentary origin of gneiss to be cared for.

In connection with the interpretation of the Wonder island conglomerate, other facts must be considered. I have already stated that large angular beams of schistic and gneissic character have floated as bodies of extraneous origin in the gneissic magma which once existed. In connection with the Basswood gneiss I have elsewhere described* many occurrences of this nature, and many others in which the schistic fragments attain such length, and with so little displacement, as to constitute a complicated interbedding of gneissic and schistic strata. I have also maintained on such evidence, the original sedimentary condition of the gneissic terranes, as against the extravagant hypothesis of a succession of almost countless "dikes" perfectly parallel with each other and with the beds of the intersected formation, and separated from each other by only a few inches or even a fraction of an inch of the formation thus wonderfully perforated by "dikes."* I have more recently, in a newly discovered region, estimated as many as five hundred alternations of uralitic schist and uralitic gneiss in the breadth of about fifty feet,† and I feel confirmed in opinion that the gneisses and crystalline schists were originally sedimentary. Thus the facts

* *Fifteenth Ann. Rep. Geol. Minn.*, pp. 40, 41, 43, 46, 54, 63, 78, 83, 84, 88, 89, 96, 97, 113, 116.

cited in reference to the Saganaga pebbles are simply corroborative of views supported by other classes of evidence on which I do not here enlarge. Though merely touching the general problem of the origin of gneisses and granites, I wish to avoid all misapprehension by stating that I recognize the important agency of heat in connection with water, in the transformation of the original sediments; I do not conceive that the characteristic features of these terranes are any legacy of sedimentary conditions; but I hold, with Scrope, de Beaumont, Scheerer, Hunt and others, that the primitive materials, through the agency of heat, water and chemism, have entered into combinations not existing in the original sediments. I hold that the transformation attained different degrees of completeness in different localities and different horizons; and I hold that pressure—especially shearing pressure—has emphasized the bedded arrangement. Thus, as I believe, the sediments were brought to a state of incipient crystallization in one place, and completer crystallization in another; while in others, the thermal action was intense enough to reduce the magma to a state of such complete fluidity or plasticity as to obliterate all traces of bedding, or allow squeezing into fissures, or even surface overflows of any such extent as observation may establish. I wish to add the important suggestion that the agencies which would transform the common magma would also transform the included pebbles. By softening and pressure, their forms have been changed; and by metamorphic action they have ceased to present, in some cases, their original mineral constitution.

Such views on the history of crystalline masses though not widely entertained, will be found supported by considerable evidence of the same nature as that afforded by the pebbles and conglomerate of the Saganaga gneiss. In 1833, Professor Edward Hitchcock called attention to certain features of a conglomerate occurring near Newport, Rhode Island.‡ The pebbles showed evidences of a former softened state, and of a partial transformation, in certain cases, to "a mica schist with a cement of talcose slate." Similar conglomerates were described by Dr.

* *Fifteenth Ann. Rep. Minn.*, 1886, p. 264.

† *Sixteenth Ann. Rep. Minn.*, 1887, p. 264.

‡ E. Hitchcock, *Report on the Geology of Massachusetts*, 1833. See also, the Reports of 1833 and 1841. The same was more particularly described by Professor C. H. Hitchcock in *Proceedings Amer. Assoc.*, 1860, pp. 112-118.

E. Hitchcock "along nearly the whole western side of the Green Mountains in Vermont."† President Hitchcock states that the Vermont conglomerate occurs on both sides of the Green Mountains. He found it "in connection with quartz rock, mica and talc schists and gneiss; sometimes merely in juxtaposition, sometimes interstratified;" and he gives a diagram showing that gneiss is sometimes superposed on the conglomerate. The pebbles are generally elongated and flattened, and give other evidence of former plasticity. At Plymouth, on the east face of the mountains, conglomeritic phenomena of a similar kind, are still more strikingly shown. Here, as in Wallingford, and in the Saganaga gneiss, the pebbles do not lie in contact with each other. Mineralogically, they are here mostly of quartz, but sometimes of granite or gneiss. Dr. Hitchcock found that the pebbles were sometimes so elongated and flattened as to reduce the conglomerate to a schistic state; and he says: "We doubted for a time, whether we could justly include gneiss among the rocks that may be originated from conglomerate; for we had not found, as yet, decided examples of pebbles in this rock." "We do not despair however, of finding pebbles in gneiss, now that we have learned how to look for them." Dr. Hitchcock argues that by metamorphic action, many of the pebbles have been mineralogically changed without destroying their character as pebbles.

In support of the doctrine of the metamorphism of pebbles, Dr. Hitchcock cites a conglomerate found along the eastern border of Vermont and southward into Massachusetts. "We define this rock," he says, "as a conglomerate with a cement of syenite or granite, or as a syenite or granite with pebbles in it, sometimes thickly and sometimes sparsely disseminated." Speaking of an outcrop of this conglomerate on the southwest point of Little Ascutney, he says, "on one side it passes without any intervening seam into a porphyry, and this into a granite, all forming one undivided ledge, so that the conclusion is forced upon us that the granite and porphyry have been formed out of the conglomerate. Most of the rock on Ascutney takes hornblende into its composition, and thus becomes syenite, and this abounds in black rounded masses which are for the most part

† *Geology of Vermont*, 1861, pp. 29-44. One of the localities is in the northeast part of Wallingford. This passage was first published by Dr. Hitchcock in *Amer. Jour. Sci.*, II, xxxi, 372-392, Mar., 1861.

crystalline hornblende with some feldspar, and which are probably pebbles transmuted."*

At Granby, in Vermont, "the pebbles, manifestly rounded, are either mica schist or white, almost hyaline, quartz * * * and the base is a fine-grained syenite, passing sometimes almost into mica schist." "When the pebbles are highly crystallized, they become so incorporated with the matrix that it is difficult to separate them with a smooth surface; and, if we are not mistaken, they pass insensibly into those rounded nodules chiefly hornblendic (augitic?) so common in syenite, especially that of Ascutney. We think those are produced from the metamorphosis of pebbles which have become crystalline since they were formed into conglomerate. * * * These facts certainly give great plausibility to the view which supposes granite and syenite to be often the results of the metamorphosis of stratified rocks."†

At the meeting of the American Association at Springfield, in 1859, Professor Hubbard, of Dartmouth College, exhibited a specimen of pure white granite from Warren, New Hampshire, in which there lay imbedded a rounded bowlder of hornblende rock more than a foot in diameter, and easily separable from the granite.‡

Dr. G. A. Hawes, in 1878,§ recorded some mica sheets at East Hanover, New Hampshire, which are "mottled by what are apparently pebbles of various sorts and sizes, that have been flattened out between the layers." He recognizes the evidences of their former plasticity and of their metamorphism, even when not carried to such a degree as to entirely obliterate all signs of the original constitution of the sedimentary mass.

None of the examples cited from America possess evidence of such strength as that afforded by the Saganagâ gneiss in reference to the former fragmental condition of the oldest crystalline rocks. The Saganaga gneiss is massive, insomuch that it is gen-

* Compare the black pebbles in the Saganaga syenite before mentioned and set down as apparently augitic; and my independent suggestion that they are the products of metamorphic action.

† The views of Dr. Charles T. Jackson on this question may be found in *Proc. Bos. Soc. Nat. His.*, 1860. Professor W. B. Rogers' views are found in same, 1861, cited in *Am. Jour. Sci.*, II, xxxi, 440-2, May, 1861.

‡ *Geology of Vermont*, p. 44. Dr. Hitchcock enumerates other localities of occurrence of conglomerates with flattened pebbles, in Bernardston, Mass., where the matrix is a mica schist. The same is true at Bellingham, Mass. These features are still more decided in bowlders near Northampton.

§ Hawes in *Geology of New Hampshire*, vol. iii, pt. iv, p. 220.

erally recognized as a syenite. It has indeed passed almost beyond the stage of alteration in which traces of sedimentary bedding remain. Nor is there any considerable mass of crystalline schists within less than five miles of Wonder island. The evidence for fragmental origins is thus carried fully into the midst of those crystalline masses so commonly regarded as centres of molten eruption.

The earliest mention which I find recorded of any analogous phenomena in the old world is by Dr. Sauer of Leipzig.* In the valley of the Mittweida near Annaberg, and about twenty-five miles south of Chemnitz, occurs a section of crushed conglomerate intercalated among the gneisses and mica-schists distributed over that part of Saxony. This appears, from the accounts, quite analogous to the pebble-bearing beds of the Green Mountains. I avail myself of a description of this occurrence recently published by Professor Hughes.† The complete sequence was not observed, but the vicinity is generally underlaid by muscovite schists and gneissic rocks. At Obermittweida, a grey feldspathic granular rock occurs, with apparently superinduced schistosity. In this were seen scattered pebbles of felsitic and quartzose rock which soon became so numerous that the rock was obviously a coarse conglomerate. "In the conglomerate were fissile sandy beds which, even when crushed, were quite unlike the mica-schists which cropped out above and below." According to a diagram given, the series of beds dip about 40°.

In theorizing on the occurrence, professor Hughes remarks that "there was plenty of room for, and strong probability of, a fault along the valley below the section." "On the whole, I was inclined to believe," he says, "from an examination of the rock in the field, that the conglomerate might belong to quite newer beds caught in a sharp synclinal fold." In support of this conclusion, he says: "The character of the two rocks, that is, of the gneissic series and the two beds associated with the

* "Ueber Conglomerate in der Glimmerschiefer-formation des Sächsischen Erzgebirges"—*Zeitschrift Für die gesammten Naturwissenschaften*, Band lii, S. 706, 1879. The occurrence is noted on the *Geologische Specialkarte von Sachen*, Massstab 1-25,000, Section Elterlein, nebst zugehörigen Erlaüterungen. Prof. Justus Roth of Berlin, published a paper on these conglomerates in 1883, in *Sitzungsberichte der Kgl. Preuss. Akad. der Wissensch.* zu Berlin, 1883, (Physikal-mathemat. Klasse,) xxviii, 14 Mai; and he later mentioned them in *Allgemeine u. Chemische Geol.*, ii, Bd., S. 427-428, Berlin, 1887. Roth gives a full account, copied from Sauer.

† *Quar. Jour. Geol. Soc. Lond.* xliv, Feb. 1, 1888, pp. 20-24.

conglomerate, is so different that I am unwilling to admit that they can both belong to one series and have been subjected to similar conditions." He mentions also, the absence of any passage from one to the other; the identification of both series with others known to be discordant to one another, and the analogy of other similar foldings in, of newer rocks, so as to produce on the surface the effect of a true sequence. The explanation was admitted however, to be purely hypothetical. In the discussion of professor Hughes' speculation before the Geological Society, every one admitted the possibility of an infolding, and could cite cases in illustration. Mr. Bauerman thought the explanation offered of the Obermittweida occurrence was probably the true one. Dr. Geikie mentioned a case of Cambrian conglomerates in Scotland, of which he was reminded, where there is "a passage from crushed conglomerates and sandstones into mica-schist."

The Obermittweida conglomerate has been discussed also microscopically by professor T. S. Bonney.* The matrix of the conglomerate, though clearly fragmental in origin, suggests that "a certain amount of metamorphism *in situ* has taken place. * * * The gneiss has a superficial resemblance to this matrix, but is rather more distinctly micaceous." The gneiss is quite characteristic and resembles one of the older Alpine gneisses. The matrix does not give evidence of much squeezing. It has essentially the constitution of gneiss, but at the same time, "the fragmental character of the rock is indubitable." He does not incline to regard it as post-Archæan, but it is probably long subsequent to the gneiss, and its appearance of consecutiveness is probably illusory.

Such an explanation, I repeat, will not apply to the case of the Saganaga conglomerate, where the matrix is absolutely of the same character as the gneiss of the contiguous region.

The German geologists, as would be expected, endeavor generally to explain the Obermittweida conglomerate without recognizing its real fragmental character. Von Hauer referred to it as only something *like* a conglomerate. J. Lehmann says the pebbles cannot be regarded as rolled stones, notwithstanding the complete rounding and smoothness of some of them.* Roth does not admit the pebbles were included rolled fragments, but

* *Quar. Jour. Geol. Soc.*, xliv, Feb. 1, 1888, pp. 25-31.

refers them to concretionary action. Dr. Sauer, while admitting the pebbles to be genuine "Gerölle," holds that the conglomerate is altogether newer than the gneiss, and that it has been "folded and faulted in." Dr Credner suggests however, that such an explanation should not be advanced as a mere hypothesis, but ought to have some facts of observation to sustain it. He gives the occurrence a common sense interpretation when he says: "Especially significant for the sedimentary origin of the fundamental gneiss formation is the presence of conglomerates embraced within it."† In this conception he includes not only cases where a conglomerate is distinctly embraced in a gneissic mass, but those where conglomerate terranes alternate with recognized crystalline masses. "In Canada" he remarks, "we find a complex of beds over 300 meters thick in which rounded fragments of syenite and diorite, of greater and less magnitude, are held together by a quartzose binding medium rich in mica." "In Michigan," he says, "several conglomerates formed of rolled fragments of gneiss, granite and quartzite are imbedded in an arenaceous talcose groundmass. In Vermont, is a similar zone of conglomerates; while near Konigsberg is a conglomeritic sandstone which alternates with gneisses and fundamental schists."

The foregoing information has been assembled for the purpose of placing before geologists a body of little known and less considered facts which must be brought into account in every attempt to reproduce the history of the oldest known crystalline rocks. The facts appear to the writer most intelligible on the hypothesis of a sedimentary origin of such rocks; but it has not been his purpose to argue that view except so far as evidence is supplied by the presence of such conglomerates as have here been passed in review.

From The American Geologist—April, 1889.

CONGLOMERATES ENCLOSED IN GNEISSIC TERRANES.

[Supplement.]

BY ALEXANDER WINCHELL.

My article on the subject above named has elicited many comments, some of which render it desirable to supplement the article with explanations and new evidences. One esteemed correspondent whose familiarity with New England geology is everywhere recognized, reminds us that the terranes from which boulders and conglomerates have been cited in Vermont, Massachusetts and Rhode Island, are post-Laurentian.[1] This was well understood in making the citations. They were not made for the purpose of proving directly the fragmental origin of Laurentian gneisses. Some of them were intended to remind geologists that certain terranes generally recognized as real crystalline gneisses—however distinguishable from Laurentian gneisses in position or petrography—inclose features incompatible with an eruptive origin. If, however, an obviously fragmental origin of any gneisses

[1] See the communication from Professor C. H. Hitchcock in the present number of the GEOLOGIST.

must be admitted, the reader may rationally infer that perhaps even Laurentian gneisses are also fragmental in origin. The evidence is that they *may* be fragmental. When therefore, in addition to this presumption, I cite similar conglomerates from the recognized Laurentian of Canada and Minnesota, we have the same evidence for a fragmental origin of Laurentian terranes as in New England, for post-Laurentian terranes.

If the gneisses of the Black Hills[2] are also post-Laurentian the fact of the association of pebbles and conglomerates has the same significance as the facts cited from New England—neither more nor less.

As to the case of included fragments which evidently are not water-worn, mention is made of them only to prove the contemporaneousness of the gneiss mentioned with processes of sedimentary rock-making. If such contemporaneity existed in New England gneisses, it may presumably have existed with Laurentian gneisses; and when I cite hundreds of similar fragments in Laurentian gneisses, the evidence rises from analogy to demonstration. Gneiss-making and sediment-forming could not be coincident in time and place, if gneiss originated from igneous fusion and sediments accumulated from watery immersion. But no one doubts that sediments so originated; gneisses associated with them, therefore, must have had an aqueous history.

As to New England granites of such character or collocation with schists as to show, as at Mount Pequawket, that they have been in a state of fusion, there is neither reason to doubt the evidence nor to be misled by it. If granites generally have resulted from metamorphism of sediments, it is extremely probable that, exceptionally, the metamorphism reached the stage of fusion, accompanied as it almost necessarily would be, by eruption and vein-filling. Many granite veins, nevertheless, may have originated from heated solutions, and others from in-squeezed plastic material in which the planes of sedimentation had not become completely obliterated.

I have cited the occurrence of pebbles in non-gneissic terranes, as in Rhode Island, regardless of their age, because the

---

[2]The allusion to the Black Hills was made only in the slip of "Errata" attached to the "Extras" of my article.

pebbles were reported as furnishing evidence of softening and distortion; and the inference would be that if metamorphic agencies had effected such changes in times as late as the Coal-Measures, it was probable that in earlier times, they had, in many situations, more completely softened once-consolidated sediments, and even reduced them to such state of molecular intermobility that crystallizing rearrangements of the molecules would have taken place.

Professor Hitchcock affirms: "There is no support to your position to be derived from any of the cases cited from the East and the Black Hills." My "position" was simply that conglomerates sometimes occur in gneissic terranes. I think when professor Hitchcock attempts to show that the gneissic terranes of New England which enclose conglomerates are not Laurentian, he yields a clear implication in his own words, to serve as support to my "position." If he conceives my position to have been that Laurentian gneisses are all sedimentary in origin, I admit that the cases cited from New England and the Black Hills do not complete the proof of it, but the inference lies so close to the facts cited that it is a mere matter of form to enunciate it.

I desire also, to notice briefly a comment communicated by the honored Director of the Canadian Survey.[3] He says, "I entirely concur in your remarks. The facts you mention, however, have been so long and so well known to us in Canada as to be considered scarcely worth discussing; and I am a little surprised that among the authorities you cite you have not referred to Logan and the "Geology of Canada," * * * That the whole complex of the Archæan or pre-Cambrian rocks is a great series of mixed igneous, clastic and pyro-clastic rocks greatly altered, physically and mineralogically, by various metamorphic agencies there can be no doubt."

To this I beg to subjoin an expression of surprise that the obvious use of facts "so well known" has been so quietly overlooked, especially in Canada, where at least one of the officials of the survey is insisting that the gneisses are eruptive, and not of sedimentary origin. If those facts are so old and familiar as to have passed the stage of appropriate com-

---

[3]This comes in a personal communication, but I assume no objection can be made to public reference to it, since it concerns a geological question of general interest.

ment, beyond the Canadian border, I feel sure that the case is different in cis-Canadian territory. It may be well, however, to ascertain from the documents precisely what has been "so well and so long known." In his description of the Laurentian system,[4] Sir William Logan says: "Notwithstanding the general crystalline condition of the Laurentian rocks, beds of an unmistakably conglomeratic character are occasionally met with among them. * * * On the twenty-fourth lot of the tenth range of Bastard (in the valley of the Ottawa) a bed of *conglomerate* is interstratified between two of the beds of limestone." The following is an abstract of the more detailed succession given changed here to descending order.

Limestone, coarse-grained, white	6 ft.
Limestone, fine-grained, arenaceous	4 in.
Sandstone, fine-grained, calcareous	2 in.
Conglomerate, coarse, of which the matrix is a fine-grained, quartzose sandstone. Contains among others, pebbles of sandstone. These are flat, and lie on their flat sides in the general plane of the stratification	1 ft. 6 in.
Quartzite, somewhat fine and calcareous	2 in.
Quartzite, coarse, granular	4 in.
Limestone, white, crystalline, coarse-grained	5 ft.

Again, he speaks of a locality north of the village of Madoc, at which, in a higher geological position, a somewhat micaceous schist occurs, which holds "numerous fragments of rock different in character from the matrix, all being without calcareous matter, and some of them resembling syenite or greenstone. North from this ridge another succeeds, consisting of micaceous schists, beyond which for 300 yards, ridges of a decided *conglomerate*, with distinctly rounded pebbles, enveloped in a matrix of micaceous schist, alternate with ridges of schist containing few or no pebbles. * * *

Still further north, another band of *conglomerate* occurs, associated with fine-grained, soft, micaceous, feldspathic schist.

The matrix of the conglomerate weathers white, and appears to be a dolomite. The pebbles, of which the largest may be six inches in diameter, are chiefly quartz, but there are also, pebbles or masses of feldspar, and a few of calc-spar. The quartz pebbles are for the most part, distinctly rounded."

It will be noticed that while these occurrences are embraced, in a wide sense, in the Laurentian system, we learn of no pebbles or conglomerates embraced directly in Laurentian gneiss. They are contained in beds whose aqueous origin

[4] Geology of Canada, 1863, pp. 22-49

would generally be admitted. It is surprising, as may be remarked in passing, that the nature of the associated beds has not been claimed as evidence of a general aqueous history of the whole Laurentian. But as long as the gneisses were free from pebbles and conglomerates the evidence of their aqueous origin was rather presumptive than direct. On the contrary, the cases which it was the main purpose of my paper to describe, presented pebbles *in the midst of gneissic masses*, and a *conglomerate imbedded completely in a gneiss* so massive as to have been commonly denominated a syenite. The matrix itself is a characteristic gneiss. I am not aware that such occurrences are "well known."

The conglomerates cited by Logan have lithologic associations quite analogous with those of the so-called Huronian conglomerates. The associations are directly with sedimentary rocks, more remotely with crystalline rocks. It was not my purpose to refer to conglomerates so situated—any further than to quote the passage from Credner in which the aggregate mass of conglomerates in the Archæan is mentioned.

In the general discussion of conglomeritic occurrences in terranes more or less crystalline, references should be made to the observations of professor W. O. Crosby.[4]

The nucleus of the Black Hills has been again and again reported granitic. But Crosby states that granites occur only as lenticular masses conformable with the stratification of the schistose rocks. This, in fact, was previously reported by N. H. Winchell and by Newton. In the eastern or newer series of Archæan rocks, occurs an important quartzite which, in places, "passes into coarse grits and conglomerate," the pebbles of which have suffered extensive deformation. Professor Crosby regards the conglomerate and associated schists as "strikingly similar to the metamorphic sediments occurring at Bellingham, Massachusetts."[5] "It is perfectly plain," he says, "that the metamorphic series consisted originally of interstratified beds of ordinary mechanical sediments—slate, sandstone and conglomerate; and the metamorphic agents have not only accomplished the chemical change implied in the fact that these rocks are now in the main, distinctly hydro-

[4] *Geology of the Black Hills of Dakota.* From the Proceedings of the Boston Society of Natural History, Vol. XXIII, pp. 488-517.

[5] Proc. Boston Soc. Nat. Hist., XX, 373-8.

micaceous, but also a very marked mechanical change, which is most apparent in the deformation of the pebbles of the conglomerate." "The fragmental nature of the conglomerate and the deformation of the pebbles are, in both regions, indisputable facts."

Even the great lenticular masses of the granite are not recognized by Crosby as eruptive. Though they sometimes branch and enclose masses of schist, the concomitant conditions are such as to furnish "a complete refutation of the view that these masses are eruptive." "True eruptive granite is probably entirely wanting in the Black Hills."

The geological conditions appear to be similar to those along the international boundary in Minnesota and Canada; and professor Crosby's conclusions appear to be entirely accordant with the facts.

Quite recently an important memoir has been issued by Dean F. R. Carpenter.[6] The conditions as found in Minnesota are accurately described in the account of the Black Hills, quoted from the report of N. H. Winchell: "The mica schists become more and more granitic by interstratification, yet the schist maintains its distinctive character, and prevails up to the very base of the granite; and appears in thin, contorted laminæ in the granite itself."[7] To these and similar views he assents. In the further details he is quite in accord with professor Crosby, and reaches the same conclusion in reference to the probable metamorphic history of the crystalline terranes.

Now that attention is particularly directed to the existence of water-worn pebbles and fully formed conglomerates in gneissic terranes, both of post-Laurentian and of Laurentian age, it is quite probable that many additional occurrences will be pointed out, and that the evidences of an early sedimentary history for most of the granitoid and gneissoid rocks will rapidly accumulate.

---

6 *Preliminary Report of the Dakota School of Mines upon Geology, Mineral Resources and Mills of the Black Hills of Dakota.* Rapid City, 1888. This was reviewed in the March number of the Geologist.

7 Ludlow's *Report of a Reconnaissance of the Black Hills of Dakota*, 1874, p. 42.

From the American Geologist, March, 1889.

TWO SYSTEMS CONFOUNDED IN THE HURONIAN. In the *Quarterly Journal of the Geological Society* for February 1, 1888, appears an important communication from professor T. G. Bonney which I have only recently found time to read with due attention. I wish now to make a note upon it. The communication is entitled, "Notes on a part of the Huronian series in the neighborhood of Sudbury, (Canada)." Professor Bonney, passing off the gneisses of recognized Laurentian age, begins his investigations on rocks supposed to be Huronian, and extends his studies westward more than fifty-nine miles beyond Sudbury—though most of his studies lie within two miles of Sudbury. The first rock encountered "is mainly composed of quartz and feldspar, with but little mica, though occasional thinnish bands of a fissile mica-schist occur. It is much jointed, and appears to have a flaggy bedding, reminding me," he says, "in its general aspect, of parts of the Highland 'eastern gneiss' in Glen Docherty, (that is where the crushing is less conspicuous) or of the schistose series on the south side of Perth Nobla, Anglesey". This zone is less than a mile wide, when "outcrops of a rock distinctly fragmental are exposed". A dark quartzose rock is observed west of Sudbury, and this grows more coarsely fragmental—the "fragments now showing very distinctly on a weathered surface, by a slight bleaching, some looking rather like a felsite, others like a holocrystalline (?gneissose) rock." Next comes a coarse breccia, looking rather like an agglomerate—the matrix a more or less fine-grained quartzite. Then follows a quartzite without fragments, and then another group of fragmental rocks, slightly reddish-gray, resembling a microgranulite with dark green spots, and these include "gneissose and schistose rocks, and a greenstone, or possibly chlorite schist." Professor Bonney erroneously, I suspect, suggests that these may be Logan's "slate conglomerate," though he leaves the matter undecided. This belt of eastern (or lower) "Huronian" rocks is obviously distinct, he says, from the Laurentian; by which I understand that the mica-schists mentioned are sufficiently distinct from the older gneisses. These older Huronian "rocks are seen under the microscope to consist chiefly of quartz, feldspar and a brownish mica." "The rock certainly exhibits a fragmental structure with secondary reconstruction."

After this, but still within two miles of Sudbury, the character of the geology plainly changes. The rocks are grouped as A. Quartzites—ordinary, conspicuously fragmental, and fine-grained-schistose; B. Agglomeratic or conglomeratic rocks. These are carefully described, but there is no occasion here for reproducing the descriptions. The quartzites possess few peculiarities. The breccias are various, but predominantly quartzose, and generally with a matrix containing quartz and feldspar. Some of these are suspected to be igneous in origin, and one seems to possess the characters of a volcanic ash. Among all the rocks described, I find no description answering the characters of the great "Plummer argillites" or "slate conglomerates" of Logan, and I am uncertain whether this member of the Huronian passed under professor Bonney's observation.

The author naturally conceived the view common to the Canadian geologist (but erroneous as I think) that the Huronian embraces the entire complex of beds to the "Laurentian gneiss." Evidently, in passing off the gneisses, he arrived at the usual belt of crystalline schists—the "Vermilion group" of the Minnesota Survey. In proceeding from these, a transition was observed toward less crystalline rocks, and in the midst of these was the condition which I have designated "nascent mica schist" in which the mica folia are exceedingly minute. Still beyond, the mica is still less conspicuous, the quartz and feldspar more soiled and much mingled with particles of "dust." This is my graywackenitic rock—though not well constituted graywacke. It escapes clearly from the group of crystalline schists. In northeastern Minnesota, this is succeeded by sundry conditions of earthy schists—argillitic, sericitic, chloritic, jaspilitic and hæmatitic. All these are wanting in the vicinity of the Thessalon, Missasagui and Blind rivers, as also the greywackenitic and crystalline-schistic rocks. It may be they are wanting in the vicinity of Sudbury. In the valley of the Thessalon, some twenty miles from its mouth, the dark, siliceous argillites appear, which lie near the bottom of the proper Huronian series. I take the liberty to say "proper" Huronian, because I find these recognized Huronian rocks, northwest of lake Superior, succeeded downwards by a break which makes them necessarily the lower limit of a system.* I do not regard therefore, as Huronian, the series of rocks succeeding the Plummer argillites (Animike slates) downward, though the Canadian geologists may so regard them. I entertain a suspicion that most of the rocks investigated by professor Bonney belong to the lower series. Even among these, as I have just stated, are two groups, before we reach the "Laurentian gneiss." Of these two, the upper sub-Huronian group, is embraced under Dr. Lawson's term "Kewatin," but is not co-extensive with it. The lower is the "Vermilion group" of the Minnesota Survey, to which Dr. Lawson applied also the designation "Couchiching group."

Now professor Bonney notes the evidence of rocks of widely different age within the compass of the series pointed out by the Canadian geologists as "Huronian." His conclusions are in part as follows:

"Among the rocks in this region at present referred to the Huronian, two groups may be distinguished, depending on the degree of alteration observed." "This distinction must indicate either (*a*) that selective meta-

* This is a stratigraphic unconformity which I have described in *American Geologist* Jan., 1888, and more in detail in the *XVIth Annual Report Minnesota Geological Survey*, pp. 256-259, 264, 323.

morphism has produced marked effects * * * (*b*) that we are dealing with a series of great thickness, the deposition of which occupied a very long time, so that the lower beds are more altered than the higher, or (*c*) that under the name of Huronian two different series are included." He concludes: "I incline to the latter opinion, viz, that the two distinct groups, of which, one at any rate, is pre-Cambrian, are included under the name Huronian."

This conclusion accords with my own convictions. Even if professor Bonney's studies did not extend to the "slate conglomerate" (Animike), he encountered two systems of rocks—the crystalline schists below, and probably the earthy schists above—the iron-bearing schists of Marquette and of Vermilion lake. If his studies embraced the Animike slates, they extended to a system stratigraphically discordant with the iron-bearing schists, and therefore, beyond question, a system of much more recent origin. Geologists who embrace under the single designation "Huronian," the entire complex of rocks from the top of the Animike slates to the "Laurentian gneiss," confound three separate systems under a single term. There "*is* a Huronian System," but not so large a one as this.

Ann Arbor, Feb. 1, 1889. ALEXANDER WINCHELL.

[From the PROCEEDINGS OF THE AMERICAN ASSOCIATION FOR THE ADVANCEMENT OF SCIENCE, Vol. XXXIV, Ann Arbor Meeting, August, 1885.]

SOURCES OF TREND AND CRUSTAL SURPLUSAGE IN MOUNTAIN STRUCTURE. By Prof. ALEXANDER WINCHELL, University of Michigan, Ann Arbor, Mich.

1. THE oldest mountain ranges and the other physiographic features depending on these exhibit, generally, a trend which is approximately north and south. That the whole terrestrial surface is marked predominantly by general trends having a submeridional direction readily appears from an inspection of a map of the world. There are, it is true, many transmeridional trends as the Himalayas; but these are late geological features and not primordial. Still, Asia is shown to be deeply impressed by meridional trends in its north and south bays and river valleys. If the continent were sunken a few hundred feet, the Arctic and the Indian oceans would meet each other along these meridional depressions.

2. The cause or causes of this meridionality must date from the earliest periods of the earth's incrustive history; since geology shows that the grand orographic and continental and oceanic features were marked out as early as the existence of the first germs of the modern saliences of the terrestrial crust, and in their trends no great changes appear to have taken place. These trends are profound and overruling features in all the geological history of the world. It is incumbent on geology to seek their causes. But since the cause lies in the remote domain of facts now obliterated and discoverable only by inference from contemporary phenomena, we have to depart from the direct inductive process in reproducing it to our cognition. By such means we are able to discover *two causes* which must have coöperated in producing meridional trends.

3. The first was *lunar tidal influence*. It is now well understood that a tide in its most general conception is a prolateness of a cosmical body resulting from the differential attractions exerted by another body upon its nearer and remoter sides. It is understood that no known matter possesses sufficient rigidity to resist this bodily deformation; and that the viscosity of matter causes some delay in the attainment, at any place, of the full prolateness due to the action of a tide-producer at that place. In other words, the tide *lags*. In a rotating tide-bearer, the tidal culmination is behind the meridian of the tide-producer. In the earth-moon couple, since the lagging is less than a quadrant, the tidal protuberance causes an excess of lunar attraction on the tidal side of the hemisphere turned toward the moon. This excess opposes the earth's rotation and perpetually diminishes its velocity. The effect of this will be considered presently. Reciprocally, the tidal protuberance acts on the moon, accelerating its velocity and necessitating its slow recession from the earth. As this recession must have continued ever since the moon existed as a separate body, we must contemplate a time when the moon was within a few thousand miles of the earth, and revolving in its orbit with a velocity proportional to the rapid rotary motion of the earth at that time.

During the ages of incipient incrustation of the earth, the moon must have been in a position to exert a vastly greater tidal influence than at present. Whatever the height of the tide, it was also a *lagging* tide. On this the moon exerted its special pull in opposition to the earth's rotation. But this pull did more. Terrestrial matter was far from rigid. The special pull caused a slight *retral slipping* of the tidal crust. The slipping extended north and south as far as the tidal prolateness — that is, 54° 44′ north and south of the moon's position. As the moon may be supposed to have attained then a declination of five degrees, the slipping action would be felt sixty degrees north and south of the equator.

The slipping action produced similar states in the disturbed crust simultaneously along the meridian passing over the crest of the tide. That is, the movements, the pressures, the accumulations, the internal arrangement of non-homogeneous materials were all distributed meridionally. With the repetition of this action at every point, at every revolution of the earth, deeply ingrained meridional structures were implanted in the forming crust. From these resulted predispositions to meridional distribution of all later physical disturbances of the crust. If through cooling and contraction of the general mass of the earth, wrinkles resulted in the crust, they became disposed longitudinally, instead of being many short wrinkles, without determinate trend. In later ages, however, oceanic pressures or other causes may have overruled the meridional predisposition, now disguised by the rigidity of the thickened crust, much of it also formed since the era of high tidal influences.

It will be noticed further, that the retral slipping would be greatest near the apex of the tidal prolateness, and would diminish north and south in proportion to the diminution in the height of the tide. In other words, the predisposition implanted would not be strictly meridional, but from the average position of the equator would trend north-northeast on the north and south-southeast on the south. This effect is traceable in the actual configurations.

4. The second cause of meridional trends was *diminution of the earth's rotational ellipticity of figure.* The equatorial protuberance subsided as rotational velocity diminished. In other words, this cause resulted in a decrease of the equatorial circumference and an increase of the polar circumference. An excess of lateral pressure was experienced about the zone involved in the equatorial protuberance. That zone was of the same width as the tidal swell. The pressure was from east to west. Simultaneous crustal conditions, therefore, trended from north to south.

This trend was necessarily imparted to all mechanical disturbances of the crust. The cause coöperated with direct tidal action in determining the trends of the great features of the earth's surface.

5. These primitive actions shed light on the problem of the *excess of surplusage in the crustal folds and plications of the mountains.* Fisher, Dutton and others have apparently shown from calculations that the cooling of the earth from the incrusting temperature to the present would not, by contraction, shorten the circumference of the earth sufficiently to supply the convolutions which exist. Claypole has indicated from measurements across a portion of the Appalachians that the convolutions reveal a very marked excess above any supply attributable to contraction from cooling. Now the secular subsidence of the equatorial protüberance may rationally be assigned as an adequate cause supplementing contractional influences.

All these results are primarily tidal, and show that in the physical history of the earth the moon has exerted a profound modifying influence; and lead to the belief that in the history of the moon the earth must have exerted an influence which has been controlling.

SALEM PRESS, January, 1886.

SYNOPTICAL VIEW

OF THE

GEOLOGICAL SUCCESSION

OF

ORGANIC TYPES.

By ALEXANDER WINCHELL, M. A.,

PROFESSOR OF GEOLOGY, ZOOLOGY, AND BOTANY IN THE UNIVERSITY OF MICHIGAN.

SECOND EDITION.

ANN ARBOR:

PRINTED AT DR. CHASE'S STEAM PRINTING HOUSE

1867.

SYNOPTICAL VIEW.

Principal Authorities consulted. F. J. PICTET : *Traite de Paleontologie*, 4 vols., 8vo., with a 4to Atlas of 110 Plates. J. D. DANA : *Manual of Geology*. A. D'ORBIGNY : *Cours elementaire de Paleontologie et de Geologie stratigraphiques*, 2 vols. in three parts, large 18mo, and a 4to Atlas of Tables. J. HALL : *Paleontology of New York*, 4 vols., 4to, with many Plates ; *Annual Reports of the Regents of the University of the State of New York on the condition of the State Cabinet*, Nos, X to XVIII ; etc. THOS. DAVIDSON : *A monograph of the Fossil Brachiopoda of Great Britain*, Parts I to VII. F. B. MEEK : *Palaeontologg of the Upper Missouri. Invertebrates*, Part I. 4to, 135 pp. ; *Palaeontology of Illinois*, Vol. I ; etc. E. BILLINGS : *Palaeozoic Fossils of Canada*, Vol. I. roy., 8vo, 426 pp., wood cuts. *Devonian fossils of Canada West*, in Canadian Jonrnal, March and May, 1860, and March, May, and July, 1861 ; *Catalogue of Silurian Fossils of Anticosti*, 93 pp. ; etc. B. F. SHUMARD : Palæontology of Missouri and Texas, in *Missouri Geological Report*, Trans. Acad. Sci., St. Louis, Am. Jour. Sci. ; *Catalogue of Palæozoic Fossils of N. A.*, I, Echinodermata. D. D. OWEN : *Geological Survey of* Wis. and Min. ; etc· R. I. MURCHISON : *Silurian System ; Siluria* ; *Introduction* to Davidson's Silurian Brachiopoda of Great Britain. J. S. NEWBERRY : *Palæontology of Illinois*, Vol. I ; Colorado Exploring Expedition ; the Scientific Journals. L. LESQUEREUX : *Geology and Palæontology of Ill.*, Vols. I and II ; Geology of Ky., Vols. III and IV ; Geology of Penn. Also, the works of T. A. CONRAD, J. LEIDY, C A. WHITE, T. M. SAFFORD, L. AGASSIZ, M. TUOMY, F. V. HAYDEN, G. C. SWALLOW, R. P. WHITFIELD, J. W. DAWSON, E. EMMONS, F. S. HOLMES.

NOTE.—Names of generic and specific value are printed in italics ; of families, in Roman letters, and of higher groups in small capitals. An asterisk affixed to the name of a species or genus indicates that it has survived to the present day.

I. PALÆOZOIC TIME.

First appearance of Organic Life.

Reign of the ancient forms of life, all the species and almost all the genera of which have become extinct.

1. LAURENTIAN AGE (Lower Azoic).

First appearance of vegetal and animal life.

Reign of PROTOZOANS and FUCOIDS.

Period of *Eozoon canadense* (FORAMINIFER) the sole organism positively known.

II. HURONIAN AGE (Upper Azoic; Cambrian).
First appearance of ZOOPHYTES, WORMS, and CRUSTACEANS.
Reign of PROTOZOANS continued.
Period of PALÆOPYGE (the sole CRUSTACEAN); *Oldhamia* (HYDROID ACALEPH); *Eozoon Bavaricum.*

III. SILURIAN AGE.

First appearance of well-preserved RADIATES, and, at last, of VERTEBRATES.

Reign of MOLLUSCS–especially Orthoceratites and BRACHIOPODS (Bivalves with central beaks and unequal valves).

Period of TRILOBITES; Orthoceratites; BRACHIOPODS; CYSTIDEANS (CRINOIDS with arms wanting, or central); GRAPTOLITES (HYDROID ACALEPHS); PROTOZOANS.

Lower Silurian. (*Silurien inferieur*)

1. ST. JOHN'S PERIOD (Lower Lingula Flags; Primordial; Etage C).
First appearance of TRILOBITES, BRACHIOPODS.
Reign of TRILOBITES.
Period of *Paradoxides, Conocephalites, Arionellus, Microdiscus, Agnostus* (TRILOBITES); *Orthis, Lingulella, Discina* * (BRACH.)

2. POTSDAM PERIOD, (Upper Lingula Flags and Lower Tremadoc).
First appearance of GASTEROPODS.
Reign of TRILOBITES continued.
Period of *Olenellus, Conocephalites, Bathyurus, Salterella,* (TRILOB.); *Obolus, Obolella, Lingula* * *Lingulepis, Lingulella, Orthisina, Camerella,* (BRACH.); *Archæocyathus* (SPONGE); *Scolithus, Palæophycus, Licrophyous* (FUCOIDS), in the Lower Potsdam; of *Dicellocephalus, Ptychaspis, Agnostus* and other TRILOBITES; *Pleurotomaria* (GASTEROP); *Orthis, Lingula* *, *Lingulepis* (BRACH.) in the upper Potsdam.

3. CALCIFEROUS PERIOD, (Probably most of the Taconic; upper Tremadoc.)
First appearance of TETRABRANCH CEPHALOPODS, LAMELLIBRANCHS, (bivalves with valves equal and beaks not central), *Receptaculites.* (FORAMINIFER).
Reign of CEPHALOPODS, GASTEROPODS, and BRACHIOPODS.
Period of *Nautilus* *, *Lituites, Orthoceras* (CEPHAL.); *Pleurotomaria, Metoptoma* (GASTER.)

4. LEVIS PERIOD, including Levis proper, Lauzon and Sillery (Lower Llandeilo); 5 CHAZY (Upper Llandeilo); 6 TTENTON; 7 NASHVILLE (Hudson River: Cincinnati).
First appearance of Spiriferidæ, Rhynchonellidæ, Strophomenidæ, (BRACH.); BRYOZOANS; CYSTIDEANS, CRINIDEANS (Fixed CRINOIDS); ECHINOIDS; GRAPTOLITES; ZOANTHARIA TABULATA; ZOANTHARIA RUGOSA (Corals with conspicuous quaternary lamellæ); disappearance of *Maclurea; Olenus, Agnostus, Ogygia, Asaphus;* decline of GRAPTOLITES.
Reign of CHAMBERED MOLLUSCS with simple septa; GASTEROPODS; BRACHIOPODS; Fixed Crinoids; ZOANTHARIA TABULATA (corals with well-developed walls and transverse diaphragms—HYDROID ACALEPHS of Agassiz); GRAPTOLITES.
Period of *Trinucleus, Asaphus, Illænus, Lichas, Calymene, Agnostus, Ampyx* (TRILOB.); *Cyrtoceras, Cryptoceras, Ormoceras, Lituites, Orthoceras,* etc. (TETRABRANCHS with simple septa) *Cyrtolites, Bucania, Maclurea, Pleurotomaria, Murchisonia, Holopea, Cyclonema, Eunema, Subulites, Metoptoma,* (GASTEROP.); *Ambonychia, Ctenodonta, Modiolopsis, Pterinea, Conocardium, Cyrtodonta,* (LAMELLIBRANCHS); *Rhynchonella, Stricklandinia, Zygospira, Orthis, Leptæna, Strophomena, Discina* *, *Trematis* (BRACH.); *Ptilodictya* (BRYOZOON); *Glyptocrinus, Heterrcrinus, Palæocrinus,* etc., with numerous CYSTIDS (CRINOIDEA);

Palæaster, Tæniaster, Pleurocystis (ECHINOIDS); *Graptolithus; Favosites, Halysites, Chætetes, Columnaria, Tetradium* (ZOAN. TAB.); *Petraia, Stromatocerium* (ZOAN. RUGOSA); *Eospongia, Astylospongia, Astræospongia*, (SPONGES) *Arthroclema* (Fucoid).

Upper Silurian (*Murchisonien*).

8. NIAGARA PERIOD; 9, SALINA (Onondaga Salt); 10, LOWER HELDERBERG.

First appearance of *Homalonotus, Phacops* (TRIL.); *Spirifera, Atrypa, Merista, Chonetes, Crania* * (BRACH.) *Actinocrinus.*

Disappearance of GRAPTOLITES; *Calymene, Illænus, Acidaspis; Halysites.* Decline of *Orthoceras*; CYSTIDEANS.

Rign of TETRABRANCHS with simple septa; BRACHIOPODS; CRINOIDS; CORAL ANIMALS.

Period of *Calymene, Lichas, Acidaspis, Illænus, Dalmania* (TRIL.); *Eurypterus* (ENTOMOSTRACAN]; *Lituites, Cyrtoceras, Gomphoceras, Orthoceras, Conularia; Platyceras, Platyostoma, Subulites, Holopea* (GASTER.); *Conocardium, Pterinea, Modiolopsis*, (LAMELL.); *Rhynchonella, Pentamerus, Sperifera, Atrypa Merista, Meristella* (BRACH.); *Fenestella, Ptilodictya, Phænopora, Helopora*, etc., (BRYOZOANS); *Caryocrinus, Ichthyocrinus, Stephanocrinus, Actinocrinus, Rhodocrinus, Eucalyptocrinus, Tentaculites* (CRINOIDS); *Favosites, Halysites, Heliolites, Cladopora, Stromatopora* (CORALS); *Ischadites, Receptaculites* (FORAMINIFERA).

In the uppermost beds of the Silurian are found, in Great Britain, the small icthyolites called *Plectrodus mirabilis* and *Onchus Murchisonii;* and on the island of Œsel in the Baltic, *Thyestes verrucosus* and *Cephalaspis Schrenkii.* No Silurian Fish-remains are known in America.

IV. DEVONIAN AGE [Old Red Sandstone; *Devonien.*]

Frst appearance of FISHES (in America) and DECAPOD (10-footed) CRUSTACEANS (in Europe). Culmination of Cyathophylloids.

Reign of FISHES and Coral-animals.

Lower Devonian. 11, ORISKANY PERIOD; 12, CORNIFEROUS.

First appearance of *Fishes* [in Corniferous]; *Productus;* broad-winged *Spirifers.*

Disappearance of CYSTIDS [in Oriskany]; *Favistella, Heliolites.* Decline of TRILOBITES and Orthoceratites.

Reign of FISHES; Coral-reef POLYPS; *Atrypa reticularis.*

Period of the Cup-corals *Cyathophyllum, Zaphrentis, Clisiophyllum, Blothrophyllum, Amplexus, Chonophyllum* [ZOAN, RUGOSA]; and the other corals, *Favosites, Michelinia, Syringopora, Aulopora, Heliolites, Haimeophyllum, Eridophyllum; Nucleocrinus; Atrypa, Spirifer, Strophomena, Chonetes, Productus, Pentamerus, Leptocœlia, Centronella, Charionella* [BRACH.]; *Conocardium trigonale, Lucina* * *proavia; Cyrtoceras, Gomphoceras; Dalmania, Proetus* [TRIL.]; *Macropetalichthys, Machæracanthus, Onychodus, Psammodus, Oracanthus, Palæoniscus* [American FISHES].

The Devonian FISHES are CESTRACIONT SHARKS * [with bony pavement teeth], and GANOIDS of the groups PLACOGANOIDS * (Sturgeon-like), RHOMBIFERS * [like the Garpike], IMBRICATES * (like *Amia*—the fresh-water Dog-fish). All have vertebrated tails; and the GANOIDS possess reptilian conformations.

Upper Devonian. 13, HAMILTON PERIOD—represented by Marcellus Shale, Hamilton proper and Genesee Shale [Black "Slate" of the West]; 14, CHEMUNG PERIOD [Huron Group of Mich.]—represented by Portage [Green Shales of Huron Gr.] and Chemung proper [argillaceous and areno-micaceous shales of Huron Gr.]

First appearance of Land Vegetation—represented by LEPIDODENDROIDS, the highest of flowerless plants, and perhaps Conifers, the lowest of flowering plants. Neither Mosses nor Grasses. Also of TETRABRANCHS with lobed septa and dorsal siphon; *Terebratula**.

Disappearance of all the old genera of TRILOBITES; *Atrypa*.

Decline of TRILOBITES, Orthoceratites, *Strophomena*, Orthis.

Reign of FISHES; *Spirifer mucronatus*, *Atrypa, reticularis*, *Spirigera concentrica*.

Period of *Lepidodendron*, *Sigillaria*, *Noeggerathia*, *Sagenaria*, *Calamites* [Land plants]; Coral-reefs; *Heliophyllum*, *Cystiphyllum*, *Diphyphyllum*, *Favosites*, *Alveolites*, *Cœnostroma*, *Idiostroma*, *Stromatopora*, *Trachypora*, *Striatopora*, *Fistulipora*, *Callopora*, *Chœtetes* [CORALS]; *Nucleocrinus*, *Dolatocrinus*, *Rhodocrinus*, [CRINOIDS]; BRYOZOA; *Atrypa*, *Chonetes*, *Productus*, *Spirigera*, *Cyrtia*, *Strophomena*, *Strophodonta*, *Spirigera*, *Retzia*, *Terebratula**, *Rhynchonella**, *Discina**, *Lingula**, *Crania** [BRACH.]; *Grammysia*, *Orthonota*, *Pterinea*, *Aviculopecten* [LAMELL.]; *Bellerophon*, *Pleurotomaria*, *Platyceras*, *Euomphalus*, *Loxonema* [GASTER]; *Goniatites*, *Orthoceras*, *Clymenia*, *Gomphoceras* [TETRABRANCHS]; *Spirorbis**; *Phacops*, *Dalmania*, *Proetus*, *Arges*, [TRILOB.] *Cypridina* [ENTOMOSTRACAN]. Also the American fishes *Macropetalichthys*, *Coccosteus ?* *Pterichthys ?* and numerous European genera.

NOTE 1. The "Catskill Group," so far as distinct from the *Chemung*, is probably included in the WAVERLY. It contains *Holoptychius* (Fish), *Euomphalus*, *Edmondia*, *Cypricardia*.

2. In Scotland, there occur, in beds generally regarded Devonian, the remains of *Telerpeton Elgininense*, an acrodont, amphicœlian, lizard-like REPTILE, associated with remains of the reptilian *Stagonolepis* and *Hyperdapodon*. These beds, however, are suspected to be Triassic.

V. CARBONIFEROUS AGE [*Carboniferien*].

First appearance of REPTILES (at least in America); INSECTEANS; BARNACLES; GYMNOSPERMS.

Reign of PLACOID and GANOID FISHES; CRINOIDS; ACROGENOUS PLANTS.

Period of Actinocrinidæ; Cyathocrinidæ; Cyathophyllidæ *Nautili**. The bizarre Fishes of the Devonian have been replaced by more normal types.

Lower Carboniferous. 15, WAVERLY PERIOD [Conglomerate of Western N. Y.; Marshall, Mich.; Chouteau, Mo.; Kinderhook, Ill.; Yellow Sandstone, Io., etc.], 16, MOUNTAIN LIMESTONE—represented by the Burlington, Keokuk, Warsaw [Chester] St. Louis and Kaskaskia Limestones [Knobstones, Ia., Ky.; Silicious Group, Tenn.]. The Waverly rocks are clearly embraced in the Mountain Limestone series of Europe.

First appearance of ~~*Palæoniscus*,~~ *Hybodus* [FISHES]; *Phillipsia*, *Griffithides* [TRILOB.]; Oysters; Comatulidæ [FREE CRINOIDS]; and in America, of REPTILES.

Disappearance of TRILOBITES, *Atrypa reticularis*, *Strophomena rhomboidalis*, *Pentamerus*.

Decline of Strophomenidæ, *Orthis*.

Reign of Productidæ, *Spirifer*, *Spirigera*; *Goniatites*; Blastoids; Palœchenoid · CRINIDS.

Period of Pentremitidæ [CRINIDS without arms]; *Actinocrinus, Platycrinus, Zeacrinus, Poteriocrinus, Strotocrinus, Steganocrinus, Gilbertsocrinus, Taxocrinus, etc.* [armed CRINIDS]; *Archæocidaris, Melonites, Palæchinus* [ECHINOIDS]; *Archimedes, Fenestella, Coscinium, Cyclopora, Polypora* [BRYOZOA]; *Lithostrotion, Zaphrentis, Sphenopoterium, Conopoterium, Favosites, Leptopora, Syringopora* [CORALS]; *Productus, Chonetes, Spirigera, Spirifera, Retzia, Syringothyris, Terebratula** [BRACH.]; *Solen **, *Mytilus **, *Myalina, Pterinea, Aviculopecten, Pernopecten, Eumicrotis, Dexiobia, Ostrea **, *Sanguinolaria, Ctenodonta, Arca** [LAMEL.]; *Straparollus, Pleurotomaria, Loxonema, Holopella, Naticopsis, Machrocheilus, Platyceras, Dentalium**, *Bellerophon* [GASTER.]; *Nautilus **, *Orthoceras, Phragmoceras, Goniatites, Cyrtoceras* [TETRABRANCHS]; *Phillipsia, Griffithides* [TRIL.]; multitudes of SELACHIAN FISHES with pavement teeth, and with sharp teeth, and GANOIDS with rhombic and with imbricated scales; *Sauropus primævus* [AMPHIBIAN, in Pa.]

Upper Carboniferous. 17, COAL MEASURES—represented by [a] false coal measures, [b] conglomerate, [Parma congl.; Bonaventure congl.]; [c] Coal Measures proper, intersected by Mahoning and Anvil Rock Sandstones; 18, PERMIAN [*Permien*].

First appearance of ENALIOSAURIAN and LACERTIAN REPTILES; INSECTS, SPIDERS, MYRIAPODS; TETRADECAPOD, and [in America] DECAPOD CRUSTACEANS; HYBODONT SHARKS.

Disappearance of TRILOBITES, Orthoceratites [in America]; Cyathophylloid corals; *Goniatites; Orthis, Productus, Chonetes, Strophomena* [BRACH.]; *Favosites.*

Decline of vertebrate-tailed GANOIDS; CRINOIDS; *Leptæna.*

Reign of ACROGENOUS PLANTS; GANOID and SELACHIAN FISHES.

Period of Coal Plants [low CONIFERS; Sigillarids; CALAMITES; ACROGENOUS CRYPTOGAMS]; *Fusulina* [PROTOZOAN]; *Cyathaxonia* CUP CORAL]; *Poteriocrinus, Actinocrinus, Erisocrinus,* etc. [CRINIDS]; *Archæocidaris* [ECHINOID]; *Fenestella* [BRY.]: *Spirifera, Spirigera* [*Athyris*], *Syntrielasma, Productus, Chonetes* [BRACH.]; *Arca, Sanguinolites, Aviculopecten, Pinna, Eumicrotis, Mytilus **, *Myalina,* [LAM.] *Bellerophon, Pleurotomaria, Naticopsis, Machrocheilus, Murchisonia, Loxonema, Orthonema, Soleniscus, Pupa **, [GASTER.]; *Nautilus **, *Goniatites, Cyrtoceras, Orthoceras* [TETRABR.]; *Spirorbis** [WORM]; *Phillipsia* [TRIL.]; *Bellinurus, Acanthotelson, Palæocaris, Anthrapalæmon* [medial and higher CRUSTACEANS]; *Beyrichia, Cypris ** [OSTRACOIDS]; *Xylobius, Anthracerpes* (MYRIAPODS); *Blattina* [ORTHOPTEROUS INSECT]; *Miamia, Hemeristia,* [NEUROPTERS]; *Palæocampa,* [LEPIDOPTER?]; in Europe a COLEOPTER; numerous GANOID, CESTRACIONT and HYBODONT, FISHES; *Raniceps, Dendrerpeton, Thenaropus, Amphibamus* [LABYRINTHODONT AMPHIBIANS]; *Hylonomus* [LACERTIAN]; *Eosaurus,* [ENALIOSAUR]. These reptiles are all American. Reptiles become more abundant in the European Permian. No ANGIOSPERMS, MOSSES, LICHENS or LIVERWORTS yet existed.

II. MESOZOIC TIME (Secondary.)

First appearance of MAMMALS; Birds; TURTLES?; TELIOST (or common) FISHES; DIBRANCHIATE CEPHALOPODS: ASTRÆOID CORALS; ANGIOSPERMS and PALMS.

Reign of REPTILES; Ammonitidæ (TETRABRANCHS with foliated septa); Belemnitidæ (DIBRANCHS); ECHINOIDS (Sea Urchins); ASTERIOIDS (Star Fishes); CYCADS.

Culmination and Decline of REPTILES, MOLLUSCS and GYMNOSPERMS.

Period of ZOANTHARIA APOROSA (foliaceous corals); ZOANTHARIA PERFORATA (corals with perforated walls).

VI. TRIASSIC AGE.

Trias: 19, BUNTER SANDSTEIN [*Conchylien* in part]; 20, MUSCHELKALK [*Conchylien* in part]; 21, KEUPER [*Saliferien*].

First appearance of MAMMALS; TURTLES?; *Ceratites*, *Ammonites*, Pycnocrinidæ [shallow cupped CRINOIDS].

Disappearance of *Orthoceras*, *Goniatites*; HETEROCERCAL GANOIDS.

Reign of SAURIAN and LABYRINTHODONT REPTILES; *Ceratites*; CYCADS.

Period of *Dromatherium*, *Microlestes* [INSECTIVOROUS MARSUPIALS, —the last European]; *Rutiodon*, *Clepsysaurus*, *Centemodon*, *Bathygnathus* [SAURIAN REPTILES]; *Nothosaurus* [a marine SAURIAN]; *Labyrinthodon* [allied to the frog and crocodile]; GANOIDS, including some with homocercal [equally lobed] tails; INSECTS; *Nautiloceras*, *Orthoceras* [in Europe], *Melia*, *Ammonites*, *Conchorhynchus*, *Ceratites* TETRABRANCHS]; numerous LAMELLIBRANCHS; *Spirifer*, *Terebratula* *.

The footprints in the Connecticut river sandstones are regarded as Triassico-jurassic.

VII. JURASSIC AGE.

Eirst appearance of DIPTEROUS and HYMENOPTEROUS INSECTS (flies and bees); SQUALODONTS.

Disappearance of vertebrate-tailed (heterocercal) GANOIDS; LABYRINTHODONTS; Spiriferidæ; Strophomenidæ.

Reign of REPTILES; HYBODONTS; Ammonitidæ; Belemnitidæ; Free Crinoids; DECAPOD and ISOPOD (equal-footed) CRUSTACEANS.

Period of *Pentacrinus*, *Apiocrinus*; CORALS; STAR-FISHES; ECHINOIDS; *Terebratula* *, *Rhynchonella* *; *Ostreidæ*; *Ammonites*, *Belemnites*; INSECTEANS; CRUSTACEANS; WORMS; GANOID SELACHIANS; ENALIOSAURS; LACERTIANS; CROCODILIANS; DEINOSAURS (the highest reptiles); PTEROSAURS (flying reptiles); TURTLES. FISHES proper (TELIOSTS) are still wanting.

22. Lias:—represented by *Sinemurien*, *Liasien* and *Toarcien*.

First appearance of PTERODACTYLS; LEPIDOIDS [mostly obtusely-toothed GANOIDS]; Sturgeons; CHIMÆROIDS [an order of Sharks]; *Belemnites*; *Thecidea* [BRACH.]; *Planorbis**, *Paludina**, *Melania**.

Disappearance of *Spirifer*, *Leptæna*.

Reign of *Ichthyosaurus* [12 species]; *Plesiosaurus* [12 species]; HYBODONTS [Sharks with conical, striated teeth].

Oolite : 24. Lower Oolite [Inferior Oolite or *Bajocien*, and Great Oolite or *Bathonien*) ; 24, Middle Oolite [Oxford Clay or *Callovien* and *Oxfordien ;* Coral Rag or *Corallien ;* 25.Upper Oolite [Kimmeridge Clay or *Kimmeridgien* and Purbeck and Portland Beds or *Portlandien*].

First appearance of Acrodont Saurians (Lizards with teeth soldered to the jaws] and, in Europe, of Free [stemless] Crinoids*.

Reign of Pterodactyls ; Ganoids ; Placoids ; Macroural [lobster-like] Decapods ; Free Crinoids ; Zoophytes.

Period of *Phascolotherium* and *Thylacotherium* [Marsupials] ; and of Ichthyosaurians.

26. Wealden [*Neocomien*].

First appearance of web-footed Birds [Natatores] culmination of the type of Reptiles.

Reign of Deinosaurians, viz : *Megalosaurus* [40 feet in length] *Iguanodon* {60 feet], *Pelorosaurus* (80 feet), and *Hylæosaurus ;* and of Crocodilians.

VIII. CRETACEOUS AGE.

First appearance of Angiosperms [more than 100 species] and Palms ; Brachyural (crab-like) Decapods ; Cycloids [soft-finned] and Ctenoid (spinny-finned) Fishes ; true *Crocodiles**; Grallatores; Whales. Decline of Cephalopods ; Icthyosaurs ; Plesiosaurs; Deinosaurs.

Reign of *Ammonites* ; Reptiles ; Rudistes ; Bryozoa ; Echinoids ; Foraminifera ; Squalodonts (sharks with sharp teeth) ; Oysters.

Earlier Cretaceous : 27, Dacota Gr. ; 28, Benton Gr. ; 29, Niobrara Gr.

Period of *Liriodendron**, *Quercus**, *Cornus**, *Fagus**, *Populus**, *Salix**, *Alnus**, *Sassafras**, *Liquidambar**, *Taxodium**, (Angiospermous trees) ; Oysters ; Asterioids ; Ammonitidæ.

Later Cretaceous : 30, Pierre Gr. ; 31, Fox Hills Gr.

Period of Ammonitidæ ; Belemnitidæ ; Oysters ; Nautilus*, *Terebratulina ; Mosasaurus* (a marine, carnivorous, acrodont lizard) ; *Crocodilus* ;* *Lamna**, *Otodus*, *Oxyrhina*, (Squalodonts) ; *Ptychodus* (Cestraciont) ; *Priscodelphinus* (Cetacean) ; Rhizopods; few corals.

[In Europe the Cretaceous is divided into GREEN SAND : consisting of Lower Green Sand (*Aptien*) ; Gault (*Albien*) ; Upper Green Sand (*Cenomanien*) and WHITE CHALK: consisting of Lower White Chalk (*Turonien*) ; Upper White Chalk (*Senonien*); Mæstricht (*Danien*). The Green Sand Stage seems to be wanting in America.]

III. CENOZOIC TIME

Dawn and culmination of the present order of nature.

Reign of Mammals.

IX. TERTIARY AGE.

First appearance of Serpents and of nearly all the orders of Mammals and Birds.

Reign of Mammals ; Sharks.

Introduction of Reptiles and Fishes approaching to existing forms. The Deinosaurs, Pterosaurs, Enaliosaurs, Ammonitidæ and Belemnitidæ have disappeared. All the mammalian species are extinct.

Period ot all the types of CRUSTACEA except the highest (MAIOIDS); TELIOST and SQUALODONT FISHES; TURTLES; CROCODILES.

32. Claiborne [Lower Eocene; *Suessonien*].

Period of ANGIOSPERMS, CONIFERS, PALMS—mostly of existing genera, and resembling Miocene plants of Europe; LAMELLIBRANCHS in great abundance.

33. Jackson [Middle Eocene; *Parisien.*]

Period of LAMELLIBRANCHS; GASTEROPODS; *Zeuglodon* (whale-like, 70 feet long).

34. Vicksburg (Upper Eocene, Lower Miocene of some; *Falunien inferieur* ou *Tongrien* and upper part of *Parisien*).

Period of Diatomaceæ (Silicious PROTOPHYTES); ANGIOSPERMS; CONIFERS; PALMS; *Orbitoides*; LAMELLIBRANCHS.

[The Eocene of Europe witnessed the first appearance of QUADRUMANA (Monkeys);Dogs (being the oldest CARNIVORA); CHEIROPTERA (bats): Squirrels; CETACEA (whale-like); of RAPTORIAL (predaceous), SCANSORIAL [climbing], RASORIAL [scratching], and INSESSORIAL [perching] BIRDS. Reign of FORAMINIFERA; SHARKS; CROCODILES. Period of *Nummulites; Palæotherium, Anoplotherium*].

35. Yorktown (Miocene; *Falunien superieur*).

First appearance of Cats; Rats; Seals; INSECTIVORA; EDENTATA; RUMINANTIA [cud-chewers]; *Mastodon.*

Reign of CARNIVORA and UNGULATA (hoofed animals).

Great increase of MAMMALS—in Europe CARNIVORA and odd-toed UNGULATES; in North America, odd and even-toed UNGULATES; in S. America TOXODONT and PROBOSCIDEAN (elephant-like) UNGULATES.

Period of the "Bad Lands" of Dakota which have afforded 8 CARNIVORES; 25 HERBIVORES, includidg 2 *Rhinoceroses* and species approaching the *Tapir*, *Peccary*, *Deer*, *Camel*, *Horse*; and 4 RODENTS. On the Atlantic coast, *Whales*, *Dolphins*, *Seal*, *Walrus*.

36. Sumter (Pliocene; Older Pliocene of Lyell; *Subappenin*).

First appearance of Bears; soft-shell Turtles; CURSORIAL [ostrich-like] BIRDS; Camelidæ.

Reign of PACHYDERMS [thick-skinned quadrupeds]; EDENTATES (incisors, and generally, canines, wanting); *Mastodon.*

Period of RHIZOPODS; *Stag; Andrias Scheuchzeri*, a Salamander once mistaken for a fossil man. In the Upper Missouri region, 27 species of MAMMALS, all extinct, including forms referred to *Camel*, *Rhinoceros*, *Mastodon*, *Elephas imperator*, *Horse*, (4 or 5 species), *Deer*, *Musk-Deer*, *Oreodon*, *Wolf*, *Fox*, *Beaver*, *Porcupine*.

X. POST-TERTIARY AGE (Quaternary).

First appearance of nearly all the existing genera of terrestrial animals. First invertebrate Fauna nearly all the species of which have continued to exist; their living representatives now inhabiting more northern latitudes. Quadrupeds nearly all extinct.

37. Glacial Epoch [Drift; Newer Pliocene or Pleistocene, Lyel; *Subappenin* in part, D'Orb.)

In America no fossil animals.

Reign, on the Eastern continent, of boreal MOLLUSCS and huge QUADRUPEDS,

Period of *Tigers*, *Hyenas*, *Bears*, *Lions*, *Wolves*, *Weasels*, *Foxes*; also of extinct species of *Elephant*, (*E. primigenius*) *Hare*, *Rhinoceros*, *Horse*, *Hippopotamus*, *Ox*, *Deer*.

38. Champlain Epoch [Laurentian, Desor; Post-Pliocene, Lyell; Pleistocene, Morris and others; *Subappenin* in part, D'Orb.]

Reign of gigantic MAMMALS and BIRDS.

Period of MOLLUSCS of northern species; *Elephas Americanus*; *Mastodon giganteus*; *Horse*, *Ox*, *Bison*, *Tapir*, gigantic *Beaver*, *Dicotyles*, *Bear*, *Lion*, *Raccoon*, *Megalonyx*; *Whale* (near lake Champlain); and probably of the pampean, Megatherioid EDENTATES, viz: *Megatherium*, *Glyptodon*, *Megalonyx*, *Mylodon*, *Scelidotherium*. The *Dinornis*, *Palapteryx* and *Aptornis*—extinct gigantic BIRDS of New Zealand, and the *Epiornis* of Madagascar, perhaps belong here. The dominant types in the Orient, were CARNIVORES; in North America, HERBIVORES; in South America, EDENTATES; in Australia, MARSUPIALS.

39. Terrace Epoch [Human; Recent; *Terrains contemporains*.]

First appearance of MAN and the Fauna and Flora contemporaneous with him. The new species were much smaller than their predecessors of the Champlain Epoch. The *Elephant*, *Rhinoceros*, *Cave Bear* and *Hyena*, *Irish Elk*, and a few other Mammals of the Champlain Epoch continued into this.

Disappearance of the *Dodo*, the great *Auk*, and perhaps of the *Dinornis*, *Epiornis*, etc., as well as *Mastodon giganteus*, *Elephas Americanus*, etc; also of *Rytina Stelleri* (a Manatee); *Bos primigenius* (Ure-Ox of Europe).

Reign of MAN.

[From the American Journal of Science, Vol. XXXIV, Nov., 1862.]

ON THE

SALIFEROUS ROCKS AND SALT SPRINGS

OF

MICHIGAN.

BY ALEXANDER WINCHELL.

The perfectly dish-shaped conformation of the strata of the lower peninsula of Michigan, has prevented the escape to the sea of such soluble substances as were originally embraced in the marine deposits from which the rocks were formed. Were there any point in the margin of one of these rocky basins, lower than its central portions, chance for escape of all its soluble contents would have existed; and it is doubtful whether in such case, brines could have been retained to the present day, in any considerable quantity. Our subterranean peninsular basins are comparable with the superficial basins in which the salt lakes of the world are located. Neither class of basins has an outlet. The basin of lake Superior was once filled with water as salt as that of the Great Salt lake. Both have received accessions of fresh water; but while one has been drained by an efflux which has continually carried away some portions of the chlorid of sodium, the other has been drained only by evaporation. The salineness of one has been reduced almost to an infinitesimal quantity;* that of the other is unimpaired, if it has not

* Given the time required for the efflux through the Straits of St. Mary, of a volume of water equal to the usual contents of Lake Superior; given also the minute percentage of chlorid of sodium still remaining in the water of the lake; it is required to determine how long the processes of dilution through meteorological precipitation and drainage through the Straits must have been continued to reduce the sea-water which originally filled the lake basin to the degree of weakness which it has now attained: disregarding the chlorids derived from the drainage waters flowing into the lake.

actually been strengthened by the loss of more water than it has received.

The subterranean basins of Michigan furnish us with three "great salt lakes." The principal one of these is shown, for the first time, in the "First Biennial Report" of the geology of the State (1860), to occupy a position between the Carboniferous limestone and the sandstones at the base of the Carboniferous system —being on a parallel with the gypsiferous formation of Nova Scotia. It is a mass of argillaceous, gypseous and pyritous shales, with thin beds of arenaceous and magnesian limestone, and beds of pure gypsum from eleven to twenty feet in thickness. The aggregate thickness is from 180 to 200 feet. Its outcrop describes an irregular circle, embracing the central portion of the peninsula. It underlies an area of 17,000 square miles, embracing the whole of 19 counties and at least half of 16 others. This assemblage of strata, though probably included in the American representation of the Mountain Limestone of the Old World, has received the local designation of Michigan Salt Group.

Seven hundred and fifty feet below this is the Onondaga salt group, the circuit of whose outcrop is traced from Monroe county to Galt in Canada West, thence to Mackinac island, Milwaukie and southward. The supply of brine in these strata has not been ascertained. They are well stocked with gypsum and are known to be saliferous.

The third saliferous horizon has but recently been recognized. It was indeed known that brine of feeble strength exists in the coal measures, but only within a few days has it been proved that the salt wells at Bay City and vicinity on the Saganaw river, are supplied from this source. It *might* have been known from the first existence of these wells, if those having the boring in charge could have been induced to preserve specimens of the rocks. The Parma sandstone below the coal measures is the reservoir of this brine, as the Napoleon sandstone beneath the Michigan salt group is the reservoir of the brine from this group. It is now known that the Bay City wells terminated at the bottom of the Parma sandstone though bored to nearly as great a depth as the wells of East Saginaw and vicinity, which pierce the Napoleon sandstone. This fact being established, a new well near Bay City has been sunk to a greater depth, and at 916 feet the Napoleon sandstone has been struck as predicted; and at the depth of 74 feet in this rock, brine has been brought up *completely saturated.* This occurrence, no less than the success of the first well bored in the valley, becomes a very gratifying confirmation of geological inferences drawn from observations extended over thousands of square miles, and in great part, hundreds of miles distant from the points where success has been attained.

When the first geological survey of the state was organized in 1837, Dr. Houghton, the superintendent, was instructed to direct his attention to the development of the "State salt springs." In pursuance of his investigations, and with the liberal coöperation of the legislature, he began, in 1838, two salt wells—one three miles west of Grand Rapids, and the other in Midland county on the Tittabawassee river. The latter, after being prosecuted at intervals for four years, had reached the depth of only 139 feet when the work seems to have been obstructed by a "quartzose" boulder. The Grand Rapids well was sunk 473 feet but without success. In the mean time Hon. Lucius Lyon of Grand Rapids sank a well 661 feet at a point further east; and, obtaining water about one-fifth saturated, succeeded in manufacturing salt for a few years, at a time when salt was selling for $3.00 per barrel.

The cause of these early failures is now apparent. Dr. Houghton entertained erroneous views of the structural geology of the peninsula. He expressed the opinion (Report, 1839, p. 9) that the strike of the rocks was northeast and southwest across the peninsula—that Saginaw bay occupied a denuded space along the outcrop of "the sandstone" just where it comes in contact with "the limestone of the north"—that the coal on the Illinois river was on the strike of the coal-bearing rocks of Michigan—and the galeniferous limestone of Wisconsin and Illinois a prolongation of "a portion of the rock formation in the northern part" of Michigan. He further supposed that the brines of the state rose to the surface through fissures in the strata overlying the salt rock (Rep., 1838, p. 21; also special Rep., 1839, pp. 2 and 3), and that the geological positions of the state wells on the Tittabawassee and Grand Rivers were about the same (Spec. Rep., 1839, p. 6); while the latter was at least 360 feet below the former and separated from it by the whole thickness of the coal measures (see also Hubbard's Geol. Rep., 1841, pp. 132, et seq.).

It now appears that while the well on the Tittabawassee was located far within the salt basin, that on the Grand River was upon the thinning out edges of the strata. The brine at the latter point, as well as in Macomb and Washtenaw counties is caused by a sort of exudation over the rim of this basin, and does not rise through fissures from a deeply seated rock.

When it became apparent that the deepest portion of the great salt basin was probably beneath the neighborhood of the confluence of the Cass, Shiawassee and Tittabawassee rivers, a boring was commenced at East Saginaw, which at 742 feet had passed through the Coal measures, Carboniferous limestone and Napoleon sandstone, and afforded a plentiful supply of brine nine-tenths saturated. This success was the signal for a general onset; and within two years, twenty-three wells have been bored along the valley of the Saginaw, and new ones are continually undertaken.

The following is an average section of the rocks passed through in the borings in the vicinity of east Saginaw:

Alluvial and Drift materials, ...	100 ft.
"Woodville sandstone," brown and coarse, ...	65 "
Coal measures, consisting of shales with some sandstones and limestones and coal, ...	130 "
"Parma sandstone" white and porous, ...	115 "
Carboniferous limestome, often highly arenaceous; generally so below, ...	75 "
"Michigan Salt Group,"	170 "
"Napoleon sandstone," light buff, rather coarse and porous,	110 "
Total,	765

The Napoleon sandstone is underlaid by a red shale which has been pierced 64 feet.

From East Saginaw the depth of the wells increases southward, toward the center of the general basin; and also northward, so that in the vicinity of Bay City the bottom of the Napoleon sandstone is found at the depth of 1000 feet. We seem therefore to have a local basin toward the mouth of the Saginaw river, although the vicinity is ten or fifteen miles nearer the outcropping margin of the salt basin, which is found at the mouth of the Pigeon river and in Tawas bay, on opposite shores of Saginaw bay.* This local basin is filled by an extraordinary thickening of the shales of the Coal measures, almost exclusively. As the Parma sandstone, which furnishes the brine of the first wells at Bay City, is probably the equivalent of the saliferous "Conglomerate" of Ohio, it seems that the supply of brine at this horizon, bears a relation to the thickness of the overlying shales of the Coal measures. It also suggests that in the deeper portions of the general basin, the Coal measures must be found similarly augmented in thickness, and the Parma sandstone similarly charged with brine. This condition should be looked for, west and northwest into Gratiot and Midland counties.

The following are analyses of Saginaw valley brines. The first is by Prof. DuBois of the University of Michigan, from the Napoleon sandstone; the second by Jas. R. Chilton & Co., from the Parma sandstone.

* On page 72, vol. i, Geolog. Rep. Wisconsin, Prof. Hall states, undoubtedly through inadvertence, that the "Hamilton group is known upon Saginaw bay." The Hamilton group strikes the lake shores in Thunder and Little Traverse bays many miles further north.

	Saginaw City.	Bay City.
Specific gravity,	1·180	1·163
Chlorid of sodium,	19·246	19·692
" calcium,	2·395	0·742
" magnesium,	1·804	0·432
" potassium,	0·127	
Sulphate of lime,	0·534	0·145
" soda,		0·116
Bromid of magnesium,		0·013
Compounds of iron,	0·064	
Total solid matter,	24·170	21·140

The difference in the composition of these brines is in accordance with their difference of origin.

The average supply of the Saginaw wells is at least 25,000 gallons each, in 24 hours.

The creation of this new branch of local industry is destined to become a matter of very great general importance. Although but two years have elapsed since the production of the first bushel of salt in the Saginaw valley, there are now (Aug. 1st) no less than 22 blocks of kettles in actual operation, turning out 1210 barrels of salt per day, or, making an allowance for the effect of winter weather, 1,980,000 bushels per year. Here is a growth, at the end of two years, equal to that attained by the Onondaga Saltworks in 1834, at the end of 38 years after the salt springs passed under the superintendence of the State. In two months, seven more blocks will come into operation, increasing by nearly one third, the foregoing figures.

Such is the strength and abundance of the brine and cheapness of fuel, that a barrel of salt is made at a cost of 64 cents. The cost of a barrel at Syracuse is at least 95 cents, so that Saginaw salt would pay the manufacturer 48 per cent of profit if the price were put down to the prime cost of the article at Syracuse. Moreover the quality of the article has proved so superior, that the market is actually clamorous for an adequate supply.

When we consider the cheapness and quality of Saginaw salt, the inexhaustibleness of the supply of brine and the excellent facilities for shipment, it would appear that there is little danger of over estimating the future development of this new resource.

University of Michigan, Aug. 4, 1862.

SYLLABUS

OF A COURSE OF

LECTURES ON GEOLOGY,

TO BE

DELIVERED IN THE UNIVERSITY OF MICHIGAN,

IN THE MONTHS OF

FEBRUARY AND MARCH, 1870.

By ALEXANDER WINCHELL, LL. D.,

PROFESSOR OF GEOLOGY, ZOOLOGY AND BOTANY.

ANN ARBOR:

COURIER STEAM PRINTING HOUSE.

1870.

NOTICE.

The following lectures are intended to embrace a popular outline of the grand conclusions based upon the data of geological science. Three lectures will be delivered per week; and the alternate days will be devoted to a fuller presentation of facts, and more rigorous discussions. The class will use Dana's Manual of Geology. A. W,

SYLLABUS.

I.—THE ANCIENT COSMOGONIES.

1. **The Hebrew**—Moses—Rabbinical Writers—Christian Fathers.
2. **The Hindoo**—
3. **The Egyptian**—Of Indian origin—Generation of Animal life.
4. **The Chaldean**—
5. **Other Oriental Cosmogonies**—Arabic—Persian—Scythian.
6. **The Greek Cosmogonies**—Homer and Hesiod—Pythagoras—Epicurus—Aristotle—Strabo, etc.
7. **The Aztec Cosmogony**—

II.—HISTORICAL SKETCH OF MODERN GEOLOGY.

1. **Italian Writers**—da Vinci—Mattiloi—Fallopio, etc., etc.
2. **Supposed Relics of the Mosiac Deluge**—Heated controversies.
3. **Specimen Authors** — Hooke — Burnet — Whiston — Scheuchzer — Moro—Buffon.
4. **The Vulcanists and Neptunists**—
5. **The Geological Society of London**—
6. **Sketch of Geological Science in America.**

III.—THE GARNERING OF THE FACTS.

Plan of the course.

1. **Footprints of the Sea.**
   1. Fossil shells far from the sea and at great altitudes.
      (*a*) Ancient opinions concerning them—"Freaks of Nature"—"Plastic Power"—Experimental "Moulds."—"Fortuitous concourse of atoms"—The Mosaic Deluge.
      (*b*) They are genuine organic *débris*—Illustration from remains of shore shells, or of human art.
   2. Sea-beaches far inland—Valley of St. Lawrence.

3. Changes of sea-level actually observed.
   (*a*) Temple of Jupiter Serapis.
   (*b*) Old Roman roads, etc.
   (*c*) Oscillations observed in America—Subsidence at St. Augustine—Elevations in Pamlico Sound—Subsidence on the Coast of New Jersey—In Nantucket harbor—Elevations along New England coast—Rotation of Grand Manan—Rotation of Nova Scotia—Submergence of site of Louisburg (Cape Breton).
   (*d*) Sea-wave on coast of Chili and Peru in 1822—The earthquake of Arica in 1868.
   (*e*) Actual emergences of new islands—In the Ægean—The Symplegades—The Aleutians.
   (*f*) Effect of a moderate depression of Illinois.

2. Traces of Fire.
1. Baked Sandstones, Limestones and Shales.
2. Refrigerated molten rocks—Traps—Porphyries—Lavas.
3. Fire visited the earth's surface before water.

3. Unextinguished Fires—Volcanoes—Hot springs—Deep mines—Artesian wells.

4. Foundation Stones of the Land—Granites, Traps and other igneous rocks.

5. Inference from the Figure of the Earth.

6. Conclusion that the Earth has cooled.

If so, from what condition?—To what do the known laws of matter conduct us?

The starting point—An igneous vapor.

7. Lessons of a pebble.

IV.—PRIMORDIAL HISTORY OF MATTER.

1. Indications of common origin of the whole Solar System.
1. Astronomical phenomena.
2. Suggestions of Leibnitz and Kant.
3. Investigations of Laplace—Conjunction of Astronomy and Geology.

2. Does Matter exist as an Igneous Vapor?
1. Nebulæ—Discoveries of Sir William Herschel—Inferences—Revelations of Lord Rosse's telescope—Contrary inferences—Irresolvable nebulæ.
2. Comets—constitution of their tails and nuclei.
3. Zodiacal Light—what is it?

4. Recent spectroscopic experiments on the *aurora borealis*.
5. The gaseous envelope of the sun.
6. The cosmos a museum illustrating every step in the process of world-making.

3. The Nebular Hypothesis—Its exposition—Our sun the residual mass.

4. Theological Opposition and its Grounds.

The "Vestiges"—All we need ask is, "Do the facts sustain it?"—The law of gravitation once a hypothesis—Every truth available for the defence of all truth.

5. The "Hypothesis" not atheistic.

1. Admissions of Whewell, Buchanan and others.
2. Science itself surrenders matter into the hands of a Creator.
3. Some thoughts on "Evolution" and the nature of "Force."

V.—THE REIGN OF FIRE AND THE WAR OF THE ELEMENTS.

1. Passage from the Gaseous to the Liquid state.

Rain of molten matter—Growth of the germinal core—An incandescent globe and a fervid atmosphere—Struggling sunbeams—Rolling tides of lava.

3. Freezing of Molten Seas.

1. The first crust—Its composition—Its frequent ruptures—Its cementation—A lava-floe—The gulf bridged.
2. Crash of the crust and its cause.

3. Appearance of Water.

1. Where had been the ocean?
2. Gathering clouds—Thickening darkness—Descending rains—The voice of thunders.

4. The "gathering together of the waters."

1. A universal ocean—Acid rains—Attacks upon the rocks—The war of chemical affinities.
2. Collapse of the ocean's floor.

5. Germs of Continents—Venerable domes.

VI.—INFERENCES TRUE AND FALSE.

The views already presented the accepted ones.

1. Not all worlds habitable—Lardner's suggestions.

1. The Fixed Stars not *known* to be centres of planetary systems—Their analogy with the sun uncertain.
   (*a*) They may possess extreme tenuity.

(*b*) Many are changing in brightness—Sirius, from red to white.

(*c*) Some have disappeared—The lost Pleiad—Other cases of disappearance.

(*d*) New stars have appeared and disappeared—The new star Hipparchus—Star of Tycho Brahe in 1572—Of Kepler in 1604—Star of 1866.

2. The remoter planets not habitable.

(*a*) Light and heat at Neptune 1-900th what we enjoy—The sun the size of Jupiter to us.

(*b*) Density of Jupiter ¼th that of the earth—A mere globe of water—But the weight of bodies 2½ times as great.

(*c*) Saturn and his liquid rings.

(*d*) What determined the existing physical conditions of the planets?

3. The moon an ancient cinder—Not inhabited and perhaps never inhabited—Density of her atmosphere 1-64th that of the earth and hence incapable of sustaining watery vapor.

4. Mercury uninhabitable.

2. Some other worlds habitable.

1. What we know of Mars and Venus—Geography, hydrography and climate of Mars.

2. Other planets formerly habitable.

3. Planets of other systems now habitable.

(*a*) No reasons against it.

(*b*) The astronomical analogies strongly favor it—Terrestrial conditions reproduced in other systems.

(*c*) Nature's economy of habitable conditions.

3. Supposition that the Earth began solidifying at the center.

1. Views of T. S. Hunt.

2. Views of N. S. Shaler.

4. Supposed necessity of great terrestrial rigidity and a nearly solid mass—Calculations of Sir William Thompson and W. Hopkins.

5. Denials of all evidence of igneous action.

1. Sir David Brewster—Evan Hopkins—Barnes—Thomas—Author of "Springs of Fresh Truth"—Prof. Tyndall.

2. Assertions of Prof. James Hall.

6. Answers to objectors.

1. All the phenomena which suggested and sustain the doctrine.

2. Analogies of water, type-metal, cold iron floating on molten iron, etc., etc.

3. Later experiments and opinions — Raillard — Delauney and Champagneul.

VII.—HOW THE CONTINENT GREW.

1. **Oceans and Continents have never changed places.**
2. **Incipient Wrinkles**—The Continent staked out.
   1. Laurentian—Appalachian—Rocky Mountain.
   2. Mostly remained submerged—The Laurentian emerged—The Adirondacs—Katahdin—Ozarks.
3. **Continent of Eozoic Time**—How we know its age—Its probable eastward extension—The "Telegraphic Plateau."
4. **The Continent at the Close of Paleozoic Time**—Its Geography.
5. **The Continent during Mesozoic Time**—Its outlines—Its rivers—Its Mediterranean Sea.
6. **The Continent at the Close of Mesozoic Time.**
7. **The Continent prepared for Man** — Its completed outlines — Its Hydrography and Topography.
8. **Continuity of Continental Growth.**
   1. Primordial prophecies.
   2. Two great water-sheds—Each with two branches—The northern branches diverge—The southern converge.
   4. Modern Geography and Hydrography an incident of remotest geological history.

VIII.—THE DAWN OF LIFE.

1. **A hypothetical Protophytic Period.**
2. **The pile of Eozoic strata.**
   1. Their position beneath other strata and above the crystalline rocks.
   2. Their enormous thickness.
   3. Their attitudes and exposures.
   4. Their lithological characters.
   5. Their richness in mineral values.
3. **Remains of Life in these strata.**
   1. Long regarded as *azoic*.
   2. Suspicions based on iron-ores and graphites (May, 1858)—Deductive discoveries, like that of Leverrier—Organisms in the Laurentian (Oct. 1858.)
   3. *Eozoön Canadense* as we find it—Description and illustrations.
   4. Its zoölogical affinities—*Amœba* and *Actinophrys*—Foraminifera in all ages—Their work in building up the continents—Nummulites and their structure—Their labors in the Pyramids.

4. **Conditions of Land and Water when Eozoon appeared.**
5. **A long pause ;through the Huronian age**—Probable future discoveries—Supposed foreign equivalents.
6. **The Advent of Silurian Life.**

IX.—LOWER SILURIAN LIFE AND SCENES.

1. **The Silurian Beach**—Its fucoidal imprints—Its sands and ripple marks—A shallow sea.
2. **A busy population**—Sudden exuberance of life.
    1. The type of Trilobites—Specimens.
    2. The type of Chambered-shells—Specimens—Even the colored nacre preserved.
    3. The type of Crinoids—Specimens.
    4. Corals and Graptolites.
    5. *Lingula* and its relations.
    6. Duration of these types—Their expansion—Peculiar per-sistence of *Lingula* and *Discina.*
3. **Chapters of Lower Silurian History**—St. Johns, Potsdam, Quebec, Trenton and Cincinnati Periods.
4. **Where we find the remains of these beings**—Cincinnanti; Richmond, Ind. ; Lexington, Ky.; Nashville, Tenn.; St. Joseph's, I.; Green Bay, Wis.; St. Anthoney's Falls.

X.—UPPER SILURIAN LIFE AND SCENES.

1. **How each act of the Drama was closed**—A collapse—a crash—an upthrow of the ocean's bottom—an obliteration of life—a new belt of land.
2. **Where were the Lands of later Silurian Time**—The desolate continent—The winding shore—The eroding waves—The teeming sea.
3. **Organization in later Silurian Times.**
    1. The perpetuated Trilobites, Orthoceratites and Crinoids—Specimens.
    2. The type of coral animals.
        (*a*) Their organization and biology—Illustrations.
        (*b*) Coral structures—Illustrations.
        (*c*) Upper Silurian corals—Specimens.
4. **Where we find the great limestone masses of this age.**
    1. Western New York; Drummond's I.; Chicago.
    2. The engineering of Niagara river.

5. The Chapters of Upper Silurian Time.
Niagara, Salina, and Lower Helderberg.

XI.—DEVONIAN LIFE AND SCENES.

1. The Reign of Coral Animals—Specimens—Coral Reefs.
2. Trilobites and Orthoceratites declining.
Cyrtoceras—Lituites—Gomphoceras.
3. The advent of Vertebrate Life.
1. Life hitherto invertebrate.
2. Advancing progress.
3. Realization of a new fundamental conception—Destined to a wonderful expansion.
4. Fishes of the Old Red Sandstone—Illustrations.
5. Devonian Fishes of Ohio and Canada—Specimens.

4. Growing continents and meagre forest growths—Glimpses of the coming age.
5. Where the Cemeteries of Devonian populations have been opened.
1. The Devonian belt of outcrops.
2. Localities—Falls of Ohio—Mackinac—Little Traverse Bay—Thunder Bay—Widder, Ont.—Delaware, O.

XII.—EARLY CARBONIFEROUS LIFE AND TIMES.

1. The Marshall Period.
1. The rocks and their exposures.
2. Fossils—Their abundance, and the testimony they give.
3. Questions as to parallelism.

2. The Reign of Crinoids.
1. A season of deep and quiet waters.
2. Crinoidal life at its culmination—Specimens.
3. Nautili and Goniatites—Illustrations.
4. Localities of the Mountain Limestone—Epochs.

3. Oscillations of Level in early Carboniferous times.

XIII.—SCENES AND INCIDENTS OF THE COAL PERIOD.

1. The destined Coal Areas.
1. Where they lay.
2. Premonitory agitations,

3. Gradual uprising of the bottom of a stormy sea—"The Conglomerate."

2. Absence of Air Breathers.

1. As yet no denizens of the land.
2. No wings to cleave the air.
3. Poison of the atmosphere.
4. Shall the progress of life be arrested?

3. The Expedient of Infinite Wisdom.

1. Upspringing vegetation.
2. Its labors upon the atmosphere.

4. Air Breathers spying out the land—Labyrinthodonts.

5. Utilization of the atmospheric poison—Man in the thought of Providence.

6. The End secured without a change of Method.

7. Provdential conjunction of luxuriant vegetation and frequent oscillations.

8. Culmination of events—Increased tension—The grand collapse—Birth of the Appalachians.

XIV.—RETROSPECT OF COAL MEASURE TIMES.

1. Scene in a coal mine.

2. Vegetation of the Coal.

1. Its modern alliances.

Classification of Plants (coal-measure types in *italics.*)

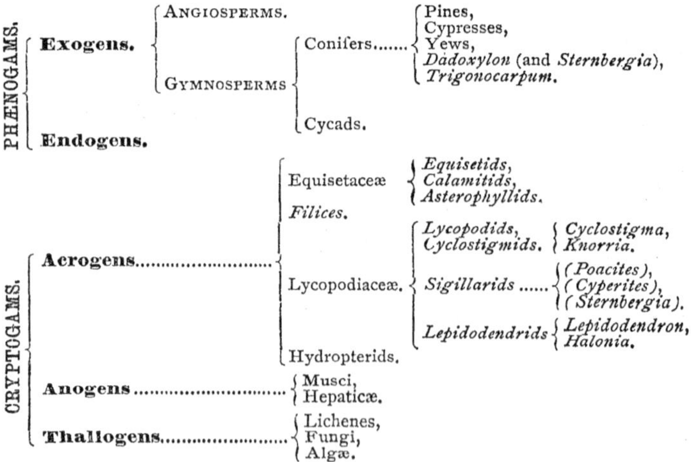

2. Picture of the landscape.

XV.—FURTHER THOUGHTS ON COAL.

1. **Varieties of Coal**—Graphite—Anthracite—Bituminous—Cannel—Brown—Peat.
2. **Six carbon-depositing ages.**
   1. Eözoic—*Plumbago*—Siberia, Greenland, United States.
   2. Silurian—*Plumbago* and *Anthracite*—Ireland, Scotland, Russia
   3. Carboniferous—*Anthracitic, bituminous* and *cannel* coal—United States, Europe.
   4. Jurassic—*Bituminous coal*—China, India, England, United States.
   5. Tertiary—*Brown coal*—Germany, United States.
   6. Post-Tertiary—*Peat*—Northern temperate countries.
3. **Coal Measures of the World**—Production—Capacity—Their final exhaustion.
4. **Total exhaustion of the sources of Fuel.**
   Limits to our occupation of the earth.

XVI.—THE REIGN OF REPTILES.

1. **Scouts of the reptile horde.**
2. **Classification of reptiles**—Enaliosaurs—Crocodiles—Pterosaurs—Deinosaurs.
3. **Chambered Shells**—Ammonites—Belemnites.
4. **Geography of the empire of reptiles**—The cotton lands of the South.

XVII.—THE REIGN OF QUADRUPEDS.

1. **Geography of the Continents.**
2. **Populations**—Elephant, Mastodon, Megalonyx, Titanotherium, Oreodon, etc.
3. **Cemetery of the Animals**—The picture of desolation.
4. **The Parisian cemetery**—What Cuvier dug out of it.
5. **The Himalayan cemeteries**—The monarch of Proboscideans.
6. **A glimmering from the Future.**

XVIII.—THE EMPIRE OF ICE.

1. **A revulsion in Nature**—Unwonted frosts—The encroaching glacier—Prostration of forests—Plowing of the rocks—Digging of lake basins—Filling of river channels—Desolation in Nature.

2. **Footprints of the glacier**—Smoothed, striated and Grooved rocks —Notable localities—"Muttoned" cliffs—Ancient moraines—Cubic miles of *débris*.
3. **What regions did the glacier invade?**

XIX.—RETURNING SPRING-TIME.

1. **Dissolution of the glacier**—The birth of torrents—The freight of sediments—Tribute of the North to the South.
2. **The last ablution in the sea.**
3. **Ascent from the bath**—Assorting and washing of the surface—The new continent.

XX.—OTHER THEORIES OF THE ICE PERIOD.

1. **Secular change in Longitude of Equinoxes.**
2. **Secular variations in eccentricity of earth's orbit and obliquity of ecliptic.**

XXI.—PRAIRIE HISTORY.

1. **Personal investigations**—New Theory.
2. **Burial of vegetable germs.**
3. **Prolonged vitality of seeds.**
4. **Correspondence of preglacial and postglacial vegetation.**
5. **How the continent was rehabilitated.**
6. **Former high tides of the lakes**—Their records.
7. **The ebb of the waters**—Uncovering of the lake-slime—Somnolence of buried germs—Encroachment of herbaceous vegetation —The shyness of the forest—Prairie fires.
8. **Theory of excessive humidity.**
9. **Theory of pulverulence of the soil.**
10. **Theory of atmospheric aridity**—Where it applies.

XXII.—MODERN CHANGES.

1. **Disappearance of species.**
2. **Filling of lakes**—Growth of Peat and Marl.
3. **Wandering of the rivers**—The Mississippi and Missouri—The rivers of Asia.
4. **Travels of the sands**—Sandy deserts—Dunes.
5. **Clearing of the forests**—Changes of climate.
6. **Excavation and deepening of river gorges.**

XXIII.—THE OLD AGE OF CONTINENTS.

1. **Popular impressions of the permanence of the land.**
2. **Changes transpiring before our eyes.**
3. **Vestiges of the Eozoic continent**—An arm extended northeastward toward the British Archipelago—another northwestward by the Aleutian islands toward the Orient—Whence the sediments which form the Alleghanies?
4. **The continent of carboniferous times.**
5. **The continent since carboniferous times**—The degradation of the Appalachians and the disposal of the sediments—The denudation of New England—The disemboweling of Tennessee—The engineering of Niagara.
6. **The worn-out "central plateau" of the continent**—Once the garden of North America—Drained to death.
7. **Revolution and renovation wrought by the great glacier**—Surface renewed for man—Its agency wanting in the Great Desert—Reflections suggested.
8. **Intimations from the decay of continents and the succssion of Faunas**—Limitations of terrestrial history.

XXIV.—THE ADVENT OF MAN.

1. **A new creation.**—Distinctive prerogatives of the human spirit.
2. **Man's birth-place a prophecy of the ages.**
3. **Man's unity**—Concurrent testimony of migrations—Relics of Oriental tribes, in America and Polynesia—The home of domesticated plants and animals—Morgan's researches in the language of consanguinity.

XXV.—MONUMENTS OF PRIMEVAL MAN.

1. **Cavern Relics**—In France—In England—In Spain—The Caucasus—United States, etc.
2. **Relics in fluviatile deposits**—The Somme—The Seine—The Tinière—The Nile—The Mississippi.
3. **Kitchen-refuse Heaps**—In Denmark—Sweden—Florida—Alabama and Massachusetts.
4. **Pile-Habitations**—Swiss lakes, &c.
5. **Tumuli, Cistvæns, Crainnoges, Dolmens and Cromlechs.**
6. **Mining and Mound relics in America.**
7. **The Three Ages of National Life**—Not Simultaneous in different parts of the world.

8. **Man in the Age of Stone in Europe**—His contemporaries—His pursuits—His Arts—His ornaments—His tastes—His religion.
9. **Primeval Man endowed with a full-orbed manhood.**

XXVI.—THE ANTIQUITY OF THE RACE.

1. **What Moses teaches and what he does not teach.**
2. **Grounds on which the opinion of a high antiquity has been rested.**
3. **Examination of these grounds**—The Mississippi delta—The gravel beds of the Somme—The cone of the Tinière.
4. **Contemporaneousness of Man and extinct Animals**—California skulls—Michigan and Missouri Mastodons—Indian traditions. —Man and the "cave-quadrupeds" of Europe.
5. **Man the witness of vast geological transformations**—The retreat of the great glacier—Assyrian, Persian and Indian traditions of deluges—Drainage of the Scythian plains—Deluges of Ogyges and Deucalion—Revolutions in the hydrographical features of China—The sundering of Isthmuses—The growth of the great prairies—Transformations of forests in Denmark, England and America.
6. **His antiquity not over 6,000 to 10,000 years.**

XXVII.—PETROLEUM.

1. **Its chemical constitution and its crude condition.**
2. **Organic origin of petroleum.**
3. **Its vertical distribution in the rocks.**
4. **Laws of its accumulation.**
5. **Formations in which it has been sought**—Fallacious indications.
6. **Formations in which it has been found in paying quantities**—Nashville Group—Hamilton Group—Genesee Group—Chemung Group—Waverly Group—Carboniferous Limestone—Parma Conglomerate—Coal Measures—Cretaceous and Tertiary rocks.

XXVIII.—EXTRACTION OF SALT AND GYPSUM.

1. **A visit to the Saginaw Salt Works**—The wells, the brine, its composition, the supply, its purification, its extraction—The bitterns—Solar evaporation.
2. **Other Salt Works.**
3. **Manufacture of Salt from Sea-water.**
4. **The mining of Salt.**

5. **Gypsum beds**—Mode of occurrence—Varieties of Gypsum—Its Uses.

XXIX.—GEOLOGY OF SALT AND GYPSUM.

1. **Primordial origin of the saltness of the Sea.**
2. **Origin of salt lakes**—Conditions of their perpetuity—History of fresh lakes.
3. **Salt lakes of former ages**—Storehouses of marine salinity—Order of superposition of products in the Salina basin—Order of deposition in the kettles.
4. **Consequences of tilting of brine-basins.**
5. **The three brine-basins of Michigan**—The Salina group—The Michigan salt group—The coal measures.
6. **The brine-basin of New York.**

XXX.—THE CIRCLE OF SEDIMENTARY DEPOSITION.

1. **Definition of the Circle.**
2. **Its rationale.**
3. **The cycles of geologic time.**
4. **The circle to be used as a key**—Application of the key—Unfolding of the epochs.
5. **Tabular exhibit from American rocks.**

XXXI.—THE METHOD OF ORGANIC HISTORY.

1. **Progression**—The five dynasties, Invertebrates, Fishes, Reptiles, Quadrupeds, Man.
2. **Progression only the general law**—Exceptions.
3. **Four fundamental conceptions**—Radiates, Molluscs, Articulates, Vertebrates.
4. **Class- and Order-Ideas and their Persistence.**
5. **Evolution of types**—Prophetic types—Retrospective forms.

XXXII.—UNITY IN THE HISTORY OF LIFE.

1. **Exposition of the Vertebrate Archetype**—Serial homologies—Class modfications.
2. **The homologies of limbs**—Fishes, Reptiles, Birds, Quadrupeds, Man.
3. **Teleology of limbs**—The feet of birds—Fundamental plan and "final cause" co-existent—Whewell's illustration from the architecture of a city.

XXXIII.—A GRASP OF GEOLOGIC TIME.

1. **Prevalent notions of the vastness of geological intervals, and** the remotness of the last terrestrial revolutions—The quantum of ground for such nations.
2. **Revolutions of the Historic Period**—The Mosaic Deluge—The Ancient Lectonia—The bursting of the Thracian Bosphorus—Former union of the Caspian and Black Seas—The subsidence of the Mediterranean—Hydrographic revolutions in China—Shifting of the bed of the Oxus—Change of climate in Ireland and Greenland—Encroachments of the Sea—Sand Floods—Recession of Niagara Falls—Drainage of Lakes—Desiccation of Swamps.
3. **Older Revolutions which our race has witnessed**—The retreating glaciers—Extinction of Quadrupeds—Revolutions of Forests—Excavation of Behring's Straits and the Straits of Dover.
4. **How we seize upon a unit of measure which can be aprehended**—Relief of the mind.

XXXIV.—PARALLELISM OF THE MOSIAC AND GEOLOGIC COSMOGONIES.

1. **Supposed conflict**--Must begin at the beginning—An original method.
2. **The Drama of Creation**—
   (*a*) **The rhythmical structure of the Mosiac narrative**—The theme—The method of its evolution.
   (*b*) **The theme** (Gen. I. 1)—What it expresses and implies—Each word significant—The vision of Moses (Ver. 2).
   (*c*) **Use of the word "yom"**—Does not mean literal "day."
      (1) The events did not transpire in six days.
      (2) The Scriptural use of the word—(Gen. ii.:4, Job xviii.:20; Isaiah xxx.:8; Job xiv.:6; Ezek. xxxi.:25; Prov. vi':34.)
      (3) Opinions of philologists—Lewis.
3. **The harmony.**

First Day (Ver. 3–5) *Creation of Light.*
The Period of Igneous Vapor.

Second Day (Ver. 6–8) *Creation of the Firmament.*
Descent of Rains—Accumulation of Sediments.

Third Day (Ver. 9–13) *Creation of Dry Land and Plants.*
Uplift of Continents—Marine Plants.

Fourth Day (Ver. 14–19) *Creation of Sun, Moon and Stars.*

["Gnasah" signifies *to appoint ;* as God said "I do *set*, my bow in the cloud." Same word used in same connexion, Ps. 104:19.

Dispersion of Clouds—Appearance of Sun, Moon and Stars—Plant growth.

Fifth day (Ver. 20–23) *Creation of Aquatic Animals and Birds*—"*Great Whales.*"

Marine Animals (Molluscs, *Paleozoic* Fishes, etc.) and Aquatic Reptiles (*Mesozoic* Enaliosaurs) and *Mesozoic* Birds.

Sixth Day (Ver. 24–31) *Creation of Land Animals and lastly, Man.*

Appearance of *Tertiary* Mammals, followed by Man.

Seventh Day (Gen. ii.:23) *God Rested—Sabbath.*

Reign of Man—Sabbath of Creation.

4. **Harmony more complete than could be expected.**
5. **Vouchers of Revelation**—Light before the Sun—Plant-life before the Sun—Man, the ruler, last instead of first. [In the Indian cosmogony higher beings were created before man, and man, before the earth.]

XXXV.—ANCIENT BELIEFS IN PERIODICAL CATASTROPHES TO THE UNIVERSE.

1. **Opinion of Dr. Reid and its untenability.**
2. **The Jews**—The Sacred Scriptures—The Rabbins—Transmitted to the Christian Fathers.
3. **The Hindoos.**
4. **The Egyptians.**
5. **The Chaldeans, Phenicians, Persians, Scythians, Arabians.**
6. **The Philosophy of Greece**—Its oriental and Egyptian origin—The Orphic Hymns—Homer and Hesiod—the Sibylline Books—Thales—Pythagoras—The Stoics—The Ionics—The Epicureans—Aristotle and the Peripatetics—Plato and the Academics.
7. **The Philosophy of Rome**—Lucretius, Lucan and Ovid—Cicero.
8. **The Celts and the modern Hindoos.**
9. **The Aztecs.**
10. **Authority of a universal belief.**
11. **Possible scientific origin of the present belief.**

XXXVI.—INHERENT LIMITATIONS OF EXISTING TERRESTRIAL ORDER.

1. **Activities which surround us**—Caused by the transformation of Force—The search for rest—The chimera of perpetual motion.
2. **Passing terrestrial changes**—Whence ? and whither ?—Behold the work of the waters—The ocean to devour the land.
3. **The wastage of terrestrial heat**—Changed climates and waning populations—Pro and Con.

XXXVII.—INHERENT LIMITATIONS OF SOLAR ENERGY.

1. **Reminiscence of the Nebular Hypothesis**—Cooling cosmical bodies.
2. **Can the Sun's heat be sustained ?**—Enormous emission of heat.
3. **The food of solar fires**—A hail of meteorites—Finitude of fuel-resources—A waning orb—Paleness of winter solstice in July —Shivering populations—Return to caves—The last men.

XXXVIII.—IN HERENT LIMITATIONS OF EXISTING COSMICAL ORDER

1. **Tidings of friction in the heavens**—The plodding comet—High testimonies.
2. **The career of planets wound up**—Conglomeration of the matter of the Solar System.
3. **A glance beyond**—Firmamental conglomeration—We pause in the presence of immensity.
4. **What then is the ferment of a planet's life-time ?**—The death of matter—Its resurrection at the mandate of Omnipotence—Cycles of matter.

X XXIX.—THE ONWARD MARCH OF MIND.

1. **The Soul's consciousness**—Unstricken with terror at the crash of worlds—"Immortal Hope."
2. **Glimpses of the achievements of mind.**
3. **The upward Struggle of the race**—Deeper penetration into the infinite—Closer communion with "the unseen"—The chrysalis bursts and the imago spreads its wings.

SYLLABUS

OF A COURSE OF

LECTURES ON GEOLOGY,

TO BE

Delivered in the Syracuse University,

DURING THE

WINTER TERM OF 1874-5.

BY

ALEXANDER WINCHELL, LL. D.,
PROFESSOR OF GEOLOGY, ZOÖLOGY AND BOTANY.

SYRACUSE:
THOS. W. DURSTON & CO., PUBLISHERS.
TRUAIR, SMITH & CO., PRINTERS.
1875.

The lectures here outlined are designed to be addressed to a class of students who have already devoted a term to the study of Dana's Manual of Geology. As they have thus dealt systematically with the details of the subject, these lectures, it is hoped, will suffice for a panoramic review of leading facts and conclusions. The presentation of themes under different aspects and combinations will have a tendency, also, to fix the most important ideas in the memory.

A. W.

SYRACUSE, January 1st, 1875.

SYLLABUS.

I. RECORDS OF PAST CONDITIONS OF THE EARTH.

We witness changes transpiring and results accomplished.

1. Traces of the former action of the Sea.

1. Fossil shells far from the sea and at great altitudes.
   (1.) Ancient opinions concerning them—"Freaks of Nature"—Plastic Power"—"Experimental Moulds"—"Fortuitous concourse of atoms"—The Mosaic Deluge.
   (2.) They are genuine *debris*—Illustration from remains of shore shells or of human art.
2. Sea-beaches far inland—Valley of St. Lawrence.
3. Changes of sea-level actually observed.
   (1.) Temple of Jupiter Serapis.
   (2.) Old Roman roads, etc.
   (3.) Oscillations observed in America—Subsidence at St. Augustine—Elevations in Pamlico Sound—Subsidence on the coast of N. J.—In Nantucket Harbor—Elevations along the New England Coast—Rotation of Grand Manan—Rotation of Nova Scotia—Submergence of site of Louisburg, (Cape Breton.)
   (4.) Sea-wave on coast of Chili and Peru in 1823—The Earthquake of Arica in 1868.
   (5.) Actual emergencies of new islands—In the Ægean—The Symplegades—The Aleutians.
   (6.) Effect of a moderate depression of Illinois.

2. Traces of the former action of Heat.

1. Baked sandstones, limestones and shales.
2. Refrigerated molten rocks—Traps, porphyries and lavas.
3. Some traces of fire older than those of water.

3. Unextinguished Fires—Volcanoes, Hot Springs—Deep Mines and Tunnels—Artesian borings.

4. Foundation Stones of the Land—Granites, gneisses and other rocks bearing marks of fire.

5. Records of Extinct Populations.

Conclusion: The earth has been the theatre of a long history, in which fire and water and animal life have each in turn, or simultaneously, enacted conspicuous parts. These forces being still active before our eyes, furnish us the means of unraveling, to some extent, the records of the remote past. And since the forces of nature must be assumed to have acted as at present at a time even earlier than the epoch of our remotest geological records, we shall be justified even on geological grounds, in deducing a history more remote than the origin of any character borne by the solid rocks.

II. NEBULAR THEORY OF WORLD-GENESIS.

1. Signs of former igneous fluidity of the earth.

1. Traces of extinguished fires upon the earth's surface.
2. Unextinguished fires within the earth.
3. Heat actually escaping from the earth.
4. Opinions on the condition of the earth's interior.
   - (1.) The solid portion but a thin crust.
   - (2.) Solidification began at the centre. Rigidity required (Sir William Thompson.) Enormous central compression (Prof. W. Hopkins) A plastic zone underneath a surface crust, (T. S. Hunt.)
   - (3.) No positive evidence of a general molten condition in the past—(Sir David Brewster, Evan Hopkins, Prof. James Hall.)
5. General agreement that the earth was once molten and underwent incrustation.
6. Answers to objections.
   - (1.) All the phenomena which suggested and sustain the doctrine.
   - (2.) Analogies of water, type metal, cold iron floating on molten iron (College Cour., 13th Apr. 1872, p. 173 and testimony of iron masters) solidified lava on molten lava, (Marsh: Man and Nature, p. 545; Kæmtz: Meteorology, p. 152.)
   - (3.) The spheroidal form of the earth.

2. Volatility of all matter.

1. The solid, liquid and gaseous conditions dependent on temperature and pressure.

2. A temperature supposable which would volatilize all mineral substances.
3. If the world has cooled from a molten, why not from a *gaseous* condition.
4. The light of *science* leads us no further back.

3. Physical constitution of the Sun.

1. The photosphere an incandescent vapor.
2. Condition of the body of the sun.
   (1.) By some considered a molten mass.
   (2.) By others, a non-luminous, intensely heated gas.
3. Terrestrial substances detected in the sun.
4. These observations confirmed and extended by what we know of the fixed stars.

5. Testimony of the Nebulæ.

Cosmical matter existing in the form postulated by the nebular theory.—Sir William Herschel—Lord Rosse.

5. Uniform action of physical forces throughout the Solar system.

1. Light permeates all parts and manifests the same phenomena everywhere.
2. Gravitation and inertia everywhere present.
   (1.) Planets all revolve about the sun—Revolve in the same direction—Revolve in elliptical orbits—Revolve in nearly one plane.
   (2.) Planets all rotate on axes—in the same direction.
   (3.) Several have satellites—which all rotate like their primaries.

6. Observed conditions of Planets and Satellites stages in a developmental history.

1. The Moon an ancient cinder—a fossil world.
2. The physical exterior of Mars.
3. The ring-condition perpetuated in Saturn.
4. Low specific gravity of the older planets.

7. Possibly a condition of matter antecedent to the fire-mist.

1. Physical constitution of the fire-mist.
2. Analogical inference of heated, non-luminous, aëriform matter.

8. **Granted the fire-mist and the known laws of matter, the solar system is a physical necessity.** Radiation—Contraction—Rotation—Acceleration—Annulation—Stratification of annuli—Ring-ruptures.

III. IMPLICATIONS OF THE NEBULAR THEORY.

1. **It does not discover the origin of things in the forces of nature.**
   1. Its starting point postulates *matter* and *force* existent.
   2. Reason, meantime, demands the origin of these existences.
   3. She feels constrained to assign self-existent primordial causation.

2. **The theory implies nothing in reference to the nature of force.**

3. **It implies that the history of our system is a history of cooling.**

4. **It implies that all cosmical history is the same.**

5. **Not all worlds habitable**—Suggestions of Whewell—Proctor.
   1. Conditions of the fixed stars.
      (1.) They possess extreme tenuity.
      (2.) Many are changing in brightness—Sirius from red to white.
      (3.) Some have disappeared—The lost Pleiad—Other cases of disappearance.
      (4.) New stars have appeared and disappeared—The new star Hipparchus—Star of Tycho Brahe in 1572—Of Kepler in 1604—Star of 1866.
      (5.) Not known to be centres of planetary systems.
   2. The remoter planets not habitable.
      (1.) Light and heat at Neptune 1-900th what we enjoy—The Sun the size of Jupiter to us.
      (2.) Density of Jupiter ¼th that of the earth—a mere globe of water—But the weight of bodies 2½ times as great.
      (3.) Saturn and his dust-like rings.
   3. The moon in a stage of senescence.
      (1.) No evidence of the presence of water.
      (2.) No indications of an atmosphere.
      (3.) These elements probably absorbed by the rocks—Volume of Moon 1-19th—surface 1-13th that of the Earth ; in cooling through 180° would create cellular space equal to 14½ millions of cubic miles—Frankland: Proc. Roy. Inst., Vol. IV, p. 175 ; Guillemin: The Heavens, p. 143; Meunier: Le Ciel Geologique.

4. Mercury uninhabitable.

6. Some other worlds habitable.

1. What we know of Mars and Venus—Geography, hydrography and climate of Mars.
2. Probably planets of other systems now habitable.
   (1.) No reasons against the supposition.
   (2.) Astronomical analogies favor it—Terrestrial conditions reproduced in other systems.
   (3.) Nature's economy of habitable conditions.

IV. PRIMORDIAL HISTORY OF THE EARTH.

1. Passage from the condition of fire-mist to the liquid state—Rain of molten matter—Growth of the germinal core—An incandescent liquid globe and a fervid atmosphere. —Struggling sunbeams—Rolling tides of lava – Central solidification.

2. Freezing of molten seas.

1. The first crust—Its composition—Its incessant ruptures and recementation—A lava-floe—Continuity established.
2. Crash of the crust, its cause and consequences.

3. Appearance of water.

1. Where had been the ocean?
2. Gathering clouds—Thickening darkness—Descending rains —Electrical disturbances—The war of fire and water.

4. The ascendancy of the waters.

1. A universal ocean—Acid rains—Attacks upon the rocks—The war of chemical affinities—Beginning of sedimentation —Chemical and mechanical deposits.
2. Collapse of the ocean's floor.

5. Germs of continents.

1. Wasted vestiges preserved to human times—Venerable domes.
2. Eroded by the elements above—Wasted by fire beneath—Ascent of isogeothermal planes—Where are the vestiges of the primitive igneous crust?

V. METHOD OF CONTINENTAL DEVELOPMENT.

1. Primordial wrinkles the germs of land-masses—
   Cause of wrinkles—Their location.

2. The Archæan germ of the North American continent.

3. The continent of Palæozoic Time.
   1. Laurentian land.
   2. Appalachian and Sierra Nevada germs.

4. The continent of Mesozoic Time.
   1. The eastern and western areas.
   2. The mediterranean channel between.
   3. Europe mostly submerged.
   4. South America still more extensively submerged.

5. The continent of Cænozoic Time.
   1. The twin areas connected.
   2. The mediterranean seas of America.
   3. The mediterranean seas of Europe.
   4. The condition of South America.

6. Unity of method in continental growth.
   1. Ultimate forms foreshadowed from the beginning—Two great water-sheds, each with two branches—The northern branches diverge, the southern converge.
   2. To what extent have continents and oceans exchanged places?
      The old idea of general exchanges.
      The later idea of no exchanges.
      The truth lies between.

7. The method of sedimentation.
   1. Constitution of a natural assemblage of strata—Conglomerate, sandstone, shale, limestone, shale.
   2. This circle corresponds to a cycle of geologic time.
   3. It seems to divide geological history into chapters and sections.
   4. Contrast between littoral and deep-sea sediments—Changes in American rocks in passing west and south-west—Less fragmental and more magnesian.

VI. THE DAWN OF LIFE.

1. A hypothetical protophytic period.

1. Mutual dependence of the kingdoms of life.
2. The vegetable the necessary forerunner of the animal.

2. The pile of Archæan strata.

1. Their position beneath all the other strata.
2. Non-discovery of the original igneous crust.
3. Enormous observed thickness of the Archæan Great System—Laurentian and Huronian.
4. Areas of exposure—Dips—Denudation.
5. Lithological characters.
6. Richness in mineral deposits.

3. Remains supposed organic in these strata.

1. Long regarded *azoic*.
2. Suspicions based on iron-ores and graphites (May, 1858)—Deductive discoveries, like that of Le Verrier—Organisms in the Laurentian (Oct., 1858).
3. *Eozoon Canadense* as we find it—Description and illustrations.
4. Its zoölogical affinities—*Amœba* and *Actinophrys*—Foraminifera in all ages—Their work in building up the continents—Nummulites and their structure—Their work in the Pyramids—*Orbitoides* in America.
5. Organic nature of *Eozoon* questioned—King and Rowney—Burbank and Perry—Carter—Confidence of Dawson, Carpenter and others.

4. Conditions of land and water when Eozoön appeared.

5. A long pause through the Huronian Period—Probable future discoveries—Supposed foreign equivalents.

6. The advent of Silurian life.

7. The method of geological classification.

In reference to Time.	In reference to Sediments.	Examples.
TIMES.	GREAT SYSTEMS....	Archæan, Palæozoic, Mesozoic, Cænozoic.
AGES.	SYSTEMS.............	Azoic, Eozoic, Silurian, Devonian, Carboniferous, etc.
Periods.	Groups...........	Primordial, Canadian, Trenton, Niagara, Salina, etc.
Epochs.	Stages..........	Acadian, Potsdam, Calciferous, Quebec, Chazy, etc.

Grounds of division and sub-division of geologic time.

VII. THE REIGN OF TRILOBITES, OR THE LOWER SILURIAN AGE.

1. **The Silurian beach**—Its fucoidal imprints—Its sands and ripple marks—A shallow sea with a sinking bottom.

2. **A busy population**—Sudden exuberance of life.
   1. The type of Trilobites, with illustrations—General structure, rank and affinities—Their antecedence of Molluscs and other lower types—Subsequent degradation.
   2. The type of Chambered shells with illustrations—General structure, rank and affinities—Permutations of septum, siphon and mode of enrollment—Glimpse of the later history of the type.
   3. The type of Crinoids with illustrations—General structure, rank and affinities—Misplaced, on the theory of genetic development—Expansion and decline of the type.
   4. Corals and Graptolites.
   5. *Lingulella* and its relations—Persistence of type illustrated—*Discina.*

3. **Chapters of Lower Silurian history**—Primordial Canadian and Trenton Periods—Grounds of division and sub-division.

4. **Where the relics of Lower Silurian life are exposed to view.**
   1. General geological section exemplifying outcrops, dips, etc
   2. Geological maps.
   3. Lower Silurian exposures.

(1.) St. Johns, N. B.; Georgia, Vt.; Braintree, Mass.; Minn. and Wis.; Black Hills, Dak.
(2.) Cincinnati; Richmond, Ind.; Lexington and Frankfort, Ky.
(3.) Nashville, Tenn.
(4.) St. Joseph's Island; Big Bay de Noquet, etc.
(5.) St. Anthony's Falls.
(6.) Trenton Falls; Watertown, N. Y., etc.

5. **Events which terminated the Lower Silurian Age**— Uplift of the Green Mountains—The Cincinnati Axis.

VIII. THE REIGN OF MOLLUSCS, OR THE UPPER SILURIAN AGE.

1. **How each act of the drama was closed**—Premonitory tremblings—A collapse, a crash, an upthrow of the ocean's bottom, an obliteration of life, a new belt of land—The work probably very gradual.

2. **Where were the lands of later Silurian Time?**—The desolate and wasting continent—The winding shore—The eroding waves—The teeming sea.

3. **Organization in later Silurian Time.**
   1. The perpetuated Trilobites, Orthoceratites and Crinoids—Specimens.
   2. The type of Polyps or true coral animals.
      (1.) Their organization and biology—Illustrations.
      (2.) Coral structures—Illustrations.
      (3.) Upper Silurian corals.
   3. Other coral secreting animals.

4. **The great limestone mass of this Age.**
   1. The system of limestone culminations in each geologic interval.
   2. The Upper Silurian mass—Western New York; Drummond's Island; Little Bay de Noquet; Chicago; Southern Ohio and Indiana.
   3. Noteworthy erosions—Niagara river; the Northern Lakes.

5. **The chapters of Upper Silurian history**—Niagara, Salina and Lower Helderberg—Economical products of each group.

6. **Geological position of Syracuse.**

IX. REIGN OF POLYPS, OR THE DEVONIAN AGE.

1. **A culmination of polyp life**—Coral reefs—Favositidæ—Cyathophyllidæ.

2. **Trilobites and Orthoceratites declining**—*Cyrtoceras—Lituites—Gomphoceras—Clymenia*—Advent of Insects and Land Plants.

3. **The advent of vertebrate life.**
   1. Organization hitherto invertebrate.
   2. The law of progress.
   3. Realization of a new fundamental conception—Destined to a wonderful expansion.
   4. Fishes of the Old Red Sandstone.
   5. Devonian fishes of Ohio and Canada—Their bulk, organization and defences.

4. **Growing continents and meagre forest coverings**—Glimpses of the coming Age—Relics of Devonian forest vegetation in New York, Ohio and Canada.

5. **Where the cemeteries of Devonian populations have been opened.**
   1. The Devonian belt of outcrops—The great limestone mass—Groups of strata—The Corniferous the culmination of the Age—The cycle of deposition well illustrated in the Devonian.
   2. Localities:—Falls of the Ohio; Columbus and Delaware, O.; Mackinac, Little Traverse Bay, and Thunder Bay, Mich.; London, Ont.; Eighteen Mile Creek, etc., N. Y.—Later Devonian along the southern part of the State of New York.

X. THE REIGN OF FISHES, OR THE CARBONIFEROUS AGE.

1. **The Marshall Period.**
   1. The rocks—Ranging with location, from olive sandstones to arenaceous and argillaceous limestones—Localities.

2. Fossils—Their abundance—Great development of Lamellibranchs and corresponding diminution of Brachiopods—Advent of Carboniferous types.
3. Questions as to parallelism—Sketch of the history of opinion—Nomenclature and equivalencies in America—Comparison with upper member of Old Red Sandstone.

2. The Carboniferous Limestone Period.

1. A season of deep and quiet waters in the west—Limestone mass—The eastern equivalents.
2. Crinoidal life at its culmination—Abundant remains in the Mississippi Valley; Burlington, Iowa; Chester, Ill.; Crawfordsville, Ind.
3. Other forms of life—Nautili—Goniatites, their structure and affinities—Fishes.
4. Oscillations of level—Successive epochs of deposition.

3. The Coal Period—Its characteristic, the development of terrestrial vegetation—The false coal measures, the conglomerate or millstone grit, the coal measures—The last replaced by limestones in the far west—Progressive change of relative sea-level implied by the wide distribution of the Conglomerate—Coal fields.

4. The Permian Period—An appendix to the coal measures—Rocks, fossils and localities.

XI. COAL MAKING.

1. Great phytogenic periods of the world's history.

1. Præzoic—Only deductively known.
2. Laurentian—Graphite in Siberia, Greenland, Canada, United States, Bavaria, Norway, Sweden.
3. Coal measures of Carboniferous time.
4. Jurassic—Richmond, Va.; China; England; Lota on south-west coast of South America.
5. Eocene—Rocky Mountains etc.; Winnipeg; Vancouver.
6. Modern—Peat-beds of Ireland, Denmark, Bavaria, the United States and elsewhere.
7. Deposits of bituminous and coaly shales.

2. The Coal Period of Carboniferous Time.

1. First in prominence and importance.
2. Three ends to be accomplished.
   (1.) To purify the air for further organic progress—The existence of method and purpose assumed as demonstrated.
   (2.) To preserve the carbon for the coming man.
   (3.) To accomplish all things under the established method of world-building.
3. Purification of the air—The poison neither annihilated nor fixed in mineral combinations—The agency of vegetation—The demand for respirable air coincident with the first time when the conditions of the land permitted the adequate development of the purifier.
4. Preservation of the Carbon—Tendency of vegetation to decomposition—Organic substances preserved only in wet accumulations—This need concurrent with the only epoch when the oscillations were sufficiently frequent.
5. Application of the historical methods to these ends.
   (1.) Oscillations of the level of the land—Foreshadowed in the False Coal Measure and Conglomerate epochs.
   (2.) Special history of this period—Oscillations—Alternate sea-bottom and verdant marsh—Number of submergences.
   (3.) The other ends demanded at the only time when the tension of the terrestrial crust could generate the requisite oscillations.
   (4.) Grand closing events—Uplift of Appalachians—Great enlargement of limits on the eastern wing of the continent—Advent of the middle ages of the world's history.

XII. RETROSPECT OF COAL-MEASURE TIMES.

1. Picture of a Coal-Measure landscape.

1. The thick, dank forest—Tree-ferns and dripping fronds—A thick jungle—Prostrate trunks and decaying stumps—Land-snails, myriapods, insects.
2. A stagnant bayou—*Archegosaurus*—*Amphibamus* and its vocal utterances—*Eosaurus* dwelling in the waters—Dragon-flies dropping their eggs—Fishes.
3. A stormy beach and a sheltered lagoon—Origin of cannel coal.

2. A change of scene—Lowering skies—Heaving sea-bottoms—Invading waves—Another submergence.

3. Results seen in modern coal beds.

1. A stony herbarium—Fairy tracery—Delicacy and perfection of features.
2. What have we represented in this coal?

   The very tissue, and cell, and pith, and root, and leaf and frond.

   The very carbon which poisoned the atmosphere æons ago.

   The very sunlight which fell upon the forest, treasured up to be disengaged again in our winter fires—Solar energy transformed and locked up to be set loose in countless steam engines of the human age.

4. Varieties of Coal and Carbonaceous deposits.

1. Caused by pressure, heat, impurities, redeposition and chemical changes.
2. A graduated series of products—The older generally most altered.

   (1.) *Peat* of the recent epoch, mostly in northern temperate countries.
   (2.) *Brown coal*, chiefly Cenozoic, in Germany, the United States, etc.
   (3.) *Bituminous coal*, Mesozoic and a portion of the Carboniferous.
   (4.) *Cannel coal*, chiefly Carboniferous—Produced by littoral attrition and redeposition.
   (5.) *Anthracite*, chiefly Carboniferous, but in limited quantities in older and newer formations—Cause of anthracitization.
   (6.) *Plumbago*, in most altered Carboniferous (Rhode Island), and in Silurian and Archæan formations.

XIII. VEGETATION OF THE COAL MEASURES.

1. Its modern alliances.

Classification of Plants, (coal-measure types in *italics*.)

PHÆNOGAMS.

ANGIOSPERMS.

Exogens, (Ordinary, trees, shrubs and herbs.)

Endogens, (Palmaceæ, Cyperaceæ, Gramineæ, etc.)

GYMNOSPERMS.

Conifers, (Pines, Cypresses, Yews, *Dadoxylon* including *Sternbergia*, *Trigonocarpum*.

Cycads.

CRYPTOGAMS.

ACROGENS.

Equisetaceæ.

Equisetids, Calamitids, Asterophyllids.

Filices.

Lycopodiaceæ.

Lycopodids.

Cyclostigmids, (*Cylostigma, Knorria.*)

Sigillarids, (*Poacites, Cyperites, Sternbergia.*)

Lepidodendrids, (*Lepidodendron* + *Sigillaria, Halonia.*)

Hydropterids.

ANOGENS, (Musci, Hepaticæ.)

THALLOGENS.

Lichens.

Fungi.

Algæ, (Confervæ, *Fucoids, Protophytes.*)

XIV. THE REIGN OF REPTILES, OR MESOZOIC TIME.

1. **The continent as shaped by the events which closed Palæozoic Time**—Its outlines—Drainage—Forests—Gulf of Mexico—Emerging western limb of the continent—Communication between the Caribbean sea and the Arctic ocean—Gulf of St. Lawrence—Lake Superior and its outlet—Niagara Falls in the olden time—Hudson river and its outlet—European Mesozoic geography.

2. **The marine populations of Mesozoic Time.**
   1. Where their remains have been exhumed—Atlantic and Gulf border—"Marl beds" of New Jersey; Prairie Bluff and Choctaw Bluff, Ala.; Western territories; California.
   2. Structure and affinities of Ammonites—Belemnites.
   3. First appearance of Osseous Fishes.

3. **The air-breathing denizens of the land and waters.**
   1. Enaliosaurs—Mosasaurs—Crocodiles—Pterosaurs—Deinosaurs—Turtles.

2. Scenes on the banks of the future Delaware.
3. Scenes in the future valley of the Connecticut—Bipedal reptiles.
4. Advent of birds—Birds with vertebrated tails—Birds with bi-concave vertebræ and sharp teeth.
5. Advent of mammals.

4. **Triassic, Jurassic and Cretaceous Periods**—Less distinguishable in America than in Europe.
5. **Disturbances**—Trias and eruptions of trap—Jurassic closed by uplift of mountains—Sierra Nevada, Wahsatch and Uintah ranges—Humboldt ranges—Cretaceous closed by northern elevations and consequent increased cold and extensive exterminations of species.

XV. THE REIGN OF QUADRUPEDS, OR THE TERTIARY AGE.

1. **The continent during the Tertiary Age**—Its approximate completeness—Intracontinental seas—Arboreal vegetation and its modern aspects.
2. **Marine animals and their approximation to modern types**—*Zeuglodon.*
3. **Decadence of the reptilian dynasty.**
4. **Rise of mammilian rule**—Mastodon, Elephant, Megalonyx, Titanotherium, Brontotherium, Dinoceras, Uintatherium, Tapir, Horses, Zeuglodon—Their possession of the continent.
5. **The cemeteries of the animals**—Why their remains are not generally distributed—The areas called Bad Lands in the west—A picture of desolation—An ancient sea freshening to a lake—The lake gradually filled with sediment—Life upon its borders—Inhumation of skeletons—Erosions of later times.
6. **The Paris basin a similar deposit**—What Cuvier dug from it—Reminiscence of the Buttes Chaumont.
7. **Himalayan deposits**—The monarch of proboscidians—*Sivatherium*—*Colossochelys.*

8. A glimmering from the future.

9. Disturbances of the Tertiary Age—Coast range in California—Rocky mountains—Pyrenees, Appenines, Carpathians, Alps.

XVI. THE REIGN OF ICE.

1. Familiar "Drift" phenomena.

1. Smoothed, striated and furrowed rocks.
2. Boulders—Drift copper and lead and iron ores.
3. Sands, clays—Old river channels—Fiords. All these phenomena connected together.

2. Sketch of continent at end of Tertiary Time—Its likeness to the modern continent in outlines, in drainage features, in forest growths. But it was comparatively worn out.

3. Wastage of continental areas—General doctrine.

4. How the preglacial continent was renovated.

1. A revulsion in nature—Northern upheaval and increasing cold—Union of lands now separated.
2. Glacier growth, movement and effects.
   (1.) Reminiscence of Alpine glaciers.
   (2.) Tremendous effects of a continental glacier—Prostration of forests—Plowing of the rocks—Digging of lake basins—Filling of river-channels and lake-outlets—Desolation in nature.
3. Extent of the ancient glaciers.
4. A gradual subsidence—Dissolution of the glaciers—Work of the torrents—The freight of sediments—Renovation of southern areas.
5. A continental submergence generally supposed.
6. A slow emergence and assorting of the materials—The assortment possibly the work of glacier-torrents without submergence.

5. Advent of man during the decline of the glaciers—Stumps of the old glaciers still in existence in the Sierra Nevadas in California and Oregon; in ice wells; in arctic and in high mountain-regions.

XVII. ICE PERIODS AND THEIR CAUSES.

1. Facts.

1. Phenomena which indicate the agency of ice—Smoothed rock-surfaces; striæ; transported fragments, etc.
2. Glaciers and their movements.
3. Icebergs—Their origin and action.
4. Glaciated condition of the southern hemisphere.
5. Ancient glacial phenomena of the northern hemisphere.
6. Supposed glacial phenomena of still older date.
7. Origin of the great New England glacier (Dana).

2. Theories.

1. Supposition that the poles and equator have changed places.
   (1.) Conflicts with the mechanical theory of terrestrial motions (Laplace).
   (2.) Also with the evidence that the oceans and continents have not been generally transposed.
2. Supposition that cold regions of space have been passed through by the earth (Agassiz) or that the sun has experienced a diminution of heat.
   Objection: This would imply simultaneous and equal lowering of temperature over all parts of the earth's surface.
3. Theory of northern elevation.
   (1.) Intended especially for the last ice-period.
   (2.) Evidences of northern uplift in America.
   (3.) But this elevation was itself an effect of the real cause—Was it merely an incident of internal cooling ?—Or was the real cause one or more of the following ?
4. Effect of change in eccentricity of the earth's orbit.
   For northern latitudes:
   Increased eccentricity increases glaciation.
   Diminished eccentricity diminishes glaciation.
5. Effect of change in obliquity of the Ecliptic.
   Increased obliquity diminishes glaciation.
   Diminished obliquity increases glaciation.
6. Effect of change in position of the Apsides.
   Winter solstice in perihelion diminishes glaciation.
   Summer solstice in perihelion increases glaciation.

3. Probability of coincidence of astronomical causes —Intervals.

4. The two polar regions glaciated alternately—Relative subsidence a consequence of glaciation.

XVIII. POST-GLACIAL HISTORY.

1. Restoration of the preglacial Flora—Was it reproduced from buried germs ?—Prolonged vitality of seeds.

2. Early condition of the Great Lakes.

1. As to altidude—Terraces—Rock erosions.
2. As to geographical extent—Outlets by Little Bay de Noquet; by the Illinois river; by the valley of the Maumeè—A channel across the lower peninsula of Michigan.

3. Subsidence of Lakes.

1. Removal of barriers—Desiccation.
2. Sites of ancient lakes.

4. Treelessness of Prairie regions.

1. The fact.
2. Certain uplands treeless from lack of moisture.
3. Some regions treeless from excess of alkali.
4. Treelessness of Illinois prairies.
   (1.) Not caused by excessive fineness of the soil; nor excessive dryness; nor excess of moisture—Trees capable of flourishing.
   (2.) Supposed explanation.
   Recession of lake waters—Uncovering of lake slime—Somnolence of buried germs—An herbless waste—Gradual encroachment of herbaceous vegetation—The shyness of the forest—Prairie fires—Arrest of the burnings.

5. Lakelets—Origin—Filling—Marl and peat.

6. These processes still going forward—Filling lakelets—Change of river beds—The Mississippi and Missouri—The great rivers of China—Deepening of river-gorges—Dissolving of sea-coasts—Travels of the sands—Sandy deserts and dunes—Clearing of forests and changes of climate—Retreating glaciers—Disappearance of species.

XIX. METHOD IN THE HISTORY OF LIFE.

1. The idea of Progress.

1. Retrospect of organic succession.
2. The progress real.
3. Expansion of types mostly upward, but partly downward.

2. The idea of Archetypes.

1. Five fundamental plans of organic structure.
   (1.) In the existing world.
   (2.) In the world of extinct life.
2. The Vertebrate Archetype in its unfolding.
   (1.) Structure of the Vertebrate Archetype.
   (2.) Homologies of parts--Limbs--Jaws, &c.
   (3.) Persistence of the Archetype.

3. Dominant Ideas.

1. They are culminating points—Rhizopods—Nautiloids—Crinoids—Acrogens-- Ammonites--Reptiles -- Mammals. Also *Orthis, Spirifera, Atrypa, Goniatites, Terebratula, &c.*
2. Retrospective and prophetic types (Penumbral types).
   (1.) Sauroid fishes prophetic of reptiles.
   (2.) Labyrinthodonts and amphicœlian reptiles retrospective toward fishes.
   (3.) Mesozoic reptiles prophetic (*a*) of birds, (*b*) of mammals.
   (4.) Birds with teeth and vertebrated tails retrospective toward reptiles.
   (5) All vertebrates prophetic of man.

4. Representatives of all prominent types still existent—Lingulidæ, Nautilidæ, Crinoids, Terebratulidæ, Gar Pikes, Alligators, Sturgeons, Cycads, Tree Ferns, Salisburia etc. and all the higher types of animals and plants.

5. The method an evolution of the idea expressed in the succession of structures—But no genealogical relationship of separate species is yet proven.

6. The human type the final culmination of the organic series.

XX. MAN IN THE LIGHT OF GEOLOGY.

1. The prophecies of the Ages.

1. Progressive improvement of organic types.
2. Prophecy of the earliest vertebrate--man in potentiality.
3. Progressive modification of limbs.

4. Promise of an intelligent being in geological adaptations having relations only to man—Coal—Metals—Wells and springs.

2. Man's birth-place foreshadowed.

1. Continental faunal characteristics.
2. These established before the advent of man.
3. The pinnacle of organization fixed in the orient.

3. Man the culmination of the organic series.

1. The erect attitude attained—progressive elevation of the longitudinal axis in older vertebrates.
2. Man a cosmopolite in opposition to the law of increasing restriction of geographical range.
3. Vast interval from brutal to human intelligence and religious capacity.
4. Nature, in man, seems to have reached a period.
5. Spiritual progress still possible and actual—Suggestion as to the balance between spiritual and corporeal vigor.

4. Man's advent has been since the last great geological revolution—Extinctions since his advent.

5. Relics of primeval man.

6. Primitive condition of man.

In possession of all the powers of modern man, but uneducated—Without the accumulated results of experience, observation and reflection.

7. Man's genealogy.

1. Mankind seems to be a family of several species—But of "one blood"—Of one moral nature.
2. These species distinct as far back as evidence leads—But possibly convergent—Only analogical evidence of the derivation of a human type (even corporeally considered) from any stock in the realm of brute animals—Yet this is not evidence as long as the analogy fails at the critical point, *a demonstrated transition from one species to another.*

XXI. RELICS OF PRIMEVAL MAN.

1. **Cavern remains in England, Belgium, France, Spain, Italy, the Caucasus and United States.**
   1. Animal remains associated with human.
   2. Human remains--Bones, implements, ashes.
2. **Relics in fluviatile deposits**—The Somme—The Seine—The Tiniere—The Nile—The Mississippi.
3. **Kitchen-refuse heaps.**
   1. Nature of the accumulations.
   2. In Denmark--Sweden--Florida--Alabama--Maine--Massachusetts.
4. **Pile-habitations.**
   1. What they are. 2. What comes from them.
5. **Tumuli, Cistvaens, Crainnoges, Dolmens and Cromlechs.**
6. **Mining and Mound relics in America.**
7. **The three or more Ages of national life.**
   1. Stone Age (Palæolithic, Reindeer and Neolithic epochs)—Bronze Age—Iron Age.
   2. Cannot be used for chronometric purposes.
      (1.) Actual progress depends on many accidents.
      (2.) Stone ages of different peoples not coincident—Nor of equal duration.
8. **Man in the Stone Age of Europe**—His contemporaries—His pursuits—His arts—His ornaments—His tastes—His religion.
9. **Primeval man endowed with a full-orbed manhood.**

XXII. THE ANTIQUITY OF THE HUMAN SPECIES.

1. **The problem is to determine (*a*) the relative and (*b*) the absolute age of the formations with which human relics are associated.**
   1. The relics may have been transferred from a formation of one age to one of another age.

(1.) By the agency of streams or waves.
(2.) By the agency of wild beasts.
(3. By human agency.

2. The relative age of the deposits is often obscure—River deposits—Cavern deposits.
3. The absolute age the most difficult part of the problem.

2. Grounds on which the opinion of a high antiquity have been rested.

1. Contemporaneousness of man with animals now extinct.
2. His presence before the conclusion of the reign of ice.
3. The belief that certain human relics are even preglacial.

3. Examination of these grounds.

1. Extinctions of species not necessarily remote.
   (1.) Some have occurred in times within the scope of history or tradition.
      (*a.*) New Zealand birds--Moa, Palapteryx and Notornis.
      (*b.*) Madagascar birds—Dodo, Solitaire, Æpyornis.
      (*c.*) Mammals--Urus--An Arctic Manatee.
   (2.) Some species visibly approaching extinction--Great Auk (thought to be already extinct), Aurochs, Sequoia--In short all species limited to regions which civilized occupation is destined to overspread.
   (3.) Some unhistoric extinctions apparently recent.
      (*a.*) Mastodons in Michigan beneath two or three feet of peat--Arrow-heads beneath seven feet--Missouri mastodon—The Irish Elk.
      (*b.*) Indian traditions of the mastodon and elephant.
2. Great geological changes do not alway imply vast periods of time.
   (1.) Changes within the scope of history or tradition.
      (*a.*) Assyrian, Persian, Indian and Jewish traditions of deluges.
      (*b.*) Deluges of Ogyges and Deucalion.
      (*c.*) The Symplegades—Drainage of the Scythian plains—The ancient Lectonia.
      (*d.*) Revolutions in the hydrographical features of China.
      (*e.*) Changes of climate in Ireland, Greenland, Germany, Egypt.
   (2.) Changes progressing whose rate may be gagued.
      (*a.*) Recession of glaciers—Mer de Glace—Glacier des Bossons, etc—Tyrolese Alps—All existing glaciers the stumps of the ancient ones.
      (*b.*) River deposits — Humphreys and Abbot on the Mississippi delta—De Lanoye on the Nile—Andrews on the cone of the Tiniere.
      (*c.*) River erosions—Niagara—Calculations.
      (*d.*) Filling and drainage of lakes—St. Clair and smaller lakes—The prairies an ancient lake-bottom—Drainage of an ancient St. Croix lake—Bergsträsser on the former union of the Caspian and Black seas.

(*e*.) Changes in rocky masses—Lowering of the Andes, Green Mountains and Coast ranges of California—Flutings by dripping water in Mammoth cave—Fossils projecting half an inch on the dome of St. Paul's.

(*f*.) Transformations of forests in Denmark, England and America.

(3.) Calculations of Adhémar on the recurrence of geologic winters—But calculations based on secular changes in eccentricity of earth's orbit exceed this result.

3. The pre-glacial age of human remains not admitted by geologists.

4. The numerical results indicated vary over wide limits.

1. A general judgment based on the rate of geological change would assign 8,000 to 50,000 years.
2. The erosions of the Niagara gorge put the Champlain epoch back 30,000 to 380,000 years.
3. The rate of coral-growths indicates 384,000 years for the age of certain reefs.
4. The age of the Mississippi Delta is placed by Humphreys and Abbot at 5,000 years.
5. The age of the Nile Delta, by de Lanoye, at 6,350 years.
6. Calculations based on movement of apsides give 21,000 years between two epochs of glaciation.
7. Those based on changes of eccentricity give about 100,000 years.

XXIII. THE OLD AGE OF CONTINENTS.

1. The mass of the sedimentary rocks a measure of past denundations.

1. Origin of marine sediments.
2. Nearly all the known rocks of sedimentary origin—Where the lands which were worn down to supply the material?
3. Their direction indicated by the gradations in the coarseness of the sediments.
4. Appalachian materials and their north-eastern origin.

2. A wasted continent older than the Archæan strata.

1. Archæan sediments manifest shore-erosions.
2. Where did those shores lie?
3. Obliterated continental areas.

(1.) North-eastward extension of American continent—The "Telegraphic Plateau"—The British archipelago answering to one on the American side.
(2.) An old West Indian continent—Now represented by the islands of the Caribbean and some adjacent portions of South America.
(3.) A wasted Mascarene continent south-east of Africa—Relics seen in Mauritius, Rodriguez, Bourbon and adjacent islands.
(4.) North-westward extension of America and connection with Asia.
(5.) These areas may have been chiefly wasted since Archæan Time.

3. **Lowering and retrenchment of the Archæan continent.**
   1. The volume of Palæozoic sediments.
   2. All abstracted from the older lands—The limestones partly chemical precipitates.

4. **Wastage of the Palæozoic continent** (in Mesozoic Time and later.)
   1. Ancient height of the Appalachians.
   2. Vast areas of coal measures swept away.
   3. Disemboweling of Tennessee.
   4. The materials gone to build the Atlantic and Gulf states.
   5. Erosions of the Niagara, Ohio, Kentucky, Cumberland, Columbia and other rivers.

5. **Wastage of Mesozoic continent** (in Cenozoic Time.)
   1. Scoring of the great central plateau of the continent—Once the garden of North America—Cañons of the Colorado.
   2. The gold-bearing gulches of California.
   3. Immense denudation in the valley of the Amazons—In Texas and Mexico.
   4. The mission of the continental glaciers—Scars concealed by its *debris*—Regions unvisited by the renovating action of these glaciers—These show the accumulated wastage of all ages since their uplift from the sea—The Great American Desert.

6. **Wastage of the actual continent**—Streams deepening their channels—Surfaces washed away—Hills lowering—Lakes filling—Marshes drying and evaporation diminishing.

7. **Each great life-period has had a fresh continent for its uses**—Faunas have disappeared with the wastage of their homes—Intimations of the limitation of the existing fauna.

XXIV. A GRASP OF GEOLOGIC TIME.

A reminiscence of the moraine-covered area at the foot of glacier des Bois and the reflections which it suggested.

1. **Oppressiveness of geological æons**--Prevalent impression that all geological intervals are vast--We seek a comprehensible unit of measure.

2. **Sir William Thompson's calculations**--Not over one hundred millions of years since the beginning of animalization.

3. **Dana's time-ratios**--Palæozoic, Mesozoic and Cenozoic time as 12 : 3 : 1--We estimate Archæan strata at 12 on this scale--Hence duration of animal life assumed at 84 millions of years, would give (dating it from beginning of Archæan) Archæan time 36 millions; Palæozoic, 36 millions; Mesozoic, 12 millions and Cenozoic 3 millions--Putting Quaternary at one-half of Cenozoic, and the Recent Period at one-half of Quaternary, the latter becomes 750,000 years, a result many times as great as that obtained from other methods of computation. (See Lecture XXII)--These intervals perfectly incomprehensible.

4. **Familiar operations of geologic forces.**
    1. Filling of lakelets--Results in a human lifetime—The period of the recent additions a measure of the whole—This takes the mind back to the Champlain epoch.
    2. Sediments of rivers—The road side torrent--Source of the sediments of the Mississippi—Annual contribution to the delta ascertained--This a unit of measure of the whole work accomplished--Thought rests back again in Champlain time.
    3. Diminution of the glaciers--Rates ascertained--Diminution in 20 years a unit of measure for the whole area vacated by the glaciers--We can think the boundaries gradually extended back to their ancient positions—This is the midst of the Glacial epoch.
    4. Species dropping out of existence—Two or three important disappearances in a human life--How long for the fifteen

or twenty since the epoch of the Cave men ?—This again is Champlain time.

5. **Twice the distance of the Champlain epoch may reach the close of Tertiary Time, and so on toward the beginning of that series of events the last terms of which we witness to-day**—Relief of the mind.

XXV. GEOLOGY OF PETROLEUM.

1. **Chemical constitution of crude petroleum**—Series of hydrocarbons—Compounds more and less volatile—Hydrogen and oxygen ratios.
2. **Organic origin of petroleum**—Indication from chemical constitution—Parallel series of compounds producible from organic substances—Association of petroleum with organic *debris*—Vegetable substances the most abundant source.
3. **Its vertical distribution in the rocks.**
4. **Laws of its accumulation.**
   1. A source situated *below* place of accumulation.
      (1.) In every actual instance, we find *a bituminous shale.*
      (2.) Some geologists believe limestones the source of the petroleum.
      (3.) Argillaceous mixtures pre-dispose to liberation of petroleum.
   2. An anticlinal axis to direct the movement of the liberated product.
   3. An impervious overlying stratum to prevent vertical escape.
5. **Inspissation of petroleum** — Asphaltum — Albertite — Grahamite.
6. **Common Fallacies.**
   1. That petroleum comes generally from coal.
   2. That a strong surface "show" is favorable.
   3. That a saturated rock insures a supply.
   4. That geological and hydrostatic principles can be disregarded—Formations explored in vain—Unproductiveness of the Corniferous and Niagara limestones—Surface shows tempting to mislead.

7. **Formations yielding paying quantities**—Cincinnati Group—Hamilton Group—Genesee Shale—Chemung Group —Marshall Group—Carboniferous Limestone—Parma Conglomerate—Coal Measures—Cretaceous and Tertiary rocks.
8. **Phenomena of "oil-wells."**
9. **Exhaustion and recuperation of oil-wells.**

XXVI. GEOLOGY OF SALT AND GYPSUM.

1. **Primordial origin of the saltness of the sea**—Early chemical reactions—Why we associate salt and gypsum.
2. **Origin of salt lakes**—Conditions of their perpetuity—Reduction of volume of Great Salt Lake in past times—History of fresh lakes.
3. **Salt Lakes of former ages**—Storehouses of marine salinity—Salt bearing formations—Rock salt not always present —Order of superposition of products in Salina basin—Order of deposition in the kettles—Origin of gypseous deposits—Not endogenous.
4. **Conditions of brine accumulation.**
   1. A source located *above.*
   2. A dish-shaped conformation—Effects of a persistent dip—Effects of proximity of outcrop to the earth's surface.
5. **The three brine-basins of Michigan**—The Salina Group The Michigan Salt Group—The Coal Measures.
6. **The brine-basin of New York**—Its general conformation —The Onondaga marshes.

XXVII. INHERENT LIMITATIONS OF THE EXISTING ORDER.

1. **The meaning of change in the natural world.**
   1. It implies a beginning.
   2. It implies an end.
   3. The idea of endless cycles physically absurd—No perpetual motion—All force seeking a state of equilibrium—No work too vast to be accomplished in finite time.

2. **The ultimate effects of erosive agencies**—Wastage of soils—Sinking of river channels—Aridity of climate—Filling of lakes and bays and the overflow of the ocean.

3. **Progressive terrestial refrigeration**—Alteration of climates—Absorption of the sea and the atmosphere—The moon a type of frozen worlds.

4. **The cooling of the sun**—Vast emission of heat—No discovered source of adequate supply—Refrigeration inevitable.

5. **A resisting medium in space**—Effect upon comets—Necessary effect upon planetary bodies—Conglomeration of the matter of the Solar System.

6. **No discovered physical cause adequate to disturb this final repose and reorganize the system**—Unscientific assumption of Spencer and his followers—Cycles of matter.

7. **This history a type of the totality of cosmical history**—How insignificant is an individuul in this immensity—How sublime is mind which can grasp the method which governs the evolutions of the universe.

XXVIII. THE LAW OF EVOLUTION.

1. **Definition and illustrations.**

2. **This law rules the physical world**—Allusion to stages of planetary genesis.

3. **The law rules in the organic world.**
   1. Embryonic development.
   2. The geological succession of organic types.
      (1.) The meaning of breaks in the series.
      (2.) The meaning of retrogressions.
      (3.) The meaning of persistence of types.
   3. The succession according to a method of evolution.

4. **The cause of evolution.**
   1. The proximate causes.
      (1.) In the physical world, physical forces.
      (2.) In the organic, physiological forces—But are these also modes of physical force?
      (3.) Theories of the mode of action of these forces.

2. The ultimate cause—This inquiry passes beyond the domain of science—But that is no reason for neglecting to seek the answer—Physical forces not self-existent nor self-acting—Only modes of activity of an ultimate cause—Physiological forces, whether transmutable or not, into physical, are not ultimate causes—Only intelligent will an ultimate cause.

XXIX. TRADITIONAL COSMOGONIES.

1. **Agreement in their general features**—Specifications.
2. **The Mosaic Cosmogony.**
   1. Its supposed conflict with science—Futility of the older attempts to effect a reconciliation.
   2. The Drama of Creation.
      (1.) The rhythmical structure of the narrative—The theme—The method of its evolution—The strophe—A vision of Moses.
      (2.) The exordium or argument, (Gen. I, 1–3,) a brief announcement of the chief facts in the history.
         (*a*.) God the Creator of the substance and forms of the universe.
         (*b*.) Terrestial chaos.
         (*c*.) Darkness on the earth.
         (*d*.) Vivification of the waters.
      (3.) Use of the word *yom*—Does not mean a literal "day."
         (*a*.) For the events did not transpire in six days.
         (*b*.) The scriptural use of the word.
         (*c*.) Opinions of the Fathers and of modern philologists.
   3. The Harmony.

First day (Ver. 3–5) *Creation of Light.*
   The Period of the Firemist.
Second day (Ver. 6–8) *Creation of the Expanse.*
   Descent of rains—Accumulation of sediments.
Third day (Ver. 9–13) *Creation of Dry Land and Plants.*
   Uplift of continents—Marine vegetation (Archæan.)
Fourth day (Ver. 14–19) *Appointment of Sun, Moon and Stars.*
   [*Gnasah* signifies to appoint; as God said, "I do *set* my bow in the cloud." Same word used in same connection, Ps. CIV, 19.] Dispersion of clouds—Appearance of Sun, Moon and Stars—Plant growth.

Fifth day (Ver. 20–23) *Creation of Aquatic Animals and Birds—"Great Monsters."*

Marine animals (Molluscs, *Palæozoic* Fishes, etc.) aquatic Reptiles (*Mesozoic* Enaliosaurs) and *Mesozoic* Birds.

Sixth day (Ver. 24-31) *Creation of Land Animals and, lastly, Man.*

Appearance of *Tertiary* Mammals, followed by Man.

Seventh day (Gen. II, 1–3) *God rested—Sabbath.*

Reign of man—Sabbath of creation.

4. Harmony more complete than could be expected.

(1.) Modern scientific discoveries anticipated—Light before the sun—Plant-life before the sun—Man, the ruler, last instead of first.

(2.) How could a historian, in the infancy of our race, pen an account of creation which should accord with the developments of the science of the following four or five thousand years?

SYLLABUS

OF

COURSES OF LECTURES AND INSTRUCTION

IN

GENERAL GEOLOGY,

WITH

REFERENCES TO SOURCES OF INFORMATION.

BY ALEXANDER WINCHELL, LL. D.,

PROFESSOR OF GEOLOGY AND PALÆONTOLOGY IN THE UNIVERSITY OF MICHIGAN.

ANN ARBOR:

SHEEHAN & COMPANY,

BOOKSELLERS AND PUBLISHERS.

1879.

SYLLABUS

OF

COURSES OF LECTURES AND INSTRUCTION

IN

GENERAL GEOLOGY,

WITH

REFERENCES TO SOURCES OF INFORMATION.

BY ALEXANDER WINCHELL, LL. D.,

PROFESSOR OF GEOLOGY AND PALÆONTOLOGY IN THE UNIVERSITY OF MICHIGAN.

ANN ARBOR:

SHEEHAN & COMPANY,

BOOKSELLERS AND PUBLISHERS,

1879.

The solid Earth whereon we tread
In tracts of fluent heat began,
And grew to seeming random forms,
And seeming prey of cyclic storms,
Till at the last arose the man."

"There rolls the deep where grew the tree.
Oh, Earth, what changes hast thou seen!
There, where the long street roars, hath been
The stillness of the central sea.

"The hills are shadows, and they flow
From form to form, and nothing stands.
They melt like mist—the solid lands
Like clouds they shape themselves and go."

In Memoriam.

Vidi ego quod fuerat quondam solidissima tellus
Esse fretum: vidi factas ex æquore terras
Et procul a pelago conchæ jacuere marinæ.

VID: *Met.*

Ann Arbor Printing and Publishing Company.

PREFACE.

In citing sources of information, the references are generally made first, to two standard text-books, Dana's "Manual of Geology," and Leconte's "Elements of Geology." Following these are frequent citations of other text-books and manuals, and some well-known popular works. Often the references extend to reports of original researches, especially those of American origin. It has been the aim, however, to quote few works not known to be generally accessible to the student. In a few cases, nevertheless, the references will be found sufficiently complete for advanced students. Thus, most of the important original sources are cited under the subjects of *Eozoön*, Fossil vegetation of America, Extinct American Reptiles and Extinct American Mammals.

Methods of minuter research are indicated in the "Supplement," and here are references to more recondite sources of information.

A. W.

UNIVERSITY OF MICHIGAN, October, 1879.

ABBREVIATIONS.

A. A. A. S.=Proceedings of the American Association for the Advancement of Science.

Ag.: *Sk.*=L. Agassiz: Geological Sketches, Boston, 1866.

Am. Jour.=American Journal of Science and Arts, New Haven, IIId Series, unless otherwise noted.

Am. Nat.=American Naturalist, Salem, Mass., now Philadelphia.

Bakewell: *Geol.*=Bakewell: An Introduction to Geology, etc., Am. ed., 8vo., 1839.

Bul. Hayd. Sur.=Bulletin of the U. S. Geological and Geographical Survey.

Bul. Nat. Mus.=Bulletin of the U. S. National Museum.

Can. Nat.=Canadian Naturalist, Montreal.

Cook; *Geol. N. J.*—Cook: Geology of New Jersey, 1868.

Cotta: *Ore Dep.*—Cotta: Treatise on Ore Deposits, New York, 1869.

Cuvier: *Discours.*=Cuvier: Discours sur les revolutions du globe, 1828.

D.=Dana, or Dana: Manual of Geelogy, 2d ed., 1874.

Darwin: *Coral Reefs.*=Charles Darwin: Structure and Distribution of Coral Reefs.

Daws.: *Story.*=Dawson: The Story of the Earth and Man, New York, 1873.

Daws.: *Dawn.*=Dawson: The Dawn of Life, New York.

De la B.: *Obs.*=De la Béche: The Geological Observer, 2d ed., London, 1853.

Fig.: *World.*=Figuier: The World before the Deluge, London ed., 1867.

Fos. & Whit.: *L. Sup.*:=Foster & Whitney: Report on the Geology of the Lake Superior Land District, 1850-1.

Hayd.: *Rep.*=Hayden: U. S. Geological and Geographical Survey of the Territories.

Hayd. *Rep.*=Contributed to Hayden's Report.

Hux.=Huxley: The Anatomy of Vertebrated Animals, Am. ed., 1872.

King: *Rep.*=King: U. S. Geological Exploration of the Fortieth Parallel.

King *Rep.*=Contributed to King's Report.

L.=Leconte: Elements of Geology, New York, 1878.

Log.: *Geol. Can.*=Logan: Geology of Canada, 1863.

Ly.: *Man.*=Lyell: Manual of Elementary Geology, 6th ed., N. Y., 1857.

Ly.: *Prin.*=Lyell: Principles of Geology, 8th ed., 1850.

Newb., *Ives' Rep.*=Newberry in Ives's Report, upon the Colorado River of the West, 1861.

Palæont. Soc.=Transactions of the Palæontographical Society, London.

P. A. N. S.=Proceedings of the Academy of Natural Sciences, Philadelphia.

P. A. P. S.=Proceedings of the American Philosophical Society, Philadelphia.

P. B. S. N. H.=Proceedings of the Boston Society of Natural History.

Pop. Sci. Mon.=Popular Science Monthly, New York.

Pow. *Rep.*=Powell: U. S. Geographical and Geological Survey of the Rocky Mountains.

Pow. *Rep.*=Contributed to Powell's Report.

Q. J. G. S., or Quar. Jour. Geol. Soc.=Quarterly Journal of the Geological Society of London.

Récl.: *Earth*=Réclus: The Earth, etc., Am. ed., 1871.

Reg. Rep.=Appendix to the Report of the Regents of the University of the State of New York on the condition of the State Cabinet of Nat. Hist.

Rep. Coast. Surv.=Report of the United States Coast Survey.

W.=Winchell: Sketches of Creation, New York, 1870.

W.: *Geol. Mich.*=Winchell: First Biennial Report of the Progress of the Geological Survey of Mich., 1861.

W.: *G. T. Reg.*=Winchell: The Grand Traverse Region, 1866.

Wheeler *Rep.*=Contributed to Wheeler's Report, U. S. Geograpical Surveys west of the 100th meridian.

Whit.: *Met. W.*=Whitney: Metallic Wealth of the United States, 1854.

W.: *Mich.*=Winchell: Michigan, being condensed Popular Sketches of the Topography, Climate, and Geology of the State, 1873

Woodw.: *Man. Mol.*=Woodward: Manual of the Mollusca.

SYLLABUS.

PART I.

INDUCTIVE OR POSITIVE GEOLOGY.

I. OUTLOOK OF THE SUBJECT.

1. **Preliminary.**
   1. Distiction between Facts, Doctrines and Speculations.
      (1.) The Facts Demonstrable to the senses of all.
      (2.) Doctrines are accepted Explanations of the Facts.
      (3.) Speculations are explanations still under discussion—Possess various degree of plausibility.
      (3.) Inductive or Positive Geology deals with Facts and Doctrines.

II. Geology is a History. (D. 4.)
   1. History of the Planet (D. 1, 2, 3) — History of its organic occupants. (D. 2, 5.)
   2. Data or Materials of the History are Relics of former conditions of the earth and its occupants. (D. 4–5.)
   3. Mineral masses — Animal remains — Vegetable remains.
   4. Mineralogy and Chemistry — Zoölogy — Botany.
   5. The earth also an Astronomical body.
   6. Its Form, Density and Movements determined by Mechanical principles — And these are Mathematical relations.
   7. Geology the Science to which all other sciences are ancillary.

III. The Starting Point of Investigation.
   1. Phenomena presented by a Drift-covered surface.
   2. Phenomena presented by an outcrop of Stratified rocks,
      (1.) The stratified condition — Sedimentation, Lect. VI.
      (2.) Relics of aquatic creatures — Fossils — Paleontology.
      (3.) Indications of marine origin.
      (4.) Wide existence of such phenomena.

3. The phenomena presented by an outcrop of Unstratified rocks. (D. 107–8, L. 205–11.)
   (1.) Crystalline — Non-fossiliferous.
   (2.) The rocks traceable to a fissure through stratified beds. (L. 205–7.)
   (3.) Indications of igneous origin.
4. Succession in superposition of rocks.
   (1.) Often seen in a high hill or mountain slope.
   (2.) Often in traveling over a level country.
   (3.) Persistence in order of superposition.
5. Discontinuity of strata. (D. 96.)
   (1.) In consequence of erosions — Illustration.
   (2.) In consequence of non-deposition.
   (3.) Land and sea-covered areas.
   (4.) Geological sections — Illustration. (D. 148, 166.)
   (5.) Geological maps — Illustrations. (D. 144.)

IV. Determination of the Normal Series of Rocks.

1. Generalization from many observations.
2. An Ideal section of the known rocks. (Chart.)
   (1.) A graduation of rocks from top to bottom.
   (2.) Indications of successive depositions.
   (3.) Indications of progressive cooling.
   (4.) Progressive changes in organization.
   (5.) General classification of the rocks. (D. 133–43; L. 269–71.)

Aqueous or Sedimentary.	Cenozoic. Mesozoic. Palæozoic.	Stratified and Fossiliferous.
	Eozoic.	Imperfectly stratified. Few fossils.

Igneous or crystalline. Of all ages. No fossils.

II. RECORDS OF PAST CONDITIONS OF THE EARTH.

I. Traces of past conditions the Material of the History.

1. Certain terrestrial changes in visible progress.
2. Similar results traceable indefinitely into the past.

II. Traces of the former action of the Sea.

1. Fossil shells far from the sea and at high altitudes.
   (1.) Ancient opinions concerning them. (Lyell: *Prin.* Bk. i, ch. iii.; Marsh. Saratoga Add. Am. Asso., 1879: Hallam: *Literature of Europe*, i., 228-30) — "Freaks of Nature"—"Plastic Power" — "Experimental Moulds" — "Fortuitous Concourse of atoms" — "The Mosaic Deluge" — "Influence of the Stars."
   (2.) They are genuine *debris* — Illustrations from the remains of shore-shells or of human industry. (W. 18–22.)
2. Sea-beaches far inland — Valley of St. Lawrence. (D. 549; Ly. *Prin.*, 178, 482; De la Bêche: *Observer*, 445-57.)
3. Changes of sea-level actually observed. (D. 582-5; L. 127; W. 19-25; De la Bêche: *Obs.*, 435-44; Réclus, 527-55, 562-7, map of upheavals and depressions.)

(1.) Scandinavia. (D. 582: L. 129; Lyell, *Prin.*, 499-511; Réclus, 531.)

(2.) Temple of Jupiter Serapis. (D. 584; Lec., 127-8; W. 19; Lyell, *Prin.*, 489.)

(3.) Old Roman roads. (Ly. *Prin.*, 493.)

(4.) Oscillations observed in America. (Cook: *Geol. N. J.*, 350-73; Dawson, *Quar. Jour. Geol. Soc.*, xi., 119; Hitchcock: *Geol. Mass.*, 307; Jackson: *Geol. N. H.*, 280; Long Island Hist. Soc., May, 1868; Réclus, ch. lxxxiv.) — Subsidence at St. Augustine, Fla. — Elevations in Pamlico Sound — Subsidence on the coast of N. J. — In Nantucket Harbor — Elevations along the New England Coast—Rotation of Grand Manan — Rotation of Nova Scotia — Submergence of the site of Louisbourg, (Cape Breton.) — Six hundred miles of the coast of Greenland sinking for 600 years. (D. 583; L. 129; Réclus, 555.)

(5.) Sea-waves on the coast of Chili and Peru in 1590, 1730, 1751, 1822, 1835; 1837, 1868· 1877. (D. 585. 662, 742; L. 130; Lyell: *Prin.*, 435, 439, 481 ; *Pop. Sci. Monthly*, Sup, Dec., 1877; *Rep. U. S. Coast Survey*, 1862, 1869.)

(6.) Actual emergences of new islands. (W. 23; Réclus, 489-96; Lyell: *Prin.*, 416) 425, 449) — Graham, I., 1831 — Sabrina in the Azores, (De la Beche: *Obs.* 100-1) — Santorin, (De la Beche: *Obs.*, 391-7.) — Aleutians, 1806, 1814 — In the Pacific. (D. 84) — Conjecture concerning the Symplegades.

(7.) Effects of a moderate depression in Illinois. (Bannister: *Geol. Ill.*. iii., 241,)

III. Traces of the former action of Heat.

1. Baked sandstones, limestones and shales.
2. Refrigerated molten rocks. — In western U. S. (L. 207; King i., 545-677; Gilbert in *Wheeler Rep.* iii., 118-131, 525-41; Howell in *id.*, 297; Stevenson in *id.*, 411-25; King, *Am. Nat.*, xi., 459. See further Lect. XXVI.)
3. Some traces of fire older than those of water.

IV. Unextinguished Fires. (D. 699.)

1. Volcanoes. (D. 702-16; L. 81-93; Ly., *Prin.*, 526-32; De la Bêche, *Observ.*, 317-48; Bakewell: *Geol.*, 311-44; Réclus, 419-52; 458-74; See further Lect. XXVI.)
2. Hot springs. (D. 692; Ly. *Prin.*, 238-49; Gilbert, *Wheeler Rep.*, iii., 150 [136 localities in U. S.]: Hayden, *Ann. Rep.*, 1871, 64-198 [Geysers]; Bakewell, *Geol.*, 443, 447-50; Réclus, 234-7. See further, Lect. XXVI.)
3. Mines and tunnels. (*Nature*, 3 Apr., 1879, 510)—Mont Cenis (Matthew, *Canad. Nat.*, vi., 96) — St. Gothard (*Geol. Rep., Italy*, 1873, *Nature*, 30 Jan. 1879, 303) — On the Comstock lode (Church, *Am. Jour.*, xvii., 289) — Sutro tunnel, *N. Y. Daily Tribune*, 6 Sept. 1879, diagrams.)
4. Artesian borings. (D. 699; Ly. *Prin.*, 236; De la Bêche: *Obs.*, 463-7 Réclus, 233, 480-8) — Alabama (W. *Proc. Am. Asso.*, 1856 — St. Louis (Litton: *Trans. St. Louis Acad.*, i., 84 ; Brodhead: *Mo. Geol. Rep.*, 34) — Sperenberg (*Nature*, 11 Jan., 1877.)

V. Foundation Stones of the Land. -- Granites, Gneisses, and other rocks bearing marks of fire. (Lect. III.)

VI. Records of Extinct Populations. (Lects. IV.-XVII.)

III. THE OLDEST KNOWN ROCKS.

On Rocks, see Von Cotta: *Rocks classified and described*, London ed., 1866; Blum: *Handbuch der Lithologie und Gesteinlehre*, Erlangen, 1860; Brooks: *Geology of Iron Region of Mich.* in *Geology of Mich.*, i, chap. iii.-iv.; Julien, in *Geol. of Mich.*, ii.; Hawes in Hitchcock's *Geol. of N. H.*, pt. iv., Mineralogy and Lithology, in vol. iii.; Foster and Whitney: *Geology of Lake Superior Land District;* Zirkel: *Lehrbuch der Petrographie*, Bonn, 1866, 2 vols., 8vo,; Zirkel: *Die Mikroskopische Beschaffenheit der Mineralien und Gesteine*, Leipzig, 1873, 8vo.; Rosenbusch: *Mikroskopische Physiographie der Mineralien und Gesteine. Ein Hulfsmittel bei mikroskopischen Gesteinstudien.* Stuttgart, 1873, 2 vols., 8vo.

I. Earliest Rocks on a cooling Planet.

1. Hypothesis of a fire-formed crust. (D. 146-7.)
1. Commencement of sedimentation. (D. 147.)
   (1.) Implies a cooled rock-surface and an ocean. (D. 147.)
   (2.) Chemical Precipitation in Primeval Ocean. (D. 147; W. 60-1; Hunt: *Chem. and Geol. Essays, iid paper*)
   (3.) Vast accumulation of stratified materials. (D 147.)
3. Cause of disappearance of fire-formed crust.
   (1.) The Isogeothermal plane.
   (2.) Ascent of isogeothermal planes as sediments accumulate.
   (3.) Progressive Melting or softening of under surface of crust.
   (4.) Progressive Metamorphism at higher levels.

II. Classification and thickness of Archæan rocks. (D. 140, 146; Hitchcock: *Geol. N. H.*, ii., 468; Hunt: *Chem. and Geol. Essays.*

ARCHÆAN	EOZOIC.	**Huronian.**	Upper. / Lower.	20,000 feet.	
		Labradorian,	10,000		30,000 feet.
		Laurentian,	20,000		
	PYROLITHIC (Hypothetical.)				

[A "Montalban" series is placed by T. S. Hunt above the Huronian, and by C. H. Hitchcock below the Labradorian.]

III. Surface exposures of Archæan Rocks.

1. The Fundamental Rocks everywhere.
2. The great nuclear area in British America, and its appendages in N. Y., Mich., and Wis. (D. 150, 160; W. 74; Daws.: *Dawn*, 7, 8; Foster and Whitney: *L. Sup.*, Pt. ii., 8; Irving: *Geol. Wis.*, 1877, 461-524.)
3. The Appalachian system of areas. (D. 150.)
4. Trans-Mississippi exposures. (King i., 15-98. See also Lects. XXIII., XXIV., XXV.

IV. Kinds of Rocks.

1. Laurentian predominantly granitoid, of both micaceous and hornblende series. (D. 151, 67-70.) — Also crystalline limestones. (D. 151; Logan: *Geol. Can.*, 1863). — Iron ores. (Perhaps those of Mich., D. 151, 159. See below.) — Graphite. (D. 151, 152; Logan: *Geol. Can.*, ch. iii. and 586-93; Daws.: *Dawn*, 18, 27-33. See also general references above.)
2. Huronian predominantly quartzose. Also diorites, limestones, iron and copper ores. (D. 159; Logan: *Geol. Can.*, ch. iv., and 594-6; 572-87; Brooks in *Geol. Mich.*, p. 1-319; Pumpelly, *Geol, Mo.*, 31-214; Moore, in *Geol. Mo.*, 1874, 638-71.)
3. Richness in Minerals. (D. 151-2.)

V. Condition of the Strata.

1. Highly disturbed. (D. 153; L. 272-3.) — Sections. (D. 148, 153; L. 273; Hitchcock: *Geol. N. H.*, ii., 15-36; King, i., Diagr., pl. i.; ch. ii., pl. ii., and Atlas, Map I., sections; Brooks: *Geol. of Mich.*, i., 184; Daws.: *Dawn*, 13; Campbell: *Am. Jour.*, xviii., 19, 121, showing relations of newer rocks.)
2. Metamorphic — Explanation. (D. 724; Bischof: *Chemical Geology;* Daubrée: *Ètudes synthetiques de Gêologie expérimentale;* Hunt: *Chemical and Geological Essays.*)
3. Subjected to enormous denudation. (Lects. XXVIII., XXIV. XXVII.)

IV. THE DAWN OF LIFE.

DAWSON: The Dawn of Life.

I. A hypothetical Protophytic period.

1. A strictly inorganic period must have existed. (D. 146.)
2. Mutual dependence of the kingdoms of life.
3. The vegetable the necessary forerunner of the animal.
4. Geological indications of early Laurentian vegetation.

II. Remains supposed Organic in Laurentian strata. Daws., as above.)

1. These strata once known as "Azoic." (Foster & Whitney: *Geol. Lake Sup.*, pt. ii., 8.)
2. Suspicions based on iron-ores and graphites. (Hunt: *Am. Jour.*, II., xxv., 431; Dawson: *Dawn*, 24-7.) — A deductive discovery as in exact science.
3. Organisms found Oct. 1858. (Logan: *Canad. Nat.*, iv., 300; *Geol. Can.*, 49; *Quar. Jour. Geol. Soc.*, Feb. 1860; W. 435-7.)

(1.) Stratigraphical position. (D. 158.) — Mineral Associations. (Daws.: 113-26; Hoffman: *Am. Jour. Sci.*, i., 378; *Jour. f. prakt. Chemie*, May, 1860.)

(2.) *Eozoon canadense* as found — Description and illustrations. (D. 158: L, 275; W. 68; Daws.: *Dawn*, 59-93.

(4.) Its zoölogical affinities. Dawson and Carpenter: *Quar. Jour. Geol., Soc.*, Feb., 1865: Daws.: *Dawn*, 59-93 — *Amœba* and *Actinophrys*. (W.. 70; Daws.: *Dawn* 60) — Compare Stromatoporidæ. (W. *Proc. Am. Asso.*, 1866.)

(4.) Its mode of Life. (Daws.: *Dawn*, 69-71.)

4. Foraminifera in all ages. (D. 131, 460, 471; Daws.: *Davon.*, 62-5, 72-6.—Their work in building up the continents. (D. 512; Daws.: *Story*, 241-3; Fig.: *World*, 241-4) — Nummulites and their structure. (D. 131, 515.) — Nummulitic limestone of the Pyramids. (D. 512; L. 485) — *Orbitoides* in America. (Daws.: *Story*, 241.)

5. Organic Nature of *Eozoön* questioned — King and Rowney. (*Quar. Jour. Geol. Soc.*, Aug., 1866; *Am. Jour. Sci.*, II., xliv., 375; *Proc. Royal Irish Acad.*, July, 1869, and Jan. and Apr., 1871; *Am. Jour.*, i., 68, 138-42; ii., 211-5.) — Burbank (*Proc. Am. Assoc.*, 1871, 262-6) — Carter. ( ) — Otto Hahn. (cited *Am. Jour. Sci.*, June, 1872, 492)—Karl Möbius. (*Palæontographica*, 1878, vol. xxv., Republished separately: see account in *Nature*, 17 and 24 July, 1879. See also Möbius in *Am. Jour. Sci.*, xviii., 177, Sep. 1879) — Otto Kuntze. (*Nature*, 28 Aug., 1879.)

6. All objections promptly met. (*Quar. Jour. Geol. Soc.*, Aug., 1866: Carpenter: *Proc. Roy. Soc.*, No. xciii., 503; Hunt: *Proc. Roy. Irish Acad.*, July 12, 1869; Carpenter: *Ann. Nat. Hist.*, June, 1874; Daws.: *Dawn*, 169-206; *Am. Jour.*, xvii., 196, March, 1879; Carpenter and Dawson: *Nature*, 31 July, 1879.

III. **Conditions of Land and Water when Eozoon appeared.**

1. No positive evidence of land. — But the Laurentian rocks are partly fragmental.

2. The sea still in a tempestuous state.

IV. **A long pause through the Huronian Age.**—Probable future discoveries — Supposed foreign equivalents.

V. GEOLOGICAL CLASSIFICATION.

I. Two Geological Conceptions, Time and Events.

1. Events or results of geological activity.

(4.) Among the Rocks: — They differ in Constitution. — Silicious, Aluminous and Calcareous. (D. 65; Lyell: *Man.*, 11-12.) — They differ in relations of Position. Unconformability. (D. 100.) — This implies changes of level of sea-bottom. — Marks boundary line in succession of deposits. (L. 269.)

(2.) Among the Fossils: — Progressive change. — Sudden transitions. — Generally corresponds with unconformability. (King: *Am. Nat.*, xi., 469.) — Transitions graduated by new discoveries. — Have cataclysms occurred? (Cuvier: *Discours;* Lyell: *Prin.*) — The truth lies between the cataclysmic, and the uniformitarian theories. (King: *Am. Nat.*, xi., 461-70; L. 288, 317, 333, 495.)

2. Time — Marked off by events — Greater and less divisions of time — Corresponding significance of the events.

II. Terms employed.

1. Rocks:—Layer, Stratum, Formation. — Formations arranged in Sub-groups or Stages, Groups, Systems and Great Systems.

2. Time: — Arranged in Epochs, Periods, Ages and Times or Æons.

3. Correlation of terms in relation to Rocks and Time.

In reference to Time.	In reference to Rocks.	Examples.
TIMES or ÆONS.	GREAT SYSTEMS.	Eozoic, Palæozoic.
AGES.	SYSTEMS.	Laurentian, Silurian.
Periods.	Groups.	Primordial, Canadian.
Epochs.	Stages.	Acadian, Potsdam.

4. Geographical origin of proper names.

III. General Historical Classification of Rocks and Geological Time. (D 140; L. 201; W. 437-8, and *Geol. Chart*; Marsh: *Am. Jour.*, xvi., pl. iv. — European Equivalents. (Cope, *Bulletin Hayden Survey*, v. 50-1; W.: *Geol. Chart.*)

IV. Intrusive Rocks. — Veins. (D. 108; L. 225-39; Whitney: *Metallic Wealth U. S.*; v. Cotta: *Ore Deposits.*) — Dikes. (D. 109, 111.) — Faulting. (D. 111; L. 222-5. See further Lect. XXVI.)

VI. SEDIMENTATION.

De La Beche: *Geological Observer*, chaps. v., vi., and vii.; Dana: *Manual*, 649, 665-674.

I. Constitution of Sediments

1. Chemical Precipitation. (De la Beche: *Obs.*, 102-111; Bischof: *Chemical Geology.*

(1.) Most active in primeval ocean. — Sketch of reactions. (W. 59-61.)

(2.) Always in progress to some extent. — Submarine emanations. — Certain mineral springs. — Evaporation. (De la Beche, 106.)

(3.) Mostly calcareous. — Often gypseous and saline. — In the primitive sea partly aluminous and silicious.

2. Organic Deposits. (De la Bêche, 112-64; D. 59-62, 606–626.)

(1.) In bulk. (D. 614.) — Exuviæ of molluscs. L. 153,) — Foraminifera. (D. 477, 671; L. 453-4; Bailey, *Smithsonian Contributions*, ii., and *Am. Jour.* II., xvii., 176, xxii., 282; Pourtales: *Trans. Am. Asso.*, 1850., 84, and *Rep. Coast Survey*, 1853, 1858, Letter to Prof. Bache, 17 May, 1862.) — Vitalized stony growths. — Corals. (D. 59, 617-26; L. 138-53; Dana: *Corals and Coral Islands.*)

3. Pulverized. — About reefs. — Disintegrated exuviæ. (D. 615, 621.)
3. Fragmental deposits. (D. 667.)
   (1.) Of Littoral origin. (D. 647; L. 31, 36.)
   (2.) Of Fluviatile origin. (D. 647; L. 20, 22.]

II. **Cementing Materials.** — Carbonate of lime. (D. 692.) — Silica. (D. 693, 725.) — Oxyd of iron. (D. 695.)

III. **Coloring Materials,** — Yellow, red and black iron oxyds. — Iron silicate. — Maganese. (D. 759.)

IV. **Sediments in relation to Distance from Shore.**

1. Littoral deposits coarser.
2. Deep-water deposits finer. (L. 40.) — Diminished in volume.
3. Deep-water deposits often calcareous. (D. 671.)
4. Local variations in the same sheet of sediments. (D. 80, 666-7. — Conglomerates, sandstones, aluminous sandstones, shales, calcareous shales, limestones. (D. 667, 669-72.) — Cross-bedding, (D. 82, 83; Hayden, *Rep.*, 1874, pl., vi,) — These variations well illustrated in North America. (D. 670, 671, *et passim.*)
5. Effect of slow submergence or emergence. -- Extension of littoral deposits. (D. 672-3.)

V. **The Sedimentary Cycle.** (W. 133-6, 1870; Newb.: *Geol. O.*, ii., 82-3, 1874; *Proc. A. A. A. S.*, 1874, 185-96; Edward Hull: *Q. Jour. G. S.*, xviii., 127-46, 1862; *Geol. Mag.*, v. 143; *Quar. Jour Sci.*, vi., 353; Dawson: *Q. J. G. S.*, xxii., 101-3, 1865; *Acadian Geol.*, 135; *Address before Nat. Hist. Soc.*, Montreal, 1865; Compare Hunt: *Geol. Can.*, 1863, 576-8; *Am. Jour. Sci.*, II., xxxv., 1863, 167; Eaton: *Geol. Text Book*, 1832, and *Am. Jour.*, II., xxiii., 281; Worthen: *Geol. Ill.*, i., 112-3, 1866.

1. Graduated intensity of action through each period.
2. Deposits graduated accordingly. — Coarse Fragmental, Fine Fragmental, Calcareous, Calcareo-fragmental. (D. 80.)
3. Each system and group presents a cycle of sediments. — Illustrate. (W. 134.)
4. Prominence of the Limestone mass in each cycle. — This a conspicuous landmark for identification, (W. 135-6.)

VII. THE REIGN OF TRILOBITES, OR THE LOWER SILURIAN AGE.

See official Geological Reports, especially those of New York, Ohio, Illinois, Canada. Murchison: *The Silurian System*, and *Siluria.*

On the general subject of Palæontology see NICHOLSON: *Manual of Palæontology*, and PICTET: *Paleontologie*, 4 vols. and Atlas of 110 plates.

For list of lower Silurian Fossils, see Miller: *The Americun Palæozoic Fossils*, 1877; Bigsby: *Thesaurus Siluricus*, 1868.

For complete bibliography, see C. A. White's, *Bibliography of North American Invertebrate Palæontology*, 1878, Hayden Survey, "Miscellaneous Publications;" No. 10, 1878, and *Supplement* to Bibliography, from "Bulletin" of the Survey, vol. 5, No. 1, 28 Feb. 1879.

I. **Lower Silurian Rocks.**

1. General aspect. — Mineral constitution and condition.
2. Relations to the Eozoic. (L. 281.) — Unconformability. — Sections. (D. 166; W. 84; L. 277; Campbell: *Am. Jour. Sci.*, xviii., 19, 121.)
3. Groups:—Primordial, Canadian and Trenton. (D. 163.) — Place of the Galena limestone. (D. 196, 197.)
4. Exposures:—(1.) St. Johns, N. B. Georgia, Vt.; Braintree, Mass.; Minn.; Wis.; Lake Superior. (W: 82-93; Foster and Whitney; *Geol. L. Sup.;* Brooks; *Geol. Mich.;* Black Hills, Dak. (N. H. Winchell: *Ludlow's Rep. on Black Hills*, 1874, 63-4, and Geol. Map.

   (2.) Cincinnati, O.; Richmond, Ind.; Lexington and Frankfort, Ky.

   (3.) Nashville, Tenn. (Geol. Tenn.)

   (4.) St. Joseph's I.; Little Bay de Noquet, etc., Mich. (W.: *Mich.*, 50.)

   (5.) St. Anthony's Falls, Minn. (N. H. Winchell: *Geol. Rep. Minn.*)

   (6.) Trenton Falls, N. Y.; Watertown, Potsdam, etc., N. Y.
5. Sections:—New York. (D. 16; Hall: *Geol. N. Y.*, 4th Dist. 27.) — Canada. (*Geol. Can.*, 847.) — Virginia. (Campbell. *Am. Jour.*, xviii., 19, 121.) — Rocky Mountains. (King: *Geol. 40th Parallel*, Atlas Map I., and "General Sections.") — Wisconsin. (Hall: *Geol. Wis.*, Plate III.; Chamberlin: *Geol. Wis.*, 1876, Atlas, Pl. XI. — Pennsylvania. (Rogers: *Geol. Penn.*, ii., 894, and Atlas, Sheet i.)
6. Economical products. (Whitney in *Geol. Io.*, 1858, i., 422-71; Brodhead: *Geol. Mo.*, 1874, 503-637; Whitney: *Wis. Geol. Rep.*, 1862, 221-420; Strong: *Wis. Rep.*, 1877, 689-752.)

II **Lower Silurian Times.** — The treeless shore. — The shelving Beach. (Ag. *Geol. Sk.*, 36.) — Its fucoidal imprints. — Its sands and ripple marks. — A shallow sea with a sinking bottom. — Another sea covering the "Great Basin."

III. **Lower Silurian Life.** (Reports cited above. Also Billings: *Palæozoic Fossils of Canada*, 1865.

1. Sudden exuberance of life. (Ag.: *Geol. Sk.*, 37.) — A busy population. (Daws.: *Story*, 40, 66, views.)
2. The type of Trilobites, with illustrattons. (D. 174-5; L. 309; Daws.: *Story*, 44-5; Barrande: *Système Silurien*, vol. i.) — General structure, rank and affinities. — Historical development and decline. — Their suddenness and zoölogical rank to be noted. (See especially Barrande: *Système Silurien du centre de la Bohême*

Tome i., and *Trilobites*, 1871, abstracted in W.: *The Doctrine of Evolution*, Appendix.)

3. The Type of Chambered Shells. (D. 124; L. 305-8; Barrande: *op. cit.*, ii., and *Distribution des Céphalopodes Siluriens.* — General structure, rank and affinities. (W.: 110-21.) — Permutations of *septum*, *siphon*, and *mode of enrollment.* (W. 119.) — Glimpse of the later history of the type. — Later than trilobites, but inferior.
4. The type of crinoids. (D. 128; L. 297-300; Billings in *Can. Geol. Surv.*, Decades iii. and iv. — General structure, rank and affinities.
5. Corals and Graptolites. (D. 199.) No polyp corals till the VIth epoch of life or Trenton. — Graptolites. (Hall, *Canad. Geol. Surv.*, Decade ii.)
6. Lingulidæ and their relations. (L. 301; Daws.: *Story*, 41-3.) — Persistence of type. — Discina.

IV. Events which terminated the Lower Silurian Age. — Uplift of Green Mts. (D. 212-16.) — The Cincinnati Axis. Newberry: *Geol. of O.*, i., 93-111; Cox: *Geol. Ind.*, 1879, 5 *seq.*

VIII. THE REIGN OF MOLLUSCS, OR THE UPPER SILURIAN AGE.

Official Geological Reports, especially those of New York, Ohio, Illinois, Michigan and Canada. Also the other references under Lect. VII.

I. How each act of the Drama was closed.

1. Premonitory tremblings. — Progressive change of sea-bottom. — Obliteration of life. — Uplift of a new belt of land.
2. Such movements generally slow. — But sometimes violent.
3. Changes of systemic value world-wide. — Perhaps not synchronous in remote regions. (D. 192.) — Minor changes progressively more local.

II. The lands of later Silurian time. — The desolate and wasting continent. — The winding shore. (D. 250-1.) — The eroding waves. — The teeming sea. — Scenes. (Fig.: *World*, 93; Daws.: *Story*, 40, 66.)

III. Organization in later Silurian time.

1. The perpetuated Trilobites, Orthoceratites and Crinoids. — Specimens. (D. 227.)
2. The type of Polyps, or true Coral-animals. (D. 617-26; ***Corals and Coral Islands; Zoöphytes***, Wilkes Expl. Exped.)

(1.) The zoölogical position of Polyps. (D. 130.)
(2.) Actinoid Polyps. (D. 130.)
(3.) Coral secretions. — Coral structures. (D. 617: L. 138-53.) — Coral reefs and islands. (D. 618–26; L. 139; De la Beche: *Observer*, 165-205; Darwin: *Coral reefs;* Beete Jukes: *Surveying Voyage of the Fly;* Reclus: *Earth*, 556-61,)
(4.) Upper Silurian Corals. — Favositidæ. — Halysites. (D. 225; L. 293.)

3. Other coral secreting animals. (D. 130.)
4. *Orthidæ.* (D. 170-2.) — *Eurypterus.* (D. 239; L. 313; Fig.: *World*, 99.)

IV. Upper Silurian Rocks.

1. Illustrative sections. (Lect. VII., I., 5.)
2. The great limestone mass of this age. — Western New York, (D. 218.) — Drummond's Island. (W.: *Geol. Mich.*, 55: *Michigan*, 52.) — Big Bay de Noquet. (W.: *Mich.*, 53.) — Chicago. (Worthen: *Geol. of Ill.*, 129-36; Winchell and Marcy, *Mem. Bos. Soc. Nat. Hist.*, 4tò., No. 2.) — Southern Ohio and Ind. (D. 221; Newb.: *Geol. O.*, iii., 7.)
3. Noteworthy Erosions. — Niagara River. (D. 219; W. 244. See Lects. XX. and XXVII.) — The Northern Lakes. (Newb.: *Geol. O.*, ii., 72-80; iii., 45-51; W. 220; Foster and Whitney: *Geol. L. Sup. Land. Dist.*)

V. Chapters of Upper Silurian History.

1. Niagara, Salina, Lower Hederberg and Oriskany. — But the Oriskany perhaps Devonian. (D. 241.)
2. Characteristic outcrops of each group.
5. Economical products of each. (D. 220, 222, 234; Foster and Whitney: *Lake Sup.*, ii., 201.)

IX. THE REIGN OF POLYPS, OR THE DEVONIAN AGE.

Official Geological Reports, especially those of New York, Ohio. Michigan, Illinois, and Canada. Also the other references under Lect. VII. On extinct organic types, see Nicholson: *Manual of Palæontology;* Pictet: *Paleontologie*, 4 vol., Atlas, 110 plates.

I. A culmination of Polyp-life.

1. Devonian coral-reefs. (D. 225; W.: *Grand. Trav. Reg.*, 41; Ly.: *Travels*, 2d vis., ii., 203.)
2. Favositidæ and Syringoporidæ in particular. (D. 204, 259; L. 293, 319.)
3. Cyathophyllidæ in particular. (D. 255, 259; L. 292. — Ancient and modern types. (Lyell: *El.*, 403.)

II. Trilobites and Orthoceratites declining. (Daws.: *Story*, 93.)

1. Representative species.
2. *Gomphoceras, Lituites, Cyrtoceras and Clymenia.*

B

3. Advent of Insects and Land Plants. (D. 258; L. 315-8; Daws.: *Story*, 101-8.)

III. The advent of Vertebrate life.

1. Organization hitherto invertebrate.
2. The law of progress.
3. Realization of a new fundamental conception. — Destined to a wonderful expansion.
4. Fishes of the Old Red Sandstone. (D. 285; L. 323-4; Fig.: *World*, 110-1; Hugh Miller: *Old Red Sandstone*, etc.; Lancaster and Powrie; *Palæont. Soc.*, 1870-1; Lyell: *El.*, 415-9.)
5. Devonian Fishes of Ohio and Canada. (D. 261-5; L. 325-7; W. 120, 127; Newb.: *Geol. O.*, Pal. i., sec. ii., 247-324; *Bulletin. Nat. Inst.*, 1857, 1-8; *Am. Jour. Sci.*, xxxiv., July, 1862.)

(1.) Their systematic position. (Newb.: *Pal. O.*, i., 247-52. — Nearest living allies (L. 327-9; Newb.: *Pal. O.*, 254-5; W. 120.)

(2.) Their bulk, organization and defences. (Newb.: *Geol. O. Pal.* i., sec. ii., 247-324.)

(3.) Many of their characters relatively embryonic. (L. 331. — Cartilaginous skeleton. — Heterocercal tail. (L.330.) — Subcephalic position of mouth. — In Placoids still other characters.

IV. Growing Continents and meagre Forest coverings.

1. Glimpse of the coming age. — Flowerless land-plants. (D. 268-71; Daws.: *Story*, 102-7; *Acadian Geol.*, 2d. ed.; *Geol. Canada*, 1871; *Q. Jour. Geol. Soc.*, xv., 483, xviii., 296, xix., 458, xxvii., 270. See also general references Lect. XIII.) — Scenes. (Fig.; *World*, 106; Daws.: *Story*, 88, 103; W. 130.)
2. Relics found in New York, Ohio and Canada. (See references under IV., 1.)

V. Chapters of Devonian History.

1. Corniferous, Hamilton, Chemung. — Oriskany perhaps belongs at bottom. (See Lect. VIII.)
2. Lithological and Palæontological distinctions.
3. The great limestone axis, Cornifero-Hamilton. — The cycle of deposition well illustrated.

VI. Geographical distribution of Outcrops.

1. Syracuse, Caledonia, Eighteen Mile Creek, and all southern N. Y. — London, Goderich, Ont. — Mackinac. (W. *Mich.*, 58; Foster and Whit.: *L. Sup.*, 164-5.) — Little Traverse Bay. (W. *Grand Traverse Region*, 40-8.) — Thunder Bay, Monroe, Mich. — Columbus, Delaware, Sandusky, O. (*Geol. O.*, i., 142-9.) — Falls of the Ohio. (D. 255.)
2. Some illustrative sections. (Rogers: *Geol. Penn.*, i., and ii., 894, 895, Atlas, Sheet 1.)

X. THE REIGN OF FISHES, OR THE CARBONIFEROUS AGE.

Official reports, especially those of Ohio, Illinois, Iowa, Kentucky, Tennessee, Indiana, Michigan. Pennsylvania, and those directed by Hayden, King, Wheeler and Powell. (See Partial List of Authorities under " Abbreviations.")

See also the other General references under Lect. VII.

I. **The Waverly Period.** (W.: *The Marshall Group*, 1870, from *Proc. Am. Phil. Soc.;* also *Am. Jour.*, II., xxxiii., 352; *ib.*, xxxv., 61; *Proc. Acad. Nat. Sci.*, Phil., Sept., 1862, 405; *ib.*, Jan., 1863, 2; *ib.*, July, 1865; *Geol. Tenn.*, 1869, 364-5, 440; Meek and Worthen: *Am. Jour. Sci.*, II., xxxii., 167-177, July, 1861.)

1. The Rocks.
   (1.) Lithological variations. (W. *Proc. Am. Phil. Soc.*, xi., 73-7.)
   (2.) Geographical distribution and outcrops. (W. *Am. Phil. Soc.*, xi., 77-82.)
2. The Fossil Remains. (W. *Proc. Am. Phil. Soc.*, xii., 385-407; White and Whitfield, *Proc. Boston Soc. Nat. Hist.*, Feb., 1862, 289-306.)
   (1.) Great development of Lamellibranchs.
      (*a.*) Their zoölogical relations. (D. 125-6; Woodward: *Man. Mol.*)
      (*b.*) Their increase with the diminution of Brachiopods. (L. 303.)
   (2.) Advent of Carboniferous types. (W. *Proc. Am. Phil. Soc.*, xii, 401-7.) — Carboniferous Crinoids. (Hall, xvii. *Reg. Rep.*)
3. Questions of Parallelism.
   (1.) Sketch of history of opinion, (W. *Proc. Am. Phil. Soc.*, xi, 57-73.)
   (2.) Nomenclature and equivalences in America. (W. *Am. Phil. Soc.*, xi, 73-82; xii, 387-401, 415.)
   (3.) Comparison with upper member of Old Red Sandstone. (W. *Am. Jour. Sci.*, xxv., 61; *Proc. Am.Phil. Soc.*, xii, 412-14.)

II. **The Carboniferous Limestone Period.**

1. A season of deep and quiet waters in the West. (D. 304-5,) — Limestone mass — Eastern equivalents. (D. 293, 295, 305.) Gypsum formation sometimes constituting the base. (D. 295, 296; W.: *Geol. of Mich.* 1861.) — The "Mountain Limestone" of Europe. (D. 306.) — Perhaps embraces the Waverly of America.
2. Crinoidal life at its Culmination (D. 297-8; L. 382-3. See Geol. Reps. Ill., Iowa, Mo., Ohio.)
   (1.) Zoölogical description of Crinoids. (D. 176, 128-9: Billings: *Geol. Can.*, Decade iv., 7-17; *Am., J. S.*, II., xlvii-l.; C. A. White, *Bost. Jour. Nat. Hist.*, Jan., 1863, 481-506.)
   (2.) Their Geological history. — Living representatives.
   (3.) Abundant remains in Mississippi Valley. — Burlington, Io. (D. 303; Lyon and Cassiday: *Am. Jour. Sci.*, xxix, 68-79.) — Kentucky. (Last ref.; Lyon, *Trans. Acad. Sci. St. Louis*, i, 628-34; *Proc. Acad. N. S. Phil.*, Dec., 1861, 409-14.)
   (4.) Other forms of life. — Large Spirifers. (D. 300; Lec. 384; *Geol. Reps. Ill., Io., etc.* — Nautili. (*Geol. Reps.*) — Goniatites. (L. 386.) — Their structure and affinities. — Fishes. (D. 301; L. 389; *Geol. Ill.*, ii, 11-134; iv. 387-74 vi. 245-488; Newberry, *Geol. O., Pal.* i. 325-55.)

3. Oscillations of Level. (D. 305, 309.) — Successive epochs of deposition. (D. 294; Hall, *Geol. Iowa,* i. 92-119; *Proc. Amer. Assoc.* 1856, pt. ii., 51.)

III. **The Coal Period.**

1. Its characteristic the development of land-vegetation.
2. The "False Coal Measures." (D. 295.) — The "Conglomerate" or Millstone Grit. (D. 311.) — The Coal Measures. (D. 311.) — The last replaced by limestones in the far West. (D. 296.) — Meaning of this fact.
3. The Coal Fields of North America. (D. 291-3, 319-21; L. 338-9; Macfarlane: *The Coal Regions of America.* See further, Lecture XI.)
4. Progressive upward movement of sea-bottom implied by the wide-spread Conglomerate. (D. 311, 320, 354, 394, 672.)

IV. **The Permian Period.** — An appendix to the Coal Measures. (Meek & Hayden, *Trans. Albany Institute,* 2 March, 1858.) — Rocks, fossils and localities. (D. 367; L. 400-4; Fig: *World,* 151-63.)

XI. COAL AND COAL MAKING.

MACFARLANE: *The Coal Regions of America,* 1873; TAYLOR: *Statistics of Coal,* 1855: JOHNSON: *Report to Congress on Coals,* 1844; LESLEY: *Coal and its Topography;* Article "Coal" in *New American Cyclopædia.*

I. **Great phytogenic periods of the world's history.**

1. Præzoic — Only deductively known.
2. Laurentian — Graphite in Siberia, Greenland, Canada, United States, Bavaria, Norway, Sweden. (Daws.: *Dawn of Life,* 27-33; *Jour. Geol. Soc., London, Feb.,* 1870.)
3. Coal Measures of Carboniferous time.
4. Permian: — Russia. (D. 370.) — Australia. (D. 370, and *Geol. Rep.,* Wilkes, *Expl. Exped.,* 1849; L. 415.)
5. Triassic:—Richmond, Va., etc. (D. 404, 406; L. 445; Lyell: *Travels,* 2d visit, ii.)
6. Jurassic:—India and China. (L. 415; Pumpelly, Smith. Contrib. xv., Art. iv.) — Lota, SW. coast of S. Amer. (L. Ag.: N. Y. Tribune, and *Am. Jour.,* iv. 143.)
7. Cretaceous:—Rocky Mts. (D. 457. Compare, however, D. 491, 493.; L. 455-6.) — Age of the Western Lignitic or Laramie formation in dispute. (See Lect. XIV.) — Winnipeg. — Vancouver. (D. 458; Whiteaves: *Mesozoic Fossils,* i, pt. ii., Geol. Sur. of Canada, 179-90.) — Queen Charlotte's islands. (Whiteaves, *Ib..* pt. i., 86-92.) — Monte Diablo, Cal. (Whitney, *Geol. Cal.* i., 27-31.)

8. Miocene:—Coos Bay, Or. (Newb.: *Bost. Jour. Nat. Hist.* vii., 506; Lesqx.: *Am. Jour. Sci.* II. xxvii., 359; Heer, *ib.* xxviii., 85.) — Qu'Appelle and North Saskatchewan rivers, B. A. (Hector, *Quar. Jour. Geol. Soc. Lond.*, xvii., pt. i., 409, etc.) — Europe.
9. Modern:—Peat-beds of Ireland, Denmark, Bavaria, United States and elsewhere. (D. 616; L. 133-6.)
10. Deposits of bituminous and coaly shales. (D. 66.)

II. Varieties of Coal and Carbonaceous deposits. (D. 314-7; *System of Mineralogy*, 755-5; Rogers: *Geol. Penn.* ii.)

1. Caused by pressure, heat, impurities, redeposition and chemical changes.
2. A graduated series of products — The older generally most altered. L. 342, 346.)
   (1.) *Peat*, of the recent epoch — Mostly in northern temperate countries. (Réclus: *Earth*, 416-8.)
   (2.) *Brown Coal* or *Lignite* — Chiefly Cenozoic, in Germany, United States, etc. (See above I., 7, 8, 9.)
   (3.) *Bituminous Coal*:—Mesozoic and a portion of the Carboniferous. (D. 315; Marvine, *Hayden's Rep.*. 1873, 110; Hayden: *Ann. Rep.*, 1870, 179-88.) — Mineral Charcoal. (D. 316; Daws.: *Story*, 118; D. *Syst. Min.*, 755.
   (4.) *Cannel Coal*:—Chiefly Carboniferous. (D. 315.) — Also Green River Eocene; (Hayden: Ann. Rep., 1870, 144.) Produced by littoral attrition and redeposition. — Torbanite, Scotland. (D. 315, 316.)
   (5.) *Anthracite*:—Chiefly Carboniferous (D. 315.) — But in limited quantities in older and newer formations — Causes of anthracitization (L. 346.) — Highly altered Carboniferous in Rhode Island. (D 319.)
   (6.) *Plumbago*:—In Silurian and Archæan formations. (See above, I., 2.)
   (7.) Prof. Rogers' Classification of Coals. (*Geol. Penn.*, ii., 988-95; Fraser, *Hayden's Rep. Wyoming*, 1870, 180.)
   (8.) Nature of Coke. (D. 61.)

III. The Vegetable Origin of Coal. (D. 351; Bischof; *Chemical Geology;* Websky in *Jour. f. Praktische Chemie*, xcii.; Hunt in *Am. Jour. Sc.*, II., xxxv., and *Canad. Nat.*, vi., 241; S. W. Johnson: *Peat and its Uses.*)

1. Chemical Composition. — Tables (D. 316, 361-2, 365: L. 343-5; D. *System. Min.*, 756-8: Rogers: *Geol. Penn.*, ii., 969-76; Marvine, Hayd. Rep., 1873, 110; Hayden: *Ann. Rep.*, 1870, 179-88; Peter, *Geol. Ky.*, 1856, 352-5, 361, 363, vol. iv., 243, 247-8, 266-9, especially 284-5; Whitney, *Geol. Cal.*, 30.) — Economical rank of Coals. (Rogers, *Geol. Penn.*, ii., 1000; Johnson, *Report to Congress.*)
2. Graduated series from wood to plumbago. (L. 343-5.)
3. Traces of vegetable structure.
   (1.) In the forms of fronds and fruits. (D. 317; Lesqx.: *Geol. Ill.*, iv., 479-89.)
   (2.) In vegetable tissue in coals themselves. (D, 318; Lesqx.: *Geol. Ill.*, iv., 478.)

4. Theories of conditions of coal-accumulation. (D. 360-4 ; L. 363.)
   (1.) A marine deposit. (Whittlesey, *Annals of Science.*)
   (2.) Formed of Drift-wood.
   (3.) Formed over sub-aërial surfaces.

IV. Stratigraphical associations of coal. (D. 311, 320; L. 335; Geol. Reports Ill., Io., O., Mo., Ky., Ind., Pa., etc.)
1. Shales. (D. 313.) — Character. — Fossil plants.
2. Clays. (D. 312.) -- Stigmaria roots. (D. 313.) Fire clays and their properties.
3. Sandstone — Often gritty or conglomeritic. — Vegetable remains.
4. Limestones — Increasing westward. (D. 313.) — Marine animals.

V. Disturbances of Coal Fields.
1. Little disturbed in the Mississippi valley — Mich., Ind., Ill. — Highly bituminous — Little disturbed in the Rocky Mts. (Hayden, *Rep.* 1870, *Wyoming,* 180.
2. Greatly disturbed in the Appalachian region. (D. 396; L. 336.) — Pennsylvania. (D. 310; L. 337; Rogers: *Geol. Penn.;* Lesley: *Coal and its Topography* and *Geol. of Penn.*, New Survey.) — Debituminized. (Rogers: *Geol.Penn.*, ii., 808-11.) — Foreign regions. (D. 344-51.)

VI. Coal Fields of the United States. — 1. Appalachian. (Rogers: *Geol. Penn.*, ii.. 954-9.) — 2. Illinois. (Rogers: *ut sup.*, 959.) — 3. Rhode Island. — 4. Michigan. — 5. Eastern and Middle Rocky Mountains. (Frazer, *Hayden's Rep. Wyoming*, 1870, 179-86. See Lect. XIV.) — 6. Monte Diablo. (See above, I., 7.) — 7. Oregon. (See above, I., 8.) — 8. Alaska. (Dall: *Alaska and its Resources.*) — On the "Coal Fields of the United States and British Provinces," see Rogers: *Geol. Penn.*, ii., 942-54.

XII. COAL MEASURE TIMES.

1. Picture of a Coal-measure landscape. (W. 149-54.)
1. The thick dank forest. (D. 352, 353,; L. 369-70; Tyndall, *Proc. Roy. Soc.*, xi., 100 [*Am, Jour. Sci.*, II., xxxvi., 99]; T. S. Hunt: *Chemical and Geolog. Essays*, 42.) — Tree Ferns and dripping fronds. — A thick jungle. (D. 354.) — Prostrate trunks and decaying stumps. (D. 356.) — Land-snails, myriapods and insects. (D. 333-6, 339; L. 385; Daws.: *Story*, 112-5, 135-42; *Geol. Ill.*, iii., 556-72.)

2. A stagnant bayou. — *Archegosaurus.* (D. 351; L. 393; Daws.: *Story,* 145; Fig.: *World,* 139; Lyell: *Elem.,* 397.) — *Amphibamus* and its vocal utterances. (D. 340.) — *Eosaurus* inhabiting the waters. (D. 340, 343; L. 393; W. 170; Daws.: *Story,* 145-6.) — Dragon-flies depositing their eggs. (D. 335.) — Fishes. (D. 336, 343.)
3. A stormy beach and a sheltered lagoon. — Origin of cannel coal.
4. Views. (Dana, 322; W., 140, 142, 144, 146, 150; Daws.: *Story,* 126, 145; Fig.: *World,* 133, 138, 142; Lyell: *Elem.,* 393.)

II. A change of Scene. — Lowering skies. — Heaving sea-bottoms. — Invading waves. — Another submergence.

III. Results seen in modern coal-beds. W. 139-48.)

1. A stony herbarium. — Fairy tracery. — Delicacy and perfection of features.
2. What have we represented in this coal?
   (1.) The very tissue and cell, and pith and root, and leaf and frond. (D. 317.)
   (2.) The very carbon which poisoned the atmosphere æons ago.
   (3.) The very sun-light which fell upon the forest, treasured up to be disengaged again in our winter fires. — Solar energy transformed and locked up, to be set loose in countless steam-engines of the human period. (Huxley, *Contemporary Review.*)

IV. Three Ends to be accomplished in Coal-making.

1. To purify the air for organic purposes. (D. 353; L. 373.) — The existence of *method* and *purpose* assumed.
   (1.) The poison neither annihilated nor fixed in mineral combinations.
   (2.) The agency of vegetation. (W. 160.)
   (3.) The demand for respirable air coincident with the first epoch when the conditions of the land permitted the adequate development of the purifier.
2. To preserve the carbon for the coming man.
   (1.) Tendency of vegetation to decomposition.
   (2.) Organic substances preserved only in wet accumulations.
   (3.) This need concurrent with the only epoch when the oscillations were sufficiently frequent.
3. To accomplish all things under the established method of world-building.
   (1.) Oscillations of the level of the land. (D. 395.) — Foreshadowed in the False Coal measure and Conglomerate epochs. (D. 354.)
   (2.) Special history of this period. (D. 354-60.) — Oscillations. (D. 357; W., 161.) — Alternate sea-bottom and verdant marsh. (D. 357-9; L. 366.) — Number of submergences. (D. 358.) — Warmth and dampness of the atmosphere. (See above, I.,1.)
   (3.) The other ends demanded at the only time when the tension of the terrestrial crust could generate the requisite oscillations.
   (4.) Grand closing events. (D. 395-401.) — Uplift of Appalachians. — Great enlargement of limits on the eastern wing of the continent. (L. 367; W. 161-2.) — Advent of the Middle Ages of the world's history. (L. 400.)

XIII. VEGETATION OF THE COAL MEASURES AND OLDER FORMATIONS.

D, especially 242, 255, 257-8, 268-71, 277, 279-80, 296-7, 321-31, 348-9; L. 346-63; W. 156-9.

DAWSON: *Story of the Earth and Man*, 121-32; *Fossil Plants of the Lower Carboniferous and Millstone Grit Formations of Canada*, Montreal, 1873.

FIGUIER: *The World Before the Deluge.*

LESQUEREUX: *Geology of Pennsylvania*, (1854), 1868, vol. ii., pt. ii., 835-84, Plates i-xx. — Synopsis in *New Amer. Cyclopædia;* Atlas to the Coal Flora of Penn., etc., 1879; Amer. Jour. Sci., Nov., 1860; *Geology of Ill.*, ii. 427-70, iv. 379-477; Pottsville Scientific Assoc., 1858, 1-23; *Fucoides in the Coal Formations*, Trans. Amer. Phil. Soc., 1866.

NEWBERRY: *Geology of Ohio*, i., 357-85; *Annals of Science*, Cleveland, 1853.

SCHIMPER: *Traité de Paléontologie végétale*, 1869.

H. C. WOOD, Jr.: *Flora of the Coal Period in the United States.* Trans. Amer. Phil. Soc., 1866.

On the Genesis and Migrations of Plants, see DAWSON, in *Princeton Review*, March, 1879, also the works there cited.

On plants older than the Carboniferous, see especially,

HALL: *Observations upon some spiral-growing Fucoidal remains in the Palæozoic Rocks of N. Y.*, xvi. Reg. Rep., 1863, 71-83; *Observations upon the genera Uphantænia, Dictyophyton, etc., op. cit.* 84-91; *The Flora of the Devonian period, op. cit.* 92-117.

DAWSON: *The Flora of the Devonian Period in Northeastern America*, Quar. Jour. Geol. Soc., xviii., 296; xvi. Reg. Rep. N. Y., 97-107; *Fossil Plants of the Devonian and Upper Silurian Formations of Canada*, Geology of Canada, 1871.

SYSTEMATIC ARRANGEMENT OF PALÆOZOIC VEGETATION.

[Extinct types in italics. Silurian, Devonian and Carboniferous types denoted respectively by S, D and C.]

PHÆNOGAMS.

ANGIOSPERMS.

Exogens. (Ordinary trees, shrubs and herbs.)

Endogens. (Palms, Sedges, Grasses, etc.)

GYMNOSPERMS.

Cycads.—*Cordaites* D. C, *Cardiocarpus* C, + *Pterophyllum* C.

Conifers D. C.—Araucariæ, Pines, Cypresses, Yews; *Prototaxites* S. D, *Pinites* C, or *Dadoxylon* (including *Sternbergia*), *Trigonocarpus* D. C, *Cardiocarpus* D. C, *Rhabdocarpus* C, *Araucaroxylon* D, *Whittleseya* C, *Annularia* C.

CRYPTOGAMS.

ACROGENS.

Equisetaceæ. (Horse-tails.)

Equisetids.

Calamitids D. C :—*Calamites* D. C, *Equisetites* C, *Annularia* C.

Asterophyllids D. C :—*Asterophyllites* C, *Sphenophyllum* C.

Filices D. C :—*Eopteris* S, *Caulopteris* D, *Neuropteris* D. C, *Cyclopteris* (*Nœggerathia* or *Palæopteris*) D. C, *Sphenopteris* D. C, *Callipteris* D. C, *Alethopteris* C, *Hymenophyllites* C, *Odontopteris* C, *Pecopteris* C, *Neriopteris* C, *Dictyopteris* C, *Alethopteris* C, *Staphylopteris* C.

Cyathaceæ—Tree Ferns,—*Caulopteris* D. C, *Psaronius* D, *Megaphytum* C.

Lycopodiaceæ—Club-mosses.

Lycopodids S. D.—*Psilophyton* S. D, *Arthrostigma* D.

Cyclostigmids :—*Cyclostigma* D, *Knorria* D. C.

Sigillarids D. C:—*Sigillaria* D. C,+ *Stigmaria* D. C, *Syringodendron* C, *Poacites*, *Cyperites*, *Sternbergia* ? C.

Lepidodendrids S. D. C:—*Sagenaria* S, *Lepidodendron* D. C, + *Lepidostrobus* C, *Halonia* C, *Selaginites* C, *Lycopodites* C, *Sahutzia* C, *Ulodendron* C, *Lepidophloios* C, *Lepidophyllum* C, *Sigillaria* + *Sigillarioides* (roots) + *Stigmaria* (floating stems) + ? *Stigmarioides* (rhizomes) C. (See under *Sigillarids*.)

ANOGENS. (Mosses, Liverworts.)

THALLOGENS.

Lichens.

Fungi.

Algæ.

Confervæ.

Fucoides S. D. C.—*Palæophycus* S, *Buthotrephis* S, *Rusophycus* S, *Arthrophycus* S, *Spirophyton* D. C, *Caulerpites* C, *Chondrites* C, *Protophyta*.

Desmids (including Xanthidia.) (D. 257, 471; M. C. White, *Amer. Jour. Sci.*, xxxiii., 385-6.

Diatoms.

XIV. THE REIGN OF REPTILES, OR MESOZOIC TIME.

On American Mesozoic geology see, besides the references below, the Geological Reports of California, the Fortieth Parallel and of the Territories, under Dr. Hayden. Also MORTON: *The Cretaceous System of the United States.*

On the Vegetation of these Ages, see LESQUEREUX: *Cretaceous Flora of the Western Territories*, Hayden Survey, Vol. vi. 4to. 1874, and *The Tertiary Flora of the Western Territories*, Hayden Surv. Vol. viii. 4to. 1878. [These "Tertiary" plants are from the Lignitic or Laramie Group regarded by many as Cretaceous.] NEWBERRY: *Rep. on the Cretac. and Tertiary Plants*, in Hayden's Explor. Yellowstone and Missouri Rivers, 1859-60, 145-74. Also FONTAINE; *Notes on the Mesozoic Strata of Virginia*, Am. Jour. Sci. III. xvii. 25, 151, 229.

On the Reptiles and Mammals, see references under Lectures XV. and XVII.

I. The Mesozoic Continent.

1. Its Geography (D. 405, 422-3, 450-1, 455-8, 478-80, 481; L. 449, 451; W. 195-8). — Outlines (L. 451-2). — Forests (D. 451). — Emerging western limb. (See Lecture XXIII). — Topography.
2. Its Hydrography. (D. 420, 423; W. 195-8). — Drainage features. — Gulf of Mexico (D. 479). — Communication between the Caribbean and the Arctic Ocean. (D. 479). — Gulf of St. Lawrence. — Lake Superior and its outlet. — Niagara Falls in the olden time. — Hudson river and its outlet. (D. 422).
3. Views. (W. 177, 179, 181; Daws.: *Story*, 194, 219; Fig.: *World*, 172, 174, 206, 213, 222, 225, 229, 240, 258, 268).
4. European Mesozoic Geography. (D. 451, 480).

II. Triassic, Jurassic and Cretaceous Ages. (D. 403; L. 404).

1. Triassic subdivisions. — Trias in the U. S.
2. Jurassic subdivisions. — Occurrence in the trans-Mississippi.
3. Cretaceous subdivisions, European and American. (Lesqx.: *The Cretaceous Flora*, Hayden Surv. Vol. vi. 4to. 14; *Ann. Rep.* 1872, 371-427; *ib.* 1874, 316-65, 8 plates, monographic; Hayden, *Ann. Rep.* 1870, 87; Cope, in *Wheeler Rep.* Vol. iv. pt. ii. 1-13.) — Question of the age of the "Lignitic" or Laramie Group. (D. 457, 491, 493; L. 455-6; Newberry, *Am. Jour.*, II., xxix., 208-18; III., vii., 90; *Boston Jour. Nat. Hist.*, vii., 506: Lesquereux, *Am. Jour. Sci.*, II., xxvii., 359; *ib.* III., vii., 546; *ib: Hayden Ann. Rep.*, 1872, 417-42; *ib.* 1873, 365-425; *ib. The Tertiary Flora of the Western Territories*, Hayd. Surv., vii., 4to., 21-31, 309-355; *ib.* 1874, 275-315; Meek, *Hayd. Ann. Rep.*, 1862, 46-9; Hayden: *Ann. Rep.*, 1872 14; 1874, ch., i.-ii; Cope. *Bull. Hayd. Sur.*, i., 10; *ib.* Report *Vert. Pal, Col.*, Hayd., Ann Rep. 1873, 431-44; Marvine. *Haydn. Ann. Rep.* 1873, 106-28, 171-6; Stevenson, *Proc. Am. Phil. Soc.*, June, 1855;

Peale, *Hayd. Ann. Rep.*, 1874, 140-55, Comparison of opinions; Endlich. *Hayd. Ann, Rep.*, 1875, 195-207; King, *Geol.*, 40*th Par.*, i., 539; iii., ch., vii., on the western cordilleras; Comstock, in Jones *Rep. N. W. Wyom.*, 132-3.)

III. Marine Populations and Plants of Mesozoic Time.

1. Where their remains have been exhumed. (D. 405-7,431.) — Atlantic and Gulf-border. (D. 455; L. 439.) — Marl-beds of New Jersey. (D. 455; Daws.: *Story*, 329.) — Prairie Bluff and Choctaw Bluff, Ala. (W., *Proc. Am. Assoc.*, 1858 and 1856.) — Western Territories. (D. 456-7; L. 440.) — Pacific border. (D. 457 L. 440.)

2. Palæozoic Types extinct:—
   (1.) Plants:—Lepido dendrids, Sigillarids Cyclostigmids, Calamites.
   (2.) Radiates:—Graptolites. (D. 384.) — Cystids. (D. 385.) — Blastids. — Favositsoid and other corals.
   (3.) Brachiopods:—Orthids, Productids.
   (4.) Cephalopods:—*Goniatites* (in Triassic), *Clymenia*, *Gomphoceras*, *Endoceras*.
   (5.) Articulates:—Trilobites, Eurypterids.
   (6.) Vertebrates:—Heterocercal Ganoids. (D. 384, 441.).

2. Palæozoic Types greatly shrunken:—
   (1.) Plants:—
   (2.) Radiates:—Cyathophylloids, Crinoids.
   (3.) Brachiopods. (Daws.: *Story* 221.)—*Spirifer*, *Leptæna*, Brachiopods generally.
   (5.) Vertebrates:—Placoderm Fishes.

4. New Types introduced or greatly developed.
   (1.) Plants:—Cycads. (D. 408; L. 416-7.) — Angiosperms. (D. 459; L. 457.) — Palms.
   (2.) Protozoans:—Rhizopods. (D. 460; L. 459.)
   (3.) Radiates:—Astræoid corals, Echinoderms. (L. 460.) — Asterioids. (L. 419-20.)
   (4.) Molluscs:—Lamellibranchs. (L. 461.) — Ammonites. (D. 439; 462-3, 467; L. 421, 464; Daws.: *Story* 221.) — Belemnites. (D. 440, 432-4.) — Structure and affinities of Ammonites. (D. 409-10; L. 422; L. Ag.: *Geol. Sk.*, 177-9, Lect., VII., III.. 3.) — Geological history of Cephalopods. (L. 425.)
   (5.) Articulates:—Macrouran Crustaceans. (D. 441.)
   (6.) Vertebrates:—Teleost Fishes. (D. 442, 462, 475; L. 466.) — Zoölogicai characters. (Huxley; *Vert.*, 130-44.)

IV. The Air-breathing denizens of the land and waters.

1. Classification of Amphibians and Reptiles.
2. Conspicuous Mesozoic types:—Ichthyopterygians. — Pythonomorphs (Mosasaurs.) — Crocodilians. — Sauropterygians. — Dinosaurs. — Ornithosaurs. — Turtles. (D. 466; W. 190.) — Geological succession among reptiles. (Cope., *Proc. Am. Acad. Boston*, xix., 194; *Am. J. S.*, ii., 217.)
3. Scenes on the banks of the future Delaware.

4. Scenes in the future valley of the Connecticut. — Bipedal Reptiles. (D. 412 ; L. 431, 443-4 ; W. 168, 183-7 ; Ag. : *Sketches*, 150-4.)
5. Advent of Birds. (D. 414, 466, 468 ; L. 470, 472 ; Daws. *Story*, 208 ; Marsh, *Am. Jour., Sci.*, March 1860 ; 1872, 56, 360, March, 1873 : Allen, *Bull. Hayd. Surv.* iv., 443, Apr., 1878.) — Birds with vertebrated tails. (D. 414, 430, 446-7, 468 ; L. 436-7, 420 ; W. 184 ; Fig. : *World*, 229 ; Mivart : *Genesis of Species.*) — Birds with biconcave vertebræ and sharp teeth. (D. 466 ; L. 470 ; Marsh, *Am. Jour.*, May 1872, 344 ; Jan., 1873, 74 ; Feb., 1873 ; x., Nov., 1875, plates ; xi., June, 1876. 509 ; xiv., July 1877, 85, plate ; xvii. 266.)
6. Advent of Mammals. (D. 415, 427, 429, 446, 449-50 ; L. 438 ; W. 188 ; Daws. : *Story*, 208. Lecture, XVII., II., i., and III., i.) — Their Marsupial affinities. (D. 415, 430 ; L. 438 ; Daws. : *Story*, 209.) — Unknown through the Cretaceous. (D. 466 ; L. 372.)

V. Disturbances. (D. 417. Lecture XX., V.)

1. Trias and eruptions of Trap. (D. 417-20, 421.)
2. Jurassic closed by uplift of mountains. (D. 452-3 ; L. 450. — Sierra Nevada and Basin ranges to the east. (D. 452, 486 ; Whitney : *Geol. Cal.* ; King : *Rep. 40th. Par.*, i., 734-54, 759. — Humboldt range. (D. 453, 486.)
3. Cretaceous closed by uplifts :—Wahsatch Range. (King : *Rep. 40th. Par.*, 745, 747, 753, not D. 453, 486.) — Uinta Range. (King : *op. cit.*, 540, not D. 453, 486. Lecture XXV., I., 7.) California west of Sierra Nevada. (D. 523.) — Part of Rocky Mts, east of Wahsatch. (Lect, XXV., I., 7.) — Increased cold and extermination of species. (D. 487 ; L. 475 ; Daws. : *Story*, 232.)

XV. SOME EXTINCT TYPES OF REPTILES.

For a completer list of extinct American Reptiles, see Supplement, "Aids to Advanced Study."

IMPORTANT REFERENCES :

E. D. Cope :—I. *Synopsis of Extinct Batrachia, Reptilia and Aves of North America.* Trans. Amer. Phil. Soc., 1869 and 1870.

II. *Vertebrata of the Cretaceous Formations of the West.* Hayden Survey, ii., 4to., 1874. For *literature* to date, see pages 51-3. For synopsis of known Cretaceous Vertebrata of N. Amer., see pp., 245-302.

III. *Report on the Vertebrate Palæontology of Colorado.* Hayden Ann. Rep., 1873, 427-533.

IV. *Descriptions of some Vertebrate Remains from the Fort Union Beds of Montana.* Proc. Acad. Nat., Sci. Phil., 31 Oct., 1876.

V. *On some Extinct Reptiles and Batrachians from the Judith River and Fox Hills beds of Montana.* Proc. Acad. Nat. Sci., Dec., 1876.

VI. *Batrachia of the Coal Measures of Ohio.* Proc. Amer. Phil. Soc., Feb., 1877.

VII. *Geology of the Judith River beds, Montana, and the Niobrara Cretaceous.* Hayden Bulletin, iii., No. 3.

VIII. Palæontological Bulletin, No. 28. Proc. Amer. Phil. Soc., 21 Dec., 1877.

IX. *Extinct Batrachia and Reptilia from the Permian Formation of Texas.* Proc. Am. Phil. Soc., 5 Apr., 1878.

X. *Report upon the Extinct Vertebrata obtained in New Mexico by parties of the Expedition of* 1874. Wheeler Survey, vol., iv., pt., ii.

Jospeh Leidy :—I. *Cretaceous Reptiles of the United States.* Smithsonian Contributions to Knowledge, 1863.

O. C. Marsh, in American Journal of Science and Arts, IIId. Series. The references denote volume and page.

Leidy and Cope are cited by the Roman numerals prefixed to their papers. The references to "Hux." signify: *A Manual of the Anatomy of Vertebrated Animals,* Am. ed., 1872.

I. Classification of Amphibians and Reptiles. (Hux., 149, 169. Compare Cope, *Bull. U. S. National Museum,* No. 1, and C. I., 4-6, 26-9.)

1. Tabular analysis of Orders of the two Classes.
2. Amphibia differentiated from Fishes. (Hux., 149.) — From Reptiles.
3. Reptiles differentiated from Amphibia. (Hux., 167-9.) — From Birds. (Hux., *Proc, Zoöl. Soc. Lond.,* Apr., 1867.)

II. Amphibians.

1. Urodela (Stegocephali, C. I., 6.)
   (1.) Salamandrids :—*Ichthycanthus.* (C. VI., 573.) — *Leptophractus.* (C. VI., 576.)
   (2.) Xenorhachia (Cope, *Geol. Ill.,* ii., 137) :—*Amphibamus.* (Cope, *P. A. N. S.* 1865, 134; *Geol. Ill.,* ii., 135-41.) — *Tuditanus.* C. VI., 577.)
   (3.) Microsauria. (Dawson,) :—*Pelion*=*Raniceps.* (Wyman, *Am. Jour. Sci.,* 1858, 158; W. 170; C., I., 9.) — *Hylonomus.* (Daws.: *Story,* 146, 148; *Can. Nat.,* viii, 167.) — *Sauropus.* (D. 302; Lea, *Trans. A. P. Soc.,* x. 1852.) — *Dendrerpeton.* (Daws.: *Story,* 146; Owen, *J. Geol. Soc.,* 1853, 81; C. I. 12.)
   (4.) Ganocephala :—*Colosteus.* (C., I., 22.) — *Rhachitomus.* (C., ix., 526.)
2. Labyrinthodonta. (Hux., 154-5; Fig.: *World,* 170.) — Characters and geological history. (L. 409; W. 172-4, 176-7.) — Footprints. (D. 412; Hitchcock : *Ichnology of New England;* L. 409.) — *Dictyocephalus.* (Leidy, *P. A. N. S.,* 1856, 256.) — *Baphetes.* (Daws.: *Story,* 145-6; Owen, *Q. J. Geol. Soc.,* 1853.)

III. Plesiosaurs. — Structure and affinities. (Hux., 180-6.) — *Plesiosaurus.* (D. 443; L. 430; W. 178-9; Ag.: *Sketches,* 160; Daws.: *Story,* 213; Fig.; 201-6.) — *Pliosaurus.* (L. 430.) — *Polycotylus.* (D. 467; C., *P. A. N. S.*, 18 June, 1869; I., 34-8; II., 70-5.)

IV. Lacertilians. — Characters. (Hux., 186-93.)

1. Rhynchocephals. (Hux., 194; Marsh, xv., 409.) — *Nothodon.* (Mh., xv., 410.) — *Cricotus.* (C., P. A. N. S., 1875, 405.) — *Clepsydrops.* (C., *P. A. N. S.*, 1875, 407.)
2. Homœosaurs. (Hux., 195-6):—Triassic *Telerpeton.* (D. 427, 428; W. 166; Hux., *Q., J. Geol. Söc.*, xxii.)
3. Protorosaurs. (Hux., 195-6.) — Permian *Protorosaurus.* — *Crematosaurus.* (C., III., 515.)
4. Monitors or Platynota. Hux., 193, 196):—*Saniva.* (Leidy. P. A. N. S., 1870, 124.) — *Thinosaurus.* (Mh., iv., 229, Oct. 1872.) — *Glyptosaurus.* (Mh., i., 456, June, 1871; iv., 302, 305.)

V. Pythonomorphs or Mosasaurs. (C., I., 182; Owen, *Q. J. G. S.*, 1879, 682; C., *Hayden Surv. Bull.* iv., No. 1; Mh. iii., June, 1872. See synopsis, C., II., 264-72.) -- *Mosasaurus.* (D. 464, 465, 468, 474; L. 469; Daws.: *Story,* 216·7; especially Fig.; *World,* 264-8; Leidy, I., 30-74. See further, *Supplement*) — *Discosaurus-Elasmosaurus,* Cope. (D. 464, 467; L. 467; Leidy, I., 22-5; W. 190; Daws.: *Story,* 217-8. See Suppl. [*D. carinatus* of Kansas had 72 cervical vertebræ; *Plesiosaurus* had 24-41.] — *Edestosaurus.* (D. 468; Mh., i., 447.) — *Cimoliasaurus.* (W. 190; C., I., 40-4; Leidy, I., 25-9.)

VI. Ichthyosaurs. (Hux., 208-14):—*Ichthyosaurus.* (D. 442-3; L. 429; W. 138-9; Ag.: *Sk.* 158-9; Daws.: *Story,* 213; Fig.: *World,* 194-200; C. I. 29.) — Resemblance to Cetaceans. (Hux., 208; D. 443; W. 178-9.) — A composite type. (Ag.: *Sk.* 159.) — *Eosaurus.* (Mh. II., xxxiv., July, 1862; W. 170.)

VII. Crocodilians. — Characters. (Hux., 214-21.) — Tabular analysis of Families.

1. Alligatoridæ:—*Alligator.* (C. *Hayd. Ann. Rep.*, 1872, 614; C. V. 15.)
2. Crocodilidæ:—*Crocodilus.* (C. *Hayd. Ann. Rep.*, 1872, 612; C. VI. 31-4; C. X, 32; Mh. i., 553.) — *Diplocynodus.* (C. *Hayd. Ann. Rep.*, 1872, 613; VI. 31, X, 60.)
3. Gavialidæ:—*Thoracosaurus.* (D. 467; Leidy, I, 5-12.)
4. Teleosauridæ:—*Teleosaurus.* (L. 431; Fig.: *World,* 225.) — *Hyposaurus.* (D. 467; Leidy, I., 18; C. I., 23; C. II., 67-80.)
5. Belodontidæ:—Belodon, perhaps a Lacertilian. (D. 428; C. I., 56-61.)

VIII Dicynodonts and Theriodonts. — Characters and history of Dicynodonts. (L. 410.) — Combined characters of crocodiles, tortoises and lizards. (Owen, .) — Characters and history of Theriodonts. (L. 411; Owen, .)

IX. Ornithoscelids. (Hux., 223-32; L. 431.) — Characters intermediate between Reptiles and Birds. (Hux., 224-6; L. 431.) — Structure of pelvis. — Position of Pubis and Postpubis. (Mh. xvi., 417, plate: xvii., 90.) — The hind-limbs. — Many bipedal. (Mh. xvii., 91.

1. Dinosaurs. (D. 413, 464; L. 431, 452; C. I., 86-90; Mh. xvi., 412.)

(1.) Permian:—*Lysrophus.* (C., P. A. N. S., 1877, 187.) — *Bolosaurus.* (C. IX., 506-8.)

(2.) Triassic:—*Thecodontosaurus.* (C. VIII., 231.) — *Palæosaurus.* (C. VIII., 232.) — *Clepsysaurus.* (D. 413; Lea, *Jour. A. N. S. Phil.*, ii., 4to. pt. 3, 1852.) — *Bathygnathus.* (D. 414; L. 447; W. 178, 184; Leidy, *Jour. A. N. S.*, 1854, 327; C. I., 119.) — *Megadactylus.* (C., I., 122 A.)

(3.) Jurassic:—*Megalosaurus.* (D. 444; L. 433; Fig.; 255.) — *Ceteosaurus.* (L. 434; Daws.: *Story*, 204.) — *Pelorosaurus.* (W. 188; Mantell, *Phil. Trans.*, 1850, pt. 2, p. 379.) — *Iguanodon.* (L. 431; W. 189; Fig.: *World*, 258; D. 445: Mantell: *Foss. of Brit. Mus.*, 224-313; *Isle of Wight*, 227-34.) — *Amphicœlias.* (C. *Pal. Bull.* 27; C. VIII., 233, 242-6. [C. says cretaceous, kangaroo-like, and *A fragillissimus* over 100 ft. in length. (C. in *San Francisco Acad. Sci.*, 1879.)]

Suborder SAUROPDA. (Atlantosauridæ, Mh. xvi., 412, Nov., 1878)—*Atlantosaurus*=*Titanosaurus*, Mh. (Mh. xiv., 87, 514; xv., 241; xvi., 412; xvii., 88; L. 468). Mh. estimates it 80 ft., in length, and says it was the largest land animal so far known.

Suborder SAURANODONTA. (Mh. xvii., 85):—*Sauranodon.* (Mh. xvii., 86.) — *Camarasaurus*=? *Chrondrosteosaurus*, Owen, *Ann. and Mag. Nat Hist.*, ii., 101, Sep., 1878, (C., P. A. N. S., 20 July, 1877, 7; C., VIII., 233-42; Mh, xvii. 89.) C. says it is Cretaceous, and *C. supremus* was 72 ft in length.

Family Allosauridæ, having affinities with Megalosauridæ. (Mh. xviii., 89): *Allosaurus.* (Mh. xiv., 515.) — *Creosaurus.* (Mh. xv., 243; xvii., 90.)

Family Nanosauridæ, having affinities with *Compsognathus.* (Mh. xv., 224; xvii., 90.) — *Nanosaurus.* (Mh. .)

(4.) Cretaceous:—*Hadrosaurus.* (.D 464, 467; L. 467 468; W. 192-3; Daws.: *Story* 202; Leidy, *Cretac. Reptiles*, U. S., 1865, 76-97; C. I., 91-8, 122I.-122 J. See references, C. II., 247.) — *Lælaps*=*Dryptosaurus*, Koch, (D. 464; W. 191; Daws.: *Story*, 203; C., P. A. N. S. June, 1866; I. 100-18; IV., 1-2; V., 1-5; Hayd. Bull. iii., 4, 805.) — *Ornithotarsus.* (D. 464: L. 468; C., P. A. N. S., 18 June, 1869; I. 120-1.) —

2. Compsognaths. (Hux., 225, 228; L. 434 — *Compsognathus.* (L. 434.)

X. Pterosaurs. (D. 464; Daws.: *Story*, 265-7; Hux., 228-32.) — General characters. — Doubtful *Ornithopterus.*

1. With fully toothed jaws — *Pterodactylus.* (D. 446, 468; W. 178, 180-1; Mh. xv. 233, Sep., 1878; xvi. 411, Nov., 1878.)
2. With jaws produced into toothless beaks. — *Rhamphorhynchus.* (D. 446, misnamed—after Goldfuss. — *Pterodactylus;* (L. 435; W. 183-4; Ag.; *Sk.* 162.)

3. With jaws entirely toothless. — *Pteranodon.* (L. 468; Mh. iii., Apr., 1872; xi. 507, June, 1876; Cope I., 169-75; II. 65.)

XI. Chelonians. — *Testudo.* (Leidy, I, 101-111; *Extinct Vert. Fanna West. Terr.*, Hayd. Surv., 339-40; C. X, 283.) — *Compsemys.* (Leidy, *Trans. A. P. S.*, 1860, 152; C. II., 91; IV. 10. — *Adocus.* (C. I., 232-3; II. 91.)

XII. Ophidians:—*Palæophis.* (C. *Geol. N. J.*, 1868, 737; P. A. N. S., 1868, 147, 234; *Trans. A. P. Soc.*, 1869, pl. xiv.) — *Dinophis.* (Mh. II., xlviii., 397.) — *Boavus.* (Mh. i., 322-4.)

XVI. THE REIGN OF MAMMALS, OR THE TERTIARY AGE.

See especially, the official geological reports of New Jersey, South Carolina, Alabama, Mississippi, Tennessee, California, British Columbia, and those conducted by Hayden, King and Wheeler. Also, CONRAD: *Tertiary Fossils of the United States;* TUOMEY and HOLMES: *Fossils of South Carolina*, 4to., 1855.

I. The Continent during the Tertiary Age.

1. Its approximate completeness. (D. 521-2.) — Outlines. (L. 479-80; W. 200.)
2. Intracontinental seas. (D. 491; L. 479, 512; W. 200-1. See Lect. XXIII.) — Relics of the Mesozoic intercontinental channel. (L. 511-2; W. 199.)
3. Arboreal vegetation and its modern aspects. (D. 497-8; L. 481-3; Lesquereux: *Tertiary Flora,* Hayden Rep., 4to. vii.; but see Lect. XIV.)
4. Stratification. (King, *Geol.* 40*th Par.* ch. v.; Lesqx. *Tert. Flor.* Hayd. Surv. vii., 10-20, 24; *Hayden Ann. Rep.* 1870, 93; 1874, 23; Marsh, xvi., Plate, iv.; *Proc. Am. Assoc. Adv. Sci.* 1877, 210.)
5. Views. (Daws.: *Story,* 253; Fig.: *World,* 288, 309, 329. Also, especially, the Reports of Hayden, King, Wheeler and Powell.)

11. Marine Animals. — Approximation to modern types. (D. 499-501; L. 486-7.) — Subdivisions based on percentages of living species. (D. 489; L. 476-7; Daws.: *Story,* 239.) — *Zeuglodon.* (D. 502; L. 500-1; W. 203; Leidy: *Extinct Mam. Dakota,* 427; *Extinct Vert. Fanna Ter.,* 1873, 337.) — *Squalodon.* (Leidy, *Extinct Mam. Dak.,* 416-24.) — Comparison of *Zeuglodon* with the Mosasaurs. — Other marine mammals.

III. Decadence of the Reptilian Dynasty.

1. Total extinctions. (L. 492): — Dinosaurs, Pterosaurs, Ichthyosaurs, Plesiosaurs, Dicynodonts.
2. Types shrunken:—Lacertilians, Crocodilians.

3. Types conserved and developed :—Chelonians. (*Colossochelys*, D. 516, 520 ; L. 493.) — Ophidians. (D. 509, 576.)

IV. Rise of Mammalian Rule.

1. Sudden abundance at the beginning of this age. (L. 495.)
2. Their predominantly placental character. (L. 495.)
3. Already considerably differentiated. (L. 495 ; Daws.: *Story*, 244.) — Types. (Mh., *Proc. Am. Assoc. Adv. Sci.*, 1877, 211-58):— Zeuglodont, Sthenorhine (both tapiroid and horned), Equine, Carnivorous, Insectivorous, Rodent, Cheiropterous, Quadrumanous. — Many of these Marsupial.
4. But these types not completely differentiated. — All the types comprehensive. (L. 508, 509-10.) — Became progressively more differentiated. — Hence supposed to have proceeded from types still more comprehensive. (L. 511.) — The Pantodont type. (L. 506-7 ; Cope, *P. A. N. S.*, Feb., 1873 ; *On the Extinct Vertebrata of the Eocene of Wyoming*, Hayd. Ann. Rep. 1872, 585-9 ; *Palæont. Bullet.*, No. 28, Proc. A. P. Soc. 21 Dec., 1877, 24-30, order AMBLYPODA proposed.)

V. The Cemeteries of the Animals. (W. 204-5.)

1. Why their remains are not generally distributed.
2. The areas called "Bad Lands." (D. 492, 494, 495 ; L. 478-9 ; W. 205-10. See also Lect. XXVII., II., 4, (4) f.) — A picture of desolation. — An ancient sea freshening to a lake. — The lake gradually filled with sediment. (D. 491.) — Life upon its borders. :— Inhumation of skeletons. — Erosions of later times.
3. Sequence of Tertiaries and names of Lakes. (King, 40th Par. i., 458 ; Mh. *A. J. S.*, III., ix., 49 ; Grinnell and Dana, *ib.*, xi., 126.) — Three geographically distinct Tertiary Basins ; probably more.

(1.) Eocene (in the middle province).

(*a.*) Vermillion Creek Group, King=Wahsatch Gr., Hayden. — Deposited in UTE LAKE. — Between Wahsatch and Rocky Mts., from Wind R. Range south to New Mexico. — The Uinta Range an island. — *Coryphodon*, *Eohippus*, *Oxyæna*, *Meniscotherium*, etc. (King, i., 376-7.)

(*b.*) Green River Group, Hayden=Elko Gr.. King. — Deposited in GOSIUTE LAKE. — Nearly the same as last, with doubled east and west dimensions. — Wahsatch and adjoining highland a peninsula ; Uinta still an island. — Fishes, Insects.

(*c.*) Bridger Group. — Deposited in WASHAKIE LAKE. — Wholly within the boundaries of Ute Lake. — *Dinoceras*, *Tinoceras*, *Uintatherium*, *Orohippus*, *Palæosyops*, etc.

(*d.*) Uinta Group. — Deposited in UINTA LAKE, south of Uinta Mts., in valley of Green and White rivers. — *Hyopsodus*, *Epihippus*, *Agriochœrus*, etc.

(2.) Miocene. — Two contemporaneous basins.

Truckee Group, King=John Day Gr., Marsh. — Deposited in PAH UTE LAKE, (Province of Nevada and Oregon.) — East of Cascade and Sierra Nevada Ranges, from Columbia river south into California. — *Rhinoceros Pacificus, Eporeodon, Diceratherium, Miohippus*, etc.

White River Group, Hayden. — Deposited in SIOUX LAKE, (Province of the Great Plains). — From Northern Kansas far into British Columbia, and west nearly to Colorado Range. — *Menodus, Brontotherium, Oreodon, Mesohippus, Poebrotherium, Dinictis*, etc.

(3.) Pliocene. — Three contemporaneous basins.

Humboldt Group, King. — Deposited in SHOSHONE LAKE, (Province of the Great Basin). — Covering Pah-Ute Lake and stretching east over the Great Basin to Wahsatch Mts. — *Protohippus, Merychippus, Dicrocerus.*

North Park Group, Hague and Hayden. — Deposited in NORTH PARK LAKE, (Middle Province). — North Park and upper valley of North Platte River. — No fossils.

Niobrara Group, Marsh. — Deposited in CHEYENNE LAKE, (Province of the Great Plains). — Superimposed on, and overlapping Sioux Lake on all sides; stretching southward to the Gulf and northward into British Columbia. — *Protohippus, Pliohippus, Procamelus, Dicrocerus*, etc.

4. Atlantic and Gulf-border Tertiaries. (D. 491, 494, 495; L. 477.)
5. Foreign Tertiary Basins. (D. 512; L. 480.) — The Paris Basin. (D. 512, 513; L. 496-8.) — What Cuvier dug from it. (D. 513, 517-8; W. 202; Daws.: *Story*, 240; Agassiz: *Sketches*, 185-90.) — Reminiscence of Montmartre and the Buttes Chaumont. — The Vienna Basin. (D. 515.) — The London Basin. (D. 511, 513; Daws.: *Story*, 245, 247.) — Himalayan deposits. — The monarch of proboscideans. — *Sivatherium*. (D. 520; L. 498-9.) — *Colossochelys*. (D. 516, 520; L. 493.)

VI. A Glimmering from the Future.

VII. Disturbances of the Tertiary Age. (L. 512; Daws.: *Story*, 236-7. See Lect. XXV.) — Some cordilleras in Wyoming, Utah and California. — Coast Range, Cal. (D. 523; L. 256.) — Enormous outflow of lava along the Pacific slope. (L. 512; See also Lects. II. and XXVI.) — Pyrenees, Appenines, Carpathians, Alps.

VIII. Parallelism of European and American Formations. (Cope, *Hayden Bulletin*, v. No. 1, 33-54; Marsh, xvi., pl. iv., Nov. 1878.)

XVII. SOME EXTINCT TYPES OF MAMMALS.

[For a completer list of Extinct American Mammals, see "Supplement."]

GENERAL REFERENCES.

LEIDY:—I. *The Ancient Fauna of Nebraska.* Smithsonian Contributions to Knowledge, 1853.

II. *Extinct Mammalia of Dakota and Nebraska*, in Jour. Acad. Nat. Sci. Phil., vol. vii., 1869.

III. *Extinct Vertebrate Fauna of the Western Territories.* Hayden Survey, 1873, vol. i., 4to.

COPE:—I. *Synopsis of the Extinct Mammalia of the Cave Formations of the United States*, Proc. Amer. Phil. Soc., July, 1869.

II. *Preliminary Report on the Vertebrata discovered in the Port Kennedy Bone Cave*, Proc. Am. Phil. Soc., Apr. 7, 1871.

III. *On the Extinct Vertebrata of the Eocene of Wyoming*, Hayden Ann. Rep., 1872.

IV. *Report on the Vertebrate Palæontology of Colorado*, Hayden Ann. Rep., 1873, 427-533.

V. *Report on the Stratigraphy and Pliocene Vertebrate Palæontology of Northern Colorado*, Bulletin, Hayden Survey, No. 1.

VI. *Descriptions of New Vertebrata from the Upper Tertiary Formations of the West*, (Palæontological Bulletin, No. 28), Proc. Am. Phil. Soc., 21 Dec., 1877.

VII. *Descriptions of new Extinct Vertebrata from the Upper Tertiary and Dakota Formations*, Hayden Survey, Bulletin, vol. iv., No. 2, May 3, 1878.

VIII. *Report upon the Extinct Vertebrata obtained in New Mexico by parties of the Expedition of* 1874, Wheeler Survey, vol. iv., pt. ii., 4to.

IX. *On some of the Characters of the Miocene Fauna of Oregon*, Proc. Amer. Phil. Soc., 15 Nov., 1878.

X. *Observations on the Faunæ of the Miocene Tertiaries of Oregon*, Hayden Surv. Bul., v. No. 1, 55-67.

XI. *On the Extinct Species of Rhinoceridæ of North America and their Allies*, Bul. Hayd. Survey, v. No. 2, 227-37.

[The general works cited above supersede many of Leidy's and Cope's numerous preliminary contributions, and hence such contributions are not quoted.]

MARSH:—Numerous papers in *American Journal of Science and Arts*, series III. These are cited by volume and page.

Leidy and Cope are cited by the Roman numerals prefixed to their publications, as above.

I. Classification of Mammals. (Hux., *Anat. Verteb. Anim.*, 273; Gill, *Smithsonian Misc. Coll.*, Nov. 1872, 8vo., 98pp.

1. Tabular analysis of the Orders.
2. The types becoming progressively differentiated through time.

II. Triassic Mammals.

1. American:—*Dromatherium sylvestre.* (D. 415, 417; Emmons: *Geol. N. C.*) — An insectivorous Marsupial. (D. 416-7.)
2. Foreign:—*Microlestes antiquus.* (D. 429.) — Related to above.

III. Jurassic Mammals.

1. American:—*Dryolestes priscus.* (Mh. xv., 459; xvi., 411.) — *D. vorax.* (Mh. xviii., 215, Sep., 1879.) — *Stylacodon gracilis.* (Mh. xviii., 60.) — *Tinodon bellus.* (Mh. xviii., 215, fig., Sep., 1879.) — All insectivorous Marsupials.
2. Foreign:—(1.) Great Oölite of Lower Oölite:—*Amphitherium, Thylacotherium.* (D. 448, 449; Fig.: *World,* 216.) — *Phascolotherium.* (D. 448, 449; Fig.: *World,* 216, 223.) — *Stereognathus.* (D. 447.)

   (2.) Purbeck beds of Upper Oölite:—*Plagiaulax.* (D. 450) — *Spalacotherium.* — *Galastes.* (D. 448.) — *Stylodon.* (Owen, *Geol. Mag.,* iii., 199; *Palæont. Soc.,* xxiv., 45.)
3. All Marsupials. — *Plagiaulax* were rodent, *Galastes* carnivorous, and all the others, insectivorous. — Seventeen European Jurassic species in all.

IV. Eocene Terrestrial Mammals.

1. American [Alabama Period. (D. 508-11.) — Green River and Vermillion Creek Groups. (King, *Geol. 40th Par.,* i., 355) + Bridger and Uinta groups.]

   (1.) MARSUPIALS:—*Triacodon.* (Mh. ii., 123; iv., 222-3; C. III.. 611.)

   (2.) AMBLYPODA:—(C. VIII., 179, 282.)

   Suborder PANTODONTA. (C. III., 187):—*Coryphodon.* (L. 502, 506-7; Mh. xi., 425, May, 1876, pl.; C. VIII., 187-250; *P. A. N. S.,* 1877, 616, brain; Owen, *Brit. Foss. Mam. and Birds,* 299.) = *Bathmodon* (C. III., 585-8; V., 8 10; VI., 24-8; VIII., 187-250.)

   Suborder DINOCERATA, Cope. [See below.]

   (3.) DINOCERATA. (Mh. v., Feb., 1873, plates; Apr., 1873, and Sup. Note; *P. A. N. S.,* 8 Apr., 1873; vii., App. June, 1873; xi., Feb., 1876, plates; C. III., 563-85; Owen, *Amer. Jour.,* xi., 401, questioning the presence of horns):—*Uintatherium.* (D. 504: Leidy, III., 93-108, 331-4; C. III., 580. — *Dinoceras.* (D. 504; L. 503, 506-7; Mh. iv., 343; v., 117, 293, 310; xi., 163, plates.) — *Tinoceras.* (Mh. iv., 322, 343; v., 293; *Am. Nat.* Jan., 1873, 52.) = *Eobasileus.* (C., *P.A.N.S.,* Jan. and Feb., 1873; C. *Am. Nat.,* vii., 1, May, 1867; C. III., 564, 575-80; C. IV., 456.) — These, with *Loxolophodon,* Cope, are thought by Leidy to represent only one genus. (L. III., 332.)

   (4.) PERISSODACTYLA. (Hux., 292):—(*a.*) Coryphodontidæ. (Mh. xi., 428; xiv., 81, plate:—[See above.] — (*b.*) Equidæ. (Hux., 295; Mh. vii., 255; viii., 288; L. 509-10):—*Eohippus.* (Mh. xii., 401.) — *Orohippus.* (Mh. iv., 207; v., 407; vi., 19-22; vii., 247; ix., 247; C. vi., 19-22.) — (*c.*) Tapiridæ. (Hux., 310; Compare Cope on *Rhinoceridæ and related Perissodactyls,* C. IX., 228.) — *Lophiodon.* (Leidy, II., 391; III, 219, 327; Mh. ii., 36.) — *Palæosyops.* (L. 504; Leidy, III., 323-6); C. III., 591; Mh. ii., 36-8.)

   (3.) ARTIODACTYLA. (Hux., 312):—Suidæ:—*Homacodon.* (Mh. iv., 126.)

   (6.) BUNOTHERIA. (C. VIII., 72.):—

   Suborder CREODONTA. (C. VIII., 85):—*Ambloctonus.* (C. VIII., 90-4.) — *Oxyæna.* (C. VIII., 95-105.) — *Didymictis.* (C. VIII., 123-6.)

   Suborder MESODONTA. (C. VIII., 85:—*Microsyops.* (Leidy, III., 82, 320.) — *Tomitherium.* (C. III., 546-8; VIII., 135-45.) — *Antiacodon.* (Mh. iv., 210.)

Suborder INSECTIVORA. (C. VIII., 85):—*Talpavus.* (Mh. iv., 128.) — *Anisacodon,* (Mh. iv., 209.) — *Esthonyx.* (C. VIII., 153.)

Suborder TILLODONTA. (C. VIII., 85):—[See below.]

Suborder TÆNIODONTA. (C. VIII., 85, 157):—*Ectoganus.* (C. VIII., 158-62.) — *Calamodon.* (C. VIII., 162-70; C. *P. A. N. S.*, March, 1876.)

(7.) TILLODONTIA. (Mh. xi., 249-51, plates):—*Tillotherium.* (L. 504; Mh. v. 485; ix., 241: xi., 249, plates; C. VIII., 84, 85.) — *Anchippodus.* (Leidy, II., 403; III., 328; Mh. ix., 241.)

(8.) RODENTIA:—*Plesiarctomys.* (C. VIII., 170-2.) — *Sciuravus.* (Mh. ii., 122; iv., 220.)

(9.) CARNIVORA:—*Limnocyon.* (Mh. iv., 126, 203.) — *Limnofelis.* (Mh. iv., 202). — *Canis.* (Mh. ii., 123.) — *Synoplotherium.* (C. III., 554-9, plates; VIII., 75, 77.)

(10.) CHEIROPTERA:—Nyctitherium. (Mh. iv., 127; v. 405.) — *Nyctilestes.* (Mh. iv. 215.)

(11.) PRIMATES:—(*a.*) Lemuravidæ. (Mh. ix., 289; xii., July, 1876):—*Lemuravus.* (Mh. ix., 239.) — (*b.*) Limnotheridæ. (Mh. ix., 239):—*Thinolestes.* (Mh. iv., 205.)

2. Foreign. (D. 516-20.)

(1.) PERISSODACTYLA:—(*a.*) Coryphodontidæ:—*Coryphodon.* (Fig.: *World,* 290.) — (*b.*) Palæotheridæ. (Hux., 212):—*Palæotherium.* (L. 497; Daws.: *Story,* 247; Fig.; *World,* 282-3.) — (*c.*) Tapiridæ:—*Lophiodon, Hyracotherium,* etc. — (*d.*) Suidæ:—*Chæropotamus.* — (*e.*) Anoplotheridæ. (Hux., 320):—*Anoplotherium.* (L. 498; Daws.: *Story,* 249; Fig.: *World,* 284-5.) — *Xiphodon.* (D. 517; Fig.: *World,* 285-6.)

(2) CARNIVORA:—*Palæocyon, Hyænodon, Arctocyon, Canis,* etc.

V. Miocene Terrestrial Mammals.

1. American, (Yorktown Period—White River, Colorado, etc.) (D. 452. For white R. Fauna of Oregon, see C. X., 55-67.)

(1.) PERISSODACTYLA:—(*a.*) Equidæ. (See under Eocene):—*Mesohippus.* (D. 505; Mh. ix., 248.) — *Miohippus.* (Mh. *A.J.S.*, III., vii., 249.)=? *Anchitherium.* (Leidy, I, 64-74; C. IV., 496-7; IX., 11-14.) — (*b.*) Tapiridæ:—*Lophiodon.* (See Eoc.; Mh. ii., 36-8.) — (*c.*) Rhinoceridæ:—*Diceratherium.* (Mh. iv., 242.) — *Rhinoceros.* (Leidy, I., 79-94.) — (*d.*) Brontotheridæ. (Mh. ix., 245; xi., 335):—*Brontotherium.* (D. 507; L., 505, 506-7; Mh., v. 486; vii., 81, plates; ix., March, 1875; xi., Apr., 1876, plates.) — *Menodus.* (Pomel, *Bib. Univ. de Geneve,* x., 75, Jan., 1849.)=*Titanotherium.* (D. 506; W. 208; Leidy, I., 72-8; II., 389; Mh. ii., 35.) — *Megacerops.* (Leidy, III., 239, 335.)

(2.) ARTIODACTYLA:—(*a.*) Suidæ:—*Elotherium.* (Leidy, I., 57-66; II., 388; III., 320; Mh. ii., 39; C. V. 27.) — *Dicotyles.* (Leidy, II., 384; III., 319.) — (*b.*) Oreodontidæ. (Leidy. III., 199):—*Oreodon.* (D. 507; L. 506; Leidy, I., 29-55; III., 201, 318.) — *Agriochœrus.* (Leidy, I., 24-8; III., 319.) — (*c.*) Hypertragulidæ. (C. X., 66):—*Hypertragulus.* (C. IV., 502; V., 26-7.) — *Leptomeryx.* (Leidy, II., 165, 383.) — (*d.*) Tragulidæ. (Hux., 326):—*Hypisodus.* C. IV., 501.) — (*e.*) Camelidæ:—*Poebrotherium.* (Leidy, I., 19-24; II., 141; C. IV., 498; V., 24; X., 59.)

(3.) PROBOSCIDEA:—? *Mastodon.* (Leidy, II., 396.)

(4.) INSECTIVORA:—*Herpetotherium.* (C. IV., 465.) — *Embassis.* (C. IV., 468.)

(5.) RODENTIA:—*Palæocastor.* (Leidy, II., 338-40, 406.) — *Sciurus.* (C. IV., 475.)

(6.) CARNIVORA:—*Drepanodon* (*Machærodus*). (Leidy, II., 54-64, 367; C. IX., 9-10.) — *Hyænodon*. (Leidy, *P. A. N. S.*, 1853, 93, 392-3; II., 38-48, 369.) — *Dinictis*. (Leidy, II., 64-8.) — *Canis*. (C. IV., 505-7; C. VIII., 301; IX., 8-9.)

(7.) PRIMATES:—*Menotherium*. (C. IV., 510; V., 22.) — *Laopithecus*. (Mh. ix., 240.)

2. Foreign. (D. 518, 519-20.)

(1.) Ungulata:—*Anchitherium*. — *Hipparion*. — *Hippotherium*. — *Equus*.— *Sus*. — *Hippopotamus*. — *Anoplotherium*. — *Camelopardalis*. — *Antilope*. — *Sivatherium*.

(2.) PROBOSCIDEA:—*Mastodon*. (Fig.: *World*, 300-6.) — *Elephas*. (L. 499; Daws.: *Story*, 254.) — *Dinotherium*. (D. 518; L. 498; Daws.: *Story*, 251-3; Ag.: *Sk.*, 189; Fig.: *World*, 298.)

(3.) INSECTIVORA:—*Erinaceus*. — *Talpa*.

(4.) CARNIVORA:—*Machærodus*. (L. 500; Daws.: *Story*, 250; Leidy, I., 94-9.) — *Felis*. — *Hyæna*. — *Canis*. — *Viverra*. — *Mustela*.

(5.) Primates:—*Pliopithecus*. — *Dryopithecus*, *Mesopithecus*. (Fig.: *World*, 307.)

VI. Pliocene Terrestrial Mammals.

1. American (Sumter Period. — Loup Fork of Platte, the Niobrara, etc.) (D. 492.)

(1.) Perissodactyla:—*Protohippus*. (Leidy, II., 274-9, 401; III., 248; C. III., 523-8; V., 15-9; VIII., 322; Mh. II., xlvi., 374; vii., 251, 253.) — *Hipparion*. (D. 506; Leidy, II., 280-92, 401; III., 247-8; C. IV., 522; V., 11; VIII, 321.) — *Pliohippus*. (Mh. *A.J.S.*, III., vii. 252.) — *Equus*. (Leidy, II., 399-400; III., 321-2; Mh. II., xlvi., 374. — *Aceratherium*. (Leidy, II., 220-8, 390; C. IV., 520.) — *Rhinoceros*. (Fig.: 316; Leidy, II., 228, 390.) — *Dicotyles*. (Mh. ii., 42.) — *Platygonus*. (Mh. ii., 40-2.) — *Merychippus*. (C. V., 19; VIII., 324.) — *Dicrocerus*, Lartet. (C. VIII., 346-60.)=*Merychodus*. (Leidy, II., 162-5. 382; III., 318; C. III., 531.)= *Cosoryx*. (Leidy, II., 173, 183; C. *Rep. Vert. Foss. N. Mex.*, 16.) — *Procamelus*. (Leidy, I., 147; II., 147-57; III., 258-9, 317; C. IV., 529-30; V., 20; VIII., 325), etc.

(3.) PROBOSCIDEA:—*Elephas*. (Leidy, II., 251-6, 397-9.) — *Mastodon*. (Fig.: *World*, 314; Leidy, II., 240-51, 392-7; C. IV., 531; VI., 225-7; VIII., 306-16.)

(4.) EDENTATA:—*Morotherium*. (Mh. xii., 61)

(5.) RODENTIA:—*Castor*, *Palæocastor*, *Hystrix*, *Taxidea*, *Arctomys*, etc.

(6.) Carnivora:—*Felis*. (Leidy, *P. A. P. S.*, 1852, 261; *Trans. A. P. S.*, 1852, 322; II., 365-6.) — *Canis*. (Leidy, II., 28-30; C. V. 11; VII., 301; Allen, *Am. Jour.*. xi,, 49.)

2. Foreign. (D. 519, 520):—*Elephas*, *Mastodon*, *Pithecus*, *Semnopithecus*, *Machærodus*, *Putorius*, *Ursus*, *Lepus*, *Arctomys*, *Arvicola*, etc.

VII. Quaternary Terrestrial-Mammals.

1. American. (D. 565-71; L. 542-7; Foster: *Prehistoric Races of U. S.*, 80.)

(1.) PERISSODACTYLA:—*Equus*. *Tapirus*. (D. 567.)

(2.) ARTIODACTYLA:—*Dicotyles*. (Leidy, II., 384.) — *Ovibos*. (Leidy, II., 373-4), and most modern genera.

(3.) PROBOSCIDEA:—*Elephas*, 2 sp., and *Mastodon*, 1 sp.

(4.) EDENTATA:—*Megatherium*. 2 sp. — *Megalonyx*, 5 sp. — *Mylodon*, 4 sp. — Glyptodon, 1 sp. (D. 520. 569; L. 545, 546, 547.)

(5.) RODENTIA:—*Castoroides* and most modern American genera. (D. 567.)

(6.) CARNIVORA:—*Felis*, *Ursus*, *Machærodus*, *Galera*.

2. Old World Species. (D. 563-5; L. 541, 547; Dawkins: *Q. Jour. Geo. Soc.*, xxv., 192, 1869, and xxviii., 410, 1872; Rau: *Early Man in Europe*, 23-30; Lubbock: *Prehistoric Times*, ch. ix.)

XVIII. THE ALPS AND THE GLACIERS.

On Glaciers, see AGASSIZ: *Systeme Glaciaire;* CHARPENTIER: *Essais sur les glaciers;* TYNDALL: *Hours of Exercise in the Alps;* RÉCLUS: *The Earth*: pp., 162-221; Payot: *Guide itineraire au Mont Blanc;* CHAMBERLIN: *Rep. Geol. Wis.*, 1876; DANA: *Man.*, 675-80; LECONTE: *Elem.*, 43-64; LYELL: *Principles*, 224-8. On the *Glacier of the Rhone traced to Lyons*, see Bibliotheque, Univ., 1870, xxxviii., 118, and *Bul. Soc. Geol. de France*, 1869, xxvi, 360. On the Glaciers of Norway, *C. de Seue, La Neve de Justedal et ses Glaciers;* 1870.

I. Geography of the Alps. (Lantern Views.)

1. Regions of the High Alps.
2. Alpine Regions and Passes.
3. The Bernese Oberland (90 miles square.)

II. Geology of the Alps.

1. General Structure of the Alps.
2. Section from Lucerne to Como.
3. Tunnel under Mont St. Gotthard.

III. Perspective Views of the Alps.

1. Mont Blanc Range from Geneva.
2. The Bernese Oberland from Bern.
3. Mont Blanc from St. Martin.
4. Les. Ouches, Mont Maudit and Pic du Midi.
5. Chamonix and the Mont Blanc from above Chamonix.
6. Mont Blanc and the valley of Chamonix, from the Flégère.
7. Mont Blanc, from the Brévent.
8. The Jungfrau from Interlaken.
9. Valley of Lauterbrunnen.
10. Valley of Lauterbrunnen and the Gletscherhorn.
11. Falls of the Staubbach.
12. The Breithorn, from the Mürren.
13. Panorama from the Mürren.
14. The Jungfrau from the Wengern Alp.
15. The Jungfrau and hotel from the Summit of the Wengern Alp.
16. The Wetterhorn from Grindelwald.
17. The Matterhorn and Gorner Glacier, near Zermatt.
18. Gorge of the Tamina at Pfeffers.

IV. The Pinnacled forms of Alpine Summits.

1. Aiguille de Charmoz, from Montanvert.
2. Aiguille de Charmoz, from the Chapeau.
3. Aiguille du Dru, from Montanvert.

4. Glacier des Bois and Aiguille du Dru.
5. Grands Mulets and Aiguille du Midi.

V. General Views of Glaciers.

1. Mer de Glace, from the Flégère.
2. Mer de Glace, from Montavert.
3. Eiger Glacer, Eiger and Monk, from the Wengern Alp.
4. Church and Glacier of Grindelwald.
5. Glacier of Rosenlauï.
6. Glacier of the Rhone.
7. Aletschhorn and Middle Aletsch Glacier from the Egischhorn.

VI. Terminations of Glaciers.

1. Arch of Ice at Source of the Arveiron.
2. Same from a different position.
3. Bridge of Ice, Glacier of Langthal, Oetzthal in Tyrol.
4. Another Bridge of Ice, Oetzthal.
5. Glacier of Langthal—ice-blocks at termination.
6. Source of the Lütschine.
7. Vault of Ice, Glacier of Rosenlauï.
8. Terminal Precipice, Gorner Glacier, Zermatt.
9. Source of the Rhine, (Hinter Rhine,) from the Rheinwald or Zapport Glacier.

VII. Phenomena of Transportation by Glaciers.

1. Village and Glacier of Argentière, showing lateral moraines.
2. Hotel Montanvert, showing moraines of Glacier of Nant Blanc.
3. Bridge des Gaillants, showing moraines of Glacier des Bossons.
4. Erratic Blocks on the Glacier of the Aar.
5. Oberaarhorn and Glacier of Viesch, from Eggischhorn, showing Median Moraines.

VIII. Glacier Motion and its Consequences. (Ref. *supra*, and Lect. XIX., III., 2.)

1. Summit of Mont Blanc, showing Firn-fields.
2. The Weissthor, the Cima of Jazzi and Monte Rosa.
3. Diagram of Crevasses, showing their cause.
4. Incipient Crevasses at entrance of "Junction" in ascent of Mont Blanc.
5. The Junction and the Plateau, showing crevasses more advanced.
6. The "Difficult Passage," Mer de Glace.
7. Another Difficult Passage.
8. Mer de Glace, from the "Mauvais Pas"—Chaos of Ice.
9. Grand Pyramids, Glacier des Bois.
10. Grand Pyramids of Ice, Glacier of Gaisberg, Oetzthal.
11. Aiguilles, Glacier des Bois.

12. Crevasse in Glacier of Grindelwald.
13. Glacier des Bossons, from Pierre Pointue.
14. Séracs before the "Junction."
15. Ladder Passage, departure from the Junction.
16. Passage of the Horizontal Ladder, Junction.
17. Aiguilles des Bossons, and the Side Wall.
18. Ladder Passage, Wall of Ice, before the Grands Mulets.
19. Precipices of Ice and Snow above the Grands Mulets.

IX. Causes of Catastrophes.

1. Great Crevasses below the Dome du Gôuter.
2. "Grande Crevasse" at the Grand Plateau, Mont Blanc.
3. Great Crevasses, impracticable passage, "Petites Montées."
4. Disaster from an Avalanche, August 20, 1820.

XIX. THE REIGN OF ICE.

GEIKIE: *The great Ice Age;* NEWBERRY *Geol., Ohio*, ch., xxx. (vol. ii), and iii., 27; *Annals of N. Y. Lyceum of Natur. Hist.*, ix.. June, 1869; *Proc. Boston Soc. N. Hist.*, x., May, 1862; N. H. Winchell, *Pop. Sci. Mon.*, June and July, 1873; *Am. Jour. Sci.*, III, i., 15-9; J. J. Dana, *Am. Jour. Sci.*, III., i., 1, 125; ii., 233, 326; E. Andrews, *Am. Jour. Sci.*, II., xlviii, 172; Jos. Leconte, *Ancient Glaciers of the Sierras, Cal. Acad. Sci.*, 16 *Sep.*, 1872; *A. J. S.*, III., v. 325-42.

I. Familiar Drift Phenomena.

1. Incoherent surface accumulations. (D. 527, 529; L. 514-6.) — Sands, pebbles, boulders, clays. (L. 514-6; W. 220 — "Hog-backs" and surface configuration.
2. Smoothed, striated and furrowed rocks. (D. 530: L. 516; W. 215, 217-8; Newberry: *Geol. of Ohio*, ii., 12-9.)
3. Fiords. (D. 533; L. 534; W 220.) — Old river channels sometimes deeply buried. (D. 552; W. 219-20; Newberry: *Geol. O.*, ii., 12, iii., 27; *Boston S. N. H.*, x, May, 1862; E. Hitchcock: *Geol. Vt.*, i., 215.)
4. All these phenomena connected together.

II. Sketch of Continent at End of Tertiary Time. (W. 213.)

1. Its Geographical Extent and Form.
2. Its Topographical and Hydrographical features.
3. Its Forest growths.
4. In many respects similar to the modern continent. (D. 525; W. 210.) — But it was an ancient and wasted surface. — Subaërial disintegration of rocks. (W. 221; also in Harper's *Geol. Rep. Miss.*, 1857; W. *Brazil in the Reign of Ice*, College Courant, June 4 and 11, 1870; Pumpelly, *Am. Jour.*, xviii., 142, etc.) — General doctrine of continental wastage.

III. How the preglacial Continent was Renovated.

1. Northern Elevation and increasing cold. (D. 539-40, 541; W. 214.) — Union of lands previously separated.
2. Glacier formation, growth, movement and effects. (On Glacier motion, see further, Mosely, *Proc. Roy. Soc.*, xvii., 202; *Phil. Mag.*, Aug., 1871; Croll, *Phil. Mag.*, March, 1869; Ball, *Phil. Mag.*, July, 1878; *A. J. S.*, III., i, 268; Mathews, *Alpine Jour.*, Feb, 1870); John Aitken, *Nature*, 13 Feb., 1873; *A. J. S.*, III., v., 305.
   - (1.) Reminiscence of Alpine glaciers. (D. 675-8; L. 43.)
   - (2.) Tremendous effects of a continental glacier. (D. 538; W. 218-9.) — Prostration of forests. — Plowing and removal of disintegrated rock-surfaces. — Smoothing and striation of hard rocks. (D. 538.) — Digging of some lake-basins. (D. 539; W. 225.) — Filling of old river-channels and lake outlets. (539; W. 219-20, 225.) — Desolation in nature. — Greenland a modern picture of continental glaciation. (D. 538.)
3. Thickness of the Continental glacier. (D. 537; *Am. Jour.*, v., 1873; L. 527.) — Limited by the thawing influence of heat escaping from the Earth. (Matthew, *Canad. Nat.*, vi., 96.) See also Dana, *ut sup.* and *A. J. S.*, III., v., 217.
4. Extent of the ancient glaciers, and directions of the ice-streams. (D. 528, 531, 537; L. 519, 526-7.) — Movement south-west along the upper valley of the St. Lawrence, Lakes Ontario and Erie, and the Maumee river. (D. 537; Gilbert, *Geol. Ohio*, i., 540-4, map); Newberry, *Geol. Ohio*, ii., 50-3, map.) — The Colorado valley supposed not glaciated. — Nor the slopes of the Rocky Mts. in the U. S. (D. 538; Hayden, *Ann. Rep.*, 1874, ch., iv.) — The western glaciers local. (King, *Geol. 40th Par.*, i. 460-1. But see R. Brown, *Am. Jour.*, II., l., 318-24.) — Glaciers in southern Colorado. (Endlich, Hayden, *Ann. Rep.*, 1875, 216-26. — Glaciation in Foreign Countries. (D. 532; L. 530-2; L. Ag.: *A. J. S.*, III., iv., 135; C. F. Hartt, *A. J. S.*, III, i., 294, Brazil.)
5. Supposed interglacial epoch. (D. 561; L. 534; S. V. Wood, *Geol. Mag.* Apr., 1872; Geikie, *Geol. Mag.*, viii., ix.; *A. J. S.*, III., iv., 231.)
6. A gradual subsidence. (D. 551, 555; L. 521.) — Dissolution of the ice-fields. (W. 222.) — Work of the torrents. (D. 553; W. 222.) — Freight of sediments. (D. 553.) — Renovation of southern areas. (D. 553; W. in Harper's Rep. on Miss., 1857, 317; W. 222-3. Compare Tuomey, *Ala. Geol. Rep.*, 1849, 2, 116, 142.) — Stumps of the glaciers still existing. (King, *Geol. 40th Par.*, i., 462; *Am. Jour.*, i., 157; Davidson, *Proc. Cal. Acad. Sci.*, iv., 1871, 161; J. Muir, *Overland Monthly*, Dec., 1872; *A. J. S.*, III., v., 69; Leconte, *Am. Jour.*, iii., 125; v., 325; x., 126; *Proc. Acad. Nat. Sci.*, Cal., iv., (pt. v.,) 259.) — Ice-wells:—Vermont.

(Hitchcock, *Geol. Vt.* i., 192.) — Oswego, N.Y., (*Am. Jour.*, I., xxxvi., 104.) — Ice-mountain in Va., (*Am. Jour.*, I, xlv., 78.) — In Wallingford, Vt. (*Am. Jour.*, I., xlvi., 331.) — Ice-caverns in Russia. (*Geol. Russia*, i., 186; Lippincott's *Gazetteer*, Art., *Yakotsk*.

7. A continental submergence generally supposed. (W. 228; C. H. Hitchcock, *Proc. A. A. A. S.*, 1871; *A. J. S.*, III., ii., 207.) — Not established for the Cordilleran region. (King, *op. cit.*, i., 466.)
8. A slow emergence and assorting of materials. (L. 524; W. 229.) — The assorting possibly the work of glacier-torrents, without submergence.

XX. POST GLACIAL HISTORY.

Newberry: *Geology of Ohio*, ii., ch. xxx; Dana, *A. J. S.*, III., v., 198.

I. Reappearance of the preglacial Flora.

1. Floral migrations under secular changes of climate. (D. 532, 543, 599.)
2. Return of preglacial types from the south. — Arctic or glacial types still lingering on mountain summits.

II. Migrations of Faunas.

(D. 542.) — A South American Fauna in the United States. (D. 569. Also Lect. XVII., VII., 1, (4).)

III. Early Condition of the Great Lakes.

1. Their present relations as to Altitude.
2. Former altitudes. (W. 241-3; 246; L. 521.) — Terraces. (W. 246-7; L. 521-2; Gilbert, *Ohio Geol. Rep.*, i., 540-4.) — Rock erosions. (W. 246-7.)
3. Former Geographical Extent. (D. 552; W. 241; W. *Michigan*, 77.) — Low lacustrine borders. (D. 552.)
4. Ancient outlets and connections. (Newberry, *Geol. Ohio*, ii., 12-9.)
   (1.) By Little Bay de Noquet. (W. *Michigan*, 28-9; N. H. Winchell, *A. J. S.*, i. 19.)
   (2.) By Green Bay, Lake Winnebago and the Wisconsin chain. (N. H. Winchell, *A. J. S.*, i., 15-9.)
   (3.) By the Illinois river. (D. 540, 552, 553; E. Andrews, *Trans. Chic. Acad. Sci.*, ii., 14.)
   (4.) By the Maumee river. (D. 540, 552; Gilbert, *A. J. S.*, i., 342-4.)
   (5.) A channel across the Lower Peninsula of Mich. (W. *Mich.*, 15-6.)
   (6.) Submerged outlets of the Connecticut and Hudson rivers. (D. 423, 540.)

IV. Subsidence of Lakes.

1. Removal of Barriers of the Great Lakes. (W. 542.) — The Niagara barrier, its effect, and the result of its degradation. (W. 235.)

2. Desiccation. — Quaternary lakes of the far west. (King, *Geol. 40th Par.*, i., 490; Stevenson, Wheeler, *Rep.*, iii., 453-71. — Lake Bonneville.) Gilbert, *Wheeler Rep.*, iii., ch. iii.; Howell, *ib.*, 250-1; Hayden: *Rep.*, *Wyom.*, 1870, 72-3; *Pacif. R. R. Rep.*, ii., 97; King, *Geol.* 40*th Par.*, i., 490-504.) — Lake Lahontan. (King, *Geol.* 40*th Par.*, i., 504-29, maps.) — Coronado's Lakes. (Endlich, *Hayd. Rep.*, 1875, 147-8.) — Other extinct lakes. (Hayden: *Ann. Rep.*, 1874, 48.) — Deposits of Marl and Peat. W. 237; King, *Geol.* 40*th Par.*, i., ch. vi.)

XXI. POST-GLACIAL HISTORY. (Continued.)

I. Aqueous Erosions.

1. The recession of Niagara Falls. (D. 553; W. 235, 244; Hall, *Geol. N. Y.*, 4*th Dist.*, 389; Foster: *Prehist. Races* U. S., 376-7.) — Data. (W. 245.) — Consequences.
2. Recession of the Falls of St. Anthony. (N. H. Winchell, *Geol. Minn.*, 1876; *Q. J. G. S.*, Lond, Nov., 1878, 886-900; Southall: *Epoch of the Mammoth*, ch. xxiii.)
3. Deepening of river gorges. (L. 529; W. 344.)
4. Changes of River channels. — The Ohio. (D. 553.) — The Hoang-Ho. (Pumpelly, *Smiths. Cont.*, xv., Art. iv.; *Am. Jour.*, II., xlv., 219; Bickmore, *Am. Jour.*, II., xlv., 209; Martin, *Am. Jour.*, II., xlvii., 100; Richthofen: *China*, 12, 85-7.) — Mississippi Bayous. (Ly.: *Prin.*, 215-7.) — The Rhine. (D. 556.) — In Vermont. (Hitchc.: *Geol. Vt.*, i., 215.)
5. Dissolution of Sea-Coasts. (L. 32-6.)

II. Fluviatile Formations. — Alluvium. (D. 649; L. 22-3, 522-4.) — Deltas. (D. 651; L. 24-7; Ly.: *Prin.*, 208-13.) — Mississippi Delta. (Ly.: *Travels*, 2d vis., ii., ch. xxi; Humphreys and Abbott: *Rep. Miss. River.*) — Bars. (D. 660; L. 30.) — Rafts. (Ly.: *Prin.*, 213.) — Terraces. (D. 558-9.) — Mud-lumps. (Hilgard, *A. J. S.*, III., i., 238, 356, 425.)

III. Sandy Deserts and Dunes. (Marsh: *Man and Nature*, ch. v.)

1. Drifting sands. (L. 520.) — Dunes of Western Europe. (Marsh: *loc. cit.*) — Of Africa. (Ly.: *Prin.*, 702; Reclus, 91.) — Of Lake Michigan. (W. *Michigan*, 13.) — Of Nebraska. (Aughey, *Hayd. Rep.*, 1874, 259.)
2. The Sahara. (Réclus: *Earth*, 90-5.) — An ancient sea-bottom. — Some portions still below the Mediterranean. — Project of inundation. (*Internat. Rev.*, iv., 138-9; *Nature*, Apr. 3, 1879, 509; Scribner's *Month.* ; *Engineering and Min. Jour.*)

3. Deserts in Poland. (Naumann: *Geognosie*, ii., 1173. — Arabian Nefouds. (Réclus: *Earth*, 95.) — Cobi. (Réclus, 95; Richthofen: *China*.) — Sandy Steppes of Tartary. (Réclus: *Earth*, 87-9.) — Grandes Landes of Gascony. (Réclus: *Earth*, 81.)

IV. Campestral Formations.

1. Prairies, grassy steppes, pampas, llaños, puszta. (W. 264; Réclus: *Earth*, 85, 98-101; Humboldt: *Aspects of Nature*, Am. ed., 25-165.) — Tundras. (Réclus, 86.) — Buried Mammoths. (W. *N. Y. Daily Trib.*, 17 Aug., 1878.) — Bogs. (Réclus: *Earth*, 83, 413-8; Ly.: *Prin.*, ch. xlvi.; Hunt: *Can. Nat.*, II., i., 426.) — Peat and Muck. (S. W. Johnson, *Trans. Conn. State Agric. Soc.*, 1857 and 1858.)
2. Loess-covered surfaces. (Pumpelly, *Amer. Jour.*, xviii., 133; Aughey, *Hayd. Rep.*, 1874, 245-50); Richthofen: *China*.

V. Post-glacial Volcanoes. (L. *Am. Jour.*, xviii., 35.)

VI. Coral Structures. — Polynesian Coral Islands. (D. 583.) — The peninsula of Florida. (W. 231.)

XXII. RELICS OF PRIMEVAL MAN.

Rau: *Early Man in Europe*, 1876; Lubbock: *Prehistoric Times*, 3d ed., London, 1872; Figuier: *Primitive Man*, Am. ed., 1870; Vogt: *Lectures on Man*, London, 1864; Foster: *Prehistoric Races of the U. S.*, Chicago, 1874.

I. Primeval Man Known to Inductive Science chiefly through European Relics.

II. Primeval Man in Europe. (L. 561, etc.)

1. Historical allusions. (Homer: *Odyss.*, ix., 113-4, 108, 122, 124, 160, 167, 244, 125-128, 271-275; Hesiod: *Theog.*, 133, 139; Aeschylus: *Prometh.*, 462-4; Aristotle: *Politica.*, l. i., c. 1.; Plato: *Leges;* Pausanias: *Descr. of Greece*, l. viii., c. 1, § 2, 5, 6; l. v., c. 17, § 1, 3; l. x., c. 17, § 2; Diod. Sic., l. v., c. 65; Virgil: *Æneid*, viii., 314-18; Tactitus: *Germ.*, c. 46.)
2. Race affinities of these men. (Vogt: *Lect.*, 370-93.)

III. Archæological Discoveries. (L. 563, etc.; W. 352.)

1. Caverns and Rock-shelters. (D. 574, 575, 576; L. 536-9, 563-5; Rau, ch. ii., iv.; Lubbock, ch. x.; Fig., 56-82, 85-90. Dawkins: *Cave Hunting*.)
   (1.) Where explored. (Rau, ch. ii., iv.)
   (2.) What they contain. (Ran, ch. ii., iv.)
2. River-Drifts. (Rau, ch. i.; Lubbock, ch. xi.)
3. Loess and Moraines.
4. Volcanic Tuff.
5. Peat Bogs. (L. 539, 542.)

6. Kitchen Middens. (D. 577 ; L. 566 ; Rau, ch. v.; Lubbock, ch. vii.; Fig., 129-34.) — On the Pacific Coast. (Schumacher, *Bul. Hayd. Surv.*, iii., 27-56.)
7. Megaliths and Tumuli. (Lubbock, ch. v.; Fig., 184-207.) — Cistvaens, Barrows, Dolmens and Cromlechs.
8. Lake Dwellings. (D. 576; L. 566: Lubbock, ch. vi; Fig., 135-7, 215-30.) — What they are. — What they yield. (Fig., 240-87.) — Crannoges. (D. 576; Lubbock, 177 ; Fig., 230-1.) — Terramares. (Fig., 232-9.)
9. Parallel facts supplied by modern savages. (Lubbock, ch. xiii-xv ; *Origin of Civilization.*)

IV. Intrepretation of the Facts.

1. Divisions of prehistoric time. (D. 574; L 561 ; Lubbock, ch. i.)
   (1.) Ages :—Stone. (Lub., ch. iv ; Fig., 1-202.) — Bronze. (Lub., ii-iii ; Fig., 205-93,) — Iron. (W. 353; Fig., 297-332.)
   (2.) Stone Age sub-divided into three epochs.
   (3.) Cannot be used for chronometric purposes. (W. 353; Rau., 12.)
2. Geological conditions in the Stone Age. (W. 361.)
3. Characters of Prehistoric Europeans. (Rau, ch. iii-iv; Lub., ch. x.)
   (1.) Physically. (Rau, 81; Lub., 337-40; Fig., 112-6 ; Vogt, 370-93.)
   (2.) Socially and Intellectually. (W. 363-5; Rau, 66-70, 83, etc , ch, v ; Lub., 586 Fig., 128, 137-83, 258-70.)
   (3.) Æsthetically. (W. 358, 355-6 ; Rau, 65-6, 71-9, 85-6, 103-5 , Lub., 29-44, 335-5.)
   (4.) Religiously. (W. 366 ; Fig., 280-3.)

V. Primeval Man in America. (Lub., ch. vii ; Foster, *op. cit.;* Squier and Davis: *Ancient Monuments Miss. Val.;* Lapham: *Antiquities of Wis.:* Haven: *Archæology of the U. S.*)

1. Mounds and Tombs. (Lub., 267-77 ; Fost., ch. iii, v, vi, viii, x.)
2. Earth-works. (Lub., 259-63 ; Lapham: *Antiq. Wis.*)
3. Mining Hammers. (Fost., ch. vii.)
4. Shell-heaps. (Fost., ch. iv.)
5. Remains beneath lava in California. (Fost., 52-6. Lect. XLVII.)
6. Mesa Ruins or Cliff-Dwellings. (Ives: *Explor. Col. Riv.*, 119, Moquis ; Jackson, *Hayd. Rep.*, 1874, 369-81, plates ; *Hayd. Rep.*, 1875, 12, 23-4.)

XXIII. METHOD OF CONTINENTAL DEVELOPMENT.

DANA, *Proc. Am. Assoc.*, 1856, pt. ii., 1-25, chart; *id.*, 1855, 1-36; *Manual Geol.*, 389-90, 591 ; *Am. Jour. Sci.*, II., xxii., 335; WINCHELL: *Sketches of Creation*, ch. xxvii.; KING: *Geol. 40th Parallel*, i., ch. vi. and viii.; GEIKIE, *Proceed. Roy. Geograp. Soc.; Popular Sci. Monthly*, Sep., 1879. On the *Geological History of the Gulf of Mexico*, see E. W. Hilgard. *Proc. A. A. A. S.*, 1871, 222 ; *A. J. Sci.*, III., ii., 391.

I. Primordial Wrinkles the Germs of Land-Masses. (Lect. XXXIX.) — Cause of wrinkles. — Their location. — The system of contraction and upheaval.

II. The Continent of Palæozoic Time.

1. Composed of Archæan sediments. (D. 161.) — These the ruins of an older, unknown land.
2. Location and Form of the Palæozoic Continent.
   (1.) The Laurentian limb. (D. 148.) — Detached insular Laurentian exposures. (D. 150; Lect. III., III., 2. Also Irving, *A. J. S.*, III., v., 284, map; J. H. Eaton, III., v., 444, map; Hind, A. J. S., II., xlix, 347-55, in Nova Scotia.)
   (2.) The Cordilleran limb. — Consisted of emerging peaks of the Cordilleran range from the Colorado to the Humboldt ranges. (King, *40th Par.* i., ch. i., *id.*, 534; Newb., *Ives Color. Exped.*, 47; Peale, *Hayd. Ann. Rep.*, 1875, 68-9.) — Thought by King to have beeen a continuous land area before Cambrian Time. (King, *40th Par.*, i., 583, 534, 729-30. Compare Newb., *Ives Col. Exp. Exped.* and Peale *Hayd. Ann. Rep.*, 1875-68.) — The Nevada Mass continued continental. (King, *40th Par.*, i., 731.) — But subsided at end of Palæozoic. (King, *40th Par.*, i., 732.)
3. Origin of sediments and supposed subsidence of Appalachian region. (D. 161, 251; L. 254-5.) — This implies a land-region to the north-east of the present continent.
4. Great thickness of Palæozoic sediments (40,000 ft.) along the border of the Nevadan continent. (King, *40th Par.*, i., 731.) — Great subsidence of Palæozoic sea-bottom. (King, 732.)
5. The configuration of America due to the topography of the Precambrian continent. (King, *40th Par.*, i., 533, 751.)
6. Europe mostly submerged during Palæozoic Time. (Geikie, *Pop. Sci. Monthly*, Sep., 1879, 599. — The Northern land of Europe and the Northern Ocean.

III. The Continent of Mesozoic Time. (D. 481.)

1. Composed of Palæozoic and Archæan sediments.
2. Its duplex constitution.
   (1.) The Laurentian limb. — Its south-eastward and south-westward growth. (D. 333, 481.) — Comparative completeness.
   (2.) The Cordilleran limb. — The Palaeozoic sea becomes dry land forming the Great Basin and the Wahsatch. (King, *40th Par.*, i., ch. ii,, Map; *id.* 536-7, 731-2 759; D. 520.) — And the Nevadan Continent sinks beneath the sea. (King, 537, 732.) — Distinction between subsidence of a lightened continental mass and of a loaded sea-bottom. — The latter gradual, the former cataclysmic. (King, i., 732.) — The western shore of this continent trended meridionally, the eastern, retreated south westward into Arizona. (King, i., 733.) — Numerous, and some extensive, islands in the Mesozoic ocean, along the Rocky mountain region.
3. The great intercontinental ocean between the Wahsatch and the Mississippi valley. (D. 481, 520; King, i., 537, 733.)
4. Europe still mostly submerged. (D. 481.) — Land growing southward. (Geikie, *Pop, Sci. Mon.*, Sep., 1876, 601.)
5. South America more extensively submerged.

IV. The Continent of Cænozoic Time. (D. 520.)

1. Composed of pre-cenozoic sediments.

2. The twin areas connected. — Uplift of Rocky Mountain region and a portion of the Great Plains. (King, 40th Par., i., 360; ch. iv., and map; D. 480.)

3· The great mediteranean seas or "Tertiary lakes" of North America. (Newb., *Hayd. Rep. Wyoming*, 1870, 329-39; Hayden: *Ann. Rep.*, 1872, 33; *id.* 1874, 47.)

(1.) Residual portions of the Mesozoic intercontinental ocean. — Shifted and enlarged, however, by regional subsidences. (King, i., 754-6.)

(2.) Their locations, extent and names. (King, i., 458; Lect. XVI.)

4. The mediterranean seas of Europe. (D. 480.)

5. The condition of South America. — The Andes under water. (D. 480.)

6. The final uplift and consummation. — But very gradual.

V. Unity of Method in Continental Growth. (D. 29-38.)

1. Ultimate forms foreshadowed from the beginning. (D. 147, 160, 393-4; King, 40*th Par.*, i., 751.) — Two great water sheds on the Laurentian limb, each with two branches. (D. 24, 160.) — The northern branches diverge, the southern converge. — The Cordilleran limb also grew from its Archæan germ.

2. To what extent have continents and oceans exchanged places? (D. 160, 250.)

(1.) The old idea of general exchanges.

(2.) The later idea of no exchanges.

(3.) The truth lies between. — Some subordinate exchanges. (King, i., 731-2, 746, 755, 756.) — Still, the Atlantic and Pacific have never been continental.

XXIV. MOUNTAIN-BUILDING.

MALLET: (See references, Lect. XXVI and Part II); HUNT: *Chemical and Geological Essays*, 241-82, 328-48; HALL: *Palæontology of New York*, iii., 1859, Introduction, 57-96: LECONTE: *Elements of Geology*, 1878, 240-60; *Am. Jour. Sci.*, III., iv., 354 and 460-72; KING: *Geology of the 40 h Parallel*, i., ch. viii., Orography; GILBERT: *Orography*, in Wheeler Report, Vol., iii., ch. i.; WHITNEY: *Mountain Building*, in N. A. Review; H. D. ROGERS: *Geology of Pennsylvania*, Vol., ii., pt. ii., 885-941; VOSE: *Orographic Geology*, Boston, 1866, 8vo., 136 pp.; BABBAGE: *Proc., Geol. Soc.*, London, ii.; SIR JOHN HERSCHEL: *Proc. Geol. Soc.*, London, ii.; NAUMAMN: *Geognosie*, I., 337-633.

Two distinct origins of Mountains. — By upheaval and by relief.

I. Mountains of Upheaval.

1. Primordial wrinkling of the terrestrial crust.

(1.) Cause of the wrinkling. (D. 739; L. 240, 252-4; see further, Part II.)

(2.) Location of some primitive wrinkles.

(*a.*) Laurentian nucleus. — Appalachian. (D. 150.) — Cordilleran, especially between lon. 105° and 115° 30'. (King, i., ch. i., and map. See also Lect. XXXIII., II., (2).) — Scandinavian. (D. 151.)

(*b.*) Perhaps Caribbean, Lemurian, Indian.

(3.) These not originally lofty mountain masses.

2. Progressive development and wear of these wrinkles.
   (1.) Source of materials for sedimentation.
   (2.) Deposition along coast-borders. (L. 254-6.)
   (3.) Parallel ranges developed successively coastward. (L. 257.)
   (4.) Simple and complex mountain folds. (L. 242-3; Whitney: *Geol. Cal.*, 121; Comstock, in Jones' *Rep. N. W. Wyom.*, 139-Wind R. Mts.) — The lowest rocks exposed along the eroded crest. (L. 242-5.)
   (5.) Indications of successive uplifts. — Section across the Adirondacs. — In the Rocky Mountains. (*Wheeler Rep.*, iii., 499.)
   (6. High inclinations and overturns of strata.
      (*a.*) Appalachians. (D. 396; Safford: *Geol. Tenn.*, 185, 190.) — Green Mts. (D. 213.)
      (*b.*) Elk Mts. Col. (D. 740; L. 176; Peale, *Hayd. Rep.*. 1873, 256, plates xvii., xviii.; Holmes, *Hayd. Rep.*, 1879, 68-71, and maps and chart of sections.)
      (*c.*) Sangre de Cristo Mts., Col. (Endlich, *Hayd. Rep.*, 1875, 121-3, plates, 125.)
      (*d.*) In foreign countries. (Murchison: *Siluria*, 96, Malvern Hills, 501, Alps. See also Rogers: *Geol. Penn.*, ii., 901-2, ideal section of Alps; and Hunt: *Op. cit.*, 328-48.)

3. The Synclinorium theory of Mountain making. (D. 748-50, 211-14, 244, 251, 275, 305; L. 252-60; Hall: *Pal. N. Y.*, iii., Introd. Comp. King, i., 731: Hunt: *Chem. and Geol. Ess.*, 49-58.) — Secular contraction of the earth pronounced inadequate. (Dutton, *Penn. Monthly*, May and June, 1876; Fisher, *Cambridge Phil. Trans.*, xii. See further, Part II.)

4. Faulting. (741; L. 258, 261, 263.)
   (1.) In Silurian rocks. (D. 214-5.)
   (2). In the Appalachians, 20,000 feet. (D. 398-400, 647; L. 261; Safford: *Geol. Tenn.*, 142, 144, 185.)
   3.) In the Colorado Range 6,000 to 7,000 feet. (King, i., 730.) — Park Range 10,000 feet. (King, i., 730.)
   (4.) In the Unita Mts, 20,000 to 25,000 ft. (L. 242, 263; King, i., 730; Powell: *Uinta Mts.*, 12, Atlas, plates i., ii., iii.)
   (5.) Along the Wahsatch Range, 3,000 to 40,000 ft. (King, i., 44, 730, 745-6-)
   (6.) Along the Basin Ranges generally, from Salt Lake to Carson Lake. (King, i., 735 and maps, x., xi. and xii.)
   (7.) The Sierra Nevada, 3,000 to 10,000 ft. (King, i., 744.)
   (8.) Disapearance of half an anticlinal by downthrow along a fault. — Sierra Nevada, Wahsatch, Unita and other Ranges. (See foregoing references.)
   (9.) Monoclinal ridges and "Kaibab structure." (Powell: *Uinta Mts.*, 10-16; also Gilbert and Howell, in *Wheeler Rep.*, iii.; Rogers: *Geol. Penn.*, ii., 920-1.)

5. Thickness of sediments in mountains of upheaval. (D. 210, 749; L. 244, 243-6; Rogers: *Geol. Penn.*, ii., 779.) — Metamorphism. (D. 750, 400; L. 357; Hunt: *op. cit.*, 18-34: Daubrée, *Annales des Mines*, V. xvi., 155-393, Trans. *Smiths. Ann. Rep.*, 1861, 228-304.)

6. The Cordilleran chain mostly formed by upheaval. (L. 241.)

7. Vertical movements generally slow. (D. 754; L. 244; Lyell; *Prin.* 159-69; Safford: *Geol Tenn.*, 183.)

II. Mountains of Relief.

1. By erosion of horizontal or slightly tilted strata. (Rogers: *Geol. Penn.*, ii., 927-33.) — Table mountains. (D. 246; Whitney: *Geol. Cal.*, 211, 248; Powell: *Uinta Mts.*, 18.)

(1.) Excavation of basins and valleys in such strata. — Central Tennessee. (W. 342; Safford: *Geol. Tenn.*, 97-104.) — The Cumberland Table Land. (W. 343; Safford: *Geol. Tenn.*, 66-79. — Amazonian valley borders. (Ag.: *Journey in Brazil*; Orton: *Andes and Amazon.*) — Uinta Mountain or Range. (Powell: *Uinta Mts.*; King, i., 9, 753.)

(2.) Removal of formations along one border. (L. 249-50.) — Appalachians. (Rogers: *Geol. Penn.*, ii., 920-1.) — Many ranges in the Great Basin. (Gilbert, *Wheeler Rep.*, iii., ch. i., sec. i.) — But these perhaps faulted anticlinals. (Howell, *Wheeler Rep.*, iii., ch. viii., sec. i.; King, i., 735, iii., 45.)

(3. Removal along both borders. — The Catskills. — The Appalachians. (L. 241.) — Mt. Dana in the Sierra Nevada. (Lec., *Am. Jour.*, June, 1873, v. 452.)

2. By erosion along anticlinals. (D. 749; L. 246; Rogers: *Geol. Penn.*, ii., 933-6.

(1.) Mountains of upheaval completed as mountains of relief. (D. 647; L. 246.)

(2.) The synclinal structure in mountains. (D. 213, 748; L. 248.)

(*a.*) Examples:—Taconic Mts. (D. 213-14, 750.) — Greylock. (D. 214.) — Green Mts. (D. 750.) — Alleghanies. (D. 398; Rogers: *Geol. Pa.*, i., 13; *ib.*, ii., 926.)

(*b.*) Coast Range. (Whitney: *Geol. Cal.*, i., 14, 144.) — Wahsatch Range. (Hayden: *Ann. Rep.*, 1872, 16.)

(3.) Anticlinal valleys. — Appalachians. (Rogers: *Geol. Penn.*, ii., 922-23.) — Valley of East Tennessee. (L. 246; Safford: *Geol. Tenn.*, 144. — Other examples. (Powell: *Color. River*, fig. 55; Murch.: *Silur.* 126.)

(4.) All sculpturing the work of erosion. (L. 245-50.) — Pinnacles and Peaks:—Castle Range, Cal. (Whitney: *Geol. Cal.*, i., 33.) — Granitic pinnacles. (*ib.*, 373.) — Mt. Brewer. (*ib.*, 380-1.) — Yo Semite. (*ib.*, 407-23.) — Other Cal. peaks. (*ib.*, 424-37.) — Wahsatch Range. (King: 40*th Par.*, i., 44, pl. i.) — Elk Mts., Col.) (Hayden: *Rep.*, 1874, ch. v., and maps; also, 1873.) — In Wyoming. (Hayden: *Rep.*, 1872, 47.) — Colorado valley. (Ives, *Explor. Col.*, 48, 49, 50, 52, 55, 62.) — "Needles" of the Swiss Alps. (Lect. XVIII., IV.)

3. Relief mountains not always metamorphic.

III. Types of Mountain Structure. (Powell: *Uinta Mts.*, 9-29; also *Explor. Color. R.*, ch. xi., and *Am. Jour.*, xii., 414-28, illus.)

XXV. PRINCIPAL EPOCHS OF OROGRAPHIC DISTURBANCE.

I. Chronological Arrangement.

1. Presilurian:—Laurentides. — Adirondacks. — Blue Ridge. — Highlands, from N. J. to Dutchess Co., N. Y. (D. 16, 211.) — Black Mts., N. C. — Black Hills. — Wind River Mts. (D. 390.) — Colorado, Medicine Bow, and Park Ranges. (King: 40*th Par.*, i., 5, 17-42; Powell: *Uinta Mts.*, 26; Marvine: *Hayd. Rep.*, 1873, 139.) — Core of the Humboldt Range. (King, *id.*, 12, 62.) — Sawatch Range. (Hayden: *Ann. Rep.*, 1873, 49-57, 246.)

2. End of Lower Silurian. — Green Mts. in part. (D. 212-14, 305, 355, 389, 390, 392.) — Northeastern U. S. (Rogers: *Geol. Penn.*, ii., 784.) — In Europe. (D. 217.)
2. End of Devonian :—Catskill Mts. (D. 290.) — New England, Eastern Canada, Nova Scotia. (D. 289, 390.)
4. End of Carboniferous :—Alleghanies. — Western portion of Great Basin, or present Nevada Plateau, with submergence of older Nevadan land on the west. (King: *40th Par.*, i., 731-2, 748.) — First displacements in Rocky Mts. (Stevenson, *Wheeler Rep.*, iii., 499-500.)
5. Between Jurassic and Cretaceous :—Trap mountains and ridges from Nova Scotia to N. Carolina. (D. 417, 486.) — Second movement in the Rocky Mts. (Stevenson, *Wheeler Rep.*, iii., 500.)
6. End of Jurassic :—Sierra Nevada, and Basin Ranges to the east. (D. 452, 486; Whitney: *Geol. Cal.;* King: *40th Par.*, i., 734-54, 759.) — Blue Mountains, Oreg. (King.) — Humboldt Range. (D. 453, 486.)
7. End of Crctaceous (i. e. in the West, post-Lignitic) :—California west of Sierra Nevada. (D. 523; King: *40th Par.*, i.) — Wahsatch Range. (King: *40th Par.*, i., 745, 747, 753. *Not* D. 453, 486; Comstock, *N. W. Wyom.*, 154.) — Part of Rocky Mts. east of Wahsatch. (D. 523; King: *40th Par.*, i., 748; Stevenson, *Wheeler Rep.*, iii., 500-1.) — Uinta Range. (King: *40th Par.*, i., 540, 753; Powell: *Uinta Mts.*, 201; Emmons, *King Rep.*, iii., 198-202, 311-6; *not* D. 453, 486.) — Cascade Range. (King.)
8. After Lower Eocene (Vermillion Creek Group) :—Formation of Wahsatch Fault, with subsidence of Central Utah. (King: *40th Par.*, 745, 755.)
9. After Middle Eocene :—Cherokee Ridge, and plications in Western Nevada. (King: *40th Par.*, i., 755.) — Pyrenees, Julian Alps. (Murchison: *Siluria*, 499.) — Appenines, Carpathians. (D. 512, 525.) — Southern Himalayas. (D. 512.)
10. End of Eocene :—Perhaps Cordilleras in Wyoming and Utah, and California. (D. 523.) — Subsidence along the East Nevada fault. (King: *40th Par.*, i., 744, 756.) — Corsican chain. (D. 525.)
11. End of Miocene :—Coast Range, Cal. (D. 523; L. 256, 512; Whitney: *Geol. Cal.*, i., 320, *seq.;* Le Conte, *Am. Jour. Sci.*, iv. 470, vii. 176.) — Rocky Mts. further raised to 11,000 ft. (D. 524.) — Subsidence of "Great Plains" and formation of "Cheyenne Lake." (King: *40th Par.*, i., 455; Lect. XVI., V. 3, (3).) — Severe crumpling in region of Pah-Ute Lake, and formation of "Sho-

shone Lake," stretching from Sierra Nevada to Wahsatch, and north, far up Columbia R. (King: 40*th Par.*, i., 456.) — San Domingo. (D. 524.) — Western Alps, including Mont Blanc, Monte Rosa, Rigi, etc. (D. 512, 525). — Antrim, Inner Hebrides and Faroe Is. (D. 525.) — Older eruptions of Auvergne and Velay. (D. 525; Ly.: *Man.*, ch. xxxii.; Scrope: *Volcanoes of Central France.*)

12. End of Pliocene:--Tilting of the Great Plains to a maximum of 7,000 ft. — Depression of east and west borders of Great Basin Pliocene, by faulting along eastern Sierra Nevada and western Wahsatch.) King: 40*th Par.*, i., 758.) — Eastern Alps, from Valais to St. Gotthard. (D. 525.)

II. Inductive Inferences.

1. The loftiest mountains developed in later geological ages.
2. The post-Carboniferous, post-Jurassic and post-Cretaceous the principal building times of the modern American continent. (King: 40*th Par.*, i., 759.)
3. Distinction of slow and paroxysmal subsidences. (King, 760.)
4. Distinction of gentle and dislocating elevations. (King, 760-1.)

XXVI. VULCANISM.

On Volcanic Phenomena, see LYELL: *Principles of Geology*, ch. xxiii.-xxvi.; DE LA BECHE: *Geological Observer*, ch. xvii.-xxi.; RÉCLUS: *The Earth*, ch. lxi.-lxxii.; ZURCHER et MARGOLLÉ: *Volcans et Tremblements de Terre*, Paris, 1866; DAUBENEY: *Description of Volcanoes*; NAUMANN: *Geognesie*, i., 76-189; HUMBOLDT: *Aspects of Nature*, Am. ed., 375-99.

On Earthquake Phenomena, see LYELL: *Principles*, ch. xxvii.-xxxii.; DE LA BECHE: *op. cit.*, ch. xxii.; RÉCLUS: *Earth*, ch. lxxiii.-lxxviii.; BAKEWELL: *Introduction to Geology*, ch. xix.; ZURCHER et MARGOLLÉ: *op. cit.*, 251-94; NAUMANN: *Geognosie*, 193-286; L. PALMIERI: *The Eruption of Vesuvius in* 1872; R. MALLET: *The Great Neapolitan Earthquake of* 1857, 2 vols., 8vo., 1862, Pt. i.; General Phenomena, Pt. ii., Phenomena of the Neapolitan Earthquake; *Facts and Theory of Earthquakes*, Reports Brit. Assoc., 1850-8.; *On Observation of Earthquake Phenomena*, Admiralty Manual of Scientific Inquiry, 3d ed., 1859, Smithsonian Ann. Rep., 1859, 408-33; *Earthquake-wave Experiments*, Phil. Trans., 1862, vol. cliii.; ALEXIS PERRY, Sundry memoirs on the earthquake and volcanic phenomena of the world, presented to *Academie Royale de Belique*, etc., 1843-1867, and subsequent years in other publications.

On volcanic Rocks, see KING: *Geology of* 40*th Parallel*, i., ch. vi.; ZIRKEL, in *Geology of* 40*th Par.*, vi., (for microscopic characters); PUMPELLY, *Geology of Mich.*, 1873, ii., pt. ii., on copper-bearing rocks; HUNT, *Geology of Canada*, 1863, ch. xx., pp. 643-70; RICHTHOFEN: *On a Natural System of Volcanic Rocks*, Mem. Cal. Acad. Sci., 1868, i., pt. ii., 4to.; LYELL: *Manual of Geology*, ch. xxviii., xxix.; DANA: *Man. of Geol.*, 76-9, and *System of Mineralogy*; also general works on Lithology, as cited in Lecture III.

[Theoretical considerations are postponed to Part II.]

Definition and explanation.

I. Volcanoes. (D. 702-16; L. 81; Lyell, Réclus, etc., as above.)

1. General description. (See above.)
2. Locations contiguous to sea-coasts. (D. 703; L. 81-2; Ly.: *Prin.*, 332-40; Réclus, *Earth*, 426-32, map; Hunt: *Chem. and Geol. Essays*, 67-9.) — Rarely far inland. (D. 704.)
3. Volcanic action perpetual or periodical. (D. 714; L. 81.) — Through craters. (D. 711; L. 82.) — Through fissures. (D. 714.)
4. Ejections:—Explosions. (D. 692; L. 82; Ly.: *Prin.*, 445.) — Molten matter. (D. 707; L. 83; Réclus, ch. lxvi.) — Volcanic bombs. (D. 709.) — Ashes and stones. (L. 83; Réclus, 468, 471.) — Mud and water. (Ly.: *Prin.*, 414; Réclus, 475.) — Vapors and gases. (D. 708; L. 85; Réclus, 433.) — Formation of Cone. (D. 704, 710, 715; L. 81, 83, 186-9; Ly.: *Prin.*, ch. xxiv.-xxvii.; *Manual*, 489.)
5. Particular examples:—(1.) Vesuvius. (D. 714; L. 88; Ly.: *Prin.*, 347-80; Réclus, 448; Zurcher et Margollé, 1-50. — Burial of cities. (L. 83; Ly.: *Prin.*, 369-80; Réclus, 470; Pliny: *Letters*; Zurcher et Margollê, 1-10; Dyer: *Pompeii*, London, 1875, and the works cited, pp. 5-9.)
   (2.) Ætna. (Ly.: *Prin.*, ch. xxvi; Réclus, 419-25; 469: Zurch. et Marg., 51-65.)
   (3.) Kilauea and Mauna Loa. (D. 708-16; Réclus, 430, 460-2; Zurch. et Marg., 200-7; Brigham: *Volcanoes of the Hawaiian Islands*, 1868; Dana, *Am. Jour.*, II., xlvi, 105-23; Coan., *ib.* xlvii., 89; III., ii., 454; III., iv., 406-6.
   (4.) Jorullo. (Ly.: *Prin.*, 411-14; Réclus, 443-4; Zurch. at Marg., 169-76.)
   (5.) Skaptar Jökul. (L. 83; Ly.: *Prin.*, 409-11; Zurcher et Marg., 80-4.)
   (6.) Tomboro. (L. 82, 83; Herschel: *Phys. Geol.*, 111; Ly,: *Prin.*, 45: Réclus, 471; Zurch. et Marg., 192-7.
   (7.) Mt. St. Elias, Shasta. (Whitney: *Geol. Cal.*, i., 332-49.) — Rainier. (L. 81.)
   (8.) Extinct Volcanoes. (D. 525; Newb., *Ives. Col. Explor.*, 65, 72; Ly.: *Man.*, ch. xxx.-xxxii.; Zurch. et. Marg., 225-37, 249.)
6. American Lavas of Post-Pliocene age. (D. 524, 753.) — Immense outflows along the Pacific slope. — Table Mountain. (Whitney: *Geol. Cal.*) — Lithological characters. (King: *40th Par.*, i., ch. vii., and Zirkel, *ib.*, vi.)
7. Comparison of Lavas of more ancient date. (Ly.: *Man.*, 486-7.)
8. Injections, Intrusions and Outflows:—Veins. (D, 108-14, 731; L. 226; Ly.: *Man.*, 567-72.) — Dikes. (D. 715, 109, 111, 722; L. 87, 207; Ly.: *Prin.*, 363; Ly.: *Man.*, 483; Hayden: *Ann. Rep.*, 1872, 37-9.) — Beds of igneous origin. (D. 717, 185, 418; L. 259; Gilbert, *Wheeler Rep.*, iii., ch. v.; Stevenson, *ib.*, ch. xiv., and p. 501; Loew, *ib.*, ch. xxiii.; Marvine, *Hayden Rep.*, 1873, 129; Peale, *Hayd. Rep.*, 1873, 318-322; Endlich, *ib.*, 345, etc.; Peale, *ib.*, 163-74; Endlich, *Hayd. Rep.*, 1874, 193-209; Peale, *Hayd. Rep.*, 1875, ch. vii.; Endlich, *ib.*, 127-36, 145-8, 212-15; Rhoda, *ib.*, 312; Crittenden, *ib.*, 364, pl. xliv.; Leconte, *Am. Jour.*, Apr., 1874; Comstock, *N. W. Wyom.*, 184.) — Basaltic columns. (D. 716, 722, 86,

87, 421; L. 209-10; Ly.: *Man.*, 483-523; Hayden: *Ann. Rep.*, 1872, 50.) — Metamorphism. (D. 724-31.) — Mountain Forms resulting from lava-outflows. (Powell: *Uinta Mts.*, 18-21; Ly.: *Prin.*, ch. xxiv-xxvii; Ly.: *Man.*, 462, 489-518.)

9. Richthofen's chronological classification. (See General Ref.) — Propylite, Andesite, Trachyte, Rhyolite, Basalt. (King: *40th Par.*, i., ch. vii.)

II. Fumaroles or Solfataras. (D. 718, 708; Ly.: *Prin.*, 347; Réclus, 434, 478, 486-8.) — About volcanic mountains. (D. 708.) — On the coast of the Bay of Naples. — At New Madrid. — New Zealand. (Zurch. et Marg., 208, 321.)

III. Thermal Waters (See Lect. II., IV. 2; Réclus, ch. lxx.)

1. Artesian waters. (Lect. II., IV. 4.) — Temperatures.
2. Deep-mine waters. (Lect. II., IV. 3.) — Temperatures.
3. Thermal springs. (D. 719; Lect. II., IV.; Whitney: *Geol. Cal.*, 93-5; Gilbert, *Wheeler Rep.*, iii., 146-55; Hague, *King Rep.*, iii., 704-7, pl. xxi., xxii.)

(1.) Their common occurrence. — In volcanic and mountainous regions. — Temperatures. (D. 719, 722.)

(2.) Geysers. (L. 94; Réclus, 482; Zurcher et Marg., 84-94.) — Phenomena. (L. 94.) — Explanation. (D. 721; L. 99-104.)

(3.) Thermal waters of Yellowstone National Park. (D. 719-21; L. 94-9; Hayden: *Ann. Rep.*, 1871, 162-98; *ib.*, 1872, 52-6; *A. J. S.*, III., iii., 105, 161, maps and views; Peale, *Hayden Rep.*, 1872, 122-158, 173-8; Bradley, *ib.*, 234-50; Jones: *Explor. N. W. Wyom.*, 1873, 24-32; Comstock, *ib.*, 189-259.)

(*a.*) Especially described and illustrated by Dr. Hayden. (Reports for 1871 and 1872. But see Comstock, *ut supra*, and *Am. Nat.*, Feb. and Mar., 1874; Richardson: *Wonders of the Yellowstone*; Taylor: *Illus. Libr., Trav. and Adventure*, 1873; Doane: *Yellowstone Exped.*, 1870, especially 24-38; also Reports of Superintendents Langford and Norris.)

(*b.*) Remarkable outbursts, and sintery deposits. (D. 719-21; L. 95-9; Jones: *N. W. Wyom.*, 25-32.)

(*c.*) Views. (D. 719, 720; L. 95-9; Hayden: *Rep.*, 1871, 66-127; *ib.*, 1872, 54, 122-5; also many photographs in "National Museum," taken by W. H. Jackson.)

(*d.*) In Colorado. (Peale, *Hayd. Rep.*, 1872, 102-3; Marvine, *Hayd. Rep.*: 1873, 205-6.)

(*e.*) Thermal Springs of New Zealand. (*Pop. Sci. Monthly*, July, 1879; Réclus, 483; Hayden: *Ann Report.*, 1871, 128; Hochstetter: *New Zeal.*, 452; Zurch. et Marg., 315-20.)

IV. Seismic phenomena.

1. Earthquakes. (D. 741, 585; L. 104-26; Ly.: *Prin.*, ch. xxviii.-xxx.; Réclus, ch. lxxiii.-lxxix.) — Destructive occurrences. (L. 120; Ly.: *Prin.*, 441, 447, 471-3, 476, 485; Réclus, ch. lxxv.; Zurch. et Margol., 251, *et seq.*; Hamilton's and Dolomieu's "*Accounts of the Great Calabrian Earthquake.*" Also, South American earthquakes as described by Humboldt, Fitzroy and Darwin; and Javan, by Stamford Raffles; also, Mallet, *ut supra.*)

2. Seismic phenomena in the United States.

(1.) The New Madrid Earthquake of 1811. (Ly.: *Prin.*, 447-9; *Travls. in U. S.*, 2d vis., ii., 172-82.)

(2.) Frequent slight shocks of later occurrence. (Twining, *Am. Jour.*, i., 47; Brigham, *Mem. Bos. Soc. N. H.*, ii., i., 227, New England earthquakes; *A. J. S.*, i., 304; J. D. Whitney, *A. J. S.*, III., iv., 316.)

3. Sea-waves. (D. 662; Lect. II., II., 3, (4); L. 119-22; *Rep. U. S. Coast Surv.*, 1855, 1862 and 1869; Ly.: *Prin.*, 478-84; Zurch. et Marg., 268, 281.) — In South America, 1868. (*Am. Jour.*, II., xlvi., 422-8.)

(1.) Caused by submarine earthquakes.

(2.) Striking examples:—Lisbon, Simoda, Arica. (D. 662; L. 120.)

(3.) Measurement of mean depth of ocean. (D. 743; L. 122; *Rep. U. S. Coast Surv.*, 1862 and 1869; Rankine, *Proc. Roy. Inst. Gt. B.*, 26 May, 1871.)

4. Submarine volcanoes and new islands. (D. 711; Ly.: *Prin.*, 415-33; Réclus, ch. lxxi.; Darwin: *Volcanic Islands;* Zurch. et Margol., 327-50; Lect. II.)

5. Slow vertical movements. (Lect. II.; Darwin: *Geol. Observ. on Coral Reefs*, etc., pt. i., 127-46; pt. ii., ch. ii. Also, Humboldt: *Aspects of Nature*, 423—shells 13,790 ft.; Somerville: *Phys. Geog.*, i., 185—shells 17,480 ft.—both cases in the Andes.)

XXVII. EROSIONS.

I. **Atmospheric Erosions.** (L. 3.)

1. By Winds. — Sand Blast. (D. 632; W. *Grand Traverse Region*, 13; Comstock, Jones' *N. W. Wyoming*, 167-70; W. P. Blake, *Pacif. R. R. Rep.*, v. 108, 230, 232; *A. J. S.*, II., xx., 180; *Proc. A. A. A. S.*, 1855, 218; Newberry, Ives' *Exped.*, 17, 24; G. K. Gilbert, *Proc. A. A. A. S.*, 1874, *B* 26.)
2. By Frost. (L. 8; Comstock, Jones' *N. W. Wyom.*, 19-80.)
3. By Atmospheric disintegration. (L. 6-8; Pumpelly, *Am. Jour.*, xviii., 133; Hayden: *Rep. Montana*, 1871, 34, 39, 43, 61; *Rep. Col.*, 1874, pl. x.; Lyell: *Travels in N. Amer.*, 2d. Visit, ii., 27; Whittaker, *Geol. Mag.*, iv., 447, *etc.*)

II. **Aqueous Erosions.** (L. ch. ii.)

1. By Rains. (D. 637; L. 9.)
2. By Ice. (See Lectures XVIII. and XIX.)
3. By Waves and Oceanic Currents. (D. 657, 661, 663, 665; L. 31-6; Ag.: *Jour. in Brazil*, 438.) — Receding shores. (D. 663; L. 33; Ly.: *Prin.*, 291-319.) — Rocky islets. (D. 663; L. 35; Ly.: *Prin.*, 287-90.) — Purgatories.
4. By running water. (Ly.: *Prin.*, ch. xiv., xv.) — Continental drainage.

(1.) Producing the great features of continental sculpture. (L. 245-50.)

(2.) Action of moving waters. (D. 638; L. 11, 18-20; Ly.: ***Prin.***, 195.) — Corrasion. — Relation to velocity. (L. 18-20; Ly.: ***Prin.***, 195. — Force of Alpine torrents. (Réclus: ***Earth***, 284-93.)

(3.) Erosions along existing river-valleys. (See Lect. XX.)

(*a.*) Ravines, Gorges, Cañons. (L. 15; Ly.: ***Prin.***, 202.)

(*b.*) The Niagara. (L. 12-13; W. 243-5; Hall: Geol. IVth Dist., N. Y.; Ly.: ***Prin.***, 203-6; ***Travels***, 1st visit; Réclus, ***Earth***, 303.)

(*c.*) The Mississippi. (Ly.: ***Prin.***, 215; Réclus, ***Earth***, 304; Humphreys and Abbot: ***Haudraulics of the Miss.***) — Upper waters. — Lower waters. (Ly.: ***Prin.***, 211.) — Ancient deeper channel and wider valley.

(*d.*) Kentucky. (W. 344.) — Cumberland, Illinois and others.

(*e.*) Green and Colorado rivers. (D. 640-3; L. Frontisp., 16 7; Newberry, ***Ives***, ***Color. Exped.***; W. 345-9; Powell: ***Rep. on Col. Riv.***)

(*f.*) The Amazons. (Ag.: *Jour. in Brazil*, 435; Orton: *Andes and Amazon.*)

(4.) Erosion of plateaux, basins and plains.

(*a.*) Colorado plateau. (D. 645; L. 16; W. 346, 348; Ives: ***Rep. Col. Exped.***, 63, 76, 80, 98-118; Newb., ***Ives' Rep.***, 45, 54-64; Wheeler: ***Prelim. Rep.***, 1871, 23; Powell: ***Color. Riv.***; Endlich, ***Bul. Hayd. Surv.***, iv., 831-64, on erosion in Col.)

(*b.*) Bridger Basin. (King's ***Rep.*** *40th* ***Par.***, iii., 238. — Bear River region. (King's ***Rep.*** *40th* ***Par.***, iii., 326-39.)

(*c.*) Plains of Texas and New Mexico. (Kimball, ***Proc. A. A. A. S., Salem***, 174.) — The "Great Plains." — The Basin of Middle Tennesee. (W. 341-3; Safford: ***Geol. Tenn.***, 134-5, and map.)

(*d.*) Bridges and Arches. (W. 248, 31, 89, 91; Endlich, ***Hayd. Rep.***, 1875, 158, pl. xx.; Réclus: ***Earth***, 240.)

(*e.*) Circumdenudation. (D. 648.) — Columns, Pyramids, Mesas. (D. 641; L. 16; W. 247; Ly.: ***Elem.***, 78, 268, 70, 556; King: ***Geol.*** *40th* ***Par.***, i., 96, Frontispiece, 396-401; Endlich, ***Hayd. Ann. Rep.***, 1874, 195, 207; Ives: ***Col. Exped.***, 76, 64; Newb., ***Ives' Col. Exped.***, 20, 30, 76-91; En dlich, ***Hayd. Ann. Rep.***, 1875, 156-8, plates xix., xx.; Holmes, ***ib.***, 256, pl. xli., xlii., 268-72, pl. xliv., xlv.; Forsyth, ***Yellowstone Exped.***, 1875, 8—"Castle Rocks." — "Garden of the gods." (Peale, ***Hayd. Ann. Rep.***, 1872, 100; 1873, 36; Marvine, ***Hayd. Ann. Rep.***, 1873, 265; Hayden: ***Ann. Rep.***, 1874, pl. viii., ix.) — "Monument Park." (D. 646; Hayden: ***Ann. Rep.***, 1873, 32; ***ib.***, 1874, 36, 40, and pl. iii., iv.) — Compare needles, columns and tables on glacier surfaces. (Réclus: ***Earth***, 193; Tyndall: ***Glaciers of the Alps***, ***Hours of Exercise in the Alps***; Lect. XVIII., V.)

(*f.*) "Bad Lands." (L. 247-8; W. 205, 206, 296; Owen: ***Geol. Northwest***, 196-9; Hayden: ***Rep. Wyom.***, 1870, 145-6; King: ***Geol.*** *40th* ***Par.***, i., Frontisp., 9, 396-401.)

(*g.*) Foreign examples. (Ly.: ***Elem.***, 67-78; ch. xix.)

(5.) Erosion of mountains. (See Lecture XXIV., II.)

(6.) Underground erosions. (D. 653-4; L. 68, 70; Réclus: ***Earth***, 245-60; Comstock, Jones' *N. W. Wyom.*, 181-2.)

III. Avalanches, mountain-downfalls and landslips. (Réclus: *Earth*, ch. xxvii.; Payot: *Guide itinéraire au Mont Blanc;* Bakewell: *Geol.*, 385; Ly.: *Prin.*, 708; D. 655.) — Lowering of Mountains. (Orton, *Am. Jour. Sci.*, ii., 267.)

XXVIII. THE OLD AGE OF CONTINENTS.

I. The Mass of the Sedimentary Rocks a measure of past denudations. (L. 263.)

1. Origin of marine sediments.
2. Nearly all the known rocks of sedimentary origin. — Where were the lands worn down to supply the material?
3. Their direction indicated by gradations in the coarseness of the sediments. (D. 373.) — Appalachian materials and their north-eastern origin. (D. 251; Hall: *Pal. N. Y.*, iii., Introduc.) — The Potsdam Sandstone a shale in Alabama.

II. The Archæan Lands of North America.

1. Archæan sediments imply shore-erosions.
2. The old Archæan surface extensively eroded *before* Cambrian time. (King: *Geol. 40th Par.*, i.)
3. These lands themselves formerly more extensive. — Eroded *during* Palæozoic time.
4. Their substance built into Palæozoic and later formations.

II. The old Caribbean Continent. (Bland, *P. A. P. S.*, xii., 56, *etc.;* Cope, *P. A. N. S.*, 1868; P. T. Cleve, *A. J. S.*, III., iv. 235.)

1. Its surviving relics.
2. Involved small areas in South America.
3. Tradition of a cataclysm in the Antilles. (Foster: *Prehistoric Races, U. S.*, 396-9; Catlin: *The Lifted and Subsided Rocks of America*, Lond., 1870.)

IV. The Lemurian Continent.

1. The Mascarene islands. (Milne-Edwards, *Comptes Rendus*, 15 Apr., 1872, 1030-4; *Ann. and Mag. Nat. Hist.*, iv., 72; *Am. Jour. Sci.*, iv., 138.)
2. Evidences of former extension to Java.

V. A Supposed Polynesian Continent. (D. 583; Leidy: *Ext. Mam. of Dak. and Neb.*, 1869, 36, 356; Huxley, *Anniversary Add.*, Lond. Geol. Soc., 1870; Cope, *P. A. P. S.*, 1871, 55, 99, and *P. A. N. S.*, 1867, 156.)

VI. The wasted Aleutian Connection. (L. 535; W. 25. See under last head.)

VII. The "fabled" Atlantis.

1. Historical reminiscences. (Plato: *Timæus* and *Critias*, Jowett's trans., ii., 462, 519-21, 588, 599-607; Theopompus, auc. Aristotle, in Plutarch: *Consolatio ad Apollonium*, § 27; Compare Preller: *Griechische Mythol.*, i., 453; Timagenes, auc. Amm. Marcellinus, in Müller's *Fragmenta Histor. Græc.*, iii., 323; Marcellus, in Müller, *op. cit.*, iv., 443.)

2. The old stump of Atlantis perhaps discovered. (Wild, in *Nature*, March 1, 1877, 377. Compare Thomson: *Voyage of the Challenger*. The *Atlantic*, i., Ch. ii., App. B., p. 93.) — Grounds for supposing a "Miocene Atlantis." (Heer: *Flora Tertiaria Helvetica*, 1855-9; Saporta, *Annales des Sci. Natur.*, 1862, and *Le Monde des Plantes*, 1878; Newberry, *Hayden's Explor. Yellowstone and Missouri Riv.*, 1859-60, 173-4; Ch. Martins, *Revue des Deux Mondes*, 1867; Cleve, *A. J. S.*, III., iv., 235. See also the palæontological generalizations of Moore, Duncan, Sowerby, Guppy, Leidy, Marsh and Cope.)

VIII. Wastage of visible areas. (D. 637-47, 663-4; L. 245-51; W. ch. xxxi. See also Lectures XXVII. and XXIV.)

1. The Alleghanies. (D. 647; L. 263; W. 339-40.)
2. The Catskills.
3. Faulting and Denudation in Wyoming Territory. (Powell: *Uinta Mts.*; L. 263.)
4. The gold-bearing gulches of California. (L. 554-7.)
5. Sundry other examples. (D. 647; L. 15; E. Hitchcock: *Geol. Vt.*, i., 226; Gilbert: *Geol. of Henry Mts.*)

IX. Rate of Continental Erosion.

1. Croll's estimate, 1 ft. in 6,000 yrs. (*Phil. Mag.*, May, 1868, 378-84; Feb., 1867, p. 1830; *Climate and Time*, ch. xx.; *Trans. Geol. Soc., Glasgow*, iii., 153.)
2. Reade's estimate, 500,000,000 yrs. since sedimentation began in Europe. (*Annual Add., Liverpool Geol. Soc.*; *Am. Jour.*, 1876, 462.)
3. Geikie's estimate, 1 ft. in 6,000 yrs. (*Proc. Roy. Geogr. Soc.*; *Pop. Sci. Monthly*, Sep., 1879, 598.)
4. These estimates apparently too low. — Erosion by the Ganges, 1 ft. in 1751 yrs., and by the Mississippi, 1 ft. in 4,640 years. (L. 10-11.)

XXIX. GEOLOGY OF PETROLEUM.

WINCHELL: *Sketches of Creation*, ch. xxv.; Dana: *System of Mineralogy*, 724-5.

I. Chemical Constitution of Crude Petroleum. (Warren: *Mem. Amer. Acad.*, II., ix., x.; *Am. Jour. Sci.*, II., xl., xlv., xlvi.)

1. Series of Hydrocarbons. (D. *Syst. Min.*, 720-2; Crosby, *Am. Nat.*, Apr., 1879, 231.) — Table. — Differential between cellulose and Petroleum. (L. 379.)
2. Compounds more and less volatile. (L. 380; W. 280.)

II. Organic Origin of Petroleum. (L. 379.)

1. Its organic constitution chemically.

2. Its producibility from organic substances and black shales. (D. 268; W. 281.)
3. Its natural association with organic *débris.*
4. The origin chiefly vegetable. — Indications. — The hypothesis of animal origin. (Hunt: *Chem. and Geol. Ess.*, 168-82; *A. J. S.*, III., i., 420-4, on Chicago limestone; *A. J. S.*, ii., 369; *Geol. Canada*, 526-8; A. J. Warner, *A. J. S.*, ii., 215.) — A controversy.

III. Its Vertical Distribution in the rocks. (L. 376-7; W. 280-1.) — In gneiss and mica schist. (*Am. Jour.*, II., xlv., 38.)

IV. Laws of Accumulation. (L. 377; W. 287.)

1. A source situated *below* the place of accumulation.
   (1.) In every actual instance we find a *bituminous shale.* (W. 282, 288; Warner, *A. J. S.*, ii., 215.)
   (2.) Limestones not an abundant source. (W. 277-8; Hunt, *Geol. Can.*, 521-6.)
   (3.) Argillaceons mixtures predispose to liberation of petroleum.
2. An anticlinal axis required to direct the movement of the liberated product.
3. A reservoir to retain the supply. (W. 287.) — Porous sandstone. (W. 293.) — Shattered rock. (W. 292.) — Cavernous limestone. (W. 292.)
4. An impervious covering to prevent escape. (W. 282, 287.)

V. Forms of Inspissated Petrolenm. (D. *Man. Min.*, 95; Peckham, *Ann. Jour.*, II., xlviii., 362, and other references there; Hunt, *Geol. Can.*, 521-6.

1. Asphalt. (D. *Syst. Min.*, 751.) — Albertite. (D. 296, 315; Wetherill, Trans., A. P. S., 1852, 353; Hitchcock, *Am. Jour.*, II., xxxix, 267.) Found in Green River Eocene and elsewhere. (Hayden: *Ann. Rep.*, 1870, 144, 181.) — Grahamite. (D. 315: L. 380; Lesley, Proc.. A. P. S., ix., 183; Wurtz, *Am. Jour.*, II., xlii., 420 — Piauzite. (D. *Syst. Min.*, 753.) — Berengelite. (D. *Syst. Min.*, 753.)
2. Pitch-lakes. (On Trinidad, Crosby, *Am. Nat.*, Apr., 1879, 239 *seq.*; Wall, *Proc. Geol. Soc.*, Lond., May 1860.) — "Gum-beds." (W. 291-2: Dana: *Syst. Min.*, 727; Crowther, *Am. Jour.*, II., xlvi., 147, in Mexico.)

VI. Common Fallacies.

1. That Petroleum comes from coal. (W. 276, 280.)
2. That a strong surface show is favorable. (W. 276.)
3. That a saturated rock insures a supply. (W. 277, 278-80.)
4. That geological and hydrostatical principles can be disregarded. (W. 275.) — Formations explored in vain. — Unproductiveness of the Corniferous and Niagara limestones. (D. 222, 256;

W. 278-80, 289-91 ; Hunt : *Chem. and Geol. Essays*, 168-82 ; Warner, *A. J. S.*, ii., 215.) — Surface shows tempting to mislead. (W. 276, 278.)

VII. Formations yielding paying quantities : — Cincinnati Group. (W. 289, 292.) — Hamilton Group. (W, 289, 292.) — Genesee Shale. (W. 288, 293.) — Chemung Group. (W. 293.) — Marshall (Waverly) Group. (W. 293.) — Carboniferous Limestone. (W. 293.) — Parma Conglomerate. (W. 293.) — Coal Measures. (W. 293.) — Cretaceous and Tertiary rocks. (B. S. Lyman, *Trans. Am. P. S.*, xv., 1, Punjab ; *A. J. S.*, III., iii., 392 ; *Report of Colonial Geologists*, London, 1860, 134, seq.; Schomburgh : *Hist. of Barbadoes*, 553, 569 ; *A. J. S.*, III., iii., 481, Santo Domingo.)

VIII. Phenomena of Oil-Wells. (W. 284.)

1. Pumping wells. (W. 285, 284.) — Spouting wells. (L. 377 ; W. 284.) — Intermittent wells. (W. 285.) — Flowing wells. (W. 285.) — Water wells. — Gas wells. (W. 283 ; Rep. on well in Knox Co., O.; Wurtz, *Am. Jour.*, II., xlix., 336 ; Newberry, *Am. Chemist*, Dec., 1870 ; *A. J. S.*, i., 146)
2. Productiveness of oil-wells. (W. 286, Appendix, Note VIII.)

IX. Exhaustion and Recuperation of Wells.

XXX. GEOLOGY OF SALT AND GYPSUM.

C. A GOESSMAN : *Chemistry of Common Salt*, Am. Jour. Sci., II., xlix., 78-89.

I. Primordial Origin of the Saltness of the Sea.

1. Early chemical reactions. (W. 59-64 ; Hunt : *Essays*, 2d paper.) — Table. (W. 61.)
2. Why we associate salt and gypsum.

II. Origin of Salt Lakes. (Compare L. 74 ; Darwin : *Geol. Obs.*, pt. ii., 75.)

1. Sometimes solutions of contiguous salt deposits. (W. 295 ; D., 630 ; L. 73.)
2. Generally residua of bodies of sea-water. (L. 73.) — Conditions of their perpetuity. — Shrinkage of most salt lakes. (W. 295 ; L. 75.) — Dead Sea. (Not as in L. 73.) — Great Salt Lake. (D. 561 : L. 75.) — Disappearance of salt lakes. (W. 295 ; Lect. XX., IV., 2.) — By drainage they may become fresh. (D. 23.)

III. Salt Lakes of Former Ages

1. Isolation and evaporation. (W. 297 ; D. 235, 696 ; Hunt : *Essays*, 104.) — Occasional accession of sea-water. (D. 236.) — Mixture of earthy sediments. (D. 235 ; L. 75.)

2. Order of deposition as evaporation proceeds. (W. 297, 302; L. 75.) — The Salina basin. — Same order in artificial evaporatlon.
3. Why gypsum always accompanies salt — Error of supposing them naturally in separated formations — Gypsum not a secondary product. (W. 297; Compare D. 234, 235; L. 75.)
4. The salt sometimes reduced again to brine. — Salt springs.
5. Thus salt formations proceed from evaporation of ancient outliers of the ocean. (W. 296; D. 235, Compare Réclus: *Earth*, 402, *seq.*)

IV. Conditions of Brine Accumulation.

1. A source located *above*. (W. 300-1.)
2. A dish-shaped conformation. (W. 298.) — Effect of a persistent dip. (W. 298.)
3. Remoteness from outcropping border of the basin. (W. 299.) — Salt springs generally marginal. (W. 299.) — Do not indicate localities where strong supplies may be sought. (W. 299.)
4. A good brine-well must be a pumping, not a flowing, well. (W. 299-300.)

V. Principal Salt-Formations of the eastern United States.

1. The Salina Formation. (W. 303.) — Its distribution. — Source of the supplies in Onondaga county, N. Y. (W. 303.) — Geological structure. (W. 303.) — Affords rock-salt in sundry localities. — Goderich, Ont. (W. 304; D. 234.) — Alpena and Mackinac, Mich. — Hope of reaching it by boring in New York. — Abingdon, Va.
2. The Michigan Salt Group. (W. 304; D. 295, 377.) — Its restriction to Mich. and perhaps Nova Scotia. — Its reservoir the Marshall sandstone. (W. 304.) — Productiveness.
3. The Coal Measures. (W. 305.) — Especially in Mich. (W. 305; *Geol. Mich.*, 165-93.) — The reservoir in the Conglomerate. (W. 305.) — Hence Michigan is underlaid by three concentric salt-basins. — General salinity of Michigan strata, and the cause. — Mineral wells of the state.
4. Other salt and brine deposits in the U. S. — The Cretaceous. (W. 306.) — Petite Anse, La. (W. 306; Hilgard, *Am. Jour.*, Jan. 1869, xlvii., 77; Goessman, *Am. Bur. Mines*, 1867.)
5. European Salt Beds mostly Triassic. (D. 424.)

XXXI. METHOD IN THE HISTORY OF LIFE.

I. The Conception of Progress. (D. 593-7.)

1. Retrospect of organic succession.
2. The progress fluctuating, but real. (D. 598.)

3. Expansion of types mostly upward, but partly downward. (D. 598.)
4. Other possible orders of organic succession.
   (1.) Unchangeability.
   (2.) Regression from primitive perfection.
   (3.) Progress by a succession of unrelated plans (Discontinuous.)

II. Persistence and Pervasiveness of Organic Types.

1. Fundamental Identity in Differentiated structures.
   (1.) Fundamental plans of organic structure. (D. 594.)
   (2.) Exemplification from the Vertebrate type.
      (a.) Generalized conception of the Vertebrate. (Hux., 25; Flower: ***Osteol. of Mam.*** 104-5; Owen: ***The Skeleton and the Teeth,*** 26-34.)
      (b.) Homologies of parts. — Limbs. — Jaws.
      (c.) Persistence of the vertebrate conception. — Pervasiveness in diversified modifications.
2. Progressive differentiation of structures fundamentally indentical. (D. 595.) — Progressive cephalization. (D. 596.)
3. The rate of this progress different along different lines of affiliation.
   (1.) Explanation.
   (2.) Hence, different stages of differentiation become contemporaneous.
   (3.) Types representative of earlier times, handed down to later. (D. 594.)
      (a.) The general type of Eozoon existed in all subsequent ages.
      (b.) All forms comparatively lower the representatives of earlier ages.

III. Apparent Breaches of the Law of Progress.

1. Persistent Forms. (Hux.: *Critiques and Addresses*, 186; *Lay Sermons*, 216-27.)
   (1. Globigerinæ. (Hux.: ***Lay Serm.***, 198; Carpenter, ***A. J. S.***, II, xlix., 415.) — Crinoids. (Sars, ***A. J. S.***, II., xlviii., 142; xlix., 130; Lovén, ***A. J. S.***, II., xlviii., 429; Pourtales, Bul. Mus. Comp. Zoöl., Cambr., No. 11; Proc, Roy. Soc., xvii., 168 and Ann. and Mag. Nat. Hist., iii., 383 and iv., 112; W. B. Carpenter, ***Phil. Trans.***, 1866, vol., clvi.) — Lingulidæ. (D. 594.) — Discinidæ — ***Rhynchonella.*** — ***Terebratulina caput-serpentis.*** (Hux.; ***Lay Serm.***, 198.) — ***Atrypa reticularis.*** — ***Strophomena rhomboidalis.*** — ***Nautilus.*** — ***Belemnoteuthis.*** — ***Ceratodus.*** (D. 594; Krefft, ***Proc. Zool. Soc.***, 1870, 221; Günther, ***Ann. Mag. N. H.***, IV., vii., 222; ***A. J. S.*** III., 387; ***Archiv. f. Naturgesch.***, 37 Jahrg., 1871, Bd., i., 321, etc.; Haeckel: ***Anthropogenie,*** 439, 442, 588, 715.) — ***Pleuracanthus.*** — Highest Lacertilians.
   (2.) All the (20) classes and 75 out of 92 fossilizable orders have persisted to the present.
2. Regressive Forms.
   (1). Among extinct species.
      (a.) From Cambrian ***Paradoxides*** to lowest Articulates, and to Molluscs, Radiates and Protozoans (if we ignore Eozoön.)
      (b.) From Cambrian Tetrabranchiates to lower orders of Molluscs and other animals.
      (c.) From Triassic Mammals to Jurassic Dinosaurs and Birds.
   (2.) Among living species.
      (a.) Proteids lower than earliest Amphibians.
      (b.) Pharyngobranchs and Marsipobranchs lower than earliest Fishes.

XXXII. METHOD IN THE HISTORY OF LIFE. (Continued.)

I. The resolution of Organic Types. (D. 597.)

1. Resolution discriminated from Differentiation.
2. Every type the potential or stock of a series of differentiations, and also of resolutions.
3. Unresolved types generally *prophetic.*
   (1.) Sauroid Fishes prophetic of Reptiles.
   (2.) Ornithoscelid Reptiles prophetic of Birds.
   (3.) Ichthyosaurian Reptiles prophetic of Cetaceans.
   (4.) The unresolved Amblypoda prophetic of modern orders of Mammals.
4. Unresolved types often *retrospective.*
   (1.) Labyrinthodonts and amphicœlian Reptiles retrospective toward Fishes.
   (2.) Birds with teeth and vertebrated tails retrospective toward Reptiles.
   (3.) Zeuglodonts and Cetaceans retrospective toward Ichthyosaurs.
5. When a higher differential is unresolved, the type is prophetic; when a lower, it is retrospective.

II. Successive Dominance of Organic Conceptions. (D. 597.)

1. Represented by highly differentiated types which continue unresolved. — As the Reptilian Type of Mesozoic Time. — Hence, it becomes *dominant* by manifestation under many modifications and in many individuals.
2. Examples:
   (1.) Rhizopods in the Eozoic.
   (2.) Nautiloids in the Silurian.
   (3.) Crinoids in the Earlier Carboniferous.
   (4.) Ammonites and Reptiles in the Mesozoic.
   (5.) Mammals in the Tertiary. — Sthenorhines amongst early mammals.
   (6.) Acrogens during the Coal Period.

III. Dominant Types Decline without Disappearing.

1. Foraminifera. — Nautilidæ. — Crinoids. — Terebratulidæ. — Ganoids. — Crocodilians. — Cycads. — Tree Ferns. — Salisburioids, etc.,
2. This results from arrest of differentiation and resolution.

IV. The Progress Ideally Continuous.

1. The same general plans of structure reproduced in successive ages and different orders.
2. This not a demonstration of material continuity.
3. But all the phenomena explicable on the hypothesis of a material or genetic continuity.

XXXIII. UNRESOLVED MAMMALIAN TYPES.

References are abbreviated as explained under Lecture XVII.

Some prominent examples of Unresolved types more particularly considered.

I. No Modern Mammalian Order definitely Isolated in the beginning of Tertiary time. (C. III., 644.)

1. Specifications of primitive ordinal types.
2. Affinities with modern Perissodactyla, Proboscidians, Rodents and Plantigrade Carnivores.

II. Common characteristics of oldest Eocene Mammals.

1. Lack of differentiation among the teeth.
2. The selenodont type of teeth entirely wanting.
3. All the ungulates had upper and lower incisors.
4. These early mammals mostly 5-toed and plantigrade.
5. Brains small and imperfectly convoluted. (Mh. viii., July, 1874.)

III. The type designated Amblypoda **by Cope.** (C. VIII., 178, 182, 273, 282.)

1. General characters. — Unites Proboscidea and Perissodactyla.
2. *Coryphodon.* — Connects most generalized Herbivores with most generalized Carnivores. (L. 502.) — Possessing affinities with Perissodactyls, Proboscidians, Carnivores and Dinocerata. (C. VIII., 187.)
3. *Dinoceras.* — Description. — Combined characters suggestive of *Rhinocerus*, Ruminants, Equidæ, *Hippopotamus* and Mastodon.
4. *Uintatherium* (?=*Dinoceras*) united characters of Proboscidians, Tapirs and especially *Dinoceras.* (L. III., 93 seq.)
5. *Orohippus* (?=*Hyracotherium*) has connections with *Palæotherium*, *Palæosyops*, *Anchitherium* and Horse. (C. VIII., 260.)

IV. The type designated Bunotheria **by Cope** (C. VIII., 72, 85,)— has affinities ranging from the gyrencephalous orders to the Prosimiæ, Quadrumana and Carnivora.

1. Creodonts :—Resemble Sarcophagous Marsupials, Dogs, Insectivora, Lemurs, and, in the tibia, *Coryphodon* — Differ from Carnivores in ungrooved upper surface of astragalus, and want of coössification of scaphoid and lunar bones. (C. VIII., 76, 78.) — Differ in certain points from all other orders. (C. VIII., 79.)
2. Mesodonts, intermediate between Creodonts and Lemurs. — Possess affinities with Simiæ, Insectivora and Ungulates.
3. Tillodonts :—*Tillotherium.* (L. 503-4.) — Description — Combined characters of Bear, Rodents, Ungulates (Palæotherium), and Insectivores (Hedgehog.)
4. Tæniodonts :—Inferior incisors like Rodents ; upper, suggestive of Edentates ; molars, like Tillodonts.

V. The type designated Brontotheridæ by Marsh. (Mh. ix., 245 ; xi., 335.)

1. *Brontotherium* :—Description. (L. 505.) — Was an odd-toed

Ungulate, but resembled *Dinoceras*, Tapir and Proboscidians. (Mh. xi., 339.)

2. *Menodus*=*Titanotherium*, related to Tapir, Palæothere, and *Dinoceras*. (D. 506-7.)

VI. **The type of Rhinoceridæ.** (C. ix., 227.) — Presents affinities with *Hyracodon*, *Tapirulus*, Lophiodonts and Tapirs; and indeed with *Palæotherium* and the Brontotheridæ.

VI. Sundry types.

1. *Oreodon* united characters of *Anoplotherium*, Deer, Peccary and Camel.
2. *Meniscotherium* united characters of *Palæosyops*, *Hyopotamus* and *Hyracotherium* (? *Orohippus*.) (C. V., 8; VIII., 251.)
3. Eocene *Diplacodon* united characters of *Limnohyus* and Miocene *Brontotherium*. (Mh. ix., 246; xi., 339.)
4. *Hypertragulus* was intermediate between Tragulidæ and typical Ruminants. (C. X., 66.)
5. *Orotherium* united Tapiroids and *Hyracotherium*.
6. *Dinotherium* (Miocene)—earliest of Proboscidioid types, united characters of Elephant, Hippopotamus, Tapir, Dugong and (in marsupial bones) Marsupials. (*Am. Jour.*, II., xxxviii., 427.)
7. Stegosauria possessed affinities with Dinosaurs, Plesiosaurs and remotely with Chelonians. (Mh. *A. J. S.*, III., xiv., 513.)

XXXIV. MISSING LINKS.

I. Unavoidable Imperfection of the Known Record.

1. Most animals that have lived have completely perished.
   - (1.) The calcareous secretions of marine forms the principal relics preserved.
   - (2.) All animals without hard secretions have perished.
   - (3.) Terrestrial Vertebrates preserved only by burial in sediments.
   - (4.) Fossils of ancient rocks destroyed by metamorphism.
2. The fossiliferous rocks very imperfectly explored.
   - (1.) No region or locality completely exhausted.
   - (2.) The greater part of the earth quite uninvestigated.
3. The known record presents many gaps in the graduated succession of organic form.
4. But the number and the breadth of the gaps continually diminishing.

II. Missing Links between Inorganic Matter and the First Known Organisms. (Dawson: *Story*, 325.)

1. Assuming Eozoön to be organic.
2. Assuming Eozoön to be inorganic.
   - (1.) Rank of first Cambrian types, Brachiopods and Trilobites.
   - (2.) Absence of Polyzoa. — Appeared in the fifth (Chazy) fauna.
   - (3.) Absence of Echinodermata, Cœlenterata and Protozoa.

III. Gap between Invertebrates and Vertebrates.

1. Appearance of Fishes in early Devonian or late Silurian.
2. Rank and distinctness from nearest related older tpyes.
   (1.) Ganoids, Placoderms and Selachians.
   (2.) *Eurypterus* and *Pterygotus*. — May be compared with the later *Pterichthys*. — But no structural resemblance.
3, The gap occupied in the modern world by Myxinoids, (Hux. 109.) Lampreys, (Hux. 110) and Lancelets. (Hux. 104.)

IV. Gap between Fishes and Amphibians and Reptiles.

1. Earliest known Amphibians, *Raniceps*, *Amphibamus*, *Baphetes*, *Anthracosaurus*.
2. Highest type of contemporaneous fishes.
3. This gap also occupied in the modern world by lower Amphibians (Salamanders and Proteids) and Dipnoans. (Hux. 145. Also Lect., XXXI., III., 1. (1).)
4. But reptilian *Eosaurus* also lived with first Amphibians.

V, Gap between Mammals and older Vertebrates.

1. First Mammals insectivorous Marsupials during Triassic. (D. 416.)
2. Not known to be preceded by Birds.
3. The highest Reptiles *followed* the first Mammals.
4. The vertebrate succession is from Lizard-like and Alligator-like Reptiles to Mammals. — No connecting links known, either extinct or living.
5. Or, it is from highest Amphibians (Triassic Labryrinthodonts) to Mammals. — Connecting links equally unknown.
6. But the mammalian line, in the living world, descends two steps lower, in *Ornithorhynchus* and *Echidna*. (Hux. 274.)

VI. No certain connecting links between Marsupial and Placental Mammals.

1. Mammals exclusively Marsupial to end of Mesozoic time.
2. Cænozoic time opens with a diversified fauna of placental mammals.

VII. The Gap between Man and Lower Mammals. (Daws.: *Story*, 328.)

1. The distinction structural, but not in respect to rank of the general structure.
   (1.) Man's organism generally not superior. — In some respects retrospective.
   (2.) But all correlations with his psychic nature a great advance. — Relative capacity of cranium. — Extreme cephalization.
2. No connecting forms as yet discovered. — Not so with existing apes and their predecessors.

VIII. A Gap between Gymnosperms and Angiosperms.

1. To the end of the Jurassic, we know only Conifers and Cycads among flowering plants.

2. With earliest Cretaceous, appear abundant Angiosperms. — These even closely akin to modern species.

XXXV. MISPLACED CONNECTING LINKS.

I. Links structurally intermediate separable into two classes.

1. Intermediate terms chronologically discordant. — Styled by Huxley "intercalary types." (*Critiques and Addreses*, 188.)
2. Intermediate terms chronologically concordant. — Styled by Huxley "linear types." (*Ibid.*)

II. Certain Living Forms intercalary between extinct forms.

1. Gregarinidae stand between *Eozöon* and inorganic matter.
2. Seven Crustacean orders between Cambrian Trilobites and *Eozoön*. — Also all Echinodermata and Cœlenterata.
3. Living Dog-Fishes between Devonian Selachians and lower forms. — Also Hag-Fishes and Lancelets. — Such examples abundant.

III. Certain Extinct Forms intercalary between forms more remotely extinct. (See references, Lecture XV.)

1. *Pterodactylus*, a reptile with wings, ornithic scapula, coracoid and other conformations. (Hux.: 229; Mivart: *Genesis of Species*, 84; Seeley, *Ann. and Mag. Nat. Hist.*, Aug. 1870, 140; *Ornithosauria*, and *Index to Foss. Rem. Woodw. Mus.*) — *Middle Oölite to later Cretaceous.* — *Ornithopsis* Seeley. (*Ann. Mag. N. H.*, IV., v. 279; *A. J. S.*, II., xlix., 393.
2. *Ramphorhynchus* and *Dimorphodon*, reptiles with wings and horny tip of mandibles, but a long tail. (Hux. 231-2.) — *Lower to Middle Oölite.*
3. *Pteranodon*, a reptile with wings, short tail, no teeth, and bird-like head. — *Later Cretaceous.*
4. *Archæopteryx*, a bird, but with long vertebrated tail and separate metacarpals. (D. 447; Mivart: *op. cit.*, 86.) — *Middle Oölite.*
5. *Ichthyornis*, a bird with good wings, but with socketed teeth and bi-concave vertebræ. — *Later Cretaceous.*
6. *Hesperornis*, a bird with poor wings, and teeth in grooves. — *Later Cretaceous.*
7. Typical aquatic and cursorial birds. — *Later Cretaceous.*
8. Remarkable showing of the preceding list of forms.
   (1.) A striking general graduation from reptile to bird.
   (2.) A strange crossing of structural affinities.
   (3.) The line runs toward "carinate" and not "struthious" birds.
   (4.) But the chronological order is not conformable to the structural.

IV. Another structural passage between Reptiles and Birds. (Hux., 225-6; C.I., 86-90. See also references, Lect. XV.) — General characters of the Ornithoscelids. — Generally regarded as showing transition toward Struthious Birds. (C. I., 86-90.)

1. *Iguanodon*, a reptile having tips of premaxillaries toothless. — *Older Cretaceous* or *Later Jurassic.*
2. *Rhynchosaurus*, with toothless mandibles. — *Trias* of Europe and America.
3. *Hadrosaurus* and *Lælaps*, with weak fore-legs and probably bipedal attitude. — *Cretaceous* of America.
4. *Anomœpus*, with four toes before, and three bird-like toes behind. — *Trias* of Connecticut valley.
5. *Compsognathus*, with light, bird-like head, and astragalus anchylosed to tibia. (Hux., 225, 228.) — *Middle Oölite.*
6. *Laosaurus* and *Hypsilophodon*, resembling last, but having ornithic ischiac and post-pubic bones, and three toes. (Mh., xvi., 415-6, pl. viii-x.)
7. *Brontozoüm*, bipedal, three-toed, with ornithic arrangement of phalanges. — *Trias* of Connecticut.
8. Typical Struthious Birds. — *Later Cretaceous.*
9. Conclusions from this showing:—The structural gradations real. — They run toward Struthious, and not Carinate, Birds. — The most bird-like Ornithoscelids the oldest. — Types connecting them with other reptiles *follow* instead of preceding. — The bulk of the reptile-fauna lived *after* the most bird-like genera. — Real birds believed to have existed simultaneously with the most bird-like reptiles. — Mammals certainly lived at the same time. — Nevertheless, the idea of *serial relations of structure* was extant in the world.

V. Inferences from misplaced links only provisional.

1. Not at liberty to infer that the real chronological order was not conformable to the structural.
2. Future discoveries may bring many of the facts into chronological adjustment.

XXXVI. CONNECTING LINKS CHRONOLOGICALLY ADJUSTED.

Besides the works cited below, see Albert Gaudry, in researches on the fossils of Pikermi and Mont Léberon; W. Kowalewsky, in investigations of the osteology of Hyopotamidæ; Huxley: *Critiques and Addresses*, 181-217, Ann. Add., 1870; New York Lectures, 1876, N. Y. Tribune Extra, No. 36; Cope: *Stratigraphic relations of the Orders of Reptilia*, in Proc. Am. Acad., Boston, xix., 194; Am. J. S., III., ii., 217. Consult, also, Haeckel: *Natürliche Schöpfungsgeschichte* and *Anthropogenie* (both in English translation. See further, Part II., of the Syllabus.)

I. **The Horse-Series.** (See Lect. XVII., IV., 1, (4) (*b*).)

1. *Equus* of the living fauna. (Hux. 293-307.) — Marked state of structural isolation.
   (1.) Structures of the fore-limb.
   (2.) Structures of the hind-limb.
   (3.) Structures of the teeth.
   (4.) Five or six American species, beginning late in Pliocene.
2. *Pliohippus*, of middle Pliocene or earlier. — Smaller size. — Central digital series more slender. — Splints more elongated. — Crown of Upper molars shorter, and crescentic areas simpler.
3. *Protohippus*, of Early Pliocene. — Size of Ass. — Central digital series still more slender. — Splints terminated by dangling hooflets. — Ulna long as arm, but slender. — Fibula rudimentary. — Crowns of molars much shorter. — *Anchippus* and European *Hipparion* (= *Hippotherium*) were closely related, and *Merychius* was probably identical. — *Anchippus*, *Hipparion* and *Stylonus* constitute a collateral series. (Cope, IX., 14.)
4. *Miohippus*, of Late Miocene of Oregon. — Size of sheep. — Three functional toes before and three behind. — Also small splint of Vth digit, before. — Ulna distinct, long as radius, but very slender distally. — Fibula co-ossified with tibia at lower end. — Molar crowns decidedly short. — Enamel folds much simpler than in horse. — The Older Miocene *Anchitherium*, the oldest equine known in Europe, is closely related, but a little more specialized.
5. *Mesohippus*, of Oldest Miocene. — Size of sheep. — Three functional toes before and three behind, but more nearly equal than in *Miohippus*. — Larger splints of Vth digit, before. — Radius and ulna distinct, and also tibia and fibula.
6. *Epihippus*, of Later Eocene. (Mh. *A. J. S.* III., xvii., 504.) — Resembled *Orohippus* in its digits, but differed in its teeth.
7. *Orohippus* of Middle Eocene of Wyoming and Utah. — Size of fox. — Four functional toes before and three behind. — Ulna complete and distinct from radius; tibia and fibula also distinct. — Molar crowns exceedingly short. — Enamel pattern simple.
8. *Eohippus*, of Oldest Eocene of New Mexico. — Size of fox. — Four functional toes before and three behind. — Rudiment of outer or Vth toe behind, and hence, probably of Ist digit before. — Hoofs mere thick, broad and blunt claws. — Molars less specialized than in *Orohippus*, without cement. —

Other structures similar. — Carpal bones eight, and somewhat similar to tapir.

II. **The Camel Series.** (See Lecture XVII, V, 1, (2), (e) and VI., 1, (1).

1. *Camelus* of the living fauna. (Hux. 329.) — Cervical vertebræ. — Metacarpals *separated only by deep cleft.* — Large canines in each jaw. — Premaxillaries each with *one incisor.*
2. *Procamelus* (=*Homocamelus*) of the Pliocene of Colorado. — Premaxillaries with full set of incisors; but *the lateral temporary.* — External incisors and canines alike. — Molars 4–3. — Lateral rudimentary metacarpals wanting. — Trapezoides wanting. — Middle metacarpals *finally united.*
3. *Protolabis* of the Pliocene of Colorado. (Cope, *P. A. N. S.*, 1876, 145; VIII., 325.) — *Full set of permanent upper incisors.* — Molars 4–3, but the posterior are sub-prismatic.
4. *Poëbrotherium* of the Miocene of Colorado. — Molars 4–3, as in primitive mammals generally. — The two metacarpals *distinct.* — Rudiments of lateral metacarpals. — The presence of a trapezium, two digits and separated metacarpals allies it with the older Anoplotheridæ.

III. **The Rhinocerus Series.** (C. XI., 227-33.)

1. *Cœlodonta* of the Pliocence had dentition $i\,\frac{0}{0\text{-}1}$, $c\,\frac{0}{0}$, and three anterior digits.
2. *Atelodus* of the Upper Miocene had the same.
3. *Ceratorhinus* of the Middle Miocene had $i\,\frac{1}{1}$, $c\,\frac{0}{1}$, and digits the same. — *Rhinocerus* of the Upper Miocene and recent fauna had the same.
4. *Aceratherium* of the Lower Miocene, had $i\,\frac{2}{1}$, $c\,\frac{0}{1}$, and *four* anterior digits, and no horn. — *Zalabis* of the Upper Miocene had $i\,\frac{3}{2}$, $c\,\frac{0}{1}$; but this genus, as known, was chronologically misplaced.
5. Other characters of the genera were correspondingly graduated.

IV. **Sundry Examples.** (See further, Huxley: *Critiques and Addresses*, 188-90; Owen: *Anat. of Vertebrates*, ch., xl., § 424; Cope, *Proc. Am. Acad.*, xix.)

1. *Dicrocerus* stands between *Antilocapra* and other mammals.
2. *Blastomeryx*, between *Cariacus* and older forms. (C. VIII., 223.)
3. Miocene *Hyracodon*, between Eocene *Hyrachyus* and modern mammals. (Mh. ix., 244.)
4. *Cercoleptes*, between Carnivora and Quadrumana.

5. *Diplacodon*, between *Limnohyus* and *Brontotherium*. (Mh. ix., 246.)
6. Pliocene *Squalodon*, between living Cetacea and Eocene *Zeuglodon*. (Hux.: *Crit.*, 190.)
7. The elephant series extends back through *Elephas*, Miocene *Dinotherium*, Eocene *Dinoceras*, Lower Eocene *Coryphodon* to ?*Oligotomus*. (C. III., 648.)
8. *Dinotherium* possessed Marsupial bones.
9. The oldest Tortoises (*Psephoderma*) intermediate between Lacertilia and typical Tortoises. (Cope, *Proc. Am. Acad.*, xix., 194.)

XXXVII. MAN IN THE LIGHT OF GEOLOGY.

I. Man the Fulfillment of the Prophecies of the Ages.

1. Meaning of the announcemont of a Law of Progress.
   (1.) Progressive improvement of organic types.
   (2.) Prophecy of the earliest Vetebrate. — Man in potentiality.
   (3.) Progressive modification of limbs.
      (*a.*) Fish. — Amphibian. — Reptile, — Bird. — Mammal.
      (*b.*) Proclamation that man must conform to the same plan.
      (*c.*) Psychic relations superadded to structural in the human arm.
2. Promise of an intelligent being in geological adaptations having relations only to man. — Coal. — Metals. — Wells and Springs.

II. Man's Birth-place Foreshadowed.

1. Faunal characteristics of the existing continents.
2. These established before the advent of Man.
3. The pinnacle of organization fixed in the Orient.
4. Corroborative evidences of Man's oriental origin.
   (1.) Human migrations, as far as known, have been eastward. (*Am. Jour.*, II. xlv., 376; Max Müller: *Chips; Atlantic Monthly*, 1878; T. Poesche: *Die Arier*. erstes Buch.; Jubainville; *Les prem. Habitants de l'Europe*, ch. iii., iv.) and westward from the Orient. (Jubainville: *ut sup.*, and generality of writers,)
   (2.) Cultivated plants have come from the East. (*Pat. Office Rep.*, 1859, 299, 361) — Of 770 plants used for food, 565 came from the Eastern hemisphere. — Of 237 amylaceous plants, 191 originated in the Old World.

III. Man the Culmination of the Organic Series.

1. The erect attitude attained. — Progressive elevation of the longitudinal axis in older vertebrates.
2. Man a cosmopolite, in opposition to the law of increasing restriction of geographical range.
3. Nature, in man, seems to have reached a period.
   (1.) Other animals his equal or superior structurally.
   (2.) Man's structure, in some respects, retrospective.
   (3.) In cephalization, far in advance.
4. Spiritual (educational) progress still possible.
5. Functional limitation of the progress of spiritualization.

IV. Man's Advent since the Last Great Geological Revolution.

1. Restriction of human relics to most superficial deposits.
2. Man of history not preglacial.
3. Man of historical regions not preglacial.
4. Geological evidence knows nothing inductively, as yet, concerning man of unhistorical races and regions.

V. Geological Man, as far as known, the Equal of Existing Races.

VI. Links Missing between Man and the animals next lower. (Lecture XXXIV, VII.)

1. Man's affinities with anthropoid apes and lower Quadrumama.
2. Not held by evolutionists as a descendent of these.
3. No known relics of his assumed line of descent.
2. Provisional inferences of Wallace as an evolutionist.
5. Consequences of the establishment of Man's derivating origin.

VII. Man's Organism bound up with the history of the Material World.

2. Identified with its inorganic history. — Always conditioned by physical surroundings.
2. Identified with its organic history. — Interwoven in every plan of organic structure and function.

VIII. Indications of a Psychic Principle correlated to the Immaterial and the Immutable.

1. The plans of nature the products of Intelligence.
2. Forms change and perish, but nature's conceptions endure.
3. Man comprehends nature, and thus thinks the thoughts of the Author of nature.
4. That which thinks as the Author of the Universe thinks, possesses a kindred nature, spiritual and imperishable.

PART II.

THEORETICAL GEOLOGY.

XXXVIII. INTERNAL CONDITION OF THE EARTH.

[The questions concerning the internal condition of the earth, metamorphism and the dynamics of volcanoes, earthquakes and mountain-making are so intimately connected that most of the works cited here, and in Lectures XXIV, XXVI and XLIV, may be advantageously consulted on each of these subjects.]

W. HOPKINS, *Transactions Royal Soc.*, 1836, p. 382; 1839, p. 38; 1840, p. 193; 1842, p. 48, maintaining existence of a very thick and completely solid crust; *On the Geological Theories of Elevation and Earthquakes*, Report Brit. Assoc. 1847, pp. 33–93, assigning vapors as a cause; Q. J. Geol. Soc., viii, 56.

HENNESEY: *Researches in Terrestrial Physics*, Phil. Trans., 1851, 545.

POULETT SCROPE: *Volcanoes*, 8vo., 2d ed., 1872; *Geol. Mag.*, Dec. 1878.

KEFERSTEIN: *Naturgeschite des Erdkorpers* 1834, vol i, 109; *Bull. Soc. geologique de France*, I. viii, 197.

CHARLES BABBAGE, *Geological Notices*, No. 36; *Proc. Geol. Soc.*, Lond., 1836 ii; *Ninth Bridgewater Treatise*, Note G, 209–220.

SIR JOHN HERSCHEL, *Proc. Geol. Soc.*, Lond., 1836, ii, 548; Babbage's *Ninth Bridgewater Treatise*, Note I, 225–247.

ROBERT MALLET, *Dynamics of Earthquakes*, Trans, Roy. Irish Acad., xxi, pt. i, 1846; *First Report* to the Brit. Assoc., 1850; *Facts and Theory of Earthquakes*, Trans. Brit. Assoc., 1857-8., Fourth Report, (Other Reports in 1851, 1852, 1853, 1854); *The Great Neapolitan Earthquake of* 1857, 2 vols., 8vo, 1862, pt. iii, Principles of Seismology; *Earthquake Wave Experiments*, Phil. Trans., 1862, vol. cliii; *Note on the History of certain recent Views on Dynamical Geology*, A. J. S. III v. 302, Apr. 1873; *Volcanic Energy: An Attempt to develop its true Origin and Cosmical Relations*, Phil. Trans., 1873, pt. i, 147, abstract, A. J. S., III, iv, 409-12, vii, 145-8; *Additions* to the foregoing memoir, Phil. Trans., 1875, vol. clxv, pt. i, (read May, 1878), abstract, A. J. S., III, viii, 140-1; *On the present state of knowledge of Terrestrial Vulcanicity, the Cosmical Nature and Relations of Volcanoes and Earthquakes*, an Introduction to Prof. L. PALMIERI's work on the *Eruption of Vesuvius in* 1872, extract, A. J. S., III, v. 219-25; *On the Mechanism of Stromboli*, Trans. Roy. Soc., 25 June, 1874, abstract, A. J. S., III, viii, 200-2; *On the Temperature attainable by Rock-crushing, and its Consequences*, Phil. Mag., July 1875 and A. J. S., III, x, 256-68; On the Origin and Mechanism of Production of Prismatic or Columnar Structure of Basalt, Proc. Roy. Soc., 21 Jan. 1875, abstract A. J. S., III, ix, 206-11.

T. S. HUNT: *Chemical and Geological Essays*, (see also, review of same by J. D. Dana, A. J. S., III, ix, 102-9), especially *Theory of Igneous Rocks and Volcanoes* (1858), pp. 1-10; *Probable Seat of Volcanic Action*, (1869), pp. 59-69; *Criticism* of Joseph Leconte's views, A. J. S., III, v. 264-70 (1875).

SIR W. THOMSON, *Phil. Trans.* May 16 and Nov. 27, 1862, xii, 103, *ib.*, 1864, on necessary rigidity of the earth; Thomson and Tait's *Natural Philosophy*. §§ 832, 833, 834, 847, 848; *Trans. Geol. Soc.*, Glasgow, iii: *Trans. Roy. Soc. Edinb.*, xxiii, pt. i, 157, on the secular cooling of the earth; *Nature*, Jan. 18 and Feb. 1, 1872, objections to Mallet's theory.

J. D. DANA, A. J. S., II, v, 423; vi, 6-14, 104-6, 161-72. (See references Lect. XLIV). Also A. J. S., II, ii, 385; iii, 94, 176 380; iv, 88; xxii, 305, 335.

E. W. HILGARD: *On some points in Mallet's' Theory of Vulcanicity*, A. J. S., III, vii, 535–46, June, 1874, and Phil. Mag., July, 1874, 41.

J. D. WHITNEY: *North American Review*, Apr. 1869.

HENRY WURTZ: *Amer. Jour. of Mining*, 25 Jan. 1868; A. J. S., III, v. 385.

DAUBRÉE: *Synthetical Studies and Experiments on Metamorphism, and on the Formation of Crystalline Rocks*, Ann. Report of the Smithsonian Institution, 1861, 228–304 trans. from *Annales des Mines*, 5 ser., xvi, 155, 393, many references appended. On *theory* see pt. iii.

O. FISHER, *Remarks upon Mr. Mallet's Theory of Volcanic Energy*, Q. J. Geol. Soc., Lond., xxxi, 469–78, 12 May, 1875; *Camb. Phil. Trans.*, xi, pt. 3, p. 489; *ib.* pt. 2, p. 18.

GEN. G. J. BARNARD, Smithsonian Contributions, No. 240, difficulties in Mallet's theory, but surmountable.

DELAUNAY, *Comptes Rendus*, July 13, 1868; *Cours elementaire d'Astronomie*, 643, 644.

STANISLAS MEUNIER: *Le Ciel Geologique*, 1871, 223.

D. FORBES, *Nature*, 6 Feb. 1872, difficulties of Mallet's theory.

F. W. HUTTON, *Nature*, 27 Nov. 1873, difficulties of Mallet's theory.

N. S. SHALER, *Proc. Bos. Soc. Nat. Hist.*, x, 237; xi, 8; *Geol. Mag.*, Nov. 1868, v. 5, 11; Atlantic Monthly.

ARCHDEACON PRATT, *Phil. Mag.*, xli, 307, 1871.

See, also, JAMES HUTTON: *Theory of the Earth, with Proofs and Illustrations*. In 4 pts. Edinb. 2 vols. 8vo., 1795; JOHN PLAYFAIR: *Illustrations of the Huttonian Theory of the Earth*, Edinb., 1802; YOUNG: *Lectures on Natural Philosophy*, i, 717, 1807; GAY-LUSSAC: *Annales de Chemie*, xxii, 428; MILNE: The Lisbon Earthquakes of 1875 and 1861, *Edinb. Phil. Jour.*, xxxi; POISSONS: *Note sur le rapport qui existe entre les refroidissements progressif de la masse du globe terrestre et celui de la surface*, Comptes Rendus, xix. 1844, and l'Institut, 1845, 32; B. TRASK, On California Earthquake of Jan. 1857, A. J. S., II, xxv, 146; J. SCHMIDT: *Das Erdbeben von 29 Juli*, 1846; and *Untersuchungen über dem Erdbeben am 15 Jan.* 1858.

I. Indications of Internal Heat. (Lects. II. and XXVI.; D. 699.)

1. Traces of former heat upon the earth's surface.
2. Deep excavations, thermal waters, volcanoes.
3. Hypothesis of intense chemical action. (Sir H. Davy, *Phil. Trans.* 1828, 1832; Lyell: *Prin.*, 527–32; Daubeney, *Jameson's Edinb. New Phil. Jour.*, liii., and *Encyc. Metrop.* pt. 40; Ennis: *Origin of the Stars.*
4. More probable inference of a long cooling process still continued.

II. Hypothesis of thin Crust and Molten or Pasty Interior. (O. Fisher, *Camb. Phil. Trans*, xii. pt. ii.; Descartes: *Principes de la Philos.*, 1644, pt. iv., §§ 2, 44, 72; Newton; *Principia Math. Phil. Nat.*, 1667; Leibnitz, *Acta Eruditorum*, Jan., 1693, and *Protogæa*, 1749; Buffon: *Les epoques de la nature*, 1778.)

1. Solidifying substances float in the molten magma. — Water, type-metal. — Solidifying iron (*College Courant*, 13 Apr. 1872, p. 173; *Nature*, 10 May, 1877, 23; 8 Aug., 1878, 397, conclusive experiments; 29 Aug., 1878, 464; xvi., 23; Mallet's apparently contradictory experiments, *Nature*, No. 156, abstr. A. J. S., III., viii., 212; A. Schmidt, A. J. S., III., viii., 287, explaining Mallet.) — Lava floating on liquid lava. (Scrope: *Volcanoes*, 84; Kaemtz: *Meteorology*, 152; Marsh: *Man and Nature*, 545.

2. Cooled terrestrial materials would float.
3. Indications of such a constitution of the earth.
   (1.) Observed rate of increase of downward temperature. (Lects. II. and XXVI.)
   (2.) Enormous lava outflows in geologic and recent periods. (Lect. XXVI., I.)
   (3.) Reputed influence of moon on earthquakes. (Lect. XXVI., IV., 1.)
4. Objected, that such a constitution gives the earth too little rigidity. (W. Hopkins, Thomson, *ut sup.*, and Barnard's reply.)

III. Hypothesis of a Solidified Interior. (W. Hopkins, W. Thomson.)

1. Enormous pressure upon the central portions of the earth. — Solidification the probable result. — This preceding superficial solidification, (Thomson.)
2. General admission of this hypothesis.

IV. The Sources of Lava Supplies.

1. Theory of a *plastic zone* between the two solidified portions, (Hunt, as above.)
   (1.) A transitional zone must probably exist. — Too hot to be congealed, and too superficial to be pressed solid.
   (2.) Zone not supposed continuous. — Contiguous volcanoes, like Mauna Loa and Kilauea, not always sympathetic, (*N. A. Review*, cviii., 598.) — Refrigeration may, in some places, reach the depth of solidification by pressure. — Hypothesis of lakes of plastic matter.
   (3.) Position and volume of the plastic zone changeable, as pressure or conductivity of overlying masses varies.
2. Theory of a semi-fluid interior combined with superheated water, (Fisher, Camb. Phil. Trans, xii., pt. ii.) — Assumes a combination not known to be possible.

(3.) Theory of melting heat as the result of lateral crushing pressure (Wurtz, Mallet, Leconte, Hilgard.)
   (1.) Terrestrial shrinkage from cooling.
   (2.) Experiments on the development of heat by crushing, (Mallet.)
   (3.) Objections made to the contractional theory, (Thomson, Fisher, Barnard, Hutton, Dutton.)

V. Denials of any Knowledge of the Earth's Interior. (Evan Hopkins; James Hall, *American Institute Lecture*, New York, 1869, cited in W. 434.

XXXIX. PRIMORDIAL HISTORY OF THE EARTH.

LEIBNITZ: *Protogæa*, 1749, (abstract in *Acta Eruditorum*, Leipzic, 1683.) or synopsis of this by CONYBEARE, in Report British Association, 1832; Buffon: *Theorie de la Terre*, 1849; *Epoques de la Nature*, 1775.

I. All Presedimentary History Reached only by Deduction.

1. The oldest known rocks sedimentary. (Lect. III.)

2. But a process of cooling implies a fire-formed crust. — This probably remelted by ascent of geisothermal planes. (Lect. III., I., 3.)
3. May reason backward, on the basis of the laws of matter and force. — This brings us to a completely molten condition. (D., 146 ; W., 28–35 ; Leibnitz, *ut supra.*) — Then to a vaporous one. (D., 146 ; W., 36–9.)
4. The fluent condition indicated by the earth's spherical form.
5. A shrinkage explanation must probably be given of the counteraction of the retarding influence of the tides on the earth's rotation during 2,000 years. (W., 403–5; Helmholtz: *Interac. Nat. Forces*, Youmans' ed., 243–7; Mayer: *The Tidal Wave*, Youm., ed., 299, and *The Earth's Internal Heat*, 312.)

II. The Volatility of all Matter.

1. The solid, liquid and gaseous conditions dependent chiefly on Temperature and Pressure. (Lyell: *Prin.*, 538.) — Familiar examples. — Volatilization of silica in the Bessimer process of steel-making. — Volatilization of iron by Dr. Elsner. — Condensation of carbonic acid by Dr. Hare. — Condensation of nitrogen, hydrogen and other gases by Pictet and Cailletet.
2. Distinction between the gaseous and the vaporous states.
   (1.) The *gaseous* a state of dry molecularization or of atomization.
   (2.) *Vapor* or *mist* consists of minute spheres of liquid matter in suspension either in a fluid or removed from the considerable action of gravity.
   (3.) Minute particles of solid matter in similar suspension form *dust.*
3. Rational to assume terrestrial cooling to have proceeded from a state of vapor, or even of gas. — Enormous volume of the planet in this condition. — This assumption sustained by our knowledge of other cosmical vapors, as sun, stars and nebulæ.

III. Passage from fire-mist to a molten globe.

1. Rain of molten matter. — Growth of the liquid core. — An incandescent liquid globe. — Central solidification by pressure.
2. A fervid and heterogeneous atmosphere. — Many substances still gaseous. — Struggling sunbeams.
3. Rolling tides of lava.

IV. Freezing of the Molten Sea. (Comp. Lect. XXXV [illegible] I., II. I.)

1. Crystallization of the most refractory substances. [illegible] Crystals of augite, leucite, mica and black garnet érupt[illegible] in great abundance in semi-fluid lava from Vesuvius. — Fo[illegible]ation of first solid film. — Its composition. — Its incessa[illegible]uptures and recementation. — A lava floe. — Contin[illegible]y established. — A crust glowing with heat.

2. Later probable ruptures and repairs. — The cause and consequences.

V. Appearance of Water, (W. 52-5.)

1. The temperature hitherto too high for its existence.
2. Gathering clouds. — Sun-light veiled out. — The still self-luminous earth. — All substances red-hot at about 977° Fah. (J. W. Draper, *A. J. S.*, Jan. 1877, 67).
3. Descending rains. — Electrical disturbances. — The war of fire and water. — The stormy period.

VI. Ascendancy of the Waters.

1. A universal ocean film. — Acid rains. — Attacks upon the rocks. — The war of chemical affinities. (W. 56-64; Hunt: *Chem. and Geol. Essays*).
2. Beginning of sedimentation. (Lect. VI.) — Chemical and mechanical deposits.
3. An age of physical violence. — Ruptures of the ocean's floor. — Explosive generation of steam. — Tepid waters and reeking skies.
4. Probable advent of marine plants. (Lect. IV., I.)

VII. Germs of Continents appearing above the waves.

1. The first mechanical sediments must have proceeded from the fire-formed crust.
2. Mechanical erosion effective only along a shore-line.
3. There must, consequently, have been a shore-line on a fire-formed land. — Such lands the germs of future continents. (Lects. XXIII, XXIV, XLIV.)

XL. NEBULAR THEORY OF WORLD—GENESIS.

EMANUEL KANT: *Allgemeine Naturgeschichte und Theorie des Himmels, oder Versuch von der Verfassung und dem Mechanischen Ursprunge des ganzen Weltgebundes, nach Newtonschen Grundsatzen abgehandelt.* Königsberg u., Leipzig, 1755. Kant's sämmtliche Werke Bd. i., S. 207.

DR. LAMBERT: *Lettres Cosmologiques*, 1761; *Cosmological Letters*, 1828.

JOHANN ELERT BODE: *Anleitung zur Kentniss des gestirnten Himmels, circa*, 1767.

PIERRE SIMON, Marquis de LAPLACE: *Exposition du Systeme du Monde*, Paris, 1796, tome ii., ch. 6. See translation in ENNIS: *The Origin of the Stars.* Appendix V.

Compare also A. WINCHELL: *Sketches of Creation*, ch. iv.; *Unity of the Physical World*, Meth. Quar. Rev., Jan., 1874; *Geology of the Stars*, 1873; FIQUIER: *The World before the Deluge*, 16-29; ENNIS: *The Origin of the Stars;* MILL: *System of Logic.* Bk. ii., ch. xiv.; L. SAEMANN: *On the Unity of Geological Phenomena in the Solar System*, Bull. de la Soc. geol. de France, 4 Feb., 1861, and Canadian Naturallst, vi., 444-51; SAIGEY: *The Unity of Natural Phenomena*, transl. 12 mo., 254 pp., Boston, 1873.

I. Common conditions pervading the Solar System.

1. Common motions. — Orbital, axial, eastward, elliptic, zodiacal. — Kepler's three laws.
2. Common forms.
3. Common substance. — Spectroscopic revelations. — Meteoric matter.
4. Laws of light. — Etherial medium. — Gravitation.
5. The bodies of the system (not including comets) must have had a common history.

II. A common primitive Fire-mist.

1. The whole solar system an ancient sphere of incandescent vapor. — Its physical constitution.
2. Probably an older condition and another form of matter. — Analogical inference of heated, non-luminous, aëriform matter.
3. Cosmical analogies of the fire-mist.
   (1) The solar photosphere. (Proctor: *The Sun;* Secchi: *Le Soleil*). — The solar nucleus perhaps a non-luminous, intensely-heated gas. (Faye: *Comptes Rendus*). — Its constituents in a state of molecular dissociation.
   (2) The fixed stars possess a similar constitution.
   (3) The nebulæ still more striking examples.
   (4) The condition of illuminated dust probably seen in the rings of Saturn and in comets and the Zodiacal light.

III. Behavior of a Sphere of Fire-mist in space.

1. It would radiate heat.
2. Through cooling it would shrink.
3. If not rotating, a rotation would be established.
   (1.) By the impinging of exterior masses against it. (Lect. XLIII.)
   (2.) By distortion of form and change of position of centre of gravity through external attractions. — Descending portions would thus pass one side of the centre of gravity and generate tangential forces.
   (3.) By the establishment of superficial currents in passing from an amorphous to a spherical form.
4. Rotation would be accelerated with shortening of diameter. — Velocity inversely as the square of the equatorial diameter.
5. The mass would become an increasingly oblate spheroid.
6. The equatorial periphery would at length become equilibrated between centripetal and centrifugal forces.
7. It would no longer descend toward the centre, and the portion within would shrink away from it, leaving a rotating ring.
8. Other rings, in succession, would be similarly detached.

IV. Behavior of a Ring of fire-mist surrounding a sphere.

1. It would continue to rotate approximately in the plane of the sphere's equator. — But its equilibrium would be unstable.

2. It might assume a stratified condition and resolve itself into a system of concentric rings. -- Influence of different velocities of rotation of outer and inner parts. — And of different densities in the substance.
3. External attractions would disturb the symmetry of its movements.
   (1) A "wobbling" motion might ensue. — This would be continually exaggerated until the ring or rings should be broken.
   (2) The centre of gravity of the ring might be drawn to one side of the centre of figure. — The matter would tend to flow to the side nearest this. — The opposite side would become progressively more tenuous.
4. However broken, the ring would gather itself spherically about one center. — This sphere would travel orbitally in the path determined by the position of the ring. — The orbit at first circular and unstable, would, through perturbations, become elliptic and stable. — The sphere would rotate axially in the same direction. (Ennis: *Origin of the Stars*, Sec. XXX). — Thus the matter of a planet would become isolated. — All the planets in succession would assume their places.
5. A stratified ring or system of rings might form a zone of planetoids.

V. Behavior of a Planetary Sphere of Fire-mist.

1. If large, it might undergo annulation — Thus matter for satellites would become isolated. — These must present the same conformities as their primaries in their motions.
2. If small, liquefaction might result without annulation. — Further history. (Lect. XXXIX.)
3. G. H. Darwin's theory of satellite origin by disruption of the primary. (*Nature*, XXI., 235-7, Jan. 8, 1880; *Phil. Trans.*, 1879.)

VI. Confirmations of these Deductions.

1. The evidences of former high temperature in the earth. (Lect. II.)
2. The community of conditions in the solar system.
3. The necessary action of physical forces.
4. The present existence of the assumed fire-mist condition.
5. The present existence of the ring condition.
   (1.) In certain nebulæ. (Lecture XLIII.)
   (2.) In the Saturnian system.
6. The experiment of Plateau. (*Taylor's Scientific Memoirs*, Nov., 1844; *Vestiges of Creation*, p. 14.)
7. The agreement of the cosmic mechanism with the requirements of the theory.
8. The present conditions of Jupiter, the sun and the moon.

9. The exterior planets generally the larger and the less dense.
10. The absence of any fatal conflicts with facts.

VII. **Difficulties of the Nebular theory as enunciated by Laplace.** (D. Kirkwood, *P. A. Phil. Soc.*, xviii., 324–6, Sep. 19, 1879; *Monthly Notices Roy. Astron. Soc.*, Jan., 1869. Comp. Slaughter: *The Modern Genesis*, 1876, and the author of *The Plurality of Worlds*, ch. vii., Am. ed., 1854.

1. Does not clearly explain breadth of intervals between planetary orbits. (Newcomb: *Pop. Astron.*, 498.) — Suggestion that the plants may be nearly of the same age. (Newcomb, 498–9, 513.)
2. Time required for spheration of a ring extravagantly large.
3. Hence, formation of satellites before cooling involved in difficulty.
4. Period of nebular rotation decreasing as square of radius, ($t : t' :: r^2 : r'^2$), the periods of the planets, ($t : t' :: r^{\frac{3}{2}} : r'^{\frac{3}{2}}$, by Kepler's third law) are *too long.* — This difficulty removed by supposing the peripheral portion rotated more rapidly than the interior, and thus suffered retardation.
5. The asteroids together (as far as known) only ¼ the earth's mass, or 1-1200 that of Jupiter, while Mars is also smaller than the earth. — But a portion of the asteroids may have been precipitated into the solar mass again,before the latter had shrunken to dimensions sufficiently within the perihelion position of the asteroidal mass. So of Mars. (Kirkwood, *A. J. S.*, III. i., 71.)
6. General agreement of opinion, nevertheless, in some kind of a nebular origin, with accompaniment of rotation. (David Trowbridge, *A. J.* S., Nov., 1864; Ennis: *Origin of the Stars;* Pierce, in *Agassiz' Contributions to Nat. His. U. S.*)

XLI. IMPLICATIONS OF THE NEBULAR THEORY.

I. **Exclusions.**

1. It is not, as here contemplated, a theory of the evolution of the universe.
2. It does not involve the comets, as the Laplacean theory did.
3. It does not deny an antecedent history for the fire-mist.
4. It does not profess to discover the origin of things, but only a stadium in material history.
   (1) Its starting point postulates *matter* and *force.*
   (2) It leaves us to search still for the *origin* of these.
   (3) It affirms nothing concerning the *nature* of matter and force.
5. It does not deny the existence of *plan* and *purpose* in the system of cosmic evolution.
6. The truth of tbe theory can be tested only by scientific evidence.

II. All the bodies of our System pass the same succession of Phases. (W. *Geology of the Stars;* Ennis: *Origin of the Stars;* Meunier: *Le Ciel géologique*).

1. The history of each of these bodies a history of cooling.
2. The phase reached at any epoch determined by the age and the mass and volume of the body.
   (1) Temperature of the Sun, (J. H. Lane, ***A. J. S.***, II. 1, 57): Secchi, 10,000,000°C, (*A. J. S.*, III. iii, 239); — Ericsson, 4,036,000°, (***Nature***, v. 344, Apr. 25, 1872; ***A. J. S.***, III. iv. 152-5). — Zöllner, 400,000°. — Spörer, 27,000° C. — Dewar, 16,000°, (***Proc. Roy. Soc., Edinb.***), vii, 697; ***A. J. S.***, III, v. 153). — W. Thomson, 14,000°, (Comp. ***A. J. S.***, III, ii, 286). — Faye, 3,000° to 10.000°, (***Comptes Rendus***). — Vicaire, 3,000° C., (***Comptes Rendus***). — Deville, 2,500 to 2,800° C, (***Comptes Rend.***). — Pouillet 1,461° to to 1,761° C.
   (2) The Earth has reached the habitable condition.
   (3) The Moon has passed this condition. — The Earth's mass being 84 times that of the Moon, it had 84 times as much heat. — Its surface being 13.4 times as great it radiatad 13.4 times as fast. — Hence the moon cooled 6¼ times as fast, and each of its stages endured 4-25 as long as the earth's corresponding stage. (Frankland: ***Proc. Roy. Ins.***, iv, 175; Guillemin: ***The Heavens***, 143; Meunier: ***Le Ciel geol.***).
   (4) Mars must be in a state of senescence. — Both older and smaller than the Earth.
   (5) Venus cannot have reached the habitable stage. — Intensity of solar heat retards its cooling and dissipates the supply of water. — The same with Mercury.
   (6) Jupiter lingers in the stormy stage. — Enveloped in aqueous vapor. — Bulk overestimated, and hence density underestimated, being placed at one-fourth that of the earth. — Indications of inherent luminosity.
   (7) The Saturnian system perpetuates the annular phase. — The rings neither solid nor fluid. (Pierce,). — They seem to be of the nature of dust.
3. The Sun's physical constitution. (Newcomb: *Popular Astronomy*, 237-82; Secchi: *Le Soleil;* S P. Langley, *A. J. S.*, III, vii, 37; ix, 192; x, 459; W. A. Norton, *A. J. S*, III, i, 395.
   (1) As old as Neptune, but less cooled in consequence of its great mass. — Will be as dense as the earth in 12,000,000 years. (Newcomb, 573).
   (2) Internal solar activities arising from the cooling process. — Spots. — Prominences. — Hydrogen flames. — Corona.
4. The Cosmical Archetype.

III. Other Worlds Habitable. (Brewster: *More Worlds than One;* Proctor: *Other Worlds than Ours;* C. Flammarion: *La Pluratité des Mondes Habités*, 8vo., 1864; *Les Mondes imaginaires et les Mondes réels*, 8vo., 1865; Fontenelle: *Dialogues on the Plurality of Worlds*, 1686, 2d ed. 1719. Also, Christian Huygens: *Cosmothereos, sive de Terris Cœlestibus, earumque ornatu, conjecturæ.* Huygenii Opera tom. ii, 645-722, Eng. trans., *The Celestial Worlds discovered, or Conjectures concerning the Inhabitants, Plants and Productions of the Worlds in the Planets*, 1698, 2d ed. 1722, Giordano Bruno:

Universo e Mondi innumerabili; Chalmers: *Astronomical Discourses*, Disc. IV; Bentley: *Boyle Lectures*, Lect. viii, ed. 1724, p. 298 *seq;* Laplace: *Sys. du Monde*, liv. 5me., ch. vi; Derham: *Astrotheology*, 3d ed. 1717, pp. xlvii, liii; liv).

1. Each planet of our system passes a habitable stage. -- Terrestrial conditions reproduced on other planets.
2. Climates and supposed vegetation of Mars.
3. Some of the larger satellites possibly habitable.
4. Planets in many other systems may have attained the habitable stage.
5. Nature's economy of habitable conditions.
6. Habitability for peculiar beings may exist where we cannot expect it. (Brewster: *More Worlds than One;* R. Owen: *On the Nature of Limbs*, 1849, Lond., 83, 84. Compare Newton: *Optics*, ed. 1721, 378, 379; Jules Boiteau: *Letters to a Materialist on the Plurality of Inhabited Worlds; The Catholic World*, Feb. 1880, 665–75 from *Revue des Questions Scientifiques*, July, 1877).
7. Some noteworthy conjectures.
   (1) D. Lardner argued the habitability of the moon and all the planets. (*Museum of Science and Art*, vol i.)
   (2) D. Brewster advances similar opinions. (*More Worlds than One*).
   (3) W. Herschel thought the solar spots the highest points (some 600 miles high) of a cool and habitable globe. — The solar heat attempered "in some mysterious way." — Earlier advocates of this opinion. (Pres. Forbes: *Reflections on the Sources of Incredulity with regard to Religion*, Edinb., 1750, p. 3; Dr. Elliot, *Edinb. Encyc.*, Art. Astron., vol. ii, p. 616; *Gentlemen's Magazine*, 1787, 636. Also works of Flammarion, Jean Reynaud, Babinet, Pioger.
8. Habitability of other worlds denied on theological grounds. Maxwell: (*Plurality of Worlds*, 1820, who holds that the Newtonian philosophy contains principles "which lie at the foundation of all atheistical systems)."
9. Denied on scientific grounds. (Whewell: *Of the Plurality of Worlds*).

IV. Many other Worlds Uninhabitable. (Faye: *Annaire du Bureau des Longitudes;* Newcomb: *Popular Astron.*, 516–19).

1. Most worlds probably too old or too recent for habitability. — At least in unsuitable stages of development.
2. All in the solar stage too intensely heated.
3. Question concerning our remoter planets.
   (1) Light and heat of Neptune 1-900th of what we enjoy. — The sun the size of Jupiter to us.
   (2) Density of Jupiter stated at one-fourth that of the earth. — A mere globe of water. — But the weight of bodies two and one-half times as great. — The density probably underestimated.
   (3) Saturn and his dust-like rings.

V. Some Cosmical Finalities.

1. Total refrigeration. (Lyell: *Prin.*, 129; Fourier: *On the Temperature of the Terrestrial Globe and the Planetary Spaces*, Annales de Chemie et de Physique, tome xxviii, 136, Oct. 1824).
   (1) A body is hot only because it has not had sufficient time to cool. — The lava of Jorullo was still ignited after twenty-one years. — That of Aetna, from 1787 to 1830, while unmelted snow remained beneath. Lyell: (*Princ.*, 396).
   (2) No assignable cause for permanent arrest of planetary cooling. — The heat radiated mostly lost to our system. (Fourier, *ut sup*). — Dissipation of energy of a system. (Sir W. Thomson. — This compatible with a total conservation of energy.
2. How uninhabibility may result.
   (1) From attainment of too low a temperature. (W., ch. xxxviii.)
   (2) From the absorption of all water and air. (L. Sæmann as in Lect. XL; S. Meunier: *Le ciel geol.*; W., *Geol. of the Stars*).
      (*a*) The volume of the ocean is only .0042 that of the earth.
      (*b*) Ordinary minerals will absorb .0127 per cent. of water. (Durocher: *Bull. Geol. Soc. France*, II, x, 431. On the porosity of rocks see Hunt: *Chem. and Geol. Ess.*, 164; Delesse: *Bull. Geol. Soc. France*, II, xix, 64: Sorby, *Q. J. Geol. Soc.*, xiv, 1858, 329, 453; D. Brewster: *Ann. de Chem. et de Phys.*, xxi, 1822, 182; *Poggendorff's Annalen*, vii, 493). — Hence the cooled earth would readily absorb all the water of the oceans, and two-thirds of its capacity would remain unfilled,
      (*c*) The volume of the air (reduced to surface density) is .0037 that of the earth. (Sæmann, *ut sup*). — Hence the cooled earth would absorb the atmosphere as well as the ocean, and if as compact as average rocks, would leave five-thirteenths of its pores still unsaturated.
   (3) The water and atmosphere of the moon thus absorbed. (Sæmann, *ut sup.*; W., *Geol. of the Stars;* Guillemin: *The Heavens*, 143; Meunier, *ut sup*). — In cooling through 180°, would create cellular space equal to fourteen and a half millions of cubic miles. (Frankland: *Proc. Roy. Inst.*, iv, 175). — Supposed recent changes on moon's surface. (Birt: *A. J. S.*, III, iv, 326).

XLII. COSMICAL DUST.

A. E. Nordenskjöld, On the Cosmical Dust which falls to the Earth with atmospheric preciptation, Poggendorff's Annalen, cli, 154, 1874; *A. J. S.*, III, ix, 145–6; H. A. Newton, *On Shooting Stars*, A. J. S., II, xxxix, 193–207; *ib*, xliii, 285: Schiaparelli, Bolletino Meteorologico Rome, v, Nos. 8, 10, 11, 12, vi, No. 2, abstract, A. J. S., II, xliii, 291–9.

I. Enlargement of the scope of our speculations.

1. Other systems of worlds to be accounted for.
2. Inquiries as to older conditions and other evolutions.
3. Gathering dust. — Examples. — Whence does it come?

II. Meteors (Newton, *as above*;) D. Kirkwood: *A Treatise on Shooting Stars, Fire-balls and Aërolites*, Phil., 1867; Newcomb, Eastman and Harkness, *Observations and Discussions of the November Meteors*, 1867, Washington, 8vo.; 40 pp, 1867.

1. The phenomena (Newton, *A. J. S.*, II, xli, 58, 192, 273, xlii, 429, xliii, 78, 276, xliv, 426, xlv, 78, 225, xlvii, 118, 399, xlix, 244; E. C. Herrick, *A. J. S.* II, xxxi, 136, xxxii, 294, xxxiii, 147, 148, 290, 291).
2. Numbers. — 7½ millions in 24 hours to the naked eye, (Newton, *A. J. S.*, II, xxix, 198). — 400 millions to telescope, (*Ib.* p. 201). — Arago says 240 millions in 3 hours in November, 1833.
3. Contribution of matter to the earth. — 28½ tons daily. — 10,000 tons yearly. — 104 million tons in 10,000 years.
4. Velocity 14 to 107 miles per second. — Meet the earth. — Consequences of penetrating the earth's atmosphere. — Composed of terrestrial substances, (J. L. Smith: *Mineralogy and Chemistry;* Meunier: *Le ciel geol*).
5. Meteoric Swarms and Orbits. (H. A. Newton, *as above;* Schiaparelli, *as above.* A. J. S., III, v, 482; *Entwurf einer Astronomischen Theorie der Sternschnuppen;* Proctor: *Other World than Ours;* D. Kirkwood: *Comets and Meteors*, 1873.
   (1) August orbit fifty times the diameter of the earth's orbit.
   (2) November orbit 33¼ years and ten times the diameter of the earth's orbit. (Newton, *as above;* Sir William Thomson, *Brit. Assoc.*, Edinb.; A. J. S., III, ii, 289, October 1871).
   (3) A hundrrd other meteoric orbits more or less known. (Kirkwood, A. J. S., III, vi 392.
6. Space filled with moving meteoroids (Newton).

III. Zodiacal Light. (Newcomb: *Pop. Astron.* 405–6).

1. The Phenomena.
2. Supposed explanation.

IV. Comets. (Newcomb: *Pop. Astron.* 365–84, 398–405; W. Thomson, *A. J. S.* III, ii, 289; Zöllner: *Ueber die Natur der Cometen*, Leipzig, 1872, 8vo., pp. c, 523; *A. J. S.*, III, iii, 476; De la Rue, *A. J. S.*, III, iv, 324; J. C. Watson: *Treatise on Comets.*

1. Conglomeration of cosmical dust. — The matter thought by W. Herschel to be derived from nebulæ. (*Phil. Trans.*, 1812, 144).
2. Not natives of our system. — Their erratic movements.
3. Periods of comets 3½ to 76, and 2,000 and even 100,000 years.
4. Tenuity of their substance.
5. Identification with meteoric swarms. (Newcomb: *Pop. Astron.*, 391–8; H. A. Newton, *A. J. S.*, II, xxxii, 449; Schiaparelli *ut sup.*, and *Monthly Notices*, Feb. 1875; *A. J. S.*, III, ix, 406. Comp. A. W. Wright, *A. J. S.*, III, ix, 459, x, 44; J. W. Mallet, *A. J. S.*, III, x, 206–7).

(1) Comet of 1862 III identified with August swarm. (Newton, Schiaparelli, Oppolzer, Schellen: Spectralanalyse, trans., 600).

(2) Comet of 1866 II. (Tempel's) identified with November swarm. (Schiaparelli, *Les Mondes*, xiii, 501, March 28, 1867; *A. J. S.*, II, xliv, 129).

(3) Biela's lost comet identified with a train intercepted by the earth, November 27, 1872. (But compare *Nature*, xxi, 240, Jan. 8, 1880.

(4) A meteoric ring only a degenerated comet. — Method of gathering cosmical matter into globes.

V. Saturnian Rings.

1. Their physical phenomena.
2. Their physical constitution.

VI. Nebulæ. (Newcomb: *Pop. Astron.* 444–52; Sir Wm. Herschel, *Phil. Trans.*, 1784, 1811, 1814).

1. Description. — Discovery. — Early opinions.
2. So-called "resolvable nebulæ."
3. True nebulæ irresolvable. — Stubborn irresolvability of many nebulæ.
4. The spectroscope. (Schellen: Spectralanalyse, also Amer. transl.; *Half Hour Recreations in Science*, Nos. 3 and 4, Boston; Roscoe: *Spectrum Analysis*, Lond., 2d. ed., 1870, 8vo., pp. 404). — Three fundamental principles of its action. — Application to nebulæ. — The spectra perhaps indicate a state of dissociation. Lockyer's conclusions touching the compound nature of so-called elements. (Nature).

SYNOPTICAL VIEW OF SPECTROSCOPIC PHENOMENA.

DESIGNATION OF SPECTRUM.		CONDITION OF MATTER.
Continuous spectrum	IMPLIES	Incandescent Solid or Liquid. (*Drummond Light.*)
Bright-line spectrum= Discontinuous spectrum= Gas spectrum.	IMPLIES	Incandescent Gas or Vapor. (*Electric Light; Solar prominences; Irresolvable nebulæ*).
Dark-line spectrum= Absorption spectrum, Reversed spectrum or Compound spectrum.	IMPLIES	Incandescent Solid or Liquid shinging through gas or vapor of lower temperature. (*Sun; Fixed Stars*).

5. Forms of Nebulæ.

(1) Amorphous. (Newcomb, 446, 450-1; Schellen: Spec. Anal, trans., 534, etc). — Great Nebula in Orion. (*Nature*, 22 Nov. 1877, 67, and 8 July, 1878, 313.

(2) Sickle-shaped. (Schellen, *op. cit*, 537).

(3) Spiral. (Schellen, *op. cit*, 537).

(4) Spiro-annular. (Schellen, *op. cit*, 540, 541).

(5) Planetary. (Schellen, *op. cit*, 544, 553).

(6) Annular. (Newcomb, *op. cit*, 448; Schellen, 540, 555, 542, also figs., 194, 195).

(7) Stellar. (Schellen, 553). — Compare Donati's comet 1858. (Watson, Newcomb, 368; Schellen, 559).

(8) Sir Wm. Herschel's suggestions:—That amorphous, planetary, annular and stellar nebulæ are successive stages in nebular life. (*Phil. Trans.*, 1811, 1814). — Ultimate condensation to a star expected. (*Ib*). — That outlying portions condense into planets. (*Ib*).

VII. General Cosmical Theory.

1. Original world-stuff pervading space. — Suggested to be the ether. (McVicar: *Sketch of a Philosophy*; Saigey: *The Unity of Nat. Phenom*).
2. Gravitational gathering of cosmical dust. — Meteoroidal, cometary and nebular accumulations.
3. Evolutions of nebulæ. — Collisions. — Heat, light, and rotation resulting.

XLIII. NEBULAR LIFE.

Sir William Herschel: *Astronomical Observations relating to the Construction of the Heavens, arranged for the purpose of a critical examination, the result of which appears to throw some new Light upon the Organization of the celestial Bodies*, Philosophical Transactions, 1811, p. 269, and 1814, p. 248. See, also, Philosophical Transactions, 1784. Synopsis of Sir W. Herschel's researches in Newcomb's *Astronomy*, pp. 465–74, 495, and fuller account in Arago's *Analyse des Travaux de Sir William Herschel* in *Annuaire du Bureau des Longitudes*, 142.

Cleveland Abbe: *The "very much extended" Nebulæ of Sir John Herschel's General Catalogue*, A. J. S., III, ix, 42–6.

I. Isolation and Sources of Nebulæ.

1. Comparative freedom of Nebulæ from perturbations from our system or our firmament.
2. The primitive materials of Nebulæ disseminated and cold. — The materials not all involved in any evolution dating from any specific beginning. — Cosmical beginnings at all times.
3. Process of conglomeration. (Compare Ennis: *Origin of the Stars*, sec. xvi).

II. Origin of Nebular Heat.

1. Theory of Nebular incandescence from condensation. (Comp. Newcomb, *Astron.*, 507, 513). — Limits of applicability of this theory.
2. Nebular amorphism an indication of nebular unions.

(1) Suggested by our theory.

(2) Amorphism probably a temporary stage. — Observed changes in nebulæ. (Newcomb: *Pop. Astron.*, 449. Compare Huggins: *On Motions of Nebulæ*, Proc. Roy. Soc., 1874; abstr. *A. J. S.*, III, xiii, 75–7).

(*a*) The Nebula in Orion. — Changes from Huygens' time to W. Herschel's. (Herschel: *Phil. Trans.*. 1811; Struve: —— ; Holden: *A. J. S.*, III, xi, 360).

(*b*) The Trifid Nebula, M. 20. (Holden: *A. J. S.*, III, xiv, 433–58, Dec. 1777; Newcomb: *Astron.*, 449–50).

(*c*) The Omega Nebula, H. 2008. (Holden: *A. J. S.*, III, xi, 341–61, May, 1876; Newcomb: *Astron.*, 450).

(*d*) The Magellanic Clouds. (Sir W. Herschel, *Phil. Trans.*, 1811).

(3) Apparent changelessness of most nebulæ due to their enormous magnitudes and distances.

3. The impact of nebulæ must generate enormous heat. — This theory, since first propounded, confirmed by James Croll. (*Nature*, Jan. 1878).

III. Origin of Nebular Rotation.

1. This an incident of collision. — The motion of two sole bodies in space. — The motion of three bodies in space.

(1) First Case.—*The centers of gravity of two nebulæ move toward one point with such velocities as to reach it simultaneously.*

(*a*) First sub-case.—*When the centres of gravity move along one straight line.*

(*b*) Second sub-case.—*When the centers of gravity do not move along one straight line.*

(2) Second Case.—*The centers of gravity move toward each other with such velocities as to pass it successively.*

(*a*) When the centers of gravity lie in one straight line.

(b) When the centres of gravity do not lie in one straight line.

2. Rotation also a consequence of superficial currents arising from the passage from an amorphous to a spherical figure. (Ennis: *Origin of the Stars*, sec. xvii; *On the Necessity of Nebular Rotation*, P. A. N. S., Phil., 1867). — How currents would be established. — Retardation by friction with the non-rotating interior. — Friction progressively augmented as density of interior increases.

IV. Origin of Regular Nebular Forms.

1. The Spiral Form may arise from the co-action of an etherial medium in a non-homogeneous nebula.
2. The Sickle Form results apparently from the orbital motion of a nebulous body in a resisting medium. — Illustration.
3. The Spheroidal Form arises in a homogeneous nebula, or from progressive homogeneity in a spiral nebula. — The nebular spheroid the normal form.

V. Differentiation of Nebulæ.

1. Non-rotating nebulæ.

(1) By a process of coagulation.

(2) By condensation about separate centers.

(3) These are possible origins of discontinuous nebulæ. — A state of stellation. — Rotation of the separate masses probable.

2. Rotating Nebulæ. (Comp., Lect. XL, II).

(1) Annulation.

(*a*) The nucleus may separate from the ring. — Example, the Stellar Nebula H. 450.

(*b*) The nucleus may adhere to the ring. — Example, the Annular Nebula in the Lyre. (Schellen: *Spect. Anal.*, 555).

(2) Spheration of annuli. (Comp. Lect. XL, III).

(*a*) By lateral loading on one or more sides.

(*b*) By perturbative rupture.

3. Each constituent mass the mother of a solar system. — The Nebula the mother of a Firmament.
4. Sublimity of these conceptions.

XLIV. OROGENY.

J. D. DANA: *On the Origin of Mountains*, A. J. S., III, v. 347, criticism of J. Hall's theory; see, also, A. J. S., II, xliii, 210. *On Some Results of the Earth's Contraction from Cooling, including a discussion of the Origin of Mountains and the Nature of the Earth's Interior:* Part I, Review of Opinions, and *Theory of Mountain Origin*, A. J. S., III, v. 423–43, June, 1873; Part II: *Condition of the Earth's Interior and Connection of Facts with Mountain-making*, and Part III, *Metamorphism*, A. J. S., III, vi, 6–14; Part IV: *Igneous Ejections, ib.*, vi, 104–6, Aug. 1873; Part V: *Formation of Continental Plateaux and Ocean-depressions, ib.*, vi, 161–72, Sept., 18 3. Earlier papers, *A. J. S.*, II, ii, 385; iii, 94 176, 380; iv, 88; vii, 379; xxii, 305, 335; also, *Geology U. S. Exploring Expedition.*

JAMES HALL: *Palæntology of New York*, iii., Introduction.

O. FISHER: *On the Elevation of Mountain Chains by Lateral Pressure*, etc. Trans. Camb. Phil. Soc., xi, pt. iii, 1869; *On Elevation and Subsidence*, Phil. Mag., 1872; *On the Formation of Mountains, and the Hypothesis of a Liquid Substratum beneath the Earth's Crust.* Proc. Camb. Phil. Soc., Feb. 22, 1875; *Mountain-making: The Inequalities of the Earth's Surface viewed in connection with Secular Cooling*, Camb. Phil. Trans., xii, pt. ii, abstr. A. J. S., x, 380-9.

J. D. WHITNEY: ***Mountain Building.***

T. S. HUNT: ***Chemical and Geological Essays***, especially, ***On Some Points in Dynamical Geology***, (1858), pp. 70–9; ***Origin of Mountains***, (1861), pp. 49–58; ***Geognosy of the Appalachians, and the Origin of Crystalline Rocks*** (1871), pp. 239–327; ***Geology of the Alps***, (1872), pp. 328–48; ***Criticism of Leconte's Views***, A. J. S., III, v., 264–70.

JOSEPH LECONTE: ***Elementary Geology***, 90–132, 252–60; ***A Theory of the formation of the Great Features of the Earth's Surface***, A. J. S., III, iv, 345 and 460, Nov. and Dec., 1872, v, 156; ***Reply to Hunt's Criticisms***, A. J. S., III, v. 448, June, 1873; ***On the Great Lava Flood of the West, and on the Structure and Age of the Cascade Mountains***, A. J.S., III, vii, 167, 259, March and Apr., 1874.

POULETT SCROPE, ***Geological Magazine***, vi, 512; F. W. HUTTON, ***Mountains***, Geol. Mag.; ***Elevation of Mountains and Volcanic Theories***, Nature. ix, 61–2; C. E. DUTTON: ***A Criticism upon the Contractional Hypothesis***, A. J. S., III, viii, 112–23. Aug. 1874; also, ***Penn Monthly***, May and June, 1876; KARL V. SEEBACH: ***Das Mitteldeutsche Erdbeben***, von 6 März, 1872, reviewed by B. K. EMERSON in A. J. S., III, viii. 405–12; FRIEDRICH PFAFF: ***Der Mechanismus der Gebirgsbildung***, mit 75 Holzsch., 8vo., 1879.

On the expansibility of rocks by heat, see DANA: ***Manual***, 700; TOTTEN: ***A. J. S.***, I, xxii, 136; ADIE: ***Trans. Roy. Soc. Edinb.***; BABBAGE, ***Ninth Bridgewater Treatise***, App. H; F. PFAFF, ***op. cit.*** and ***A. J. S.***, III. x, 235. On contraction in passing from the liquid to the glassy and the stony states, see MALLET, ***Trans, Roy. Soc.***, 1872; DELESSE ***Bull. Soc. geol. de France***, II, iv, 1380, 1847.

See also references under Lectures XXIV, XXVI, XXVIII and XXXVIII.

I. Theory of Upheaval by Subterranean Forces. (Studer: *Geologie der Schweiz*).

1. Steam, gases, molten matter or other agents. (Strabo: *Geographia, lib.* vi). — Chemical explanation. (Sir H. Davy, etc.; W. Hopkins, *Report Brit. Assoc.*, 1848; Lect. XXXVIII).

2. Explanation inadequate. (Suess: *Die Enstehung der Alpen*, 165 pp., Wien, 1875, abstr. A. J. S., III, x, 446–51). — These forces too local, and not sustaining. — Mountains do not rest on aëriform foundations. (D., 739). — Nor are they upheld by cores of igneous rocks. (*Nature*, xxi, 177, 25 Dec. 1879). — Nor is the maximum pressure of steam adequate to elevate the crust, or a column of lava in a volcano. (Whitney, *N. Amer. Rev.*, cxiii, 255).

3. Laccolitic mountains a quasi-exception. (G. K. Gilbert: *Rep. on the Geol. of the Henry Mts.*, Powell Surv., 1877; *Nature*, xxi, 177) — Bubbles or blisters raised by intrusive trachytes.

II. Theory of Wrinkling by Lateral Pressure. (Dana. *ut sup.*, and *Man.*, 735, 745; Descartes; *Principes de la Philos.*, pt. iv, § 42.

1. Cause of incipient wrinkles in the earth's crust. — Attributable to lateral pressure. — Effects observed in motion of rocks in quarries. (W. H. Niles, *A. J. S.*, III, iii, 222).

2. Tendency to continual subsequent development.
   (1) Their crests become lines of weakness.
   (2) Lateral pressure would continue to fold in the same direction.
   (3) Influence of deep ocean waters. (Dana). This would tend to parallelize mountain ranges with continental shores.
   (4) Formation of continents and ocean basins. (D. 738).

3. The presence of one fold would predispose to contiguous parallel folds. — Mechanical illustration. — Hence a chain of parallel ranges.

4. The ocean's pressure would result in an excess of thrust away from the shore. (D. 745). — Hence the folds might altitudinally incline continent-ward. — Or might become tilted over. — This possibility often realized. (Lect. XXIV, I, 2,(6)).

5. This theory fulfills requirements of many facts. — But does not explain enormous thickening of strata in mountain-ranges. (Lect. XXIV, I, 5). — Accepted so far as it goes, but requires to be supplemented.

III. Theory of Wrinkling by Mashing Together. (L. 252; Wurtz, A. J. Mining, 25 Jan. 1868, read Aug. 1866; Dana, Mallet, *ut sup.*; Ramsay, Addr. Geol. Sec, Brit. Assoc., 1866).

1. Assumes all the positions of the above theory.

2. Assumes also a thickening of mountain-strata by mashing together. (L. 253).
3. The theory tends to explain metamorphism and igneous phenomena. — Compression the source of heat. (Mallet, Leconte).
4. Mashing might also result from lateral crowding of fluid matter thrust up under the fold. — Attended by thinning along the crest of the fold.
5. This theory explains the thickened strata. — But does not explain their more coarsely fragmental character, and the deficiency of calcareous constituents.
6. The adequacy of secular cooling from shrinkage denied. — Shrinkage insufficient and corrugation too much localized. (Dutton, *A. J. S.*, III, viii, 113; *Penn Monthly*, May and June, 1870). — Shrinkage insufficient and frictional heat too much diffused. (Fisher, *Camb. Phil. Trans.*, xii, pt. ii: *Q. J. G. Soc.*, xxxi, 471–2, 473–6). — But some shrinkage is a fact, whatever the cause, and great tangential strain hardly disputable. (L. 260). — Suggestions that the molten interior was at first combined with superheated water, and thus more bulky. (Fisher, *Camb. Phil. Trans*, xii, pt. ii).

IV. **The Synclinorium Theory**. (D., 748–50, 211–14, 244, 251, 275, 305; L. 252-6. Comp. King, 40 *Par.* i, 731; Hunt, *A. J. S.*, II, xxi, 392, 1861; *Chem. and Geol. Ess.*, 49–58; Vose: *Orographic Geol.*; Whitney, *N. A. Review*, cxiii, 265).

1. Starts from the evidences of excessive sedimentation along mountain axes. (Hall: *Pal. N. Y.*, iii, Introd., 69 *seq*).
   (1) These evidences generally admitted conclusive.
   (2) Character of mountain-sediments implies excessive deposition, and proximity of a continental shore. — Principle of distribution of sediments. (Lect. VI, iv.)
2. And recognizes the proofs of progressive subsidence during accumulation.
   (1) Without subsidence, the sea along the axis of deposition would become so shallowed that deposition would cease.
   (2) Subsidence often regarded a mechanical effect of local loading of the crust. (Hall: *ut sup.*).
   (3) But this view untenable. (Fisher, *Geograph. Mag.*, x, 248). — A belt of crust yielding under a foot of sediments would not uphold a mountain mass. — Subsidence, in some cases, has accompanied unloading, and upheaval has accompanied loading. (King: 40 *Par.*, 537, 732).
3. It admits whatever mashing together may have been possible.
4. It admits the mechanical origin of more or less heat, as manifest in the phenomena of vulcanicity.
5. And, finally, it recognizes inherent internal heat as a probable factor.

6. The mechanics of the final uplift of a synclinorium not fully understood. (D. 749 ; Leconte).
   (1) The synclinorium seems to have been a fact.
   (2) The uplift seems to have been a fact. (L. 242-4, 255-6). — Hall's theory does not provide for this. (Dana, *A. J. S.*)
   (3) Softening or fusion of lower portion of synclinorium a suggested condition of upheaval. (Dana). — But the very condition of softening is the existence of an overlying accumulation. maintaining the original thickness and consequent rigidity.
   (4) Consideration of the mechanical conditions existing about a synclinorium.
      (*a*) Structural arrangement on completion of the synclinorium.
      (*b*) Structural arrangement after uplift of the synclinorium into an anticlinal.
      (*c*) The problem is to ascertain the mechanical conditions of passage from the one to other.
      (*d*) Possibility of a synclinal mountain-mass resulting from mashing together without upheaval of synclinorium.

XLIV. THEORY OF CONTINENTAL GLACIATION.

L. AGASSIZ: *Systeme Glaciare*; JAMES CROLL: *Climate and Time*, 12mo., 577 pp., Am. ed. 1875; (Criticism of this by S. Newcomb, *A. J. S.*, III, xi, 263). LEHON: *L'Homme Fossile*, Part II; COL. DRAYSON: *Probable Cause, Date and Duration of Glacial Epoch*, Philosophical Magazine, 1871, abstr. A. J. S., III, ii, 304.

I. Recurrence of Phenomena of Glaciation. (Croll, *Climate and Time*, ch. xviii).

1. Summary of phenomena of last glaciation.
2. Similar phenomena of remoter date.
   (1) Worn and transported boulders in the Cambrian. (Jas. Thomson, *Brit. Assoc.*, 1870, 88).
   (2) Lower Silurian indications. (J. Carrick *Q. J. G. S.*, v. 10; *Phil. Mag.*, Apr., 1865, 289; Geikie: *Great Ice Age*, 512; Jukes: *Manual of Geol.*, 421; Haughton. in McClintock's *Narrative of Arctic Discoveries*; *Q. J. G. S.* xi, 510.
   (3) Smoothed rock-sufaces and shingle in Medina Epoch. (Hall).
   (4) Devonian indications. (Ramsay, *Reader*, 12 Aug. 1865; Cumming: *History of I. of Man*, 86; Selwyn: *Phys. Geog. and Geol. of Victoria*. 1866, 15-16; Taylor and Etheridge, *Geol. Surv. Victoria*, Quarter-Sheet 13 NE)
   (5) Similar phenomena in the Permian. (D. 431; *Amer. Nat.*, iv, 560; Ramsay, *Q. J. G. Soc.*, xi, 197; Sutherland, *Q. J. G. Soc.*, xxvi. 514; Daintree: *Geol. Dist. Ballan, Victoria*. 1866, 11).
   (6) In the Triassic. (T. A. Conrad and H. Wurtz, 1869; Dana, *A. J. S.*, III, ix, 315; Fontaine, *A. J. S.*, III, xvi, 236).
   (7) In the Jurassic. (Fontaine, *A. J. S.*, III, xvi, 236). — In the Upper Oölite of Scotland. (Judd, *Q. J. G. Soc.*, xxix; *Phil. Mag.*, xxix, 290).
   (8) Between Middle Cretaceous and Lower Eocene. (Dawson, *Princeton Rev.* March, 1879, 284). — In English Cretaceous. (Godwin Austen, *Q. J. G. Soc.*, xiv. 262; *Brit. Assoc. Rep.*, 1857, 62; *Q. J. G. Soc.*, xvi, 327; *Geologist*, 1860, 38).
   (9) A cold period at base of English Eocene. (*Nature*, 10 July, 1879, 258). — The *Flysch* of Switzerland. (Lyell: *Prin*).
   (10) In the Miocene. (Gastaldi, *Mem. Acad. Sci. Turin*, II, xx).

(11) Croll's extension of the idea to the Coal Measures. (*Op. cit.*, 296–8, and ch. xxvi.)

II. Hypothesis of passage through cold regions of space. (Lyell: *Prin.*, 127; Poisson: *Théorie math. de la chaleur*, Comptes Rendus, 30 Jan. 1837; Agassiz: *A Journey in Brazil*, 399, 425). — Or that the sun has experienced a diminution of heat. (Lyell: *Prin.*, 128; Sir John Herschel, *Proc. Roy. Astron. Soc*, No. iii, Jan., 1840; Balfour Stewart). — Both would involve simultaneous lowering of temperature over all parts of the earth. (D. 542. Compare Hopkins, *Q. J. G. Soc.*, viii).

III. Theory of the varying distribution of land and water; and consequent changes of marine currents. (D. 541: Lyell: *Prin.*, ch. vii, viii; Dawson, *Princeton Rev.*, Mar. 1879). — Northern elevation. (D. 541; *A. J. S.*, III, ix, 314-5, II, xxii, 346). Closing of Behring's Strait and submergence of Isthmus of Panama. (D. 541). — A true cause, but, to be of sufficient magnitude, would conflict with evidence of permanence of oceanic and continental areas. — The requisite distribution of northern land to produce the known glaciation, difficult to conceive. — The effect of placing all the land along the equator would be the opposite of what Lyell supposed. — The theory not suited to explain a succession of ice periods at secular intervals. — Northern elevation itself perhaps an effect of the real cause.

IV. Suggested change in the power of the atmosphere to transmit terrestrial heat. (D. 542; Tyndall; Hunt). — Cold of mountain elevations. — This, also, would affect all regions similarly.

V. Astronomical Theories. — Secular variations in the elements of the earth's orbit. (Stockwell, *A. J. S.*, II, xlvi, 87. See, also, *A. J. S.*, II, l, 147. Also, Meech, *Smithsonian Contributions*, ix, Art. i, Sec. vii). — Discussion in reference to Northern Hemisphere. — Researches of Humboldt, Arago, Sir J. Herschel, Lyell and Croll.

1. Effect of changes in the obliquity of the ecliptic. (Drayson, *Q. J. Geol. Soc.*, xxvii, 232; *The last glacial epoch of geology;* Thos. Belt, *Q. J. G. Soc*, Oct. 1874, abstr. *A. J. S.*, III, ix, 313–5).

   (1) Increased obliquity diminishes glaciation.
   (2) Diminished obliquity increases glaciation.
   (3) This cause insignificant, and now abandoned. (Croll: *Clim. and Time*, ch. xxv; George Darwin).

2. Possible shifting of position of terrestrial poles. (Sir W. Thomson, *Brit. Assoc. Rep.*, 1876, pt. ii, p. 11; *Trans. Glasgow Geol. Soc.*, iv, 313; Haughton, *Proc. Roy. Soc.*, xxvi, 51: Geo. Darwin,

Trans. Roy. Soc., clxvii, pt. i ; I. F. Twisden, *Q. J. G. Soc.*, Feb. 1878 ; Airy, *Athenæum*, 22 Sep. 1869).

(1) This also an insignificant cause. — To displace the pole 1° 46′, one-twentieth the surface of the earth must be lifted 10,000 ft. (G. H. Darwin).

(2) Since the glacial epoch, no physical changes have occurred which could move the pole six miles. (Cr ll, *Geol. Mag.*, Sept. 1878).

(3) Geological evidences exist that the pole has not changed since Silurian time. (Haughton, *Proc. Roy. Soc.*, Apr. 4, 1878; *Nature*. July 4, 1878 ; E. Hill, *Geol. Mag.*, June, 1878 ; Croll, *Geol. Mag.*, Sep. 1878; W. Thomson, *ut sup*).

(4) Dynamical principles show the present axis a necessary permanency. (Sir W. Thomson, *ut sup ; Brit. Assoc.*, 1874).

3. Effect of precession of the equinoxes, or change in position of the apsides. (Adhémar : *Revolutions de la mer ;* Le Hon : Periodicité des Grandes Déluges, 1858).

(1) Winter solstice in perihelion diminishes glaciation. — Opposite view entertained by J. J. Murphy. (*Q. J. G. Soc.*, xxv, 350).

(2) Summer solstice in perihelion increases glaciation.

(3) This cause alone also insufficient. — Croll now says null. (*Clim. and Time*, 83 ; *Phil. Mag.*, Sep. 1869 ; Arago, *Edinb. New Phil. Jour.*, vi, 1834).

1. Effect of change in eccentricity of earth's orbit.

(1) Increased eccentricity increases glaciation.

(2) Diminished eccentricity dimishes glaciation.

(3) This cause alone regarded as inefficient. (Sir J. Herschel, *Treatise on Astronomy*, § 315; *Outlines of Astronomy*, § 368; Arago, *Annuaire* for 1834, p. 199; *Edinb. New Phil. Jour.*, Apr. 1834, p. 244; Humboldt: *Cosmos*, iv, 459, Bohn's ed.; *Phys. Descrip. Heavens*, 336).

(4) Croll connects this with consequent changes in ocean currents. (Croll : *Clim. and Time*, etc. See brief abstract by Croll in *A. J. S.*, III, xvi, 389, and a fuller one by A. Winchell in *International Review*, July-Aug., 1876).

(*a*) Changes in eccentricity produce little or no *direct* effect.

(*b*) Increased eccentricity produces diminished winter heat and this promotes snowy precipitation. — The prolongation of the winter thus only increases the snow. — The short, hot summer would not diminish it. — Heat absorbed in liquefaction. — Fogs and vapors exclude solar rays.

(*c*) Effect of this upon ocean currents:—Prevailing winds the cause of ocean currents. (Croll : *op cit.*, ch. ii, iii, xiii). — Maury's theory. (Maury : *Phys. Geog. Sea*, § 24). — Appears to be untenable. (Croll: *op cit.*, ch. vi, vii). — Carpenter's theory. (Carpenter, *Proc. Roy. Soc.*, Dec. 1868, Nov. 1869 ; *Nature*, i, 490; *Proc. Roy. Geogr. Soc.*, xv). — Also untenable. (Croll; *op cit.*, ch. viii, xi).

Why the region of calms is now north of the equator. — The condition supposed would place it south. — This would direct the Gulf-Stream southward. (Croll: *op cit.*, ch xiv).

(*d*) European cold caused by diversion of Gulf-Stream.

(5) Such a theory when established would furnish a clew to geological time. (Croll : *op cit*,, ch. xix. Lecture LIII, IV).

(8) Criticisms of Croll's theory. (J. J. Murphy, *Q. J. G. Soc.*, xxv, 350, 1869, abstr. *A. J. S.*, II, xlix, 115-8; S. Newcomb, *A. J. S.*, III, xi, 263 ; Chas. Martins, *Revue des deux Mondes*, 1867).

VI. Displacement of Earth's centre of gravity by an ice-cap. (Croll, *op. cit.*, ch. xxiii, xxiv; Adhémar: *Revolutions de la mer.* Comp. Shaler, *Mem. Bos. Soc. Nat. Hist.*, ii, 322). — Submergence an incident of glaciation.

XLVI. MOTION OF GLACIERS.

L. AGASSIZ: *Systeme Glaciare*, 1847; JAMES CROLL, *Philosoph. Mag.*, March, 869, Sep. 1870; *A. J. S*, III, i, 65–68; *Climate and Time*, ch. xxx, xxxi; Canon MOSELEY, *Proc. Roy. Soc.*, 7 Jan. 1869; *Phil. Mag.*, May, 1769, Jan, 1870, Aug. 1871; *A. J. S.*, III, ii, 304; ALBERT HEIM, *Poggendorff's Annalen*; *Phil. Mag.*, June, 1871; *A. J. S.*, III, ii, 145; W. MATHEWS, *Alpine Journal*, Feb, 1870; *L., E. and D., Phil. Mag.*, Dec. 1871, Jan. 1872; *A. J. S.*, III, iii, 99; BALL, *Phil. Mag.*, July, 1870, Feb. 1871; *A. J. S.*, III, i, 268; JAMES D. FORBES: *Occasional Papers on the Theory of Glaciers*; JOHN TYNDALL: *The Glaciers of the Alps*, 1860; *The Forms of Water*, 1872; JOHN AITKEN, *Nature*, 13 Feb. 1873; *A. J. S.*, III, v, 305.

I. Nature of the motions of Glaciers. (Ref. Lect. XVIII).

1. More rapid in the middle than along the borders.
2. More rapid at the surface than at the bottom.
3. More rapid by day than by night.
4. And twice as fast in summer as in winter.
5. The glacier adapts itself to the inequalities of the channel.

II. Theory that the Glacier moves by Expansion and Contraction. (L. Agassiz; Charpentier; Moseley, *Proc. Bristol Naturalists' Soc.*, 1869).

1. Effect of expansion of a slab on an inclined plane.
2. Effect of contraction of the same.

III. Theory that it moves as a Viscous Body. (D. 682; L. 57; Bordier, 1773; Rendu; *Mem. Acad. Sci., Savoy*, 1841; J. D. Forbes: *Travels in the Alps*, 1843; *Occasional Papers*).

1. Arguments for this theory.
2. This does not explain seasonal and diurnal variations in the rate of motion.

IV. Theory of motion by Regelation. (L. 58; Tyndall, *Phil. Trans.*, cxlvii, 327; *Glaciers of the Alps;* James D. Forbes, *Proc. Roy. Soc.*, viii, 455; Helmholtz: *Popular Lectures*, 133, *seq*).

1. Definition of regelation. (Tyndall: *Heat as a mode of motion*, 167–72).
2. Faraday's explanation of regelation. (Tyndall: *Forms of Water*, 173). — Molecular attractions more solidifying in the centre than at the surface. — Hence two liquefying surfaces brought together solidify because made internal.
3. James Thomson's explanation. (*Proc. Roy. Soc., Edinb.*, Feb. 1850; Tyndall: *Hours of Exercise*, 383, *seq.*; Jamin: *Traité de Physique*, ii, 105; Helmholtz: *Popular Sci. Lectures*, Am. ed., 107–152, es-

pecially 133). — Pressure, consequent melting, and refreezing on removal of pressure. — Requisite pressure is in some cases absent.

4. Final explanation. (Croll: *Clim. and Time*, 557; Tyndall: *Hours of Exercise*, 365, 384). — Two melting surfaces brought into contact assume the condition of an *interior* film, where the icy state is maintained.

5. Regelation explains persistent continuity of the ice, but not the *motion* which *precedes*, and is the condition of regelation.

V. Theory of Motion by Molecular Melting and Refreezing.

(Croll: *Phil. Mag.*, March, 1866, Sep. 1870; *Clim. and Time*, ch. xxxi).

1. A molecule at the instant of receiving heat above 32°, liquefies and flows into the most accessible interstice.
2. But it instantly transmits its heat to the next molecule and refreezes. — In refreezing it requires more space, and creates an expansive tendency of the mass.
3. This next molecule similarly liquefies, flows, transmits and refreezes. — Each succeeding molecule, in turn, behaves similarly.
4. Thus the ice-mass is transferred molecularly to lower levels. — Erosion is effected by the molecular transfer, and by the molar motion resulting from expansion.
5. Difficulties of this theory.

   (1) The proof cited to establish transmission of heat through ice confounds diathermancy with conductivity.

   (2) When one molecule melts, a whole layer would melt simultaneously. On transmitting their heat to the next layer, that would melt; but the first layer would *not* recongeal, in consequence of a new accession of heat. Thus the *conduction* of heat through a mass at 32° would liquefy it wholly or partially, and it would *not* recongeal.

   (3) Molecular movements would not produce geological denudation.

VI. Present state of Theory.

1. Ice, like wax, molasses-candy and many other substances, is brittle under a momentary force, but yields moleculary under a continued pressure. — It is so far a fluid, and like all fluids would adapt itself to inequalities.

2. It has not been shown that a *slight* pressure, even its own gravity, is not sufficient to produce the phenomenon of "shear," or molecular over-slipping. — It may be presumed that gravity would suffice. — Canon Mosely's assumption of a high "index of shear" not admitted.

3. The residual molecular cohesion would tend to cause the ice to move, to a partial extent, as a rigid mass. — It would therefore *erode*.
4. All refreezing or regelation in the interior spaces and interstices would develop an expansive tendency which would augment both terminal motion and erosive action, and would help the freer border of the ice over hindrances to motion. — Hence more rapid motion when thawing introduces water into the icy spaces.
5. Crevassing results from an abrupt strain which the waxiness of the ice has not *time* to respond to. — A gentler change of slope affords more time, and may avoid crevassing. (Comp. Aitken, *A. J. S.*, III, v. 305). — Tyndall's contrary opinion. (L. 59; Tyndall: *Hours of Exercise*, etc).
6. Grains of truth in most of the theories.

XLVII. CAMPESTRAL FORMATIONS.

Superficial deposits spread out in generally treeless, but sometimes forest-covered, plains.

I. Loess.

1. Review of geographical distribution. (Pumpelly, *A. J. S.*, III, viii, 133; Aughey, *Hayden Ann. Rep.*, 1874, 245–50; *Sketches of Nebraska*, 1880, 280–4); v. Richthofen: *China*, 56–74, 152–189.
2. Its geological position.
3. Physical characters. (v. Richthofen). — Color. — Fineness. — Calcareity. — Cylindrical perforations. — Fossil remains.
4. Theories of sedimentary origin, marine, lacustrine or fluviatile. (Aughey, *ut sup.*; Kingsmill, *Q. J. G. Soc.*, 1871, 376; v. Richthofen, 162–8).
   (1) Grounds. (Gümbel: *Geognost.Beschreibung des Bair. Alpengebirges*, 1861, 798; 805, 852, 872; Fallou: *Ueber den loess*, Jahrb. f. Min., 1867. 143–58).
   (2) Difficulties of these theories.
5. Theory of glacial and torrent origin. (Lyell: *Antiquity of Man*, ch. xvi).
6. Theory of sub-aërial origin. (Richthofen: *China*, 74–84; Pumpelly, *A. J. S.*, III, viii, 133). — This theory opposed. (Jos. Leconte, *A. J. S.*, III).

II. Arid Plains.

1. The "Great Plains" of the trans-Mississippi.
   (1) Their physical characters.
   (2) Their topography.

2. Treelessness generally due to aridity.
   (1) Meteorological data.
   (2) Results of irrigation.
3. Influence of alkalinity in the soil.
4. The plains of the "Plateau" and "Basin" regions of the U.S.

III. Marshes, Bogs, Wet Plains, Swamps, Heaths.

1. American Bogs or Swales.
   (1) Treeless. — Grass-covered. — Level. — Peaty. — Generally underlaid by marl.
   (2) These evidently the beds of ancient lakes. — Wetness the residuum of the lake-water. — Destined to be expelled by further additions of solid matters.
2. Wet lands underlaid by "hard-pan."
   (1) The "Landes" of Gascony, the "Campine" of Belgium, the Heaths of Holland and Germany. (Reclus: *Earth*, ch. xiii; Emil de Lavaleye, *Revue des Deux Mondes*, June, 1861). — Some pine-covered plains in Prussia and the United States.
   (2) Regions underlaid by a ferruginous film of concreted sand. ("alios" of Gascony or "jernal" of Jutland). — Sufficiently elevated, but being without slope, and impervious below.

IV. Sandy Steppes and Tundras. (Comp. Humboldt: *Steppes and Deserts*, in *Views of Nature*).

1. Steppes of the Dnieper. — Steppes of the Caspian and their aridity. (v. Baer: *Kaspische Studien*; Zaleski; *La vie des steppes Kirghizes*). — Winter aspect. — Tundras of northern Siberia.
2. These regions recently sea-covered. — Brackish and alkaline. — In northern Siberia permanently frozen at shallow depths.

V. Treeless Prairies, Savannas, Grassy Steppes.

1. Prairies of Illinois. — The "Polders" along the coast of the German Ocean. — The Magyar "Puszta." — The "Tchornosjom" or Black Earth of Russia, stretching from the Black Sea northeast, and covering an area twice the size of France. (Ruprecht: *Bullet. de l'Académie de St. Petersbourg*, vii, No 5). — Plains or "Steppes" of southern Siberia. (Humboldt: *Asie Centrale and Tableaux de la Nature*). — "Llanos" of Columbia. — "Pampas" of the La Plata. (Humboldt: *Tableaux; Voyage dans les Regions equinoxiales*).
2. Theories of Origin of Illinois Prairies. (W., 264–72; *A. J. S.*, II, Nov. 1864).
   (1) Treelessness caused by annual burnings. (*A. J. S.*, I, i, 331). — Generally abandoned.
   (2) Caused by choking out by the tangled roots of cane. (*A. J. S.*, I, xxiii, 40), — Cane does not grow in Illinois.
   (3) Caused by excessive dryness of climate. (D., 44; Cooper, *Smithson. Ann. Rep.*, 1858, 276; Newberry, *Ohio Agric. Rep.*, 1859; Lambert, *Pacific R. R. Rep.*, i. 166). — The treeless plains of the west probably originated, in part, from such cause. — But in Illinois, trees grow when planted.

(4) Caused by excessive humidity of soil. (Atwater, *A. J. S.*, I, i, 116; Bourne, *ib.*, ii, 30; Lesquereux, *2d Ark. Geol. Rep.* Also, *Western Monthly Mag.*, Feb. 1836; Engelmann, *A. J. S.*, II, xxxvi, 384). — Objected that the Illinois prairies are *not* generally wet. — That certain appropriate trees often occupy wet situations. — That in Illinois trees grow when introduced.

(5) Caused by extreme fineness of the soil. (J. D. Whitney, *Iowa Geol. Rep.*, i, 24; *New Amer. Cyclopæd.*, Prairies). — Wanting in evidence. — Trees do grow when introduced. (Wells, *A. J. S.*, I, i, 331; Engelmann, *ib.*, II, xxxvi, 389; Edwards, *Dep. of Agric.*, 1862, 495; C. A. White, *Geol. Iowa*, 1868, 166. See also, *Prairie Farmer*, Chicago, *passim*; Gerhard: *Illinois as it is*, 277).

(6) Geological theory. (W., 241-72; *A. J. S.*, II, Nov. 1864).

(*a*) The prairie soil a lacustrine formation. — Physical characters. — Fresh-water shells. — Former high level of the Great Lakes. (Lect. XX, III, 2).

(*b*) Lacustrine sediments inclose but few living germs. (W., *ut sup*).

(*c*) The drift deposits seem to be replete with living germs. — Sudden appearance of unwonted species. (W., *ut sup*).

(*d*) These living germs buried during glacial epoch.

Approximation of Tertiary and even Cretaceous vegetation to modern types. (Lesquereux, *A. J. S.*, II, xxvii, 363; Newberry, *A. J. S.*, II, xxix, 215, *seq.*).

Glacial action must have buried innumerable living germs.

Prolonged preservation of woody tissue. — Maul handles in ancient mines of L. Superior. — Piles of London Bridge and Old Savoy Place, and the city of Venice. — Piles of Trajan's bridge over the Danube. — Piles in the Swiss lakes. — Wheels in Roman mines of San Domingo. — Cedar timbers in N. J. Swamps. (Cook: *Geol. N. J.*, 343, *seq*; Lyell: *Travels in N. A.*, 2d Vis., i, 34). — Timber in saliferous sandstone in S. A. (Orton: *Andes and Amazon*, 116, note). — Found buried with Cohoes Mastodon. (Hall, *App. Rep. N. Y. Regents*). — Prostrate forests beneath diluvium. (Locke, *Trans. Assoc. Amer. Nat. and Geol.*, 240; Worthen: *Geol. Ill.*; *A. J. S.*, II, i, 54). — In the Danish bogs. (*Mem. Acad. Sci.*, Copenhagen, ix, 1842; *Smithson. Ann. Rep.*, 1860, 305, *seq.*; Whittlesey, *Proc. Amer. Assoc.*, 1866, 49). — Wood in Cretaceous sandstone in Ala.

Persistence of vitality of seeds. (W., *ut sup.*; *Amer. Exchange and Rev.*, June, 1870; *Gardener's Chronicle*, Lond.; *Patent Off. Rep.*, 1857, Agric., 256). — Indications of latent seeds in the soil. (*Hist. Brit. Dominions in Amer.*, Lond., 1773; Marsh: *Man and Nature*, 285, *seq.*; Darwin: *Origin of Species*, Am. ed., 69). — Dr. Lindley's raspberry seeds from Hadrian's time. — Wheat from Egyptian mummies. (Carpenter: *Elem. Physiol.*, Am. ed., 41; Draper: *Intellect. Devel. Europe*, 72; L. Agass.: *Prin. Zool.*, 136). — The account doubted. (Asa Gray, *A. J. S.*; Lyell: *Prin.*, 565). — Fresh grape seeds with Cohoes Mastodon. (Hall). — New species of poppy from soil beneath the refuse of the Laurium silver mines in Greece. (Theod. v. Heldreich, Univ. Athens).

(*e*) Flora of the preglacial period reproduced from these germs.

(*f*) But the flora of the prairies must have come from surrounding regions.

(*g*) Coöperation of Indian burnings.

(*h*) This theory criticized. (Geo. Vasey, *Amer. Entomol. and Botanist*, July-August, 1870; Dana, *Amer. J. S.*, II; Lesquereux).

XLVIII. THE QUESTION OF EVOLUTION IN GEOLOGY.

I. Prolegomena.

1. Evolution the progressive differentiation of an identical existence. — The progress of heterogeneity out of homogeneity. — Based on the principle of continuity. (Leibnitz).
2. It is a method, a *mode*, a relation in the terms of succession.
3. A question of *fact*. not of causation or of consequences. — The fact to be ascertained by observation. — The philosophy of causation may be consulted when the fact is known.

II. The Principle of Continuity in the Inorganic World. (W., *The Doctrine of Evolution*, 18–27).

1. All consecutive conditions mutually connected by an infinity of intermediate conditions.
   - (1) The formation of a river-delta. — Its growth inch by inch, millimetre by millimetre.
   - (2) The development of a continent. — Its surface expanded by infinitesimal stages. —Its final highly differentiated condition reached by passage through all lower degrees of differentiation.
   - (2) The formation of the earth. — Differentially progressive in its mode of cooling. — In its process of solidification. — In its sedimentations. — In its denudations. — In its diversification.
   - (3) Indications that a material continuity runs back from the present condition of the earth through its cosmical history, and thence through the cosmical history of all the planets, and thence through the totality of cosmical history. (Lects. XXXIX-XLIII).
2. Discontinuity of process inconceivable, except through new creative beginnings.
3. General admission that inorganic history exemplifies the principle of evolution.

III. The Principle of Evolution in Palæontology.

1. Are successive organic types materially (genetically) connected?
2. The general graduation of organic forms. (Lect. XXXI).
   - (1) The general tenor of palæontological history.
   - (2) The nicely graduated successions in certain instances. (Lect. XXXVI).
3. Apparent breaches of the principle of progress.
   - (1) Missing links. (Lect. XXXIV).
   - (2) Graduated structures chronologically misplaced. (Lect. XXXV).
   - (3) The misplacement sometimes amounting to apparent regress in respect to rank. (Lect. XXXI).
4. These appearances perhaps attributable to the imperfections of our knowledge. (Lect. XXXIV, I).
   - (1) Successional gaps may be filled by future discoveries. — The constant tendency of discovery to fill the gaps.
   - (2) Chronological misplacements perhaps only local. — In another region the lower terms may have appeared earlier. — Appearances of regression similarly explicable.

(3) The palæontological consequences of changes in ancient faunal distributions.

(*a*) Illustrated by changes now in progress.

(*b*) The record must present for single localities or regions, abrupt transitions, chronologica misplacements and taxonomic regressions.

(4) Palæontological consequences of relapses in the material environment of life.

(*a*) Correlation between structure and environment.

(*b*) Strctural progress keeps pace with inorganic progress.

(*c*) Cataclysms and local pauses in inorganic progress would condition arrest or regress in organic history.

(*d*) So, sudden improvements in environment might condition secularly sudden improvements in organic structure.

IV. A Material Continuity not proved by Palæontology.

1. Erroneous opinion that palæontology furnishes a "demonstration." (Huxley: *New York Lectures*, 1876; O. C. Marsh: *Nashville Address*, 1877).

2. A perfect graduation of terms compatible with a method of universal discontinuity.

(1) Illustration from products of human efforts. — Wheeled vehicles. — Aquatic vehicles.

(2) Illustrated in the law of chemical homologues.

(4) In the family groups of crystallography.

(5) And even in geometrical forms, as the " conic sections " and the family of triangles.

(5) Hence, each form of life may be conceived an independent origination.

3. But an evolution of the concept palæontologically demonstrated. — And this proves unity of plan, and hence, unity of intelligence.

V. A Material Continuity rendered probable by Palæontology.

1. This hypothesis compatible with all the phenomena.

2. We have the right to reason from the *tenor* of observed facts, as well as from the facts actually known. — Such reasoning implies that apparent gaps were actually filled. — That the graduation was continuous, and that the relation of the terms was genetic.

XLIX. THE QUESTION OF EVOLUTION AT LARGE.

CHARLES DARWIN: *Jour. Linnæan Soc.*, Lond., 1858; *The Origin of Species by means of Natural Selection*, (1758), N. Y., 1860; *The Variation of Animals and Plants under Domestication*, 2 vols., N. Y., 1868; *Expression of the Emotions in Man and Animals*, N. Y., 1873; *The Descent of Man, and Selection in relation to Sex*, N. Y., 1877.

ALFRED R. WALLACE: *Ann. and Mag. N. Hist.*, Sep. 1855; *Jour. Linn. Soc.*, Lond. 1858; *Contributions to the Theory of Natural Selection*, N. Y., 1871.

HERBERT SPENCER: *First Principles of Philosophy*, N. Y., 1865; *Principles of Biology*, 2 vols., N. Y., 1866.

ST. GEORGE MIVART: *On the Genesis of Species*, N. Y., 1871; *Lessons from Nature as manifested in Mind and Matter*, N. Y., 1876; *Contemporary Evolution*, N. Y., 1876: *Man and Apes*, N. Y., 1874.

ASA GRAY: *Darwiniana: Essays and Reviews pertaining to Darwinism*, N. Y., 1878.

T. H. HUXLEY: *On the Origin of Species, or the Causes of the Phenomena of Organic Nature.* N. Y., 1866.

ERNST HAECKEL: *Naturliche Schopfungsgeschichte*, 4th ed., Berlin, 1873, trans. *Nat. History of Creation*, N. Y; *Anthropogenie: Entwickelungsgeschichte des Menschen*, Leipzig, 1874, trans. *The Origin of Man*, N. Y.

H. S. CHAPMAN: *Evolution of Life*, 2d ed., Philadelphia, 1873.

A. WINCHELL: *The Doctrine of Evolution*, N. Y., 1874.

Also DEMAILLET: *Telliamed, ou entretiens*, etc., Amsterdam, 1748, also transl.; LAMARCK: *Philosophique Zoologique*, etc., nouv.-ed., 1873; NAEGELI: *Enstehung und Begriff der Art*; A. KÖLLIKER: *Ueber die Darwin'sche Schopfungsgeschichte*, 1864; E. D. COPE: *Origin of Genera*, Proc. A. N. S., Phil, Oct. 1868; *The Hypothesis of Evolution*, Lippincott's Mag., 1870, and "University S ries," New Haven, 1873; *The Method of Creation of Organic Types*, Proc. A. A. A. Sci., 1871; *A Review of the Modern Doctrine of Evolution*. Amer. Nat., Mar. and April, 1880, 166; T. PARSONS, *A. J. S.*, II, xxx, i, July, 1860; R. OWEN: *Anatomy of Vertebrates*, ch. xl; *A. J. S.*, II, xlvii, 33; A. HYATT: *Mem. Bos. Soc. N. Hist.*, I, pt. ii, 1867; *Amer. Nat.*, iv, 230–7, June, 1870; J. D. HOOKER: *Flora of Tasmania*, Introduc. Essay; *A. J. S.*, II, xxix, 1 and 305, Jan. 1860.

I. The Palæontological Evidence. (Lect. XLVIII).

II. The Morphological Evidence.

1. Familiar indications of blood-relationship. — Eminently morphological.
2. Structural relations in the organic kingdoms. — Basis of classification.
   - (1) Fundamental plans of structure.
     - (*a*) As to ultimate structures. — Cells, membranes, fibres, tissues.
     - (*b*) As to general structure. (Lect. XXXI, II; XXXVII, I).
   - (2) Fundamental physiological conceptions. — Nutrition, Respiration, Circulation, Neuration, Musculation, Wastage and Repair.
3. Rudimental structures. — Rudiments of structures morphologically interpretable, but functionally useless. — "Dysteleology" of Haeckel.
2. These all indications of genetic connection and common origin.
5. But not a demonstration of such.

III. The Variational Evidence.

1. Arising from Geographical Position.
   - (1) As to plants. — Juniper, Paper Birch, Chestnut Oak, Hackberry, Beach Plum, Black Thorn, June Berry, Wild Rose. — Confluence of genera, as *Cardamine* with *Dentaria* on one hand, and *Arabis* on the other.
   - (2) As to animals.
     - (*a*) Echinoderms. (L. Agassiz, *Proc. Amer. Acad.*, v. 72). — Sponges, (Haeckel: *Die Kalkschwamme*).
     - (*b*) Molluscs. (Cooper, *Proc. Cal. Acad. N. Sci.*, v. 28; Barber, *Amer. Nat.*, Sep., 1876, 529; Weatherby, *Proc. Cincinnati Soc. Nat. Sci.*, No. 1, June, 1876; Lewis, *Proc. Bos. Soc. Nat. Hist.*, v. 121–8).
     - (*c*) Insects. (A. S. Packard, *Geometrid Moths*. Hayden Surv., x, 42–3; W. H. Edwards: *Butterflies of N. A.*, pt. ix; Walsh, *Proc. Entmol. Soc., Phil.*, iii, 403).

(*d*) Fishes. — Blind fishes of caverns. (F. W. Putnam: ***Life in the Mammoth Cave***).

(*e*) Birds. (S. F. Baird, ***Pacif. R. R. Rep.***, ix, 1858; ***Mem. Nat. Acad.***, Jan. 1863; ***A. J. S.***, II, xli, Jan., Mar. and May; J. A. Allen, ***Proc. Bos. Soc. Nat. Hist.***, xv, 156; ***Bull. Mus. Comp. Zool.***, ii, No. 3, pp. 229-49; ***ib.***, iii, July. 1872; ***Bull. Hayden Surv.***, ii, No. 4, 345 Aug. 1876, repub. ***Amer. Nat.***, Oct. 1876, 625; R. Ridgeway, ***A. J. S.***, III, iv, 454, Dec. 1872, v. 39, Jan., 1873, and ***Bull. Hayden Surv.***, No. 2, 1875, 58; ***Amer. Nat.***, vii, 415, July, 1873. Comp., also, Coues, ***Proc. A. N. S.***, July, 1872, 60; ***Key to N. Amer. Birds***, Oct. 1872). — Generalizations drawn by Baird, Allen and Ridgeway.

(*f*) Mammals. (Baird, ***Pacif. R. R. Rep.*** viii, 1857: Allen, ***Proc. Boston Soc. N. H.***, xvi, 276; ***Rad. Review***, i. No. 1, May, 1877; ***Leporidæ:*** Hayden Rep., xi. 4to., 269, 304-323, 645-52; E. Coues, ***Muridæ***, Hayden Rep., xi, 4to., 29-31, 32, 40, 65, 73, 75, 185, 189, 240; H. C. Yarrow, ***Wheeler Rep.*** 4to., v, ch. i).

(3) These variant forms as good species as ever. — The error of abandoning them as species.

2. Arising from changed environment.

(1) The Axolotl or ***Siredon lichenoides***. (Duméril; Marsh, ***A. J. S.***, II, xlvi, 364; ***Tribune Extra***, No. 8).

(2) ***Branchipus*** and ***Artemia***, (Schmaukevitch; Hagen, ***Proc. A. A.***, 1876). — These results, however, to be received with caution. (Verrill, ***Proc. A. A.***, 1869, 230..

3. Arising from hybridity.

(1) Repeated assertion that hybridity has originated no permanent forms.

(2) Hybrid species of trees enumerated in Floras. (Gray: ***Man. Bot. North. U. S***). — Vegetable hybridity fully established. (A. DeCandolle, ***Treatise on Oaks***; Naudin: ***Hybridity in the Veg. Kingdom***).

(3) Fertile hybrids of Common and Chinese geese in Mt. Auburn Cemetery, (Youmans, in Quatrefage's ***Nat. Hist. of Man***, 143). — Very common in India, and occurring in England, (C. Darwin, ***Nature***, xxi, 207, Jan. 1, 1880).

(4) Fertile hybrids of hare and rabbit. (Gindre, ***Bull. de la Soc. imp. Zool. d'Acclimation***, 1870, 659-67).

4 Examples among fossil remains.

(1) ***Orthis biforata***, with varieties ***lynx, laticosta, dentata, acutilirata***. (Meek: ***Pal. Ohio***, i, pl. x; Hall: ***Pal. N. Y.***, i, 133, pl. xxxii D).

(2) ***Spirifera disjuncta***, with eighteen varieties. (Hall: ***Pal. N. Y.***, iv, pl. xli, xlii).

(3) ***Spirifera mucronata***. (Hall: ***Pal. N. Y.***, iv, pl. xxiv). — ***Atrypa reticularis***, with sixteen varieties. (Hall: ***Pal. N. Y.***, pl. li-liii; Whitfield, ***XIX Rep. N. Y. Regents***). — ***Pentamerus Knightii***. (Davidson: ***Brit. Foss. Brachiop***).

5. Rudimentary structures result from variation.

6. The facts of Variability demonstrate the *possibility* of a material continuity between species.

IV. The Embryological Evidence.

1. Nature of the embryological succession. — We can indicate twenty-two, or more, stages in the development of highest mammals. (Hæckel: *Anthropogenie*).

2. Parallelism of all embryonic series. — Lower forms arrested at earlier stages. — The parallelism suggests descent from common ancestors.
3. Parallelism with geological succession. — Earlier geological types were comparatively embryonic.
4. Parallelism with the morphologically graduated series.
5. An identical order of succession three times occurring. — The first *ontogenetic* and rapid. — The second *palæontological* and slow. — The third *taxonomic* and simultaneous.
6. Embryological history proves that transition by material continuity, from term to term of this succession, is a *fact*. — If a fact in the embryological series, it is probably a fact in the almost identical palæontological and taxonomic series. — The derivation of species by material continuity must therefore be admitted as a general law of nature.

L. EVOLUTION THEORIES.

[Authorities as in Lecture XLIX].

I. Necessary Discriminations in the discussion of Evolution.

1. Is a universal Method of Evolution a *fact* in nature?
2. What are the *conditions* under which an evolution arises?
3. What are the *instruments* and *agencies* for effecting it?
4. What is the *efficient cause* employing the agencies, under the requisite conditions, in producing the fact?
5. These discriminations often overlooked. — The Fact sometimes regarded the ultimate goal of science. — Conditions often regarded a full explanation. — Instruments or agencies often set down as "true causes."

II. Suggestions recorded in the history of Science.

1. As to the Fact. — A frequently recurring doctrine in all ages. — Always met with denials, under the impression that it precludes divine agency.
2. As to the Conditions.
   (1) Modes of the organism.
      (*a*) Inheritance, or transmission of identity. — Centripetal.
      (*b*) Variability, or capacity for change. — Centrifugal.
      (*c*) Prolonged embryonic development. (*Vestiges of Creation*).
      (*d*) Acceleration of development. (Hyatt, as in Lect. XLIX).
      (*e*) Acceleration and retardation of development and growth. (Cope: ***Method of Creation***; *Origin of Genera*).
      (*f*) Repetitive addition. (Cope: *Method of Creation*).
      (*g*) Relation to grade of organ or animal. — Cope's "grade influence."
      (*h*) Frequency of exercise. — Equivalent to "use and effort," (Cope), and

"use and disuse," (DeMaillet, Lamarck, Darwin). — Includes "animal motion," suggested by Cope as "cause of animal evolution." (Cope, *P. Amer. A. A. Sci.*, Aug., 1877; *Penn Monthly*, Jan. 1878; *Origin of the specialized teeth of Carnivora*, Am. Nat., Mar. 1879). — This not a cause, since whatever change ensues is caused directly (instrumentally) by the physiological action.

(2) Modes of the environment. — Determining the "struggle for existence." (Darwin: *Origin of species*).

(a) Physical surroundings. — (DeMaillet: *Telliamed*; Lamarck: *Philos. Zool*).

(b) Competition with fellow-beings.

(c) Extermination of unfittest. — Whereby "fittest," *i. e.* best, survive, to continue the species and perpetuate acquired modifications. — The characteristic conception of "Darwinism," which thus leaves all *causation* of variation untouched.

3. As to instrumentalities and agencies.

(1) Reproductive activities. — Normal. — With saltative progress. (Huxley). — *Parthenogenesis.* (Kölliker).

(2) Influence of enviroment. — This a misapprehension.

(3) Physiological activities, organizing material into forms correlated to the environment. — The "growth-force" of Cope.

(4) Inherent conation toward certain modifications of structure. (Lamarck). — Hardly distinguishable from the coördinative force in physiological work. (See next point).

(5) Intelligent selection. (Cope: *Method of Creation*, 29; *Consciousness in Evolution*, Penn Monthly, Aug., 1875. Compare *Origin of the Will*, Penn Monthly, June, 1877).

(a) Automatic or unconscious. — A directive influence exerted upon physiological activities.

(b) Voluntary or conscious. — Choice of means by which the animal seeks its own well-being. — Part origin of "struggle for existence."

4. As to causes.

(1) Environment, Natural Selection, Use, etc. — These not real causes. but subcauses. — *Environment* only the condition of a certain kind of physiological activity. — *Natural Selection* only the outcome or remainder, after active cause has made certain snbtractions. — *Use* only the condition of more intense physiological action in certain organs.

(2) Inherent tendency to improve or change. — Either coöperative or all-underlying and all-conditioning. — In either case, only an effect which conditions other effects.

(3) The Unknowable. (Spencer: *First Principles*, etc).

(4) A Supernatural Power.

(a) The real cause is something which cannot be construed as an effect.

(b) It acts *in the organism*, through physiological processes, and not at a distance, in the environment.

(c) It acts with discernment, cognizing a certain correlation as an end, and directing the eperations of life toward that end. — Cognition implies *intelligence;* direction, *will* and *motive* for willing; the cause is therefore, a personality.

(d) The cause is not the animal or plant in which the modification takes place. — Nor any other animal. — It is, therefore, a supernatural Cause.

2. ·Theories are based principally on views in reference to conditions and instrumentalities, and the scope of application of the principle of evolution.

III. Conspectus of Theories of the Origin of Species.

1. Immediate Creation. (Material Discontinuity).

   (1) In single Pairs, ... { *Linnæus, Cuvier.* *Popular Opinion.*

   (2) In Colonies, ... *L. Agassiz*, etc.

2. Mediate Creation or Derivation. (Material Continuity or Evolution).

   (1) Through a Force which is a mode of the Unknowable. . . . *Spencer.*

   (2) Through so-called external influences or forces acting on the generative system.

   (*a*) Physical surroundings. (Transmutation). . . . . *De Maillet*

   (*b*) The same and conflicts of individuals (Natural Selection) with use and disuse.

   (*aa*) Embracing the psychic nature of man.

   (*aaa*) By insensible gradations (Variative). . . *Darwin, Haeckel.*

   (*bbb*) With occasional leaps (Saltative) and with a molecular selection. . . . . *Huxley.*

   (*bb*) Excluding the body and mind of man, ... *Wallace.*

   (3) Through an internal force, conditioned by the environment, and by use and disuse.

   (*a*) An inherent nisus toward improvement. (Conative-variative). { *Lamarck.* *St. Hilaire.*

   (*b*) Genetic processes exclusively. (Filiative).

   (*aa*) Prolonged embryonic development. (Variative-filiative). "*Vestiges.*"

   (*aaa*) Heterogeneous generation. . . . . . *Kœlliker, Ferris.*

   (*bbb*) Homogeneous generation. . . . . . . *Parsons, Owen.*

   (*c*) An immaterial force, genetic processes being the instrument. Saltations admitted.

   (*aa*) Excluding the psychic nature of man. . . . *Mivart, Nægeli.*

   (*bb*) Including the psychic nature of man.

   (*aaa*) Through ordinary generation. . . . . . . *Huxley.*

   (*bbb*) Accelerated development, ... *Hyatt.*

   (*ccc*) Accelerated and retarded development. . . . . *Cope.*

IV. Conclusions eliminated.

1. Evolution is the designation of a general method employed in nature for the effectuation of results. — "Development" employed in nearly the same sense.

2. "Darwinism" is the designation of a particular theory of the instrumentalities by which the evolution is effected. — Therefore not synonymous with evolution. — May be a false or insufficient doctrine, while evolution is a true one. — Cannot, by any means, claim to be an adequate explanation of the phenomena of organic life.

LI. PRIMITIVE MEN,

THEIR ETHNOLOGY, AFFILIATIONS AND DISPERSION.

A. WINCHELL: *Preadamites*, 8vo., Chicago, 1880, ch. vi, x, xi, xiv, xix-xxv; O. PESCHEL: *The Races of Man*, N. Y,, 1876; P. TOPINARD: *Anthropology*, London, 1878; C. VOGT: *Lectures on Man*, London, 1864.

I. The terms Archæology, Ethnology and Anthropology. — Prehistoric Anthropology to be investigated on the same basis as extinct life in general. — The Archæological data discussed in Part I, (Lecture XXII).

II. Primitive Types of Mankind.

2. Existing races of men. (Peschel).
   (1) The Black Races.
      (*a*) Australians and Tasmanians. — (*b*) Papuans and Negritos. — (*c*) Hottentots and Bushmen. — (*d*) Negroes.
   (2) The Brown Races.
      (*a*) Mongoloids: Malays, Chinese, Altaians, Japanese, Americans.
      (*b*) Dravidians.
   (3) The White Race or Mediterraneans.
      (*a*) Hamites. — (*b*) Semites. — (*c*) Japhetites or Aryans.
2. Affinities among ethnic types. — Gradations. — The lower not descended from the higher.
3. The primitive races low in rank. — Australians probably approximate the earliest men. — Higher races later in appearance.

III. Hypothetical continent of Lemuria.

1. Evidences of its former existence.
   (1) Zoölogical. — Lemurs. — Birds. — Men.
   (2) Botanical. — Palms.
   (3) Geological. — Shoals in Indian Ocean. — The entire area in process of subsidence.
2. Here was perhaps the cradle of mankind.

IV. Dispersion of Mankind from Lemuria.

1. Primordial bifurcation of the human stock. — Australian and African stems. — Why not assigned to distinct origins.
2. Dispersion of the Australian branch.
   (1) Australians. — Connection with India. — The Tasmanian differentiation.
   (2) Papuans. — Retral movement to the Andamans. — Divergence to Luzon, Formosa, and perhaps Japan. — Melanesian expansion. — Oceanic improvement of the type.
3. Dispersion of the African branch. (Ulotrichs).
   (1) The Hottentot type. — Moved from eastern equatorial Africa.
   (2) The Negro type. — Kaffir Bantus drove Hottentots southward. — The Soudans spread westward.
   (3) Many Africans not of these races.
4. Rise and dispersion of Mongoloids.

(1) Malayan stem. — Regress to Madagascar. — Pacific expansion. — Micronesian type. — Polynesian type. — Extreme eastward advances.
(2) Thibeto-Burmese stem.
(3) Chinese stem. -- Primitive seat. — Migration.
(4) Altaian stem. — The northeastward stream. — Divergence of Turks, Mandchus, Tunguses, Samoyeds and Ural-Altaics.
(5) Troglodytic stem. — Dispersion in N. Africa and in Europe.
(6) American Sedentes. — Access from Asia. — Their characteristics. — Their dispersion over N. America, Mexico, Central America, Granada, Peru, Chile and Patagonia. — Copper-mining, mounds, mesa-ruins, Mexican and Peruvian civilizations.
(7) American Vagantes. — Contrasted with Sedentes. — Compared with Malays. — Access by Polynesia. — Indications of former continental connection. — Spread over the plains of S. America. — Drove back Sedentes in N. America.

5. Rise and dispersion of Dravidians.
6. Rise and dispersion of Mediterraneans.
(1) Hamitic Family. — Displaced Mongoloids everywhere. — Possessed all Western Asia, N. Africa and Southern Europe.
(2) Semitic Family. — Absorbed Hamites in Asia. — Semitic empires. — Maritime Phœnicians.
(3) Aryan Family. — Asiatic branch. — European branch. — Ultra-Euxine and cis-Euxine streams. — Ulterior ramifications.

LII. THE ANTIQUITY OF MAN.

A. WINCHELL: *Preadamites*, ch. xxvii; SIR C. LYELL: *The Geological Antiquity of Mankind*; J. C. SOUTHALL: *The Recent Origin of Man*, Phil., 1875; *The Epoch of the Mammoth*, Phil., 1878; E. ANDREWS, *A. J. S.*, II, xlv, 180; *Meth. Quar. Rev.*, Dec. 1876, Jan. 1877.

Three aspects of discussion on this question.

I. Epoch of the First Men.
1. No positive data bearing directly on the question.
2. They probably appeared in Tertiary time.

II. Epoch of the Stone Folk of Europe. — Their antiquity long exaggerated. (Haeckel: *Natuerlich. Schœpf.*, 595, *etc*). — Grounds of such opinions.
1. Preglacial remains of other animals mistaken for human remains.
(1) Notched bones found at St. Prest, France, with Pliocene elephant. — Marks made by a contemporary rodent.
(2) Cut bones of Léognan, of Miocene age. — Marked by a carnivorous fish.
(3) Flints in Miocene of Thenay. (*Congr. Internat.*, 1867, 67). — Not artificially produced.
2. Human remains erroneously supposed preglacial.
(1) The Guadeloupe skeletons. (D. 579; C. König, *Phil. Trans.*, 1814, 107).
(2) Human skeleton with Pliocene elephant at Le Puy-en-Velay. (Topinard: *Anthropology*, 436; Caspari: *Urgesch. der Menschheit*, i, 84). — Skeleton *not* in same lava as elephant, but a later lava.
(3) Flints in the gravels of the Somme. — But these gravels prove to be post-glacial.

(4) Human skull from Pliocene of Colle del Vento. (Issel, *Cong. Internat.*, 1867, 75, 156). — The fact not scientifically established.

(5) Human pelvis in a preglacial deposit at Natchez. — The bone fell down from the top of a bluff. (Lyell: *Antiq. Man.*)

(6) Remains in Victoria cave, Eng. (Geike). — The deposits probably not preglacial. (J. Evans, *Add. Geol. Soc. Lond.*, 19 Feb., 1875; *A. J. S.*, III, x, 229-32).

3. Man not preglacial in Europe. (Huxley, *Nature*, 22 Aug., 1878, 448. Comp. Haeckel, *op cit.*, 594). — But he witnessed the decline of the glaciers.

4. Man probably of Pliocene age in California. (J. D. Whitney). — Probably of Mongoloid type.

5. Remoteness of the glacial decline in Europe.

(1) Human history and movements in glacial and preglacial times.

(2) Grounds of belief in high antiquity of glacial epoch.

(*a*) Astronomical hypothesis of glacial periods. (Lect. XLV, V).

(*b*) Cotemporaneousness of man with extinct animals. (Lect. XXII). — Extinctions not necessarily remote.

(*aa*) Gigantic extinct birds of New Zealand and the Mascarenes. (D. 580-1; L. 558-60; *Encyc. Brit.*, 9th ed., iii, 731; A. Milne-Edwards, *Comptes Rendus*, May, 1875; *A. J. S.*, III, x, 233. Comp. A. Günther, *Nature*, 28 July, 1874). — *Rytina Stelleri*, *Balæna Biscayensis*, Trojan shells.

(*bb*) Species approaching extinction. — Great auk, Labrador duck, capercailzee, great aurochs, sequoia and many familiar species.

(*cc*) Extinctions apparently recent. — Mammoth, Mastodon, (*Am. Nat.*, April, 1879, 269. — Irish elk.

(3) Magnitude of geological changes since man's advent. — Real greatness of those changes.

(*a*) Remoteness in time produces an illusion. — Historic times record great geologic events. — Geographical changes in China. (Pumpelly, *Smiths. Contr.*, 4to., xv, art. iv; Von Richthofen: *China*, 285-7). — Changes in basin of Black and Caspian seas. (W.: *Pread.*, 440 and *ref.*).

(*b*) Retreat of Alpine glaciers. (Tyndall: *Hours of Exercise in the Alps*; W.: *Pread.*, 437-8). — Existing stumps in America. (Lect. XIX, III, 6).

6. Estimates of prehistoric archæologists. — Appearance of Iron in the West 2700 years ago. — Age of Bronze, 2700 to 4000 years. — Age of Polished Stone, 4000 to 6000 years. — Age of Reindeer, 7000. — These results accordant with traditional indications. (W.: *Pread.*, 442).

III. **Epoch of Mediterranean Race.** — Must exceed somewhat the historic antiquity of Egypt. — Era of Menes according to Lepsius, 3892 B. C. — According to Mariette and Lenormant, 5004 B. C.

LIII. ESTIMATION OF GEOLOGICAL TIME.

I. Oppressiveness of Geological Æons.

1. Geological changelessness of some historic spots. — Plymouth Rock. — The Acropolis. — Mont Blanc.

2. Permanence of the aspects of the heavens.
3. Slowness of shore-erosions and of sedimentary processes.
4. Time required for material of a bed of coal.
4. Such facts tend to produce an exaggerated impression of the vastness of geological periods. — We need some comprehensible unit of measure.

II. Cosmical Limitations of Terrestrial past Duration.

1. Age of the Sun's heat. (Sir W. Thomson, *Phil. Mag.*, viii, 1854; *Macmillan's Mag.*, March, 1862; *Address Brit. Assoc.*, Edinb., reprint, *A. J. S.*, III, ii, 286, Oct. 1861; Croll: *Climate and Time*, ch. xxi).
   (1) Meteoric theory of solar heat, (Mayer: *Celestial Dynamics*, Youmans' ed., 261).
   (2) Contractional theory. (Helmholtz, *Phil. Mag.*, xi, 1856; W. Thomson, *Phil. Mag.*, viii).
   (3) Solar heat probably, in large part, a residuum of the primitive temperature. (W., *Sketches*, ch. xxxviii; Croll: *Clim. and Time*, 349, *seq*).
2. Duration of the secular cooling of the earth. — A maximum of 100,000,000 years since commencement of incrustation. (Thomson and Tait: *Nat. Phil.*; Croll: *Clim. and Time*, 335). — Actual calculation results in 80,000,000 years. — Reade demands 500,000,000 years since sedimentation began in Europe. (*Ann. Addr. Liverpool Geol. Soc.*, 1876; *A. J. S.*, 1876, 462).
3. Duration of tidal retardation of earth's rotation. — The investigation not yet made.

III. Calculation based on relative thickness of Sediments. (D., 381, 481, 585).

1. Account cannot be taken of relative energy of geologic forces. — Probably greatest in the world's early history.
2. Maximum thickness of sediments, limestone being multiplied five-fold. (D., 381): Archæan, 230,000 ft.; Palæozoic, 153,000; Mesozoic, 38,300; Cænozoic, 12,800. — Joining palæontological with stratigraphical evidences, **Devonian + Triassic = Jurassic + Cretaceous + Cænozoic.** (Ramsay, *Proc. Roy. Soc.*, No. 152, 1874).
3. The Pyrolithic æon probably as long as the Archæan.
4. Distribution of the Earth's incrusted life-time. (Comp. D., 591).

	Percentages.	*Years.*
PYROLITHIC ÆON. (Fire-crust),	34.6	34,600,000
ARCHÆAN ÆON. (Strata),	34.6	34,600,000
PALÆOZOIC ÆON,	23.1	23,100,000
Silurian,	15.6	15,600,000
Lower Silurian, (Cambrian),	13.2	13,200,000

	Percentages.	Years.
Potsdam Sandstone,	1.9	1,900,000
Rest of Lower Silurian,	11.3	11,300,000
Upper Silurian,	2.4	2,400,000
Devonian,	3.8	3,800,000
Carboniferous,	3.8	3,800,000
Mesozoic Æon,	5.8	5,800,000
Triassic,	1.78	1,780,000
Jurassic,	2.22	2,220,000
Cretaceous,	1.78	1,780,000
Cænozoic Æon,	1.9	1,900,000
Tertiary,	1.5	1,500,000
Post-Tertiary,	0.4	400,000
Glacial,	0.2	200,000
Champlain,	0.2	200,000

5. This result for post-glacial time perhaps too great. — One hundred millions too high an aggregate, and Pyrolithic and Archæan relatively longer than assumed.

IV. Calculation based on Eccentricity of Earth's Orbit.

1. Supposes maximum eccentricity the indirect cause of northern glacial periods. (Lect. XLV, V, 4).

2. Last occurring epochs of maximum eccentricity before 1800 A. D.:— 100,000 years (.0473), 210,000 years (.0575), 310,000 years, (.0424), 750,000 years (.0575), 850,000 years (0747). — Those at 210,000 and 850,000 years the most striking.

3. Croll regards last Glacial Period as extending from 240,000 to 80,000 years ago. (Croll: *Clim. and Time*, 325, 355). — The Miocene glaciation he puts at 850,000 years ago, and the Eocene at 2,500,000 years. (Croll: *op cit.*, 358–9). — These figures apparently too high. — The last mid-glacial epoch perhaps 100,000 years ago. — Then, since decline of glaciers, say 50,000 years.

V. Calculations based on Erosion and Deposition.

1. Gorge of Niagara. (D., 219, 590; L. 14; Hall: *Geol. N. Y.*, iv, ch. xx; R. Bakewell: *Geol.*, 260; J. Marcou, *Bull. Soc. Geol. de France*, II, xxii, 190, 529; Ramsay, *Q. J. G. Soc.*, xv, 1859; T. Belt, *Q. J. Sci.*, April, 1875). — Assuming rate of Erosion uniform.
   (1) R. Bakewell, 3 feet per year, 12,300 years.
   (2) Lyell and Hall, 1 foot per year, 35,000 years.
   (3) E. Desor, .03 foot per year, 1,232,000 years.
   (4) J. Marcou, .52 foot per year, 71,000 years.

(5) T. Belt, 0.1 foot per year, 200,000 years for whole gorge, but only 20,000 for that below the whirlpool. — The remainder of the gorge, and all the old one, being considered preglacial. — Last result accords best with limits of time at our disposal for terrestrial history.

2. Gorge of Mississippi, at St. Anthony. (N. H. Winchell, *Q. J. G. Soc.*, Lond., Nov. 1878, 880). — Rate from 1680 to 1856, 5.15 feet per year; time from Fort Snellling, 8202 years. — This a post-glacial erosion.
3. Deltas of rivers.
   (1) The Mississippi delta about 5000 years. (Humphreys and Abbot, *Hydraulics of the Miss.*, 1861. Comp. L. 28).
   (2) The Nile delta, 6350 years. (De Lanoye: *Rameses the Great.* Comp. L. 28).
4. Terraces of Lake Michigan. (E. Andrews, *Trans. Chic. Acad. Sci.*, ii; Southall: *Epoch of the Mammoth*, ch. xxii). — Total time since Glacial Period, 5300 to 7500 years.
5. General continental erosion. (L., 10–11; Croll: *Clim. and Time*, ch. xx; Geikie, *Trans. Geol. Soc. Glasgow*, iii; Jukes and Geike: *Man. Geol.*, ch. xxv; A. Tylor, *Phil. Mag.*, 1850). — Subsidence in basin of Danube, one foot in 6846 years; of Mississippi, 4640; of Nile, 4723; Ganges, 1751; Rhone, 1528; Hoang-Ho, 1464; Po, 729 years.

LIV. LIMITATIONS OF THE EXISTING ORDER.

I. Meaning of Change in the natural World.

1. It implies a beginning.
2. It implies an end.
3. The idea of endless cycles physically absurd. (W., *Sketches*, ch. xxxv). — Perpetual motion equally impossible in human and in the cosmic mechanism. — All force seeking a state of equilibrium. — Finite time suffices for the accomplishment of any work, however vast.
4. Recognized principle of degradation of physical organisms. — Dissipation of energy. (W., *Mich. Jour. Educ.*, Aug. 1860, 273; *Ladies' Repos.*, Cin., Jan., 1864; *College Courant*, New Haven, Jul. 12 and 17, 1869; *Sketches of Creation*, 1870; Sir. W. Thomson; Helmholtz; Spencer: *First Prin.*, 450, *etc*).

II. Ultimate tendencies of Terrestrial Erosions. (Lect. XXVII, XXVIII; W., *Sketches*, ch. xxxvi).

1. Wastage of soils. — Disappearance of vegetation and aridity of climate. — Sinking of river-channels. (D., 641–2). — Filling of lakes and seas. — Transfer of elevations to deltas and sea-bottoms. — Great American Desert. (Wheeler, *Prelim. Rep.*, 1871, 20; Powell: *Colorado*).

2. Growth of Delta of Mississippi river. (D., 651–2; Humphreys and Abbot: *Hydraul. Miss*,, 141, 418, *etc*). Total annual contribution, one square mile 268 feet deep. — Annual advance of delta, 338 feet. — Inevitable destruction of the upland.

4. Lowering of continental surfaces.
   (1) Sundry estimates. (Lect. XXVIII, LIII).
   (2) Relative masses of continents and oceans.
      (*a*) Mean height of land. (Krümmel, *Gottingen Acad.;* G. Leipoldt, *Petermann's Mittheilungen*, April, 1875; *Nature*, 15 April, 1875; *A. J. S.*, III, ix, 482; *Nature*, 3 Feb., 1879, 348-9). — Europe, 300 m.; Asia and Africa, 500 m.; America, 330 m.; Australia, 250 m.; mean, 426 m., or 0.0566 mile. — Surface ratio of land to water, 1:2.75. — Ratio of volume of land to water, 1:22.4.
      (*b*) Continents above sea-level transferred to sea-basin would raise the sea 112.4 m., or 368.2 ft. above the land. — This doctrine enunciated by Buffon. (*Theorie de la Terre.*) — But denounced by the Sorbonne. (Lyell: *Prin.*, 41; Buffon: *Hist. Nat.*, tome v, ed. de l'Imp. royale, Paris, 1769.

III. Progressive Terrestrial Refrigeration. (Lect. XLI).

IV. Absorption of Sea And Atmosphere. (Lect. XLI, V.2). — Observed secular desiccation of the continents. (J. D. Whitney, *Amer. Nat.*, x, 513, Sep., 1876).

V. Coincidence of Axial and Orbital Periods of the Earth. (Helmholtz: *Interaction Nat. For.*, Youmans' ed., 243). — Six months insufferable heat and six months insufferable cold.

VI. Solar Refrigeration. (Lect. XLI). — Vast emission of heat. — No known source of adequate supply.

VII. Final Aggregation of Matter. (W., ch. xxxix; Spencer: *First Prin.*, 480, *seq.*; Fiske: *Cosmic Philos*).

1. Conditions of Stability of our System. (Laplace). — The planets solid and their motions *in vacuo.* — Neither condition fulfilled.
2. A resisting medium in space. (B. Stewart: *Conservation of Energy*, 96; Fiske: *Cosmic Phil.* Also, Spencer, Cousin, etc.).
3. Shortening of periods of rotation. — Encke's comet. — The fact denied. — Illustration from meteoroids in our atmosphere. — Inevitable precipitation of planetary matter.
4. Process of aggregation in other systems.

VIII. Glimpses Beyond.

1. Question of final aggregation of all matter. — The result inconceivable.
2. There must be a reorganizing principle active in nature. — But the forces of matter incapable of effecting a cosmic resurrection.
3. Cycles of matter. (W., ch. xl).

LV. WORLD-LIFE.

A. WINCHELL: *Geology of the Stars*, Half-Hour Recreations in Popular Science, 279-82; ENNIS: *Origin of the Stars.*

I. General Cosmic Morphology.

1. The deepest principle of change in cosmic existence is expressed by the word *cooling.* — Other activities come into play concomitantly.
2. The three great cosmic forces are *heat* and atomic and molar *attractions.*
3. A world's life-time is but a progressive cooling, with its incidents and consequents. — It passes successively through all the phases and stages known to cosmogony.
4. Cosmic life-times have begun at different epochs, and proceed at different rates. — Probably beginning and ending continually. — Hence, contemporary cosmic existence, analogously to the kingdoms of organic life, presents a simultaneous panorama of a world's life-time. — The taxonomy of the heavens is therefore a cosmic embryology and a cosmic palæontology. (Lect. XLIX, IV, 5).

II. Nebular Stage.

1. Diffused Phase or Cosmical Dust. (Lect. XLII). — Cosmic atoms gathering, condensing and developing heat. — An antecedent phase of matter supposable, in the form of a continuous, cold, or heated gas. (Ennis: *Origin of the Stars*, sec. xvi). — But the conception not yet correlated to the normal nebulous condition.
2. Normal Nebular Phase. — Mineral mist floating in a gaseous medium. — Spectrum of one, two or three bright lines. (Lect. XLII, VI, 4). — *Some of the irresolvable nebulæ.*
3 Continuous Fire-mist Phase. — Mineral mist increased in quantity, but the mass remaining homogeneous and mostly gaseous. — Spectrum of bright lines superposed on an extremely faint, continuous spectrum of scarcely appreciable breadth. — *Certain irresolvable nebulæ;* also, *a few* "*stars.*"

   Annulations perhaps take place in this phase. The primitive nebula is resolved into solar nebulæ, in which other annulations succeed. — Annular, and probably spiral and curved nebulæ. — Saturnian rings persisting like a preserved embryo.
4. Discontinuous Fire-mist Phase. — Segregation and accumulation around local nuclei, without annulation. — Fire-mist or photospheric matter still in small proportion to gaseous. —

K

Bright line spectrum superposed on a faint continuous spectrum. — *Certain resolvable nebulæ.* — Compare nebula in Draco.

III. Stellar Stage.

1. Nucleating Phase. — Increasing amount of photospheric matter. — Nuclear condensation apparent. — Sun systems and planetary segregations past the phase of annulation. — Bright lines over a continuous spectrum. — *Planetary Nebulæ* and *Nebulous Stars.*
2. Nucleated Phase. — Liquid precipitate increased. — Temperature and luminosity so diminished that the absorbent capacity of the still gaseous atmosphere just equals the emissive power of the nucleus and photosphere. — Spectrum continuous. — Certain *star clusters* and most *resolvable nebulæ.*
3. Sirian Phase. — Atmosphere of great depth and tension. — Absorbent capacity exceeds emissive. — Spectrum of dark lines of extraordinary breadth. — *White stars.*
4. Arcturan Phase. — Atmosphere diminished in depth and tension. — Spectrum the normal solar spectrum. — *Yellow Stars.*
   (1) Some fixed stars in the last two stages the centres of cosmic systems.
   (2) Some have their attendant worlds still luminous.
      (*a*) Sirius a sun with four still luminous *planets.*
      (*b*) Procyon, Rigel, Aldebaran, Arcturus, Antares, Zeta Cancri, etc., have each one or more.
      (*c*) Some of these companions have still smaller attendants, as Mu Lupi, Eta Lyræ, Xi Cancri, 12 Lyncis, Theta Orionis. — These are still-luminous *satellites.*
5. Solar Phase. — Photosphere thinned to point of eruption by upward vortical movements. — Maculation by condensation of the cooled vapors. — Incipient variability. — *Our sun.*
6. Variable Phase. — Photosphere periodically darkened by the great amount of macular matter floating on photosphere. — Approaching total liquefaction. — *Periodic* and *Irregular Stars.* — Their periods from a few hours to 500 days, and range of brightness from fourth to ninth magnitude. (Argelander in Humboldt's *Cosmos*, iii).
7. Molten Phase. — Photospheric matter exhausted. — A molten globe. — Spectrum continuous. — Some *star clusters* and *resolvable nebulæ.*
8. Incrustive Phase. — Primitive crust. — The light ruddy. — Incipient darkening. — Spectrum of dark lines, but giving the *ensemble* of vaporosity. — *Red Stars.*

9. Eruptive Phase. — Crust darkened, but disrupted at intervals, giving spasmodic luminosity. (Lect. XXXIX, IV). — Spectrum returns to vaporous or other earlier indications. — *Temporary Stars.* (Ennis : *Origin of the Stars,* 123–8).

IV. Planetary Stage.

1. Jovian Phase. — The stormy condition. (Lect. XXXIX, IV–VI).
2. Terrestrial Phase. — Culmination of organic career. — Movements of atmosphere comparable with those of solar photosphere. — Earth and some satellites of Jupiter and Saturn.
3. Martial Phase. — Planetary senescence. — *Mars* and *some satellites* of older planets.
4. Retarded Rotary Phase. — Work of tidal retardation far advanced. (Lect. LIV, V). — *Moon, Mars* and some *older satellites.*
5. Lunar Phase. — Planetary death. (Lect. XLI, II, 2, V). — *Moon* and some *older satellites.*

V. Unity of Cosmical Phenomena.

[From the American Journal of Science and Arts, Vol. XL, Nov., 1865.]

SOME INDICATIONS OF A NORTHWARD TRANSPORTATION OF DRIFT MATERIALS IN THE LOWER PENINSULA OF MICHIGAN.

By Professor ALEXANDER WINCHELL.

THROUGHOUT the northern part of Lenawee and Hillsdale counties, the southern and eastern parts of Jackson, and the southern and western parts of Washtenaw county, are found numerous tabular, detached masses of limestone, sometimes cropping out on a hill side, like a ledge in place, and sometimes imbedded two or three feet in the sand and gravel at the summit. The position of these masses is generally nearly horizontal, though for the greater part slightly tilted in one direction or another. They sometimes present an extent of six, eight, or twelve feet square; and in occasional instances even more, so as to offer every appearance of an outcropping formation. In some cases many hundred bushels of lime have been burned from them before exhaustion. Underneath them we find the semi-stratified drift materials so characteristic of the general surface of the peninsula. At the bottom of the drift, which in some places is not over ten or twenty feet deep, we find the rocks of the Huron, or more frequently the Marshall group, in place. Many patches, nevertheless, occur as far north as the outcrops of the Carboniferous limestone, and create great confusion in tracing the latter formation unless the fossils are strictly attended to. Smaller fragments of the same limestone are still more abundant throughout the same limits; and, by their disintegration, have imparted a highly calcareous element to the soil, even along the arenaceous belts. The percolation of meteoric waters, in turn, has given rise, in great abundance, to calcareous springs, and deposits of marl, tufa and travertin.

In the southwestern part of the peninsula, in the counties of Berrien, Van Buren and Ottawa, similar phenomena are again observed. The calcareous element of the soil is even more abundant; and large patches of sand have become firmly cemented, so as to present the consistency and appearance of ledges of sandstone. It really requires an extended series of observations to convince one's self that the region does not furnish considerable outcrops of a sandstone formation—especially as numerous blocks of undoubted Marshall sandstone occur upon the surface.

Some examples of these phenomena may be more definitely cited. On the S.W. ¼ S.E. ¼ sec. 13, Woodstock, Lenawee County, (221),[1] in the side of "Prospect Hill," limestone occurs in tabular masses six by twenty feet, and seven feet thick. An old lime-kiln stands near. Similar limestone occurs on the S.E. ¼ S.W. ¼ sec. 12, Woodstock (223) and S.W. ¼ S.E. ¼ sec. 1. From the latter locality several hundred bushels of lime have been burned. On sec. 3 of the same township, the Marshall sandstone is reached at the depth of 4 to 12 feet from the surface. On sec. 4 the sandstone is known to be over 75 feet thick; so that there can be no mistake in assuming it to be in place. On the N.E. ¼ N.W. ¼ sec. 6, Woodstock (230), is a large tabular mass 10 feet long and known to be over 6 feet broad. The dip is toward the east.

On the N.W. ¼ N.W. ¼, sec. 32, Columbia, Jackson county, (233) is a mass of limestone. Sixty rods north of here the sand-rock is known to be within 20 feet of the surface, and has been penetrated 44 feet. On sec. 30 it has been penetrated 60 feet. On the N.W. ¼ N.W. ¼ sec. 26, Liberty, Jackson county, (235), masses of limestone are so abundant that a kiln has been constructed and several hundred bushels of lime manufactured. At the time of my visit, about 35 cords of wood were piled by the kiln, indicating considerable confidence in the resources of the quarry. Fragments of Marshall sandstone, with its fossils, are abundant, mingled with the fragments of limestone. Similar masses of limestone may be seen again on N.W. ¼ N.E. ¼ sec. 26, Hanover, (239), and on the S.W. ¼ N.E. ¼ same section, (240). Several wagon loads of fragments have been removed from the subsoil over the principal mass at the latter place. On the S.E. ¼ S.E. ¼, same section, a common well reached the Marshall sandstone at the depth of 35 feet, and was excavated 40 feet in the rock. The hills on N.E. ¼ N.E. ¼ sec. 33, same township,

[1] These numbers designate the localities.

(243), are filled with fragments of limestone, while the Marshall sandstone is struck at the depth of 50 feet on sec. 35, and at 30 feet on sec. 27. Farther north, on secs. 10 and 11, Leoni, (92 and 206), similar fragments again occur. Also on sec. 25, Grass Lake, (208). At a place one mile northeast of Franciscoville, (209), 20,000 bushels of lime have been manufactured in ten or twelve years.

In the adjoining parts of Washtenaw county, several kilns proclaim the presence of extensive nests of limestone. Even within the corporate limits of the city of Ann Arbor an extensive deposit has been quarried; and just beyond the limits, on the east, are the ruins of a limekiln which, many years ago, exhausted still another deposit.

Similar masses of limestone occur in Hillsdale county, one half mile southwest of Jonesville, (270); on S.W. ¼ N.W. ¼ sec. 21, Allen, (274); N.E. ¼ N.W. ¼ sec. 21, Adams, (289); S.E. ¼ N.E. ¼ sec. 22, Adams, (291); N.E. ¼ N.E. ¼ sec. 24, Adams, (292); S.W. ¼ N.W. ¼ sec. 19, Woodbridge, (296), and in many other localities.

In the southwestern part of the state, on the S.E. ¼ N.W. ¼ sec. 11, Hartford, Van Buren county, (415), limestone is found within two feet of the surface over the space of three or four square rods. One hundred rods north of here the wells are from 40 to 100 feet deep, without reaching any native rock—though thick beds of cemented sand and gravel are frequently encountered.

On the S.W. ¼ sec. 17, T. 7 N.R. 13 W, Ottawa county, (438) is the last occurrence that will be cited. Several slabs 3 or 4 feet long have been removed, and others remain, over an area of at least a square rod.

It is quite evident that such masses of stratified limestone have not been rolled to the same extent as the quartzose and gneissoid boulders which constitute the most striking feature of the "northern drift" of the same regions. By some agency these tables have been lifted gently from their original sites and carefully deposited where we find them. Paying no regard to their included fossil remains, it might be imagined that they constitute the ruins of the Carboniferous limestone formation, whose place is between these fragments and the centre of the peninsula. This formation gently rises toward the periphery of the peninsula, and at certain distances from its present outcrops would intersect the highest diluvial hills in the places occupied by the fragments which I have described; and which, for this reason, might be imagined as marking the outermost limits of a once continuous formation of Carboniferous limestone. The abundant fossil remains contained in these fragments, however, not to speak of their lithological characters, convince us that the rock belongs to a much earlier epoch.

In short, no doubt could be entertained by one who has examined the subject, that these fragments appertain to the age of the Corniferous limestone. The rock, in structure, is irregular, often brecciated, with streaks and nests of bituminous and argillaceous matter. At other times it is compact and massive. Not unfrequently it presents the peculiar structure known as "lignilites." All these characters belong to the Corniferous limestone as exposed along the western shore of Lake Erie, and at numerous points throughout the county of Monroe.

Turning to the more reliable evidence of the fossil remains, it may be stated that the following are examples of the more frequent identifications:

At 92, *Heliophyllum Canadense* Billings, *Clisiophyllum Oneidaënse* Bill., *Acervularia Davidsoni* E. & H., *Conocardium trigonale* Hall, *Proetus crassimarginatus* Hall, *Amplexus* and *Favosites.*

At 182, *Lucina proavia* Goldf., *Conocardium trigonale*, *Dentalium* and *Fenestella.*

At 208, *Lucina proavia* and three species of Bryozoa.

At 230, *Strophomena rhomboidalis* Wahl, *Chonetes glabra* Hall, *Spirifera gregaria* Clapp, *Atrypa reticularis* Dal.

At 233, *Chonetes hemispherica* Hall, *Atrypa reticularis*, *Cyrtodonta* (*Vanuxemia*) *Tompkinsi* Bill, *Pleurotomaria rotunda*, Hall.

At 270, *Chonetes lineata* Hall, *Atrypa reticularis.*

At 289, *Chonetes lineata*, *C. glabra* Hall, *Atrypa reticularis*, *Leiorhynchus multicosta* Hall, *Rhynchonella Thalia* Bill., *Lucina proavia*, *Proetus crassimarginatas* Hall, *Platyceras and Proetus* sp.?

At 291, *Cyathophyllum Zenkeri* Bill, *Chonetes lineata*, *C. glabra*, *Orthis Vanuxemi* Hall, *Strophomena hemispherica*, *S. rhomboidalis*, *Spirifera varicosa* Hall, *S. gregaria*, *Atrypa reticularis*, *Charionella scitula* Bill., *Rhynchonella Thalia*, *Lucina proavia*, *Conocardium trigonale*, *Proetus crassimarginatus*, *Fenestella*, *Producta* (two species), *Streptorhynchus*, *Athyris*, *Platyceras.*

At 292, *Orthis Vanuxemi*, *O. propinqua* Hall.

At 296, *Chonetes glabra*, *C. arcuata* Hall, *Stricklandia elongata* Bill.

At 298, *Strophomena hemispherica.*

The following are the more common Corniferous fossils occurring in the Drift at Ann Arbor:

Favosites Gothlandica Goldf., *F. cervicornis* De Blainv., *F. turbinata* Bill., *F. polymorpha* Goldf., *F.* (*Emmonsia*) *hemispherica* Y. & S. sp., *Fistulipora Canadensis* Bill., *Michelinia convexa* D'Orb., *M. favosoidea* Bill., *Alveolites labiosa* Bill., *A. Rœmeri*[2] Bill., *Syringopora perelegans* Bill., *S. Hisingeri* Bill., *S. Maclurei* Bill., *S. nobilis* Bill, *Stromatopora concentrica* Lonsd., *Cyathophyllum Zenkeri* Bill., *Zaphrentis prolifica* Bill., *Clisiophyllum Oneidaënse* Bill.,

Heliophyllum Eriense Bill., *H. exiguum* Bill., *Cystiphyllum Americanum* E. & H., *Blothrophyllum decoricatum* Bill., *Diphyphyllum Archiaci*[2] Bill., *Phillipsastræa Verneuili* E. & H., *P. gigas* Owen, sp., *Acervularia Davidsoni*[2] E. & H., *Tentaculites scalaris* Schlot., *Chonetes glabra* Hall, *C. hemispherica* Hall, *Strophomena hemispherica* H., *S. perplana* Con., *S. inæquiradiata* H., *S. demissa* Con., *Orthis propinqua* H., *O. Eryna* H., *Ambocœlia umbonata* Con., sp., *Spirifera gregaria* Clapp, *S. varicosa* H., *S. acuminata* Con., sp., *Leiorhynchus multicosta*[2] Hall, *Nucleospira concinna*[2] Hall, *Charionella scitula* Hall, sp., *Atrypa reticularis* Dal., *A. impressa* H., *A. aspera?* Hall, *Meristella unisulcata* Con., sp., *M. nasuta* Con., sp., *Leptocœlia concava* H., *Pentamerus aratus* Con., sp., *Stricklandia elongata* Vanux., sp., *Centronella glansfagea* Hall, sp., *Rhynchonella Thalia* Bill., *Lucina proavia* Goldf., *Conocardium trigonale* Hall, sp., *Platyceras Thetis* H., *P. crassum* H., *P. dumosum* Con., *Platyostoma strophius* H., *Murchisona Leda* H., *Proetus crassimarginatus* H., and more than two dozen species which seem to be undescribed.

If no reasonable doubt exists that these detached masses belong to the Corniferous limestone, the next question which presents itself relates to the region whence they have been derived. In view of the facts cited, it is evidently absurd to assume that no transportation has taken place; for these masses of Corniferous limestone are found resting over the Hamilton group, the Marshall group and the Carboniferous limestone—and, I am pretty well convinced, even in some cases, as far north as the Coal measures. There are insuperable objections to assuming that they have been transported with the great mass of drift materials from the northern outcrops of the rocks of this age at Mackinac and the surrounding region. *First*, the transporting agency has not moved masses of other kinds of rocks which attain to anything like the same dimensions. *Secondly*, That agency, if we may judge from the condition of the siliceous, trappean and gneissoid boulders of admitted northern origin, would have ground to powder so fragile and friable a rock as these limestones; or at least would have broken them into small fragments, and deposited them in a worn and rounded condition. *Thirdly*, If the Corniferous limestone could have been transported in such masses from its northern outcrops to southern Michigan, much more would the harder and more massive Niagara limestone of the same regions have been similarly

[2] These species of the Hamilton group are here included, because occurring in the same fragments with admitted Corniferous (and Schoharie grit) species. The Lower Helderberg *Leptocœlia concava* is included for the same reason. In none of the cases just referred to, however, do we experience any difficulty in discovering slight constant peculiarities in the Corniferous species. The richness of the exotic Drift fauna of this locality, in the number and state of preservation of its remains, far exceeds any that has been signalized by the geologists of the Old World.

transported. The same may be said of the Trenton limestone. We find, however, that fragments of these limestones are of rare occurrence; and the fossils of Silurian age scarcely sustain to those of the Corniferous limestone the ratio of one to one hundred, in the drift deposits of the southern portion of the state. Even the Carboniferous limestone, whose outcrop extends through Kent, Eaton, Jackson and Oakland counties, is scarcely represented among the drift materials of the region in question. It is apparent that we must look in another direction for the origin of these lost rocks.

The nearest outcrop of the Corniferous limestone is in northern Indiana and Ohio, and the southeastern corner of Michigan[3]. Every fossil cited above is found in place in some part of that region. The formation dips under the peninsula of Michigan; and, throughout the area occupied by the lost masses in question, it lies from one hundred to twelve hundred feet beneath the surface—the depth of course increasing toward the center of the Carboniferous area. The circumstances suggest the exertion of some powerful agency acting northward with tremendous energy, but with a gentle and equable movement. It would seem as if the summit of the low anticlinal in the Corniferous limestone to the southeast of Michigan had been immersed in a shallow sea or lake, the freezing of which had incorporated the upper layers of the rock in an immense thickness of ice, which, by a rise in the water, had floated off as enormous ice-floes, bearing their cargoes of limestone northward till deeper and milder water loosened their icy hold, or they became stranded on the bosses which mark the belt of the Marshall sandstone. From the position of these masses in the "Modified Drift," as well as from the direction and gentleness of the movement, it would seem impossible that the events should have been contemporaneous with the actions which characterized the great glacial epoch.

Additional facts exist which seem to lead the mind further toward a belief in a northward acting post-glacial agency. The fossils of the Hamilton group, whose outcrop is along a belt lying somewhat farther north than the Corniferous limestone, are scattered through the soil of the region lying still farther north, in a degree of abundance which bears about the same ratio to that of the Corniferous fossils as the attenuated Hamilton rocks bear to the Corniferous. Indeed it may be said that *Spirifera mucronata* is the most abundant single species in our drift; as it was certainly the most abundant species that lived in these parts of the Lower Devonian sea. Other common species of the Hamilton group are *Ambocœlia umbonata* Hall, *Cyrtia Hamilton-*

[3] It probably underlies the drift materials of the southwestern angle of the state and the adjacent parts of Indiana, but no actual outcrops are known to exist.

ensis Hall, *Spirifera Marcyi* Hall, *Spirigera concentrica* Brown, sp., *Platyceras attenuatum* Hall, *Dalmania Boothi* Green, sp., and many others. These species exist in an admirable state of preservation, quite incompatible with the theory of their transportation from the far north; and they occur across a belt of the state reaching at least thirty miles north of the outcrop of the Hamilton rocks.

Again, above the identifiable Hamilton rocks, we find, in this state, a great thickness of argillaceous and bituminous shales, destitute of fossils, but freighted with Kidney iron ore. Nodules of this ore are strewn not only over the region of the outcrop of these "Huron" shales, but throughout Washtenaw and other counties lying over the upper Devonian and lower Carboniferous strata—to say nothing of the occurrence of such nodules within the limits of the Coal measures, where, by some geologists, they might preferably be referred to the indigenous strata.

Still again, the well marked fossiliferous beds of the Marshall sandstone, lying next above the Huron shales, and outcropping along a belt still farther north, is represented by a series of enormous fragments resting over the non-fossiliferous upper portions and the Carboniferous limestone. The lower, or fossiliferous portions of this formation do not outcrop farther north than Moscow, in Hillsdale county, while fragments of it have been transported in great abundance into the southern townships of Jackson county. The most notable example occurs in a deep railroad cut three miles north of Napoleon, where the abundant fossiliferous fragments led me for some time to suppose the actual outcrop must be in the immediate vicinity; although I had found the non-fossiliferous Napoleon sandstone intervening between the locality and the most northern known outcrop of the fossiliferous beds at Moscow. I collected here a large proportion of the common fossils of the Marshall group such as *Rhynchonella Sageriana*, *Chonetes pulchella*, *Myalina Michiganensis*, *Cardiomorpha modiolaris*, *Tellinomya Hubbardi*, *T. Stella*, *Pterinea crenistriata*, *Cardium Napoleonense*, *Solen scalpriformis*, *Bellerophon galericulatus*, *Orthoceras Indianense*, *Goniatites Marshallensis*, and numerous other species. The fossiliferous layers of the Marshall sandstone are decidedly friable—insomuch that it is in little request for building purposes—and it would seem absurd to suppose that these large fragments had been moved two hundred miles from the northern outcrop of the formation, when a transfer of ten or fifteen miles from the southern outcrop would bring them to the position which they occupy. We should expect, also, if derived from the north, that some contrast in the organic facies, due to local, if not to climatic causes, would present itself; but on the contrary, we find the fauna of the fragments strictly identical with that of the nearest indigenous rocks of the same age.

The facts above cited recall some observations made several years since in Alabama, and which led at that time to impressions similar to those just set forth. My observations were made especially upon the neighborhood of the junction of the "Rotten Limestone" of the Upper Cretaceous, with the argillaceous and arenaceous strata of the Lower Cretaceous. The "Red Loam" of the central belt of the state, which I have evidences to prove to be but the Rotten Limestone altered *in situ*, or with slight transportation, has in many cases along the junction of the upper and lower strata, been moved northward over the clayey and sandy region appertaining to the lower Cretaceous; where, by its admixture with diluvial sand and pebbles, it is proved to be an exotic formation.

I forbear to express any belief in reference to the former existence of a transporting agency acting from the south to the north, over all or any portion of the interior of the continent; but such facts as I have cited cannot fail to call to mind the suggestions made some years since by President W. Hopkins, touching the course the Gulf Stream would necessarily pursue, in case of the subsidence of the North American Continent[4]. The facts are of sufficient importance to merit investigation; and it is to be hoped that other observers will inform us whether they are exceptional phenomena, or correspond, in connection with others, to some ancient, glacial or hydrographical area.

University of Michigan, August 4, 1865.

www.ingramcontent.com/pod-product-compliance
Lightning Source LLC
LaVergne TN
LVHW021313110826
845150LV00003B/556

* 9 7 8 1 4 2 5 5 5 8 4 8 2 *